See overleaf. Ben Campanale at the Milwaukee Mile in 1938

HARLEY~ DAVIDSON

THE MILWAUKEE MARVEL

HARRY V. SUCHER

Foulis

Haynes

ISBN 0 85429 936 X

© Harry V. Sucher 1990

First published August 1981

2nd Revised Edition March 1982
2nd Revised Edition reprinted March 1983
3rd Revised Edition September 1985
4th Revised Edition July 1988
Reprinted February 1989.
Reprinted March 1990 with updating material.
Reprinted July 1991 with further updating material.

A FOULIS Motorcycling book

Published by
Haynes Publishing Group Ltd
Sparkford, Yeovil, Somerset BA22 7JJ, England

Haynes Publications Inc
861 Lawrence Drive, Newbury Park, California 91320 USA

A Catalogue record for this book is available from the British Library

Library of Congress Catalog Card Number

88 81754

Editor: **Jeff Clew**
Cover design: **Phill Jennings**
Layout design: **Lynne J.Blackburn**

Printed in England by J.H. Haynes & Co. Ltd.

Dedication

Dedicated to the memories of Arthur Davidson and William S.Harley who, starting out with little more than an idea, and in the American free enterprise tradition, founded an organization that was to become of historical significance to American transportation.

Foreword

Any Publisher who proposes to produce a factual and readable book on the early history of motorcycling in America at this late date must find an Author who is a motorcycle enthusiast, blessed with amazing perception, literary ability, and insatiable desire, before it becomes too late, to record for posterity this sector of American transportation history. He will need a number of old-time motor-cycling friends, who, in turn have old-time motorcycling friends, engineers, mechanics and champions. Then, in order to get started, he must have the time, the available funds, the energy to write to, travel to, visit with and pick the recollections and brains of those few remaining 'old timers' (of which he himself will desirably be one) to collect and collate over a period of months and possibly years, the varied memories and opinions of informed, uninformed, prejudiced, or sometimes spiteful persons. Finally, and most importantly, he must wind up the job by 'sifting the wheat from the chaff', giving the benefit of the doubt to those deceased and defenseless persons, many of whose actions, while controversial, were of necessity created by the natural desire for economic survival.

The publisher of this book is fortunate to have as the Author, Dr.Harry V.Sucher of Garden Grove, California, who measures up to the features suggested in the above paragraph.

While I have not found it easy to agree with the opinion of all of Dr.Sucher's informants, which is quite understandable, he has done an excellent job of sifting the wheat from the chaff and has come up with a book which, in spite of the time lapse and the demise of practically all of the principals, matches or betters his 'Iron Redskin' book of a year or two ago, which covered in detail the founding and development of the Indian motorcycle, the great competitor that Harley-Davidson contended with all through the years.

My long-time personal association, friendship with, and admiration for Bill, Walter, and Arthur Davidson, Bill Harley and their sons and grandsons, and the previously inadequate record of their achievements, caused me to offer my co-operation to Doctor Sucher. I can recommend this book to all would-be and should-be owners, and to all the 'Old Timers' who like myself, even before the days of Mr.Ford's 'Tin Lizzie', enjoyed the thrill of twisting the right grip of a 'Silent Gray Fellow' on an open road, experiencing for the first time the never-to-be-forgotten thrill of the sport of motorcycling.

Alfred Rich Child

Contents

Author's Preface   10
Acknowledgements   11

Chapter 1 William S. Harley and the Davidsons   13
Chapter 2 Success and Disappointment   33
Chapter 3 The Roaring Twenties   65
Chapter 4 Oriental Interlude   79
Chapter 5 Disappointment and Disaster   89
Chapter 6 The Great Depression   113
Chapter 7 World War II   175
Chapter 8 Post War Problems   185
Chapter 9 A Time of Change   213
Chapter 10 The AMF Era   237
Chapter 11 A New Beginning   277
Chapter 12 The Rebirth of Harley-Davidson   304
Appendix 1 The Excelsior Motorcycle   335
Appendix 2 A General Guide to the Descriptive Designation of Harley-Davidson
             Models   345
Bibliography   358
Index   360

Author`s Preface

From the backyard of a modest home in Milwaukee, when the uncertain clatter of the first Harley-Davidson motorcycle first pierced the air, to the lusty roar of a modern chopper as it rockets through the streets of Las Vegas, Harley-Davidson has ever been a dominant force on the American motorcycle scene.

As one of the pioneers of the industry, Harley-Davidson experienced the initial triumph and then the near demise of American motorcycle manufacturing. In the period between the wars, the motorcycle became an insignificant entity within the domestic transportation scene, due to the complexity of certain socio-economic factors which we will examine. With their backs to the wall, the surviving makes struggled on, maintaining a brave front to the world, but perforce existing through subterfuge and deception. As an already controversial entity, the motorcycle industry, through its business relationships and marketing methods, became even more controversial. As the sole surviving member of that industry, (a remarkable achievement in itself), Harley-Davidson has lived on in the eye of the storm.

Strangely enough, the true story of the life and times of Harley-Davidson has never been thoroughly explored. Through the years we have been exposed to both the fictionalized and self-laudatory 'histories' published by the factory, as well as many unfounded excoriations by critics whose writings were based on unsound evidence.

It now appears that never before has the history of Harley-Davidson been subjected to professional journalistic research. The author hopes that this effort will fill this void, and at the same time offer an interesting portion of the saga of American transportation history.

Harry V Sucher

Acknowledgements

THEY SAID IT COULDN'T BE DONE. THE AUTHOR WAS WARNED BY COMPETENT advisers that to attempt the writing of the history of Harley-Davidson could only result in a dead end. No help would be forthcoming from surviving Company personnel, they said, nothing but adamant opposition to the telling of the REAL story of Harley-Davidson. But this proved not to be the case. Certain former AMF executives, whose Company were at one time the owners of Harley-Davidson, were, if anonymously, willing to comment upon the happenings of an era that proved to be a somewhat unfortunate period. But the doomsayers were right in one respect: certain of the Company's old timers, including former President William H. Davidson, and certain serving remnants of the old Milwaukee staff, gave official notice that they wanted no part of any such revelation. The traditional veil of silence that ever surrounded the internal affairs of the American motorcycle industry was still to be reckoned with. This condition appears to have been brought about by the precarious state of the industry in the critical between-the-wars years. In Harley-Davidson's case, it may also be attributed to the fact that the Company's long control of the activities of the American Motorcycle Association, and the bitter on-going controversy that attended it, may well be a factor. Then too, as later events proved, the Company's actual intent in more recent years was diametrically opposed to the public image it wished to present.

But in starting the project, it was soon found that a vast store of information was forthcoming from many hundreds of people who were interested in seeing that this vital segment of American transportation history be recorded for posterity. These included both past and present dealers, owners, and most fortunately, a large group of one-time Company employees, as well as many former competition stars whose various recollections and impressions could be distilled to provide the essence of the story. This reporting involved hundreds of interviews and literally thousands of conversations with the people involved. As time went on, the project demanded much extensive travel on the part of the author, not only throughout the United States and Canada, but in nearly every country in the free world, not only to gather material on past and present Harley-Davidson activities, but to correlate these to the ever-changing aspects of the world's motorcycle market.

Additionally, certain elements of the middle and later period of the history are autobiographical, as the author, a veteran motorcycle owner and rider, fortunately possesses a first-hand knowledge of many of the events that took place, as well as personal experience involving many of the models that Harley-Davidson produced through the years. All in all, and with the author's life-long interest in recording the history of the American motorcycle industry, the project has been going on continuously for well over fifty years now. As Harley-Davidson is still, at this writing, an ongoing activity, it was necessary to update the original work, revising where necessary as later research revealed, and otherwise keeping abreast of the current picture.

It is impossible to mention all the people whose valued contribution made the work possible, and space considerations allow only the mention of those whose historical position is more familiar to students of our motorcycling heritage.

Some of the more prominent people whose help is gratefully acknowledged are Hap Alzina, Nelson Bettencourt, Floyd Clymer, Charles Cook, Joe Frugoli, Dudley Perkins, Angelo Rossi, Claude Salmon, and Tom Sifton.

At a later date there were Paul Albrecht, John and Jean Burdette, Skip Fordyce, Orrin Hall, Armano Magri, Frank J. Murray, Gene Rhyne, Joe Sarkees, Francis 'Shorty' Thompkins, and John Underwood.

During the years when I was actively engaged in collecting and restoring old machines, there were Bruce Aiken, the late J. Worth Alexander, Maury and Beverly Biggs, P.T. Boone, John Cameron, Del Du Chene, the late Russell Harmon, the late Elmo Looper, the late Sam Pierce, Bob and Pat Ross, Ernest Skelton, Bob Stark, and Gerald and Ted Williams. As such activities involve much sentimental interest, these people not only helped revive it but are revered for their personal friendship as well.

Former Competition stars who added much to the story include Bud Ekins, Ed Kretz, the late Fred Ludlow, the late Erwin G. 'Cannonball' Baker, and the late Joe Petrali. Former veteran race mechanics whose help is acknowledged include the late Jud Carriker, Marvin 'Red' Fenwicke, and 'Pop' Schunk, as well as the contributions of the late Joe Walker. The latter, a long time Harley-Davidson dealer, was a valued friend for many years, and generously allowed me to test ride many old machines that passed through his hands, as well as ensuing new models as they appeared. I am grateful to his widow, Edith, for allowing me access to certain of his private papers dealing with his long-time association with the Company.

I am also grateful for the kind encouragement of two Honored Founders of the Antique Motorcycle Club of America, Emmett Moore and Theodore A. 'Ted' Hodgdon, and Arthur Segal, a Past President. I would also like to thank Frank Conley, Secretary of the Classic and Antique Motorcycle Association, Jeff Clew of the Vintage Motor Cycle Club of Great Britain, and Ed Youngblood, present President of the American Motorcyclist Association. I have also welcomed the friendship of Carl T. Wicks, President of the Harley-Davidson Owners' Association, and its Technical Director, E.L. Stillman.

I also express my appreciation for the valuable contributions of the late Leslie D. Richards concerning government procurements, sales and marketing trends, information on the Federation of American Motorcyclists, and details of the founding of the American Motorcyclist Association in the period between 1919 and 1925. I would also like to thank the late Thomas Callahan Butler for additional information on the same period, together with his comments on the Shidle marketing reports.

I am grateful to Bud Ekins for allowing me access to his very impressive collection of antique motorcycles, as well as to the late Steve McQueen who also possessed a very large collection.

A most outstanding contributor was Alfred Rich Child, the patriach of Harley-Davidson, a very wonderful gentleman who passed away in his 95th year on February 18th, 1986. As an ageless and articulate individual, his keen mind provides a total recall of both his long time association with the four Founders, as well as many others connected with Company affairs. The complex history of his representation and association in the Orient for many years is now fortunately revealed for the first time.

I am particularly grateful for the helpful advice of two very dear friends of many years standing, Dewey Bonkrud and Johnny Eagles. Both are highly expert mechanics and practical engineers. Not only do I appreciate their valued friendship, but their valuable technical advice gained from years of practical experience and observation.

In the current economic significance of the rapidly growing accessory market, or 'aftermarket' of motorcycle components, I have benefited from on-going conferences with representatives of four of the larger firms involved, Gary Bang, Drag Specialities, Jammers, and Motorcycle Nostalgia. Steve Iorio, owner of the last firm, renders me regular reports on the status of this market. The proprietors of smaller specialist firms manufacturing single components have also been co-operative in providing information. I have also enjoyed the confidences of the owners and proprietors of various firms in Taiwan, Korea, and Japan who manufacture a myriad of motorcycle parts and accessories, and who supply much of those imported for resale in the United States, and who also have kept me abreast of the current state of their markets.

I must also acknowledge my pleasant acquaintanceship with large numbers of representative Harley-Davidson dealers, both in the United States and Canada as well as many in foreign countries. Through their kindness I have been able to ascertain contemporary marketing trends, as well as the on-going state of their relationship and reactions to current Company policies.

I also extend my thanks to the many photographers who have provided the generally excellent illustrations that accompany the text, and whose names appear with the appropriate photo credits.

Not to be forgotten is my Editor, Jeff Clew, who is also the Executive Editorial Director of the publishers of this book. As a noted motorcycle expert and author of a large number of technical works on the subject, he is also a recognized historian, and has published a number of valuable works in this field. Not only do I appreciate his warm personal friendship through the years, but also his helpful guidance in the execution of a very difficult and demanding task.

To my wife, Margery, who helped to edit, type, pore over and comment on the manuscript, and who supported me in loving concern through many years of creative endeavor, I acknowledge my eternal love and gratitude.

Harry V. Sucher
Garden Grove, California
1985

Chapter 1

William S. Harley and the Davidsons

THE DIRECTION OF PUBLIC ATTENTION TO THE MOTOR BICYCLE IN THE USA CAME about in a somewhat indirect manner through the medium of professional bicycle racing which, at the close of the 19th century, was of great interest to a vast bicycling public. In certain competitive events held at the many indoor board tracks or velodromes located in the larger cities throughout the country, tandem machines propelled by two riders were used to pace or precede competitors in sprint events in order to 'cut the wind' or otherwise allow the racers to ride in their slipstream. This was to make for faster times and to give the effect of a more accurate or 'pure' indication of the rider's speed capabilities. Such tandem pacers had already been in use in Europe, and particularly in France, on some of the larger velodromes since 1894 or 95. A couple of seasons later, motor powered machines came into use, some being roadster-type powered bicycles, and some being rather large machines with big, slow-turning engines specially built for this purpose. Motor powered pacers were first seen in the United States in 1899, when a one-time bicycle racer, Kenneth Skinner, and the manager of bicycle racing events at New York's famous Madison Square Garden, imported about a dozen small De Dion type engines for this use. Various cycle mechanics adapted several tandem pedal pacers for this use, but reliability was sometimes a problem because an engine failure could terminate an event. A young bicycle mechanic named Carl Oscar Hedstrom made a name for himself at this point by refining and improving Skinner's engines for better performance and he designed and built his own version of a powered tandem. His efforts later resulted in the founding of the giant Indian motorcycle company.

During this period the several leading bicycle journals featured continuing articles on the progress of powered bicycle design, most of which was then taking place in England and Europe, although a few native experimenters had entered the field. The first American of note was one E.J.Pennington, of Trenton, New Jersey. In 1894 he had built a rather unorthodox machine based on pedal cycle frames but fitted with very large diameter tyres. A two cylinder engine was fitted on an outrigger frame behind the rear wheel, the drive to the axle being by means of a pair of cranks. While the machine could be made to run after a fashion, it appeared that its inventor was more of a promoter than an engineer. He endeavored to create a paper empire by offering large blocks of stock for public sale. After interest in the project in the United States was not forthcoming, he journeyed to England where he was able to found the Great Horseless Carriage Company through the co-operation of a bicycle financier, H.J.Lawson. The latter was able to sell about 100,000 worth of stock before the venture predictably collapsed in 1899.

In the meantime, the world wide bicycle boom flourished unabated, with hundreds of large and small factories operating at peak capacity. In June of 1898, the Waltham Manufacturing Company, of

Waltham, Massachusetts, makers of the famous Orient Bicycles, announced their intention of marketing motor bicycles. They had adapted their heavyweight roadster bicycle for the fitting of a small De Dion type engine built in France by the newly founded Aster concern, and proposed to name it the Orient-Aster. The first models were offered for sale in the spring of 1899. The Marsh Cycle Company of nearby Brockton built a similar machine, also powered with a De Dion type engine, which was first offered for sale in January of 1900. The following spring, Colonel Pope announced that proto-type motorbicycles were being tested at his Hartford factory. In the spring of 1901, Carl Oscar Hedstrom and George M.Hendee formed the Hendee Manufacturing Company, following the successful public demonstration of the former's prototype machine in Springfield. The E.R.Thomas Company of Buffalo, New York, announced the introduction of their soon-to-be-famous 'Auto-Bi' a few months later. By the turn of the century, the American motorcycle industry had become a reality.

Around the turn of the century, two young men who had been close friends since their early grammar school days in Milwaukee, Wisconsin, and who were both bicycling enthusiasts, turned their attention to the design of a practical motor bicycle. William S.Harley was born in Milwaukee in 1880 to working-class parents who had recently emigrated from England. The origins of the Harley family are somewhat obscure, but it is known that they came from the vicinity of Manchester. When young Harley had completed his education at the age of fifteen, he found employment as an apprentice bi-cycle fitter in a small cycle factory in North Milwaukee. He was described by contemporaries as having a natural aptitude for mechanics and, paradoxically, he was also interested in the out-of-doors, natural history, and drawing and sketching. Two years later he decided to broaden his technical capabilities by becoming an apprentice draftsman in a small metal fabricating plant in Milwaukee, where his boy-hood friend, Arthur Davidson, was also employed as a pattern maker. A year younger than Harley, he was the younger son of a family of three boys and two girls who had emigrated to the States from Aberdeen, Scotland, sometime in 1871 or 1872.

It is at this point that the true events of their mutual interest in the developing gasoline engine diverge somewhat according to several slightly differing accounts that subsequently appeared in Harley-Davidson Company literature in later years. The official version has been that their initial ex-periments with small gasoline engines were directly concerned with powering bicycles. However, two contemporaries of both Harley and Davidson independently told the author in the early 1950s that their first efforts were directed toward the development of small engines for powering rowboats. It seems that Harley, with his aforementioned interest in nature, was also a dedicated trout fisherman, and frequently, with young Davidson, fished many of the lakes that abounded in the Milwaukee region. As a powerboat could obviously vastly enhance a fisherman's scope of activity, it is not sur-prising that it should capture the young outdoorsman's interest.

It appears that with their preoccupation with gasoline engines, the two read all of the current literature on the subject they could lay their hands on, which included the leading scientific journals of the day, as well as automotive publications that were now becoming widely circulated, and material in the popular cycling magazines dealing with the now emerging motor bicycle.

Harley and Davidson's interest was also enhanced through their recent acquaintanceship with a newly-emigrated German draftsman who was employed in the same shop, one Emil Kroeger (or Kruger) who had in his possession some actual shop drawings of some small De Dion type gas engines acquired from the Aster concern in Paris, where he had lately been employed. It is known that the pair built three small prototype engines, the last being of sufficient power to propel a small rowboat, fitted with a propellor and installation equipment also built by the partners of their own designs. Unfortunately, no photographs or other specific details of their excursion into marine engineering sur-vive.

During the fall of 1900, Harley and Davidson next turned to the study of motor bicycle engines, and during the ensuing winter made the patterns for the castings of a small engine based on the Aster drawings with a 2⅛ inch bore and 2⅞ inch stroke. Working in their spare time during the evenings and weekends they assembled three or four of these engines and tested them in standard heavyweight, utility type, pedal cycle frames. Their main technical difficulties at this time appeared to be with car-buretion, and they finally settled on a primitive spray type instrument that offered little if any throttle control, limited engine speed variations being effected by altering the dry-battery-activated spark control setting. After much experimentation, a fairly satisfactory carburetor was subsequently evolved.

It was during this time that Arthur undertook another and unrelated after-hours venture (no doubt to earn extra funds to finance the engine experiments) involving the making of job patterns. This was in association with another young mechanic named Ole Evinrude, who was later to win fame and fortune as the developer and promoter of the first practical outboard marine engine.

As this was the day of the primitive 'clip-on' motor bicycle, Harley and Davidson had ample opportunity to observe the technical details of the various makes of machines already in commercial production. Some of these, such as the Indian, Marsh, Orient, Pope, Thor, and Wagner, to name the most prominent, were of fairly substantial construction. But as is too often the case when a new product is capturing public attention, about a dozen fly-by-night concerns were producing flimsy and inferior machines in order to make a quick profit.

Sometime during 1902, Arthur's 26 year old brother Walter, who had been an apprentice machinist in one of the railroad shops in Milwaukee, but who was then employed in its shops in Missouri, Kansas, and Texas Railroad in Parsons, Kansas, moved back to Milwaukee and secured a similar position with the Chicago, Milwaukee, and St.Paul Railroad. He had been in touch with the powerboat and motor bicycle engine experiments through correspondence with Arthur, and now offered to lend a hand with the project in his own spare time.

As the work advanced, the lack of suitable shop equipment at the Davidson family home at the corner of 38th Street and Highland Avenue made further progress most difficult. Fortunately, Harley was now able to secure the use of a small shop owned by a mutual friend of his and the Davidsons that was equipped with a small lathe and a drill press, together with a fairly comprehensive set of hand tools.

The first prototype model was finally completed early in the Spring of 1903. During the initial road tests the engine ran well and appeared to be acceptably reliable, producing a top speed of about 25 mph, but lacking sufficient power for serious hill climbing. During extended testing on the usual muddy and rutted roads of the Milwaukee suburbs, the weakness of the standard pedal cycle frame became all too apparent, with frame breakages, distortions, and the repeated failure of the steering head bearings.

The ancestor of the H-D big twins: The 1911 magneto-equipped twin.

Realizing the immediate need for a more powerful engine, Harley designed a new and larger model, following the now almost standard De Dion configuration, but with a 3 inch bore and a 3½ inch stroke, heavier castings and flywheels, and a swept volume of 25 cubic inches. After the drawings were made, Arthur again made up the casting patterns.

With a more powerful engine, fitted into another pedal cycle frame, chassis failures were intensified, and both Harley and Davidson at once agreed that in order to produce a practical machine, the whole had to be conceived as a motorcycle and not a converted bicycle. The new frame was a frank copy of the best in contemporary practice. It was brazed up from heavy gauge tubing, with a lengthened wheelbase to allow for a loop to house the engine case just ahead of the pedal bracket. The fuel tank was carried in the modern position on the top tube; the tool case and battery box being positioned on the frame to give the best balance. The fork, while unsprung, was made from extra heavy tubing and carried a triple crown, supported by extra heavy bearings and races in the head lug. The drive was by a flat leather belt, with a spring-loaded pulley as a tensioning device bearing against the lower run that was activated by a ratcheted hand lever. This last was a fitting common to nearly all the more successful contemporary machines, as it could be used as a primitive clutch when a momentary halt was expedient. It also helped when getting underway, which was accomplished by vigorous pedalling along with a gradual manual tightening of the belt.

The original and later enlarged shop housing the initial H-D assembly. It was situated at the rear of the Davidson home at 38th St. and Highland Avenue in Milwaukee.

While the belt drive in both flat and V type form was the drive fitting of choice in most pioneer motorcycles, exponents of chain drive were already questioning its efficiency, citing slipping problems when wet and the vulnerability of the necessarily large diameter rear wheel pulley to clogging with mud, which resulted in reduced tractive power on anything other than gentle gradients. On the other side of the coin, belt drive was cheap and economical to assemble. and provided 'soft' power through its flexibility that lessened the possibility of frame distortion from the torque of the engine. Then there was the added advantage that the manual control of slipping the belt through the use of the idler pulley could somewhat mitigate the 'all-or-nothing' speeds of these early machines that universally possessed a somewhat vague regulation of the engine revolutions. While some early contemporaries, such as Indian, Reading-Standard, and Thor fitted chain drives, early chains were prone to breakage under hard going, and the power transmission was somewhat harsh and led to much chain snatch at low speeds. It was not until friction discs and spring loaded shock absorbing devices came into being that chain drive became more satisfactory.

Harley and Davidson at long last found themselves with a machine which they considered suitable for commercial sale. The improved engine and drive train had proved sufficiently reliable after exhaustive testing, and the frame and forks appeared sturdy enough to contend with the universally bad roads then existing. Another point in question that was satisfactorily solved was the fitting of very sturdy wheels. Most pioneer designs featured heavy pedal cycle wheels which soon failed through fractured spokes and broken bearings. Harley had designed his own heavy duty type with large hubs and heavyweight annular bearings that appeared to last indefinitely if kept well greased. While the machine was not innovative in the fitting of the standard De Dion type engine or in its overall configuration, its massive components ensured that it would not disintegrate during the first few dozen miles of travel as would many of its contemporaries. It may well be noted that the rugged construction of the developed prototype presaged generally sturdy and heavyweight constructions that have ever been the hallmark of Harley-Davidson products.

In the beginning both Harley and Davidson had agreed that the new machine would be named 'Harley-Davidson', as confirmed both from their own later statements, and in the recollection of several contemporaries. The mention of Harley first was in recognition of his original concept of the overall design and of his development of the prototypes. The opinion was later reinforced by the other Davidson brothers who later joined in the formal founding of the company. In any case, the wording 'Harley-Davidson' was more agreeably euphonious than 'Davidson-Harley'.

Now that the ultimate design had been finalized, it was at once painfully apparent to Harley and Davidson that they lacked sufficient capital to undertake any semblance of commercial production. In fact, through economic necessity, they were still committed to their regular employment to pay their own living expenses, the whole project being a very limited 'backyard' type of venture.

At this juncture, the elder Davidson, William C., the Scottish immigrant carpenter, erected a 10 x 15 foot wooden shed in the backyard of the family home, which housed a lathe and a drill press, both bought second-hand, and powered by a small gasoline engine. The legend 'Harley-Davidson Motor Co.' was painted on the door as an optimistic announcement that a new name was being added to the ranks of American transportation history.

What with the completion of the prototype machine, Harley decided that he would greatly benefit from additional training in the formal study of automotive engineering. While it was obvious that he possessed the natural mechanical ability to create a practical motor vehicle, it was still more obvious, most of all to himself, that he could have arrived at his ultimate goal much more quickly had he enjoyed a more formal background in the subject. He was also rightly convinced that he could better serve the now infant company's projected future with a more solid foundation of expanded engineering knowledge. Therefore, in the fall of 1903, he enrolled in the Engineering Department of the nearby University of Wisconsin at Madison. With but meager cash reserves, he paid his expenses by waiting on tables at a fraternity house and undertaking small, part-time engineering assignments at local manufacturing concerns. In the meantime, Arthur carried on at home with the individual hand assembly of motorcycles, with the aid of a few part-time helpers who were paid a small salary on a piecework basis. When technical problems arose, Harley was able to advise his partner as his own knowledge progressed. Arthur built two motorcycles that winter to special order, the assembly being financed by charging half the purchase price as a down payment, with the balance on delivery.

With more orders being placed by interested customers, who had learned of the new make's reliability by word of mouth, Walter Davidson quit his job at the railroad shop in the spring of 1904 to devote his full time to motorcycle production. Up until this time, Arthur had been in full charge of the shop in addition to his regular employment, and both he and Harley agreed that another hand was needed if the project was to move forward. Also, with more orders coming in, it was now expedient to fill them as quickly as possible, otherwise the whole venture would readily die on the vine. The size of the shed was now doubled to 10 x 30 feet, and four part-time helpers were taken on to assist Walter in machine building. Arthur, who still remained in his regular employment, now devoted all his spare time to sales promotion of the new machine. Three machines were built and sold during the summer and fall of 1904, five more being assembled during the following year.

It now became evident that the backyard shed at the Davidson home was too small to permit further expansion, so it was decided to purchase a factory site in the industrial area of Milwaukee. Still hampered by lack of working capital, yet with an inbred Scottish aversion to paying high risk interest rates to commercial banks, the partners were fortunate in being able to enlist the aid of a well-to-do relative. James McLay, a maternal uncle, who had emigrated to the States some years before the Davidson family, agreed to loan the money for the purchase of the land. At that time residing near Madison, Wisconsin, he had reputedly prospered handsomely in land speculation, and also followed the avocation of bee keeping. In due course a large lot was secured at the corner of 27th and Chestnut Streets, conveniently adjacent to a spur line of the Chicago, Milwaukee and St.Paul Railroad. The name of the latter street was ultimately changed to Juneau Avenue, giving it later world wide significance as the traditional home of Harley-Davidson. A small, two-storey wooden building was erected on the rear of the property which afforded a considerable expansion of working area. Production facilities were greatly enhanced with the acquisition of more tooling. The result was that 49 machines were built and sold to residents of the Milwaukee area during 1906.

This encouraging increase in sales prompted Arthur to at long last quit his job as a pattern maker and to devote his full time to sales promotion. During 1907 his efforts in canvassing individual potential customers as well as the inducing of several local bicycle dealers to take up franchises saw sales triple to 152 units for that year.

It might well be mentioned that while public interest in motorcycles had increased steadily since the initial appearance of the first pioneer machines at the turn of the century, their sales and marketing were as yet a somewhat uncertain proposition. By this time there were a number of fairly soundly conceived designs on the market and also a number of very inferior products. Some were placed on the market without adequate prototype testing, while others were cheap copies of already successful machines. As the extension of the bicycle, the earliest motorcycle dealers were quite naturally for the most part proprietors of established bicycle shops. While obviously thoroughly familiar with bicycle mechanics, only a few of these had little more than a rudimentary knowledge concerning the intricacies of the gasoline engine. Their ability to aid their customers in the upkeep or repair of their machines was frequently woefully inadequate.

On the other hand, the widespread public interest in the newly emerging automobile was of direct benefit to motorcycle sales, as most of the young men of the time, yearning for personal transportation, had not the means to purchase the former. The cheap mass-produced car had yet to appear on the market.

During the years of their prototype experiments, both Harley and Davidson had become well aware of the emerging problems of sales and marketing, and it was Arthur's early conclusion that the building of a strong retail dealer's organization to support any projected mass production of the product was essential.

The earliest successful motorcycle manufacturer to build a strong dealership was George M.Hendee of Indian, who had already gained much experience in the field as bicycle manufacturer. In the promotion of motorcycles, he not only relied on his own bicycle dealerships for a nucleus, but made sure that they possessed the mechanical aptitude to quickly adapt to the servicing and repair of motorcycles. Other early manufacturers who followed this same well tried formula were the Pope concern, already with a vast sales network of bicycle dealers, and the George N.Pierce Company, who shared the same background.

Arthur wisely followed these well-proven procedures in his promotional activities in the Milwaukee area. He was particularly careful to make a thorough investigation of a prospective dealer. He not only gained a first hand opinion of his personality, but could observe his work habits, his ability to handle customers, as well as the extent of his standing and reputation in his immediate community.

Now that he had thoroughly convinced himself that he had arrived at the proper formula for retail expansion, Arthur next suggested that the company be incorporated under the laws of the state of Wisconsin. Harley and his brother Walter immediately agreed to his proposal, and so on September 22, 1907, the Harley-Davidson Motor Company of Milwaukee became a corporate body. In the still infant organization, Walter was named President and General Manager, Arthur was Secretary and General Sales Manager, and the still absent Harley, pursuing his studies at the University, was named Chief Engineer and Designer, as well as filling the post of Treasurer.

In order to strengthen their manufacturing procedure, the eldest Davidson brother, William A., then thirty six years of age, was invited to join the company as Vice President and Works Manager. As expert tool maker and metal fabricator, and possessing an extensive practical knowledge of metallurgy, he had also accumulated valuable experience in shop practice as the toolroom foreman for the local

A representation of an early 1903 H-D single. Now on view in the Rodney C.Gott Museum at the AMF-H-D assembly plant at York, Pennsylvania.

repair branch of the Chicago, Milwaukee and St.Paul Railroad. Described as a large, heavily built man, slow of speech and deliberate of thought, he was known to possess the qualities needed to handle and oversee the activities of the usual rough-hewn, hard-drinking men that characteristically manned the industrial and manufacturing plants of that era. As a paradox to his later stature within the industry he remained a lifelong non-motorcyclist.

As an aside to William A.'s joining the company, the incident of his birth later became an interesting vignette of H-D history. Born in 1870, he was wont to refer proudly to close associates about his Scottish ancestry and to his birth in Aberdeen. In later years, copy writers for company literature solemnly affirmed that the Davidsons had all been born in the United States, specifically in Milwaukee. This somewhat trivial point became the focal point of testimony in a government tariff hearing some forty years later.

During the first year of corporate organization, titles meant little, with all of the partners lending a hand along with their staff in whatever undertaking demanded attention. In later years, all four were referred to in company literature as the Founders of the company, apparently as a courtesy to their joint participation in corporate organization that more or less officially marked the entrance of the company into the industry.

The machine with which the company now proposed to seriously attempt a penetration of the soon-to-be stormy American motorcycle market, was still the basic 1903 model that had been produced in very small numbers up to that time with but a few very minor improvements as indicated by trial and error in actual use. It was wisely decided to continue manufacture with a one-model program, in spite of the fact that most of the several dozen concerns now in the field offered different sizes of machine. Arthur was adamant in reminding possible critics that the present model was a sound all-around machine capable of a variety of applications and employment, and that concentration on one model rationalized manufacturing procedures and helped to keep costs and consequent retail pricing highly competitive. This proved to be sound reasoning, as what with many small and lightly financed manufacturers in the field, the building of too many diverse models often proved their undoing. Coupled with this, the science of costing, production control and marketing analysis was still highly underdeveloped.

To the bewilderment and confusion of potential buyers, the motorcycle market was overcrowded with a myriad of small manufacturers, many of whom were making extravagant claims for their products. Added to this, a brisk component part and supply trade had come into being, and it was possible at that time to purchase sufficient frames, forks, wheels, fuel tanks, and even several types of engines, often of doubtful quality, to actually assemble complete motorcycles. These were supplied by firms such as the Harry O. Geer Company of St. Louis or the Rochester Cycle Supply of New York. The availability allowed almost anyone who could purchase a few part sets to produce his own make with a few hand tools, with his own name affixed to the fuel tank. Mostly flimsy affairs, these were seemingly always able to attract a few buyers.

With an already established if limited reputation for building a sound machine, the infant company next grappled with the most pressing technical problem now facing the industry, namely that of front suspension. Almost without exception, the pioneer machines of the 'clip-on' era utilized conventional unsprung pedal cycle forks, with a single crown passing through the head lug. This, of course, made for a very harsh ride, considering the roads of the period, the comfort of the rider being inadequately taken care of by the doubtful resiliency of a standard bicycle-type saddle. These problems were later compounded by the increasing weight and the increased power of the more latterly developed machines. Perhaps the most serious complication was that the enhanced stresses and increased vibration syndromes made more imminent the danger of fracture of the fork legs from the molecular disintegration of the metal.

William Harley was evidently quite familiar with these problems, as the 1903 prototype model was fitted with very strong forks. Numerous other designers, such as Carl Oscar Hedstrom of Indian, fitted cartridge-type forks, as did some of his imitators, which offered a fair degree of spring travel. Their disadvantage, however, was the constantly varying wheelbase which made for uncertain handling on rough roads, and in cornering. Harley's answer to the problem was conceived while he was in his senior year at the University, and was ultimately based on the leading link principle. It consisted of a pair of solid unsprung legs supported by a triple crown lug at the steering head. The sprung legs were positioned just ahead and parallel to these, and were attached to the steering head above by a single crown just above the triple crown of the fixed legs. The two sets of legs were connected at the bottom by a pair of forged steel links to form the pivot joint. The sprung legs were joined over the top of the mudguard by a steel forging that formed a bridge. The spring action was controlled by four long coil springs enclosed within the tubes forming the moveable fork, the upper pair for load, the lower for rebound. The wheel axle carried just forward of the sprung blades lower attachment designated the descriptive term of the system.

The advantage of this arrangement was its rigidity, made as it was from sturdy heavy gauge components, low stress factors on the springs, adequate wheel travel on impact, and a non-varying wheelbase. While the device worked very well during the years when high speeds were not yet attained, certain deficiencies appeared during the classic era when high performance models were developed. The handling could become uncertain in the event of even slight misalignment, and a positively dangerous wheel wobble occurred in certain subsequent models. As the original design was carried forward on nearly all of the production machines for the ensuing four decades, it was this single feature that ultimately became the subject of perhaps more controversy than any other facet of H-D design.

With the formal incorporation of the company, it was now obvious that an effective advertising campaign must be instituted. The story is told that one Walter Dunlap, a member of a newly organized Milwaukee advertising firm of Klaus, Van Peterson and Dunlap, was contacted with this end in view. As neither firm was as yet in a strong financial position, the work was contracted for an a pay-as-we-go basis. The Company continued to retain this firm for the next fifty years, not only to provide media exposure, but in the preparation of catalogs and dealer aids as well.

Factory floor space was slightly enlarged in the spring of 1908 to 4,760 square feet, and production was tripled over the previous year with 456 machines assembled by 36 production employees. In order to keep abreast of the latest manufacturing methods, Walter Davidson enrolled in a local trade school to learn the latest test methods of heat treating metal, in turn imparting these to the production staff. He next journeyed to Chicago, in company with William Harley, to acquire the latest techniques of oxygen-acetylene welding, which were also incorporated into production.

Arthur had by this time traveled extensively throughout the Eastern United States demonstrating the latest H-D which now incorporated the new spring fork. Dealerships in New York, Chicago, Philadelphia, Atlanta, Newark, and other large cities had now been franchised. The West Coast was well covered by active dealerships in Los Angeles, San Francisco, and Seattle. With characteristic Scottish caution, he was careful to select only those to represent the company who, in his estimation, possessed the mechanical aptitude to set up and manage repair and service facilities, as well as the necessary business acumen to insure success in the venture. It has been reported that Arthur on numerous occasions expressed anguish that he often felt obliged to refuse certain H-D enthusiasts who clamoured for franchises but who in his judgment lacked the necessary qualifications properly to represent the company or service the product.

It was about this time that a range of bicycles was added to the line, the machines being built under contract with the H-D label and color by the famous Butler Brothers, who were wholesale suppliers located in Chicago. It was reasoned that as long as most motorcycle dealers also handled bicycles, the company could enlarge its representation and add to sales volume by supplying pedal cycles as well. As the large supplier could furnish the bicycles at a lower cost, and as the H-D Company had insufficient space to fabricate bicycles anyway, the arrangement proved both advantageous and profitable.

By this time there were about 36 significant motorcycle manufacturers in the United States. Indian, sparked by the able management of George M. Hendee, was the largest, and was complementing its expanding sales with continuous factory expansion. Excelsior, backed by the Schwinn Bicycle empire and Pope, with similar backing, ranked next, followed by Iver Johnson, Merkel, Reading Standard and Wagner, all of whom built good quality machines. The day of the flimsy 'clip on' was now happily past, and the motorcycle was at long last coming into its own as everyman's personal transportation, the cheap car as yet still in the future. Mechanical innovations such as the cam operated inlet valve and all-chain drive, together with reliable clutches, were now appearing, although most makes adhered to the V or flat belt drive. The motorcycle was still mainly a utilitarian vehicle, and H-D, whose origins lay within this concept, sought to enhance the ruggedness and reliability of their product. A commendable sidelight to this dedication was their desire to make the motorcycle more acceptable to the general non-motoring public, and to this end they endeavored to remove the main public objection to powered two wheelers: the usually offensive exhaust note. Even the earliest models were fitted with efficient silencers and in keeping with their now traditional light gray color, came to be known as 'The Silent Gray Fellow'.

In line with this early utilitarian concept of H-D machines, Arthur spent much time in canvassing various commercial and government agencies where the use of motorcycles could be applicable. In 1909 he attended the annual convention of the Rural Free Delivery Mail Carriers of America held that year in Chicago. Motorcycles had recently found favor in rural mail delivery, due to their economy and ability to negotiate the country roads of the period. Up until this time, Iver-Johnson, Jefferson, and the Wagner machines, all simple but sturdy conventional types with belt drive, had been the favored makes for this employment. Arthur took a demonstration machine to the meeting, which was favorably received, and the Advertising Department subsequently contracted for large advertising displays in the monthly *RFD News* magazine. These efforts resulted in H-D machines being purchased in large numbers by the mail carriers. Clarence Chamberlain, who was later to gain fame as a transatlantic aviator, was for a time a mail carrier in Dennison, Iowa, and rode H-D machines for several years. Other large commercial organizations, such as the Bell Telephone Company, who eventually put 700 machines into service, and numerous other public utility organizations and law enforcement groups purchased H-D machines.

While at its inception the motorcycle was essentially a utility vehicle, the growth of motorcycle sport was inevitable, due if nothing else to the inherent form of the machine. Even during the earliest pioneer days, sporting bicyclists and clubmen projected its suitability for competition events, such as

The classic photograph of Walter C.Davidson after winning the 1908 Long Island Endurance Run. The machine is almost identical to the first 1903 models except for the sprung leading link fork.

speed and reliability trials, endurance runs, as well as out-and-out racing. As early as 1903, members of the New York Motorcycle Club, first formed as an auxiliary to the New York Bicycle Club, met with members of the nearby Alpha Motorcycle Club to found the Federation of American Motorcyclists. It was projected that this organization could serve the interests of motorcyclists at the national level, as well as to organize and regulate various competition events in the future. While the foundations of a national organization were now formally inaugurated, it was not until 1908 or 1909 that the FAM had any real influence, when significant numbers of motorcyclists were active to give it impetus.

Up until this time, the H-D Company ignored all types of competition, although numbers of H-D machines were entered in various events by private enthusiasts. There are numerous accounts of H-D victories in early issues of bicycle magazines, most of which by this time contained a motorcycle section. Their successes were generally due to their inherent ruggedness and dependability even though they were certainly not the fastest when compared with contemporary makes. Many of these early speed or reliability contests were of the hare-and-hound variety. A pack of fast but not too reliable machines out-distanced the field at the start, only to be ultimately passed when stranded at the roadside by a plodding H-D.

In June 1908, the FAM announced the first large event of its kind to be held in the United States, billed simply as the 'Endurance Run'. Planned as a two-day affair, it was to start at Catskill, New York, proceed to Brooklyn, and finish with the 180 mile circuit of Long Island. It was at this juncture that President Walter Davidson decided that H-D could not afford to ignore any form of competition any longer, especially as the other factories were boasting of competition victories in the trade press. Feeling confident of being able to make at least a good showing, and with an eye to the possible advertising value, he shipped a standard model to New York as an official entrant. No less than eighty four riders representing twenty two makers of machines were flagged off at dawn on June 29th. Stiff gradients and badly rutted country roads eliminated nearly half the field by the first day. Walter was still in the running by nightfall, however, and the next morning checked out with the other survivors for the circuit of Long Island. Timing his arrival at the various check points with meticulous care, he successfully completed the run. When the final scores were tabulated, he was found to have made a perfect 1000 point record. As a complimentary gesture, the competition committee awarded him five additional points, making a perfect score plus five.

Not content with this outstanding victory, Walter remained in New York to compete in the FAM Economy Run which was staged the following week in a hilly country area adjacent to Roslyn, Long

Island. Walter again racked up a sensational victory, as with a quart of fuel in the tank, he won with a calculated 188 miles to the gallon average. Much was made of these two victories in the trade press, both for their own merits, but especially in view of the fact that it was the first time that the company had officially supported formal competition. Established dealers reported increased sales as a result, and several new franchises were awarded on the Eastern seaboard.

Meanwhile, back in Milwaukee, William Harley returned to the factory after graduating with honors from the University with his degree in Automotive Engineering. He was gratified that both sales and production had materially increased since the previous season, augmented in no small degree by the recent inauguration of the spring fork which greatly enhanced rider comfort. In the anticipation of further plant expansion, the Production Department personnel was expanded with the hiring of George Nordberg, an experienced tool and die maker, as William Davidson's production assistant. His association was almost immediately reinforced by the addition of another associate, one Frederick Barr, another competent machinist and shop expert. Both men were to figure prominently in H-D affairs for some years thereafter.

Harley's immediate plans now called for the updating of the original 1903 prototype machine which had been in continuous production for the past five seasons with but minor improvements. The new prototype was laid out with a longer and heavier frame, together with a strengthened spring fork, which increased the wheelbase from 51 inches to 57 inches. It also featured a larger single cylinder engine of 3-5/16 inch bore and a 4 inch stroke for an increased piston displacement of 35 cubic inches, still based on the original De Dion principle with an atmospheric inlet valve. The new engine was rated at 5 hp and now increased the top speed to 50 mph. Designated as the Model 5-35, it was to be introduced for the 1909 sales season.

Also subjected to prototype development was a new V twin model. The identical 5-35 cylinders were fitted, but with a slightly reduced bore to give it a rating of 7 hp. Belt drive was retained for both models, control still being effected by the standard idler pulley working against its lower run, just behind the engine pulley.

Then, as now, there was a constant search for more speed and power. What with the now substantial increase in motorcycle sales generally, the leaders in the industry rightly concluded that the vast distances and generally bad roads still in existence in most parts of the United States indicated the development of heavier and more powerful machines.

An interesting feature of the prototype twin was the fitting of a mechanical inlet valve. This fitting was a modification of the overhead De Dion type, the action being activated by a tappet running off a timing pinion in the engine case. The cylinders were set at a 45° angle, establishing the H-D commitment to this configuration in all subsequent V twins.

It was during this period that most of the American manufacturers of any consequence were offering V twin models, most of which soon centered on the single liter or 61 cubic inch displacement. Many subsequent American motorcycle historians somewhat lightly described the V twin configuration as the most handy expedient to produce a larger engine than the single cylinder type that would be most easily accommodated in the standard bicycle type frame still in use, but the arrangement had much to recommend it. With the addition of a mere 30 to 35 pounds of extra weight (the poundage of most of the single cylinder assemblies of these days), the hp output could be more than doubled. In addition, the relatively narrow angle of the cylinders allowed for a short manifold coupling for the carburetor intake, which simplified induction problems. On the other hand, the almost universal adoption of the V twin by American motorcycle engineers that set the fashion for the industry at once imposed certain technical limitations. The first was that the narrow angle of the cylinders made for an unequal firing sequence, that of 42, 45, or 50° plus or minus the 360° of crankshaft rotation that inevitably led to an inbuilt vibration syndrome that was almost impossible to counteract. In addition, the narrow cylinder angle reduced the possibility of a large cylinder bore, increased piston displacement and subsequent better power output until then being inexorably mated to lengthening the stroke. The ultimate result was that critical piston speeds of over 4,000 feet per minute were imposed on this type of engine. In practice, few V twin engines could be run at speeds much over 7,000 rpm without encountering critical inertial forces, and the American designers at once limited the ultimate power development by following this type of design. On the other side of the coin, the V twin engine showed remarkable torque development at very moderate engine speeds, characteristically in the 2,300-4,000 rpm range, which made for a slow turning, long lasting engine, that was better suited for usage over long distances and would provide a high mileage between overhauls as demanded by American operating conditions.

The prototype twin was subjected to thorough testing, and as cleared for production was finalized with an engine whose displacement was slightly enlarged to the now standard 61 cubic inch piston displacement. For the 1909 season a Schebler carburetor was used, a proprietary instrument fitted to most American motorcycles, to replace the former H-D type. The high production rate of the

Schebler carburetor allowed it to be fitted with a considerable saving in cost. Both the single and twin for 1909 were now fitted with a more gracefully contoured fuel tank formed of two halves that enclosed the top frame tubes, and all engine controls were of the Bowden wire type, enclosed within the handlebars.

The company's official competition activities for that year included the entry of Walter Davidson and three other riders, Crolius Lacey, Frank Ollerman, and Robert E. Underhill in the FAM-sponsored endurance run from Cleveland, Ohio, to Indianapolis, Indiana. All four experienced no mechanical troubles and ended the run with perfect scores, winning the Team Prize for the company.

By the summer of 1910, motorcycle sport had become a fixture in the motoring scene. Out-and-out racing events had been held in many of the short 1/8th and 1/6th mile indoor board tracks or velodromes that had been previously built for bicycle racing. As the power and speed of the racing motorcycles increased, these proved unsuitable, if not downright dangerous. To improve matters, Jack Prince, the New Jersey engineer who had superintended the construction of many of the early velodromes, built now 1/4 or 1/3 mile 'motordromes' in most of the country's larger cities during the next decade. Racing circuits were established in various geographical sections of the country and a point system enabled regional championships to be established. As the motion picture was still a limited form of entertainment, radio was as yet undeveloped, and professional athletics were as yet not well organized, motor sport contests were now at the height of their popularity, especially as both the automobile and the motorcycle were still somewhat of a novelty for most people.

Dirt track racing at many of the county fair horse tracks also became soaringly popular, as fair-attending patrons offered a captive audience to the race promoters. This condition also explains why road racing never became popular in the United States, as there was no practical means of crowd control to create a paying audience along a spreadout road course.

Motorcycle racing continued to gain in popularity, and the leading factories supporting it with both specialied machines and paid professional riders included Excelsior, Indian, Pope, Merkel, Reading Standard, and Thor. Other than supporting endurance runs and reliability trials, H-D continued to withhold support from this type of competition.

A 1910 H-D 9-35 Model single at the 1974 Classic and Antique Motorcycle club rally at Visalia, California. *(George Hays)*.

A 1910 9-35 Model in original condition from the Bud Ekins collection. The belt pulleys and belt are missing. *(Alisha Tamburri).*

To cater to the burgeoning interest in motorcycling, numerous trade publications came into being. During the pioneer era, most bicycle magazines featured sections devoted to motorcycling. Among these were *Bicycling World* which later sponsored *Motorcycling Review.* Then there was *The Motorcycle Illustrated* and *Motorcycling,* published in Chicago. *The Western Bicyclist and Motorcyclist,* published in Los Angeles, later became *The Motorcyclist,* and ultimately became the last surviving trade publication during the lean years of US motorcycling in the 1930s. During their heyday, all of the trade journals were well supported by the various motorcycle and accessory manufacturers through their voluminous advertising.

H-D continued their two model single and twin line through 1910 and 1911, but for the 1912 season an innovation offered for both models was the fitting of an optional all-chain drive, although the belt was still available for a couple of more years. Also, the single was now fitted with a mechanical inlet valve, already standard on the original twin, which offered the advantage of higher engine speeds and enhanced power development. This change in design, while still based on the pioneer De Dion-Bouton configuration, was now to be seen in several leading American makes, and with the overhead rocker mechanism, became popularly known as the 'pocket valve' type. The side-by-side valve arrangement, offered by Indian after 1915 along with other makes, became known as the 'flat head' — terminology which persisted in domestic parlance for many years thereafter.

In reference to the chain drive, William Harley, who had come to recognize its mechanical superiority, refused to incorporate it into his designs until he had perfected what he considered to be a reliable clutch. While some competitive designs had sought to eliminate the all-or-nothing aspect of the best drive by fitting various examples of the proprietory Eclipse clutch which was designed to be fitted to the engine pulley, it was of somewhat light construction and its longevity questionable. Harley's answer to the problem was the fitting of a sturdy multiplate clutch with some 76 square inches of plate surface, inside the rear wheel hub, which was activated by a rod and bell crank arrangement whose control lever was mounted on the right tank side.

To start the engine, the machine was placed on the rear stand and the engine cranked by turning the rear wheel with the pedalling gear. After warming up, the clutch was disengaged, and the machine was rolled off the stand. The rider then got under way by manipulating the throttle and clutch lever. The new clutch proved rugged enough to stand up to the demands of heavy start-and-stop traffic, and was a decisive factor in making the new model a popular seller, especially for commercial work. The new model was designated the 9-35 — the 9 referring to the chronological year of development, and 35 to the cubic inches of engine displacement.

Another 1912 innovation for the enhancement of rider comfort was the introduction of the patent 'Ful-Floteing' seat post. While the negotiation of rough roads, (usually the rule of that day rather than the exception,) had been lately aided by the now universal fitting of some type of spring fork, the usual bicycle type saddle offered but little resiliency to the rider's posterior. The new H-D system included the spring loading of the seat post with a 14 inch coil spring inside the seat tube, the usual saddle springs being retained for initial deflection and rebound.

In the meantime, Arthur Davidson had been devoting most of his time to the further building of a strong dealer organization. An additional intensive visit to the Far West during 1912 and 1913 resulted in enhanced representation in California, Oregon, and Washington, as well as in Arizona and New Mexico, where the possibilities of nearly all-season riding enhanced motorcycling popularity. The im-

An official Company photograph of the Founders, taken about 1910. From left: William A.Davidson, Walter C.Davidson, Arthur Davidson, and William S.Harley. *(The H-D Motor Company).*

proved twin was especially popular in the West, due to the vast distances in that area. In order to improve communication between the factory and the dealers, a house organ called *The Dealer* was circulated in leaflet form. Hints on selling techniques were discussed together with lavish praise of the various features of H-D machines in comparison with other makes. Couched in rather quaint and florid Victorian prose, the effort was an initial attempt to standardize factory sales policies. Very few copies of this publication survive today, as a large supply of back issues surviving in storage at the factory were destroyed in 1926.

By 1913, motorcycling in the United States was approaching the zenith of its popularity. About 35 makes were represented, offering both touring and utility type machines, including a couple of well-designed fours, the Henderson and the Pierce, together with the previously developed V-twins and singles, and a few ultralightweights of the two and four-stroke type. Indian was still the acknowledged sales leader of the industry, producing over 31,000 of the 71,000-odd machines made that year. H-D was already mounting a strong challenge, however. In 1911, H-D had enlarged its factory space to 80,000 square feet, and with 480 production employees had assembled over 6,000 machines. With its now strengthened financial position through increasing sales, the management, overcoming their original aversion toward paying bankers' interest rates, obtained a substantial loan from Milwaukee's Marshall and Illsley Bank to effect this expansion. During 1912, the Company again increased its floor area to 187,000 square feet and with over 1,000 production employees on the payroll produced over 11,000 units.

Aside from the soaring popularity of motorcycle sport at the motordromes, board tracks, and county fair tracks, the motorcycle was now well entrenched in the transportation scene for both utility and commercial purposes. Although automobile production was steadily increasing, most makes were still too expensive for the man of average means. While Henry Ford had launched his immortal Model T in 1909, its production had not yet attained its later volume, and the selling price of $850 was still nearly three times that of the average good solo motorcycle. In addition, the sidecar was now coming into popularity, and for an additional $75.00 or so it could offer limited transport for the family man. Furthermore, the early automobile still offered a formidable mechanical challenge, both in operation and maintenance. A motorcycle, much less complicated and with exposed moving parts, remained as a less complex form of motoring.

While the H-D factory still declined to provide private owners with official sponsorship in competition, personal machines were now being entered by private owners in numerous endurance and road racing contests, often with very creditable results.

The San Jose California Road Race held on December 8th 1912, saw Ray Watkins and Ben Torres on standard twins fitted with Flexi sidecars, a proprietary make having a hinged chassis that allowed the wheel to bank with the machine on corners. Both contestants averaged better than 49 mph over a rain-drenched and very muddy course.

In the 3rd annual running of the Bakersfield California Road Race, Frank Lightner took another standard twin over a very rough course for first place, arriving at the finish nearly an hour ahead of the next competitor.

A prominent Eastern fixture in those days was the 225 mile Harrisburg to Philadelphia and return contest. Entrants included factory teams sponsored by Indian, Merkel, Pope and Thor. The private H-D entrants, again without any official support, totaled eight riders. All finished the course with a 1-2-3 win, all the others placing.

In the Fall of 1913, the first of a series of desert road races through the Southwest was scheduled under official FAM sponsorship. Announced as an endurance event, the course was laid out over what has been aptly described as the worst roads on the North American continent. The route selected was between San Diego, California and Phoenix, Arizona, approximately 445 miles. It followed the isolated desert tracks first travelled by the covered wagons of the pioneer immigrants 65 years before, the only really passable one being the last leg from Caliente to Phoenix, a distance of 94 miles. In addition to the almost impassable condition of the road, if it could be called such, the contestants risked hunger, thirst, heat prostration and possible death from exposure in case of a breakdown. There was also a real danger of annihilation at the hands of roving bands of renegade Apache Indians who still roamed the region, as well as from Mexican guerillas who often raided the isolated ranches north of the border to steal cattle. The coming contest was given much publicity in the trade press, and was the object of much comment in the general media. After all, the earlier frontier days were still a timely topic of general interest, as many people yet living had participated in the great westward migration as children or young adults.

The first race was planned as a three day event, starting on October 31st with overnight stops at Yuma, 116 miles from San Diego, Caliente, 110 miles to the east, the last leg being the 94 miles to Phoenix. Eighteen riders representing Excelsior, Harley-Davidson, Indian, and Thor were flagged off at 2 minute intervals from the public square in San Diego. The H-D riders, Arthur Holmes and Frank Meock, were the only private entrants.

The first fifty miles offered little difficulty, as the track here was in fair condition. Ahead lay the dreaded Mammoth Wash, the sandy desert area that was the graveyard of many immigrant wagons whose remains still could be seen. Cannonball Baker on his two-speed Indian was eliminated here by engine failure. His teammate, Paul Derkum, forged on, aided by the fact that he had cemented small section car tires on his wheel rims, and made the first leg to Yuma in 7 hours 11 minutes. He also was first into Phoenix, followed by Indian riders Ray Smith and Harry Weitzell. John Long, Excelsior, and Roy Artley, Thor, placed 4th, followed by Lorenzo Boido, Indian. Art Holmes and Frank Meock trailed in together in last place.

Much was made of the results in the trade press. It was pointed out that almost all of the machines finished, in spite of the severity of both the course and the heat. Indeed, the modern machines of today would be hard pressed to duplicate their performance under such arduous conditions. While Holmes and Meock placed last, they were severely handicapped by the fact that their standard machines were single geared. Both were quick to inform the factory of this fact, together with the

June 1912   Cosmopolitan Magazine

This Harley-Davidson Does the Work of Three Horses

THE Home Telephone Company, of Portland, Indiana, say in part:—"*Used our Harley-Davidson Motorcycle in trouble Department for two months, doing the work of three horses. It has traveled 2,400 miles, has given entire satisfaction, and the expense of gasoline and oil is so small as to hardly be worth consideration.*"
HOME TELEPHONE CO.

We have a large number of similar expressions from Butchers, Grocers, Jewelers, Department Stores, Gas and Electric Companies, etc. These firms have found the Harley-Davidson the most rapid and economical means of delivery and transportation. What the Harley-Davidson is doing for them, it will do for you. THE

Harley-Davidson

Is the Most Desirable Motorcycle for General Use

It is the Most Comfortable. It is the only motorcycle built with a Ful-Floteing Seat. This seat floats or suspends the weight of the rider between 24 inches of concealed springs. These springs assimilate all the vibrations, jolts and jars.

It is the Most Economical. The Harley-Davidson holds the World's official economy record, established at the National F. A. M. Meet, July 3, 1908.

It is the Most Reliable. The Harley-Davidson is the only machine ever awarded a diamond medal and a perfect score of one thousand points with a plus five points additional for its super-excellent performance by the Federation of American Motorcyclists.

It is the Most Durable. Harley-Davidson Motorcycles sold ten years ago are still running and giving satisfaction.

Easiest Starting. It is the only machine fitted with Free-Wheel Control. This control permits starting and stopping by the mere shifting of a lever. In writing for catalog state whether for commercial or private use, and we will send additional data.

HARLEY-DAVIDSON MOTOR COMPANY
249 B. STREET :: MILWAUKEE :: WISCONSIN

An example of the large scale advertising campaign launched by the H-D Company during 1911 and 1912.

opinion that their engines were somewhat short on power when compared to the others, although they ran faultlesly over the entire distance. Holmes, in later commenting on the lack of factory support, bitterly castigated Walter Davidson as 'too tight fisted to even offer to pay for their fuel, oil and tires . . . .'

H-D quite naturally received much publicity in regard to this and other contemporary contests, especially where private entrants often made a very good showing, even if first place wins were not forthcoming in all cases. As a paradox, the factory still piously proclaimed in their advertising that they did not support racing or competition in any form. In the September, 1913 issue of *Pacific Motorcyclist,* it was stated in a full page advertisement — 'Don't blame us when Harley-Davidson wins a race meet, because we do not believe in racing. We do not employ any racing men. We build no special racing machines, but the results speak for themselves.'

This somewhat high-handed attitude quite naturally antagonized substantial numbers of H-D enthusiasts who were competition minded. They had lately been entering various contests at their own expense, without the usual complimentary spare parts, fuel, oil, and tires that were generously supplied to the entrants of other competing makes, who also often enjoyed the help of factory mechanics in preparing their machines. During the winter of 1913, a few franchised H-D dealers began offering certain subsidies out of their own pocket to mollify those riders who were helping to glorify the marque.

At the same moment, and as later events proved, it was during the Company's public protestations against participating in competition that the top management was actually debating the advisability of offering official support to racing. It was now all too apparent that a large segment of the motorcycling public was competition-minded, as witness the large crowds generally seen at most race meets, and whether or not the bread-and-butter roadsters resembled the racing machines, the name of a winner on the tank sides was a powerful sales stimulator.

According to the composite recollections of several veteran Company employees, Harley and the Davidsons actually decided to take affirmative action during the late spring of 1913. The erstwhile plodding H-D was at long last to be committed to the perilous arena of motorcycle sport. To implement this decision, William Harley as Chief Engineer, offered one William (Bill) Ottaway the position of Assistant Engineer in his department. Ottaway was then employed by The Aurora Automatic Machine Company of Aurora, Illinois, as Chief Engineer in charge of design and development in their Thor Motorcycle Division. A pioneer automobile and motorcycle owner, as a natural mechanic and practical engineer he quickly became a self-taught innovator in engine design and tuning. Joining the Aurora organization in 1909 following their emergence from the clip-on period, he was responsible for the development of the famous 'White Thors', which were not only respectable road machines but in racing form quickly made a name for themselves in the early motordrome and horse tracks. One of Ottaway's assistants in the engineering department was one Albert G. Crocker, a former student of automotive engineering at the University of Illinois, subsequently to be employed in a similar capacity with Indian, and a later figure in the motorcycle industry whom we shall meet again.

There has been much speculation among serious motorcycle historians concerning the relative positions of both Harley and Ottaway during this period of H-D history. As the original developer and later official corporate head of the Company's Engineering Department, Harley was quite naturally responsible for the development of the H-D motorcycle up to this point in time. On this basis, it would appear that he might well have had the technical ability to proceed with the subsequent evolvement of more powerful and sophisticated engines with which to meet the challenge of the now spirited competition activities within the industry. On the other hand, he has been described by contemporaries as a plodding and methodical technician, proceeding cautiously, and indeed, up to this point, still preoccupied with refining the original concepts of De Dion Bouton. Although capable of turning out refined creations built on the work of others, it is evident that he lacked that certain flair of originality that has historically accompanied the efforts of less orthodox but more flamboyant engineers. To his lasting credit, Harley was at least able personally to face his own limitations in the matter, and seek association with another designer who had, in four short seasons, made an enviable position for himself as the designer of potent racing machinery.

The story goes that Ottaway accepted the offer immediately, agreeing to limit his efforts to the improvement of the basic and well tried H-D engines, without the option of putting the factory to the expense of tooling up for entirely new designs.

While Ottaway undertook immediate experiments in the engine department with speed tuning, Harley set about the task of developing an improved transmission system. The single gear concept for a high powered heavyweight V twin that had become the accepted American motorcycle design was now obsolete, as no engine could be expected to make efficient use of its potential power development without change speed gears. Then there was the added onus that with the now growing popularity of the sidecar, the single gear could not be successfully applied where an extra load was imposed, without

A 1912 belt drive 35 cu.in. single in original condition. The Company now was manufacturing two models, with the twin in limited production. (*George Hays*).

lowering the sprocket ratios to the point where the overall performance would be nothing short of pathetic. Harley's answer to the problem was a heavyweight, cluster-type, two-speed gear located in the rear wheel hub, which was combined with his already successful clutch, whose efficiency had done much to enhance the make's reputation during the past two seasons. The gear was offered for both the twin and single cylinder models, and with characteristic H-D caution, single gearing on both was still available at the buyer's option.

In the meantime, sales were increasing, due to a growing public demand and an ever expanding dealership resulting from the tireless efforts of Arthur Davidson. Outlets were now to be found in most of the country's larger cities, and the New England area. Now the rest of the North Eastern states, once an Indian stronghold, were well represented.

Plant area was again expanded, with a rearrangement of production facilities under the capable hand of William Davidson, assisted by George Nordberg and Fred Barr, with an eye to an anticipated 30% increase in production.

An innovation for 1915 was the introduction of the step starter, which replaced the bicycle type pedalling gear. This consisted of a pair of pedals with their shaft inserted through the countershaft hub. With the clutch disengaged, the rider could start or restart the engine at rest without the need of dismounting and placing the machine on the rear stand. Another progressive feature was the fitting of a hand lever that was connected to the rocker-type foot pedal controlling the clutch.

The sidecar really came into its own during 1914, both to enhance the motorcycle's usefulness to the family man, as well as in numerous commercial uses with various types of box or platform bodies. As H-D did not then have the production space to inaugurate sidecar production, they negotiated an agreement with the Rogers Company, a Chicago-based manufacturing firm organized in 1910, to supply sidecars to the trade. H-D accepted their standard single seat body, but specified a specially-designed heavyweight chassis that was more rugged than Rogers' original type and carried the standard H-D front wheel with its extra heavy annular-type bearings. An initial order of 2,500 units for 1914 was increased to 5,000 in 1915, when Rogers augmented their somewhat limited production facilities to supply this order.

The cyclecar appeared on the American scene in credible numbers during 1914, inspired by the popularity of the motorcycle, and attempted to appeal to the buyer by offering a lightweight four wheeled vehicle possessing initial stability. All of the larger motorcycle manufacturers were approached at varying times by the embryo builders of such machines to supply them with engine and transmission units. Most of these were by this time running at full capacity to service their own market, and most of them, including H-D, declined.

In the Fall of 1913, H-D's management decided that their production was such that they could now attempt to enter the export market. American machines of their characteristic rugged design had already been well accepted overseas, starting with Indian, who had established a foothold in the United Kingdom in 1908, and was now well entrenched in the European and Australasian markets, along with lesser numbers of Excelsiors, Hendersons, and Popes. H-D's first efforts in this direction were made in England, where one Duncan Watson, a Scot whose family was already engaged in the import-export trade, agreed to set up a distributorship in London.

To facilitate the hoped-for expansion of these markets, an Export Department was set up, and was headed initially by one Eric von Gumpert, who is said to have had some experience in the field through former employment in an import-export firm in New York City. The story is told that the Davidsons, who were reportedly staunchly anti-semitic, questioned von Gumpert's ethnic background. When it was discovered, upon investigation, that he was a member of a solid German immigrant family with proper Milwaukee antecedents, his appointment was confirmed.

With the consummation of the export agreement with Watson, who immediately set up facilities in London as an initial retail outlet and service agency, the first shipment of machines was received in April. It is reported that sales were brisk from the start, as heavyweight American V-twins had already made a place for themselves in the United Kingdom. They proved popular with both fast solo riders as well as sidecar enthusiasts through their previous exposure to Indian machines imported by Billy Wells since 1908, as well as lesser numbers of Excelsiors. Watson also took steps to set up dealerships in Paris, Amsterdam, Brussels, and Copenhagen, but the outbreak of the World War and the almost immediate dislocation of shipping activities halted these efforts for the time being. In all, about 350 machines were received before the declaration of war in August 1914. While the improved 5-35 single cylinder model was made available, very few of these were sold, as most buyers of American machines were quite obviously V-twin enthusiasts.

In the meantime, Bill Ottaway was well on his way to improving the efficiency of William Harley's already well proved 61 cubic inch twin. With modifications in the porting of the exhaust and intake manifolds, altered combustion chamber contours, and improved valve action, a considerable increase in the power of the standard roadster models was achieved. Ottaway also spent considerable time in studying the possibilities of lessening the inherent vibration characteristics of the engines through both static and dynamic balancing of the crankshaft and flywheel assemblies. While it was, of course, impossible to overcome this built-in design weakness entirely, the engines ran more smoothly as the result of his efforts.

In addition, Ottaway designed a special racing model for limited production. Catalogued as the Model II-K, the many H-D enthusiasts who had longed for an out-and-out competition machine now at long last saw their dream come true. Fitted with the one-liter 61 cubic inch 'pocket valve' engine that was basically the standard H-D roadster engine, it featured special cams and special intake and exhaust porting. Mounted in a short coupled racing frame with 51 inch wheelbase, it followed the fashion of the day by having countershaft gearing, as no gearboxes were ever fitted to the early track racers. It weighed slightly under 300 pounds with a gallon of oil and 3 gallons of fuel aboard.

Ottaway subjected several prototypes to rigorous testing on out-of-the-way fairground horse tracks, paying particular attention to steering and handling characteristics. Old time employees in the Engineering Department have recalled that one of the first problems was the handling of the machine with the use of the now standard H-D pattern leading link fork. While no serious problems had been noted in previous roadster machines, whose top speeds barely exceeded 60 mph, the 90 mph plus speeds of the II-K were something else again. The first prototype machine was seen to take the rider into a tank-slapping wobble before it reached 80 mph. Ottaway at once suggested that a new fork be designed, and was heard to voice the opinion that a trailing link type be substituted. The Company's top management vetoed this suggestion at once, stating that any racing machine should at least incorporate all of H-D's traditional design features, and Ottaway had to content himself with further modifications to the rake, trail, bottom link configuration, and spring tension rates which, after considerable trial and error experimentation, at least partially corrected the trouble.

The Model II-K was now set to open a new and thrilling chapter in H-D history.

Chapter 2

Success and Disappointment

HARLEY-DAVIDSON'S FIRST BID FOR COMPETITION SUPREMACY CAME ON JULY 14th 1914, at the soon-to-be famous two mile country fair horse track at Dodge City, Kansas, a well-known frontier town of the old West, which was subsequently to become the Indianapolis of American motorcycle racing.

The course had been selected for a projected 300 mile classic the year before, when FAM President, Dr.W.S.Patterson and a group of fellow motorcyclists visited the area while en route to their annual convention in Denver, Colorado. Being impressed with both the suitability of the track and the high state of competition enthusiasm evidenced by two wheel devotees in Dodge City, the competition committee began making plans for the event to be held there the following year.

The first 300 Miler saw six makes represented: Excelsior, H-D, Indian, Merkel, Pope, and Thor. The H-D team consisted of Walter Cunningham, Paul Garst, Paul Gott, 'Red' Parkhurst, and Alvin Stratton, all mounted on the new II-K models, carefully selected from the twelve initial machines produced, and personally tuned by Bill Ottaway. Excelsior fielded its now famous 'Big Valve' racers, a pocket valve type with 2½ inch valves developed the previous season. Indian relied on their very fast 8 valvers perfected in 1911 by Carl Oscar Hedrom, although they brought along three standard pocket valve machines as a reserve.

The race was flagged off promptly at noon under a strong summer sun, the 36 contestants being lined up in six rows of 6 machines for a rolling start, behind the pace car carrying Dr.Patterson, who held the checkered flag. Lee Taylor on a Flying Merkel blasted into an early lead which he held for the first sixty miles for a time of 51 minutes 39 seconds. Behind him by twelve seconds was H-D's Walter Cunningham, who clocked a blistering hour and 28 minutes for the first hundred miles, to pass Lee Taylor on the north turn. A stretched rear chain and a fouled spark plug put him out of action at the 181st mile, ending H-D's chances of victory as he was the only member of the team with sufficient lead to put him in position for a possible victory. Glen 'Slivers' Boyd, on a very fast 8 valve Indian, roared ahead to win at 68 mph, closely followed by Bill Briar on a White Thor, who was second, and Carl Goudy, Excelsior, finished third. While the balance of the H-D team trailed the back, they all finished the course, and Cunningham's early scintillating performance created much excitement in the crowded stands. An added interest was the first public appearance of the usually staid H-D machines in racing trim, and with special machines at that!

On November 26th the second annual running of the 300 Mile Savannah Road Race was scheduled, comprising 27 laps over an 11½ mile circuit of varied curves and straights. H-D again entered six machines, ridden by Irving Jahnke, Maldwyn Jones, Alvin Stratton, Martin Schroeder, Ray Weishaar, and A.W.Yerks.

Schroeder took an early lead in the second lap, followed by Bob Perry, Excelsior, Erle 'Red' Armstrong on an Indian, who in turn was followed by Ray Weishaar and Erwin G. 'Cannonball' Baker on a stock Indian.

Lee Taylor, now with the Wigwam on an 8 valve Indian, took the lead at the 14th lap, and ran away from the field to win at 61 mph, garnering the $800.00 winner's purse. Joe Wolter, Excelsior, was a far second, with Irving Jahnke, H-D a close third, with his three teammates close behind. While victory again eluded H-D, they made a very strong showing that was not lost on the fans, and the sports writers noted it as a promise of better things to come from Milwaukee.

It was also noted that Bill Ottaway's careful team organization and attention to reduced pit stop time had much to do with H-D's excellent showing, a factor not heretofore too prominent in American track racing.

In the Fall of 1914, the Company announced an improved version of their past season's two speeder, now catalogued as the 'J' model, for the 1915 sales season. This new machine was to be the forerunner of their Big Twin 'Top-of-the-Line' model that would continue in production with but detail changes for the next fifteen years. While identical in most respects to the two-speeder, it now featured a rugged three-speed all-enclosed sliding gear-type transmission, with a sturdy multiple plate clutch mounted on the countershaft. While the former two-speed hub gear had proved acceptably reliable, its lack of a third ratio had somewhat limited full utilization of the engine's power band, particularly in sidecar work. Then, too, while the in-hub unit was not particularly heavy, its weight, combined with that of the standard heavyweight hub bearing assembly, produced a certain amount of rear wheel hammering, especially in the rough roads of the period. With the necessarily heavy transmission now

A 1914 61 cu.in. twin two-speeder from the Bud Ekins collection, picture taken at Visalia in 1974. Note the rod control mechanism extending to the gears in the rear hub. This device was the invention of Charles H. Lang, early H-D dealer as well as Company shareholder. It was fitted for two seasons only, being replaced by a conventional three-speed sliding gear unit mounted in the frame behind the engine. *(George Hays)*

mounted in a more conventional position just behind the engine, the overall weight of the machine was in better balance.

Noting the problems that had been encountered in some contemporary makes with clutches of insufficient strength and consequent reliability, William Harley carefully considered this aspect of his new transmission system and experimented with several possible variations. He ultimately settled on a rather massive heavyweight multiplate design that closely followed that of the proprietary Bendix type that had been manufactured for some years as an accessory and could be adapted to the engine shafts of earlier belt drivers. When Ottaway, who had been closely following the proceedings, noted that Harley had incorporated Bendix's screw-type release mechanism, he suggested that this feature might entail patent infringement, as Victor Bendix of the Bendix Manufacturing Company had purchased the manufacturing rights the year before with the intention of incorporating the clutch into his own range of products. For reasons known only to himself, Harley was adamant concerning the finalization of his design as planned, but Ottaway's opinion was later vindicated.

The new model was well received, and with sales of over 8,000 machines in 1914, President Walter Davidson was confident that this could be topped in 1915.

The popular step starter was retained in the new model, as it worked well in conjunction with the new transmission. While the company had ordered 5,000 sidecars from the Rogers Company for the new season, they received only 3,000 units, due to production problems. H-D still lacked the floor space to add their own sidecar manufacture, concentrating their efforts on enhancing motorcycle production.

While a slightly updated 5-35 single was still offered, with both single gearing either by chain or belt, or the 1913 two-speed hub as an option for utility and commercial work, most of the production centered on the Big Twins, as American buyers now favored heavyweight models.

The 1915 three-speed model exemplified the more or less standardized heavyweight American motorcycle now produced by Excelsior, Emblem, Indian, Dayton, Michealson, Reading Standard, and others less prominent. H-D was in a very excellent competitive position at this point of domestic motorcycle history. Fabricated from the best of available materials, its products now earned a well deserved reputation for general excellence. With the improvements in engine design by William Ottaway, together with the lessons learned in speed tuning incidental to racing, the standard twin now developed 37% more power than previously, with enlarged breathing porting, improved valve action, and an enhanced lubrication system.

In spite of the generally high enthusiasm for motorcycling, production for 1914 dropped from a high of 71,000 units for the previous year to just under 60,000 machines. The onset of the war in Europe had shut off the supply of many components previously imported from overseas, such as bearing sets, magnetos, and certain cycle parts. The inevitable inflationary effect of war had substantially raised the cost of iron, steel, tires and other rubber parts, as well as electrical equipment. These factors, of course, forced an immediate rise in retail prices, which inevitably resulted in some buyer resistance, as wages and salaries had yet to keep pace with the inflationary spiral.

Another disquieting event in American industrial history was the recent raise in wages granted by Henry Ford to his many thousands of production employees, who were now paid $5.00 for a ten hour working day, double that formerly paid, as $2.50 per day had for years been the standard for industrial production workers. Ford's enormously growing production and his consequent profits not only enabled him to afford this increase, but he cannily envisioned that the repercussions from this move throughout industry would enable more working people to purchase Ford cars. His action, of course, brought forth a storm of protest from most of the country's industrial leaders, who condemned it as inflationary, socialistic, and a potent danger to the economic stability of the country. Nevertheless, most of them subsequently followed suit, and wages generally kept pace with inflation. This condition had a significant effect on the domestic motorcycle industry. Many of the smaller manufacturers who, through limited production, enjoyed only a regional market adjacent to their factories, were already feeling the effects of inflation on their production costs. The total effect was that many of these makes of acceptable quality and loyal popularity simply ceased their operations, or converted to other products more closely associated with the changing times.

William Ottaway's improvements to the new H-D machines created no small interest on the part of their chief competitors, Excelsior and Indian. The former introduced a new variation of their famous 'Big Valve' models, and Indian's Charles B.Franklin hurriedly designed a more potent side valve model to replace the original pocket valve design of their founder, Carl Oscar Hedstrom. The once plodding H-D utility type image was now changed to that of a high performance machine!

The Fall of 1914 saw the first formal organization of the American Motorcycle industry with the founding of the American Motorcycle Manufacturers Association having headquarters in Manhattan. Its Board of Directors included W.G.Schrack of Angola, New York, Arthur Davidson of Milwaukee, Thomas W.Henderson of Detroit, K.H.Jacobs of Middleton, Ohio, and L.D.Hadden, of Hartford,

An intrepid traveler pauses to check his route map. The machine is a 1914 two-speeder. Note the large Solar acetylene headlamp. *(The H-D Motor Company)*.

Connecticut. This body was later to become the American Motorcycle and Allied Trades Association.

On the competition scene, H-D inaugurated their opening challenge to their chief rivals, Excelsior and Indian, by entering the FAM sponsored road races scheduled at Venice, California, in the spring of 1915. As a small seaside resort town southwest of the city of Los Angeles, co-operative city officials agreed to close some of the public streets for the running of the event. Strong factory support included teams sponsored by Dayton, Excelsior, H-D, Indian, Pope and Thor. The H-D team was captained by an emerging midwest racing star, Otto Walker, and featured improved engines developed by Bill Ottaway the previous winter. Walker covered the 300 mile course through the city streets at an average speed of 68.31 mph, to win the $800.00 first place purse. His teammate, Red Parkhurst, was a close second. Carl Goudy and Bob Perry on Excelsiors were third and fourth. A new rider whom we shall meet again, the youthful Fred Ludlow, was fifth on an Indian, followed by Morty Graves, also Indian mounted, for sixth place.

On July 4th, the Dodge City 300 Miler saw twenty nine riders on seven makes of factory sponsored machines, representing Cyclone, Emblem, Excelsior, H-D, Indian, Pope, and Thor, lined up for the start. Don Johns, on a Cyclone of very advanced design, set a terrific pace at the start and nearly lapped the field during the first three laps. While still far ahead at the 101st mile, he went out with a broken chain, leaving Carl Goudy and Morty Graves on Excelsiors in second and third places. Ill luck felled both the Excelsior and Indian teams during the 90th lap, leaving Walker and his five teammates to finish the race, the Walker taking the checkered flag at 79.84 mph, nearly nine miles faster than the previous year.

In August, teams from Excelsior, H-D, and Indian met at Tacoma, Washington, for the inaugural race at the newly completed board track just constructed by Jack Prince. Erle Armstrong won the main event at 79.84 mph, closely followed by Otto Walker on his H-D, who crossed the finish line just a wheel length behind, and barely ahead of, Don Johns on another Indian. The thrilling duel of these three riders during the final laps had a capacity crowd on its feet at the finish.

The following September the H-D team, again headed by Otto Walker, joined Excelsior and Indian at yet another of Jack Prince's new board ovals at Maywood, a suburb of Chicago. Walker won a signal victory, this time riding the new famous II-K model, which was now fitted with a new prototype engine designed by Bill Ottaway featuring 8 valves. In spite of some handling problems, Walker's win at 89.11 mph was an all-time record on the boards up to that time.

The favourable publicity resulting from these outstanding racing successes was such that nearly all of H-D's dealers reported increased sales, and a production target of 15,000 units was set for the 1916 sales season. The standard single and twin models were now offered with full electrical equipment specially engineered by the Remy concern. In addition, the step start was eliminated in favor of a more modern kickstart mechanism enclosed within the gearbox. The emphasis was now on the V twin, with very few singles being produced, most of these being sold for commercial use, such as for mail carriers or public utility service.

The most important item of H-D's ever-expanding competition program was the development of the soon-to-be-famous Model 17 racing 8 valver. While Ottaway had been able to greatly increase the power of the basic pocket valve models, it was obvious that the ohv four-valve per cylinder could greatly enhance the breathing capabilities and provide more efficient combustion chamber configuration if both intake and exhaust valves could be positioned within the cylinder head, as already proved by Indian's Carl Oscar Hedstrom.

Under Ottaway's direction, several prototype engines were built and tested, but preignition problems and spark plug failures were encountered, even though the interior shapes of the cylinder heads closely followed profiles recently developed by Ricardo in his epoch making experiments in cylinder head design. After continuing difficulties, Ottaway finally suggested to Walter Davidson that the Company engage Harry Ricardo himself to facilitate the development of the new engine. The story goes that Davidson demurred, citing the high cost of Ricardo's round trip steamship fare from England, together with the fee for his services. He ultimately relented, however, when Ottaway pointed out that the $25,000 already expended on the preliminary development would be lost entirely unless winning engines could be forthcoming. After several weeks of experimentation Ricardo at last came up with acceptable results, the new engines turning out a credible 55 hp from the standard 61 cubic inch configuration. And this in 1915!

The limited production racers were offered in both single cylinder 30-50 cubic inch and twin 61 cubic inch models, the former being produced by merely deleting the front cylinder and altering the timing sequence. The machines were at first intended only for the factory team, but it was later decided to sell a few to specially favored private competitors who had already proved their ability. The number of these singles built is not known, but veteran factory employees have stated that about 30 of the latter were ultimately produced. Some have ventured the opinion that only a few were made as Ricardo, by prior agreement, was to receive a small royalty on each machine completed.

As Competition Manager, Ottaway now organized the factory racing for the coming Dodge City 300 Mile Classic. Captained again by Otto Walker, the lineup consisted of Harry Brant, Floyd Clymer, Sam Corrento, Harry Crandall, Paul Gott, Irving Jahnke, and Ray Weishaar. In preparation for the coming season, Ottaway, now assisted by E.E. Welborn, drilled his riders in team tactics, practiced pit stops with the factory mechanics who were to accompany them, and perfected the flag signaling system, all of which had already paid such rewarding dividends during the past season. Team members were groomed to a razor edge of tactical readiness by physical conditioning, and good food and regular hours were also demanded from each member.

In commenting on these events in an interview with the author in 1965, the late Floyd Clymer, who had won a place on the team through some local wins in his native Colorado a couple of seasons before, stated that Ottaway was a stern taskmaster, and demanded total co-operation from all team members during an intensive six week training period. In commenting on the machines themselves, Clymer stated that the Model 17 was almost identical to the II-K models that preceded it, except that the wheelbase was lengthened slightly to 54 inches. According to his statements, this change created a number of steering and handling problems, not only from the changed frame dimensions, but also from the increased weight of the new engines. As with the II-K, each rider encountered steering and handling problems at high speeds, which were dealt with in various ways. With some riders, moving the seats either backward or forward to alter the weight distribution appeared to correct most of the troubles, but in the end, Ottaway also increased the rake in the forks of all the machines. In his own machine, Clymer recalled that the compression springs were shortened to lower the position of the pivot, and with the wheel axle now slightly above it, high speed stability was improved. This modification provided the limited fork travel so necessary in high speed track work.

37

At the third running of the Dodge City Classic on July 11th, the local Chamber of Commerce and the merchants' association went all out to make the affair a gala event for an anticipated crowd of 30,000 visitors. The main street was decorated with flags and bunting, and a parade featuring several marching bands and military units was held just before the race. Several floors of Dodge City's largest hotel, The Harvey House, were set aside as the official race headquarters. Riders, team managers and their personnel, motorcycle manufacturers and accessory and tire suppliers were in attendance.

The official starter manning the pace car was T.S.Sullivan, Automotive Editor of the *Boston Globe* newspaper, who waved off the contestants at 11.00am. Otto Walker was a non-starter due to a sudden illness and Ottaway substituted twenty-one year old Floyd Clymer. While many in the crowd were somewhat surprised at the change in the line up, Clymer was not exactly an unknown to many fans, due to his many recent racing victories in the Colorado area. It was also rumored that he was soon to take up an H-D franchise in Denver.

On the first lap, Don Johns took an early lead on his Indian, but was overhauled by Clymer in the second lap. Johns dropped back to third when passed by Bob Perry on a very fast big valve Excelsior, but was forced out in the fifth lap by a broken valve. Clymer now widened his lead, with nineteen year old Irving Jahnke coming up from the rear of the pack on a signal from the pits to close in behind. Clymer stayed ahead for the first hundred miles, pulling Jahnke along just behind him in his slip stream, setting a new record of 83.62 mph for the first hundred miles. At the one hundred and first mile, Jahnke pulled ahead, acting on pit signals, as Clymer's engine was noted to be overheating. After that they changed places every few laps, until at the 150th mile the timekeeper announced that their elapsed times were identical.

Don Johns dropped out at the 200th mile with a blown engine, leaving Clymer and Jahnke to alternate between first and second place. Clymer ultimately dropped out at the 296th mile with a blown rear tire. Joe Wolter, Excelsior, was a distant second, with Ray Weishaar, H-D, third. Paul Warner and Gene Walker on Indians were fourth and fifth, with Morty Graves on an Excelsior trailing in sixth. Jahnke's winning speed was a record 79.79 mph, for which he collected $800.00 in prize money together with an additional $200.00 bonus for his lap times.

On July 25th, the H-D team entered the races at the newly-opened board track at Sheepshead Bay, Long Island, New York, winning first, second, third, fourth and sixth places. Don Johns, Indian's star rider of the season, was the only member of his team to finish in a place, garnering the fifth spot. Red Parkhurst, the H-D winner, made the very fast time of 89.01 mph, in spite of a pit stop to change a fouled spark plug, and a very unnerving speed wobble in next to the last lap which nearly brought him down. In the National Championship races held on the same course, M.K.'Curly' Fredricks, Bill Briar, and Alvin Barclay won all three first places for H-D at speeds of well over 90 mph.

Space considerations preclude further accounts of H-D's phenomenal successes during 1916, but suffice it to say that the team criss-crossed the country during the balance of the season to win no less than fifteen National Championships.

The late Floyd Clymer, in recounting his experiences with the H-D racing team, told the author that while the machines were in most cases only fractionally faster than those fielded by Excelsior and Indian, it was Ottaway's tireless attention to pit stop timing and constant drilling of the riders in track strategy and signal techniques that had the most critical effect on their continuing successes.

H-D's showing in the 1916 desert races were somewhat of a disappointment. H-D enthusiasts Harry Crandall and R.J.Orput requested, but were denied, any factory support, and entered the contest on their own 1914 two-speeders which had obvious limitations as to both power output and speed.

The race was flagged off at Springerville at dawn on November 6th, the riders being started at two minute intervals. Roy Artley was first into Flagstaff, closely followed by Alan Bedell. Jack Dodds limped in two hours later, having had to stop at intervals to clean sand from his carburetor. R.J.Orput, on his H-D, was reported as having been stalled somewhere behind, with a broken fork spring. Just before reaching Winslow, Cannonball Baker was closely following Harry Crandall on his H-D when the latter went over a rise and skidded to a fall in loose sand just over the crest. Baker put his machine into a slide to avoid hitting Crandall, and both went into a ravine. They managed to make minor repairs to their battered machines and carried on. Al Meacham was the next casualty, buckling his front wheel on a large rock. Bedell took a header over his handlebars when fouled in a deep rut, and cut his forehead severely, but managed to remount and carry on. Roy Artley finished first for a time of 13 hours 12 minutes. A rather bloody Bedell was second, with Joe Wolter, Excelsior, third, and Dodds, Indian, fourth. Indian took three out of the first four places, with a dejected Crandall and Orput arriving hours behind. Orput was heard to denounce bitterly the parsimony of the factory for not supplying three-speed machines, and reportedly soon deserted Milwaukee for the Wigwam.

1916 was a year of attrition for the United States motorcycle industry. While a large number of manufacturers showed machines at the annual Motorcycle Show staged in January in Chicago, most of

The immortal 'Red' Parkhurst at Dodge City, Kansas, in 1915. The machine is an updated K-11 Model fitted with William Ottaway's improved pocket valve engine. *(The H-D Motor Company)*.

these did not continue with actual production. While this may appear as a paradox to the soaring popularity of motorcycling since 1910, with now more than 200,000 machines registered on the North American continent, the fall came not without reason. Most of the early manufacturers were lightly financed, and operated with modest facilities and with a minimum of tooling. This necessarily limited their production, and most of them were never able to expand to the point of gaining a substantial dealer representation. In fact, many of them appeared to cater largely to a local market. The European war had caused a dramatic rise in the cost of materials, many imported accessories were now unavailable, and labor was demanding higher wages due to the effect of the continuing inflation. Added to these problems was the fact that in those days the science of industrial management, techniques of marketing, internal cost and inventory control, the essence of successful manufacturing, was as yet undeveloped. Many firms producing sound machines were haphazardly organised and ineptly managed.

Indian, still the leader of the industry was in sound financial condition, due to its high production and still growing sales position. Excelsior, backed by the astute Ignatz Schwinn, and financed through his fabulously successful bicycle empire, was also quite secure. H-D, through its cautious development and conservative growth, and now enjoying an expanding sales position, was also well in the black. Much of its soundness was due to the production expertise of William Davidson, whose tireless search for greater efficiency and ruthless methods of internal cost cutting consistent with quality control, were now a byword in the industry.

Other than these leading concerns, now known in the trade as the 'Big Three', the second string manufacturers were far less fortunate. Pope, a once viable operation, integral with its parent automobile and bicycle empire, was now faltering due to managerial difficulties encountered following the death of Colonel Pope in 1910. The brilliant Merkel was foundering on problems of quality and costing control, and the management of Thor, somewhat disheartened by the defection of William Ottaway, were now showing more interest in their highly profitable home appliance production. Lesser concerns, such as Dayton, Minneapolis, Feilbach, Flanders, Yale, and others, simply expired due to a variety or combination of the causes mentioned. Other than the Big Three, the principal survivors were Iver-Johnson, a favorite with rural mail carriers, and supported by their extensive fire arms manufacture, Reading Standard, Emblem, soon to become an export-only operation, and Schickel, a 500 cc two stroke with a rather unconventional cast aluminum frame. With conditions of attrition, and with the very low production of the secondary makes, domestic production had now fallen to slightly over 50,000 units.

While some of the factory and sales personnel of the surviving factories were jubilant over the decline of competition, wiser and more knowledgeable people within the industry viewed their now thinning ranks with foreboding, and as a dire portent of things to come.

1916 also saw the first employment of motorcycles in the U.S. Army's combat units. In the spring of that year, the War Department dispatched a punitive expedition of about 20,000 men into northern Mexico under the command of General John J.Pershing, in pursuit of General Francisco (Pancho) Villa. A participant in the Mexican Revolution of 1910, Villa's military activities in the north were seen to get out of hand, and acting on his own initiative, he began raiding U.S. territory north of the border. His depredations ultimately included the attack on the town of Columbus, Arizona, killing 19 Americans. Mexico's President, Francisco I.Madera, whose government forces were insufficient to cope with the wily ex-bandit, gave the US government permission to enter the country in hopes of capturing him. While Pershing was unable to find either Villa or any of his tattered army in the vastness of his own territory, the campaign was significant in that it was the first time that motorized units, including aircraft, trucks, automobiles, and motorcycles, had been used in a military operation in North America under actual combat conditions. Equal numbers of H-D's and Indians, together with lesser numbers of Excelsior big twins were employed, in both solo and sidecar form. These machines were standard roadster models, the only concession to military use being the fitting of slightly lower gear ratios. All the heavyweight twins acquitted themselves nobly, providing both adequate performance and dependability, often under appalling field conditions and with but minimum maintenance. It was this somewhat limited campaign that had much to do with revising the thinking of the US Army's General Staff concerning the mechanization of warfare, which heretofore had been based entirely on cavalry operations or horse drawn transport.

In the field of endurance runs, H-D's 1916 records were no less outstanding. In the FAM-sponsored 24 hour Poughkeepsie run, solo and sidecar teams of three entrants each won perfect scores for team prizes. In the Worcester, Massachusetts 24 hour run, two H-D sidecar teams won gold medals for perfect 1000 point scores. A 450 mile endurance run held in the vicinity of Omaha, Nebraska, sponsored by the FAM with trophies donated by the *World Herald* newspaper, saw H-D entrants winning first and second places. Eight out of ten H-D riders made perfect scores in the Portland, Oregon to Roseburg run.

In an attempt to publicize the all-electric Remy equipped models, H-D's factory sponsored team all featured this equipment in the 400 mile run. While the electric models had been introduced the preceding year, the reliability of the contemporary batteries were sometimes in doubt, and many veteran riders still preferred the reduced illumination of the well known Solar acetylene or in-unit carbide systems which, up to this point, had proved more dependable. Among the H-D competitors were Julian C. 'Hap' Scherer, whom we shall meet again, and A.W.Herrington, later to be associated with both the once famous Marmon car, as well as the Indianapolis speedway. He was, for a time, employed in the H-D engineering department.

A disappointing setback in August was H-D's failure to win the much publicized Pike's Peak hill climb, scheduled by the FAM a month after the official opening of the first passable auto road to the top of the 14,000 foot mountain. Excelsior, H-D, Indian, and Thor all fielded strong teams. In an all out effort, Indian mounted 8 valve track engines in roadster frames with three-speed gearboxes. It was Floyd Clymer, however, who stole the show, with an ultralight cut-down track frame and a specially tuned engine, made up especially for him by the local Excelsior dealer. The H-D contingent could take some comfort, however, by Van Vanderkoff and Harold Boyd winning the sidecar event in a specially tuned 1915 three-speed outfit.

In the Fall of 1916, Arthur Davidson announced that a new sales innovation would be the implementation of a new system of factory-dealer liaison by the division of the country into geographical districts, each with a factory represenative. These representatives would report directly to the factory concerning any sales or delivery problems encountered in the retail outlets. While this new policy would undoubtedly facilitate dealer factory communication more effectively, critics noted that it would at once tighten control of the H-D management over their dealers, as Arthur Davidson was already noted for keeping what is known as a very tight ship.

To this end, the often quaintly composed factory dealer communique, *The Dealer,* was withdrawn, and in its place, a new publication named *The Enthusiast* was published under factory auspices. It was sent broadcast to all registered H-D owners, including the dealers themselves, on an infrequent basis.

Former Enduro Champion and latter day motion picture stunt rider Bud Ekins with his 1915 'J' Model. This was the last year of the step starter and the first year a three-speed transmission was fitted. *(Alisha Tamburri).*

Johnny Eagles (left) and Bud Ekins fire up the latter's 1915 'J'. The cloud of blue smoke indicates that the total loss lubrication system is functioning satisfactorily. *(Alisha Tamburri).*

In the Fall of 1916, all formal competition activities were suspended, both through the mandate of the FAM and through mutual agreement by the manufacturers, due to the increasingly troubled international complications brought on by the war in Europe. The position of the United States since the beginning of the War in August, 1914, was to remain neutral. In fact, President Woodrow Wilson in his 1916 campaign for re-election promised to keep the country out of the war. But the sinking of the Lusitania, followed by continued attack on American shipping by German U-boats, had aroused much sentiment for the Allied cause, augmented by the harrowing stories told by newsmen concerning alleged German atrocities against Belgian civilians. After his re-election in 1916, President Wilson received permission from a now compliant congress to place the country on a preparedness footing. As a result, a large number of manufacturing firms readied themselves to fulfill war department contracts for materiel.

After the successful demonstration of the motorcycle's role in the Mexican campaign, all of the Big Three's management held themselves in readiness to produce machines for the government, and instituted individual prototype experiments with military models.

It was this now sudden preoccupation with military machines, and the subsequent war department contracts consummated, that was to have a most significant effect upon the future of the H-D Company.

The Indian Company, whose fortunes since 1913 had come under the control of a non-motorcycling board of directors who were more interested in profits than in the long term future of motorcycling, decided at this point to go all-out in the securing of military contracts. They reasoned that it would be more economical to supply the armed forces than to continue to compete in the civilian market, for the duration of the war at least. To this end, and in an effort to corner the military orders, they offered government purchasing agents the opportunity to buy solo machines for $187.50, with $49.50 for sidecars. In addition, Indian boldly offered to supply 20,000 machines at this price. This price cut profits dangerously thin, and at the same time allowed no margin for the very real prospect that the inevitable war-time inflation could suddenly drive production costs higher.

H-D's management at once saw the folly of neglecting the civilian market, especially as they themselves were just now gaining a strong second place as compared with Indian. While the dictates of maintaining a patriotic stance in the matter precluded their seeking a unit price per machine or sidecar unit higher than that of Indian, they prudently made their offer on the supplying of 7,000 machines, projecting at the same time a 10,000 machine output for civilian consumption.

Accordingly, and while widely announcing H-D's contribution to the war effort, Arthur Davidson inaugurated a blitz sales campaign to recruit new dealers, especially in areas where Indian had been the strongest, and where motorcycle sales in general had been flourishing. As the supply of new Indian machines and accompanying spare parts now slowed to a trickle, not a few Indian dealers switched their allegiance to Milwaukee.

Late in 1917, H-D again offered 50% of their production to the government, which ultimately totaled approximately another 7,000 units, and received, together with Indian, a slightly better price due to the inflationary rise in production costing. At the same moment, H-D was able to more firmly entrench themselves in the civilian market at Indian's expense, and their 17,000 unit production for the 1916-1917 year enabled them to challenge Indian's usual annual 20,000 plus production that they had enjoyed for several seasons past.

The 'J' models were greatly improved, both in the military and civilian versions which were almost identical, largely as the result of the engine modifications learned from the past racing seasons. With new high velocity intake manifolds, altered cam profiles, strengthened valve gear, and a larger oil pump, about 25% more power was available. In addition, the front forks were improved with larger diameter tubes for greater strength, and better spring action. The clutch and gearbox were now fitted with heavier plates and enlarged shaft bearings. The appearance of the machine was enhanced by altering the dies that stamped out the fuel and oil tank halves, the slab sided razor edged profile seen since 1909 now giving way to a more pleasingly rounded shape.

As their contribution to the war effort, the American motorcycle industry supplied 15,000 H-D's, 2,600 Excelsiors, 41,000 Indians, and about 200 Cleveland lightweight two-strokes. In common with other types of war material produced in vast numbers, large numbers of these machines never reached the fighting front. Many machines which ultimately survived the hard usage of active service were left behind in vehicle dumps, a few of which later found their way into native civilian hands. Most of the machines remained in the States, where they were employed in training and staging centers. Most of the new machines received but not used were declared surplus, and came onto the civilian market through agents, who bought them in quantity through competitive bidding. Many of the machines which saw but limited service through these channels remained in active service for several years thereafter. Some of these could still be seen in daily use in stateside posts or in such far flung areas as the Philippine Islands or at the Panama Canal Zone until well into the 1930s.

In referring to H-D's role in the war effort, an anecdote often repeated with varying details in subsequent issues of the *Enthusiast* was how Corporal Roy Holtz, mounted on a sidecar outfit, was the first American soldier to enter Germany at the cessation of hostilities. With his company captain as a passenger, Holtz set out on a mission near the German border close to his base in northern Belgium. After a series of blunders where they lost their way during a heavy rain storm, they inadvertently crossed into Germany on November 9th 1918, and were immediately captured by a German patrol billeted at a farmhouse where they stopped to ask their way. They were released at noon on November 11th, with directions on how to return to their home base. Now united with their infantry unit, they re-entered Germany on November 12th, where a Signal Corps photographer snapped the now famous picture. Holtz remained in Germany with the army of occupation for another eight months, and his sidecar outfit reportedly gave flawless service during the balance of his tour of duty.

The maintenance of service motorcycles of all participating makes was under the direction of Thomas Calahan Butler, a member of Indian's sales force on leave of absence, who was said to have received his appointment from President Wilson. Butler recruited about 3,000 mechanics from the various factories, and several service departments were established on the East Coast. Only a small number of this force actually saw overseas service, however, as the war ended before the maintenance system had been fully organized. As an outgrowth of this effort, all of the Big Three manufacturers subsequently established their own service schools after the war to train dealers and their personnel. H-D's service school was under the capable direction of Joseph Ryan for some years thereafter. The rugged American V twins had established an enviable record of service under conditions of hard wartime use, giving outstanding performance in scouting and liaison assignments, as well as in dispatch carrying or in maintenance of telephone and telegraph lines at various points along the front.

By virtue of their somewhat limited war production and continued attention to the civilian market, H-D found themselves in a strong position at the close of hostilities, as their long-time rival, Indian, discovered their once strong dealer organization in disarray due to an almost total commitment to War Department contracts.

Arthur Davidson at once moved to strengthen his own dealerships by weeding out ineffectual or

A 1917 'J' Model sidecar outfit from the Bud Ekins collection. The sidecar bodies were built for H-D by the Rogers Company of Chicago. Their style was practically identical from 1915 through 1924. *(George Hays)*.

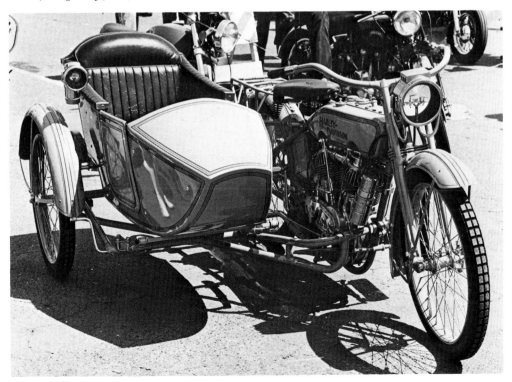

non-aggressive outlets. He also stepped up H-D's traditional strong advertising policy by instructing the Company advertising agencies to contract for additional space in a variety of other than the usual trade journals, such as hobby and mechanics publications, hunting and outdoor periodicals, and other media particularly directed to youthful readers. He was able to implement his previous intention of stationing factory representatives in various regions of the country to keep in closer contact with the dealers.

Of signal advantage to the company's continuing good fortune was the knowledge and experience gained in the production department during the enforced pressures put upon it to supply both the military and civilian markets. Efficiency had been improved through the tireless efforts of William Davidson, together with enhanced quality control and continuing excellence of the product through the employment of advanced metallurgy. Production efficiency was also aided by the fact that the company was still concentrating on mainly a one model range. While the older type singles and twins with both single gears or the 1914 type two-speed rear hub were still available on special order, most of their ancillary parts were identical with the 61 cubic inch 'J' type. Of this, the two principal variations were either the magneto equipped 'F' models, or the fully electric 'J' with a generator battery system.

In a burst of optimism over the company's prospects of assuming a dominant role in the industry during the coming post war years, the founders decided to update their production facilities with the building of a vast new addition to the factory. With construction commencing in the late fall of 1918, the new quarters were ready for occupancy by April of 1920, and were laid out as an L shaped multi-story edifice affording a total of nearly 600,000 square feet of floor area. With working space for 2,400 employees in 96 departments, it now surpassed the Springfield plant built by Indian some years before as the largest motorcycle facility of its kind in the world. Overcoming their earlier reluctance to pay bank interest rates, the founders were said to have borrowed over $3,000,000 from Marshall & Illsley to construct not only the building itself, but to add nearly $500,000 worth of the latest type of machine tooling. The company was now in a position to double their present production to a total of 35,000 machines per year.

The industry was electrified in April 1919, when as a complete surprise an entirely new and radically different type of machine was announced by H-D. Designated the Model 'W', and called the 'Sport Twin', it was a rather small and compact machine on a 53½ inch wheelbase, weighing about 275 pounds ready for the road, and powered by a horizontally-opposed side valve engine of 37 cubic inches displacement, with an SAE rating of 6 hp.

A rare 1917 'J' type single as restored by Bud Ekins. Designated as the Model 'C', this 35 cu.in. machine was in limited production through 1920. They were mostly used in commercial applications. *(Alisha Tamburri).*

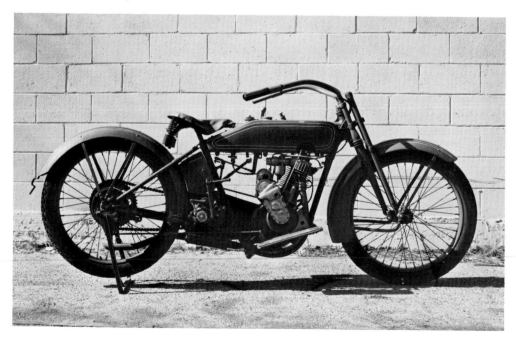

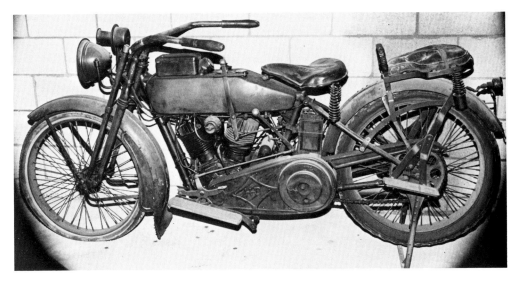

An electrically-equipped 1917 military 'J' Model in original condition from the Steve McQueen collection. The 61 cu.in. and later 1922 74 cu.in. 'Js' were identical in appearance from 1917 through 1924. *(Alisha Tamburri)*.

A three-speed sliding gear-type transmission was mounted just behind and slightly to the rear of the crankcase, the primary drive being by helically cut gears to a multiplate clutch running in oil. The final drive was by chain completely enclosed in a dust-proof sheet metal case. The footboards, clutch and brake lever attachments were carried on brackets fitted to the bottom of an open bottomed diamond or 'Keystone' type frame.

A marked departure from the now traditional H-D leading link front suspension was the fitting of a trailing link strut braced fork activated by a single barrel coil spring attached to the head lug. The initial 'W' type featured magneto ignition, with an optional acetylene lighting set. Also offered later was a 'WJ' type with battery and coil ignition and electric lighting.

Frankly based on the contemporary English Douglas, whose several models of horizontally-opposed twins had been popular sellers in the United Kingdom and elsewhere for several seasons past, the new model was easy to start, possessed almost no vibration at any speed, and had a top speed of 48-50 mph, with a comfortable cruising speed of about 40. As subsequent performance tests were to prove, it was a machine that, under somewhat different domestic social and economic conditions, might well have become an economical everyman's motorcycle.

While the domestic industry had for the past several seasons concentrated almost entirely on filling the now well-established public demand for heavyweight V-twins, the new model was, of course, at complete variance with current fashion. However, some knowledgeable motorcyclists, highly placed within the industry, had been heard to question the general lack of mediumweight and more moderately powered models. While possessed of high power and with speed capabilities that usually far exceeded the road facilities extant at that time, most big twins were rather difficult to start and awkward to manhandle within a confined space. By necessity they attracted mainly speed enthusiasts who were perforce mostly athletic young men. The medium and lightweight utility type of machine would, of course, have had an appeal to an actually larger and more broad spectrum of the potential transportation market, if properly introduced and promoted. As a paradox, a recent attempt by the Indian company to penetrate this market with the ultralight two-stroke model K single and later a medium weight opposed twin Model O met with failure. This was in large part due to the new model's rejection by many of the Indian dealers themselves, who were big twin enthusiasts for the most part, and appeared either unready or unwilling to promote a new model within another segment of a previously untapped market.

On the other hand, the only enduring model to find favor with a rather limited utility market was the two-stroke Cleveland, launched in 1915. However, it had been marketed by established bicycle dealers and sporting goods or allied retailers, whose main preoccupation was point-to-point utility transportation and who had no interest in high speed travel or competition activities. Almost unnoticed by the general motorcycling public, Cleveland managed to produce and sell about 5,000 machines each year, half of which went to export markets.

H-D's top management must have carefully charted their course with the introduction of the W Sport Twin, offering a well made and substantial non-sporting type machine that was easy to ride and maintain. In its sales promotion, Arthur Davidson sought to interest certain potential dealers who were already known to be partial to the potentials of the utility market, coupled with an accelerated advertising campaign to acquaint the general public with a new type of motorcycle. To this end, he engaged one Walter Klemenheimer, a former newspaper advertising specialist, and Julian C. ('Hap') Scherer, a former sales manager for the Firestone Tire Company. The latter was both a pioneer motorist and motorcyclist and had already gone on record as favoring lightweight machines as the logical answer to the average man's transportation needs. Described by contemporaries as a genial and ebullient personality, he was apparently well fitted to fill the newly-created post of Publicity Manager.

An expert and experienced rider, Scherer immediately set out to prove the Sport Twin's mettle, setting some notable records. On June 21st 1919, he rode a factory-prepared machine from the Canadian border to Tijuana, Mexico, for a new Three Flag record of 64 hours, 58 minutes for the 1,689 mile distance. This bettered the previous time set by Wells Bennett on a 61 cubic inch Excelsior twin by 5½ hours.

The following Spring Scherer attacked the Denver to Chicago record made by Floyd Clymer on a Henderson Four in 64 hours for the 1,224 miles during May 1920. With the aid of Denver's enthusiastic H-D dealer, Walter W. Whiting, Scherer made the run in the opposite direction during the following month, beating Clymer's time by 16½ hours. H-D's advertisements in the trade press concerning this exploit pointedly emphasized that the Sport Twin had less than half the cylinder displacement of the Henderson. In all fairness, however, it must be pointed out that the roads of that day gave a medium weight machine a distinct advantage, providing its engine produced effective low speed torque (which the Sport Twin's did). Deep ruts, the presence of many large stones, viscous mud during rain storms, and the necessity for many off-the-road detours, all tended to put a heavyweight machine at a disadvantage under road conditions where full power could not be used, and the excess weight became an actual disadvantage.

Another well publicized performance of the Sport Twin was the ride of one Edwin Hogg, a leading naturalist and conservationist of the day, and one time disciple of the noted John Muir, on a survey trip through California's notorious Death Valley. Hogg's expedition was sponsored through the joint efforts of the Pacific Coast Borax Company, The Tonopah and Tidewater Railroad, and the Death Valley Railroad, who were considering the establishment of three resort hotels and rail lines to serve them in this scenic but extremely primitive area.

A most inhospitable region, Death Valley is a vast sunken area some 150 miles long and 10 to 40 miles wide, surrounded by granite mountains of 8,500 to 15,000 foot elevation. Arid and forbidding, with scant rainfall and summer temperatures of up to 140°F and few watering holes or springs, countless travellers have died of exposure and starvation within its confines since its discovery in the mid-1800s.

As an amateur motorcyclist dedicated to the lightweight concept, Hogg rightly concluded that a two-wheeled vehicle could better traverse the primitive trails of the region. After surveying the motorcycle market, Hogg purchased a Sport Twin from Harley Rathbun's San Bernardino agency which was then carefully tuned after its running-in period by mechanic Jack Fletcher. Starting from his home in Los Angeles, Hogg made the 1,200 mile round trip through Death Valley, completed his survey, and returned two weeks later. He reported that the Sport Twin performed faultlessly under extremely strenuous use, his only problem being with numerous tire failures that included wearing out of a set of them during the journey.

In the Spring of 1919, H-D renewed its export efforts in the United Kingdom, and the 1914 agreement with Duncan Watson was reactivated. The latter established a large salesroom at 74 Newman Street in London, and made plans to set up satellite dealerships in other areas of the British Isles. The actual details were worked out through the efforts of Eric von Gumpert, who was to reactivate the Company's export program now that the war was over. During the war effort, von Gumpert had been occupied as Traffic Manager, with duties involving the routing of dealers' machine and parts orders via the nation's now extensive network of railroads, which were then the only means of public, personal or commercial transport. Incidental to these duties, von Gumpert did not leave Milwaukee, but conducted his assignment through voluminous correspondence. An export branch was established in Australasia, to serve the Australian and New Zealand markets, which were finalized by Arthur Davidson himself on a personal tour to this area where he met with numerous prospective dealers and enthusiasts.

In the initial shipment of 50 machines to the United Kingdom, 15 were Sport Twins, which reportedly met with a good response from British buyers. They were to receive good acceptance from sales efforts in Belgium, Holland, and the Scandinavian countries, Norway, Denmark, and Sweden.

During the spring of 1919, the Company reactivated their now dormant competition program, under the continuing direction of Bill Ottaway, assisted by R.W.Enos, who now proceeded to organize what was to be perhaps the most formidable array of racing talent yet seen in the United States. Soon to be known as the 'Wrecking Crew', its more prominent members included Jim Davis, Ralph Hepburn, Walter Higley, Fred Ludlow, Otto Walker, and Ray Weishaar. All were skilled competition riders of proven abilities, and their formidability was enhanced by their expertise in team tactics and pit stop techniques, implanted by Ottaway and Enos.

Excelsior and Indian had also committed themselves to a strong post-war competition program, and together with H-D, were shortly to inaugurate the so-called Golden Age of motorcycle competition in the United States.

Indeed, all forms of motor sport were now recapturing the wide public interest that it enjoyed during the immediate prewar years. Both the automobile and the motorcycle were still a relatively recent development in the transportation field, and manufacturers of both supported competition activities to advertise their products. Then too, it must be recalled that during this period in history, professional athletics in general were as yet somewhat limited in scope. Professional football and basketball were as yet undeveloped, and the beginnings of professional baseball had just been given a

The classic photograph of Corporal Roy Holtz — 'The first Yank to enter Germany' — November 12, 1918. *(U.S. Army Signal Corps).*

setback and were tainted in the public mind by the Black Sox scandal in Chicago where an alert sports reporter exposed the fact that certain games were fixed for the benefit of certain gambling interests. The only other competitive sport to capture public attention was prize fighting, which often was too brutal for general public taste.

Most of the board tracks built just prior to the war had been rebuilt and repaired. Jack Prince, the principal builder, undertook most of these projects, as well as construction of a number of new tracks adjacent to several of the country's larger cities. In addition, many of the nation's hundreds of county fair horse tracks were altered to better accommodate auto and motorcycle racing.

The Wrecking Crew, now ready for the opening of the 1919 season, proceeded to duplicate their impressive 1916 record with an almost unbroken series of victories. 'Red' Parkhurst, a newcomer to the H-D team, won the 200 Mile International Road Race Championship at Marion, Indiana. Otto Walker headed the H-D team at Los Angeles Ascot Speedway on November 30th to win all three first places. At the next race, held on January 4th 1920, before a capacity crowd of 26,000 enthusiastic spectators, the H-D team took four first places in the 100 Mile Main Event. Walker, the winner, racked up

Two views of William Ottaway's 61 cu.in. pocket valve racer developed for H-D's post-WW I racing program. The prototype as shown was fitted with unsprung strutted girder forks. Subsequent machines were fitted with modified H-D leading link sprung types *(C.May)*.

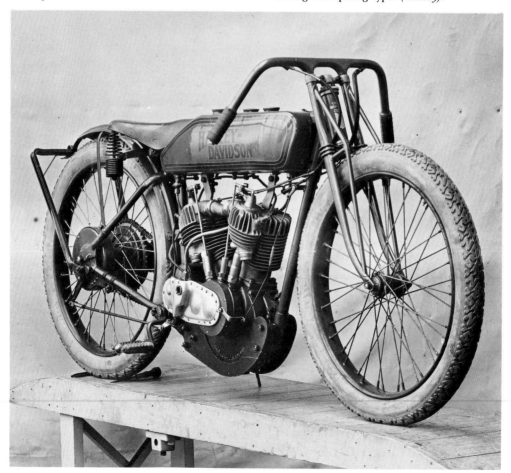

a time of 77 minutes, 42 seconds, for a new course record of 77.25 mph. Hepburn, Parkhurst, and Ludlow captured all the succeeding places at speeds exceeding 74 mph.

As an interesting aside to these victories, an article in the *Western Motorcyclist* and *Bicyclist* described the extensive preparations carried out by Ottaway in order to save valuable time during pit stops. The mechanics had advance notice of individual rider's needs via a telephone line that extended along the track to a lookout. At the pits, quick axle release nuts facilitated 10 second wheel changes, along with special fuel and oil containers which allowed almost instantaneous topping up of fuel and oil tanks through extra large tank orifices. Pit stops also included a fresh pair of goggles for the rider, and a refreshing drink of water or fruit juice. After intensive drilling, such pit stops could be accomplished and the rider pushed off within 55 to 60 seconds.

During the early part of the 1920 season, the H-D racing team was provided with newly developed pocket valve engines which replaced the former 8 valve types. H-D's management reasoned that the advanced development of the standard roadster engine configuration could not only lead to enhanced performance of these models, but that potential buyers would be more impressed if the racing machines appeared to be using engines similar to types offered for public sale.

On January 11th, the H-D team swept the field at the 50 Mile Ascot Championships, with Walker again winning, this time at 80 mph, with team-mates Ludlow taking second, Parkhurst fourth, and Hepburn fifth.

Hap Scherer's Three Flag record of 1919 had just been broken by Cannonball Baker on a 61 cubic inch Indian Powerplus on July 15th, and a few days later it was broken again by Wells Bennett on a 61 cubic inch Excelsior, for a new time of 53 hours 28 minutes.

On September 15th, Al Hadfield, as a private entrant without factory support, riding a standard 61 cubic inch H-D standard twin, left the Canadian border at dawn, arriving at Tijuana 51 hours and 22 minutes later. This record stood for a year, only to be bested by Wells Bennett on an Excelsior, shaving Hadfield's record by 18 minutes. Hadfield again challenged this record in November, beating Bennett with a flat 49 hour run. This exploit was given much publicity by the trade press, as heavy rains slowed progress through Washington, Oregon and Northern California, necessitating much high speed running in central and southern California toward the end to make up for lost time.

As an aside to the numerous competitive long distance runs of the 1915-1920 periods in the transcontinental and Three Flag categories, it will be noted that H-D was never represented by the most famous of the long distance riders, namely Cannonball Baker. The author, who was researching various historical aspects of the American motorcycle industry during 1955 and 1956, interviewed Baker regarding this during Baker's visit to the West Coast for the annual meeting of the Trailblazers, an organization of pioneer motorcyclists. Baker said that he was in the habit of representing any make of machine whose manufacturer would offer $500.00 to $1,000.00 appearance money, together with a stipulated bonus for lowering the elapsed time of a previous run. He said that on two or three occasions H-D's President, Walter Davidson, contacted him about the possibility of setting up an attack on record runs for certain distances held by competing makes. In each case, Baker reported that Davidson balked at the paying of the appearance money, stipulating that bonuses be paid only if the run in question set a new record. As Baker's reputation was already well established, he insisted that an appearance fee be paid. Since the two could never come to terms, no agreement was ever consummated.

H-D offered three basic roadster models during this period: The magneto-equipped 'JF' with optional acetylene lighting, the electrically equipped Model 'J', and the Sport Twin. During the late summer of 1919, the Model 20 J was announced with the Company's own make of electrical equipment, featuring their version of generators, horns, batteries, and lighting sets. While the batteries were furnished by outside suppliers, the balance of the system was offered on the premise that Remy's equipment no longer measured up to H-D's standards of reliability. While this new policy freed the company's reliance on Remy, in reality their first units were not wholly satisfactory and many dealers were forced to supply Remy equipment to owners who experienced difficulties with the Company's own products. It was not until the fall of 1920 that the Company solved the problem of their ailing electrical units. It is said that a former electrical engineer in Remy's employ, one George Appel, was hired to superintend their improvement.

An important event in the history of American motorcycling in the summer of 1919 was the dissolution of the Federation of American Motorcyclists. Never a really strong organization, either numerically or financially even in 1916 when domestic registrations topped 200,000 machines, its strength was further eroded during the war years when most of its active members joined the armed forces. Indeed by the time the Armistice was concluded, FAM had lost fully half of its membership. Supported by a $2.00 annual subscription from members, often collected haphazardly through the regional chapters, its officers served on a voluntary basis, and in many cases were not reimbursed for expenses incurred in carrying out their duties.

The generally weakened condition of the FAM was first publicized in the trade press by Leslie D. (Dick) Richards, a pioneer motorcyclist Associate Editor of a leading journal of the day, *Motorcyclist and Bicyclist Illustrated* in the March 6th issue. Richards pointed out the general weaknesses of the organization at all levels, particularly in the matter of governing competition, which at this point was almost out of hand. He suggested that for proper functioning, a strong membership and efficient management were required if the interests of motorcycling in general were to be served by a national organization. It was also noted that with the general dissatisfaction with the present FAM, a splinter group on the West coast had recently been organized, known as the Federation of Western Motorcyclists.

Irwin D. Allen, of Akron, Ohio, the national President of the FAM, responded to Richards' comments through a series of letters sent to other trade journals. He admitted the current weaknesses of the organization, particularly in the areas of enforcement of competition rules, and the difficulty of carrying on FAM affairs generally in the face of declining membership and consequent impaired financial resources. During the course of his correspondence, he wrote that, in his opinion, if motorcyclists in general did not wish to support the organization in its present form, the formation of a new body was now most definitely in order, and that the present FAM management would be more than willing to step aside or offer to resign if such a step were considered necessary.

At this point, H. W. Parsons, the Editor and owner of *Motorcyclist and Bicyclist Illustrated*, published an editorial suggesting that Allen's suggestions should be acted on imemdiately in order to preserve a national organization dedicated to the best interests of motorcycling in general. Parsons then attended the annual meeting of the American Motorcycle Manufacturers Association, which was held in Chicago during the first week in July. He spoke at length on the need for a better organization, pointing out that among other matters, the chaotic lack of efficient enforcement of competition rules was now relegating such activities to an 'outlaw' basis, where much rule bending and gamesmanship were making a mockery out of motorcycle sport. He ultimately moved, and was seconded, that the manufacturers take over the functions of the FAM until such time as a new governing body could be organized. Parsons was promptly nominated and elected to serve as Chairman to carry out this edict. During subsequent meetings, and under the guidance of the Manufacturer's Executive Committee, the FAM was reorganized to form the American Motorcycle Association. It was originally intended to operate independently of trade influence, and to be a democratic organization, freely governed by officers elected from the ranks of the general membership.

At the annual Motorcycle Show held in Chicago in January 1920, the control of competition activities, the most controversial item within the membership of the former FAM, was placed in the hands of one A. B. Coffman, named as Competition Chairman. Although Coffman was a dedicated and capable administrator, and was able through herculean efforts to sort out and authenticate a large number of recent competition records, he was not popular with many of the members due to his alleged arrogant and dictatorial manner. He was replaced the following year by one Douglas Hobart, an Indian dealer in Hartford, Connecticut, who had at one time been employed in Indian's Engineering Department. He was shortly to serve for a time as the AMA's *de facto* President, and the official headquarters were moved to Hartford. In the meantime, Hobart received some strong support from many interested members in the final structuring of the AMA, especially from Dick Richards, who had now become Publicity Manager for the Indian company.

While the AMA was initially a private owner's organization, trade influence in various forms ultimately became an important factor in it, and its bearing on the subsequent turbulent history of American motorcycling will presently be noted.

During the early months of 1920, following the alleviation of the worst of the world wide economic chaos after the war, H-D became firmly established in the United Kingdom under the capable direction of Duncan Watson. It was about this time that Watson became Lord Mayor of London and was shortly afterwards knighted by King George V. While there was much enthusiasm among British riders for American heavyweight V twins, sales were modest due to the lower per capita income in the British Isles as compared to America. Regarded by most as a sidecar machine, many British sporting riders were quite taken with the high speed capabilities not found in contemporary domestic makes. A number of machines, many highly modified, began to make their appearance at Brooklands race track, where post-war speed competition was now in full swing. Prominent H-D enthusiasts included T. R. Allchin, Douglas Davidson (no relation to the Founders), Freddie Dixon, Frank Longman, and Claude Temple.

Davidson gained immediate notoriety for being the first British rider to attain 100 mph, although this record had already been established in the United States. His mount was one of two factory specials ordered from the factory by Duncan Watson for this express purpose, which were set up by Watson's mechanics in November 1920. In their original form, they were board track machines with short wheelbases and solid single gear countershaft drive, powered by specially tuned standard pocket

Two H-D riders duel on the famous Maywood Speedway near Chicago in 1920. Note the vast expanse of 2in x 4in laid-on-edge decking. *(C.May).*

valve engines with polished manifold passages and high lift cam gears. During initial practicing, winter weather permitting, it was found that the short wheelbase frames were difficult to control on Brooklands' rough surface. The machines were disassembled, and during the winter, were rebuilt with standard wheelbase roadster frames, which proved more suitable. This change resulted in Davidson's subsequent record. Claude Temple, riding the second machine, rode in the famous duel with Herbert Le Vack on his well-known 1911 8 valve Indian factory racer. On April 29th, just 24 hours after Davidson's 100 mph run, Le Vack, on his Indian, topped Davidson's record with a timed speed of 106.52 mph.

The noted Freddie Dixon, long a Yankee big twin enthusiast, riding a 1916 board track type Model 17 with an 8 valve engine, nosed out I.P.Riddoch on a 994 cc Zenith Blackburne at the Clipson Speed Trials by over 3 mph, his speed being 101.12 mph. He subsequently raced the same machine at Brooklands, when, on October 20th 1923, he won the British Motor Cycle Racing Club Championship at 100.00 mph.

Claude Temple, for several seasons past a big twin enthusiast, had already duelled with Davidson for the 100 mph record, being beaten by only one-fifth of a second during the latter's classic run. He was still second best three weeks later, when on April 21st 1921, he again ran second to Davidson at the BMCRC meeting in the three lap Senior Race. He finally gained a signal victory for himself when he lapped Brooklands' giant oval at 90.09 mph, the first over 90 mph time recorded on this famous circuit.

During the Member's Meeting in July, Temple won the Five Lap Championship for the Club and the Harry Smith Cup at 91 mph.

With one of the new specially-tuned pocket valve engines just developed by Ottaway as a replacement for the Model 17 8-valvers, Temple raised the Classic Hour record two weeks later to 87 miles 922 yards. In September he recorded 99.86 mph for the flying start kilometer, at the same time making a mile record at exactly 100 mph.

These Brooklands records received much attention from the British motorcycle press, and did much to enhance H-D's prestige, as well as to bring about a healthy increase in sales, although due to economic reasons previously mentioned, American V twins could capture only a small segment of the English market. The big 'Yanks' were always the beau ideal of sporting riders and aspiring boy racers.

Meanwhile, back home in the States, the Big Three readied themselves for the 'Golden Age of American competition'.

On February 10th, and as a prelude to the 1920 racing season, Bill Ottaway, Racing Team Manager R.W.Enos, and Publicity Manager Hap Scherer, went to Daytona Beach, Florida, along with star riders Fred Ludlow, Red Parkhurst and Otto Walker, two mechanics, several 8 valve racers, a couple of pocket valve specials, and a bullet-bodied racing sidecar. Their object was to attempt to set some new straight-away records on the now famous sand course. Now that the Competition Committee of the newly organized AMA had established definitive racing categories, it was obvious that priceless advertising for the marque could be forthcoming if the projected records could be established.

Upon the party's arrival, the condition of the course was scarcely promising. Heavy storms had ravished the Eastern seaboard, unusually high tides had softened the sand, and a lack of sunshine left the outer surface mushy. In spite of this and in defiance of superstition, Ludlow made a trial run on Friday 13th, making a one-way kilometer run in 21.75 seconds for an average speed of 103 mph, a remarkable speed for a pocket valve engine. Bad weather prevented further runs until the 15th, when Red Parkhurst, on an 8 valver, averaged 110.94 mph and set up a five mile distance in 3 minutes 32 seconds. The following day, under drier conditions, he raised his mile time to 112.61 mph and the three mile time to 2 minutes 46 seconds. With the weather now clear, Parkhurst rolled the sidecar outfit, with Ludlow as his passenger, at 82.09 mph for the mile and 83.9 mph for the five miles.

While these records were impressive, and were substantially faster than any others racked up in the United States up to that time, they became open to question, even though timed by admittedly accurate Stewart-Warner timing devices supervised by an official of the Motorcycle and Allied Trades Association. They were all tabulated on one way runs, and not the up-and-back traverse of the course, as was the usual practice even in those days for the establishing of timed speed records. Enos and his assistants carefully surveyed the wind conditions before each run, and quite naturally ran with the wind in each case. It was for this reason, and the glowing reports of the so-called 'records' reported in current issues of the *Enthusiast* that the international body governing motorcycle sport, the FIM, did not accept them as official.

Before returning to Milwaukee, the mechanics carefully tuned a bored and stroked version of the standard 61 cubic inch roadster engine that now boasted 68 cubic inches, and Parkhurst made several test runs with it, although its times were not recorded. This was a prototype of the new 74 cubic inch 'J' engine that was placed in production in 1921, no doubt as an answer to Indian's 74 cubic inch version of the popular 'Powerplus' model announced a few months earlier.

In the meantime, board track racing continued to capture popular spectator interest in all parts of the country. Jack Prince had built several new tracks adjacent to many of the nation's larger cities, and huge crowds thronged the grandstands at the weekly or bi-monthly meetings held during the summer racing season. Board track racing is an extremely hazardous sport, and many thoughtful people were appalled at the increasing number of gory accidents now decimating the ranks of the popular ace riders. In many instances, both the national and local press attacked auto and motorcycle racing as a murderous spectacle. While large numbers of people were by this time avowed racing fans, the sport was producing a very definite negative attitude toward motorcycling in general. While the tracks offered the vicarious thrill of a gladiatorial contest, the spindly and overly fast racing machines, with their short fire belching exhaust stacks emitting clouds of pungent burned castor oil fumes, were scarcely calculated to inspire the fans to acquire a motorcycle for their personal transport.

Both trade and spectator interest in motorcycle competition narrowed somewhat after 1920, when Ignatz Schwinn formally announced that henceforth the Excelsior Motor Company was officially supporting no more competition activities. Its engineering department had developed a fantastically powerful ohc 61 cubic inch racing engine late in 1919, and had built about six machines, together with a spare engine for each, for use by the factory team. Their star rider, Bob Perry, was tragically killed while testing one of these machines at Los Angeles Ascot Speedway on January 3rd. The story is told that in his grief at receiving the news Schwinn, who had come to regard Perry as a son, rushed to the racing shop and smashed several of the spare engines with a sledge hammer. A single machine with a spare engine remained at large in the hands of Waldo Korn, who proceeded to ride it as a private entrant for two succeeding seasons.

Meanwhile, at Dodge City, now hailed by the trade press as the motorcycling Indianapolis, plans were being made to revive the formerly popular pre-war 300 Mile Classic. Traditionally held on July 4th, it was scheduled this year for the 5th, as the 4th fell on a Sunday and the Race Committee thought it best not to risk the wrath of the stern midwest fundamental religious organizations. The town readied itself for an anticipated crowd of 30,000 fans, and the streets and many of the shops were again decorated with flags and bunting. The factory teams and private entrants had arrived a few days earlier for practicing and review of the course, as well as a final drill in pit stop procedures.

On the day of the race, H-D's now famous 'Wrecking Crew' was ready for action, manned by Roy Artley, Leonard Buckner, Jim Davis, Ralph Hepburn, Maldwyn Jones, Walter Higley, Don Marks, and Ray Weishaar.

The official Indian Team consisted of Albert 'Shrimp' Burns, M.K. 'Curley' Fredericks, now riding for the Wigwam, Bob Newman, and Gene Walker.

The H-D machines were all of the pocket valve type, but Indian fielded two 8 valvers first raced in 1919, together with the new side valve specials designed by Charles B.Franklin. The race was started behind a pace car, which pulled off the track after the first lap, to a rolling start. Gene Walker blasted into the lead with his 8 valver, closely followed by Burns on a similar model, with H-D's Jones and Hepburn coming up behind. The leaders went to the pits in the 31st lap, and Jones took the lead on his H-D to set a new 100 mile time of one hour 11 minutes and 12 seconds for an 84.22 mph average. Jones went to the pits at lap 57, with Ludlow now going into the lead and into a seesaw contest with Burns for the next 80 miles. At Jones' pit stop, Higley and Davis alternated in the lead in response to orders from the pits, with Jones returning in the 267th mile to set a new lap record of 81.76 mph for the 300 mile distance. This shaved a few minutes off the great Ralph Hepburn's distance record hung up at the Ascot Speedway the preceding June.

Burns and Jones then alternated in the lead until both were stopped by blown engines. Davis took the lead at the 119th lap and held it to the finish, taking the checkered flag. He crossed the line 2½ laps ahead of Gene Walker, who was followed by Weishaar on his H-D for third place, with Speck Warner, Indian, fourth. Davis averaged 81.8 mph for a new record. Eleven laps were recorded at over 90 mph, with Bob Newman on one of the new side valve Indians topping the field with an incredible 96 mph run. The fastest H-D lap was by Weishaar at 92.25. The Excelsior contingent, all riding as private owners, now without factory support, failed to finish.

The National Motorcycle Road Race of 1920 held at Marion, Indiana, has been described by motorcycle historians as the last large event of its kind to be held in the United States. Road racing in this country had never been popular, as local prejudice against both the machines and the sport precluded closing public roads suitable for the purpose. Then too, such contests were never attractive to potential promoters, as it was next to impossible to control a paying crowd within any sort of enclosure that could afford a satisfactory view of the contest.

The Marion Chamber of Commerce, in anticipation of vast crowds visiting the city, donated $5,000 to help grade and repair the five mile course, and to lay a coat of dust-inhibiting oil on the surface. A visitor's bureau was set up to co-ordinate the filling of available accommodations, and much advertising space was purchased in various publications to announce the event. The city government also co-operated to the extend of adding $2,200 to the winners' purses, already subsidized by accessory manufacturers.

Under clear skies the race was rolled off behind a pace car, with Shrimp Burns on a side valve Indian jumping to an early lead within a few seconds. Clearing a small mound of earth at the foot of the stands with both wheels in the air, he blasted around the course in 4 minutes and .02 seconds for a new lap record of 77 mph.

The H-D team kept well behind, on orders from the pits, in order to save their engines for the finish. The five Excelsior riders, now riding as private entrants, all followed suit. Burns rode on at full throttle, and in the 13th lap set a new course record of 4.01. On the 24th lap he broke his chain, and Ray Weishaar of the Wrecking Crew took the lead. Burns soon returned with a new chain, and with another desperate full throttle ride managed to overhaul Weishaar, racking up a 75.8 mph average for the first 100 miles, the fastest speed yet recorded in the world on a road course.

On the 32nd lap Burns again lost a chain, the flailing end of which tore off his fuel pipe and grounded him permanently. Weishaar continued at a somewhat restrained pace, winning at 71 mph. Leonard Buckner on a side valve Indian was a close second, with Jim Davis, H-D, just behind. A trio of Excelsior riders finished almost in a dead heat for fourth, fifth, and sixth places. With an attendance of over 20,000 spectators positioned around the five mile rectangular course, AMA-sponsored road racing in America was not seen for another three decades. Prize money of $1,000, $500, $300, and $100 was paid for the first four places, together with bonus lap money provided by accessory manufacturers. At the end of the race, Weishaar commented that he could have made better time had he not been afraid of blowing his engine or breaking a chain. William Harley and Arthur Davidson, together with a contingent of factory personnel, were on hand to applaud the winner, and all received the congratulations of Indian's General Manager, Frank Weshler, who was ever a generous loser as well as a formidable opponent.

That Fall, H-D machines swept the board at the National Championship Sidecar races held at Greeley, Colorado on September 18th to 20th. Lester Foote and Frank Kunce captured all eleven first places between them, with twenty major places. These victories were somewhat hollow, however, as neither Excelsior or Indian fielded factory-supported teams. The competition offered by the private entrants at the event was so futile that it was described as nothing short of pathetic by the trade press.

Motorcycling activities and registration of machines in proportion to the population since the end of the war was now centered in the Far Western and Southwestern region of the United States. This was due to the all-weather riding climate that usually prevailed, coupled with the fact that the vast distances prompted the need for private transport due to the lack of public facilities. While the

The immortal 'Wrecking Crew' at Dodge City, on July 4, 1920. From left: Maldwyn Jones, Fred Ludlow, Ralph Hepburn, Jim Davis, Ray Weishaar, Otto Walker, and Walter Higley. (*C. May*).

The new Juneau Avenue factory building nearing completion, in 1920.

Eastern part of the country had a vastly more dense population, motoring was usually confined to the spring and summer months due to the rigors of the climate. Up to this time, Indian was far and away the sales leader, largely due to the efforts of such aggressive dealers as Guy Urquehardt in San Diego, C. Will Risdon in Los Angeles, and Hap Alzina in Oakland. In addition, many smaller but equally successful satellite dealers were to be found in the smaller cities. Excelsior was also well represented, as were a few less prominent makes such as Reading Standard and the utility type Cleveland. H-D's interests were well looked after in the San Francisco Bay area by Dudley Perkins, but the situation farther south was less fortunate. H-D's representatives in both San Diego and Los Angeles were, for various reasons, delivering only a token number of machines. Arthur Davidson, in appraising the situation, ordered the company's Northwestern factory representative, Verne Guthrie, to round up new dealers for the area. The story goes that Guthrie had recently become acquainted with one Rich Budelier, a pioneer motorcyclist and presently an instructor in Economics at the University of Utah. Guthrie was somehow able to induce the latter to move to San Diego and take over the ailing dealership. Budelier, a genial six foot giant of a man with an engaging manner and a persuasive personality, while possessed of no mechanical ability, was able within a short time to make the San Diego franchise a resounding success.

In spite of substantial public support of motorcycle competition, members of the industry now noted with alarm the sudden drop in motorcycle sales during the 1921 season.

At the close of the war, both H-D and Indian, as the leading manufacturers, each had the potential capacity of producing 35,000 units per year. Excelsior, with somewhat smaller facilities, could assemble about 25,000 machines per year. The third string firms had possibly a cumulative capacity of turning out some 6,000 machines per year, which matched their somewhat limited dealer representation. But with a production potentiality of 100,000 machines per year, the industry actually shipped only a third of this at the year's end. H-D, with its giant Juneau Avenue complex now fully implemented, could ship only slightly over 17,000 machines in response to dealers' orders. Indian, the production leader for the last decade and a half, shipped only 19,000 machines, far below the 30,000 projection, most of these being their popular 37 cubic inch Scout.

Many of the industry's executives at once blamed the soaring production of the cheap car, which was now coming to the fore in the US transportation scene. Henry Ford's production of his immortal Model T was such that he could lower its price to $400 at the factory gate, and boast that the company was now adding one new dealership every day. General Motors Chevrolet Division halted production of the large 'Baby Grand' model, and a new small model appeared that sold for only $25 more than the Model T. The ebullient William Crapo Durant was shortly to introduce his Star car, which would add some three million units to the low cost car parade. With their modest prices and their dealer representation now blanketing the country, the family man promptly ignored the sidecar combination, and opted for the stability of four wheels, full weather protection, and four to five passenger carrying capacity.

While this turn of events had ominous portent, the factories themselves chose publicly to ignore what was happening, and continued to issue glowing releases to the trade press containing highly exaggerated production and sales figures. It may be recalled that flamboyant publicity for well over the past decade had now, by tradition, become an almost inseparable adjunct to the motorcycle industry. This trend was undoubtedly inaugurated by one John J.O'Conner, a turn-of-the-century bicycle racer with a flair for journalism and a long time friend of George M.Hendee. The latter had appointed him Indian's Publicity Manager in 1909, and his subsequent exaggerated Victorian prose was to regale the motorcycling public for the next two generations. Other company house organ scribes followed suit, and motorcycle reporting assumed the literary stature of a vaudeville handbill. O'Conner's florid pronouncements of Indian's excellence paralleled Biblical prophesies, and in H-D's house publication, *The Dealer,* were such masterpieces of hyperbole that most surviving copies were ashamedly destroyed by company orders in later years.

In addition, the trade press now assumed a head-in-the-sand attitude toward the motorcycle's falling popularity. With the alarming rate of attrition among its manufacturers since 1916, advertising revenues had dropped accordingly. Haunted by the spectre of declining circulation, they lived in mortal fear of antagonizing those firms who were left. Outside of a few cautious editorials commenting on the need in some areas for cleaner dealer premises and the use of more advanced sales techniques, the

Ralph Hepburn receiving the congratulations of his fans upon winning the 200 mile Championship race at the Los Angeles Ascot Speedway, June 22, 1919. *(C. May)*.

abrupt decline in motorcycle sales was never mentioned. Definitive or objective road tests of newly in-troduced models were never aired, and the offering of unsuitable machines or glaringly apparent faults in existing machines were suffered in silence. This state of affairs was particularly confusing to the possible aspiring novice buyer, who, in reading either company advertising matter or descriptions of currently offered machines in the trade press, could only conclude that the industry produced pluperfect machines. Added to this was the editorial inference that the American motoring public was on the verge of abandoning four wheels for two!

The only exception to this journalistic fairyland was the editorial offerings of H.W.Parsons, of *Motorcycle and Bicycle Illustrated,* the sole gadfly of the industry. He noted that the motorcycle was now no longer a medium of transport, and was becoming the toy of the wealthy sportsman. Due to the ever increasing costs of high performance machines, motorcycling was fast becoming an expensive form of entertainment. As an extension of this supposition, it was also becoming a 'gentleman's sport'. Shortly afterwards, Parsons emphasized how motorcycling was now appealing to an ever-shrinking minority. Compounding this problem, he became further concerned with the antisocial behavior of a growing minority within a minority, and was perhaps the first to express apprehension about motor-cycling's potential image.

The artificial veil of silence thrown over the current state of the motorcycle market was at long last flung aside, not by the sycophantic trade press, but through the pages of a trade paper newly published for the benefit of the automobile industry. It came about when Norman G.Shidle, a young automotive engineer with a journalistic flair, founded in January 1919 a trade paper which he called *Automotive Industries.* Aside from his interest in the technical development of the automobile, he had recently become concerned with the problems of sales and marketing.

While automotive design and engineering improvements had done much to enhance the depen-dability of the post-war car, together with improved production techniques resulting in the registration of over eight million automobiles in the United States by 1920 (more than two thirds of all motor vehicles registered in the world), all was not well within a supposedly healthy industry. Nearly five hun-dred individual makes of vehicle were being offered to the market, yet the number of firms going into bankruptcy had become alarming. Most of these failures were due to the various manufacturers' failure correctly to predict the types and designs that would appeal to potential buyers.

In a series of articles, Shidle endeavored to point out the solutions to these problems through methods of marketing analysis, which were a forerunner of the science of market analysis which is to-day an integral part of all manufacturing endeavor. These articles also included data on setting up costing schedules for production planning.

At this point, Leslie D. (Dick) Richards, whom we have met before as the Associate Editor of *Motorcyclist and Bicyclist Illustrated,* filled the position of Publicity Manager for Indian in January 1920. Almost at once he became highly concerned with the problem of diminished motorcycle sales. An inveterate student of the transportation industry, he had lately been studying Shidle's articles on automotive marketing, and at length wrote him a letter suggesting that a similar inquiry be made into the motorcycle problem.

At the same time, and quite coincidentally, Hap Scherer, H-D's Publicity Manager, who was currently engaged in promoting the company's 37 cubic inch Sport Twin model, was also giving serious thought to the general public rejection of the motorcycle. It was later noted that Charles Cleland, Reading Standard's Publicity Manager, as well as the Publicity Manager of Excelsior, whose name is now forgotten, were exploring the same problem. During an interview in 1974, Richards told the author that Shidle had told him of his correspondence with representatives of the other factories during the summer and fall of 1920.

The upshot of the matter was that Shidle attended the National Motorcycle Show held that year in New York's Madison Square Gardens. During the ten day meeting he arranged a conference at the Algonquin Hotel with Richards, Scherer, Cleland, and the Excelsior representative. The object of the conference was to obtain from the various members of the industry certain data including recent pro-duction figures that comprised the number of units and types of models, together with their methods of projecting production, future sales prospects, and methods of determining material acquisitions. In return, Shidle and his staff agreed to conduct a marketing analysis for the benefit of the motorcycle in-dustry. He also revealed that a member of his staff, one Raymond Prescott, was currently being subsi-dized as a student in advanced economics at Columbia University, probably the first scientific inquiry into domestic transportation marketing analysis.

During the course of the meeting, Shidle found that he was working in a rather sensitive area, as with the general declining motorcycle sales, each manufacturer had been careful to conceal actual sales or production figures, continuing to issue optimistic and highly exaggerated reports for the benefit of the trade press reporters.

While the motorcycle representatives were initially skeptical of Shidle's motives in the matter,

HARLEY-DAVIDSON WINNING ROCKY MOUNTAIN CHAMPIONSHIP
OVERLAND PARK RACE TRACK, DENVER, COLORADO.

See photo caption on picture. *(C.May)*.

(for, after all, he had been originally preoccupied with their four-wheel competitors), his evident sincerity ultimately won their confidence, and all co-operated fully with his requests for information on their individual operations. At the same moment, all present agreed that for the time being at least, their deliberations must be kept secret, as if their respective factory top management were to learn of their divulging such data to one another or to an outsider, they would all no doubt be subject to instant dismissal.

Several additional meetings were held in various New York hotels that Fall, the motorcycle representatives journeying to that city on the pretext of other business commitments. After a few of such gatherings, the Excelsior representative elected to withdraw from the group, leaving Richards, Scherer, and Cleland to carry on.

Shidle's ultimate conclusions in the matter, aided by Prescott and the rest of his research staff, ultimately coincided with those already arrived at by Richards and Scherer, who had become warm personal friends. They concluded that the industry's emphasis on the heavyweight V twin models, together with extensive commitments to racing, had alienated the majority of potential American transportation buyers. The typical American motorcycle had grown progressively heavier, was consequently difficult to manhandle within a confined space, required much muscular energy to start, possessed an offensively loud exhaust note, and appealed almost exclusively to athletic young men whose interest was very likely to diminish with advancing age.

Shidle was particularly critical of the general emphasis on racing and competition, which, while enjoying a rather broad public appeal as a spectator sport to those craving thrills and excitement, had now firmly planted in the public mind the idea that motorcycling was essentially a dangerous undertaking. This simply led to the conclusion that most of the people attending race meets could never be

OTTO WALKER ON HARLEY-DAVIDSON
EIGHT VALVE MACHINE WHICH AVERAGED
104.43 M. P. H. IN 25 MILE RACE AT
BEVERLY, CALIFORNIA, APRIL 24, 1921

See photo caption on picture. *(C. May)*.

interested in the motorcycle as their own personal transport. The further conclusion was that a potentially vast market for low-powered, low-cost utility machines, originally the target of the turn-of-the-century experimenters seeking to offer mass low cost transportation, had been totally ignored for at least the past decade.

For the manufacturers whose representatives had participated in supplying data, Shidle and his staff offered their confidential conclusions: H-D had an efficient production capability, enhanced by their limited model variation, and a strong dealer representation; Indian suffered from a lack of co-ordination between yearly sales projections and the acquisition of raw and component materials, but also enjoyed a strong dealer representation; Excelsior offered limited production, but had the artificial cushion of a vast bicycle market to offset any production inefficiencies; Reading Standard offered nearly a dozen different models with a yearly production of under 2,000 units which seriously impaired production efficiency and was further hampered by insufficient capitalization.

Shidle subsequently published these conclusions in a two-part article in his own publication, *Automotive Industries,* without reference to his confidential meetings with the motorcycle representatives. Entitled 'Where is the Motorcycle Going?' copies were mailed for reprinting to the motorcycle trade press. The first part appeared in his April 27th, 1921 issue, the second on May 4th. The only motorcycle editor with the courage to reprint Shidle's article was H.W. Parsons, Richards' former employer, of *Motorcyclist and Bicyclist Illustrated.*

Hap Scherer was particularly gratified at Shidle's conclusions, as he, like Richards, had for some time been convinced that the domestic motorcycle industry had for too long been catering to a much limited segment of the motorcycle market. His willingness to assume the position of Publicity Manager at H-D was inspired by the hope that he could in some way focus public attention on the genuine merits of the mediumweight Sport Twin model, which could have a broad appeal to people seeking dependable low cost utility transportation that was not related to high speed travel or competition activities. Since the introdution of that model, he had been able to convince H-D's management of the need to devote much space in the *Enthusiast* to articles on it, embracing touring and utility activities, as well as its suitability for both youthful and feminine riders. At the same moment, he felt somewhat reticent about revealing his part in Shidle's searching investigation into the matter, knowing full well of President Walter Davidson's almost paranoic aversion to any co-operation with competitors, even if such could be of benefit to the general industry.

Following the publication of Shidle's reports in his own publication, and the exposition of the same by Parsons, Richards decided to take a bold step and reveal the extent of his participation in the matter to his chief at Indian, Frank J. Weschler. After some deliberation the latter, although somewhat taken aback, gave him full authority to take over the management of Indians' material procurement facilities based on marketing projections, a move which was later credited with saving Indian during an extremely critical period of its survival history. Scherer, who had been in close touch with Richards since the meetings with Shidle, and after much soul searching, decided to take up the matter with President Davidson. In later years, Scherer revealed to intimates that Davidson's reaction was almost predictable. In a stormy session in his executive offices, he berated Scherer for acting without authorization from H-D's top management, for revealing critical company secrets, and for generally proceeding in a disloyal if not downright traitorous manner. Following a lively three-hour meeting, during which Scherer futilely attempted to defend his position and explain his concern for the current depressed state of the industry, he was summarily discharged with his salary terminated as of that date.

When word of the incident reached H-D's now widespread dealer organization there was much sympathy for Scherer's position in the matter. Not a few of the dealers who were aware of the industry's problems were in agreement with him, and all conceded that his promotional efforts on behalf of the company and in the promotion of the Sport Twin were all headed in the right direction. To add fuel to the fire, Scherer almost at once was offered the position of Sales Manager in Rich Budelier's newly organized dealership in Los Angeles, another controversial aspect of H-D history which subsequently will be considered.

As an aftermath of this rather turbulent affair, it will be noticed that in no subsequent issues of the *Enthusiast* are individual employees or their doings ever given undue exposure, the emphasis being on the activities of the Founders themselves. Brief personal items were allocated only to current competition stars, sales personnel or dealers, with no continuing coverage given to any individual. What with the sympathy within the trade for Hap Scherer, and the general consternation generated by his dismissal, the Company was apparently taking no chances on creating any more anti-heroes.

In spite of falling sales, the H-D Company entered the 1921 racing season with renewed efforts. Their first memorable win of the season saw the now immortal 'Wrecking Crew' become the first factory team anywhere in the world to win a contest at over 100 mph. This occurred at the new post-war Fresno, California board track, where both H-D and Indian fielded their best professional talent, riding ohv, side valve, and pocket valve machines. Out of four main events, Team Captain Otto Walker placed first, with his teammates taking nine out of twelve 1-2-3 places. Walker's wins were all run at speeds of well of 100 mph.

In the Fifty Mile Race, Walker, in a terrific burst of speed on the third lap, made the mile oval in 33 seconds for a time of 108.7 mph. His teammates all finished with 102-103 mph averages, as did second place winner, Gene Walker, on a side valve Indian.

A month later, on April 24th, Walker won the 25 mile race at 104.4 mph on the very fast Beverly Hills boards, with teammate Jim Davis a very close second. Davis went on to win the 50 mile race at 97.3 mph, with another teammate a fractional second, a machine length behind. Shrimp Burns, on a side valve Indian, won the fifteen mile Consolation Race at 102.5 mph.

At the fifth running of the Dodge City 300 Mile Classic, the three major manufacturers were represented, although the Excelsior contingent were now running as private entrants and had to supply their own fuel, spare parts, and pit organization. The track was opened for practicing a week before the race. Shrimp Burns racked up a new lap record of 1 minute 14 seconds, on an old 8 valve Indian at 97.4 mph, with a second lap in 1 minute 16.5 seconds, with most of his Milwaukee teammates turning out averages only fractionally slower.

Rain and thunderstorms muddied the track a couple of days before the race, but clearing skies and warmer weather soon dried it up, to the relief of all concerned. H-D's starting group now consisted of Jim Davis, Ralph Hepburn, Walter Higley, Fred Ludlow, Otto Walker, Team Captain, and Ray Weishaar. All were mounted on pocket valve machines, except Hepburn, who rode a specially tuned 8 valver.

Indian's team included Shrimp Burns, Floyd Dreyer, Curley Fredericks, Don Pope, Johnny Seymour, Hammond Springs, and Speck Warner.

Del Du Chene with his authentically-restored 1920 magneto-equipped 37 cu.in. horizontally opposed Sport Twin model. This machine is identical to one acquired by the author as a schoolboy in 1927. *(John R. Stinson).*

Excelsior was represented by Wells Bennett, Warren Cropp, Waldo Korn, Les Parkhurst, and Joe Wolter. All were riding rebuilt big valve models from previous seasons, as the fantastically fast ohc engines had been destroyed by Schwinn, and the few remaining examples had already exhausted their spare part supply.

The race was flagged off at 11.00 am, the riders pushing out in rows of four behind a pace car. Hepburn gunned his fantastically fast 8 valve H-D into the lead, and held a blistering pace through the 103rd mile, when he went to the pits for fuel and oil. Fredericks, Indian, and Cropp, Excelsior, with Otto Walker, had been dueling for the second spot, all well ahead of the pack in second, third, and fourth positions. Walker was now narrowly ahead during Hepburn's pit stop, but the latter pulled out to regain the lead position. Cropp and Fredericks next dropped out with blown engines, allowing Bennett, Excelsior, to gain a close second to Hepburn, making the best showing of the Chicago contingent. His advantage was short lived, however, as he went out in the 83rd lap with a dropped valve. Hepburn bored on to widen his lead to the finish, setting a new record of 87 mph at the 200th mile. Team Manager Ottaway attempted to flag Hepburn into reducing his speed somewhat to save his engine, but was ignored by the latter who forged on to ride a 103.5 mph 149th lap, the next to the last before he took the checkered flag. He finished twelve minutes ahead of Indian's Johnny Seymour who was second, with Ludlow, H-D, a close third, with Weishaar and Walker fourth and fifth just barely ahead of Indian mounted Don Pope.

T.R.Allchin and his modified 584 cc
Sport Twin at Brooklands in 1921.
With twin carburettors and increased
compression ratio he was able to
attain a speed of 68.90 mph. *(The
Motor Cycle)*.

Hepburn collected $1,300 in prize money, $1,000 for his win and the balance for record lap times. He also took the Schebler Carburetor Award for the winning machine.

The last big race of 1921 was the Grand National, held at the New York State Fairground track at Syracuse. It was here that Fred Ludlow made his name immortal in the annals of American racing by winning in one race the National Five, Ten, Twenty Five, and Fifty Mile Championships. Noting his faultlessly running engine, Ludlow was carefully shepherded through the pack by Team Manager Ottaway, aided in keeping his proper position by fellow members of the Wrecking Crew. At the proper moment, Ludlow forged into the lead, much to the delight of a capacity crowd who were on their feet for most of the contest. He racked up record speeds for the distance of 81.8 mph for the mile to 77.6 mph for the fifty miles.

While Ludlow had not been a consistent front runner in previous contests, he was a key member of the team through his faultless riding, and his ability, along with the others, to follow prearranged team tactics that made H-D the spectacular winner in most of the great races.

In spite of the sweeping victories achieved during the imemdiate pre-war and subsequent post-war racing seasons, and the invaluable prestige that inevitably resulted, H-D's management at last decided to terminate all official sponsorship of competition activities. It was all too apparent, then as now, that victories in any category of motor sport accrue to the organization willing to spend the most money, and the cost had been tremendous. The costs of the Company's final racing season were said to amount to about $200,000, comparable to a million dollars at today's reporting, with salaries of $15,000 to $20,000 for the star riders, as well as the mechanics' wages, the cost and maintenance of the machines, plus the expenses of travel and lodging while on the circuit.

It was also apparent that in spite of H-D's spectacular wins in most of the big national races, a total domination of the sport by one make was practically impossible. On the many hundreds of county fair horse tracks throughout the country, local Excelsior and Indian enthusiasts with either personal skills in speed tuning, or access to dealers or mechanics with such ability, racked up creditable victories. Then too, sectional loyalties were such that these competing makes might well dominate the market in any given area.

In a formal release to the trade press in December, President Davidson stated 'We find that we have become engaged in two distinct businesses at the factory: one the business of racing, with a complete separate organization, and the other the legitimate business of making and selling motorcycles.'

Chief Engineer Harley further elaborated on the change in company policy stating 'We found that instead of racing activities consuming only a small portion of the attention of the engineering department, the demands had gradually increased until it was all out of proportion to the results ob-

D.H.Davidson (no relation to the Founders) on this 989 cc H-D was the first rider ever to exceed 100 mph at Brooklands. The machine was originally fitted with a short wheelbase board track racing frame. When this proved unmanageable on the rough surface, a standard roadster frame was substituted. *(The Motor Cycle).*

tained. With the new arrangement, the entire Engineering Department will be devoting all its time to the solving of production and engineering problems connected with the production of standard roadster machines, and the purchaser will benefit accordingly'.

It was emphasized, however, that a very limited number of racing machines would be produced for the benefit of qualified competitors, but without any official financial subsidizing of their maintenance.

The actual reason for the termination of factory-sponsored competition was, of course, the fact that sales had fallen to the point that only 11,000 machines were shipped in 1920, as compared to slightly over 17,000 ordered during 1918 and 1919.

William Davidson now streamlined the production lines for lesser production and better efficiency, trimming back the work force to about a thousand from a war time high of 2,500. The extra production facility adjacent to the main factory was now disposed of and the company tightened its belt for whatever might lie ahead. It was also coincidentally announced that henceforth the company would distribute no more bicycles, once thought to be an indispensable adjunct to a successful motorcycle dealership. As the bicycles had not been made in Milwaukee, but bought out from large manufacturing concerns such as Butler Brothers, the change saved the distribution costs, and these were now transferred to the Davis Sewing Machine Company, whose already intact bicycle subsidiary would now handle the spare parts for all machines formerly marketed under the H-D label.

The Indian company was in an even more dire situation. Its 1920-1921 production had now fallen to about 7,000 units, pathetically below the 20,000 figure of 1920. Due to the heroic efforts of General Manager Frank Weschler, the aid of Dick Richards' marketing and procurement data from the Shidle reports, and the popularity of Charles Franklin's immortal Scout, the company muddled through.

The Excelsior company merely cut back production on its once popular 61 cubic inch big twin, and concentrated on its newly-acquired four cylinder Henderson, which was now becoming the most popular mount for law enforcement use. Cushioned by its vast bicycle empire, the economic losses in motorcycle manufacture were scarcely noticed.

Cleveland, Emblem, Iver-Johnson, Reading Standard, and Schickel limped on with miniscule production, and an industry capable of producing 100,000 machines annually now turned out a bare 25,000.

The trade press continued to ignore the industry's crisis, except for Parsons' reports on the Shidle marketing survey. The only other exposure of the matter was from L.E.Fowler, an automotive engineer who edited the Chicago based *Motorcycling and Bicycling,* and who had designed the Cleveland 63 lightweight two-stroke in 1914. This was aired by means of an interview between Fowler and James Ward Packard, the then retired designer and one time Chief Engineer of the prestigious Packard Motor Car Company. Packard, who had been a pioneer bicyclist during the high wheel days, predicted not only a revival of interest in bicycling, but a possible vast market in lightweight utility-type motorcycles, provided they could be mass produced to sell at reasonable prices, be dependable, and above all, be easy to start. Prophetic words from an automotive pioneer, which would become a reality four decades later through the efforts of Japanese motorcycle engineers!

An unfortunate aside to the H-D Company's rather abrupt announcement concerning the termination of factory sponsored racing occurred at the State Fair races at Phoenix, Arizona in September. The Wrecking Crew had been sent to the Southwest following the Nationals at Syracuse, with high hopes of rounding out the season with another victory. While the team swept the field, as predicted, it now found to its consternation that the factory had not forwarded the necessary funds to pay for their train fare to their respective homes, as was the usual procedure. While the mechanics apparently had the means of returning to Milwaukee, along with the costs of shipping the machines, the Wrecking Crew, who were mostly lightly funded on arrival in anticipation of their usual salaries and expenses, now found themselves stranded. They were ultimately able to raise the train fare by pawning their watches and floating a small loan from the local H-D dealer. Varying reports of the matter were furnished in later years by surviving team members. Some have stated that President Davidson refused to accept collect long distance telephone calls in Milwaukee and that he ultimately dispatched a terse telegram, instructing them to return to their own homes without visiting Milwaukee!

Fred Ludlow, as H-D's top star at the termination of their official racing participation, was particularly bitter concerning the treatment meted out to him by Walter Davidson. A natural born rider, he was also a skilled mechanic and tuner, and had hoped for a future position with the company in the engineering department. Davidson had been noncommittal concerning his requests in the matter, but according to Ludlow he had not given a negative answer. After he had returned to his home in Los Angeles, Ludlow, with no other employment immediately in view, acquired a 'J' model sidecar outfit, together with some spectacular motion picture racing film footage, and toured the country giving film shows and lectures dealing with past racing seasons. Ludlow's presentation was generally well recieved, but on a subsequent trip to Milwaukee and a meeting with Walter Davidson, the latter castigated him quite severely concerning the subject matter of his films, stating that as much footage was devoted to Excelsior and Indian competitors as was allocated to H-D. In spite of Ludlow's protestations that any race by necessity featured competition, Davidson was adamant, and Ludlow hurriedly departed. He then defected to the Wigwam, to become shop foreman in C. Will Risdon's prosperous Indian agency in Los Angeles. He subsequently became a motorcycle traffic officer for the city of South Pasadena, retiring at the age of 60 in 1955. During the same period, he took part in various speed events on both Indian and Henderson machines, racking up numerous records that are still well remembered. At this writing he resides in a convalescent home in Pasadena, a much revered figure in American motorcycle competition history.

H-D engines and other components were utilized in two rather divergent efforts at producing cycle cars during the 1920-1921 season. The Grey Light Car Company, a miniscule operation in Denver, Colorado, built two prototypes of a light roadster fitted with H-D 61 cubic inch 'J' type engines and gearboxes and motorcycle wheels. Bearing a close resemblance to the later Austin Seven, it was rather heavily built to withstand the rough country roads of the Denver area. With 800 lbs of empty weight, it was of necessity geared rather low, and, while it ran satisfactorily, it proved to be too limited in overall performance to satisfy its buyers. The other effort took place in France, where Automobiles Rally, Colombes, Seine, put together a Bedelia type cycle car with a narrow wheel track and tandem seating. A standard 61 cubic inch 'J' type twin and gearbox were fitted, the final drive being through a pair of belts to the rear wheels. A somewhat archaic vehicle in concept, it gave way to a more conventional light car with a four cylinder water-cooled engine after three or four prototypes were built. The original components were purchased from H-D's Paris representative.

Chapter 3

The Roaring Twenties

AFTER A MINOR ECONOMIC DISLOCATION DURING THE FALL OF 1920 AND THE LATE Spring of 1921 due to a general reorganization of the country's post-war production facilities, the United States entered an era of almost unprecedented prosperity. Physically unscathed by the war, and sustaining but minimal casualties as compared with their European allies, the country had few problems in converting the economy to peacetime pursuits. With the rest of the world's producing nations still prostrate from the war's devastation, the United States quickly became the world leader in manufacturing. Yankee ingenuity now turned its attention to applying enhanced production knowledge to the development of new products for a seemingly inexhaustible consumer market.

The social order had also undergone rapid changes. Many of the young men who grew up in sectionalized rural isolation had gained new sophistication on foreign wartime assignments. Women now found a new freedom in the employment opportunities opened to them when male help was not available. Coupled with these factors, there was a growing public disillusionment with the government and political system when it soon became apparent that the 'war-to-end war' and 'peace without victory' was a myth when the realities of Versailles were critically examined. Added to this, the futility of attempting to legislate morality through the passage of the Prohibition amendment and the consequent growth of organized crime to supply the thirst for alcoholic spirits, further nurtured national disillusionment.

The newly inaugurated President, former Ohio senator Warren G.Harding, was a sensual man who was as corrupt as he was handsome. Succinctly he stated that 'normalcy' was now the order of the day, which was translated by the man in the street to mean the pursuit of happiness and the almighty dollar.

The most sought-after commodity, after a part of the general demand for time and labor saving household appliances was met, was now the automobile, as both an escape from isolation and to satisfy the natural human urge to travel. By 1921, over 400 distinct makes of cars weere on the market, ranging from undistinguished machines assembled from proprietary parts in localized areas, to the vast series production from industrial giants like Ford and General Motors. The former's production soon increased to the point where every other car on the road was a Ford, together with a host of small Chevrolets and a dozen lesser makes of similar size. With prices of such vehicles now hovering around $400.00 at the factory gate, the casual shopper for transportation would now no longer seriously consider the typical American motorcycle. This particularly applied to the family sidecar market, which disappeared almost overnight.

In consequence of this turn of events, the way in which motorcycles were marketed changed drastically. Following the 1913-1914 boom in two wheelers, many prospering dealers in the larger cities had acquired extensive and attractive premises, often rivaling those of adjoining automobile sales establishments. With the falling off of sales, not a few of these dealers dropped motorcycles in favor of cars. Other dealers, in being forced to operate on a reduced scale, left their large quarters in prime business locations in favor of smaller and less pretentious premises in less prestigious locations. Many dealers in smaller cities and towns found themselves forced into low rent unpretentious or even ramshackle quarters, which further diminished the marketing status of motorcycles.

As the motorcycle declined as a pure transportation entity, the character of the rider also changed. The typical motorcycle owner of the early 1920s was now more than likely to be a blue collar artisan or cowboy type, with a predilection for high speeds or adventure. He was complimented in some degree by a more prosperous, if iconoclastic sporting type, the thrill-seeking undergraduate, an occasional budget-minded commuter and, here and there, an adventuresome feminine enthusiast. Generally speaking, the riding of a motorcycle was now not considered to be entirely socially respectable. The scene was compounded by the rowdy speed demon who rammed a crowbar up his silencer system to destroy its effectiveness, and proceeded to further alienate the general public against motorcycling in any form.

Arthur Davidson, as General Sales Manager, was at once cognizant of the industry's mounting problems, and took steps to remedy them wherever possible. The obvious approach was to strengthen dealership representation. As all franchises were subject to yearly confirmation, wavering or ineffectual dealerships were cancelled, and more promising prospects were solicited to replace them. The regional Factory representatives responsible for covering the various geographical areas of the country were given crash courses in retail sales techniques and ordered to relay their knowledge to the individual dealers in their respective territories. Particular emphasis was directed toward encouraging individual dealers to clean up their premises, as too often new machines were displayed in windows so obscured by dirt and cobwebs that a prospective buyer could scarcely examine the machine displayed behind it!

While H-D production was concentrated on the now refined 'J' models, single cylinder Model 35 production having been terminated, much effort was also made to emphasize the Sport Twin, although much of its sales impetus was missing due to the loss of its most enthusiastic exponent, former Publicity Manager Hap Scherer. Orders were disappointing, in spite of its sales to such diverse nonmotorcycling types as famous theatrical impressario, Daniel Froman, and Norway's dignified Crown Prince Olaf. Much space in the *Enthusiast* was devoted to its promotion, no doubt inspired by both the critical state of the motorcycle market and the admonitions of Dick Richards of Indian and the now absent Hap Scherer.

The 61 cubic inch 'J' model remained the backbone of H-D's sales efforts, and retained a hard core of loyal followers, mostly young riders in whose short span of memory the 'J' remained as THE classical H-D model. In response to the demand for more power, especially in heavy duty side-car or commercial box body outfits, a 74 cubic inch model was now offered. While it obviously offered an improvement for this use, its slightly higher top speed and enhanced low speed torque for faster acceleration was an immediate attraction to solo enthusiasts. The new model was also widely used as a sidecar outfit by transporters of illicit spirits, as such an outfit, in a good state of tune, could usually outrun pursuing law enforcement units who mostly used automobiles. It also offered strong competition to the newly introduced Indian Chief which, as a complement to the already popular Scout, was also a favorite transport in the now lucrative illicit liquor business.

As a paradox to the seriously depleted domestic sales, the American manufacturers, in the Big Three category at least, now found that their products were in strong demand overseas. While Great Britain up to this point was leading the world in the production of the largest number of makes and diversity of types, most were not generally suited to the stern demands of colonial service over bad roads in underdeveloped countries. The rugged Yankee V twins, with their massive construction and simple and easily maintained engines, fitted with rugged clutches and gearboxes, developed sufficient power to haul either a large sidecar or heavily loaded commercial body which greatly enhanced their usefulness. By 1924, fully 50% of domestic production of all makes was now allocated to overseas outlets. The Emblem Motorcycle Company, a relatively small concern with modest production facilities located in a small manufacturing facility at Angola, New York, now completely abandoned their domestic market, and dispatched all their production to Europe, where the make was particularly popular in Holland and Belgium.

As a paradox to their now weakened position in the industry, Indian's indomitable Frank Weschler announced that the company would continue to support professional racing competition. As a result, some of H-D's former stars such as Jim Davis and Ralph Hepburn, joined the Wigwam's contingent. For the following seasons, Indian quite naturally dominated professional racing competition, which was still centered on the country's numerous board tracks, even in the face of declining public support and the deteriorating condition of these vast timbered speed temples.

With the growing importance of the export market, H-D's top management turned their attention abroad. Eric von Gumpert, still technically the company's Export Manager but functioning as Traffic Manager, kept in close touch with company overseas operations, particularly with Duncan Watson. The latter, selling a substantial number of machines in the United Kingdom, within the limits of the British big twin market, had expanded his scope of operations by establishing dealer outlets on the continent of Europe and in the Scandinavian countries. The Jones Brothers of Christchurch, New Zealand, whose activities were enhanced by a favorable agreement with the factory negotiated by Arthur Davidson during a visit to New Zealand during 1920, had already established a viable dealership on that continent.

On the domestic scene, H-D was now the acknowledged leader, with a projected production of

Freddie Dixon with his H-D eight valve special. Assembled on a short wheelbase frame, Dixon rode it in the British Motor Cycle Racing Club meeting at Brooklands on April 23, 1923, winning three races, including the Three Lap Race at 94.5 mph. *(The Motor Cycle).*

about 12,000 units for the 1923-24 sales season. Indian was second with a production of about 8,000 units, with Excelsior trailing with about 5,000 units, most of which were the steadily popular Henderson Four. Schickel and Iver Johnson had now almost retired from the struggle, with Cleveland and Neracar, a latecomer to the utility market, in very limited production.

In spite of its leadership in production, the dealer representation of H-D was virtually the same as Indian on the domestic scene, each now having about 1,100 dealers in the United States and Canada. H-D's excess production was allocated to the export market.

In line with the increasing importance of export sales, and with an eye to possibly bolstering the failing domestic sales of sidecar outfits, H-D's top management prevailed on the Rogers Company to build a widebodied sidecar body, capable of carrying not only two adult passengers, but an enhanced commercial load as well. The wheel track was necessarily extended to the then standard US automobile gauge of 56½ inches. While the enlarged body was favorably received in some quarters overseas, it was regarded only as a novelty on the domestic market, where it had the disadvantage of being difficult to handle at anything more than moderate speeds due to its wide track.

In the meantime, Arthur Davidson turned his attention to H-D's critical position in the now important Southwest and Far West markets, where the vast distances and all-weather riding conditions, not to mention the existence of a healthy number of sporting riders, was now absorbing fully one half of all domestic motorcycle sales.

It will be recalled that H-D's position in this area had been seriously weakened by inept dealer representation in both San Diego and the Los Angeles area following the war. The situation had been greatly improved in the San Diego area by the fortuitous appointment of Rich Budelier, but matters in Los Angeles were still critical, where C.Will Risdon of Indian, together with aggressive representatives of Excelsior, and to a minor degree, Reading Standard and a few other makes, were holding a wide sales lead.

The problem appeared to lie with the Appeal Manufacturing and Jobbing Company, which had held the Los Angeles franchise since early in 1918, and had fallen on evil days.

With no planned sales campaign, a refusal to purchase any local advertising, and a general lack of aggressive management, the concern was selling only a minimal number of machines in comparison to its competitors. A further impediment to success, although in no way their fault, was the presence, almost adjacent to the Main Street location, of several rather disreputable nonfranchise motorcycle repair shops which were repeatedly under surveillance by the Los Angeles Police Department for allegedly dealing in stolen machines and spare parts. As Sales Manager and titular head of the Company's dealer organization, Arthur Davidson was well aware of the problem, having made a personal survey of the situation during an inspection tour of the West earlier that Spring. In a subsequent meeting with factory representative Verne Guthrie, Davidson suggested that perhaps Rich Budelier

F.A.Longman, an H-D enthusiast, was a consistent winner in various Brooklands events from 1923 through 1926. *(The Motor Cycle)*.

could be persuaded to move to Los Angeles. The Sales Department would, of course, revoke the Appeal Company's franchise in favor of Budelier, should he accept the proposed offer. To further implement sales on the West coast, the Company was already in process of negotiating an agreement with two warehousing facilities for the distribution of parts and machines. This was at once a departure from usual company practice of assembling and shipping machines and dispatching them from the factory only on dealer's orders. The new system would entail more expense in assembling and shipping machines before firm orders were received, but apparently the importance of the growing Western market was such that the Company considered it worth the extra capitalization involved. Agreements with the Santa Fe Warehouse Company in Los Angeles and the San Francisco Warehouse Company were consummated to receive and ship goods dispatched from Milwaukee.

It is reported that Budelier readily agreed to accept the Los Angeles dealership, as the largest city in prosperous California could most certainly offer more scope and opportunity. The now-booming San Diego franchise was then taken over by Roy Artley, the noted competition rider, and William J.Ruhle, a pioneer motorcyclist and a long time H-D enthusiast who was well acquainted in the San Diego area. Artley, coincidentally, was doubly related in law to Fred Ludlow, as the two had married sisters.

Budelier moved to Los Angeles, and after the Appeal Company closed out their operations, he opened up temporary headquarters at Main and Adams Streets, some distance from the notorious 'Motorcycle Row', and planned the construction of a large new facility. As a long time friend of Hap Scherer, and noting that he was now unemployed, Budelier immediately offered him the position of Sales Manager in his new venture. It has been reported by long time factory employees that Walter Davidson was so enraged that Scherer was about to rejoin H-D operations outside his immediate jurisdiction that he at once proposed to force Budelier to withdraw his job offer. It is also reported that Arthur Davidson intervened at this point, suggesting that Hap Scherer's popularity and broad acquaintanceship among H-D enthusiasts would be of significant benefit to the critical Western Sales effort.

Another significant milestone in this period of H-D history was the addition of Arthur R. Constantine to the Company's Engineering Department. Constantine was a graduate engineer who had lately been employed in the Development and Design Department of General Motors' Buick Division.

At this juncture, Alfred Rich Child enters the story; a most remarkable man whose subsequent connection with the H-D Company and whose later activities within the industry were to have a significant bearing on the course of the country's motorcycling history. He was born in Chichester, Sussex, England on May 20 1891, the son of a retired officer in the British Navy who had later returned to service with the Coast Guard. In common with many other sons of naval personnel, he had spent his early youth as a cadet in the Greenwich Royal Naval School, from which he had graduated in 1907. It was during this period that he first became familiar with motorcycles, as one of the instructors rode an early Ormonde machine. Following his graduation, Child's father proposed that he should apprentice himself to a corn broker, but young Child demurred at the confinements of a desk job and the limited future of an office clerk. The elder Child insisted, and in the ensuing family conflict engendered by his refusal, he ran away from home and took passage to New York City on a Cunard liner, working his passage as a mess steward. Arriving at his destination with but $3.00 in his pocket, he immediately obtained a job in an office building as maintenance man and elevator operator. Passing through a series of varied employments, he was, for a time, butler and handyman on the Long Island Estate of William Thaw, whose son Harry was involved in the noted shooting fray with architect Sanford White over the favors of Evelyn Nesbet, a well known New York courtesan. During this period, Child rode an early 'camel back' Indian owned by William.

Noting the lack of opportunity in being a servant, Child conceived the idea of establishing a travelling clothing supply and haberdashery business to serve the house staffs of the great Long Island estates, as their isolation and lack of transportation made it difficult for them to travel to stores. Child's transport for this enterprise was a 1914 H-D sidecar outfit, purchased from a dealer in New York City.

A short time later, soon after the start of the war in Europe, he obtained his first substantial employment as a petty officer in the US Coast Guard, based on his experience as a naval cadet. His initial assignment was aboard a cutter whose function was to carry personnel to board and search cargo and passenger ships leaving New York harbor for Europe for possible contraband that would aid the Central Powers, as even at this early stage of the war, US sympathies were for the Allies.

It was at this time that Child contracted a severe case of influenza, a world wide scourge of the later war period, and after he recovered sufficiently to return to duty, he was posted to the Passport Office. In those days the Coast Guard had the sole government jurisdiction not only for the issuing of passports, but also was empowered to collect income taxes from departing aliens who at that time were forced to declare any income derived during their stay in the United States.

It was in the performance of these duties that Child met David Weistrich, an English Jew who 69 owned a wholesale bicycle parts supply concern in New York City. The latter urgently required a quick passport to enable him to make a trip to Holland to collect a $50,000 debt owed him by a firm in that country. As the proposed journey was most critical to Weistrich's fortunes, and as Child was able to expedite the clearance of his passport, the two struck up an immediate friendship. Noting Child's obvious executive abilities, Weistrich told Child to look him up following his return from Europe. Child joined the Weistrich sales force as a traveling representative in the late fall of 1918. His initial travels were scheduled through the Southern states, and Child elected to utilize a 'J' model H-D sidecar outfit which could also carry his samples. As Weistrich had, in the meantime, acquired the franchise for the wholesaling of New Departure coaster brakes and other bicycle parts, Child could now offer a broad line of highly saleable products. In addition, he carried a line of small oil lanterns made of copper, which sold for a dollar, and were very popular sellers where rural electrification was still two decades away. Then Weistrich became ill, and turned the management of the business over to his brother-in-law. Child recalls that he did not get along too well with the man, as the latter proposed to reduce his formerly lucrative commission agreement. Casting about for a new selling opportunity, and after some reflection, he decided to apply to the H-D Company for a sales position, being by this time favorably impressed with the ruggedness and dependability of their machines.

Child contacted the factory, and soon received a telegram from Sales Manager Arthur Davidson. The two ultimately met in the old Algonquin Hotel on 28th Street in New York City. Davidson was initially concerned about Child's ethnic background, particularly relating to whether or not he was Jewish! (Child still had his broad British accent.) Upon being assured of his pure Aryan background, Davidson next inquired whether his business and ethical concepts had been unfavorably influenced by his late connection with a Jewish owned firm, and if such might render him unfit to become associated with a strictly gentile-owned company. While this episode might appear preposterous in the light of today's racial and ethnic toleration, such was not the case in the United States in the early 1920's. As white Protestant Anglo-Saxon culture was predominant in America, most people were suspicious of foreigners, particularly following the victory of social radicals in Russia. The swarming ghettos of foreign races caused native apprehension in many of the nation's larger cities, particularly concerning the threat of job displacement. These emotions were heightened by the popular sentiment of isolationalism following the war. The often prosperous foreigners, particularly Jews, were generally barred from membership in social clubs, country clubs, and many of the country's leading hotels and summer resorts. The reactivated Ku Klux Klan boasted over three million members, all dedicated to preserving the purity of America, and in some areas Jews, Catholics, and black people were subject to persecution. Henry Ford was soon to publish his infamous protocols of Zion, purporting to expose a widespread Jewish conspiracy to control the world's money supply. Racial and ethnic pejudice did not materially abate until well after World War II.

After some discussion, Child was able to convince Davidson not only of his pure Aryan background, but of his fitness to undertake a job, and he was put to work under Theodore A. (Ted) Miller, Arthur Davidson's assistant in charge of domestic sales. His first base of operation was from his home in Garden City, Long Island, from which he operated as a company Sales Representative and Area Supervisor for the States of New York, New Jersey, New England and Eastern Canada. Following this, he was reassigned to the Southern States. Child recalls that he was no doubt sent to this territory because of his previous experience in the area, and because H-D sales in the deep south up to this point had not been spectacular. As in the case of other factory representatives, he was provided with vouchers for his expenses for fuel, oil, food and lodging. With characteristic Scottish thrift, Arthur Davidson informed him that due to the exigencies of post-war inflation, the company was now forced to allow up to 80 cents a day for meals and up to $1.50 per night for hotel rooms, but in no case were these figures to be exceeded! Child's assignment was to personally call on the approximately 48 dealers presently franchised in the Old Confederacy, offer them help with sales promotion and sales techniques, and act to iron out any real or imagined problems they might have with their relations with the factory. He was also ordered to see to it that the dealers take delivery of crated machines languishing in railroad freight depots, as, in line with the company's strict pay-on-delivery policy, a sight draft from the local bank had to be presented to take delivery. It was his idea to take photographs of each dealer and his premises with his own camera, so the management could correlate their sales performance with their public image. This was a factor in determining the annual dealer review for the yearly franchise renewal.

In the Spring of 1921, Child was next assigned to Milwaukee, where he was still involved in the Sales Department, and he accordingly moved his family from Long Island to that city.

Arthur Davidson next projected a selling mission to South Africa, where Indian, and secondly Excelsior, were particularly strong, and where H-D's representation up to this point had not been effectual. Child, selected to make the journey, was provided with a new electrically-equipped 'J' sidecar outfit, fitted with a wide-bodied Rogers built unit for enhanced carrying capacity. He left Milwaukee early that Spring for New York, where he embarked on the Mauretania for Southampton. He first visited his parents in England, and then embarked on a Castle Line steamer, the Windsor Castle, for Capetown. His initial visit was with A.R.Callow Limited, who had taken a H-D franchise a year and a half previously, and to date had sold 39 machines, mostly sidecar outfits. Child remained in Capetown for a few weeks, aiding Callow to inaugurate a more aggressive sales campaign, which resulted in their selling more machines and enlarging their operation. He next journeyed to Johannesburg, calling on bicycle dealers in both that city and in adjacent territories. He recalls that his main problem was to locate such dealers with the requisite mechanical ability to undertake the service and repair of machines sold, which was a highly necessary adjunct to a successful dealership. Along the way, Child was able to undertake numerous sightseeing trips, implemented by the fact that Arthur Davidson had instructed him to stay at the best hotels and to entertain prospective dealers without reference to rigid economy, all backed with a $5,000 letter of credit from the Marshall and Illsley bank in Milwaukee. In this case, the traditional H-D Scottish thrift was subordinated to management's desire to appear before the South Africans as an outstandingly affluent organization.

Along the way, Child visited the famous de Beers diamond mine as well as the scenic Victoria Falls, and his subsequent travels through South Africa could provide enough subject matter for a separate book in itself. He traveled over nearly impassable or non-existent roads, sold 50 machines to a native dictator in Mombassa, and was transported over streams and rivers by large companies of native warriors, who carried the outfit bodily on a pair of long poles positioned under the sidecar chassis. After a series of incredible adventures which are now a part of Child's extensive personal memoirs, he ultimately arrived in Cairo, where he transhipped his outfit to Italy. In all, he booked orders for over 400 machines, and added a number of dealers to the Company's roster. In spite of his efforts, Indian continued to be the most popular big twin machine on the African continent.

Meanwhile, back at the factory, the H-D Company was in process of contending with the shrinking domestic market. The Company now had about 1,200 dealers franchised, producing about 11,000 machines for the 1921 sales season. Indian shipped about 7,000 units that year, due to numerous production and financial problems, but still serviced well over 1,000 dealers. While H-D led in production, its domestic sales still were about on a par with Indian, the difference being that H-D's export shipments to Europe and South America were ahead of the Wigwam. Excelsior was a poor third, with about 300 dealers who now concentrated on the four-cylinder Henderson. Cleveland, Iver-Johnson, Reading Standard, Shickel, and Neracar, the last a rather curious utility model with center-pivot steering, were still in evidence, but cumulatively sold only about 4,000 machines.

In order to beef up dealer confidence, H-D announced a general dealers' meeting to be held at the factory in the early spring of 1922. The event was billed as a dedication ceremony for the new factory, which in itself was a rather anticlimatic gesture, as the new facilities had been in operation for nearly two years. Invitations were extended to all dealers in the United States and Canada, but the bulk of the attendance was from the adjacent Midwestern region. Aside from a tour of the factory, whose production and assembly facilities were now drastically reduced, the general meetings were conducted in a large garage facility at the rear of the Juneau Avenue complex. The main conference featured the appearance of the Chairman of the Board of Directors of the Marshall and Illsley Bank, who in a somewhat florid speech, (the author's informant who was there states that in his opinion, it was written by the company's Publicity Department), extolled the merits of the Company and its products, and informed the assemblage that President Walter Davidson's credit rating was such that he could obtain a million dollar loan at any time by just signing his name for it. The meeting also featured the first official appearance of William H.Davidson, Vice President William A.Davidson's son, presently enrolled as a student at the University of Wisconsin in Business Administration, who gave an address on the promising future of the motorcycle industry.

The Company's labor force, now drastically reduced from the industry's salad days, consisted mostly of veteran employees from the Company's original incorporation in 1907, when production of H-Ds had begun in earnest. But few had been added since the drastic retrenchment a year or two before, and these only when needed through natural deaths or attrition.

William Davidson, always in charge of production, was ever the stern taskmaster, ruthlessly discharging on the spot any worker who was caught shirking his duties or whose efforts could not measure up to his exacting standards of excellence. On the other hand, any good worker who was experiencing personal, domestic, or financial problems, could find a readily sympathetic ear from 'Big Bill', as he was affectionately called. The latter always carried with him a sizable roll of money, and any worker in genuine need could always count on a $50.00 or $100.00 advance on his salary if the occasion demanded. These 'loans' could be paid back at the worker's option, but no formal demands were ever made for repayment. While the wages paid to H-D's production crew were always somewhat below that of the prevailing standard, they came to be a hard core of loyal enthusiasts whose term of service in many cases was measured in decades rather than years.

71

Claude Temple, a consistent winner at various Brooklands events. He is here seen winning the BMCRC Championship on October 7, 1921 at 92.37 mph. *(The Motor Cycle).*

The Company's sales efforts were now directed toward the refined electrically equipped 'J' model, lately offered in 74 cubic inch as well as the traditional 61 cubic inch categories. The Company had dropped the original Remy electrical equipment shortly after the war, not only to save the cost of buying proprietary equipment, but also to free themselves from dependence on outside suppliers. The first factory built units had in some cases proved unreliable, however, and many an owner had replaced factory equipment with still existing Remy components. The factory had made haste to rectify the matter, and by 1922 these were now functioning with acceptable reliability. What with the termination of factory-sponsored competition, the sales emphasis was now on reliability rather than speed, and the suitability of H-D products for individual transport, as well as commercial and law enforcement uses.

Touring articles were now featured in the *Enthusiast,* and they ran a series of continuing articles on the adventures of two ex-servicemen, or 'doughboys' as they were then called, Royal Gerberick and Roy Kerle, who with a 1920 electrically-equipped 'J' sidecar outfit covered 19,000 miles on a circuitous trip through the midwestern and western areas of the country. In spite of universally bad roads and a heavily overloaded outfit, the two intrepid travelers experienced but minimal mechanical trouble.

Meanwhile, H-D's management was in process of its continuing evaluation of the shrinking domestic motorcycle market. At midseason of 1922, President Walter Davidson ordered the phasing out of the production of the Sport Twin. Motorcycle historians have long speculated about the reasons for the dis-continuance of this very sound model. Outside of a few initial problems with overheating of the rear cylinder, which were solved by minor improvement to the lubrication system, the model had been eminently satisfactory within its sphere of employment. One logical theory is that the domestic middleweight market had up to that time been dominated by Indian's very popular Indian Scout. While of the same cylinder displacement, its V twin configuration afforded it superior torque and pulling power, and its hill climbing abilities and top speed were somewhat superior to the 'W' as a result. Then too, it was of the now traditional American V twin design, where the former was of rather unorthodox type, to American riders at least. There was also a certain resistance to the model from the dealers themselves, already firmly orientated to heavyweight machines offering a high speed capability, and in many cases loath to promote a model that offered mild, but dependable performance to utility riders. Another possible alternative was the fact that H-D production was currently organized to manufacture the 'J' models, long the backbone of Milwaukee's organization, and the relatively low volume of 'W' production added to the costing that William Davidson was constantly seeking to rationalize.

While the machine was an attraction to schoolboys, rural mail carriers, cautious utility riders, and a few intrepid feminine enthusiasts, it was not a model that fitted in with the current high speed macho image fancied by the majority of fans who sought to emulate the racing star's image. Furthermore, its former principal exponent at the factory, Hap Scherer, was no longer engaged in promoting medium performance motorcycling on the West Coast. The Sport Twin was always more popular overseas than at home, being well accepted in England, Europe, Australia and New Zealand. The flat twin was already well thought of in these areas, where the type had been pioneered by Douglas as well as lesser makes. When production finally ended in 1922, about 6,000 units had come off the assembly lines. A few examples are known to have been shipped to Duncan Watson on special order during 1923 and 1924, presumably built up from remaining spare parts in stock. While the machine had created a mild sensation among utility riders a couple of years earlier, its death knell had probably been sounded by the cheap car, whose recent high production was now bringing vast numbers to the used market to sell at very low prices.

The author's first motorcycle was a weathered but sound 1920 'W' magneto-equipped model purchased in the Spring of 1927 in partnership with a schoolboy friend, who put up half of the $10.00 purchase price. A new set of spark plugs restored its inherent easy starting and smooth running capabilities, and it afforded many pleasurable short journeys into the countryside, adding much to the fascination of boyhood search for adventure. It was subsequently sold to make possible the acquisition of a more powerful 61 cubic inch 'J' model, which later added another facet to the author's H-D experiences.

In the Fall of 1922, Arthur Davidson and Indian's General Manager Frank Weschler inaugurated the first of a series of clandestine meetings between the top management of both factories.

The Temple-Anzani Special. The specially-designed 61 inch 998 cc ohc engine was fitted to a chassis built by the Osborne Engineering Company, utilizing many H-D parts. *(The Motor Cycle).*

The object appeared to be a general discussion of the many problems besetting the industry, but the main reason was to equalize the retail prices of their comparable models. While such agreements had long been illegal in business and industry under the Sherman and Clayton Antitrust Acts against restraint of trade, it was still an almost universal practice among like segments of American industry. While the Davidsons, with their usual Scottish caution, had ever been wary of any sort of fraternization with the personnel of competing companies, they had enjoyed a somewhat ambiguous relationship with Frank Weschler ever since he was Indian's unofficial manager in 1916. At all the big National Races since that time, when H-D was the more frequent winner, Weschler had always made it a point to cordially congratulate both riders and management on their victories. Then too, he had earned their natural, if grudging, admiration for his almost single handed heroism in saving the company during its dark days of 1921. With the current state of the motorcycle market, it now appeared expedient to at least remove any retail price differential between the two makes.

At the meeting in question, held in a suite in New York City's Astor Hotel, the author's informant, then a young member of the sales staff, stated that the two dined in private in an adjacent room. Savoring crepe suzettes and lobster thermidor in an atmosphere of somewhat strained conviviality, it was decided that as Indian had undercut by $5.00 on similar models in 1921, Indian would add a $5.00 premium to their 1922 models. It was then agreed that, henceforth, similar models in each case would carry the same price tag through a continuing yearly gentlemen's agreement.

By 1922, the more or less continuous attempts at long distance record breaking on the part of both car drivers and motorcycle riders had come to an end. By this time the surface of most of the principal continental and important regional routes had been improved to the point that ordinary travel had become commonplace. Through energetic lobbying on the part of various regional and national automobile clubs, the main transcontinental highway, now known as the Lincoln Highway, had been improved to the point that the adventurous motorist could now undertake its traverse without fear of

A 1926 Zenith-JAP Special at Brooklands. In common with many other large V twin Specials, this machine had fitted H-D forks. *(The Motor Cycle)*.

either wandering from its well marked route, getting mired in axle-deep mud or sustaining physical damage from large rocks and boulders.

The principal long distance exponent for spectacular record attempts up to this period in US motoring history had been Erwin G. 'Cannonball' Baker, who had at one time or another ridden most leading makes of motorcycles as well as piloting several makes of popular automobiles over the country's nearly impossible routes. In the motorcycle sphere, at one time or another he competed for Ace, Excelsior, Henderson, and Indian, the notable exception being Harley-Davidson. In an interview with the author in 1957, when queried about this descrepancy, Baker stated that while he had several tentative contacts with H-D President Walter Davidson regarding both transcontinental and Three Flag record attempts on the West Coast, the two could never agree on Baker's financial terms for such appearances. Baker, after his reputation as a record breaker was well established, usually charged the sponsor of the make in question $1,000 for his appearance on the course, plus $25.00 per hour for each hour shaved from the current record. In his negotiations with Davidson, the latter demurred at the high initial fee, and instead countered with an offer of $250.00 for the appearance and $50.00 for each record hour. Baker stated that his own expenses for fuel, oil, and comfort stops en route at stated intervals usually cost more than this amount, mostly for fees for the persons involved in implementing them, and that Davidson's offer could give him only a modest fee for what was usually a herculean effort. It was for this reason that Baker never made any serious record attempts on H-D machines, as according to his own statements, Davidson was not sporting enough to invest any real money in Baker's now proven abilities of endurance.

An interesting footnote to long distance record breaking during the swashbuckling days of motorcycle was the experience related by Wells Bennett, the noted Excelsior exponent, incidental to his attempt in the early summer of 1921 to break the existing Three Flag record. Starting from the usual jumping off place at Blaine, Washington, he made phenomenal time from there through Oregon, due to unusually good weather conditions. His luck still held through California's great valley until he reached Fresno, when he was flagged down by a local motorcycle policeman for speeding. Bennett managed to put up bail to insure his return to fight the citation, but lost two valuable hours of riding time in the process. Upon reaching Bakersfield some distance south, he was again apprehended for allegedly exceeding the speed limit, and was incarcerated in the local jail for the night, obviously terminating his record attempt.

In later years, Bennett was fond of recounting this adventure, and offered evidence that the H-D dealers along the route from San Jose south had importuned the law enforcement officers to impede and ultimately to terminate his run, which was certain to have set a new running time.

During the 1923 competition at the great Brooklands oval in England, H-D entrants continued to rack up impressive records. On April 7th 1923, at a meeting sponsored by the BMCRC, Freddie Dixon won the Three Lap Solo Race on an 8 valve H-D Special, provided by Duncan Watson, at the record speed of 94.5 mph. That same Fall he won the 1,000 cc Championship Race with the same machine, at 100.10 mph. Taking it to France the month before, he had won the flying start kilometer record on the Bois de Boulogne at 106.8 m.p.h.

Brooklands speedman Claude Temple, during the early months of 1923, had put together a machine of his own design which he named the British Anzani Special, utilizing a specially built 998 cc 57 degree V twin with overhead camshafts. This machine, a wonder in its day at Brooklands, with H-D frame, forks, and wheels, hung up a number of speed records that stood for several seasons. This historic machine happily still exists in the hands of M.N.Mavrogordato, a British racing motorcycle enthusiast.

The high speed steering characteristics of earlier model H-Ds with their traditional leading link forks has long been a matter of controversy among motorcycle historians and vintage enthusiasts. Even the author has been preoccupied with the results of their effect on the early Brooklands record breakers. A more or less satisfactory answer to this question was ultimately forthcoming from the late Harry Coulter, a one-time mechanic who aided in the preparation of both H-D and other big V twins fitted with similar types of fork. In an interview with the author in 1959, Coulter stated that most of the H-D record breakers modified the steering geometry to form a greater rake at the head lug, and shortened the compression springs to bring the axle pivot well above its attachment to the fixed fork leg. This modification steadied the steering at high speeds, although it imparted a rather disconcerting roll when the machine was set to turn at speeds below 50 mph. While this effect could be of some consequence in touring or utility use, it was obviously unimportant at the 90-100 mph speeds attained in record breaking attempts.

A somewhat battered but mechanically sound 1924 magneto equipped 'J' model was the author's second machine, acquired in the summer of 1929 as the result of the sale of the originally owned 1920 Sport Twin. Purchased for $20.00, and enhanced by an $11.00 valve-and-ring overhaul by local Santa Rosa dealer Joe Frugoli's mechanic, Charles Cook, the machine provided many hours of pleasurable motorcycling adventure. In addition, it afforded first hand experience of the vagaries of H-D's classic steering at high speeds.

Somewhat north of the author's home in Santa Rosa, just outside the village of Cloverdale to the north, there was a long hill whose gentle gravel gradient provided a fairly smooth surface. Boy racers were wont to utilize this course, as it offered an enhanced simulation of motorcycle or car high speed capabilities. The author's 61, as overhauled and run in, had a top speed of about 64 mph. At this speed, the steering was steady. On the slight downgrade, at full throttle, this capability increased to about 72 mph, and at this rate of travel an annoying, if not dangerous, wobble made itself felt. A very slight acceleration then produced a tank-slapping gyration that was down-right frightening. The machine was subsequently examined by Dealer Joe Frugoli, who checked the frame and forks for cor-

John Cameron's 1920 eight valve Special. The engine was located in England, and John completed the machine with authentic period parts. *(George Hays)*.

rect alignment, and found all in order. His ultimate suggestion was that the forks be dismantled and the compression springs shortened to decrease the angle of the bottom links, apparently even in those days the time honored cure. As the cost of this modification was $5.00, and the author was an impecunious schoolboy, the conversion was declined, and thereafter his riding was confined to speeds under 65 mph.

In the early spring of 1923, Indian's General Manager, Frank J. Weschler, journeyed from Springfield to Chicago, taking with him funds to pay off a short term loan negotiated from a bank in that city during one of Indian's recurring financial crises. As the Springfield banks had become somewhat wary of Indian, with their recent boom-and-bust history of performance, Weschler had been forced to travel far afield to raise capital to carry on operations. His terminus near Milwaukee then prompted him to arrange another policy meeting with H-D's management, subsequently held in the Blackstone Hotel, Chicago, on April 3rd and 4th.

With the usual price fixing on parallel models concluded, President Walter Davidson next suggested that another matter be settled, namely that franchised H-D and Indian dealers be forbidden to handle any other make of machine. Up to this time, it must be noted that some of the larger dealers handling both H-D and Indian frequently also held franchises for Excelsior, Cleveland, Iver Johnson, Reading Standard, and Neracar. While H-D and Indian were not particularly amenable to this arrangement, they often hesitated to interfere too far in the dealer's private affairs, especially if he had taken on either of the large manufacturer's makes after he had already undertaken business with other makes. Walter Davidson's reasoning and that of his brother Arthur was that with the critical condition of the domestic market, it was now illogical that the showrooms of the largest two surviving manufacturers should feature competitive machines. Weschler was reported to have disagreed, stating that

motorcycling in general might attract more potential converts if a wider choice of makes and models were available. The author's informant in the matter, a young clerk in Indian's accounting department who had accompanied his chief to Chicago, stated that Walter Davidson was adamant in the matter, and after a time, Weschler capitulated. The enforcement of the new edict was once placed in the hands of the regional traveling representatives of both factories, who would at once report any infraction of the ruling to the top management, so that the matter could be reviewed when the yearly franchise reviews came up. H-D, of course, would brook no flouting of their authority, but Indian's management sometimes looked the other way in cases where a few of their dealers had enjoyed previous successes with the Cleveland. The virtual phasing out of Excelsior's once-popular 61 cubic inch twin in favor of their more successful Henderson Four somewhat simplified the problem for both, as many new dealerships were being established to handle that model exclusively. H-D and Indian's enhanced 'gentleman's agreement' sounded the death knell of such marginal makes as Reading Standard,

Schickel, Iver Johnson, and pushed the mildly popular utility Cleveland out of the market. The clandestine Chicago meeting, while probably known to less than half a dozen people within the industry at the time, was ultimately to have far reaching effects upon the continuing decline of motorcycling interest in the United States.

All three of the domestic motorcycle factories now turned their attention to export markets, which were buying sufficient volume of production to ensure the survival of the industry.

Chapter 4

Oriental Interlude

THE EXPORT OF HARLEY-DAVIDSON MACHINES TO JAPAN AND THE ORIENT DURING the early 1920's involves a most complex set of circumstances, and therefore requires a separate chapter in itself. At the outset, it is sufficient to say that it was not only critical as a necessary adjunct to an export program necessary for the company's survival due to a depressed domestic market, but was also instrumental in Japan's development of its own future auto and motorcycle industries. It may be noted that Indian was already entrenched in Japan, with an active agency in Tokyo importing 600-700 machines per year, about 40% of them being sidecar outfits. Prince (later Emperor) Hirohito rode such an outfit for some years.

A handful of H-D machines were imported to Japan by the Army during the years 1912-1917, but, curiously enough, no spare parts were ever ordered. No doubt the Army officers involved believed quite literally the H-D advertising statements that their machines were largely trouble-free! Early in 1922, an import firm in Tokyo, Nippon Jidoshe K.K., headed by the young Baron Okura, which had been importing limited numbers of American automobiles since 1919, sent Milwaukee an order for a small trial order of 74 cubic inch 'J' model electrically-equipped machines in the Spring of 1922. During the following year they imported about a further dozen machines. During the following year they imported about a further dozen machines, ignoring company suggestions that they stock a few of the more critical categories of spare parts.

It was during this period that the Charles Cable Company, an import-export firm in San Francisco, wrote to Milwaukee stating that they were presently doing business with a merchant in Ulan Bator, the capital of Inner Mongolia. They suggested that if they could obtain the distributorship for all H-D products in Inner and Outer Mongolia, they would place substantial orders with the company, and pay against documents placed in San Francisco banks.

In the meantime, the Charles Cable Company placed some substantial orders for H-D machines that same year. Payments were made on delivery from funds deposited in San Francisco banks, and for some reason it was thought in Milwaukee that somehow the Charles Cable Company was supplying machines and other commodities to Ulan Bator. However, it soon became some cause for concern that no spare parts were ever ordered. Charles Cable insisted that the Mongolians had their own spare parts, although it was difficult to imagine that an area encompassed by the Gobi Desert and, under an economy based on the breeding of goats and camels, could possess machine shop facilities to carry on such work!

At this point, Alfred Rich Child, who had just returned from his epic journey on H-D's behalf through South Africa, was informed by the Company that he should soon be preparing himself for a survey of the Japanese and far Eastern situation regarding a potential motorcycle market.

On September 1, 1923, the Kanto or Eastern area of Japan was devastated by a catastrophic earthquake that killed or injured hundreds of thousands of people and left millions homeless. During this period, Charles Cable visited Milwaukee and had a conference with Eric von Gumpert, still H-D's titular head of the Export Department, but more properly functioning as Traffic Manager. Cable suggested that the time was ripe for appointing him H-D distributor for Japan, Korea, and Manchuria. On orders from management, von Gumpert informed them that at the moment, the Japan Automobile Company of Nippon Jidosha were the official distributors of the Company's products in Japan, and that pending a survey by Alfred Rich Child as Export Sales Representative, they would make no other appointments.

To further complicate the situation, in the Spring of 1924 the Congress of the United States passed a rigid immigration law severely limiting the immigration of Asiatics into the United States, which included Japanese. This was a tremendous blow to Japanese pride, and the Japanese Ambassador in Washington D.C. immediately demanded an exception to the ruling for his countrymen, on the threat of 'serious consequences'. When such a ruling was not forthcoming, violent demonstrations erupted in every Japanese city from Hokodate to Kagashima.

It was in this hostile atmosphere that Alfred Rich Child disembarked at Yokohama in July 1924, from the Canadian Pacific liner 'Empress of Canada', and registered at Tokoyo's Imperial Hotel. It became evident that Charles Cable had contacts in Japan as well as in Ulan Bator, as Child was invited a few days later to dine with the Baron Okura, who had been educated in both England and the United States, and spoke excellent English.

During the subsequent meeting with Okura, Child pointed out that H-D's management were dissatisfied with the sales results so far achieved by his staff of Nippon Jidosha, as well as their total disregard for the necessity for maintaining a stock of spare parts. Okura, on the other hand, continued to defend both his own and his employees' sales policies, and demanded that Nippon Jidosha be granted a continuation of their present yearly contract. After several futile attempts to resolve the matter, Child ultimately broke off all negotiations with this group.

It was at this juncture that an English speaking native named Yamada, who had once represented the Izu Peninsula Tea Growers as a lobbyist in Washington, introduced Child to one Genijiro Fukui, a US-educated individual who was one of the three founders of a now prestigious pharmaceutical manufacturing concern, the Sankyo Company Limited of Muromachi, Tokyo. Its President, Matasaku Shiohara, was presently in negotiation with Dr. Baekeland, the inventor of 'Bakelite', to secure the rights to manufacture products made from this material in Japan. During Child's conversations with Fukui, it was revealed that he and one Ichita Taguchi headed the Koto Trading Company, an import and export subsidiary of the Sankyo Company Limited.

It then became apparent to Child that Charles Cable had been secretly diverting some of the H-D motorcycle shipments, originally consigned to Mongolia, to Japan, and in effect 'bootlegging' them to the Koto Trading Co. right under Nippon Jidosha's nose, in spite of their so-called exclusive sales rights to act as H-D agents.

Perceiving the duplicity of the Koto organization, Child then opened negotiations with the three principals of the Sankyo Company in view of appointing them H-D distributors from Japan, subject to certain conditions which would be laid down by Milwaukee. It was obvious that in view of the earthquake devastated Japanese roads, a 1200 cc H-D sidecar, sidevan, or three-wheeled rear car would be for several years an ideal vehicle to use under these conditions.

During an exchange of cablegrams between Child and Milwaukee, it was decided that Child should be the titualar head of the agency, in view of the double-dealing that had been experienced between Cable and the Koto organization. During this time Baron Okura attempted to intervene on his own behalf, but was ultimately informed that his company would receive no more H-D machines. At this point, the three principals of the Sankyo organization were agreeable to the condition that Child remain in Japan to act as liaison between themselves and Milwaukee. To this end Child produced a letter of credit from the National City Bank of New York to cover the purchase of 350 Big Twin H-D machines, mostly with sidecars. Also included were $20,000 worth of replacement parts and $3,000 worth of dealers' repair tools. In addition, the whole transaction was covered by an agreement that Child would be the Managing Director of a newly formed 'Harley-Davidson Sales Company of Japan', his recompense to be 5% of the landed cost of all H-D products. The wholesale cost of the machines was augmented by freight, crating, and excise duties paid at the port of entry.

Following the consummation by cable of the details of his export agreement, Child sailed for the States on the Empress of Canada, whereon landing at Vancouver he met Arthur Davidson who was just returning from a sales trip to Australia and New Zealand. Arthur was justly congratulatory of Child's Japanese effort, as he had originally discouraged the initial sales attempts in that country due to the current anti-American sentiment following the Asiatic Exclusion Act.

Child met with the Founders in Milwaukee to finalize the details of the export of machines to

Ray Weishaar's 1923 61 cu.in.
pocket valve racer. In original
condition, it is a part of the
Bud Ekins collection.
Weishaar cut his name on the
timing case cover. *(Alisha
Tamburri).*

Japan. In August, 1924, he returned to Tokyo to organize the import machinery. He had previously hired Harry Devine, the factory H-D Parts Manager who had already enjoyed nearly twenty years of experience with the parent firm, to accompany him.

The H-D Motorcycle Sales Company of Japan, now its official title, set up headquarters in a rented building just off the Ginza at the Kyobashi crossing in Tokyo. One of the earliest native employees was Yamada, who became Child's right-hand man, along with Morikichi Sakurai who was not only a skilled mechanic but an ardent motorcycle enthusiast. Most of the subsequent staff became enthusiasts as time went one. Capitalization for the agency was provided by Genjiro Fukui of the Sankyo Pharmaceutical Company.

The first shipments of H-D machines to Kyobashi were the 1925 models as designed by Arthur Constantine, much to Child's peace of mind, as the earlier sheet metal soldered tanks from the flat tank era were prone to leak.

When the new bulbous tank models were imported during January 1925, there were few motorcycles manufactured in Japan, as at that time they had no such industry. Competition was provided by Indian, who were at this time marketing 800 to 1,000 machines per year. Various production and financial problems in Springfield had been making shipments somewhat erratic, however, and within a couple of years H-D imports exceeded those of Indian. Other makes concurrently being imported included AJS, Matchless and Norton from England, Husqvarna from Sweden, Moto-Guzzi from Italy, and after 1927, BMW from Germany. Realizing that the prime transportation requirement in Japan at this time was in the commercial sphere, Child wisely concluded that the rugged 74 cubic inch models could be best utilized as sidecar, sidevan or for the powering of rear cars. Morikichi Sakurai designed both the heavyweight and light duty rear cars, the latter for use with the newly introduced 21 cubic inch side valve singles in 1925-26.

Limited competition from a native manufacturer subsequently appeared in the form of a rear car powered with a 500 cc proprietary side valve engine supplied by J.A. Prestwich of Great Britain. Another contemporary Japanese firm entered the rear car field with an exact copy of the 21 cubic inch H-D design, built by a company that ultimately produced the contemporary rotary engine Mazda.

As the Sankyo Company's original activity was the manufacture of pharmaceutical products, it quite naturally participated in contract sales of these products to certain government agencies, namely the Army and Navy. Following up these contacts it also secured contracts for the sale of H-D motorcycles to the armed forces, and these machines became the standard military vehicles.

In addition, district police prefectures and the Post Office department purchased hundreds of H-Ds. Through the Outer Mongolian contacts, numerous H-Ds were sold to various Chinese and Manchurian War Lords, after 1929, such as Chang Tso Lin. His son Chang Hsu Liang, as well as Chiang Kai-shek, purchased as many as 200 machines at a time, mostly sidecar outfits.

A typical small town rural motorcycle dealer's premises in the deep South. This was apparently the time before H-D exerted its single-make mandate over their franchisees. *(Alfred Rich Child).*

A typical Southern sheriff with his trusty 'J' Model. Charged with suppressing the illicit
liquor traffic, law enforcement officers frequently encountered rum runners using identical
equipment! *(Alfred Rich Child)*.

As the business expanded, branch sales offices were opened in Osaka and Fukuoka in Japan, and
Darien, Manchuria. In addition, a new four story structure was built in the Temeike district of Tokyo
containing a large spare parts warehouse and service facility. This building was used until 1973 when it
was replaced by a larger edifice. Spare parts distribution was handled from Tokyo, which allocated
them throughout Japan and Manchuria, as required.

In addition, about 400 service and dealer outlets were established throughout the islands of
Japan itself. Some of these were substantial operations, but the majority were characteristic Oriental
single family enterprises, where the mechanic's family lived and worked in a one room makeshift
building on dirt floors. Such was characteristic of all engine and mechanical repair work undertaken in
the Orient during those days, and Child reports that it was difficult to induce the mechanics to utilize
the conventional work benches that he later provided from company workshops.

Subsequent to the inauguration of H-D sales in Japan, Child made at least one journey a year to
Milwaukee to maintain a close contact with the company, and to suggest improvements in shipping
methods. A particular problem of this period was the rough handling accorded crated machines in
transit, and Child had to insist on extra heavy packing of shipments to avoid damage, which in many
cases in the past had been extreme. It was during this period that Child underwent treatment for a
cancerous condition in the bones of his left hand. He was first treated in Milwaukee General Hospital,
but shortly afterwards sustained an amputation in Saint Lukes Hospital in Tokyo.

A critical problem for all importers of American products into Japan arose in the Fall of 1929
when the yen, which, in 1924, was the equivalent of 49¼ American cents, suddenly dropped to 20 to
30 cents. This meant that the ultimate retail price of H-D machines would by necessity be doubled. In
discussing this matter with the author in an interview in the fall of 1978, Child stated that this new state
of affairs indicated that either the export of H-D machines to Japan be terminated, or else an agreement be effected with the Company whereby manufacturing rights to H-D machines be secured for
Japan. Not wishing to give up his by this time lucrative business in Japan, Child conferred at length
with the management of H-D for the securing of such rights, along with the necessary blueprints,
material lists and specifications, heat-treating formulae, machine tool and die sequences, plus all other
necessary data.

Sankyo's management at length agreed to Child's proposal, as well as offering the requisite
financial backing, and Child set sail from Yokohama on the Asama Maru in company with Shiohara's
son-in-law, who was to act as liaison representative for Milwaukee.

At the initial meeting in Milwaukee, the Founders were all skeptical of the engineering and
mechanical abilities of the Japanese to produce workable copies of H-D machines, and further expressed their surprise at Child's temerity for suggesting such an undertaking. After some considerable

negotiating, however, and no doubt motivated by the sudden inauguration of a world wide depression, together with the payment of $75,000 as a royalty, they agreed to conclude an agreement with the Sankyo group for the manufacture of H-D machines in Japan. The Company agreed to provide all necessary blueprints, material lists, metallurgy schedules, and all other directions for motorcycle manufacture, in return for an agreement that no Japanese-built H-D machines would be exported. It was also agreed that while tooling up for production, and prior to the actual manufacture of machines, Sankyo would continue to import and market the Milwaukee-made product.

As a part of the transaction, Child was able to hire Fred Barr, H-D's Assistant Factory Superintendent under George Nordberg, to supervise the setting up of Sankyo's manufacturing operation in Japan. Barr's title was now that of Chief Engineer, and he was offered a lucrative tax-free contract for three years. While Barr was a key man in the Milwaukee operation, Child believes that the Company was willing to let him resign due to the fact that they were already feeling the effect of the depression and were coincidentally cutting down on staff and production personnel.

Barr proved to be the key official in the new Japanese operation as subsequent events were soon to show. Together with Mr.A.Sakurai, Sankyo's first engineering supervisor at the Kyobashi crossing in 1925, Barr put together a group of capable young engineering personnel and mechanics who had friends and acquaintances in allied mechanical lines who ultimately became subcontractors to produce various component parts of H-D machines from the blueprints supplied from Milwaukee. These were submitted to the Shinagawa plant for inspection and evaluation by Fred Barr before their incorporation into prototype models for final testing before production was inaugurated.

In retrospect, and in view of the fact that in 1929 the Shinagawa factory was the very first complete motorcycle manufacturing plant in Japan, it may well be said that Sankyo's effort here was the forerunner of the great Japanese motorcycle industry which today dominates the world markets.

Incidental to the inauguration of Japanese production, the first shipments of the first of the initially ill-fated VL side valve 74 cubic inch models began arriving in Yokohama as per the original licensing agreement. Of the initial production of the first 1,300-odd defective machines, Child ultimately was obliged to make good some 73 units, the details of which unfortunate episode in H-D history will subsequently be described.

In the meantime, and while Barr was co-ordinating Japanese production of component parts, certain surplus machine tooling was purchased from the parent factory, some of which no doubt being declared surplus in Milwaukee due to the decline of US motorcycle production following the onset of the depression. Additional tooling was purchased from other US manufacturers, as well as from Germany, due to the favorable exchange rate.

No Japanese personnel were ever sent to Milwaukee for training in the factory's Service School, due to language difficulties. Additionally, none of the four Founders or any members of the Export Department's staff ever visited Japan, except for a brief visit from Walter Davidson, Jr., President Davidson's son, who passed through Japan on a brief pre-college tour before the Shinagawa factory commenced formal operation.

The only company representative to ever visit Japan before the consummation of the Sankyo agreement was Joseph Ryan, the Company Service and Parts Manager, who made the journey at Child's request in 1925 when Child requested some official aid in setting up his spare parts dispersal system incidental to his first export agreement with the factory itself.

As H-D machines fabricated completely from Japanese-made parts were not assembled and sold until early in 1935, Child continued to import substantial yearly shipments of Milwaukee-made machines. In recalling this phase of H-D history, Child told the author in 1978 that the existence of the continuing 5% landed cost commission from the factory on such shipments was a potent factor in his continuation of his 1924 export agreement.

During the early negotiations for Sankyo acquisition of H-D manufacturing rights, and in the subsequent complete manufacture of H-D machines in Japan, the H-D company carefully avoided any public disclosure of either their dealings with Sankyo or the fact that their machines were subsequently built under license by a Japanese concern. This was no doubt prompted by the growing awareness in the US of the buildup of Japanese military power, together with the general public disapproval of the Japanese military adventures in Manchuria.

As most motorcycle applications were still in the field of commercial transportation, most of the imported Milwaukee models were of the 74 cubic inch big twins, and 21 cubic inch and 30.50 cubic inch singles. These were shipped for adaptation to various types of Japanese manufactured rear cars, and consisted of complete machines, but with the rear wheel and mudguard omitted. The 45 cubic inch twin was not imported, as its general configuration and power development was considered not suited to rear car applications.

After the final production of Japanese H-Ds was finalized by 1935, and, as at this point, the Japanese engineering crew had production well in hand, Fred Barr's contract was terminated. He and

The Traffic Squad for the city of Winston-Salem, North Carolina. Photograph taken by Alfred Rich Child when he was a traveling H-D representative for the Southern States. *(Alfred Rich Child)*.

H-D Export Manager Eric von Gumpert (center, hands in pockets) attends a club rally in Christchurch, New Zealand, in 1927.

his family were showered with expensive presents by Shiohara and Fukui, and they were presented with first class steamer tickets for a world tour that ended back in Milwaukee.

At this point in time, a problem in Japanese-Milwaukee relations appeared which presented diverse difficulties in the relations between Sankyo and the parent company. H-D had just finalized the design of their new cradle framed 61E model, a 61 cubic inch ohv model offering higher performance than the long popular VL side valve machines. The Founders now proposed that the Sankyo Company, together with the payment of a very substantial license fee, acquire the manufacturing rights of the new ohv model.

As Child was, and had been, importing substantial numbers of Milwaukee-built H-D machines, his own organization quite naturally received one of the first of the new 61E models. Child's son, Richard, took this machine on a 400 mile test ride to the south of the main island of Japan, and ultimately returned to report the journey as nothing short of a disaster. The engine constantly leaked oil, the ohv rocker mechanism required continual adjustment, and the valve springs remained intact for only limited mileages.

Alfred Rich Child, his wife, Eleanor, and children, with the 'J' sidecar outfit. *(Alfred Rich Child)*.

In due time improved examples of the 61E arrived in Japan, following the Milwaukee factory's strenuous efforts to make the necessary improvements in the initial production run of some 1900 machines. Many of these had shown valve gear defects, and were thoroughly tested by Child and his staff regarding their suitability for Japanese application.

It was ultimately decided that the new model was less suited than the contemporarily produced side valve models, which possessed more tractive power at lesser and more economical engine speeds and were more suitable for sidecar and rear car applications.

As the result of these conclusions, at a meeting in the Muromachi Sankyo Building, Mr.Fukui and a half dozen of the company's financial backers, together with a group of the auditors, finally decided against any further negotiations with Milwaukee regarding the obtaining of a license to manufacture the new ohv machines.

As a further development of this discussion, which had become somewhat heated, one of the auditors took it upon himself to send a cable to a Mr.Kusanobu, the New York representative of Sankyo Pharmaceuticals, and suggested that he proceed to Milwaukee and contact the four Founders to advise them that Sankyo would no longer finance future shipments of H-D machines to Japan if

Child were to continue as Company representative in that country. He was also to emphasize the fact that Sankyo was not at all interested in producing any of the new ohv 61E machines, but would continue to produce at the Shinagawa plant the well proved side valve (now UL Model) machines which were by this time well proved and more suited to Japanese conditions. It was further intimated that these were to be produced under the name 'Rikuo', literally translated as 'King of the Road'.

Kusanobu, acting now as Sankyo's agent, was well chosen as an emissary as he had been born in Canada, educated in the United States, had married a Canadian and was well versed in American business methods as well as having a command of fluent English. His approach to the Founders was not well timed, however, and after a stormy meeting during which the Founders firmly rejected his proposal, it was reported by a reliable witness that burly young Walter Davidson Jr. (the son of the late Walter C.) came near to ejecting Kusanobu from the premises.

In the meantime, Child was in continuous communication with Milwaukee and Arthur Davidson over his own status with the Company, as well as the marketing situation of Milwaukee-built machines. The ultimate decision was that the factory would terminate all its agreements with Sankyo and the Shinagawa operation, and that Child would now head a new sales organization with himself as exclusive agent, with his own sales office, spare parts depot, and shipping arrangements. In addition, and for the first time in H-D history, the factory agreed to ship machines and parts on open account, with payment due 90 days after landed delivery.

Child immediately established a new headquarters in Tokyo under the name 'Nichiman H-D Sales', which was now, of course, a distinctly separate organization having no connection with the Japanese manufacture of native-built Rikuos. At the same moment, Mr.Fukui remained on friendly terms with Child, and purchased several hundred sidecar outfits from him during 1936.

As an aside to this rather bizarre reorganization, Child was not offered any financial remuneration from Milwaukee for his efforts in the Sankyo negotiations, no doubt in view of the fact that he had prospered handsomely during the past decade from his original company association.

Child emerged from the new agreement as the exclusive H-D sales agent for the whole of Japan, Korea, North China, and Manchuria, with access to both the 74 and 80 cubic inch side valve and 61E ohv machines and their concommitant spare parts. In addition, Fukui, the former Tameike Sales Department Manager, continued to sell Milwaukee machines, which they purchased from Child, to fill out their Rikuo line.

This budding and profitable venture was suddenly terminated, however, when in January, 1937, the National Diet, by this time a puppet organization of the newly-emerging militaristic government of Japan, announced that certain import tariffs, motorcycles among them would increase from Y74 to Y560.

This incredible increase in import duty appeared to have resulted from a previous conference regarding the importation of motorcycles between Child and one Colonel Fujii, who acted as liaison between civilian manufacturers and the military procurement apparatus. Fujii had at that time advised Child to dispose of his Japanese assets, terminate his commercial activities, and return to the United States with his family at the earliest possible moment. He was further advised tht Mr.Fujii would now purchase Child's present stocks of machines and spare parts, as well as arriving shipments in transit. As a further means of expediting the liquidation of Child's holdings, Col.Fujii stated that the purchase could be made with gold US dollars, which at that point in time were very difficult to export from Japan.

Child's first reaction to this proposal was to refuse. By his own admission he enjoyed his life in Japan, had made many firm friendships, developed a keen interest in Oriental art, and owned three palatial homes located in Yokohama, Kamakura, and Karuiziwa. On the other hand, the now politically powerful military regime was in firm control of the government, and it was futile to contemplate that they would make any concessions to aid any single individual. He therefore closed out his business and sold his remaining stocks of machines and parts to Mr.Fujii, which included those both on order and en route to Japan.

In order to minimize the effect of the termination of his franchise, Child cabled Milwaukee the details of Colonel Fujii's ultimatum, and at the same time requested that they dispatch at once up to 300 more machines in addition to those already on order and en route. The management was justifiably cautious, however, and advised Child to liquidate his holdings now in hand with all dispatch. Child complied, and leaving his wife and children in his home at Karaizawa, sold the Kamakura residence, and set sail for Milwaukee. He had hoped to obtain a domestic position in the Milwaukee Sales Department, but on his arrival and following an interview with Arthur Davidson, the latter informed him that the Company had no such position to offer him. He further stated that as Child had already amassed a tidy fortune from his Japanese operation, he could scarcely be satisfied with a salaried position in the Company which of necessity could offer him only a comparatively modest return.

Child next obtained a position with the Bendix Manufacturing Company of South Bend, Indiana, as their Sales Representative for North China, on the basis of his wide knowledge and familiarity with general business and marketing conditions in that area.

Due to the militaristic makeup of the new Japanese government, the Sankyo Company was not able to negotiate a new contract with H-D for either Japan or Manchuria. The Shinagawa factory continued to manufacture Rikuo machines during the war and shortly thereafter, but production declined greatly after 1946. The company concurrently manufactured naval torpedoes shortly before the attack on Pearl Harbor, some of which no doubt were used against the US Pacific Fleet.

H-D's Oriental interlude and the complex details involving Milwaukee's connection both with Child and the Rikuo machines was never publicized, either officially or unofficially. Due to the general growing apprehension in the United States, both within military and upper echelon government officials, the company no doubt thought it expedient to suppress any details of their connection with the building of Japan's war machine. There are, in fact, perhaps only a handful of men yet living at this writing who are conversant with the true facts of the matter.

Child's son, Richard, who assisted him in setting up the Nichiman-Harley-Davidson import agreement in 1935 and 1936, founded the Balcom Trading Company after World War II, with headquarters in Takanawa, Tokyo, and is at this writing the sole importer of H-D motorcycles, along with German BMW automobiles. In spite of the present state of world leadership in motorcycle manufacture now enjoyed by Japan, several hundred Milwaukee-built H-Ds are sold in Japan each year.

Child's contribution to the transportation economy of Japan long before any such industries were ever developed in that country, his influence upon the ultimate domestic establishment of such industries, as well as his contribution to the survival of the H-D Company during the difficult years of the US motorcycle industry, well deserve to be remembered. According to Child's own records, his organization imported an average of 2,000 machines each year from 1924 through 1936. In addition, several thousand Rikuas were built during the latter period after 1930. Added to this should be the 800-1,000 machines per year imported into Australia and New Zealand. Thus, the total Japanese and Australasian sales formed a very important and vital part of H-D's continuing fortunes.

While Child mentions many problems with the H-D Company incidental to his import operations, in his reminiscences he recalls that the management was ever co-operative and, in every case, treated him fairly.

The ultimate fate of the Rikuo, while not strictly a part of H-D history, is here added for general interest from information supplied by Charles D. Bohon, a motorcycle journalist who has travelled in Japan.

The Sankyo organization, under direction from the military government, carried on production of the original VL based model after 1937, which was subsequently designated as the Type 97 Military Model. It was usually built as a sidecar machine with an integral shaft drive to the sidecar wheel. About 18,000 examples were built between 1937 and 1942. In addition, some conventional solo models were built, with optional sidecars. Some of these were made with elongated fuel tanks to increase their range, resulting in a somewhat awkward appearance. Some units were built as rearcars. All of the above were said to have been designed by Sakari.

After the recovery of the Japanese economy in 1950, 750 and 1200 cc models were built as copies of H-D's current panhead model. In the late 1950s these were built with H-D type rear suspension and hydraulic forks. They were said to have been intended for law enforcement use. Production was limited to 1,500 to 2,000 units per year.

A shaft drive single cylinder machine patterned after the prewar 30.50 Model C was built in very limited numbers after 1950.

The Kurogane Company, a separate concern with no official connection with Rikuo, also built near exact copies of VL models from 1937 through 1945. As this firm was located in Hiroshima, its operation was obliterated by the dropping of the atomic bomb by the U.S Air Force.

The production of all Rikuo type machines ceased after 1959. The late Takashi Moromatsu, one-time member of Japan's Internal Trade Commission, has stated that Richard Child's reactivated H-D import program was responsible as Japanese enthusiasts appeared to have preferred the Milwaukee-built product.

Chapter 5

Disappointment and Disaster

SINCE ITS EARLIEST DEVELOPMENT THE MOTORCYCLE SOON BECAME A PRIME TOOL of law enforcement. It was apparently first employed in the nation's larger cities to catch runaway horses, but soon figured in the apprehension of speeding car drivers, even in the days when the average automobile had the frightening top speed of 30 mph. Indian, as the earliest leader of the industry, reaped the initial harvest of law enforcement sales, to be challenged by Excelsior and H-D as soon as their production became significant. H-D began a vigorous campaign for the law enforcement business after 1912, and this was intensified during the post WWI days when their production ultimately equaled and then surpassed that of Indian. While large numbers of both 'J' type H-Ds and Indian Chiefs and Scouts were now utilized by various law enforcement bodies, most motorcycle officers preferred the four cylinder machines built by Excelsior, as well as the newly-introduced Ace. The obvious reasons were that the fours were less prone to vibration, started more readily and, for their day, had rapid acceleration. It was much less physically tiring to ride a machine that was inherently immune to vibration for an 8 or 10-hour shift. Consequently the Henderson, and latterly, the Ace, became the favorite police machines, at least in areas where the authorities involved in purchasing were willing to expend public funds for a somewhat higher priced machine. In some areas where, in those days, officers were allowed to supply their own machines for official use on a contract basis, fours were almost universally the machine of choice.

With the demise of the Ace in the Fall of 1924, through unfortunate financial difficulties suffered by their maker, Schwinn immediately increased Henderson production, as well as substantially raising its retail price, now that he had a monopoly on the type. H-D's top management, ever cognizant of the now critical motorcycle market, at once foresaw the opportunity to compete in a new, if limited market, with a four cylinder model of their own.

In a private meeting, the Founders at once decided that the Engineering Department should set about developing prototype designs of such a model. William Harley initiated a survey of the matter, and after some deliberation, suggested that an outside consultant more conversant with four cylinder design should be engaged to assist in the matter. While some of Harley's contemporary critics within the industry had in the past offered the opinion that the latter's engineering abilities extended but little beyond that of making minor variations in the original works of DeDion Bouton, it was at least obvious that his prompt seeking of outside advice had in the past saved the Company much valuable time in the development of new designs.

Everett O.DeLong, formerly in charge of Ace's Engineering and Design, and currently at liberty with the collapse of that Company, was retained as a consultant with a six month's contract. DeLong's retention was obviously a good choice. A graduate automotive engineer, he had at once developed an absorbing interest in four cylinder motorcycle design. He was fully conversant with the type, throughout its F.N-Pierce-Henderson evolvement, and had first attracted the attention of the industry with a 90 in V-type four that he had designed in collaboration with Cannonball Baker in 1920. A promising design that had actually undergone prototype testing in an Indian Powerplus frame, only capitalization difficulties had prevented its initial manufacture. He had next become Henderson's protegé, and had worked with Arthur Lemon in the Ace Company, where the two had turned out some rather potent competition engines.

DeLong readily accepted H-D's offer, and sworn to strict secrecy in the matter, was installed in an office in an out-of-the-way area of the factory. As a top secret project within the Engineering Department, only the principals, George Nordberg, and two other trusted members of the staff were aware of what was underway.

Proceeding with a strict admonition that the new design should be rationalized within the present production schedule as closely as possible, DeLong suggested that an Ace-type F head engine be fitted into the standard J chassis. The front down tube was cranked forward to follow the wheel arc, and a rectangular tubular frame was set horizontally to accommodate the engine case. As the design work proceeded, William Davidson at once rejected it on the grounds that such an engine would be too costly to produce, so the project only progressed through the preliminary drawings.

DeLong's next effort, with some help from Harley, was perhaps more practical from the production standpoint. Again based on the standard J chassis, it was fitted with what was in essence two J-type engines placed side-by-side, utilizing a common crankcase. Standard J cylinder assemblies were incorporated, but the barrels were sleeved down to produce an engine that was of about 80 cu. in. displacement. A slightly modified three-speed J transmission was fitted, the countershaft being extended on additional outrigger bearings to accommodate the slightly widened drive line to the engine sprocket. The standard J clutch was fitted, but with extra plates and somewhat stronger springs.

Both Harley and DeLong were now quite enthusiastic about the design's possibilities, both from its rationalized production capabilities, and for the fact that such an engine would undoubtedly have fewer cooling problems, long the inherent weakness of the more familiar in-line type.

In the ensuing conferences with the Founders, William Davidson again rejected the proposal, stating that production costs could well price the finished machine out of the market. While both George Nordberg and the other Davidsons were reportedly favorable toward the project, William was adamant, and the project was cancelled. It was later reported that the wooden mockup of the engine made by DeLong was hurriedly destroyed to erase all evidence of its projected development.

Veteran H-D employees have long speculated about the projected four affair and most especially concerning William Davidson's role in its rejection. Some members of the engineering department informed the Author in later years that, in their opinion, the V-four as designed by DeLong had distinct possibilities, both as to its superior cooling capabilities, and in its possible economies in manufacture due to its utilization of the currently produced 'J' cylinder assemblies. Others have stated that, in their opinion, more in-depth costing studies might well have shown that the model's production was economically feasible.

Other old time or retired members of H-D's engineering staff have stated that William Davidson's opinions carried great weight within the Company's hierarchy, both from his position as Head of Production, and his financial interest in the Company. It has been ascertained from numerous knowledgable sources within the H-D organization that, due to the original terms of their corporate agreement, both William J.Harley and the Davidsons shared equally in the profits of the Company. However, while the other Founders had seen fit through the years to invest a part of their earnings in other ventures outside the Company, William Davidson had reinvested all of his shares within the Company itself, and had by this means now become its principal share holder. Holding as he did now, a commanding financial position, it is obvious that his decisions regarding general company policy would carry great weight. In addition, William's preoccupation with production efficiencies was by now a traditional byword at H-D, and the emphasis on production of the 'J' model had enabled him to rationalize its manufacture to the point that a very high quality machine could be assembled to sell at a very competitive price. It is also known that William was also firmly opposed to diversification of models and the consequent production disruption, and it may well have been that this was one important reason for his rejection of the four. While the details of the many closed meetings held by the Founders regarding on going Company policy could never be publicly revealed, the matter of the four remains as a challenging mystery in the complexities of H-D history.

After his contract with H-D was terminated, DeLong was subsequently retained by Cleveland to update the somewhat archaic T-headed four-cylinder model manufactured briefly in small numbers by that company after they terminated production of their long popular two-stroke lightweight model. He designed two high performance models of advanced design, one of 45 cubic inches, which was later

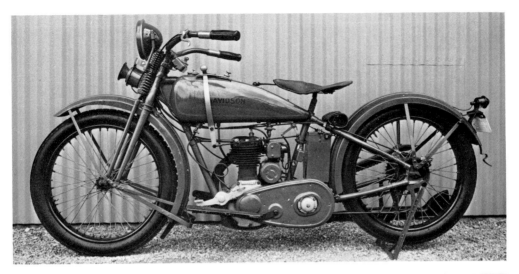

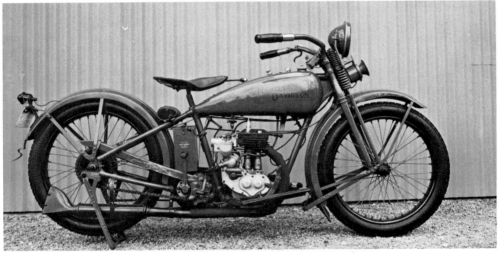

Del Du Chene's
authentically-
restored 1926 Model
'B' single. *(Alisha
Tamburri).*

dropped to make way for a 61 cubic inch model that was capable of over 100 mph. This latter was a sensation during 1928 and 1929, but the Company's mounting financial problems due to its limited retail outlets caused it to suspend production after only a few hundred machines had been produced. DeLong himself was to die tragically a few years later, hopelessly insane from an inoperable brain tumor.

H-D's participation in competitive sport was severly curtailed after the close of the 1921 season due to the official termination of factory support. The disposition of the remaining factory-owned racing machines remains an historical mystery. Some accounts have it that the former Wrecking Crew members were allowed to purchase them for $1,500 each. Others state that the Founders presented some of them with their mounts as a gift. A few Excelsior riders did the same, in line with Excelsior's similar policy, but without factory support neither group was able to do much better than second or third place wins. Indian, under Frank J.Weschler's dedicated management, elected to continue the Company's traditional support of competition in the traditions laid down by Carl Oscar Hedstrom and George M.Hendee. Several prominent members of the Wrecking Crew, including Jim Davis, Curly Fredericks, and Ralph Hepburn, transferred their allegiance to the Wigwam, and cumulatively racked up a string of impressive victories during subsequent seasons.

The numerous board tracks near the larger cities continued to attract large crowds, as public resentment against such often gory spectacles was gradually waning. Wind and weather was now taking its toll of the vast wooden structures, and encroaching residential and industrial expansion were already forcing some of them out of the picture. The death of Jack Prince, their principal exponent and promoter, from a sudden heart attack, had now eliminated their repair and renovation. In addition, the position of the motorcycle in the transportation field was now further eroded by the fact that the Model T Ford, due to its overwhelming production, could advertise the retail price of its two seater roadster at $265 without an electric starter, the self-starting model being but $20 more in similar stark form at the factory gate. Chevrolet and Star, vigorously competing in the same market, were also being offered for a few dollars more.

In the Spring of 1924, William Ottaway's warning to William Harley regarding the latter's pirating of the basic design of the Bendix clutch came true when Victor Bendix, its inventor and President of the Bendix Manufacturing Company of Indianapolis, Indiana, filed legal action against the H-D Company, charging patent infringement. Following a couple of hearings in Superior Court, H-D, on the advice of Counsel, capitulated with a confession of judgement. They subsequently paid Bendix damages in the amount of what was reported as $18,000. H-D's Engineering Department then immediately revised the basic H-D clutch design to include a cam type release that differed sufficiently from the basic Bendix design to terminate the infringement problem.

In the early Spring of 1924, H-D's management decided that an updating of the now classic 'J' model was in order. While the 'J' model had been much refined during the decade since its inception, with many improvements to the engine that made the model a high quality product, its appearance

Geoffrey Hockley, a New Zealand enthusiast, restored this 1926 ohv AA single. The side and ohv models were identical except for the engine.
(The Antique Motorcycle Club of America).

Famed competition rider Eddie Brinck with his 1926 'Peashooter'. Note the Flying Merkel-type telescopic fork. *(C.May).*

was still that of a somewhat spindly motorcycle little changed in appearance since 1914. In the meantime, Ace, Henderson, and Indian had gradually updated their styling to offer a more streamlined appearance, which was most definitely more attractive. Chief Engineer William Harley now commissioned Arthur Constantine to redesign the new venerable 'J', with strict orders to execute the revision with as little increase in production costs as possible. Under the stern eye of William Davidson, Constantine was able to modernize the silhouette of the 'J' with a minimum of structural alteration. The frame was lowered at the seat post, giving a 3 inch reduction of saddle height, and a somewhat bulbous two-piece fuel and oil tank configuration was instituted which supplanted the former, now archaic design. In addition, the mudguards were widened slightly and given somewhat deeper valances, resulting in a more modernized and attractive appearance.

Constantine, on his own initiative, also undertook two other projects, one on behalf of the Company, the other as a private venture, which were to have ultimate far-reaching effects on his own career in the domestic motorcycle scene. The first was the order for a specially-designed 74 cubic inch 'J'

93

model for a local missionary and friend of his, home on leave from an overseas assignment. His friend had written a letter to the Company asking for a specially-designed machine which would include some type of cleats attached to the wheel rims to give him additional tractive power when riding the machine off the roads in desert sand. Constantine designed a special machine with cranked seat and chain stays which, along with similar alteration to the fork tubes, would permit the fitting of metal cleats to the wheel rims to obviate the sand problem. In addition to this special one-off model, Constantine also designed an entirely new motorcycle. Based on the standard 'J' model, it featured a lowered and more compact profile on a 57 inch wheelbase, having redesigned front forks, and a new pocket valve engine with 45 cubic inch displacement. When he showed the results of his work to William and Arthur Davidson, the latter at once dismissed the proposed new model as an unneeded complication to H-D's standard 'J' production. The former condemned it as both an unauthorized undertaking and a waste of valuable company time. In the resultant recriminations, Constantine resigned from his position as an assistant engineer, and subsequently took a position in the Excelsior Company, which event was to later form a subsequent chapter in American motorcycle history which will be explored later.

Another complication in subsequent 'J' models was the traditional valve cam arrangement, which due to the increased power developed caused undue stress on the cam followers, which were activated by a single roller carried on a single outrigger bearing. The traditional configuration was subjected to much wear due to the side thrust imposed by the inlet tappets to the overhead intake valve. Practical mechanics almost immediately found a solution to the problem by fitting Indian cam followers, which had a forked arrangement subject to less wear, the assembly being slightly modified to fit the standard factory fitting. This practice at once caused much consternation at the factory, and the Engineering Department at once issued directives condemning their use, which was emphasized by the traveling factory representatives. Knowledgable tuners and many dealers' mechanics persisted in the matter, however, and the author has observed many old 'J' engines in the hands of antique 'J' owners still fitted with reworked Indian adaptations that were resurrected in later years! The Company attempted to solve the problem by increasing the thickness of the original cam followers, but the problem of side thrust and consequent rapid wear was never totally overcome before the 'J' was supplanted by the later 'VL' models.

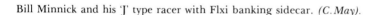

Bill Minnick and his 'J' type racer with Flxi banking sidecar. *(C. May)*.

The H-D Company was forced to manufacture their own sidecar models in both the passenger and commercial box body models late in 1925 when the Rogers Company suspended their production. With the death of the company founder, B.F.Rogers, the concern was eventually sold by the heirs to one B.F.Leopold of the Eros Manufacturing Company, another Chicago-based company previously engaged in the fabrication of sheet metal products and other metallic extrusions. Walter Davidson had made a couple of attempts, after 1920, to force the original Rogers Company to agree to supply the H-D Company with sidecar units exclusively, the idea apparently being to give H-D a monopoly on the supply of Rogers' products during the general decline of the motorcycle market. Rogers had refused, as his organization had been engaged since 1914 in supplying such units to the general motorcycle trade, including Ace and Excelsior, which now also included the popular Henderson. The story goes that Rogers refused to comply with this request even under threat of having the contract with H-D terminated. The same ultimatum was extended to Leopold, who not only refused to comply, but shortly afterwards terminated all sidecar production in favor of more lucrative commitments outside the motorcycle industry. As a result, the H-D Company initiated production of their own sidecar units, and set up a separate production facility.

Due to the general decline in motorcycle sales, various accessory manufacturers producing such ancillary items as lighting sets, rear mudguard carriers, speedometers, spotlights, heavy duty electric generators, and other items, gradually disappeared from the market. In consequence, the surviving three manufacturers at once were forced to supply such items to their dealers. The H-D Company set aside a large wing of the factory for the manufacture of these products, and within a short time had the largest such facility within the industry. A separate retail catalog was produced to advertise accessory items, along with confidential wholesale price lists for the dealers. The factory representatives were continually urging the enhanced stocking of accessories, emphasizing that the 40% to 60% retail markup was an important adjunct to dealer profits.

At the annual sub rosa meeting between Indian's Frank J.Weschler and Arthur Davidson, held in the summer of 1924 at the Astor Hotel in New York City, the retail prices for the H-D's 61s and 74s and the corresponding Indian Chiefs and Big Chief models were set at parity.

During the Spring of that year, an unsubstantiated rumor circulating through the Big Three factories had it that an unnamed import-export concern in New York City had formulated tentative plans to import a line of lightweight utility and mediumweight roadster machines from England. It has been reported that neither the Excelsior or Indian management were greatly concerned about the matter, but that Walter Davidson immediately took steps to track it down. After numerous inquiries, he decided to launch a frontal attack on the possible threat of a foreign motorcycle invasion by contacting Wisconsin's senior Senator, Robert M.LaFollette, a long time leading figure in the state's political scene, concerning the current tariff situation on imported vehicles. He learned to his dismay that the Tariff Commission had set a rate on them at a minimal 5%, as up to this time the importation of foreign vehicles had been almost non-existent except for a few Rolls Royce cars. Before the Senator had time to follow through with Davidson's request, he died suddenly on June 10th from a heart attack. His seat in the United States Senate was then taken over by his son, Robert Jr., who was to continue the LaFollette dynasty in Wisconsin. The latter who was, coincidentally, a distant relative of the author, in recalling the incident in later years, stated that he had informed Davidson that it would require substantial political effort and the expenditure of a sizable sum of money to lobby the Tariff Commission into extending the rates on foreign vehicles, especially as there was presently not sufficient imports of such to offer a threat to the American industry. After some reflection, Davidson is reported to have abandoned his efforts to pursue the matter further.

Another interesting vignette of H-D history during these years was the matter of the Pacific Motors affair in Los Angeles, and the alleged role played in it by the now very active H-D representative in that city, Rich Budelier. To begin the story, it is a matter of record that Indian machines were first selected by the Purchasing Department of the City of Los Angeles for law enforcement use, and had been the sole make in police department work since 1920. After he revitalized H-D's role in Los Angeles, Budelier quite naturally sought to break Indian's monopoly. During the annual performance tests conducted on the San Bernardino highway, Budelier readied a carefully run-in 61 cubic inch 'J' model to enter the contest. Upon hearing of Budelier's intention, C.Will Risdon, of Indian, put his ace tuners at work on a 61 cubic inch Chief, which model had been selected during the two previous years by the motor officers as their favorite. This machine was carefully honed to perfection with assistance, we are told, from Fred Ludlow. The Indian attained a speed of 92 mph against a 69 mph from the H-D, and Risdon was soon gleefully affixing police insignia to 25 new Chiefs for their official delivery to the Department.

Shortly afterwards, Risdon announced his intention to retire, and a prospective buyer in the form of one A.F.Van Order, arrived on the scene. It seems that Van Order had lately been the Sales Manager for Budelier, being frequently seen about the city on a pristine H-D sidecar outfit. In his

Johnny Eagles with his 1926 JD. The machine is authentically restored except for the fitting of a 1929 front wheel with brake assembly to better cope with modern traffic conditions. *(Alisha Tamburri)*.

representations to Risdon, however, Van Order stated that he had just been fired by Budelier for some trivial reason, and as a dedicated motorcyclist he was anxious to transfer his allegiance to the Wigwam. The story goes that Risdon was not entirely satisfied with Van Order's offer, but was finally persuaded to sell him the franchise on the strength of the fact that Van Order had established a holding corporation which he had designated as Pacific Motors, and which had substantial monetary backing. Van Order took over Risdon's extensive premises, which included several dozen new and used machines, a well equipped workshop, and a comprehensive spare parts inventory. Van Order's next step was to increase the fire insurance coverage of both the buildings and contents to its ultimate maximum. The following month, the entire premises was suddenly engulfed in a massive conflagration, it taking six engine companies several hours to extinguish the flames that leveled both the motorcycle shop and two adjacent buildings. At this point the story becomes somewhat confused, as varying versions of the incident have been related by early day motorcyclists, some claiming that it was Budelier himself who set the fire, others implicating Van Order. The author, who has delved into the matter for some years, has

Harvey Mummert's 1925-1926 ultra-light monoplane with a geared-down 61 cu.in. 'J' type engine.

Close up of Mummert's chain reduction propellor drive.

Sarter Tiffany's ultra-light biplane fitted with a 61 cu.in. H-D engine.

come up with what may be the most authentic evidence from the statements of the late Harold McClellan, then an investigator with the Los Angeles Fire Department's Arson Squad. He told him in 1958 that his agency had received a call from one of Risdon's ex-employees, now working for Van Order, that he somehow suspected an imminent catastrophy, and he called the arson investigators as the fire started. Officers immediately launched an investigation, dispatching detectives to both Van Order's and Budelier's homes. The former was not to be found, the statements from his family being that he was out of town on a business trip. Another squad of detectives who entered Budelier's home found him in bed, but fully clothed and with his shoes on! The late J.Harold Louderback, then a young legal assistant in the Los Angeles County District Attorney's office, later stated that while both Budelier and Van Order were somehow involved in the matter, investigators could not turn up sufficient hard evidence to sustain criminal charges that would hold up in court. Louderback went on in later years to become a distinguished judge in the state's Apellate Court.

H-D was without competition in downtown Los Angeles for two years until Albert G.Crocker   97 came out west from Kansas City to activate a very aggressive dealership, although Indian was still well represented in the surrounding cities in the Los Angeles basin. Budelier continued to expand his own extensive dealership, and Van Order remained in various capacities on the fringes of the industry. He later founded the Trailblazers, an organization of pioneer motorcyclists that still holds annual meetings in the Los Angeles area.

The now updated 'J' was well received by H-D enthusiasts, not only from its somewhat moderniz- ed appearance, but from further improved cam and valve action and a larger capacity oiling system which enhanced its performance as well as its already well-deserved reputation for reliability. Company-built sidecar models in both passenger and commercial carriers were also offered, along with a wide two-passenger type based on the original Rogers design that was built in limited numbers for export use.

In the Spring of 1925 the export of American machines to Great Britain received a severe setback when the Chancellor of the Exchequer announced the imposition of a 33⅓% import tax on foreign motorcycles. Growing economic and labor troubles were said to have inspired this action, as the cur- rent government was attempting to stabilize domestic marketing conditions. Its effect was the almost immediate cessation of Yankee imports, and Duncan Watson terminated his operations by canceling his H-D franchise agreement. The factory maintained a small parts and service outlet in London until 1930 for the benefit of British enthusiasts, many of whom were still riding 1914 and 1915 models. Repairs and maintenance were subsequently undertaken by several specialist shops operated by en- thusiasts through the early 1930's. In later years, F.H. Warr, who maintained premises in the London suburb of Fulham, became H-D distributor for the United Kingdom, selling new machines thereafter in very limited numbers, as the artificially high retail price now mandated by the newly imposed tariff, plus the shipping costs, priced new machines out of sight.

During the mid-1920's the total motorcycle production in the United States was substantially less than 25,000 machines. H-D production leveled out to approximately 11,000 to 12,000 units per year, with Indian making from 6,000 to 8,000 and Excelsior turning out about 3,500, most of which were their still popular four cylinder Henderson. In most of these years, over 50% of all domestic production was exported to overseas markets.

With this state of affairs, dealer morale in many cases was at a very low ebb, especially in the smaller towns and cities. H-D's factory representatives were circulating through their various territories offering encouragement through suggesting new sales and advertising techniques. In addition the Company bravely continued its extensive national advertising campaign, not only in the pages of the now dwindling trade press, but in mechanical and hobby magazines, outdoor and nature publications, and occasionally in local newspapers. Perhaps the greatest problem the industry faced during these dif-

An authentically-restored 1927 JD from the Bud Ekins collection. The 'J' models were updated in 1925 by Arthur Constantine, and were identical in detail until 1930. *(Alisha Tamburri)*.

Three views of the Juneau
Avenue factory complex
in the late 1920s.

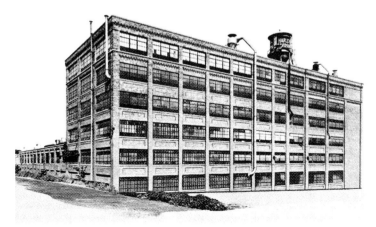

ficult years was the public image of motorcycling as reflected in their often dingy and rundown premises. The factory representatives were constantly exhorting dealers to clean up and to refurbish these establishments, an often impractical suggestion in the face of limited sales.

The now static condition of the domestic market quite naturally weakened the position of the AMA, together with the fact that public interest in competition was waning, following the gradual deterioration of the board tracks. There was also a certain monotony in these contests, as Indian had by this time become the dominant make in such contests due to continuing factory support of racing. While motorcycle registrations still numbered about 150,000 machines throughout the country, only a minority of their owners were willing to pay the $2.00 yearly membership dues to support the organization. In the Fall of 1925, AMA President Douglas Hobart, called a meeting of the Motorcycle and Allied Trades Association in New York City, which included representatives of the Big Three manufacturers, together with the now decimated ranks of the accessory manufacturers and the tire companies. Stating the obvious lack of support from the general motorcycling public, Hobart pointed out that the AMA was now in the same unfortunate position that the former AFM had found itself following the war. After some lengthy discussion, it was decided that each of the sustaining M & ATA members should contribute funds to the AMA on a pro-rata basis, as it was now obvious that the AMA would otherwise collapse. This was finally agreed upon, but at the same time it was decided that the factories, both directly and through their dealer outlets, would continue to solicit support from motorcycle owners at large. Hobart resigned his office shortly thereafter to take up an Indian franchise, and George T. Briggs, President of the Wheeler-Schebler Carburetor Company, was elected from within the ranks of the M & ATA to take his place, serving until the Fall of 1928.

During this period, the Excelsior Company decided to re-enter its official support of competition in the 21 cubic inch class, at the urging of one Joseph (Joe) Petrali, a budding competition rider. At the same time, Indian expressed interest in this competition category, as they were then in process of testing prototype ohv versions of their 21 cubic inch Prince model, placed in production the year before. Hobart's last official act, on his own initiative, was to give official AMA sanction to the recognition of this new competition class. This greatly angered President Walter Davidson, as up to this point, H-D had no 21 cubic inch machines in production. It was later alleged that he concluded that Hobart, being an Indian enthusiast, had attempted to place H-D at a disadvantage. When H-D took the dominant role in AMA affairs in later years, Hobart's name and his role in AMA history was stricken from the organisation's official records.

In spite of H-D's withholding of official support of competition during these years, H-D machines continued to figure prominently in many regional competition activities. Many racing enthusiasts and clubmen determined to individually keep Milwaukee's flag flying, and many racing specials, mostly personally built up from stock parts, emerged from both dealers' shops or the backyards of mechanically-inclined enthusiasts. While H-D could quite naturally not challenge Indian in either the big National Races or on the boards, they racked up credible wins at rural county fairs and out-of-the-way horse tracks. As the now weakened status of the AMA did not give them the power to put an end to unsanctioned or 'outlaw' events, H-D was still a potent force in official competition.

It was during this period that H-D engines figured somewhat prominently in the powering of ultra-light aircraft. While the recent World War had given great impetus to aircraft design progress, most of the machines produced for the war effort were too costly to be maintained by either private owners or commercial operators. Added to this, most of their engines were designed with but a short duration service life, which added to their general unreliability. At the same moment, the availability of large numbers of war surplus aircraft at give-away prices had up to this time effectively strangled private efforts at instigating general aircraft manufacture. Then too, the highly publicized exploits of the wartime aces featuring the 'knights of the air' concept could scarcely be related to an interest in flying on the part of the ordinary citizen. Most of the aircraft observed by the general public during the immediate post-war era were the exhibition flights and stunts performed at county fairs or during the course of patriotic celebrations — scarcely calculated to impress the public that flying could be other than a daredevil undertaking.

In an effort to stimulate public interest in private flying and at the same time to encourage the development of low cost aviation, a newspaper in England, the Daily Mail, sponsored a design contest for ultra-light aircraft at Lympne Aerodrome in the south of England in the Summer of 1923. In deference to the total lack of suitable professionally-designed small aircraft engines, the power plants were limited to a cubic displacement of 750 cc, or 45 cubic inches, which could include the converted motorcycle engines already utilized by the early experimenters. While the overall results of the contest were inconclusive, the meeting attracted world wide attention among aviation enthusiasts. In the United States, numerous experimenters had already been at work, such as Etiene Dormoy, Ed Heath, B.H. Petienpol, Weston Farmer, and Jean Roche. In addition to these, one Harvey Mummert, an aeronautical engineer employed by the Curtis Wright Aviation Company, who was also an H-D enthusiast, was engaged in building a small wood framed, low winged monoplane with a 26 foot wingspan. For power, he utilized a converted 61 cubic inch 'J' model engine. Entering it in the National Air Races held in the Summers of 1924 and 1925, he managed to attain second place wins.

While V twin engines were generally not well suited to ultralight aircraft due to the characteristic uneven firing angle causing sufficient vibration to shake the light airframes to pieces after a few flights, Mummert's results were somewhat more satisfactory, as he statically and dynamically balanced his engine for the 1,600 to 1,800 rate of revolutions that gave optimum propellor efficiency. He later built a small racing biplane for Sarter Tiffany powered by an inverted 'J' engine which competed successfully in the 1926 National contest. Most subsequent light aircraft were powered with Henderson or Indian Four conversions, due to their smoother running capabilities.

Production of the only mildly successful domestic lightweight motorcycle, the Cleveland, was phased out by its makers early in 1925, supposedly to make way for the assembly of their projected four cylinder models. The management of Indian, with possibly some inside knowledge of Cleveland's plans, hastened to produce a 21 cubic inch side valve model which was designated as the 'Prince', its designer, Charles Franklin, basing it on contemporary English models.

H-D's management immediately rose to the challenge, and the Engineering Department was at once put to work to develop a machine of similar size. During the prototype development, an Indian Prince, as well as a 350 cc BSA and a New Imperial imported from England were secured for evaluation. The outcome was what was essentially a scaled down 'J' model with the option of two engine types: a 21 cubic inch side valve model designated as the Model 'A', and an ohv model of the same displacement designated as the 'AA'. The economy models without electric lighting were priced at $210 and $250 respectively. The all-electric 'B' and 'BA' models sold for $235 and $275. The machines were well-balanced, handled and steered satisfactorily, and were capable of top speeds of about 50 and 65 mph respectively. The patented H-D spring seat post afforded acceptable comfort for the rider over rough roads, much superior to that offered in either the now defunct Cleveland or the current Indian Prince.

The side valve 'A' model enjoyed mild popularity with utility riders, such as newspaper delivery carriers and Western Union messenger boys. The performance capabilities were, however, somewhat limited by the fact that if the machine was ridden for any length of time over 45 mph the cast iron piston fitted to the earlier model was prone to seizure, the usual result being a broken piston. Practical dealers' mechanics and backyard motorcycle engineers were quick to ascertain that the pistons of a once popular Oldsmobile automobile could be substituted for the genuine factory article, and prudent dealers usually stocked such as they could be sold to the usually impecunious schoolboys for $1.50, a distinct saving over the H-D retail price of $4.50. This glaring defect was somewhat of an anachronism, as the cylinder head had been designed for the factory by Harry Ricardo, who was paid a small royalty for each machine produced.

The ohv model was somewhat more successful, and offered more sprightly performance, with a 65 mph top speed, and could actually produce a steady 60 mph cruising speed without trouble, providing suitable roads could be found to maintain this rate of travel. The exposed rocker gear, which was provided with only sketchy lubrication, wore rapidly however, and required frequent adjustment to keep the engine in tune.

The inherent possibilities of both models for economical transport in the United States was somewhat blunted by the universal availability of serviceable used Ford and Chevrolet cars, which were then selling on the used car market for $50 to $75. While the fuel mileages of both the A and B models was fantastic, such economies were unimportant in an era when gasoline was sold for 18 to 20 cents a gallon.

The principal market for the new singles was, of course, overseas, although the increased import tariff in England effectively cut off the anticipated sales in the United Kingdom which H-D had hoped to penetrate on the strength of the already established position of the big twin 'J's'. Both models were fairly well received both in Europe and in the Scandinavian countries, where the demand for economical transportation wss paramount due to the high price of gasoline. On the home front, dealer resistance was still a factor, as most of these were still big twin orientated and were not overly inclined to promote a model that did not offer excessive power and speed.

In the meantime, flat track racing, which had been initiated in New Zealand, became a popular spectator sport in both Australia and England, and eventually received mild recognition in the United States. The high performance 'AA' ohv single was a natural for such competition, and due to its small size and displacement was compared to the usual heavyweight big twins, to become known as the 'Peashooter'. In consequence, the factory now offered a lightened competition version with a shortened frame to reduce the wheelbase, together with strutted telescopic forks based on an earlier successful design by Joseph Merkel for his once noted 'Flying Merkel' machines. With a high power-to-weight ratio and in competition form having a weight of only 215 pounds, the Peashooter had good handling characteristics and made an enviable reputation for itself on the short tracks, both in Australasia and

The Model C 30.50 single. Known as the 'Baby Harley', its side valve engine of modest power output was mated with an ultra-heavy chassis shared with the newly introduced 45 cu.in. side valve. Its main sales were in the export market.

in the United States during the late 1920's. Its popularity was only eclipsed when later highly developed Rudge and J.A.Prestwich speedway specials finally surpassed it.

The ohv Peashooter received a well deserved notoriety in its own country, on both short tracks and as a hill climber. The new 21 cubic inch competition class, as approved by the AMA through the efforts of Douglas Hobart, became a show case for the H-D Company, as Indian reneged on its offerings in this class due to its very limited production of the 21 cubic inch ohv Prince Models, said to have been caused by the company's now current financial troubles. In consequence, H-D now swept the board in 21 cubic inch competition, through the efforts of Joe Petrali, whose role in H-D history will be subsequently discussed.

In the meantime, Excelsior scooped the industry with the surprise introduction of a new 45 cubic inch middleweight motorcycle which was named the 'Super X'. This new model was a twin, as the formerly popular 61 cubic inch model had been phased out two years before to make way for enhanced production of the Henderson Four. It featured both in-unit construction of the engine and gearbox through a geared drive, as in the popular Indian Scout, with the pocket valve arrangement of the classic 'J' H-D. The few H-D employees who had access to the company's drafting room immediately noted that it was Constantine's 45 cubic inch model that had been rejected two and one half years before by Walter Davidson, shortly before Constantine resigned from the Company. The new machine was somewhat dissimilar in that instead of the rather bulbous fuel and oil tank, it utilized mostly Henderson components, no doubt to rationalize production, the frame being shortened and its bottom modified to fit the twin's crankcase.

H-D immediately rose to the challenge by commencing prototype work on their own 45 cubic inch model, and Indian's Charles B.Franklin designed an enlarged Scout engine to also fill this category. Early day riders have stated that the 'X' proved to be a very potent performer, although the quality of its general metallurgical components was not up to that offered in H-D machines, and it possessed a somewhat less-than-rugged lower bearing assembly.

At the annual secret price fixing meeting between Indian's Frank J.Weschler and Arthur Davidson, held in 1926 at the St.Regis Hotel in New York City, the retail price of the Prince was raised from $185 to $195. The $210 price of the side valve Peashooter was dropped to the same figure. As the 61 cubic inch Chief had now been dropped from the Indian line in favor of the more popular 74 cubic inch model formerly known as the 'Big Chief', the retail price of this and the HD-74 model were set at a $325 parity.

In the Fall of 1926, for the 1927 sales year, H-D introduced a new ignition system that featured a field coil generator to dispense with the more usual distributor and utilized a single coil that fired the spark plugs on both ignition and exhaust sequences. Although this split the sparking output and often caused minor explosions within the silencing system if unburned residual gases were present, the system proved reliable and was subsequently fitted to later models. In addition, standard Alemite lubrication fittings were installed as a replacement for the now obsolete cup-type formerly used. This made for more effective pressure lubrication of critical bearing surfaces, but enabled the rider to service the cycle parts of his machine at automotive garages or service stations.

A surprise offering which was of signal importance to the many thousands of 'J' enthusiasts was the new 'JD-H' model which featured a 'two cam' exhaust and intake configuration for the valve mechanism in 1928. The standard 'J's' of course, had long appeared with a single lobe arrangement for each cylinder, and while offering satisfactory power output, also somewhat limited the possibilities of more sophisticated tuning for high performance. In common with the sporting 'J' model offered in 1925, the option of smaller 25 inch wheels was available, giving a somewhat lowered center of gravity. But without a reduced arc to the mudguards from the standard design the descrepancy between the two produced a somewhat shortened appearance on the overall silhouette of the machine.

This 'Two Cam' model, as it came to be called, quite naturally was an attraction to speed enthusiasts. The position of the valve lifting mechanism was such, however, that a side thrust was imposed from the cam gear, which produced somewhat rapid tappet wear, although this was of small consequence to the average handy owner who was usually something of a mechanic who could effect his own tappet replacement with little difficulty. Its high selling price of about $375 was somewhat of a sales handicap as it represented a $50 premium over that of the standard model, this in the days when a dollar could purchase vastly more than it can at this writing.

The two cammer was in the ultimate sense a very satisfactory model, both in terms of performance and reliability, and it has often been described by experienced old time H-D enthusiasts as one of the best models the factory ever produced.

In the Fall of 1927, AMA President George Briggs called a special meeting of the M & ATA directors and informed them that he was unable to implement the proposed programs of the organization due to lack of proper funding. Contributions from ordinary private riders had fallen far short of the director's original projections, due to lack of support. Co-incidental to this major crisis within the AMA, a new member of the M & ATA now entered the picture in the form of one James A. (Jim) Wright, a dedicated motorcycling enthusiast who had just joined the Indian Company as General Sales Manager. His fortuitous appearance was due to shake up Indian's management, wherein one Louis J.Bauer had lately assumed control of Indian following the resignation of Frank J.Weschler. Wright, who was already aware of the AMA's mounting troubles, had lately written a letter to President Walter Davidson, suggesting ways and means of alleviating the present difficulties. In later years, an old time H-D executive, who enjoyed certain confidences with Walter Davidson, told the author that the latter at first was somewhat hesitant to meet with Wright, who was a newcomer to the industry as well as employed by H-D's principal competitor. But realizing at the same moment the urgent necessity for strengthening the national motorcycle organization in the face of the industry's critical marketing position, he agreed to meet with Wright at the Blackstone Hotel in Chicago. The results of this conference were that the two were able to arrive at an understanding regarding the need for both a concerted drive

Harley-Davidson's finest hour. The immortal 'Two Cam' JD and JDH 61 and 74 cu.in. models. Only their necessarily high selling price prevented them from being runaway best sellers.

to induce more private owners to join and support the AMA, together with the need for enhanced financial subsidization on the part of both the Big Three producers and accessory manufacturers as well.

At the same moment, Wright was placed in a somewhat embarrassing position. The Indian Company was now undergoing financial difficulties because of President Bauer's proposal to diversify and manufacture non-motorcycle products. This lessened his inclination to put up more money for AMA support. Angry at being forced to provide the extra funds for the AMA, Walter Davidson reluctantly agreed to increase H-D's subsidy. Therefore, H-D became in fact, the controlling contributor to the AMA. This resulted in abolition of democratic control of the organization, and enabled the H-D Company literally to dictate future AMA policy.

As an aside to Davidson's and Wright's deliberations, it was also privately agreed that Davidson would now back Wright as the next incoming President of the M & ATA, as Briggs was in process of resigning. It was also agreed that the two would continue to meet annually to fix prices as it had now become an industry tradition. Oldtime members of the M & ATA have stated that Wright's main qualification for this office, other than his wholehearted dedication to motorcycling, was that he was one of the few men within the industry who could get along with Walter Davidson.

Early in 1928, the 'J' models were further modernized by the fitting of a front wheel brake. This was an innovation on the part of the American manufacturers, and lately had been added to the newly introduced Indian Scout and Indian-Ace four. While foreign motorcycles had featured a front wheel brake for nearly a decade. American designers had been tardy in accepting the idea. As it was, Yankee riders in many cases viewed the matter with suspicion, many claiming disastrous results where the front wheel might lock up on sudden braking, especially in a skid. Not a few of these diehards simply disconnected the control cable on new models just purchased, and proceeded with the rear brake as of yore.

In the Fall of that year, the 'JD' was further improved by fitting a larger capacity oil pump which was now interconnected with the throttle, the effect of which was to force more oil into the engine as the speed increased. This new system was not entirely satisfactory, as over-oiling was often experienced, such as in the ascent of a long gradient, when plug fouling occurred.

Another addition was a somewhat strengthened frame, which was made substantially heavier by the addition of more gussets at strategic points, such as at the steering head and beneath the gearbox. While the improved 'J' was now some 100 pounds heavier than its 1914 ancestor, the engine turned out double the original horsepower through evolved improvements. The 74 cubic inch model was now almost universally preferred by domestic riders, the 61 being more favored by overseas customers where the price of gasoline was a factor.

In the Summer of 1928, two entirely new H-D models were introduced and this brings us to a complex and almost unfathomable period in the Company's history.

In an apparent attempt to gain the best of both worlds, H-D introduced a larger capacity single to complement its 21 cubic inch single which was popular overseas, and a 45 cubic inch twin which was to offer needed competition to both Indian's soaringly popular 101 Scout and Excelsior's new Super X model. In an obvious attempt to rationalize production, both models were to share the same frame and cycle parts, the only difference being in the size of the engine. Built to a 56½ inch wheelbase, the new model was basically a scaled down 'J', as redesigned by Arthur Constantine in 1925. The single, with a long stroke side valve engine that displaced 30.50 cubic inches, was similar to the 21 cubic inch model and was fitted with the same clutch and gearbox. The 45 cubic inch differed only as to the engine. The immediate problem of these models was that both weighed substantially over 400 pounds, which seriously taxed the performance capacity of the single, whose top speed was cataloged at 60 mph. At the same moment, the twin's long stroke motor, initiating the classic 2¾ x 3 13/16 inch cylinder dimensions, was long on torque but short on acceleration capabilities. This, coupled with a ⅞ inch carburetor and restricted manifold breathing, severely limited its performance capabilities. While the single possessed adequate torque, its Ricardo-type cylinder head at once proved susceptible to overheating when driven hard, with consequent piston seizure, coupled with the fact that it was harnessed to an overly heavy frame. Its performance was best described as mediocre. The twin was hampered by the fact that its torque development was somewhat high for being mated with a light pattern single cylinder clutch and gearbox, which impaired its reliability. The twin, as competition for the Indians and Super X's, failed miserably in this respect, as its top speed in original form was but 56 mph. In addition, its light pattern forks seemed insufficiently strong to cope with ordinary road shocks, and were subject to distortion on collision with curbs or rocks.

Its most glaring defect, however, was the shape of the down tube of the frame, common to its companion single, as its straight line offered no space in the twin for the fitting of the electric generator in front of the crankcase, the only position available. To correct this, the standard H-D generator, utilizing the now well-proved H-D field coil system, was mounted above the crankcase on the left-hand side and set at an angle parallel to the front cylinder. This became known as the 'three cylinder

The author after a test ride on Bud Ekin's 1929 74 cu. in. two cammer. Note the twin bullet headlights that were fitted to all models during 1929 and 1930. *(Alisha Tamburri)*.

William Hoecker's authentically-restored 1930-31 DLD 45 cu.in. side valve model, first introduced for the 1929 season. Known as the 'three cylinder Harley', it was fitted with an unorthodox vertically-driven generator. *(Alisha Tamburri)*.

Harley'. This instrument was activated by a rather unorthodox bevel gear drive taken off one of the forward timing pinions, and was soon to show its weakness under hard driving.

A new lightweight sidecar was offered to complement the new model; a disastrous decision. The purchasing agent of the Department of the Interior was induced to supply twenty five 'R' model sidecar outfits for use by the National Park Service Rangers in both Yellowstone and Zion National Parks, to provide both handy and economical patrol units for the Rangers. The late Thomas L.Rasmussen, then a Ranger in Yellowstone, told the author in 1958 that the 45's were unable to develop sufficient power to haul a rider and passenger over even normal gradients. The sidecars were detached as a result, and the motorcycles were then employed as solo mounts, retaining their rather low sidecar gearing in order to negotiate the undulating terrain of the Parks.

The author was fortunate to experience some first hand observations of the model through his friendship with a schoolmate, Charles Cook, who was employed by the local H-D dealer, Joseph (Joe) Frugoli, as a part time mechanic. Frugoli ordered one of the early 45 models, intending it for use as his personal mount and as a sales demonstrator, as its $295 selling price was substantially lower than that of the now classic 'J' big twin. After setting up the machine and subjecting it to a brief breaking-in period, he found that its top speed was no more than 56 mph — nearly 20 mph slower than its intended rival, the 101 Indian Scout. Frugoli and Cook were able to coax a slight increase in speed after fitting a larger intake manifold and a larger carburetor, along with alterations to the cam profiles. After some 800 miles, the generator drive shaft broke, and Frugoli relegated the machine to storage, vowing to order no more 45's. It languished there for some years, being finally resurrected for a utility rider during World War II.

After numerous complaints from disgruntled dealers, the factory made haste to rectify matters by fitting larger carburetors and installing larger bearings in the generator drive shaft. While these improvements ultimately boosted the top speed to about 62 mph, many otherwise enthusiastic dealers and riders asked the factory representatives and management why the Engineering Department had not subjected the model to extensive road testing before clearing it for production. In the meantime, the appearance and usefulness of the machine was somewhat improved during the Spring of 1929, by fitting a somewhat larger fuel and oil tank with more pleasing lines.

In the meantime, President Walter Davidson, in a series of meetings with Indian's Jim Wright, now installed as President of the M & ATA, and the Executive Committee, finalized plans to implement the administration of the AMA. E.C.Smith, a casual H-D sidecar rider formerly employed as an automobile accessory salesman, was installed as Executive Secretary, with the head office of the AMA now based in Columbus, Ohio. Smith was to serve in this capacity until 1954.

The improved 45 now evidenced further defects in that its light pattern clutch and gearbox, transplanted to both the new 30.50 as well as from the current 21 single, showed certain defects under hard usage, a somewhat sad surprise to one time 'J' owners who had become accustomed to H-D drive train infallibility.

The new 'C' series single, also known as the 'Baby Harley', fared but little better on the domestic scene, as the mildly-tuned side valve engine developed insufficient power in its heavyweight chassis to offer much in the way of performance. While cataloged as a machine capable of steady mile-a-minute speeds, prolonged running at over 50 mph repeatedly caused overheating and consequent piston seizures. Somewhat of a mystery machine, it was apparently produced only in small numbers, most going to export utility markets. The Company's Far Eastern Representative in Japan, Alfred Rich Child, placed orders for substantial numbers of the single cylinder 'C' model, as its low speed torque characteristics were well suited for use in the commercial rear car units in Japan. Most of the machines were ordered without rear mudguards or wheels, but with a lengthened rear chain to facilitate this usage. The Factory kept the model in production until 1937, especially for Child's benefit.

The author has first-hand knowledge of but two of the 'C' models. One was observed in Claude Salmon's Oakland, California showroom in 1936 as a used machine said to have been lately brought to this country by an Australian immigrant. The other was in the hands of the late J.Worth Alexander in dismantled condition, and following his death in 1977, it passed to other hands as a basket case. It is currently awaiting restoration. H-D enthusiast Robert Ross, of Los Angeles, has related his utilization of an old stripped down 'C' model in the once popular desert races and enduros held in the Southern California area in the early 1950's. He has stated that while the engine was generally reliable and exhibited good torque characteristics in hill climbing, it overheated badly under full throttle running. The author has attempted several times to obtain data on the 'C's history from the factory but encountered the usual H-D wall of silence. It may be assumed that the machine enjoyed but limited production, and that only a few models were ever sold on the domestic market. About a dozen 'C' models still survive, in varying states of original condition, in the hands of several members of the Antique Motorcycle Club of America.

Coincidental to the development of the new 'R' and 'C' models, a new 74 cubic inch machine was announced in August of 1929. An entirely new machine with heavier frame and forks and a lowered riding position, it was offered to supersede the venerable 'J' type, the mainstay of H-D production since 1914. Generally characterized by massive construction, the 'VL', as it was cataloged, weighed about 550 pounds with fuel and oil. The engine was of the side valve type, with a bore and stroke of 3 7/16 x 4 inches, and with a 5:1 compression ratio stated to produce 26 - 28 hp. Critics were quick to note that the total loss lubrication system was still fitted, albeit enhanced by a variable oiling system interconnected with the throttle, as in the last of the 'J's.

The reversion to the side valve type was thought by many knowledgable H-D enthusiasts to have been influenced by Indian's long standing success with that type. It was also much cheaper to manufacture due to the employment of detachable cylinder heads. The power output was hopefully to be enhanced by the utilization of combustion chamber profiles developed by Ricardo. The side valve design also facilitated maintenance, as decarbonization of the cylinder head and piston crown and valve grinding could be effected without having to remove the engine from the frame, a practice not possible in the former 'J' models. Motorcycle historians conversant with design evolution noted that the new engines marked the end of H-D's last direct connection with the configuration of De Dion and Bouton.

A further interesting innovation in the 'VL' was the fitting of quickly detachable and interchangeable wheels and the introduction of a more stylishly streamlined sidecar unit. This improvement was suggested a couple of years before by Alfred Rich Child, who had already noted that certain British-built competitors on the export market, such as the AJS, were already so fitted. In addition, provision was made for carrying a spare wheel on the back of both the passenger sidecar body as well as the various types of commercial bodies now offered.

When the first production examples of the 'VL's reached dealers' showrooms, many enthusiasts did not take kindly to the overall aspect of the new model. Conditioned as they were to the classic 'J', they noted at once that the new machine was not only about 100 pounds heavier than its predecessor, but that the power rating over the last 'J's had not been increased. In fact, the dealers and the factory were besieged by requests for the continued manufacture of the two cam 'JH' model, which not only represented the ultimate development of that type, but whose overall performance was still superior.

In addition to these first-hand criticisms, the first production 'VL's proved to be an almost fatal disaster. While a well-finished machine built from the finest available materials, the engine had been designed with inordinately small flywheels. Old time factory employees have reported that these had been fitted in order to produce more rapid acceleration together with higher revving capabilities, presumably to give the 'VL' a more competitive performance, in comparison with the highly popular 'K' model Hendersons and Indian Fours which were still the machine of choice with most law enforcement bodies.

An offside view of Bud Ekins' 1929 two cammer. Note the distinctive disposition of the push rods. *(Alisha Tamburri).*

While the 'VL' in fact possessed vivid acceleration up to about 50 mph, the power output subsequently fell off badly due to the reduced torque effect of the small flywheels. Hill climbing and load carrying ability were thus greatly impaired, and the overall performance with a sidecar unit attached could only be described as unacceptable. The author was fortunate to have the opportunity to take a ride on Joe Frugoli's first 'VL' which was to be used as a demonstrator. He noted at once that the performance was impressive up to speeds of about 50 mph. After that, the power curve fell off badly, and the engine vibration above that speed was of an intolerable teeth-loosening and wrist-shattering variety.

There was, of course, immediate consternation both among domestic and export dealers when the initial 'VL's were uncrated and given test runs. The factory was besieged with telegrams, cablegrams, and telephone calls inquiring why the model was placed in production without prototype testing, which would have certainly revealed its initial weaknesses. In addition, many of these communications elaborated on the general dealer dissatisfaction with the recently produced 45 twins, again asking why the factory was releasing new designs without subjecting them to even nominal road testing.

Old time factory employees have described both the consternation at the factory as well as the general chaos in the field. There is no record of any official communication to the dealers regarding the solution to the problem, but the factory representatives in each of the country's geographical areas immediately contacted the dealers under their jurisdiction to assure them that matters would be shortly rectified. The dealers were exhorted to remain loyal to the factory, and to assure their customers that H-D's management would make good the defects in design. Such prompt action on the part of the factory was, of course, most expedient, as many customers who had received initial 'VL's were now either demanding that their machines be turned in and their purchase price refunded. To further complicate the problem, many law enforcement buyers had canceled their orders after testing their machines, and a number of dealers terminated their franchises, either quitting the game or defecting to Indian or Excelsior.

The Engineering Department at once embarked in a round-the-clock crash program of building and testing a revised engine design, and within a few weeks finalized production of a new engine. The original small flywheels were replaced with those of larger diameter, necessitating the fitting of larger crankcases. The design was further re-engineered with altered cam and valve action. While these modifications resulted in an engine of more acceptable all-around performance, the larger cases now required a deeper frame loop to accommodate them, and a new design was hastily jigged up and assembled to replace the original.

The factory next notified their dealers that the revised component parts would be shipped to them without charge, with the mandate that the dealers dismantle the machines either already in customers' hands or on order and rebuild them at their own facilities. This, of course, meant considerable expense to the dealers, as anyone familiar with motorcycles is well aware that to completely dismantle and reassemble a machine requires a considerable amount of shop time. Dealers who were adamant in demanding further financial compensation for this work were summarily advised by the area representatives to comply with the Company mandate or surrender their franchises. A number of dealers, disgruntled by what they considered high handed and arbitrary treatment by H-D's management, did just that.

This debacle quite naturally cost the factory a great deal of money. The composite statements of several old time factory employees indicate that the Company ultimately was forced to make good on about 1,326 machines. It has also been reported that the $75,000 received from Alfred Rich Child for the rights to manufacture H-D's in Japan was soon exhausted, and that an additional $35,000 was allocated from Reserve Company funds before all the new parts were ultimately placed in the dealers' hands.

In addition, the factory was still besieged by numerous dealers and 'J' enthusiasts for the resumption of production of a limited number of these models, especially the popular two cam 'JH' model, of which only about 1,900 units were built during 1928 and early 1929. Management's answer was that as the production facilities of the factory had by now been changed over to assembling current models, it was economically impossible for them to resume 'J' production. Upon receiving this rebuff, many dealers and not a few riders who were implacable 'J' enthusiasts, ordered large quantities of spare parts, stockpiling them to service the many thousands of 'J's still on the road, and which remained in active service for another two decades.

Incidental to the revamping of the 'VL's, the frame of the 21 inch single was shortened and the saddle post was lowered to give a somewhat more cobby appearance. Production of the ohv model was terminated, although in deference to the latter's competition successes, a large quantity of spare parts were continued in production. In addition, the performance of the ailing 45 twin was enhanced somewhat by the fitting of improved cam and valve action, and a strengthening of the generator drive mechanism which was giving constant trouble.

Nels Groftholdt's authentically-restored two-cammer. This machine is said to have once been in California Highway Patrol service. The two cam engine was designed during 1923-1924 by Arthur A. Constantine and William Ottaway. It was first produced in limited numbers as a fuel burner for factory hill climb machines. *(Steve Nelson)*

As an advertising gimmick in the Spring of 1929, the younger Davidson generation, Gordon, Walter, and Allan, were dispatched on a cross-country trip from Milwaukee to Los Angeles. Mounted on the improved and pristine 45 twins, and nattily attired in well-cut English-style riding boots and breeches, the trio set out from their home base, typifying clean-cut young America on two wheels. Veteran dealers and their mechanics subsequently reported that lengthy stops along the way for repairs and adjustment to their machines made the journey unduly long, and an extensive publicity campaign heralding the event was canceled.

The chaos at H-D was paralleled at Indian, where a quick succession of management changes to executives who were not interested in motorcycling almost wrecked the company.

During the same period, Excelsior made a surprising comeback in the middleweight twin market with Arthur Constantine's brilliantly redesigned 45 cubic inch Super X, which at once outclassed the similar H-D model, and offered strong competition to Indian's now immortal 101 Scout, as it had a top speed of 90 mph.

At the annual general policy and price fixing meeting between Arthur Davidson and Indian's Jim Wright held at Columbus, Ohio in the Spring of 1929, Davidson urged a strong reaffirmation of the formerly sanctioned agreement between the two organizations to mandate the retail sale of only H-D and Indian. An observer at this meeting reported that Davidson's emphasis in the matter was due to the motorcycle sales activities of one Reggie Pink, who had a modest establishment in the Bronx in New York City for the sale of British machines. Starting on a small scale in the Spring of 1927, he had been able to build up a successful business handling Douglas, Norton, Velocette, and Ariel machines. Although Pink had not been successful in establishing satellite dealerships, Davidson apparently considered his activities as a possible threat to present Yankee supremacy.

As a paradox to Indian's greatly weakened position in the late 1920's, their professionals swept the board in 1928 and 1929 by winning all of the big National races. In spite of hard times, Indian was able to scrape together enough funds to continue factory support of competition. However, Indian's

Robert Ross's 1929 74 cu.in. two cammer in its more familiar Western guise as a 'California Bobber'. *(George Hays)*.

position in AMA policy matters was greatly weakened as their management was willing to offer only token financial support to the organization. As a result, H-D remained as the largest contributor, its majority funding being augmented by minimal support from a few accessory manufacturers and tire companies.

The late 1920's saw the emergence of the sport of hill climbing as a somewhat minor sporting fixture. Uphill races had long been popular in motorcycling circles, but later developments saw the contests relegated to unclimbable off-the-road gradients. H-D's C.W.Hemmis in the East, and Windy Lindstrom, Joe Herb, and later Joe Petrali and Sam Arena in the West, vied with Indian's 'TNT' Terpenning and Orrie Steele. Excelsior found a potent champion in Gene Rhyne, who won all the big Nationals for Super X in 1930 and 1931.

During the 1930's nearly every edition of the popular Fox and Movietone newsreels shown in motion picture theaters featured a 30 to 60 second sequence of daredevil riders climbing nearly perpendicular hillsides.

Most of the factories built a few special machines for such use, loaning them out to favored competitors who had previously proved their mettle on homebrewed machines. H-D produced a limited number of these interesting specials, some of which were designed for methanol fuels.

Surprisingly, 1929 turned out to be a banner year for the long-ailing domestic motorcycle industry, with a total output of over 31,000 machines. This was the industry's best year since 1919, when 62,000 units came off the production lines. Over half of this output was exported, however, and in proportion to population growth and now soaring automobile production, the industry assumed an even more redundant position in the domestic transportation field.

A further interesting facet of H-D history during the middle and late 1920 period was the gradual establishment of a company museum, featuring a collection representing a model of each machine ever produced by the company. Many of the earlier types were already in company hands from the numerous prototype experiments conducted by the Engineering Department. Later models were sometimes asembled from old parts still on hand, and some were acquired from dealers who had either owned them outright, or acquired them from various private owners. This collection has come to play an important role in securing for future generations a first hand view of domestic motorcycle history, and is presently housed in a special building at H-D's American Foundry complex in York, Pennsylvania.

Unlike Excelsior and Indian, H-D machines were never directly available for retail sale from a dealership within the Milwaukee factory complex. Such sales were by company mandate only from franchised dealers who did business on their own account. While it was always possible for a purchaser to travel to Milwaukee to take delivery of his machine, and save freight charges, the financial details were always handled through the rider's local dealer. As an encouragement to enthusiasts to visit the factory, guided one-hour tours of the plant were traditionally held twice daily, except for the annual vacation period in the late Summer, when production was suspended for about two weeks.

During the late 1920's certain events occurred on the international economic scene which caused further problems for the troubled domestic motorcycle industry. The United States, as has been mentioned, emerged virtually unscathed from the World War holocaust, and was almost at once able to concentrate on industrial development that made it the leading manufacturer of all manner of products. The resultant prosperity made it possible to retire all of the national indebtedness incurred in the war effort, and the country was enjoying unprecedented prosperity. Wage earners, professionals and business owners, not to mention the myriad of corporations, were prospering handsomely. The only exception to this happy state of affairs were farmers. The mechanization of farming brought about a large surplus of foodstuffs. This kept farm prices down, while the costs of operation advanced along with a continuing rise in inflation. As domestic agricultural producers were not then protected by tariffs, they were in constant competition with foreign products usually priced lower.

As a result, there was much pressure upon Congress, especially from the midwest farm bloc, to institute protective tariffs for the benefit of agriculture. This situation caused the drafting of the McNary-Haugen bill, named for its congressional sponsors. This bill provided, in addition to high tariff walls, price supports for domestically-produced footstuffs, together with government purchase of surplus food products for resale on foreign markets wherever a demand might be forthcoming.

As a politically expedient bill which enjoyed much popular support in both houses of Congress by large majorities, it was presented to President Coolidge in the Fall of 1926 for his signature. It was immediately vetoed by Coolidge, who was adamantly opposed to any government interference with private economic matters. The bill was subsequently presented to him 1927 and 1928, with the same result. But in 1929, it was presented to the newly-elected President Hoover, who had effectively made his promised acceptance of it an issue in his campaign, and it was duly signed into law with much popular acclaim.

The immediate result of this legislation was the instant retaliation by many foreign governments in the erection of formidable tariff barriers against the import of American manufactured goods. This state of affairs was particularly critical in the Australasian markets, where both American cars and motorcycles had enjoyed substantial sales during the past decade. Similar high tariffs were established throughout Europe, as many economists had already concluded that the growing influx of American goods had hampered post-war development of their own industries. The principal export markets remaining that offered favorable trading conditions to US products were South Africa, various South American countries, parts of Africa, Belgium, Holland, and the Scandinavian countries which up to this time had no significant vehicular manufacture.

Now faced with the curtailment of the crucial export sales, the American factories were forced to make the best of their domestic position, previously only marginal.

H-D's management, headed in this instance, by General Sales Manager Arthur Davidson, immediately sought ways and means to strengthen their dealership organization. A few incompetent and wavering individuals had their franchises canceled, and their places filled by more erudite and progressive individuals. The Factory Representatives for the various areas were given updated information on the latest marketing techniques, and were exhorted to do their utmost to stimulate their dealers' sales efforts. Particular emphasis was centered on the proper maintenance and cleaning up of premises, as dingy retail quarters were still the bane of both the domestic manufacturers.

In addition, H-D's management had been continually increasing the size and scope of their accessory department. Dealers were constantly urged to stock more of these items: rear carriers, leg shields, windshields, speedometers, saddle covers, spotlights, as well as a comprehensive line of clothing, all obtained by the factory through outside wholesale jobbers.

It was during this period that the factory put increased pressure on the dealers to handle only accessory items supplied through the Company, the factory representatives reporting to Milwaukee when dealers were not fully co-operative in this policy.

With the sudden curtailment of the export market, the matter of domestic sales to law enforcement bodies now received increased attention. While in the public mind the purchase of any particular make of vehicle for this use might tend to indicate that the make was chosen for its superior qualities, in actuality nothing could have been farther from the truth. A particular make was often chosen if the local dealer in question was willing to make a financial sacrifice to have his product receive the consequent advertising value, and at the same time satisfy the dictates of a tight-fisted government purchasing agent. In other cases, where certain local political considerations had to be met, two or three favored makes would be placed in service on a yearly rotational basis, and thus subjected to a ruinous trade-in allowance to make way for a successor. In some cases dealers or suppliers had to contend with whatever political connivance or corruption was going on in their particular area, and often scheming politicians or corrupt civil servants had to be paid off under the table to consummate a sale.

The Henderson and Indian Fours were usually the choice of the officers, and after the newly introduced Henderson 'K' models were much desired. In cases where the purchasing organization did not wish to pay the high prices for these models, the choice was then between the H-D 74 and the Indian Chief. 45 inch machines were employed in limited numbers for this work, but the higher powered models were generally preferred. A few Indian Scouts were used, but the H-D 45 was never favored, as, in its early years, it was scarcely able to overhaul the contemporary family sedan.

All things considered, the supplying of law enforcement machines was generally considered to be a somewhat less than pleasant aspect of the business, and was treated by most dealers as a necessary evil.

As the decade grew to a close, the dealer representation of the two larger factories was reduced to about a thousand retail outlets each. Excelsior, always the underdog, had less than two hundred, and emphasized the Henderson in sales promotions over their limited production Super X.

The era of the great motorcycling spectacles was now over, as the board tracks were gone, the last survivor being the vast oval at Rockingham, New Hampshire, which saw a few races in the Spring of 1929 before being dismantled that Summer.

While the past two seasons had seen a slight upsurge in motorcycle sales, impending economic events were now drastically to change any hopes of a still rising market.

Chapter 6

The Great Depression

THE WORLD-WIDE ECONOMIC DEPRESSION WHICH HAD ITS BEGINNING IN THE United States with the infamous Black Friday on Wall Street in October, 1929, produced a catastrophic impact upon nearly every inhabitant of the country. One third of the nation's work force, estimated at between 13 and 15 million people, ultimately found themselves unemployed. One third of the country's railroads were in bankruptcy, and over 5,000 banks failed. In the rural areas, farmers and others in related agricultural pursuits were particularly hard hit, and in some parts of the country over one fourth of the real estate was under foreclosure. With many people facing actual starvation, many counties and municipalities stretched their diminishing tax dollars to set up soup kitchens to feed the hungry and homeless. Countless business enterprises, both large and small, were failing everywhere, swelling the ranks of those already plunged into abject poverty. An inquiry into the causes of this tragedy are beyond the scope of this work, but it was largely the result of world-wide financial speculation and the attendant inflation in the decade following the close of the war. In the United States, the lack of any government control over the trading of stocks and securities enabled speculators to buy on margin, with as little as 10% of face value. The crash came when traders were unable to come up with enough hard cash to cover their purchases when the demand was made. The average citizen, generally unfamiliar with the laws of economics, at once blamed President Hoover and the Republican Party then in power. It was then inevitable that the voters next turned to the Democrat Party and Franklin D. Roosevelt, who proposed to lead the country back to prosperity by way of Keynesian Socialism already popular in both England and Europe.

The sales of motorcycles, in common with all other consumer goods, fell alarmingly, and, as a now historically marginal industry, probably suffered to a greater degree than many others.

While motorcycles were obviously capable of being operated much more economically than automobiles, they never attained the status of a depression vehicle simple because there was such a vast number of used cars now available at give-away prices. Model T Fords, which had accounted for nearly one half of the domestic production during the 1920's, now sold for from $15.00 to $75.00, according to condition. Originally high-priced cars such as the stately Packards, Cadillacs, Pierce Arrows, or Peerless's could be had for from $100 to $300 and most of these were junked when no buyers could be found. In addition, with gasoline retailing at from 15 to 20 cents a gallon, economical operation was never too much of a consideration in a country where thousands of producing oil wells were now capped in a vain attempt to keep the price somewhere near a profitable margin.

Motorcycle dealers in many of the smaller towns and cities simply disappeared. Some formerly prosperous dealers in larger trading areas made further retrenchment from the salad days of 1920, and 113 moved to less favored business locations, where garages or other buildings could often be rented for $25.00 per month. Others survived by taking on additional lines of commerce, such as sporting goods, outboard motors, or became fix-it shops undertaking household appliance repair or saw filing. Both H-D and Indian, once united against such practices by their dealers, now looked the other way, as any outlet that placed an order for the odd new machine or who ordered a minimal trickle of parts and accessories was now an increasingly desirable asset.

At the same time, President Walter Davidson, through the factory representatives, bluntly informed the dealership that they could expect no help from Milwaukee, even if their survival was at stake. They were further informed that in the face of the country's mounting economic troubles, no-holds-barred competition tactics were now the order of the day, the target being their mortal enemy, Indian.

The grip of the H-D Company over their dealers' daily fortunes is well illustrated by the so-called Denver incident. This involved their long time retail outlet in that city, owned by one Walter W. Whiting, and was a lively topic of discussion among pioneer western motorcyclists for many years after. Whiting, a pioneer motorcycle enthusiast had taken the Denver franchise in 1918, following its relinquishment by Floyd Clymer, who had obtained it in 1916. Through aggressive sales campaigns, coupled with fair dealing, Whiting had built up a very lucrative business with one of the highest sales volumes in the West. His chief competitor after 1921 was Floyd Clymer, who had re-entered the motorcycle trade with both Indian and Excelsior franchises. Clymer subsequently allowed his agency to languish in favor of the promotion of his then famous hole-in-the-windshield automobile spotlight, and in 1925 it was taken up by Leslie D. Richards, one time Publicity Manager for Indian. Richards and Whiting, in spite of being business competitors, struck up a warm personal friendship, and worked together to promote the cause of motorcycling in the Denver area. Both acted as co-sponsors for a very active motorcycle club, and also promoted tours, picnics, and gymkhanas to which riders of all makes were cordially invited. In addition, both Whiting and Richards were lightweight enthusiasts, and unlike many of their confreres, made a special point of promoting this class of machine. Another motorcyclist, O.B. Senter, who as Whiting's Sales Manager, also joined to help inaugurate what was a mild boom in motorcycling in the Denver area. When the news of the Denver situation reached the ear of Walter Davidson, he at once took issue with Whiting over his close association with Richards, and through the district factory representative, Whiting was warned that his close co-operation with his competition was most definitely against H-D Company policy. When confronted with this news, Whiting defended his position by calling attention to his impressive sales record, together with the relatively large numbers of motorcycles registered throughout the Denver area and the state of Colorado. He said that, in his opinion, what was good for motorcycling in general was in the best interests of all concerned. A further complication to Whiting's difficulties with the H-D Company was Floyd

The redesigned 45 cu.in. twin for 1932. A heavier frame and forks were fitted, along with a new engine with conventionally-positioned generator, and a strengthened drive train.

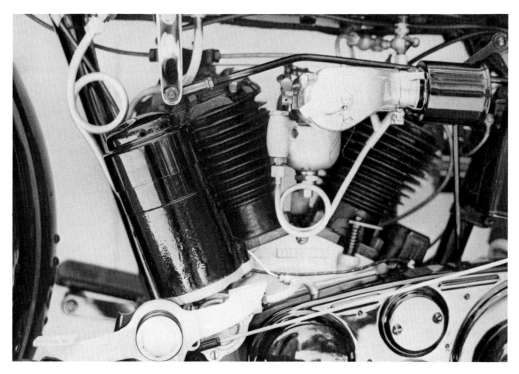

Close up view of the early DLD near vertical generator. Bearing failures were experienced under high speed running. *(Alisha Tamburri)*.

Clymer, who proposed to again re-enter the motorcycle business following the now failing popularity of his automobile spotlight. As Dick Richards was presently the well-entrenched Indian dealer, the only other obvious alternative was H-D. Clymer, who by this time was well aware of Whiting's difficulties with H-D's management, proposed that the Denver franchise be taken over by himself. It was decided that the dealership not be under his own name, but in the name of H.D.Cooper, who had previously been associated with him in the spotlight venture, the financing to be provided by Clymer.

H-D's management at once revoked Whiting's franchise accepting, it is said, a substantial sum of money for the transfer to Cooper. An embittered Whiting, as the story was recounted to the author by Whiting's nephew in 1967, deserted the motorcycle trade in favor of the automotive accessory field. Cooper immediately zeroed in on Richards' Indian business.

At this point, Indian's financial difficulties were causing many embarrassing delays in the delivery of new machines and spare parts. Cooper capitalized on this situation to sell Indian parts at greatly reduced rates, from part stocks still held by Clymer from his previous Indian dealership, with H-D's apparent blessing. In spite of the fact that Whiting's former Sales Manager, O.B.Senter, defected from the H-D camp to accept a like position with Richards' Indian agency, Richards was forced into bankruptcy. This most unfortunate affair, still well remembered by surviving pioneer motorcyclists, while of momentary advantage to H-D's cause in the Denver area, aroused the ire of many right thinking motorcyclists as the news of the matter spread throughout the West. Both Whiting and Richards were well respected, and they received widespread sympathy in their resulting financial losses.

Ironically, Clymer realized only small financial gain for his efforts. He was shortly afterwards convicted in Denver's Federal District Court for mail fraud, and was sentenced to serve an intermediate term in Leavenworth Federal Prison.

The 1929-1930 period of domestic motorcycle history, aside from the ominous overtones of the impending economic depression, was a time of crisis for all three of the surviving manufacturers. H-D was still smarting from the technical failures of both the initial new 45 inch models, as well as the newly introduced 'VL's. Indian was tottering on the brink of financial disaster, both from the general decline in motorcycle sales as well as from the inept management of three successive presidents. Only the continued production of their 101 Scout and a continuing infusion of capital generated by West Coast

115

distributor Hap Alzina kept it perilously afloat. Added to this, there were continuing rumors that Ignatz Schwinn, the eccentric founder of the bicycle empire and the owner of Excelsior, was now contemplating the termination of motorcycle manufacture due to its minimal profit picture.

This somewhat dismal picture was somewhat relieved when on April 23rd, 1930, an article in the *New York Times* announced that E. Paul du Pont, scion of the noted du Pont de Nemours family, had just purchased the controlling interest in the Indian Motocycle Company. This news was viewed with mixed emotions by H-D's management, as Indian's shaky financial position was public knowledge, and many well informed people in the trade had for some time considered that with Indian's expected demise, H-D would now become the only significant domestic motorcycle manufacturer.

At the outset, it was common knowledge that du Pont, while a sporting motorist and pioneer motorcyclist with genuine interest in keeping Indian alive, was also interested in utilizing a part of the company's vast unused facilities for the manufacture of aircraft engines, as he had lately developed a consuming preoccupation with aviation. It was also now evident that Indian was in a very sound financial condition, as the multi-millionaire du Pont was not only enjoying fabulous profits from his Ball

The 1932 Big Twin sidecar outfit, with quickly detachable and interchangeable wheels, sidecar brake, and optional reverse gear was popular with overseas military and police establishments.

Grain Powder Company, but from his additional holdings in various du Pont de Nemours subsidiaries as well as his bulging portfolio of blue chip stocks and bonds acquired for him through his brother Francis I. du Pont, owner of a prestigious brokerage firm on Wall Street. When du Pont took control of Indian, the production of diverse products was discontinued, and the company's somewhat disheartened dealers were now assured that motorcycle manufacture would be the order of the day, and that every effort would be made to regain Indian's once formidable sales position.

With H-D's management now considering this new turn of events in relation to their own marketing position, the industry's picture changed again late in the following Spring with Ignatz Schwinn suddenly announcing that he was was terminating the manufacture of Excelsiors and Hendersons. The current economic depression and indications of its severity and long duration have long been reported by various motorcycle historians as being behind Schwinn's decision. Other events, however, which were to now directly concern the future fortunes of H-D, were a critical factor in the demise of Excelsior.

As it may be recalled, the noted Henderson Four had long been the favored mount of law enforcement officers, and its prestige was enhanced by the introduction in 1929 of the newly designed 'K'

A youthful William Herbert Davidson, the son of Founder William A., winning the Jack Pine
Enduro on a 1930 DLD model.

models from the board of Arthur Constantine. These superb models, far and away superior to the contemporary Indian Four models which still utilized the only slightly updated 1919 Ace type engines, almost immediately accelerated law enforcement sales. Much of this added interest in the Henderson was quite naturally enhanced by the fact that many of H-D's law enforcement orders were canceled subsequent to the initial 'VL' fiasco, not to mention the added strengthening of Indian's position with their Four and Chief models for such use.

To further strengthen Excelsior's advantageous position in the matter, the canny Schwinn ordered accelerated Henderson production, and in an attempt to lower the somewhat non-competitive price of the new 'K' models made what proved to be a fatal blunder. The standard Splitdorf and Delco magneto and electrical systems were repalced in the Fall of 1930 with cheaper units, specially devised for the Henderson by some obscure manufacturer.

With outstanding law enforcement orders throughout the country, estimated by old time Excelsior employees as being nearly 450 units, an order for 150 machines was placed by the purchasing department of the State of California, for its State Highway Patrol. This large order, obtained by devious means, as described in the author's companion book on Indian, the *IRON REDSKIN*, was no more than delivered when Schwinn's fatal decision began to have its telling effect. The cheapjack magnetos were prone to cause misfiring during high speed running, and the generators were unable to function properly if the lighting sets, red warning spotlights, and sirens were operated simultaneously. California State Highway Patrol Chief, E.Raymond Cato, at once contacted Schwinn, and threatened legal action against Excelsior unless the ailing ignition and lighting systems of the initial 75 machines were replaced. Schwinn at once contacted the five principal Henderson dealers in the Los Angeles basin, where the first increment of Highway Patrol machines was in use, but to his consternation, all refused to participate in any validation of the usual factory guarantees regarding faulty factory equipment.

At this point, an Excelsior factory representative made a hurried trip to Los Angeles, and after a futile attempt to enlist Henderson dealer support in the matter, effected a contractual agreement with one Harley Rathbun, a San Bernardino H-D dealer, to replace the ailing electrical units on the initial 75 Highway Patrol Hendersons. Rathbun and his brother were long time H-D enthusiasts and dealers in the Los Angeles basin, and currently held franchises in Los Angeles, Santa Ana, and San Bernardino.

When the H-D factory got wind of the matter, they immediately contacted Rathbun, officially advising him not to enter into any contractual agreements with Schwinn, stating in effect that it was not proper for an H-D representative to pull Schwinn's chestnuts out of the fire. Rathbun's immediate reply to these top management directives was that in the face of the current depressed state of motorcycle sales, he was not about to turn down a somewhat lucrative repair contract, even it if were outside his usual H-D sales and service activities. Noting that Rathbun was adamant, and no doubt taking into consideration that Rathbun and Rich Budelier were the most prominent H-D sales representatives in the critical Southern California market, H-D's management relented and no official reprisals were instigated against Rathbun. As a matter of record, Rathbun ultimately repaired only about half of the ailing Hendersons, and many of these were later condemned out of service by the California State Highway Patrol. Rathbun later sold a number of these as second-hand machines. Of the twenty or more 'K' model Hendersons still existing in the hands of antique enthusiasts in the Southern California area, most are relics of Excelsior's California debacle.

Following the cessation of Excelsior production, the limited domestic market was at long last reduced to two manufacturers, who, during the ensuing decade, became locked in what became a fratricidal war rather than normal marketing competition.

E.Paul du Pont's acquisition of Indian had put the company back on its feet. This laid to rest the rumors that the Wigwam was shortly to suspend production. It was not only backed by du Pont's vast industrial empire, but benefitted from his general interest in sporting motoring. William Crapo (Billy) Durant, the ebullient automotive pioneer who had originally formed General Motors, only to have it wrested from him by E.Paul's uncle, Pierre S.du Pont, told the author in an interview shortly before his death that E.Paul du Pont's interest in motoring, together with his inherent pride in his present financial successes, would have never allowed Indian to fail, no matter what its depression losses.

At the same moment, the H-D Company, while currently enjoying the largest domestic production, and possessed of a strong background of financial solvency, had never been favored with any such outside cushion of financial reserve, and its only cash surpluses through the years had been accumulated by internally generated profits.

With the indeterminate position of Excelsior, it now appeared that the battle lines between Milwaukee and the Wigwam were shortly to be drawn. Whatever private thoughts the Founders may have had regarding the matter will, of course, never be known, but it was subsequently reported that there had been much jubilation among some of H-D's factory personnel in prospect of the industry

Two views of an interesting Factory Special. A 30.50 cu. in. road racing machine exported to Japan. It featured dry sump lubrication and was intended for use with blended fuels. About twenty five examples were assembled during 1930, but none were made available in the USA.

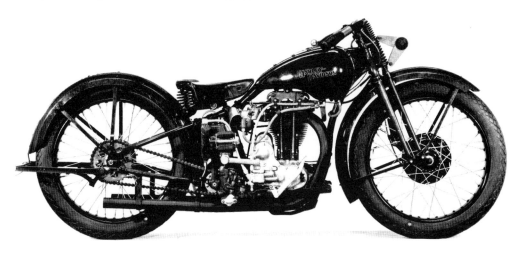

becoming a one-make monopoly. The new strength of Indian now changed the picture, together with the fact that the number of domestic dealers handling both makes was nearly equal, and domestic sales showed H-D held but a slight edge.

With the new turn of events, several old time H-D dealers have recalled that sentiment against du Pont was running high at Milwaukee. There were reportedly widespread derisive allusions to him as 'that New Jersey Jew', a patent misnomer as du Pont's ethnic background was Aryan French, and his historic home was in the state of Delaware.

Whether the Founders approved of these slanderous allegations is not a matter of record, but it is well known that the factory representatives in the various regions of the country put increasing pressure on their dealers to intensify their sales efforts in order to swamp the competition. Dealers were urged to junk any over-age Excelsiors or Indians that might come into their hands, either through trade-ins or outright purchase. It has long been a rumor, though unsubstantiated by any surviving documentary evidence, that any H-D dealer junking such machines could receive a $20.00 cash rebate from the factory, provided that the machine's registration papers were surrendered to the factory representative.

President Walter Davidson now conceived another sales campaign to strengthen H-D's position in the alarmingly shrinking law enforcement market. It was to make available to qualified buyers the Police Model 'VL' at a knock-down price of $195.00, only slightly more than its net production cost, 119

A limited edition 45 cu.in. ohv road racing machine intended for the European market only. None were available in the USA.

together with the trade-in of any other machines on hand, whether H-D, Indian, or Excelsior's Henderson. Furthermore, such sales were to be made directly from the factory by special sales agents, in itself a complete reversal of the company's lifelong policy of retailing machines only through their regular dealers. In addition, any and all of the trade-in machines were to be summarily junked. When the news of this proposal reached the dealers, there was a natural storm of protest, as these now beleagured individuals were being bypassed by the factory sales, and would not receive the usual dealer's markup. The factory representatives attempted to placate the dealers with the assurance that they would continue to receive the usual factory co-operation in the servicing and upkeep of whatever Police Specials were sold in their respective areas, but most of the dealers remained unmollified. Several cancelled their franchises, as many of them were by this time in straitened financial circumstances. A limited number transferred their allegiance to Indian, as the still popular 101 Scout was now being produced in slightly greater numbers due to Indian's revitalized management.

In spite of strong dealer protest, the program was carried on for another six months, and it was noted that several hundred machines of competing makes were junked in the process. While the company momentarily enjoyed a sales victory, the general bitterness within the trade, and indeed the revulsion felt within the company's own dealer organization at the cold bloodedness of the program, caused President Davidson to reluctantly terminate the offer.

Motorcycle historians are in almost universal agreement that it was this single episode in H-D history that precipitated the bitter war between the two factories that was most harmful to the whole domestic motorcycling movement, and of ultimate detriment to the progress of the industry as a whole. The country's Indian dealers were quite naturally outraged, especially as many aged but still serviceable Indians were reduced to scrap. The situation was particularly unfortunate at the retail sales level. Competitive dealers in the same or adjacent cities and towns, who had once enjoyed at least friendly rivalry, were often no longer on speaking terms. The effect upon private owners was even more tragic. In many cases a distressed rider requiring such necessities as lubricating oil, a tire or an inner tube or even a spark plug, would be refused service by the dealer of the opposite make.

The impact on club activities was also most unfortunate. Many such organizations, their numbers already decimated by the growing depression, were forced to disband, as the owners of the two rival makes now refused to meet or ride with their opposite numbers. In some instances, one-make splinter groups were formed from former members of formerly congenial clubs. Fights often resulted when they encountered their opposite numbers at race meets or even along public roads. Many thoughtful riders deserted motorcycling in disgust, and the public image of the sport, already somewhat tarnished, hit a new low.

The seemingly paranoic hatred on the part of H-D's top management, and especially that of President Davidson, for any competitive make of motorcycle, has long been the subject of speculation by both riders and motorcycle historians. Much of it was known to have centered on E.Paul du Pont, who was erroneously dismissed by some as a richly endowed dilitant playboy, when in realty he was a shrewd businessman and a highly knowledgeable industrialist. Also, the Davidsons may have harbored the somewhat natural resentment by people of working class backgrounds for those of inherited wealth and position. Coupled with this, there was still the rankling matter of the initial technical failures of the newly introduced 45 inch twin, and the disastrous debacle of the early 'VL' models. In addition, the now discontinued 'J' models still enjoyed a loyal following who had yet to accept the 'VL', and the factory was still being besieged by requests to resume production of the immortal two cammer 'JH'.

The ohv 'Peashooter' flat track racer. It was widely used in US events during 1928 through 1934. It was ultimately outclassed by the more refined English JAP machines.

With the depressed state of the industry, most of the once popular trade magazines had folded. The sole survivor by 1931 was the *Pacific Motorcyclist and Bicyclist,* which was now known as *The Motorcyclist.* Its new owner was one A.E.Welch, who had purchased the publishing rights for a mere pittance, and found that the general circulation had fallen to 15,000 copies per year. Even at a nominal one dollar per year subscription price, few riders appeared to support it.

Concurrently, the position of the AMA became reduced to pathetic proportions. With declining rider support, Secretary-Manager E.C.Smith eked out his own and the organization's existence from a handful of private owners' membership dues and from the very minimal donations now emanating from the trade, operating his office in Columbus almost singlehanded.

Due to the economic stress of the times, motorcycle competition was but a shadow of its former greatness. The great board tracks had all disappeared. Any thoughts of reviving them were now dashed by the final public rejection of their gory spectacles, and there appeared to be no promoters left with enough money to finance such contests. Dirt track racing events appeared sporadically at various county fair grounds, and were more often than not of the unsanctioned 'outlaw' variety, due to the impotent position of the AMA, whose once active Competition Committee now had no funds to furnish referees for such contests. Flat track racing was still mildly popular, riding on impetus derived from Australia and New Zealand, and was still drawing crowds in impoverished Great Britain. Its survival was no doubt largely due to the fact that a track could be prepared on any handy field by a few hours work with a road grader.

In spite of hard times, the Founders decided that H-D should re-enter the competition field, at least on a limited basis, by utilizing its still popular 21 cubic inch 'Peashooter' model that was racking up impressive records in Australia, New Zealand, and the United Kingdom. Up to this time, the 21 inch class had received but scant attention from either American competition riders or from the AMA. What action there had been was mostly dominated by H-D, as Indian had produced but few such models, and only during 1926. They decided to revive the class, and the now nearly powerless AMA Competition Committee readily assented, apparently to offer the sport and the public at least a token revival of American motorcycling's past glories. The H-D factory now hired a single professional at the munificent depression salary of $40 per week, one Joseph (Joe) Petrali.

This remarkable man, who was single-handedly to offer so much color to subsequent motorcycle history, was born February 22nd 1904, in San Francisco, California, the son of Italian immigrants. The family moved to nearby Sacramento in April 1906, just days before the tragic earthquake that leveled San Francisco. Young Joe's childhood interest in things mechanical was sparked by a neighbor, Dewey Houghton, a local cycle mechanic who owned a 1910 belt drive 30.40 cubic inch Flanders single. Sensing Joe's engrossing fascination with the machine, Houghton allowed him to clean it periodically, as well as to observe and later assist in its constant tuning up and overhaul. Along the way he frequently took young Joe to see such major pioneer competitors as Don Johns and Ray Seymour race at the old Sacramento Fair Grounds. At the age of 12, Houghton allowed him to ride the Flanders, and the following year Joe was able to persuade his father to allow him to purchase a well worn Hedstrom Indian 30.50 single.

A 1930 factory built 21 cu.in. hill climber. It was built for Herb Reiber, who was joined a year later by Joe Petrali.

A 1923 'J' type hill climber ridden by Oscar Hostetter in AMA events during the 1928-1931 seasons. Note the strutted front forks.

Abandoning any thoughts of higher education, Joe next went to work at Archie Rife's Indian agency, where Rife was amazed at Joe's natural mechanical ability. During slack times at the shop he allowed Joe to convert his own machine to racing specification, and he entered several novice and club competition events at the local fair grounds. He later won an economy run for single cylinder machines, covering 176 miles on a gallon of fuel, which made the 1918 National Record book.

Still running his Hedstrom single, he competed with much success in many of the outlaw events being held at various county fair tracks throughout Northern California. His many victories came to the attention of Jud Carriker, Santa Ana Indian dealer and the factory's West Coast Competition Manager, who attempted to secure for him a factory racer from Springfield. Due to Indian's post-war financial difficulties, no new racing machines were then being assembled, although Frank J. Weschler was aware of Petrali's budding potential as a competition star. Upon the tragic death of Shrimp Burns at Toledo, Ohio, in the early Spring of 1920, Weschler shipped his machine to Carriker for Petrali to enter the board track racing, which was opening in Fresno for the 1920 season. Carriker decided to experiment with alcohol fuel at the opening event, there then being no restrictions against its use, in order to give his protégé at least a fighting chance against the formidable factory-sponsored H-D Wrecking Crew, which that season consisted of Jim Davis, Fred Ludlow, Ralph Hepburn, Otto Walker, and Ray Weishaar.

In recounting the events of that day to the author in an interview in 1968, Petrali recalled that his carburetor had not yet been correctly adjusted to alcohol fuel. While his 8 valve engine ran erratically, he was able to work well up among the leaders early in the contest, and the now alarmed members of the Wrecking Crew maneuvered their machines to box him in. Through heroic efforts and a hair-raising burst of speed, he was able to finish second, a truly magnificent achievement for a 16 year old novice.

That Winter, Indian's Kansas City distributor, Albert G. Crocker, made Joe a most lucrative offer to work for him in his shop, his fame as a mechanic already established, and Joe moved to that midwestern city.

In the Spring of 1921, the first big National Race that brought him instant fame was on the great board oval at Altoona, Pennsylvania. Although billed as a starter, he was unable to enter, as by some mixup his machine had been shipped to Pittsburgh. H-D's great Ralph Hepburn, who fell during practice and injured his hand, noticed young Joe sitting disconsolately by the pits. He generously offered to let Joe ride his 8 valver and offered him a 50-50 split on any winnings he could garner. The machine had thrown Hepburn when the rear wheel locked up as its engine seized, so Joe, then totally unfamiliar with either the standard 'J' model H-D's or their special 8 valvers, quickly dismantled the engine and converted it to run on high test tetraethyl lead aviation fuel, a small supply of which H-D entrant Eddie Brinck had just obtained from the nearby Wright Aviation Company airfield. Although Brinck and some of the other Indian riders had originally considered using this fuel, they decided, just before practicing got underway, that it was too volatile and dangerous and did not attempt to have their engines adjusted for its use.

Joe converted Hepburn's engine and at the same time cured its overheating problems in time for the first race. When the main event was started, Jim Davis blasted his way into an early lead, but dropped out on the 11th lap due to a broken valve, but not before he had lapped the field. Eddie Brinck took the lead on his Indian, and Joe worked his way up behind him. In a terrific see-saw battle that brought the crowd to its feet, Brinck took the lead in the north turn. In his intense concentration, Joe had overlooked the fact that Brinck had lost two laps during an enforced pit stop to change a front wheel, and did not notice the checkered flag. After completing the two extra and unneeded laps at breakneck speed, Joe coasted into the pits in a state of exhaustion. It was only then that he realized that he had won!

Joe received Hepburn's congratulations, and left immediately for Kansas City. In the meantime, H-D factory officials attempted to contact him in the pit area after the race, in hopes of signing him up as a rider, but no one appeared to know that he had left abruptly. When they ultimately traced him to Kansas City, they were unaware of his association with Crocker. He finally agreed to ride for them on a part time basis, as H-D, of course, no longer fielded factory teams. Crocker generously allowed him to continue in his present position as his Shop Foreman, servicing and repairing Indians, although he was subject to some criticism by neighboring Indian dealers for keeping Joe in his employ.

Joe next purchased an 8 valve from the H-D factory, his machine being built up from remaining parts in the Racing Department. He raced all through what limited events were scheduled during the 1925 season. He received strong competition from Indian, who were still officially supporting racing. The only concession the H-D factory offered was free spare parts and pit crews, where needed.

Joe's first big victory for H-D as a contract rider was on the very fast fairground track at Laurel, Maryland. He won the Ten Mile event at an elapsed time of 109 mph, and hung up a new record for the Twenty Five Miler. A naturally gifted rider, he was now rated as a top racing star, having at one time or another bested such outstanding contemporaries as Eddie Brinck, Jim Davis, Curly Fredericks, Bill Minnick, and Johnny Seymour.

At the close of the 1925 season, H-D decided to withdraw their previously limited support for competition, and Joe subsequently established a connection with Excelsior. While Schwinn had immediately terminated all factory-sponsored competition at the time of Bob Perry's death at Ascot in 1920, Joe felt that he might somehow persuade the latter to sponsor limited competition in the 21 cubic inch class in which the lower power and lightweight machines were far less hazardous to ride than the more usual 61 twins. Joe also wished to work with Arthur Constantine who, since his discharge from H-D, had headed Excelsior's Engineering and Design Department. During the initial conference at Chicago with Schwinn and Constantine, Schwinn expressed his confidence in Joe's competition and design capabilities, and agreed to offer limited sponsorship in the development of a new 21 inch class racer.

Constantine immediately set to work, and with considerable help from Joe, produced a very fast racing prototype. Before all the bugs had been worked out of the new design, the big initial competition event of 1927 was held at Springfield, Illinois. With the new Excelsior not yet ready to race, Joe accepted an offer from Indian to ride one of their specially prepared ohv 21 cubic inch Prince models, in company with Eddie Brinck and Al Pechar. Pechar had just returned from a very successful tour of New Zealand and Australia, where he had hung up several new records. A last minute addition to the team was the redoubtable Bill Minnick.

On the first lap of the race, Brinck went wide in the first turn, caromed off the fence, and went down just ahead of Joe. In the resulting crash, Brinck was killed instantly with all of his neck vertebrae fractured, and Joe sustained his first major competition injuries, a broken jaw, nose, and collarbone.

He made several spectacular victories during the ensuing season, and next joined H-D when the Excelsior factory closed in the Summer of 1931. For several seasons thereafter, he functioned as H-D's one-man competition team, competing in numerous races and hill climbs on the now immortal 'Peashooter'.

The year of 1931 opened with continuing economic stress, as the full effect of the depression was now felt world wide. The current H-D model range for 1931 was to be carried on in limited production for the 1932 sales year. The 21 and 30.50 cubic inch singles were continued unchanged. The now improved 74 cubic inch Big Twin was also carried forward, with minor improvements to the lubricating system and the fitting of a more massive clutch assembly. This model had by this time gained general acceptance through its improved performance and reliability, although it was still not wholly accepted by many dyed-in-the wool 'J' enthusiasts.

Windy Lindstrom, West Coast hill climb expert, with his factory built ohv model. Indian fans were amused at the fitting of the trailing link forks.

The ill-fated 45 was now redesigned, with a new engine that carried the generator in the more conventional position, just ahead of the crankcases, and was driven by the valve cam mechanism. It featured a new and heavier frame to fit the contours of the new engine, together with heavier forks which were seldom prone to misalignment. A further improvement was the fitting of a heavyweight gearbox and clutch assembly, these no longer being shared with the two single cylinder models. Offered as the 'D', 'DL', or 'DLD' model depending on whether it was in commercial, touring or sporting state of tune, its performance was still somewhat less than spectacular, although it has been described as being able to overtake the popular Model A Ford sedan. A rugged and reliable machine, it was still overshadowed by the Indian 101 Scout, which was discontinued for the 1932 season in the interest of rationalized production.

As a paradox to the continuing bitter rivalry between the two barely surviving factories, and the unrelenting savage enmity for the Wigwam on the part of President Walter Davidson, representatives of the two factories met that fall in New York's Waldorf Astoria Hotel for their annual price fixing meeting. The assemblage was reported as being somewhat gloomy, following a meeting of members of the directors of the M & ATA the day before in which the country's economic trends were under serious discussion. Present were General Sales Manager Arthur Davidson, together with his opposite number, James Wright of Indian, and along with each were a couple of trusted associates. In assessing the general condition of the market, it was mutually agreed to set prices of all machines at rock bottom levels. The H-D Big Twin and Indian Chief were priced at $320 at the factory, the H-D 45 and Indian

Bud Ekins' 1931 74 cu.in. VL model. The first 1326 machines built had to be dismantled and fitted with improved engines when the original design showed insufficient power. *(Alisha Tamburri).*

Scout at $295. As Indian presently produced no singles, the $195 and $235 prices of the two H-D singles were not at issue. James Wright made a confidential announcement that Indian was provisionally planning to market a 30.50 cubic inch twin the following spring, and Arthur Davidson then suggested that it should be priced at $250. Wright acceded to the fairness of this suggestion, but stated that the final costing estimates had yet to be made.

A surprise visitor at the meeting was Indian's President E.Paul du Pont, who arrived at the suite of rooms reserved for the occasion where the dinner was already in progress. Declining an invitation to break bread with the assembled guests, he began addressing the meeting with tight lipped restraint, his subject being the bitter competition between the two organizations which had lately reached almost untenable proportions. Addressing his next remarks to Arthur Davidson, he castigated him for the Big Twin sales campaign in the law enforcement matter, and stated that it was a flagrant abrogation of the former gentleman's agreement between the two factories to fix prices in advance of each sales season. He further warned that all parties concerned should continue to use great care to ensure the complete secrecy of the meetings. He said that if the knowledge of the meetings ever leaked out, all parties concerned would be subject to Federal prosecution. He next went on to express indignation at the fact that certain H-D factory personnel had characterized him as a despicable 'New Jersey Jew', and that he greatly resented such implications as being both insulting to himself and other allied du Pont organizations.

The author's informant, who was present at the meeting and who recalled its details in an interview in 1961, stated that Davidson was abjectly speechless during and sometime after du Pont's restrained but impassioned utterances. After several minutes he appeared to have somewhat recovered his composure, and spoke briefly in defense of his company's actions in the matters in question. He stated that H-D had recently been in critical financial straits, not only from the rapidly worsening depression, but had also suffered heavily in both the 45 twin and 'VL' debacles. He further pointed out that his company had not the financial backing of any related corporate organizations as did du Pont, and that H-D faced further marketing problems with the threatened loss of additional export markets due to present world wide economic conditions. He was next reported to have offered his personal apologies to du Pont for any alleged personal insults through company channels, and further stipulated that any future price fixing agreements between the two companies would be honored without any reservations. He added that he hoped that the present recriminations in the matter would be both forgiven and forgotten. du Pont then reportedly shook hands with Davidson, extended his own assurances of future friendship and co-operation together with his own personal regards, and immediately left the meeting.

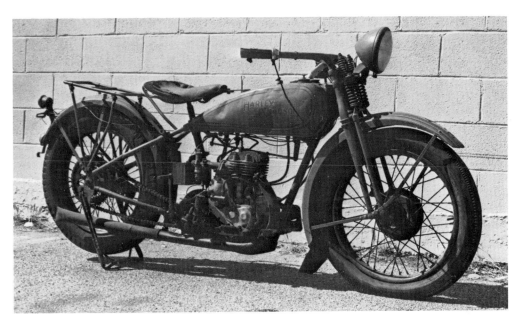

A 1931 21 cu.in. single in original condition. This machine, found in Australia, had been fitted with oversized tires, English-type bars, and an Amal carburetor and controls. *(Alisha Tamburri)*.

Arthur Davidson's apprehension regarding the immediate future of the American motorcycle industry's export market soon proved to be well founded. A 10% import tax on all motor vehicles was imposed by all of the British Commonwealth nations in the spring of 1932, which included Canada and Australasia. This action was initiated by pleas from Great Britain who, as the mother country, solicited co-operation in its now most critical economic situation to institute a 'Buy British' program. As American machines had long been exported to these areas in substantial numbers, the added tax posed a formidable marketing barrier.

It was about this time that H-D engines again became associated with the ultra-light airplane movement when one Lester (Les) Long, an enthusiast from Beaverton, Oregon, built up an engine utilising 1924-1927 'J' cylinder and piston assemblies. Mindful of the inherent unsuitability of conventional V twin motorcycle engines for their use, Long devised a horizontally-opposed twin, using crankcases of his own design, fitting an oil pump and other ancillary fittings from readily available stock automobile parts. The result was a well-balanced engine that displaced 80 cu.in, the result of fitting a specially fabricated crankshaft that gave a slightly than longer stock 'J' stroke. Turning out about 30 hp and with the ability to spin a 5'2" propellor at a useful 2750 rpm, the engine provided a much needed power plant for light airplane design that heretofore had needed to make do with less satisfactory engines.

Long made a tentative appointment to meet with President Walter Davidson to discuss the possibilities of its limited production by H-D. In later years, Long stated that Davidson in the end refused to meet with him, citing the press of more important Company matters. In the end, Long made up about 50 engines, both in his own shop and through castings being ordered and fabricated by other enthusiasts. A few of these engines still survive in the hands of ultra-light airplane enthusiasts.

In contrast to the doom and gloom of 1932, H-D machines in all models were now offered in a series of attractive color combinations, a distinct departure from the former olive or Brewster green which had been the rule ever since the close of the first World War. This not only added a more stylish touch to the machines, but also offered additional competition to Indian, which by this time was, quite naturally, using various color combinations featuring du Pont de Nemours paint.

By 1933, the economic plight of both the United States and the entire civilized world had reached its lowest ebb. Newly elected United States President, Franklin D.Roosevelt, a Democrat, was swept into office by a disheartened electorate with an overwhelming majority, on the promise that the New Deal could solve the nation's ills. Roosevelt promptly assured the American people that all they had to fear was fear itself, and subsequently dragooned a compliant Congress to authorize the inauguration of a vast network of government agencies to control all phases of the nation's economic life. For the next

127

Somewhere in China. Motorized units of Generalissimo Chiang Kai-shek's Eighth Route Army with VL sidecar outfits. Note the left-hand fitted sidecars. *(Alfred Rich Child)*.

two years, the country flirted with national socialism, the more flagrant aspects of which were declared unconstitutional by a conservative Supreme Court, whose tenure of appointment harked back to the days of more orthodox free enterprise.

During the late Spring of 1932, H-D introduced their Servi-car, a three wheeled rickshaw-like vehicle that was a frank copy of the rear car commercial units already produced for nearly a decade in Japan and the Far East. H-D's version was based on the currently produced 'D' model 45 cubic inch twin, fitted with a low compression commercial-type engine, a car type rear end with a differential axle activated by the extended final chain drive of the motorcycle.

This type of machine was pioneered in the US by Indian, when Charles B.Franklin designed several prototype units based on the 101 Scout. The initial employment in the United States was aimed at the automotive repair and service market, as the machine, named the Dispatch-Tow, was used to pick up and deliver automobiles for repair or service, the motorcycle unit being towed behind the car on a tow bar. As Indian suspended production of the 101 late in 1931, H-D remained as the sole manufacturer of these useful units until 1935, when Indian introduced a new Scout model.

The Servi-car not only filled the original automotive purpose of the original Dispatch-Tow, but soon found favor as a law enforcement unit to enforce auto parking time in congested urban areas. The officer assigned to this duty could proceed at low speeds through municipal parking areas with time limit mandates, marking the rear wheel of the parked cars with a chalk fitted staff. On the return time check, vehicles already marked could be issued citations for overtime parking. The machines could be readily and safely operated by otherwise non-motorcycling personnel, often feminine officers, giving rise to the popular appelation of 'Meter-Maids'. The Servi-car also found favor with commercial operators requiring light delivery duties, and were very effective in other utility use under low temperatures, snow and ice.

During 1933, the domestic motorcycle industry produced a total of 7,418 machines, 5,689 of which were built by H-D. The dealer representation of both H-D and Indian now stood at about 800 outlets each. Both companies sold about the same numbers domestically, H-D's disproportionate share being shipped to export markets still enjoyed in South America, Japan, and to a lesser extent in Spain, Germany, the Low Countries, and Scandinavia.

During the Spring of 1933, H-D's position on antisemitism was again aired in the Zimmermann affair, centered in Rochester, New York, a highly controversial issue long debated by pioneer motorcyclists in the Upstate region.

Harry A.Zimmermann, an early day motorcycling enthusiast and one time Pope exponent, obtained an H-D franchise in 1922 through the offices of the area factory representative, who was later thought to be either oblivious of the fact that Zimmermann was Jewish, or somehow inexplicably unaware of long established Milwaukee policy in the matter of excluding Semites from participation in company affairs. Reportedly an individual of pleasing personality, Zimmermann had, by shrewd business tactics, coupled with innate attributes of honesty and fair dealing, built up a thriving business in the Rochester area. His particular interest had lately centered on the high performance two cam 'JH' models after their introduction in 1928. He subsequently sold a number of these superb models to sporting enthusiasts, as well as a few sidecar units based on this model and used by rum runners transpor-

The H-D-Indian hybrid. This 1929-1931 Excelsior Super-X was originally designed by Arthur Constantine as a prototype H-D just before his discharge by President Walter Davidson in 1925.

ting illicit liquor landed on New York's North Lake shore by high speed motor launches based in Canada. As the potent 'JH's could easily outdistance the stodgy Fords and Dodges then utilized by local Treasury agents, even when somewhat penalized by sidecar gearing and a heavy load of bottled spirits, their high speed performance soon became a local legend. Only after Treasury agents were able to secure a pair of the magnificent Model K Lincoln Police Flyers were any of the rum-running Harleys apprehended.

Zimmermann, in the meantime, had enjoyed the dubious distinction of not only selling and servicing the night running "JH's', but later maintained them for the Treasury agents, who used them in their law enforcement activities after they had been legally confiscated.

The story is told that an unnamed deposed Excelsior agent had coveted Zimmermann's franchise for some time, and ultimately approached Milwaukee for information concerning the present status of Zimmermann's franchise. Whatever the facts of the latter's ethnic background, or what previous exceptions H-D's Sales Department may have taken to his conduct of his dealership will, of course, never be known. It was alleged that the Company instituted an obstructive campaign against Zimmermann, old time riders of the Rochester area reporting that his orders for spare parts and accessories began going mysteriously astray, with orders for even new machines being delayed for no accountable reason. In addition, the factory was also alleged to have ceased to answer his correspondence, and the area representative no longer made his usual personal calls. After some three months had elapsed, and with no possibility of redress apparently in sight, Zimmermann regretfully terminated his franchise and almost immediately secured the representation of Indian, as there was at that time no Wigwam outlet in the Rochester area.

Zimmermann's initial motorcycle dealership had been opened under the registered name of 'Rochester Harley-Davidson Company'. With his assumption of the Indian franchise, Zimmermann saw fit not to change the title of his business, and casual callers not familiar with Zimmermann's past difficulties with H-D were now amazed to enter his premises and to encounter a showroom full of gleaming red Indians!

H-D's management was almost immediately apprised of the matter, and through the offices of their legal counsel, filed a lawsuit against him and in their pleading, they sought to forbid him to use the H-D name henceforth in any manner.

The matter subsequently came to trial in the Superior Court of Monroe County. Upon hearing the evidence presented, Judge Callahan ruled in favor of the defendant, stating that Zimmermann had entered into his original franchise agreement in good faith, and that if H-D chose to terminate the agreement, as a Wisconsin-based organization, they had no further legal connection with Zimmermann who operated his business in the state of New York, and that he was free to conduct his business under any name he chose.

During the Winter of 1932 and 1933, Indian offered H-D strong competition in the miniscule utility motorcycle market by introducing the Pony Scout, a small twin of 30.50 cubic inch displacement which, while introduced at an initial retail price of $225, was ultimately offered at $195, abrogating the previous year's price fixing agreement between H-D and Indian. While H-D's management was somewhat perturbed at this model's introduction, it was by this time painfully obvious that American riders had already rejected the single as being both too lightly powered and not in keeping with the established macho image of the fast and rorty big twin machine that was long the established model on the North American continent. Most of H-D's singles were sold on the export market, the 30.50 being imported by Alfred Rich Child in Japan in fair numbers to power his now popular line of commercial rear car models.

During the Winter of 1933, the officers and Directors of the M & ATA and the AMA met in Columbus, Ohio, to discuss the current dire state of motorcycling. With registrations for the whole North American continent at an all-time low of 96,000 machines, sales of new machines, due to the now devastating effect of the depression, were at an all-time low too. Motorcycle sport was now almost non-existent. Professional racing was almost at a standstill, with H-D's Joe Petrali the sole surviving $40 per week employee carrying the flag for that class of competition. What with Excelsior out of the picture, and Indian no longer supporting professional riders, H-D's domination of the 21 cubic inch class was indeed a hollow triumph, as competition in this category was relegated to occasional appearances of one make.

After some discussion, it was ultimately decided that a whole new set of competition rules be promulgated, emphasizing the role of the private owner as a competitor in rather mildly conceived sports events.

Competition was divided into three categories, with Class A and B designating professional riders employed by factories, and Class C to include private owners. In order to compete in this class, a private owner was mandated to ride his machine in street trim to competition events. At this point, the headlight and rear tail light, which nominally included the hinged rear mudguard section, could be removed, along with the chainguard, and the entrant could then proceed with whatever type of competitive event was being staged. (Most privateers in practice habitually rode without a front fender). Stringent rules were laid down forbidding the radical alteration of engine specifications from stock specification, and competitors were barred from transporting their machines to competitive events by truck or trailer.

In addition, a new (to the US) type of sporting event was the English-type trial, introduced to the AMA Competition Committee by Theodore A. (Ted) Hodgdon, Indian's resigning Advertising Manager. This provided a sporting alternative to the more casual private owner who was not interested in high speed events, and indeed, could be entered without recourse to removing any of his machine's standard fittings.

By common consent, the AMA Competition Committee also decided that most of the Class C events be tailored to the use of 45 cubic inches in machines, an emerging popular class. It came within the purchase limitations of depression riders, which also more or less mandated a milder power output as compared with the more formidable 61 cubic inch class which, in the public mind, had already been established as capable of lethal top speeds. In this latter class, and including 74 cubic inch models, now the standard US big twin, certain other mild competition trials and hillclimb events were also undertaken.

This new official AMA sports classification was entirely in accord with H-D's Management wishes, as in their improved 45 cubic inch model they now theorized they had a production machine capable of competing with Indian's 101 Scout.

In addition, the country was again re-districted into various geographical competition areas, with an official referee with broad discretionary powers to both conduct and enforce the newly instituted rules of competition. In the practical sense, this latter innovation ultimately proved to offer some additional advantage to H-D, as in advancing the greater share of financial support to both the M & ATA and the AMA, the majority of the district referees were H-D enthusiasts. While many of these officials tended to handle competition matters fairly and objectively, certain favoritism and gamesmanship ultimately worked to H-D's competition advantage in future years, as will be seen.

The now burning question of the fratricidal warfare between H-D and Indian and its obvious detrimental impact on motorcycling as a whole, next occupied the attention of Arthur Davidson and Indian's James Wright. Noting that club life, the life blood of private motorcycling, had been unfortunately affected, the two agreed in a later private meeting that steps should be taken to calm the seriously troubled waters. AMA Secretary Manager, E.C.Smith, was next dispatched, riding an H-D Big Twin sidecar outfit supplied by H-D, on a truce-making tour of the country with the intent of remedying the situation. Smith accordingly set up in advance a series of meetings with the various once-active clubs across the country, and was ultimately successful in reactivating a number of them, even though their loyalties were divided between the two competing makes. His journeys were also oriented toward making the membership of each club 100% sustaining members of the AMA. His main selling point was that an active but mild competition program, including participation by each individual club member, could do much to resurrect renewed interest in the movement as a whole. While his efforts were generally successful, some riders remained unconvinced, pointing out that Smith was a life long H-D enthusiast and that most of the District Referees were H-D oriented.

As a further step in an attempt to strengthen the AMA, and to save money as well in very difficult times, the *Motorcyclist* magazine was designated as the official AMA publication. Those riders contributing the nominal $1.00 per year subscription fee would now receive an AMA membership card.

While the AMA was quite obviously a non-democratic trade-dominated organization, most club members at least saw the wisdom of having some sort of national motorcycling body, and in the end both the AMA and club activities received a needed shot in the arm.

During the deliberations of the AMA Competition Committee, a somewhat obscure and brief ruling was placed on the books that allowed 30.50 cubic inch ohv machines to compete on equal terms with side valve 45 cubic inch models, provided that their compression ratio was not over 7.5:1. This was a somewhat left-handed offer to include the very limited number of English machines then in the hands of American riders (probably not over 250 examples) and in later years this became the subject of most bitter controversy.

In the Fall of 1934, the single cylinder models were no longer shown in the domestic catalogues. A limited number of side valve 21s were manufactured for the export market until 1936, however, and fair numbers of the 30.50 model were exported to Japan for the benefit of Alfred Rich Child where they mostly formed the motive power for his specially-fabricated rear car units. This was carried on until 1937, when Child was forced to terminate his activities there by the newly instituted militaristic government. Emphasis was now on the 74 cubic inch Big Twin and 45 cubic inch models. Furthermore, the Servi-car and various sidecar models, both passenger and commercial, were emphasized. In

A VL rear car as manufactured in Japan for commercial use. The machines were ordered without rear wheels or mudguards, but with extra length rear chains. *(Alfred Rich Child)*.

An enclosed VL rear car as built for the Tokyo Branch of the Singer Sewing Machine Company. *(Alfred Rich Child)*.

A VL box-bodied rear car used by the National Cash Register Company's Japanese sales outlet.
(Alfred Rich Child).

addition to detail improvements in the lubrication systems and drive trains, the appearance of the machines was enhanced by the fitting of more pleasingly contoured mudguards, in line with current automotive practice. A new Big Twin model was announced with the enlarged piston displacement of 80 cubic inches, effected by slightly increasing the bore of the standard 74. This latter was marketed primarily as a law enforcement model, together with a comprehensive line of extra equipment from the Accessory Department, such as heavy duty spotlights and sirens.

By this time, the Big Twin 'VL' model had evolved into a very rugged and dependable machine, easily started by means of its improved field coil generator which proved very reliable and was admirably suited to both private and commercial uses. For 1935, a four-speed transmission with optional three forward speeds and reverse for sidecar use was offered, although most dealers held back on offering orders for this due to persistent rumors of a new Big Twin model that might leave them with an extra spare parts demand.

The idea of the extra displacement of the new 80 model was generally well received, as it offered a slight power advantage in serious hill climbing as well as an edge for heavy duty sidecar work. Its drawback, however, was a somewhat enhanced vibration problem due to the inherent imbalance of the V twin configuration.

While now an admirably rugged and trouble-free machine, the Big Twin was still possessed of one serious weakness, namely the very real possibility of overheating and piston seizure during prolonged full throttle running, especially during high summer temperatures. While the improved 'VL' was said to have a slight top speed advantage over its traditional rival, the Indian Chief, the latter appeared to be less susceptible to overheating, a telling factor in law enforcement use during high speed highway pursuit of speeding motorists. Although the Chief, especially when fitted with the still optional magneto, was a formidable competitor, it was almost impossible to start during cold weather unless parked in a well-heated garage overnight.

Due to slightly improving economic conditions, H-D production for 1935 totaled 10,398 units, a marked improvement over the 7,897 figure for the previous year. The sales improvement was due to enhanced export markets, mostly in Japan, South America, Southern Europe and Australasia.

In an attempt to revive the now flagging interest in professional Class A, flat track racing, H-D's engineering department brought forth another 'Peashooter' type model fitted with a 30.50 cubic inch engine. A frank copy of the contemporarily successful J.A.Prestwich-engined models (more simply known as JAPs) its development was largely the work of Joe Petrali, who designed and tested the new engine largely on his own time. He was encouraged in the effort by President Walter Davidson, who now hoped for a more potent machine to compete with the current crop of JAPs and Rudge Specials

133

which had lately dominated flat track competition. Petrali recalled to the author that Davidson had offered him a $1,000 bonus to oversee the design and limited production of H-D's entrance into the now popular 500 cc class. About a dozen machines were ultimately built in the racing department, but several bugs appeared and the machine's performance in the initial events entered did not prove encouraging. Walter Davidson subsequently ordered their production terminated, citing financial reasons for not subjecting the prototype design to further development. Petrali somewhat bitterly recalled later that Walter Davidson refused to pay him the previously stipulated bonus, again calling attention to the financial exigency of the times.

H-D production now centered on three twin models, the updated 45, the familiar 74 cubic inch VL, and the new 80 cubic inch twin, which was identical to the 74 except for the bored out cylinders. In addition, a line of sidecars and various commercial sidecar bodies were offered, as well as the Servicar. In regard to the 74, H-D enthusiasts were now saying that it had taken the company five seasons to develop the 'VL' to the point that it could perform as well as the now defunct 'J' models. 'J' enthusiasts still referred longingly to the now immortal two cam 'JH'.

With an encouraging upturn in the nation's economy, H-D somewhat enhanced their advertising program, as well as both the content and distribution of the *Enthusiast* magazine. In addition, the activities of the accessory department were enlarged, and an important item was the introduction of the 'buddy seat', an elongated saddle that accommodated two riders. The passenger's feet were provided for by the fitting of either extentions to the rear of the footboards, also a new accessory item, or by means of a pair of foot pegs that could be bolted to the lower frame rails. This arrangement not only offered a safe riding position for two riders, but added the zestful possibility of very close contact between the driver and wife or girlfriend. In addition, the area over the rear wheel was clear for the fitting of either a rear carrier or saddle-bags, or both, and opened up enhanced possibilities for carrying luggage on extended tours.

Sporting motorcycling received a welcome infusion of renewed interest as well as providing some interesting competition to H-D in the 45 cubic inch class with the introduction of Indian's newly designed Sport Scout in the fall of 1934 for the 1935 sales season. While the late lamented 101 model had been dropped from the line for 1932, it was still the machine of choice for the majority of sporting riders. The new model was of approximatley the same size and weight as the H-D 45, and was possessed of a somewhat better speed potential due to its shorter piston stroke with consequently wider bore.

With a slight increase in public motorcycling interest due to the now encouraging economic upturn, the AMA Competition Committee now planned a somewhat expanded program of National Races in the early spring of 1935.

As an opening event, and with perhaps an attempt to revive the early post-war glories of the Marion Road Races, the Committee selected a fast road course at Camp Foster, an inactive military base near Jacksonville, Florida. Billed as a 200 Mile National, it was the first long distance event of its type since 1920. The course was eminently suitable, as it was fenced in to allow for crowd control, insuring a paying gate for the expected 10,000 spectators, as well as a reasonably safe road surface. In addition, it was also to serve as a showcase for the newly revised competition Class C rules that mandated the entrance of nearly stock machines.

A heavy duty VL rear car with artillery-type wheels. *(Alfred Rich Child)*.

An elaborate VL rear car conversion with enclosed cab and car-type steering wheel controls. *(Alfred Rich Child)*.

A large field of 68 riders was flagged at noon on February 24th, a most unseasonably hot day under the blistering Florida sun. As the only domestic makes entered, H-D and Indian were evenly divided, together with single entries by riders of Ariel, Norton, Rudge and Velocette.

Red House, of Washington, D.C. took an early lead on his Sport Scout. A formidable contender, he was touted as a sure winner, but a blown tire in the 23rd lap of the 1.6 mile course ended his ride. Bill Carpenter, of Lancaster, Ohio, next took the lead on his H-D, and began a give-and-take battle with Rody Rodenburg of Indianapolis on a Sport Scout. The two switched first and second positions several times, with Rodenburg blasting into the lead at the finish when Carpenter ran out of fuel in sight of the finish.

To add color to the affair, National Class A Champion Joe Petrali acted as the official referee, with Indianapolis auto racing star 'Wild Bill' Cummings as the starter, and Cannonball Baker acting as one of the judges. Creditable rides were also made by an up and coming H-D star from San Jose, California, Sam Arena, as well as R.D.Johnson, from Savannah, Georgia.

Rodenburg's winning time was 3 hours, 51 minutes 31 seconds, with Carpenter just 6 seconds behind as he coasted across the line with a dead engine. A significant third place winner was George Pepper, of Belleville, Ontario, Canada, who was 2 minutes behind the winner on a 500 cc ohc International Norton. His remarkable performance was not lost on the large crowd of spectators, most of whom were unfamiliar with foreign machines. It also added further laurels to Norton's already distinguished position in international races, although the United States was now fully isolated from such competition.

At a subsequent meeting of the AMA Competition Committee, President Walter Davidson is reported to have urged that International Norton models should henceforth be barred from Class C Competition. He was subsequently overruled by the majority led by James Wright, who cited the fact that Pepper's machine came within established Class C specification, both as a catalogued model, and present state of tune. He further argued that with only five known International models being extant on the North American continent, such action would not only be unsporting but would amount in the public's eye as an overkill.

A few critics were quick to note that in the race report appearing in a subsequent issue of the *Motorcyclist* Pepper's closely placing 3rd was carefully glossed over, its focus being mainly in the tabulation of the various rider's times at the end of the article. When queried later about the matter, the then Editor, Chet Billings, was reported to have succinctly stated that as the presently official AMA publication, the magazine was mainly concerned with promoting 'American' motorcycling!

Numbers of American big twins saw military service in the Spanish Civil War. H-D had already become well established in Spain, with franchised dealers in Madrid, Seville, and Barcelona. Machines already in military service were used by both sides, with numbers of civilian models being impressed for whichever side was able to commandeer them. As the war was viewed with much apprehension, through the intervention of both Communist Russia and Fascist Germany, neither faction received much sympathy either in Europe or in the United States, all observers seemingly aware of the war's ominous import. It is probably for this reason that both American factories did their utmost to conceal the fact that their machines were being used in the conflict. A 1933 'VL' gained some notoriety, however, during the famous siege of the Alcazar. It was here that several hundred Loyalist military cadets were besieged for several weeks before being annihilated by Franco's forces. With its rear mudguard and tire removed, the machine was attached to a belt which activated an electric generator to supply lighting throughout the ancient fortress. As the machine was necessarily clamped in a stationary position, the engine was cooled by directing air to the cylinders by means of two household electric fans. The author has in his possession, among his considerable collection of H-D memorabilia, a newspaper photograph of this machine, which is unfortunately now too faded for photographic reproduction.

The Class C competition category was by this time receiving increased attention from many otherwise casual riders, as Class A racing was now all but dead. Most of the latter events centered around certain of the larger county fairground circuits, and were limited to the 21 cubic inch 'Peashooter' class. These events were dominated by H-D's sole professional, Joe Petrali. After his peak year of 1931, he was still a high point winner from 1932 through 1936. H-D's performances were almost a one-make show, as Indian virtually abandoned this class in favor of the further development of their Sport Scout for the more popular Class C competition. Aside from Petrali, Lou Balinski and Fred Toscani were active with their 'Peashooters', and received limited factory support for their efforts.

In the earlier days of Class C competition, H-D's 45s were more often than not outclassed by Indian riders. The discontinued 101 was still the favored sporting mount, as it could be stripped to weigh less than 300 pounds, and was equipped with magneto ignition as standard equipment. The H-D was not only heavier, but was further handicapped by not having magneto ignition available, and was forced to assume the weight penalty of a coil and battery. In addition, H-D's condensers were prone to overheat and fail under prolonged high speed running. Many enthusiasts wired up their condensers in series, and fitted a series of switches which would enable them to activate a new one when a failed unit cut out in a hard run. The long stroke H-D motor was unable to turn as fast as the Indian, which had a more equal configuration, although the torque output of the former was formidable once the revs had been built up. To counteract this disadvantage, some enthusiasts blanked out second gear, and thus could move into top gear from low without having to drop revs while going through second. The Sport Scout's engine could run even faster than the 101, which was of great advantage when coming out of a turn. Whatever the differences, the countless dirt track and TT duels between the two makes was the lifeblood of American motorcycle competition for the next two decades.

The AMA Competition Committee attempted to continue the enforcement of the strictly stock mandate for Class C Competition, but it appeared that by common consent, both factories soon abandoned such restrictions, and the AMA looked the other way.

In conjunction with the saga of H-D's 45 competition, and in the gradual development of H-D engines into more potent competitors, the marque's racing fortunes became explicitly interwoven with the career of Tom Sifton. An early day H-D enthusiast, noted for his mechanical skill, he became a sub-dealer in San Francisco in 1929 under the sponsorship of Dudley Perkins. He next obtained his own full dealership in nearby San Jose in 1933. Becoming increasingly involved in competition, in common with most dealers of those days, Sifton set about to breathe life into the admittedly anachronistic 45 engine.

It is by this time an almost legendary fact in motorcycle history that it was more often than not a practical engineer outside the factory that really made the make go. Ariel had its L.W.E.Hartley, Rudge its Roland Pike, Indian its Red Fenwicke and Pop Schunk, Norton its Francis Beart; and so it was that H-D had Tom Sifton.

By what alchemy these mechanical geniuses were able to breathe more life into powerplants not of their own original design, has long been a matter of historic speculation. It may well be that development engineers grow stale on a project perhaps too long on a drawing board. Or it may well be that long periods in the forest blot out the sight of the trees. At any rate, Sifton, by extensive modifications to porting, valve action, and other details, was ultimately able to make the long stroke 45 into a frequent winner.

The first competitor Sifton sponsored was Louis Guanella, who soon made a name for himself in the far west circuit, followed by Sam Arena, who was ultimately to become one of the most noted H-D contestants in the middle and late 1930's. He was able to mount formidable opposition to Indian's legendary Ed Kretz, who usually swept the board if his hell-for-leather riding style didn't blow his long suffering engine. Sifton importuned the factory to modernize and update the 45, but met with a cool reception from both William H.Harley and William Ottaway when he suggested that a modernization was in order. Sifton retired to his shop, and ultimately came up with a machine that enabled Sam Arena to win the Oakland 200, clipping 17 minutes off the previous record into the bargain.

In again referring to Sifton's wizardry, most H-D riders were convinced, mostly through sad experience, that one couldn't run an engine wide open for a whole lap without snapping the throttle shut at least twice to bring oil up into the cylinder walls. Sifton experimented with various oil control piston rings and eventually came forth with a lubrication system that would allow the cylinders to run wet. Critics, noting Arena's wide open running, warned Sifton that if he were not ordered to slow down, he risked certain seizure. Sifton's answer was, to himself at least, that if Arena slowed down, the clandestine oiling system would allow too much oil to come up and foul the spark plugs!

Sifton ultimately came into much conflict with H-D's management in the late 1930's when their Racing Department was in process of developing their later standard WR racer. Through direct contact with the factory representatives in person, the factory practically demanded that Sifton make known to them his heretofore secret modifications. It was alleged by H-D management that Sifton was conducting a competition with Sifton rather than H-D machines. The latter, however, remained adamant, and he did not reveal his tuning secrets to the factory until 1947, the year Sam Arena retired and took over Sifton's San Jose dealership.

H-D's official position in the matter of Class C competition remained critical during the late 1930's, due to the pre-eminence of Indian's Sport Scout. Rollie Free, a veteran Indian dealer in Indianapolis for many years, told the author in 1976 that following a spectacular race meet in that city in 1936 that ended in a sweeping Indian victory, a group of H-D factory personnel approached him to find out just why the Sport Scout could be tuned to deliver such outstanding performance. In the course of the meeting, held in an opulent Indianapolis watering place, the latter recounted both their problems in developing a really potent H-D racer, and their inability to persuade Tom Sifton to reveal his tuning secrets. Free related that he was able to both commiserate with them in their dilemma, accept their hospitality with grace, but at the same moment reveal none of his own private knowledge of just how the Sport Scout was tuned by knowledgable mechanics to deliver its winning performances.

Persistent rumors within the industry regarding experimental work at Milwaukee regarding the introduction of a new model H-D finally came to light in the spring of 1936 with the announcement of an entirely new model, the 61E, a massive V twin with overhead valves. The new machine, which bore no direct relationship to the previous 'VL' series, featured a cradle-type frame with twin down tubes, heavier forks, and incorporated a number of innovative features to both current H-D practice and to contemporary American motorcycle design. While maintaining the bore and stroke of $3^5/16$ x $3^1/2$ inch stroke of the classic 61 cubic inch 'J' models, the new engine featured overhead valve configuration that doubled that engine's hp output to 36. With a compression ratio of 6:1 and a top gear ratio of 3.73 to 1, the theoretical top speed was projected at well over 90 mph. In addition, the new engine featured dry sump lubrication, already seen on Indian, and long a standard item on foreign designs. At last it brought H-D into the middle period of the twentieth century.

In addition, a wide ratio four-speed gear box with gears in constant mesh, coupled with a new massive multiplate-clutch mechanism, was to carry on H-D's established reputation of a trouble-free drive train. The overall appearance of the new model, which weighed slightly over 600 pounds with fuel and oil aboard, was enhanced with the fitting of an entirely new streamlined fuel tank, in two halves, the lubricating oil being carried in a gallon capacity tank fitted behind the seat post.

As the first domestic machine ever to be offered with overhead valves, the 61E featured push rods of unequal length running off a single lobe from the timing chest.

While ostensibly the work of H-D's design department, headed by William S.Harley and augmented by the efforts of Bill Ottaway, much of the practical development was effected by Joe Petrali and Hank Syvertson, a long time member of the Racing Department. In addition, much of the testing of the initial prototype models was carried out by William Harley's son, William J. The latter, born in 1912, had joined the Company at the age of 19. Expected to prove himself, he was started at the bottom as an apprentice. He also studied engineering at the University of Wisconsin, as his father before him, and gained his degree in 1935. While his formal duties were now that of a draftsman in the engineering department, he had much to do with the road testing of the two 61E prototypes. In later years, he confided to intimates that the latter models required extensive modifications to the original

One of the last Rikuos, an RT II 750 cc model. Weight, 230 kg, top speed 120 kph. It is fitted with a four-speed transmission. The last of this series was built between 1956 and 1960. *(Charles D. Bohon)*

The three wheeled Servi-car introduced in 1932. The small town petroleum products outlet advertises regular and high octane gasoline at 18 and 20 cents per gallon.

Official factory photograph of a 30.50 cu.in. short track machine as originally designed by Joe Petrali.

steering geometry, as he narrowly missed several crashes when testing the new model in extensive runs in the country adjacent to Milwaukee.

While the new model appeared basically sound, there were certain defects in the ohv system which were found to leak oil excessively. Petrali, who was well aware of these problems, told the author in 1968 that he cautioned H-D's management not to release the new model for production until the matter had been solved. President Walter Davidson, however, had set the target date at June 1936, and gave the go-ahead for production in spite of Petrali's warnings, the outcome of which will be subsequently discussed.

Concurrent to the development of the 61E, Petrali conferred with President Walter Davidson concerning the problem of updating or improving the current 45 model to make it more competitive with Indian's Sport Scout model, which by this time had proved itself to be a definitely superior machine. He suggested that the company take the initiative in bringing out a high performance ohv model, which would entail the design of an entirely new engine. His reasoning was that the H-D Company, due to its majority financial support of the AMA, could now dictate a new set of competition rules in the 45 cubic inch class that could not only obtain AMA approval of such a new model for Class C competition, but could force Indian to redesign their Sport Scout in order to compete with H-D. President Walter Davidson's answer was that the cost of such a project would probably entail the expenditure of at least $100,000 and with the present state of both the general motorcycle market and the company's current financial status, it was out of the question. He further stated to Petrali that the project could be instituted only if Alfred Rich Child could be induced to purchase the manufacturing rights of the 61E for this figure.

In the meantime, under the direction of William A. Davidson, the 61E was placed in production, and of a total of 8,879 machines projected for production in 1936, 1,926 were of the new model. While the 61E was basically a sound and rugged machine built from the best available materials in the time tried H-D tradition, early models showed certain defects in the valve gear. These included valve spring breakage, insufficient lubrication for the rocker mechanism, from massive oil leakage from the rocker boxes and subsequent loss of correct timing sequence with a resultant loss of power. The author, as a young man, recalls being allowed a test ride on Joe Frugoli's personal 61E which had been ordered for demonstration purposes. While the machine in the author's opinion offered decidedly better performance than the last 'VL' models, even including the briefly produced 80 inch model, upon his returning the machine to the shop he noted that his legs from the knees down were heavily saturated with lubricating oil.

With the official announcement that the 61E was a high performance machine of advanced design, (at least as far as the American market was concerned), many dealers were somewhat hesitant initially either to order the new model or to unconditionally recommend it to favored customers, due to their unfortunate experiences with the early 45 and 'VL' models during 1929 and 1930. When the obvious defects of the new ohv valve model became painfully apparent, both dealers and knowledgable riders again questioned the factory's judgment in releasing a new design for production before all the bugs had been thoroughly worked out.

In commenting upon this most critical phase of H-D history, Joe Petrali told the author that while he had had much to do with the basic design of the 61E, he had certain reservations regarding the ultimate reliability of the first prototype models. He then suggested to President Walter Davidson that more time be allotted to further testing with a view to correcting these faults, and that any official announcements regarding the release of the model for sale should be held in abeyance until such had been completed. Davidson's reply was that what with the relatively large sums of money that had already been expended on prototype development, the company was now forced to place the model on the market in order to recoup as soon as possible.

While the sychophantic motorcycling press, now solely represented by the AMA-backed *Motorcyclist,* offered lavish editorial praise to the 61E without reference to any concommitant road tests, its debut was somewhat overshadowed from an almost unexpected quarter.

Albert G. Crocker, whom we have met before as a one time colleague of William Ottaway's in the old Thor organization, had for the past few seasons been building a limited number of Class A speedway machines for use on short tracks. What with the recent ascendancy of the more highly developed JAP and Rudge-engined machines, he had ceased assembly of the latter to concentrate his activities on the production of a machine that had long been an unrealized ambition: a high performance heavyweight V twin the classic Yankee tradition. The result, with the collaboration of another heavyweight enthusiast, a practical engineer and skilled mechanic, Paul A. Bigsby, was a rather noisy and hard-to-start rorty big twin that offered sensational performance. Due to its more nearly 'square' bore and stroke configuration, moderate weight for its size and rather 'tall' gearing, its 100 mph plus top speed was at least ten miles better than the well tuned Big Twin H-D's and Indian Chiefs. During the initial speed trials held on the old Lake Muroc race course in the Spring of 1936, the newly-introduced Crocker beat everthing in sight. With the local sensation created by the new make, the *Motorcyclist* was literally forced to publish a graphic report of its achievements.

Old time H-D factory employees and dealers in various discussions of the matter through the years have attested to management's chagrin over both the results of Crocker's efforts and the attendant, though somewhat grudgingly accorded, publicity. Their subsequent reaction to the matter ultimately took a somewhat surprising turn, which we shall see.

Following the natural disappointment of many H-D dealers and riders over the initial shortcomings of the 61E, the Engineering Department at once inaugurated a crash program to rectify the matter. The metallurgy of the valve springs was improved, and a new supplier ultimately provided more long-lasting components. The rocker gear was redesigned for improved oiling capabilities, together with an improved bearing arrangement. Repair kits containing the new parts were dispatched to the dealers, with instructions to make good on any of the initial 1,900 machines that showed defects.

As a publicity stunt, and in an effort to publicly demonstrate the capabilities of the 61E, plans were formulated to attack the existing straight-away mile records long held by Indian rung up on the famous beach course at Daytona. Hank Syvertson of the Racing Department, with the help of Joe

Another version of the 1934 short tracker from the Bud Ekins collection. Note the Merkel-type forks and the similarity of the engine to the contemporary JAP design. It was quickly outclassed by the latter's later models. *(Alisha Tamburri)*.

Petrali, built up a special machine around a stock engine. Modifications included twin carburetors, a high tension magneto, increased compression, modified breathing capabilities, and high lift cams. Set with a high 3:1 top gear ratio, the machine was calculated to show a top speed of 160 mph. To reduce weight, a special frame of lightweight tubing was built up and high pressure racing tires were fitted, the wheels being provided with faired aluminum discs. A streamline tail section, reminiscent of contemporary racing car practice, extended from the rear of the saddle to cover the rear wheel.

After a number of studio pictures of the machine were taken by the Publicity Department photographer, including several with Petrali aboard wearing a clean white shirt and necktie, the 61, along with a stripped stock 45 inch model supposedly tuned to Class C rules, was loaded on a truck for the trip to Daytona Beach. A three mile course had been laid out under the direction of John La Tour, who had recently acted as the official timer for Sir Malcolm Campbell's recent record race car runs on the same stretch. One mile was used to get up speed before hitting the trap for the record, the third mile being required to bring the machine to a stop.

On March 13th, defying superstition, Petrali warmed up the 45 and made several runs through the course. What with problems experienced with carburetion and burned out spark plugs, the best average was a somewhat disappointing 102.04 mph. The 61 was next rolled out for a preliminary run, 141

Two views of Edward Carlson and his 1936 74 cu.in. VL. 1940 and later 16 inch rear wheels were often fitted to give a softer ride. *(George Hays).*

but when a speed of approximately 100 mph was reached, the machine suddenly became unmanageable. Hoping that a quick burst of speed might correct the difficulty, Petrali opened the throttle, whereupon the front wheel started to aviate, and at the same time swung back and forth over the course. Due to his consummate riding skill, Petrali was able to wrestle the 61 to a standstill. Noting at once the unfavorable aerodynamic qualities of the wheel discs and tail fairings, Petrali ordered the pit crew to remove them. In stripped condition, the machine now stayed on course, and three full throttle runs were made, the best average being 136.18 mph, for a new record. This was a rather hollow triumph, as it was only 10 mph faster than Johnny Seymour's 1932 record time made on a modified board track Indian racer with a slightly modified 8 valve engine that was one of six assembled by the factory in 1924.

While the H-D factory quite naturally made much out of the victory, it did not mention in the publicity reports that the machine did not make its record run as a streamliner. Only one photograph of the 61 on its actual running run was surreptitiously taken by a local newspaper photographer. The actual machine is presently on view at William Tuthill's Museum of Speed at Daytona Beach.

In commenting on the matter in an interview with the author in 1967, Petrali stated that in his opinion the 61 would have performed much better if it had been lighter, as even in stripped form it weighed nearly 400 pounds, some 125 pounds heavier than Seymour's earlier Indian. He also was of the opinion that if it had weighed 100 pounds less, it could have been fitted with taller gearing, and might then have attained the 150 mph figure envisioned by President Walter Davidson. The latter's hopes for this speed were centered on his offer to Petrali of a $1,000 bonus if he could reach this figure. Upon his return to Milwaukee, Petrali attempted to induce Davidson to award him at least half of the promised bonus, citing the problems experienced with the machine and his near disaster when the machine went out of control. Davidson was adamant, however, and no bonus payment was forthcoming.

In the Fall of 1936, the now venerable 'J' model was retired from Class C competition in the TT and hill climb categories by a change in the rules mandated by the AMA Competition Committee, which effectively barred the model from future events. This action was, of course, instigated by H-D's top management, which now decided that for too long the 'J's had overshadowed the 'VL's', which were now to be superseded by the 61E and the soon-to-be announced 'U' series. While no official announcements were forthcoming from the factory, the Competition Committee announced that henceforth pocket valve engines and machines with exposed external compression type rear brakes were to be barred from competition. This arbitrary action quite naturally angered the many die-hard 'J' enthusiasts, including its two leading exponents who had already racked up an impressive set of wins during the past several seasons, Hap Jones and Fred Toscani. These two, in company with a number of other sporting 'J' enthusiasts, were particularly chagrined, as they had collected an impressive array of

The Buddy Seat. An important adjunct to social motorcycling.

The crash guard as pioneered by H-D in the mid-1930s.

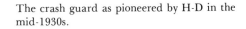

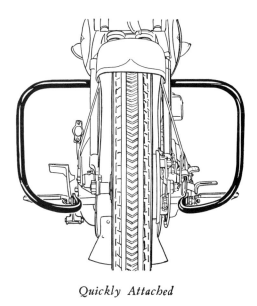

FINEST MENS' AND LADIES' RIDING BREECHES
POLO STYLE WHIPCORD
Dark Oxford or Police Blue

Our leader in riding breeches. The nifty Polo Style is dressy. Here is a strong closely woven pre-shrunk cotton whipcord material that wears like iron. Double thickness on inside of knees and seat. Five roomy pockets. Sizes 28 to 40 in standard lengths, 30 to 38 in extra longs, 28 to 32 in extra shorts.

		Code
11097-34—Oxford Whipcord	.........$3.95	bykah
11097-35—Police Blue Whipcord	...... 3.95	byepr

Polo Style Breeches

ENGLISH MILITARY STYLE

Style plus utility. The last word in style and quality—these extra high grade, part wool breeches will appeal to the most critical buyer. Made from a new closely woven tan material, both distinctive and long wearing. Full grain leather facings are used at the knees. You cannot duplicate these high quality breeches at our low price. Sizes 28 to 40 in standard lengths, 30 to 38 in extra longs, 28 to 32 in extra shorts.

English Military Style Breeches

		Code
11099-X—Tan only	....$7.50	bajox

MEN'S WHITE OR BROWN SUMMER WEIGHT

These light, summer-weight gabardine breeches are styled after a popular pattern, they are neat and attractive. Made of the best pre-shrunk, washable material. Five pockets. In white or rich brown. Available in sizes: 28 to 42 waist in standard lengths; 28 to 38 waist in extra shorts; 28 to 36 waist in extra longs.

		Code
11094-36—White Gabardine	$3.75	byede
11098-36—Brown Gabardine.....	3.75	byeef

CLASSY LADIES' BREECHES and JODHPURS

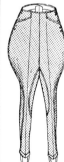

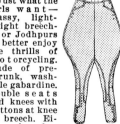

Just what the girls want — classy, light-weight breeches or Jodhpurs to better enjoy the thrills of motorcycling. Made of pre-shrunk, washable gabardine. Double seats and knees with buttons at knee on breech. Either breeches or Jodhpurs are attractively styled, beautifully fitting, excellent tailored garments with high-rise back and liberal waist and leg outlets. All points of strain reinforced for longer wear. Available in standard lengths only. Sizes 24 to 34 waist measure.

Jodhpurs

Ladies' Breeches

		Code
11092-36—Ladies' White Riding Breeches	.................$3.50	byczy
11093-36—Ladies' Rich Brown Jodhpurs	.... 3.75	byeab

GENUINE HORSEHIDE

Leather riding breeches were made originally for the competition rider, as they are quite a protection against injury in case of a spill.

These well tailored horsehide breeches are really weather-proof. They are made from fine, soft, black, front quarter horsehide and are fully lined. Have five pockets and belt loops.

		Code
11068-X—Black Horsehide Breeches	..............$12.50	bahio

HIGH GRADE RIDING BOOTS

The field boot style, as illustrated, is the style desired by motorcycle riders. The lacings at the instep and the calf make it easy to put on and take off this style of boot. We can supply dress boots or ladies boots on special order, but the field boot is the most practical and is carried in stock.

Harley-Davidson boots are made from high grade calfskin that will give long service. They are fully lined and have excellent soles. Can be supplied in sizes 6 to 12, and all standard widths. Get your proper measurement from your shoe dealer. Stocked in black only.

		Code
11090-34—Field Boots	.....$12.25	buryh

5

A part of the extensive line of motorcycle clothing from H-D's extensive accessory offerings.

machines and spare parts, mostly of the two cam 'JH' type. Jones subsequently abandoned Milwaukee in disgust, and shortly afterward joined forces with Indian by taking a dealership in San Francisco. This action also removed the surviving Super Xs that were still active in Class C competition, as their pocket valve engines and rear brakes were identical with H-D 'Js'. As highly tuned Xs, many with strengthened lower ends were ever formidable contenders in any sort of competition, H-D's management, working through the AMA hierarchy, must have felt greatly relieved in disqualifying them.

The introduction of the 61E was followed that fall by two newly designed side valve machines, the 74 and 80 cubic inch 'UL' and 'ULH' models. These were practically identical to the former as to cycle parts, and in addition were fitted with a circulation oil pump and dry sump lubrication, the oil being carried in a four quart tank under the saddle, as in the 61E. In contrast with the early teething troubles of the latter, these two 600 pound heavyweights proved entirely successful from their beginning. They were further distinguished by the fact that they were probably the most rugged, durable, and trouble-free motorcycles ever produced by the American industry. They had the added advantage of being quickly and easily serviced, as a top overhaul, only required after high mileages, could be effected without removing the engine from the frame. With their massive high torque engines that turned out well over 30 hp at moderate revolutions, both models were well suited to heavy duty sidecar or commercial use. While their fork geometry was such that they steered somewhat heavily, they could be easily handled in city traffic as their massive multiplate dry type clutches could be slipped without harm, and even prolonged operation in this use produced but little wear in the mechanism. In addition, their fuel consumption was moderate if cruising speeds were held below 60 mph.

While well accepted by American riders, they were particularly successful on the export market, being utilized mostly for sidecar or commercial sidevan uses. Due to their ruggedness and longevity they were also popular for law enforcement use. They found almost universal acceptance by the Government of Mexico, as well as in various countries in Central and South America in military and constabulary units. Their ruggedness and low maintenance costs were advantageous, particularly in areas where highly skilled mechanics were lacking, as well as the fact that they could stand up to misuse and abuse meted out to them by inexperienced riders.

In short, the 'U' models offered a broader based appeal than did the high performance 61E, and their only real weakness was their inability to stand up to high speed running, especially in hot climatic

The 1936 VL 80 cu.in. model with four-speed transmission, the last year of the VL. The police accessory group is shown.

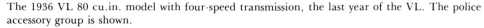

conditions. If operated at speeds over 70 mph, the cylinders and heads were much more prone to overheating and distortion, usually resulting in piston seizure. They suffered in comparison with the contemporary Indian Chief, their main competitor, as the latter's combustion chamber profile and cooling fin designed by James Hill appeared better able to cope with high speed operation. On the other side of the coin, Indian's oil immersed clutch and archaic sliding gear transmission suffered greatly in comparison to H-D's new heavyweight constant mesh gear set and multiple dry plate clutch configuration.

The 45 cubic inch model 'D' was also updated for 1937, and was fitted with the same mudguards and fuel tank pressings of the larger twins to rationalize production. In addition, its engine now had improved cooling and lubrication with the fitting of dry sump oiling, the latter being carried in a chamber in one of the tank halves. While the high compression engine option offered to riders seeking mild sporting performance gave somewhat more spirit to the formerly sedate model, its advantage was somewhat offset by the increased overall weight of the machine, which was now well over 500 pounds in road-going trim. It was no match for the more highly developed Indian Sport Scout and its appeal to sporting riders was further diminished by the fact that due to H-D's big twin parts sequence so that it was not possible to easily 'stroke' it to an increased piston displacement. On the other hand, its lower bearing and flywheel assembly was more rugged than that of the Scout, and practical mechanics almost at once began adapting these parts to the Scout engine, which then resulted in a highly potent machine with the displacement increased to 52 cubic inches.

A further weakness of the new model, especially when fitted with the high compression engine, was that under fierce acceleration the single frame tube that supported the engine base was prone to flexing and many riders found that this distortion caused the outer run of the double chain drive to run off the sprockets. The diameter of the tube and the thickness of the mounting flanges were inceased the following year in hopes of curing the trouble, but this was only partially successful. While a cradle type frame, such as seen in the current big twin models, would have undoubtedly corrected the fault, the resultant weight penalty would have been formidable in a machine already overly heavy for its power development. Nevertheless, the 45 remained as a popular utility mount for many riders, as well as for elderly or feminine types who did not opt for high performance and appreciated its easy starting capabilities as well as its usually unfailing reliability. It was widely exported to many undeveloped countries for utility or commercial use. It was also seen as a military mount, particularly in countries where universally poor roads ruled out high speed travel. In the United States, its most familiar guise was as the basis for the popular Servi-car, widely used as a commercial carrier or in law enforcement traffic and parking control.

The Winter of 1936 and 1937 saw the nation's industries encountering increasing problems with labor. Sociological historians may recall that the labor union movement had gained impetus during the closing years of the 19th century and the opening years of the 20th. Public sympathy was aroused with the exposure of the often appalling working conditions and low wages suffered by many of the production workers following the rise of industrialism in the United States following the Civil War. The problem was complicated by the hordes of immigrants that had been allowed to enter the country from Europe with the blessings of the industrialists who foresaw the need for a vast pool of exploitable labor. With the leadership of union organizers such as Samuel Gompers and John L. Lewis, trade unionism gained strength after the First World War, but much ground was lost during the depression when jobs were scarce and the general economic picture was such that any employment offering even minimal wages was at a premium. In 1934, the Populist President Franklin D. Roosevelt induced a compliant Congress to pass the Wagner Labor Relations Act, which encouraged union organization among workers, and which could now offer the hope of raising the then current 30 to 35 cent hourly stipend.

In the Midwest, and subsequent to the passage of the Wagner Act, several drives were instituted by union organizers to recruit members, one of which was led by one Charles Travis, one of the founders of the United Auto Workers. After some resistance, he was able to organize General Motors workers in 1935, and shortly afterwards, Chrysler. The giant Ford Motor Company was a much tougher nut to crack, as old Henry had long been an ardent foe of unionism. Union organizers fought a number of pitched battles outside the Dearborn plant, and two young labor organizers named Walter Reuther and Charles Frankenstein were badly beaten in one encounter with Company police units. After Ford ultimately capitulated, other related and sometimes unrelated manufacturers such as Caterpillar Tractor, John Deere, Libby-Owens Ford, and International Harvester, recognized the United Auto Workers as their labor bargaining agent.

The organizers next turned their attention to H-D, whose management had been historically opposed to unionization ever since the Company's incorporation in 1907. On the other hand, H-D had never held to a policy of sweatshop labor, and had habitually paid production workers from 40 to 75 cents per hour, according to their skills and abilities. As Head of Production, William A. Davidson, as has been seen, ran a very tight ship, but his paternalistic treatment of his work force and his sympathy

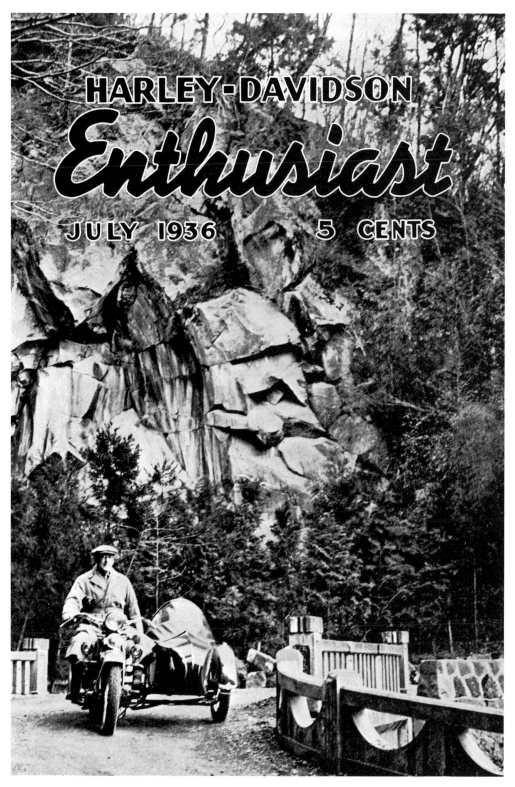

Alfred Rich Child, the perennial sidecar enthusiast, graces the cover of the July 1936 *Enthusiast*. The scene is typical of the Japanese countryside.

for their personal problems engendered a strong feeling of camaraderie and company loyalty. It has often been stated by many veteran H-D employees that while many of them could command slightly higher wages elsewhere in the Milwaukee area, their loyalty to 'Big Bill', the H-D Company, and the product, made it unthinkable for them to remotely consider any other employment.

At the same moment, the feeling for unionism was growing, and in the Fall of 1936, Walter Reuther ordered union organizers posted at the gates of the Juneau Avenue plant to hand out leaflets and otherwise announce that H-D workers were now being solicited to demand a union shop.

During this campaign, William Davidson tended to ignore the matter, sure of the loyalty of his staff. When warned of the dangers of possible impending violence, he shrugged the matter off with the terse statement: 'Let them try'.

The matter dragged on throughout the Winter, but events came to a head in the early months of 1937 with William Davidson's sudden failing health. A large, hearty man, with an appetitie for good food and drink, his weight had at long last attained rather alarming proportions. Shortly afterwards he sustained painful swellings in his lower legs which made mobility difficult. Early in March, he was confined to the hospital for several weeks, and was subsequently released by his doctors on the condition that he confine himself to his residence and make substantial efforts to reduce his weight. He patently ignored this advice, continued to consume his usual generous intake of food, along with his daily ration of strong German lager beer supplied to him by his lifelong friend, Fritz Gettelman, the brewmaster of a local brewery, for which Milwaukee was long justly famous. Late in March he was again confined to hospital, but in spite of intensive treatment his legs continued to swell alarmingly. At length gangrene set in, and in a desperate attempt to save his life, both legs were amputated. He never regained consciousness after this surgery, and died April 21st, 1937, in his 67th year. Mourned by his family, his brothers, company associates, dealers and H-D enthusiasts, his passing marked the end of yet another era in American motorcycling history.

The contributions of William Davidson to H-D's ultimate success were most substantial. In charge of production ever since the formal incorporation of the company, his previous knowledge of industrial procedures and general plant management were of inestimable value during the critical years when the company sought to penetrate an already well established industry. His competence in this field enabled the company to build a superior product, with Davidson's practical knowledge of materials and metallurgy, as well as to efficiently produce the products at rock bottom costing. It was this factor that enabled H-D to survive during an era when the often sound designs of the originator foundered on the inability of plant managers to translate them into production realities. While Davidson was known to be ruthless when it came down to the ultimate control of production line procedures, this factor, combined with his intimate knowledge of the materials involved, enabled H-D to produce a superior product at a competitive price.

It has further been noted that in addition to his initial ability to translate the original sound designs of William Harley into a practical product, his influence in design development and much of overall company policy was also due to the fact that of the four Founders, he held the largest individual block of company stock. While the others invested much of their individual profits back into the company, they also purchased shares in other enterprises unrelated to the motorcycle industry. Not so with William Davidson, whose sole efforts were orientated toward the company itself. A somewhat plain and rough hewn man, who was more at home on the production line than in the boardroom, his personal influence through the first three decades of the company's existence was perhaps greater than that of any of the other Founders.

In the interim following Davidson's death, William Ottaway took over production supervision. Faced with reorganizing and updating these facilities, together with the ever increasing pressure from the union organizers, and now abetted by certain of the younger members of the production force who favored unionization, Ottaway capitulated, and the company at long last signed an agreement with the United Auto Workers Union to submit to collective bargaining.

In the meantime, the local Milwaukee press, in reporting the progress of the proceedings at the H-D factory, noted that certain of the production staff favored unionization. While the media was now able to generate some public sympathy for the union, in the now highly industrialized state of Wisconsin, there was little enthusiasm for organized labor's victory. As a result of a series of meetings between union representatives and H-D's top management, there was an increase of 15 cents per hour for production personnel, along with certain fringe benefits. The consequent rise in production costs was reflected in a 10% increase in the retail price of machines.

Incidental to these events, the company's management next retaliated against certain members of the production force who had, in the later and more critical bargaining procedures, voted for unionization. Most of these were either relatively recently employed or apprentices, and were thus in the younger age group. In open defiance of the recently negotiated union contract most of these dissidents were at once discharged. Among them was one Johnny Speigelhoff, a Milwaukee resident

A typical hill climb course in the mid-1930s.

who had lately gained recognition as a formidable competition rider. He almost at once obtained employment as a mechanic at a nearby Indian agency, and for the next decade figured prominently in motorcycle sport on an Indian Scout.

Following this rather critical period in H-D history, veteran factory employees subsequently reported that never again did the former happy family atmosphere pervade the production department. The now mandatory presence of union stewards induced a somewhat dampening effect on the former spirit of camaraderie.

During the Summer and Fall of 1937, a series of articles in the *Enthusiast* offered tributes to William Davidson's many contributions to Company progress. It was pointed out that under his direction the factory's tool fabrication department produced nearly all of the necessary tools, jigs, dies and other equipment used on the production lines. The factory was also provided with over 100 automatic machines that produced various sizes of screws and bolt stock, and that other similar devices could turn out stock bars up to 4 inch in diameter. Other machines turned out various sizes of roller bearings in the millions. A giant hundred ton press, twenty feet high with eight foot wheels, could be inter-

149

changeably fitted with the various dies that stamped out fuel tank halves, mudguard shells, tool box and oil tank components, as well as the various sizes of sprockets. A number of the famous Bullard Multimatic machines were also utilized which carried out numerous individual machining operations automatically.

In the General Inspection Department, sample parts from each production run were checked against Rockwell Hardness in tempering. Bearings were checked to one ten thousandth of an inch, gear teeth being checked to half this gauge. Gear pitch was checked to one thousandth. As a master check on all inspection procedures, a set of the famous Johansen measuring blocks were utilized, which insured accuracy to one millionth of an inch.

In spite of the employment of such sophisticated machinery, visitors to the plant familiar with industrial production procedures often noted that the overall operation was a curious mixture of both ancient and modern. After component parts were fabricated and stocked, much of the final assembly was carried on by somewhat laborious hand fitting. Much of this work was effected by veteran craftsmen working in various small cubbyholes throughout the plant.

The H-D Company was long noted in the industry by its almost complete manufacture of all component parts. The management cited that supply difficulties had been experienced in former years when outside contractors, such as those furnishing electrical equipment, sometimes failed to make deliveries on time as promised, thus delaying production and order filling.

In common with most vehicle manufacturers, H-D assembled machines only on orders received, following the customer's orders to the dealer as to model, paint finish options, and accessory groups. This practice facilitated the saving of storage space, as large numbers of finished machines would have taken up much floor room.

During the mid-1930s, transcontinental record breaking again became popular, although the presence of much improved road surfaces now made it a much less heroic undertaking. In the Spring of 1934, Randolph Whiting on an Indian Chief set a new New York to Los Angeles record of 5 days 3½ hours. With no immediate challengers, Whiting broke his own record the following year, this time on a Sport Scout, racking up an impressive 4 days 19 hours. That Fall, Earl Robinson, the very enthusiastic Detroit H-D dealer, riding a specially tuned 45 model, made the 3,005 mile run in 3 days 6½ hours, an average speed of 39 mph. His record was shortly afterward challenged by Rody Rodenburg on a Sport Scout, who shaved 7 hours off his time in June 1936, averaging 42.9 mph.

A new transcontinental sidecar record was hung up for H-D by two experienced enthusiasts, William Connelly and Fred Dauria, in October 1936. Both had independently attempted solo crossings the Spring before, on 74 inch VL machines, but each had been put out of the running by both illness and mechanical troubles before reaching the Mississippi River. In order to insure success, they decided to team up on a sidecar outfit, and selected one of the new 1936 'U' models for the attempt. Their exhaustive preparations included the fitting of an auxiliary 15 gallon fuel tank in the sidecar to extend their cruising range, along with carrying numerous spare parts and extra tires and tubes. The total weight of the outfit totaled nearly 1,800 pounds, which cut their top speed to about 58 mph. Over the great plains country they cruised flat out, averaging 52 mph. To reduce fatigue, each drove 300 mile segments, with fuel stops scheduled at 600 mile intervals. H-D dealers along the route kept their shops open to provide both food and fuel.

Starting as they did rather late in the season, the pair encountered freezing weather over the Rocky Mountain passes in Wyoming. Halting briefly in Cheyenne to replace their now nearly bald tires and to obtain new spares, they next encountered unseasonably hot weather in Western Utah and Eastern Nevada. This caused their engine to vapor lock, and the subsequent fuel starvation reduced their top speed to 30 mph. Cooler weather corrected the problem about 100 miles east of Las Vegas, and as they sped into the suburbs of Los Angeles, they were met by a contingent of Los Angeles motorcycle officers who escorted them to the Selig Zoo, the official termination point, where an AMA timer clocked their finish. Their elapsed time was 69 hours 46 minutes for the 3,100 mile distance, nearly two hours off the previous solo record, with an average speed of 45 mph. Their record was not broken for another twenty years, until John Penton, on a BMW, set a new time of 52 hours as a solo entrant in the Summer of 1959. In the absence of other sidecar challengers, Connelly and Duaria's record still stands in the sidecar category. At the finish, their outfit was somewhat travel stained, but in generally good mechanical condition with the exception of some corrosion of the exhaust valves. Much was made of their very creditable exploit, both in the pages of the *Enthusiast* as well as the trade press. Their record was even more impressive when viewed as a private effort without any factory sponsorship. It also provided much well deserved publicity for the stamina of the now 80 inch model, which was to be continued the following season as the new 'U' cradle frame model.

In the Fall of 1936, Fred Ham, a Pasadena motorcycle police officer who was both a long time H-D enthusiast and a physical culture devotee, broke the Three Flag record previously set by Paul Rameley on a 21 'Peashooter', ten years earlier. For his run, Ham selected a new 74 inch side valve

Joe Petrali and Jim Davis (both mounted) together with their pit crew at Syracuse, New York, where the former won the National Dirt Track Championship in 1936. Famed tuner Hank Syvertson at left.

The start of the 1936 Dirt Track National, with winner Joe Petrali.

model, and after a careful 1,200 mile break-in period, prepared to assault the record from the Canadian end of the course. Making the northward journey in leisurely fashion, he selected his route and made arrangements with dealers along the way to supply food, fuel, and spare parts if needed.

The return run for the record was started at Blaine, Washington, which was situated on the International border. He started at 3.00 am, in order to provide two days and one night of riding. Clad in leather breeches and jacket to combat the cold in the Washington mountains, he was able to average 50 mph for the first leg of the journey. Shedding these for the heat of California's great Central Valley, he was plagued by great swarms of insects which literally plastered the front of his machine, otherwise proceeding without incident. On the final stretch from Los Angeles to Tijuana he was escorted by San Diego H-D dealer, Roy Artley, himself a record breaker of an earlier era, who mounted a similar model. His elapsed time was 28 hours 7 minutes, some 10 hours off the old record. He experienced no mechanical troubles other than a broken throttle cable, the sturdy side valver never missing a beat for the entire distance.

Ham's next triumph for himself and H-D was the racking up of numerous new AMA records for a non-stop 24 hour run at the Muroc dry lake course on April 8th and 9th 1937. This time he selected a new 61E ohv model, which was prepared by Pasadena H-D dealer Bill Graves after a careful 1,200 mile break-in period. The latter installed factory supplied improved ohv fittings and springs and a reworked oiling system to correct the earlier 61E faults. Ham was determined to make the run as a solo undertaking, and already in superb physical condition, he underwent further taining by swimming several hours each days before the event. With his machine tuned to stock specification his only modifications were the removal of the front mudguard to enhance the flow of cooling air to the front cylinder and the addition of a specially-designed shroud to cover the carburetor air intake to keep out the fine sand of the lake bed. His efforts at preparation were aided by the advice of Fred Ludlow, the well known H-D racing star of an earlier era, who was now a motorcycle officer in the Pasadena Police Department.

The course was laid out in the center of Lake Muroc, a five mile circle outlined with both flags and flare pots for day and night running. While the smooth surface was ideal for safe high speed travel, the 2,680 foot altitude presented carburetion problems with 100 plus degree daytime temperatures and below freezing nights. At Ludlow's suggestion, Ham fitted a buddy seat which enabled him to 'tuck in' his considerable bulk, and he commenced his tireless circling of the course. Stopping only for fuel, oil, and drinks of fruit juices, he managed to cover an incredible 1,825 miles during the 24 hours for an elapsed time of 76.02 mph and 83.25 mph for actual running time, setting 43 new AMA records in the process.

The 61E ran faultlessly during the grueling 24 hour run, requiring only a replacement of the rear chain at the 1,400th mile that was effected within a three minute pit stop. Much was made of Ham's exploit, both in the pages of the *Enthusiast* and in the trade press. It was not only a tribute to Ham's superb physical endurance, but also did much to enhance the somewhat original tarnished image of the 61E now fitted with improved valve gear.

As an indication of slightly improved economic conditions, H-D production rose from 8,879 units in 1936 to 11,674 in 1937. But the relatively soft state of the domestic market was emphasized by the fact that the combined output of both US factories for both years was but 13,907 and 17,704 respectively. Of these totals, over 50% of the output was exported.

The late 1930's saw an encouraging resurgence of motorcycle club activities, which were subjected to continuing attention by AMA Secretary Manager E.C.Smith through orders of the M & ATA's Board of Directors. Some of the clubs in the larger cities saw a membership of owners of both H-D's and Indians, together with a few surviving Hendersons and Super X's. In centers of smaller population, the clubs tended to be more of the one-make variety, dependent upon the willingness or ability of the individual dealers to offer support to owners of their own particular make of machine. The heavyweight models tended to be the favorites of clubmen, as these machines were better suited to long distance rides and offered the option of inviting wife or girlfriend, as well as being able to carry the requisite amount of luggage.

The touring family-oriented clubs, which usually had substantial numbers of sidecar enthusiasts, generally tended to favor H-D machines, while the sporting type clubs more often than not were mainly composed of Indian Scout owners who favored competition events as opposed to touring. In any case, the predominant machine was usually a big twin, now fitted with a dualseat, windshield, saddle bags, luggage carrier, together with whatever extra lighting and accessories the owners elected to install. Such machines later became known as being 'Full Dress', or 'Dressers', as opposed to those who favored stripped down sporting machines, usually of 45 inch displacement. Whatever the individual club's orientation, the AMA endeavored to see that all members were AMA affiliated, and as such received designation as an official AMA group.

It was during this period that the H-D Company enhanced its advertising program, and

augmented the size and content of the *Enthusiast*. This was in direct competition with Indian's counterpart, *The Indian News*. Both companies engaged photographers to attend various club runs and contests to take pictures for future publicity and advertising campaigns, the latter then being made available to both the dealers and the trade press. It was usually a source of amusement at large motorcycle gatherings to witness the photographers persuading owners of the competing makes of machine to form into individual groups for such picture taking.

The editors of each house organ quite naturally gave exclusive prominence to their own make. Important regional sports events or big National races were featured only if the marque in question was the victor. By seemingly mutual consent, the opposite competitor was never mentioned by name. Tabulated race results at the end of each article inevitably left a blank space whenever the competitor was involved. A casual extra-terrestrial visitor from Outer Space, if he chose to investigate the current motorcycle scene, could well conclude that there was only one make of American motorcycle, depending upon which house organ he happened to peruse!

Another facet of this now somewhat amusing situation was that in the tabulation of official AMA records, precedence to H-D wins and placings was often noted, due to the fact that that company, through its top heavy financial support, historically dominated AMA affairs. Critics have been quick to note that upon close analysis, Indian wins or close placings in many cases were either distorted or omitted entirely from official tabulation. Indeed, much of the historic antagonism between enthusiasts of both makes can be traced to H-D's domination of AMA affairs. This rather unfortunate situation had its origins in the selection of the official referees and competition officials who, in a majority of cases, were H-D enthusiasts. In all fairness, it must be stated that many of these men went out of their way to be both objective and fair in conducting competition meetings, though there were many cases where this was not so. In recounting motorcycle history of an earlier era, many veteran riders have cited cases where, in some instances, a Sport Scout could lap the field, but then be awarded second place upon the citation of an obscure rules infraction! Several pioneer riders of the Midwest have recalled the July 4th race meet at Des Moines, Iowa, in 1936, where a Sport Scout and a resurrected Super X lapped the field in a twenty five mile main event race, only to be awarded second and third places behind an H-D due to an obscure technical infraction of the rules called by the referee. It was this sort of gamesmanship that often precipitated near riots at racemeets, and further tarnished motorcycling's image as a roughneck sport.

The four Founders inspect one of the first ohv 61E models to come off the line. *(H-D Motor Company)*.

A factory-built 45 cu.in. ohv hill climber as used in the West during 1934 through 1940. The engine is the same type as noted in the 1930 European Road Racer. *(Alisha Tamburri)*.

In the Fall of 1937, and in an effort to correct this often unfortunate situation, a number of Indian dealers, together with a few of the more prominent Indian competitors, approached AMA President James Wright, Indian Sales Manager, concerning the problem of the imbalance of H-D enthusiasts filling official AMA competition committees. Wright's answer was to bring the matter to the attention of his boss, Indian's President E.Paul du Pont. The crux of the matter was, of course, H-D's overwhelming part in AMA financing, which had overshadowed that of Indian ever since 1929. The substance of their deliberations was never officially revealed, but Wright at length did report back to his Indian cohorts that du Pont remained adamant in his refusal to increase the amount of Indian's AMA subsidy. Some years later, however, in 1943, after Wright had resigned from the Indian Company, he revealed some of the details of the matter to a close personal friend, the late Paul A.Dunlop. Dunlop informed the author, in an interview in 1959, that during Wright's discussions with du Pont, he told Wright that he considered Indian's $20,000 per year AMA subsidy more than adequate, and that he was not prepared to increase it. He is reported to have further stated that with the acknowledged competition superiority of the current Sport Scout models over the opposite H-D model in the Class C category, he felt that this fact could well counteract H-D's advantage in having a preponderance of their own adherents in the AMA competition hierarchy. While Wright was not in total agreement with du Pont's conclusions in the matter, it was his own opinion that du Pont was still harboring hostile feelings toward H-D's top management in countenancing the attitudes of some of their employees in the 'New Jersey Jew' affair, and he was not prepared to enter into any negotiations with AMA's Competition Committee regarding changes in current AMA policies. Wright further stated that du Pont, while still vitally interested in Indian's welfare as its President and principal stockholder, was at the same time much preoccupied with the management of the Ball Grain Powder Company and his other industrial holdings which were then providing him with very substantial profits, not the case with his Indian interests. The total extent of H-D's financial subsidy of the AMA has, of course, never been revealed, but a composite summation of the reports of various former H-D employees indicate that it was, through the 1930's, at least $75,000 per year. The upshot of the matter was, as variously reported by old Indian enthusiasts, that Indian competitors received somewhat of a vicarious thrill in winning many events through the sheer merit of the Sport Scout, in spite of the fact that in certain of the competition events, they entered with the knowledge that the referees and officials were prejudiced against them at the start.

The almost traditional two make monotony that had pervaded the domestic motorcycle scene was somewhat relieved in the mid-1930's by the very limited appearance of a few British machines. Many of these were supplied by Reggie Pink, the Bronx entrepreneur, who imported small numbers of Ariel, Douglas, Norton, Rudge, and Velocette machines since 1927. His clientele appeared to represent a limited number of affluent enthusiasts who also favored foreign automobiles of the sporting type, which appeared in miniscule numbers during the depression days. In 1936, William E.Johnson, a Pasadena, California motorcycling enthusiast who was a successful attorney, established Johnson Motors, which imported Ariel and Triumph machines. Encouraged by his initial efforts, Johnson then established a branch outlet in San Francisco. His successes with such imports was largely based on the prowess of Edward Turner's noted Speed Twin, which offered outstanding performance in a machine that was essentially no larger than the standard British single, and which had created no little interest in its home country where the single had long reigned supreme. In addition, he offered the Ariel Red Hunter model, a mediumweight single which could often show a clean pair of heels to heavyweight domestic 'V' twins, although its longevity suffered from excessive high speed running. Jack Frodsham, an expatriate Englishman, opened a Velocette dealership in Los Angeles in 1935, and the rather surprising capabilities of the 21 cubic inch ohc KSS model were an eye opener to enthusiasts who formerly considered the 'one lunger' as a novelty not well suited to serious motorcycling.

While the scope of the foreign invasion was initially minimal, a grand total of 67 machines being imported during 1936, both domestic factories, in line with their traditional on-going gentleman's agreements, officially reminded their respective dealers, both from direct factory communication and through their traveling representatives, that under no circumstances would either of them countenance any of their franchises taking on sales agreements for any other makes.

At the same time, the H-D Company announced to both their dealers and customers that an expanded range of motorcycle accessories as well as clothing items were now to be offered from the Accessory Department. They also informed the dealers, through traveling factory representatives, that only accessories and sundry items obtained through factory sources could be sold by franchise holders. While this now established policy was, of course, a ploy to enhance the company's monopoly over their dealership's retail outlets, it was also obviously calculated to keep out any possible competition from foreign motorcycle accessory items that might somehow penetrate the American market along with the entrance of foreign machines.

A departure from H-D's ironclad ruling regarding the handling of other manufacturer's products, was the company's attitude toward the emergence of a limited number of motor scooters in the late 1930's. The most prominent were produced by the Cushman Motor Company of Lincoln, Nebraska, who for some years marketed a line of powered two wheelers, together with those built by Salsbury, Powell, Gladding, and a few other more obscure makes. A number of dealers, especially in the larger cities, handled some of these products, with the apparent blessing of both H-D's management and the ever-watchful factory representatives. While the domestic scooters of those days were basically somewhat crudely conceived, and rather indifferently powered with small industrial type, four-cycle, air cooled engines built by Briggs and Stratton or Lauson, they represented basic transportation at a $75 to $150 initial cost, a figure no conventional motorcycle of even primitive type could hope to match. Many dealers quite rightly theorized that they could very well give aspiring but impecunious schoolboy riders their first taste of motorcycling. As most states in those far off days allowed driving licensing to youths at the age of fourteen, the lowly scooter was usually the first powered vehicle purchased by adventurous newsboy types.

In contrast to their almost amused tolerance of the scooter, H-D's management was now thoroughly irritated by the justly-famous Crocker motorcycle. Based and sold in its greatest numbers in its home Southern California area, it continued to attract more than passing attention by its stellar performances, particularly at the usual speed trials continually being held both formally and informally at the Muroc dry lake course. Old time Crocker enthusiast Herbert Fagan relates countless incidents where the Crockers regularly beat specially tuned H-D and Indian Chief Big Twins in such trials, usually winning with a 10 to 15 mph edge. By the Spring of 1938, Crocker's miniscule production totaled but 36 units, and this in its second season of manufacture.

In casting about for ways to deal with this upstart in high performance motorcycling, President Walter Davidson, with the somewhat guarded advice of the Company's legal counsel, decided to explore the possibilities of bringing suit against Albert G.Crocker for patent infringement, the object being to put him out of business.

Accordingly, on March 7th 1938, Joe Petrali, together with an un-named factory mechanic and a commercial photographer named Austin Barnes met in a small automotive garage located in Chicago's south side under Walter Davidson's orders. Their mission was to dismantle the engine, clutch, and transmission of a 61 cubic inch Crocker that had been borrowed for the purpose, to ascertain if any of the Crocker's design features in any way resembled any aspects of the regularly produced H-D machines.

One of the first 61Es to arrive in Japan is delivered to a Tokyo enthusiast. Alfred Rich Child at right.

In recounting the details of this rather bizarre event to the author, Petrali stated that he remembered the machine as being finished in black with red trim, and that it carried a very low engine number, being described as a 61 cubic inch model purchased by a Midwest enthusiast sometime during the month of January 1938. The appropriate engine parts were dismantled and Barnes took a number of photographs, which were then forwarded to Milwaukee for evaluation. The Engineering Department ultimately reported that the Crocker's internal parts did not resemble those of H-D in details, but only in principal, and that in their opinion, there was no plagerization or copying of H-D's design. The Company's legal counsel, who was in close touch with the proceedings, concurred in this opinion, and Walter Davidson is reported to have at long last abandoned, if somewhat reluctantly, his plans to file a patent infringement suit against Crocker.

While following the advice of the company's legal counsel in abandoning his formal attempts to eliminate the Crocker, its continuing presence still rankled Walter Davidson. The following year, he unofficially informed both the Budd and Kelsey-Hayes concerns, then the principal supplier of domestic motorcycle wheel rims, that if they continued to supply such to Crocker, the H-D Company would subsequently cancel their contracts and undertake to build their own. Whether these companies took Davidson's threat seriously is not known, but at any rate they informed Crocker of the situation after supplying him with some sixty sets of rims. What alternatives were offered are today not known, but henceforth riders ordering Crockers were advised to bring along their own rims, purchased as a part item from some sympathetic H-D or Indian dealer.

As Crocker was now fitting Linkert carburetors to his currently produced machines, which for some seasons past had been fitted to some H-D models, the Company issued the same warning to Linkert, as it had to Budd and Kelsey-Hayes. According to a number of veteran motorcyclists, Linkert chose to ignore this edict and H-D, in spite of this, continued to fit Linkert units.

By a strange turn of fate, the author acquired a somewhat derelict Crocker from a Midwestern collector, R.J.Hicketheir, in 1967. In original condition, it carried black paint with Chinese red trim, and bore engine number 31. Joe Petrali subsequently came to the opinion that this machine was in fact the same one that was the subject of his examination twenty nine years before, especially as it was reported to have originated in the Chicago area and was registered in the State of Illinois.

At the close of the 1937 season, H-D's line of big twin machines was perfected to the point that it formed the main basis for H-D production for the next three decades. The 61E, following the correction of its initial faults, later became known as the 'FL' or 'FLH' model. In modifying its initial ohv mechanism its once potent top end performance was reduced somewhat, due to the adoption of an altered cam profile. Old time riders have reported that the later 'FL's' were more sedate, but vastly more reliable. The rugged side valve models continued to be popular sellers, both at home and overseas, their dependability enhanced with detail improvements to the electrical and lubrication systems. Perhaps the outstanding feature of both types was the literally indestructible clutch and gearbox assemblies which made them outstanding in continuous heavy traffic work. While the side valvers were still vulnerable to piston seizure under prolonged high speed running, the 'FL' and later high compression 'FLH' models were not, and came into wide use in law enforcement, not to mention their appeal to the more sporting riders and distance tourists.

The updated 45 model still had limited appeal, but had some adherents in the utility field. Its chief domestic role now appeared to be as the basis for the Servi-car. In addition to the four twin models, the usual range of passenger and commercial sidecar types were carried forward each succeeding year.

The domestic American big twin, whether H-D or Indian, had by this time attained a state of reliability which was at least equal to, and in many cases better than, that of the contemporary automobile. Vast mileages could now be covered with but routine maintenance. In fact, the enthusiast could now plan a transcontinental journey with the expectation of an uninterrupted trip, except for perhaps one oil change and a couple of adjustments to the rear chain. Added to this, the Big Twins had the ability to carry a passenger with comfort and safety on a dual seat, together with space in the long wheelbase for necessary luggage.

The 1936-1937 61E, 45 inch and 'U' models featured a new type chronometric speedometer which was fitted integrally with an attractively streamlined instrument nacelle placed over the forward portion of the fuel tank halves. This not only afforded a more attractive fitting than the former accessory-type Corbin instrument that was carried on a protruding bracket, but was much easier to read under way due to a much larger diameter face. While the instrument was acceptably accurate as to recorded travel, it was characteristically adjusted at the factory to an optimistic speed setting and ultimately gave rise to the somewhat derisive 'Harley Speedometer' appellation. The author, who in later years acquired a pristine 1950 'FL' model, was quick to note that in the upper speed ranges his instrument was about 13 mph fast, a timed 75 mph being indicated as 88 mph. An inquiring letter to the factory elicited a somewhat vague and ambiguous reply, but a later conversation with a factory rep-

Vintage Motor Cycle Club member Colin Light's 1930 Model C single. Found in Spain, it was said to have been ridden by a member of Francisco Franco's bodyguard. The chrome wheel rims and exhaust system is non-standard. Note the twin bullet headlights. While not cataloged in the U.S. after 1934, it was actually built through 1937 for the export market. *(Jeff Clew)*

resentative brought forth the somewhat reluctant comment that the practice was a definite safety factory. In essence, a speed enthusiast who noted a 100 mph speed on the clock was officially being protected from himself and his own folly with a more realistic 86-87 mph. In addition, the high compression 'FLH' models, in the days of the classic leading link fork, could often exhibit an alarming speed wobble at 90 mph plus travel, and the indication of a 100 mph speed on the clock would usually satisfy the most rabid aspiring boy racer, as well as minimizing another controversial aspect of H-D design.

An interesting aspect of middle and late 1930 period motorcycling was the two-wheeler interest of many of Hollywood motion picture stars in Southern California where much of the country's interest in the sport was centered due to the all season riding potential. Much publicity was centered on the participation of such virile actors as Clark Gable, Ward Bond, Keenan Wynn, Robert Taylor, and Randolph Scott, together with a number of leading directors such as Victor Flemming, as well as lesser lights in the film making community. Beverly Roberts, a current B-grade thriller actress and 45 twin rider was featured in several issues of the *Enthusiast*. A favorite ploy of Hollywood press agents was the posing of some budding starlet astride a motorcycle, the pulchritudinous effect being emphasized, though the girl in question often appeared fearful, even on a stationary machine!

The most prominent Hollywood rider of the era was undoubtedly Clark Gable, then at the height of his popularity and fame as Rhett Butler in the epic 'Gone With The Wind'. A UL and FLH enthusiast, Gable purchased his first UL from Budelier in the Fall of 1937. He once informed a friend that he rehearsed his movie lines while enjoying leisurely long weekend country rides in the Southern California area.

H-D machines did not enjoy as much feature film coverage as did Indian, due no doubt to the indefatigable Floyd Clymer, Los Angeles Indian dealer, who made various Redskin models available as either outright gifts or on a no-cost loan basis to the leading studios. This obvious advantage was somewhat tempored by the fact that on occasion H-D enthusiasts among film production crews often made their own personal machines available for certain picture sequences where traffic scenes were featured. It is reported that Rich Budelier once approached President Walter Davidson regarding Company subsidization of a number of H-D models for loan or gift to film companies for such use, citing the incalculable publicity for the marque, together with the possibility of neutralizing Indian's already overwhelming exposure through Clymer's efforts. Davidson is said to have expressed disapproval of Hollywood's 'extravagant goings-on', and declined to expend company funds on such frivolity!

In the late 1930's the H-D Company inaugurated a program to foster closer relations between the factory and its dealers by organizing regional H-D dealer's associations throughout the geographical areas of the United States. One of the objects, as President Walter Davidson was quoted as stating, was "to discourage any H-D dealers from fraternizing with Indian people." Another advantage to the Company was that a ready made captive audience was available on the occasion of the meetings to push advanced sales techniques and to further reinforce the philosophy, in the minds of the dealers at least, that H-D produced the country's pre-eminent motorcycles.

While the Company was only able to sponsor twice yearly meetings in each locality, it offered a golden opportunity for the factory to reinforce 'brand name' loyalty.

One of the most notable money making schemes in the retail sale of used motorcycles, and a most potent factor in dealer survivorship in depression days, was that of the 'stripping' and re-equipping of such machines. This practice involved the removal of the usual 'dresser' accessories, such as windshields, spotlights, dualseats, saddle bags, and other extras, and the machine was displayed in stripped condition with the standard solo saddle in place. As many riders now subscribed to the 'dresser' mode, in most cases they would then purchase the standard accessory items from new stock as extras. The equipment removed from the later model machine was then kept on hand, usually in a back room, for sale to the purchaser of an older used machine who wished to conform to the contemporary style. The factory also encouraged this policy, as they profited from accessory sales to the tune of at least a 40% markup on wholesale costs to dealers, with the latter enjoying the same benefit from their retail markup. The accessory market, just before WW II, was such that special competition classes for 'dresser' machines became an almost standard club event in meets where H-D machines were the most popular. This was the so called 'Best Equipped' machine, which could well mean that some enthusiast attached some two hundred pounds of extra spot and tail lights, various sorts of luggage carriers, mudguard moldings, various chrome plated novelties, and other bric-a-brac, the whole festooned with a myriad of small colored electric lights that gave the total effect of an over-decorated Christmas tree.

The Professional or Class A competition category was almost non-existent since the inauguration of Class C competition, except for the sponsorship of the 21 'Peashooter' that was ridden by the country's sole surviving factory rider, Joe Petrali. He won almost all of the events in this class that were held concurrently during the big AMA national races. His usual opponents were Fred Toscani and Art Schaeffer, riding similar Indians. What with factory support, professional mechanics, and his own tuning ability, victory was almost always a foregone conclusion. In addition, the Indian contingent was forced to compete on ten year old machines, the engines of which had undergone but scant refinement before the factory terminated their limited production in 1927. According to a veteran Indian employee, Indian had decided some time before to concentrate their main engineering improvements on the very successful Sport Scout, rather than on a racing version of the single which had long been out of production.

Petrali's wins during his professional competition career were impressive. He was high point man in the AMA record books from 1931 through 1936. He was National Hill Climb Champion from 1932 through 1938, riding various factory-built specials. In these far western meets, he had in his pit crew, an enthusiastic teenager, one Earl Flanders who, later in post WW II years, owned a highly successful BMW dealership and large motorcycle accessory business. More recently, he has been prominent in the affairs of the Trailblazer's organization, and has also long been a member of the AMA Competition Committee.

A very rare 1938 45 cu.in. model from the Steve McQueen collection. Note the sports-type handlebars and period cowhide saddle bags. *(Alisha Tamburri)*

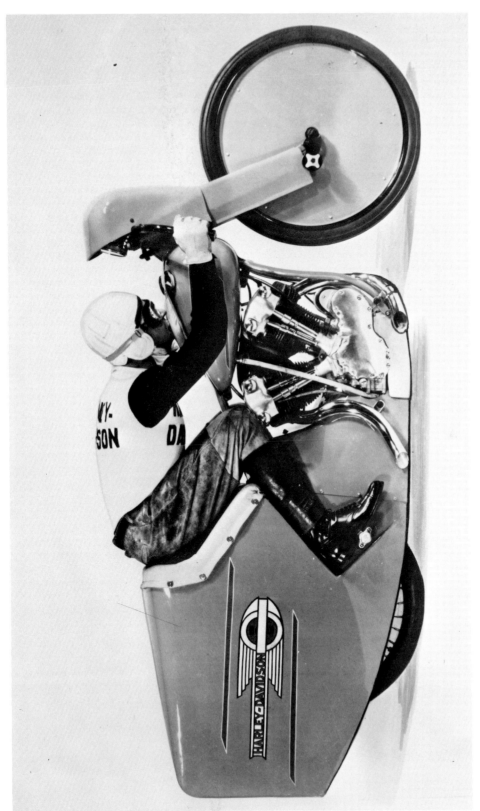

A posed studio portrait of Joe Petrali and the 61 ohv Special built by himself and Hank Syvertson for an attack on the World's Land Speed Record at Daytona Beach, Florida. The photographer insisted that Joe wear a white shirt and necktie! *(H-D Motor Company).*

Early in 1938, the AMA Competition Committee decided to suspend Class A activities due to lack of public interest. It was further mandated that the main emphasis should be on Class C as this group, made up mostly of private owners, was quite naturally the largest, and included Novice, Amateur, and Expert categories. Petrali, who was by this time receiving a salary of $240 per month, met with President Walter Davidson and proposed that he be tendered a new position in the Experimental Department, along with a substantial increase in pay, recalling Davidson's refusal to make good on his promised bonuses for the design of the 1934 short tracker and his appearance on the 61E Daytona Special. Davidson countered with an offer of employment in the Experimental Department, but refused either to increase the pay rate, or to pay any bonuses. Following a somewhat stormy confrontation between the two, Petrali, with no little bitterness, resigned from the Company immediately. Shortly afterwards, he entered a few Class C races on the West Coast on one of Tom Sifton's famous modified 45's. After a series of creditable victories, he hung up his goggles for good after missing death by inches during the Oakland 200 Miler when Dick Ince, on another H-D, skidded in front of him and was instantly killed, going through the fence. He next became associated with Art Sparks, at Thorne Engineering, where his vast mechanical knowhow was valuable in the building of race car engines. His work with Thorne was subsequently noticed by the famous Howard Hughes, who put him in charge of his flight services and service management at his Culver City, California plant. Petrali learned to fly at once, and in later years regaled audiences with tales of Howard Hughes's eccentricities, like being aroused in the middle of the night to fly to Phoenix, Arixona for a hamburger! In all, he was with Hughes for about ten years, and flew with him in the one and only hop the famous 'Spruce Goose' ever made over the Long Beach harbor in 1947. He later became the Chairman of the Certification Committee of the United States Auto Club, and at one time or another certified most of the land speed record attempts at Lake Bonneville, Utah, as well as those held in other parts of the country. He also, on occasion, acted as an official timer for both the AMA and the international FIM.

Petrali ever enjoyed the reliving of his competition days, and was a frequent speaker at various motorcycle clubs, as well as at meetings of old timers, such as the annual dinner of the Trailblazers. He once told the author that the most fearless rider he ever competed against was Jim Davis, and that his most formidable hill climb opponents were Indian stars Howard Mitzell and Orrie Steele. He died suddenly in the Spring of 1974, as the result of a cerebral haemorrhage said to have been caused by a

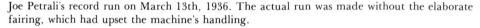

Joe Petrali's record run on March 13th, 1936. The actual run was made without the elaborate fairing, which had upset the machine's handling.

heat stroke sustained in the excessive temperature at a speed trial at Lake Bonneville. Mourned by all motor sports enthusiasts, he was truly one of the all time immortals of competition motorcycling.

The principal motorcycle events of the later 1930's were, of course, in Class C, and the far-sightedness of the AMA Competition Committee in establishing the Novice-Amateur-Expert categories paid off in bringing aspiring stars along in an orderly manner. After 1936, National AMA competition was largely dominated by the great Ed Kretz, Indian's star rider, whose unconventional but spectacular hell-for-leather riding style created a new era in American two-wheeled sport. In recounting the competition events of the period, most old timers agree that Kretz's winning of any contest was assured as long as his machine held up, but in many cases he was simply too much for his mount.

Kretz launched his spectacular career by winning the 200 Mile National, then held at Savannah, Georgia. Babe Tancrede, a seasoned H-D competitor from Rhode Island, a pre-race favorite, gave Kretz strong competition, along with veterans Ted Edwards and Ray Long. A surprise top finisher was George Pepper, the Canadian ace from Toronto, riding a 500 cc ohc Norton International. In keeping with the now established AMA position in regard to denigrating foreign competition, the report of the event in the *Motorcyclist,* still the official AMA publication, limited mention of Pepper's victory to the summary column at the end of the article!

H-D's racing star in the Class C category who ran Kretz a very close second in riding ability was Sam Arena. Surviving old time competitors, including Kretz himself, rate Arena as a very close contender. In addition, he was more versatile than Kretz, as he also excelled in hill climbing and Class A short track competition.

Starting out as a young boy with a bicycle powered with a Smith Motor Wheel, Arena progressed through the usual series of derelict motorcycles until 1933, when his budding mechanical ability won him a job, (this in the depth of the depression), at $18.00 a week as an apprentice mechanic at Tom Sifton's H-D shop in San Jose, California. With a 500 cc ohv flat track special obtained for him from the H-D factory by Sifton, he entered the limited professional B Class events for such competition on the short flat tracks then becoming a mildly popular spectator sport on the West Coast. After many consistent wins of the 1/5th mile ovals, he was transferred to the A Class, and was next awarded his soon-to-be-famous 79 competition number. In his first major TT race, which was held incidental to the 1934 Southern California Gypsy Tour at Lake Tahoe, he won handily on a stock machine over a large field of experienced riders.

Receiving some factory support in 1935, he entered a number of the big Nationals, and won many creditable victories in Class C on a potent 45 inch that had been tuned with uncanny skill by the wizard of San Jose, Tom Sifton. Sifton was already well into his perennial love-hate affair with the factory. As he adamantly refused to co-operate, the factory in the light of his remarkable results dared not cancel his franchise and the matter was shelved for the next decade.

Back to Sam Arena who, late in 1935, signed with Putt Mossman for a season for flat track racing in New Zealand and Australia, where he enjoyed much success. He returned to the West Coast the following year for another season of short tracking, and next rejoined Mossman in England where he was a member of the latter's team at Hackney Wick.

Again returning to the States in 1936, he rejoined Class C competition and was able to garner several second and third places in the big Nationals. He attained further triumphs in 1938, where he racked up consistent weekly wins at the Neptune Beach TT course. At the final big Pacific Coast event of the year, the Oakland 200 Miler, he not only won but broke all existing records in the Class C 100 and 200 Mile category. His average speed was 83 mph, 9 mph over the record!

In 1939, he was well on his way to winning the Daytona 200 Mile classic when a fall on the south turn filled his carburetor with sand and put him out of the running at the 183rd mile, the noted Ben Campanale then being the winner.

Returning to the Bay area, he entered the night races at the San Francisco motordrome, and was a consistent winner both there and at Neptune Beach in the B Class. He took second place at the Oakland 50 Miler, as well as being top man from 1939 through 1941 in the Professional B Class hill climbs. In these he competed against such well established local H-D stars as Joe Hern, of Modesto, and Windy Lindstrom of San Jose. He won 26 of such local events in both the 45 inch and 80 inch categories.

In 1940, the AMA Competition Committee chose to encourage Class C hill climbing, as it widened the field to more aspiring amateurs and made for larger cards of entrants. Special engines requiring blended fuels were now barred, as were special rear wheel traction devices. Arena shifted his interest to this competition, and was a consistent winner in events scheduled at the better known contest hills adjacent to Berkeley, Watsonville, Fresno, San Jose and Skyline.

He continued his short track racing as well, regularly sweeping the field at Sacramento, Riverside, and other West Coast courses. His only injury to date was a broken arm, sustained at Lakeport where he laid his machine down to miss a fallen competitor.

The author with his authentically-restored 31st Crocker. Both he and the late Joe Petrali believe that this was the same machine dismantled by the latter in Chicago in 1938, under orders from Walter Davidson who was contemplating a patent infringement action against Albert G.Crocker. *(George Hays).*

A blown tire cost him the Oakland 200 Miler in 1940, as did a similar incident at Hollister, where a win would have given him permanent ownership of the trophy. During this season he was also a regular entrant on the half mile tracks at Galt, Dixon, and Emeryville, where he was a consistent winner with almost monotonous regularity.

It was Arena's good fortune to sustain a miraculous escape from critical injury or death in August 1941, at the Oakland 200 Miler which saw perhaps one of the most tragic accidents in the annals of American motorcycle competition. Ed Kretz, flogging his Scout along at his usual blistering pace, had already lapped the field, and was well ahead at the 38th lap. Tommy Hayes, H-D star from Texas was second, and Kretz, coming up behind him, had just opened his throttle. At that moment Hayes overtook H-D mounted Ben Campanale in the north turn, but entered the corner too fast. Swinging to the outer edge of the track from the centrifugal force of his full throttle turn, he hit a rough area and was thrown from his machine, dying instantly from the impact. Campanale, immediately behind him, also went down, but at this moment, Hayes's riderless machine, its throttle still wide open, charged into the gap. All three riders following Kretz, June McCall, Jimmy Kelly, and Sam Arena, all H-D mounted, entered the resultant pile up in 1-2-3 order. McCall was killed instantly, and Kelly and Campanale each spent nearly a year in the hospital suffering from multiple fractures and extensive internal injuries. Arena was unhurt through some miracle, and was able to remount his machine and carry on. Trailing Kretz, he caught up with the latter just 32 miles from the finish when Kretz sustained a broken rear chain, and, in spite of a buckled rear wheel, Arena came in 7th.

Still undaunted, Arena entered other California flat track races with continuing success, together with numerous B and C Class hill climbs during the same period. At the TT race at Lodi, which proved to be the last pre-war competition meet, he took first in all events.

While the Indian Scout appeared to have a definite edge in various competition events during the late 1930's and early 1940's, just before WW II, the net results, as gathered from a myriad of reports on the sporting events of the period, saw both makes nearly equal as to wins. As the majority of the contests were in the Class C category, and as most of the riders were in the Amateur class, reaching for Expert status, their cumulative riding abilities were roughly equal. The overall results were greatly affected by track conditions, as county fair horse ovals were more often than not in rough and rutted condition. Then there was the matter of the degree of tuning skills available to the riders, whether performed by themselves, by either a local dealer or an independent handy mechanic. Added to this was the often reported gamesmanship on the part of a local AMA official, who more often than not was prejudiced in favor of H-D, although the odd Indian devotee with similar proclivities was not unknown. While the general run of competition under the prevailing Class C rules has been described by knowledgeable critics as somewhat ragged, the system was at least sufficient to keep the flag flying in the days when US motorcycling was far and away a minority sport.

One of the more significant reasons for the lack of general public knowledge of domestic motorcycle affairs or a recognition of its sporting events was the lack of any effective press coverage. Motorcycle historians have lately pondered over the possible reason the AMA hierarchy never made a conscious effort to hire public relations representatives, or to make any visible efforts to interest the leading sports reporters of the day in motorcycle affairs. Local news coverage of club events, social meetings, rallies, field meets, or any other such activities was never given, even in areas where motorcycling was mildly popular.

As far as the big National races were concerned, even these were limited to a few lines buried somewhere in the back pages of the sporting section. The only front page references appear to have been in cases where some bloody traffic accident involving motorcycles occurred, often with an editorial comment on the dangers of riding such vehicles. This most unfortunate situation is today considered by some historians to be responsible for the inferiority complex of the management of the surviving factories and translated itself into an almost paranoic fear of publicizing their minority position within the otherwise burgeoning transportation scene. It was almost as though the factories withdrew into their own cocoon of endeavor, and took their devotees with them. As it was, the average rider of those days often appeared as a defender, rather than an advocate, of motorcycle ownership.

On a happier note, the motorcycling scene was enlivened by the activities of a limited number of

John Coursey with his 80 cu.in. ULH model. The headlight, footboards, seat and rear carrier are of later manufacture. This and the companion 74 cu.in. model are considered by many motorcyclists as the most rugged and durable ever built. *(George Hays)*.

motorcycle drill teams that made their appearance in various parts of the country. The most noted was the organization sponsored by a popular motion picture star of the day, Victor McLaglan, who originally financed the formation of one as an outgrowth of his sponsorship of a horseman's troupe of parade riders. Its usual complement was about thirty six riders, elements of which performed various maneuvers in groups of sixteen to twenty four. Offering precision drills in often intricate patterns, the performances provided safety for the participants as no high speed stunt type riding was allowed. To join the troupe, an applicant's riding skills were carefully evaluated, and a criterion for membership was the ownership of a big twin H-D machine painted in black-on-white police colors. The H-D machines were selected as standard, as the oversize dry plate clutches enabled faultless low speed control. The troupe was featured in many parades as well as sports events and other civic gatherings in the Southern California area. The troupe remained active until the late 1940's.

The Nobles of the Mystic Shrine, an elite order of the Masonic Fraternity, formed numerous drill teams in several of the country's larger cities, largely patterned after the original McLaglan concept. Most of these groups also used H-D big twins. Another group of noted H-D riders were the famous drill unit from South of the border, the Mexico City Police Team.

This troupe, already well known in Central America, made several trips to the States to exhibit their talents at various holiday events. These organizations formed an effective showcase to exhibit the better aspects of motorcycling, and were popular favorites wherever they appeared. In recent times many of the old time drill units have faded from the picture, largely due to the increased cost of the machines, as well as the spiraling promotion expenses of staging such events. A leading survivor of these spactacular units is the Cossack Drill Team based in Seattle. A group of H-D enthusiasts, some of the members perform on meticulously restored classic 'VL' models.

Another organization of private riders that brought much-needed glamor to motorcycling in the late 1930's was the Motor Maids of America, a feminine contingent of motorcyclists organized by Verna Griffith. Chapters of this body, who immediately gained recognition as an officially chartered AMA group, were formed in many of the larger cities of the country. Most were organized as auxiliaries to already established AMA clubs, although a few were formed as autonomous bodies. As the founder, Verna Griffith was an H-D enthusiast, and her cohort and later perennial National President was Dorothy Robinson, the wife of the popular Detroit H-D dealer, Earl Robinson, the tone of the Motor Maids organization was largely orientated toward H-D machines, although a few rode Indian Sport Scouts. Aside from their attractive appearance in smart uniforms at club outings, Gypsy Tours, and holiday celebrations, they commanded much attention from their ability to handle their heavyweight mounts. The fact that a petite 100 pound rider could readily start a 600 pound 61E or side valve 'U' model was a lasting tribute to the efficiency of the H-D field coil generator ignition system.

Motorcycle sales to law enforcement organizations received increasing attention from both of the surviving factories after 1930. The Henderson and Indian four cylinder models were the machine of choice in most of the larger cities, such as New York, Chicago, San Francisco, Oakland, Vancouver, and New Orleans due to their smooth running capabilities and general suitability for suburban patrol duties. While the 'K' model Henderson was eminently suited to the needs of long distance highway patrol duties due to its ability to maintain high speeds under the stress of long pursuits, the Indian Four, still carrying its 1919 Ace type engine was not, and for such duties the less costly big twins, both H-D's and Indian Chiefs were found to be far more suitable. The H-D Company's Sales Department developed a particularly aggressive campaign to penetrate this market, and as a result, by the end of the decade, the nationwide sale of H-D's topped Indian in this field by about two to one. H-D's selling emphasis was that their indestructive heavyweight clutch and gear box could stand up to more hard usage than the oil-immersed opposite on Indian, still fitted with the obsolete sliding gear arrangement.

H-D's factory representatives were given special training at the factory into the intricacies of promoting and consummating law enforcement sales for the benefit of the dealers in their respective areas. What many of the dealers were often to learn, however, was that the ultimate sale of any type of law enforcement vehicle was always involved in political gamesmanship. The transaction almost always meant dealing through corrupt politicians or avaricious tenured civil servants who inevitably demanded either a financial kickback or other special favors. The traffic officers who rode such machines often further complicated the picture by demanding special favors from the dealers who supplied the motorcycles, expecting them to service and maintain them. Often they requested goggles, gloves, or other riding equipment, which were to be supplied free of charge and billed to the regular service cost. In some cases, the officers were enthusiasts who also owned private machines, and the dealer was often expected to maintain these as well and add the charges to the law enforcement maintenance. While the dealer in question could invariably count on a steady source of income from the after sales service, many of them rightly concluded that having to deal with law enforcement bodies, as well as the often corrupt administration governing them, was in the end not worth all the complications involved.

Another ploy in law enforcement sales was the inclusion of specifications of either make into the

Ben Campanale, who won the Daytona Classic for Milwaukee in 1938 and 1939.

Another late 1930s Champion, Paul Goldsmith.

One of the most versatile of H-D's 1930s stars, Sam Arena was at home on either the track, TT course, or at hill climbing.

A 61E 'Knucklehead' as a 'California Bobber' — the forerunner of the post-war 'Chopper'. *(George Hays).*

procurement ordinances that set forth the type of machine that could be presented to the so-called competitive bidding system which was a part of most law enforcement charters. This practice, if it could be initiated, could assure the continuing purchase of the same make of machine. For instance, if the official specification for a machine called for in the bidding were described as 'a 74 or 80 cubic inch 'V' twin American-made motorcycle with a four speed transmission with left handed gear shift mechanism and right hand throttle control', it was obvious that only H-D machines could be offered. The H-D Company is said to have inaugurated this practice in the late 1920's. Dealers who possessed some local political influence, were urged by the factory representative to take advantage of their situation to see that H-D specifications were written into purchase ordinances. The factory's legal department also stood ready to offer both help and advice in giving effect to this intent. This is most probably the reason why H-D machines were predominent in law enforcement use throughout the country after 1935, although some large cities whose law enforcement organizations favored Indian, had similar ordinances favoring that make. H-D's notable failure to penetrate both the city of New Orleans and the State of Louisiana is a case in point. Indian's pioneer dealer, George Gonzales, who owned extensive sales premises on New Orlean's famous Canal Street, had in the early 1930's forged a strong political alliance with the notorious Governor, Huey P. Long. Gonzales's power was such that Indian specifications in both state and municipal ordinances effectively kept H-D out of the bidding. Gonzales continued his association with other members of the powerful Long family for many years afterward, and it has only been in relatively recent times that an H-D dealer could hope to prosper in the State of Louisiana!

H-D's signal advantage throughout this morass of political intrigue, was the fact that its massive dry plate clutch and rugged transmission was more suited to standing up to the hard usage meted out to the drive train under continuous service than was the oil-immersed clutch and archaic sliding gear transmission traditionally fitted to Indians.

In 1940, H-D, in common with Indian, offered the option of 16 inch wheels and 5 inch section tires on all models, the former 18 inch x 4 inch or 4½ inch type being retained if desired by individual customers. This new feature, together with H-D's effectively sprung seat post, made for an exceptionally smooth ride. On the now generally smooth highways, the actual need for a sprung rear end was all

Bud Ekins' 1940 61 EL. It has been fitted with a 1941 tank badge and a 1947 tail light. This was the first year of the optional 16 inch wheels and 5 inch section tires. (*Alisha Tamburri*).

but eliminated. On the other hand, many enthusiasts claimed that the larger diameter tires made the handling and steering less accurate, especially at high speeds. H-D's management, through confidential instructions to the factory representatives, put the word out to the dealers that the new tires could make for a much safer machine, due to the lessening of road shocks, and that H-D's now traditionally 'fast' speedometer aided in this premise by making the rider think he was going much faster than he actually was. The high speed wobble still encountered with the now classic girder fork, appeared now to be less of a problem. In the case of the 45 inch model, the new option added a further weight penalty, although the softer ride was an attraction to utility riders as well as export buyers who still had to contend with inferior road surfaces.

The retail selling price parity between H-D and Indian now tended to be somewhat divergent, due to the fact that Indian's model range had become more extensive. Their Four now sold at nearly $1,000, with the 30.50 Junior Scout offered at a modest $250. H-D's ohv 61E retailing at $475 had no counterpart with Indian, whose side valve 74 inch Chief was now $400. H-D's 74 inch side valver had a similar price tag, the 80 inch being $25 higher. The H-D 45 and Indian's Sport Scout continued at parity at $325. It has been reported that Arthur Davidson's last price fixing meeting with Jim Wright was held in Columbus, Ohio, incidental to a meeting of AMA officials to discuss general business matters.

It was during this latter period that individual brand name loyalty for either make had progressed to the point that a few dollars difference in cost became less important. At any rate, the economic picture of the country had now vastly improved. Times were generally better, as unemployment was lessened, due to the inflationary effect of the war in Europe. The United States at long last was enjoying a modicum of prosperity, not from the complex planning of a socialized government, but from external economic forces from abroad.

Domestic motorcycle production had become somewhat stabilized during the late 1930's. H-D's production of 8,158, 8,312, and 10,461 for the years of 1938, 1939, and 1940 almost paralleled that of Indian. The loss of H-D's production lead was no doubt due to their now shrinking wartime export market, although the domestic industry was still exporting about 50% of its output. The United States showed a national registration of 126,233 machines in 1939, which was only a slight increase over the 96,401 figure reported in 1935. These figures attest to the gradual decline of motorcycling interest throughout the decade, as the overall population of the United States had increased by one-third since 1930, and automobile registrations during the same period had tripled. There were now so few motorcycles amid such a vast horde of automobiles, that in the minds of many motorists, the motorcycle was now almost wholly associated with law enforcement.

At the same moment, American motorcycling was characterized by a very loyal, if small, following. Each factory kept in close contact with its respective adherents through their individual house organs. Each still quite naturally offered its own version of the motorcycling picture, reporting only sporting events where the make in question won, and totally ignoring those in which it did not. 'Brand Name' loyalty was paramount, and any defection to the rival make was the epitome of heresy. The *Motorcyclist* continued to offer bland platitudes concerning the joys of the sport, but without any objective policy regarding the road testing of the limited range of machines offered. News regarding the activities of a corporal's guard of dealers handling foreign machines was actively suppressed, as were their wins in field trials or club sporting events.

A pleasant adjunct to the end of a somewhat gracious decade as far as motorcycling was concerned was the club activities. Many of these, often sponsored by H-D dealers, stressed the family aspect by including many mixed social events as well as weekend picnic type outings. The emphasis on 'well equipped' machines that were sometimes overloaded with useless accessories, at least led to the criterion of clean, well-silenced machines. Most of the clubs adopted smart uniforms, mandatory at all club functions. Such activities did much to enhance the public image of motorcycling, as did the commendable policy of sponsoring or assisting in local charity drives or in acting as police auxiliary units or search and rescue teams in times of natural disasters.

To aid in sales, H-D sponsored a finance facility, officially known as the Kilbourne Finance Company, along with an auxiliary company that specialized in motorcycle insurance. Up to this time, the public image of motorcycling had been such that no usual bank or finance company would consider the public financing or insuring of machines. These organizations' activities quite naturally aided the sales picture, and dealers were extended further help by being able to finance the flooring of new machines through the Kilbourne organization.

The position of the clubs was strengthened by the fact that District AMA officials offered aid in either the formation of new groups or the strengthening of those already in existence. In return, all club members were expected to join as individuals. While some grumbled about the non-democratic character of the AMA and its trade management, it was generally conceded that the AMA was the only viable force in holding organized motorcycling together.

Robert Ross's superbly-restored 1940 61 EL sidecar outfit. This model is fitted with the 18 inch wheels of past models.

The sporting side of motorcycling during the late 1930's continued to attract a dedicated, if limited, following. Numerous clubs were formed whose membership was made up of sporting types, the majority favoring the Sport Scout. A serious impediment to enhanced public recognition of motorcycle sport was the general lack of publicity in the news media accorded to race meets, hill climbs, TT events and other competition. When approached about the matter on several occasions by concerned AMA members, President Jim Wright simply stated that a lack of funds prevented the implementation of a full scale publicity department within the AMA organization. As Indian's E. Paul du Pont had already gone on record as refusing to augment his company's minimal AMA contribution, coupled with President Walter Davidson's adamant stand against increasing H-D's already majority contribution to the organization's treasury, no effective steps were then taken to obtain expanded press coverage. It was later reported that Executive Secretary E.C. Smith, acting on orders from Davidson, shortly afterward informed the AMA Directors that organized American motorcycling existed principally for the benefit of its card carrying members, and that an extended publicity campaign would cost too much for the AMA's current financial resources. With this head-in-the-sand pronouncement, American motorcycling further retreated into its own inbred sphere of activity. While some of the big National races received limited space in some of the larger newspapers, most regional or local events were largely unreported.

The Class C sporting scene during the 1940-1941 season was largely dominated by the spectacular performance of the now legendary Ed Kretz. While he was more often than not a non-finisher, due to his explosive riding tactics which led to mechanical failure of his Sport Scout, his hell-for-leather tactics made him a first rate crowd pleaser. He was especially popular with the non-riding spectator contingent that had at long last found motorcycle racing as a new diversion. A popular sports rider of the day once reported that Kretz was a sure winner in any contest entered, providing his machinery held out, and the only question was who might come in second! Kretz relates that on numerous occasions he was approached by Milwaukee to desert the Wigwam and ride for H-D. He remained a steadfast Redskin, however, until Indian's last days. While his loyalty in this regard was unquestioned, there was also in the back of his mind the memory of the somewhat cavalier treatment that Walter Davidson meted out to such past heroes as Fred Ludlow and Joe Petrali.

In the Fall of 1940, H-D announced a 74 cubic inch version of the 61 cubic inch 61E that was now known as 74F, although the original version was still continued in the line. The new model, indistinguishable from its parent machine except for the engine, gained its increased displacement through cylinder enlargement by boring and stroking, the new configuration measuring 3 7/16 by 3 31/32 inch. Developing 45-48 hp on standard fuel, it was capable of a top speed of close to 100 mph with 3.73 solo gearing.

The new machine was quite naturally welcomed by speed enthusiasts, and sidecar owners at once noted its enhanced pulling power, especially in steep gradients. 61E enthusiasts were quick to note that the larger displacement machine was noticeably less smooth than its parent, and the characteristic rocking couple of the latter could at some engine speeds be most pronounced.

As H-D now entered a new decade, its products can well be stated as representative machines of their type; they were exemplary models of the American big twin concept. Built of the finest materials, with proper attention to rust proofing (long a bugbear of motorcycle finish), they bespoke both quality of product and meticulous attention to detail. With continually improved refinements in both lubrication and electrical systems, they offered automobile-type dependability, and usually required but three-kick starts in any weather, provided the correct drill was carried out to set them in motion. The now standard American control system of foot controlled clutch and hand controlled gearchange, later to be the source of much adverse comment, proved to be more than adequate for proper control of the massive drive train that was itself now a legend of dependability. Built without visable changes from 1938 through 1948, this series of machines, in the opinion of many veteran enthusiasts, implemented the so-called 'Golden Age' of H-D perfection. Many meticulously restored machines of this vintage are still providing their proud owners with yeoman service, and bring eight or ten times their original price when bought on today's market.

The last pre-war sporting event of 1941 was the 200 Mile National. This premier feature, inaugurated originally at the big county fair horse track at Savannah, Georgia in 1934, was moved to Daytona Beach, Florida, in 1937. The course was rather unorthodox, in the annals of American competition at least, as it offered a combination of both sand and road racing. The long legs of the track consisted of a portion of the beach, connected at either end by steeply banked turns to a rather uneven road course that was surfaced with clay and asphalt. The AMA Contest Committee decided that such a speedway could offer a more challenging terrain than the more prosaic horse tracks, and the road type course could produce higher speeds.

If the new course was an innovation compared to the classic American broadsliding style of competition, the results of the contest to both the AMA hierarchy and American motorcyclists alike were even greater, as it was won by one Billy Mathews, of Ontario, Canada, that country's budding racing star, on a single cylinder 500 cc ohc Manx Norton model.

The story behind Mathews' spectacular win is no less interesting. Motorcycling and motorcycle racing in the United States had long been almost completely isolated from International competition. There had never been an interchange of racing talent, and American competition affairs were totally divorced from the FIM ever since 1923, when Indian's British importer, Billy Wells, was removed as their representative to the international body. The foreign racing scene was never reported in the AMA-controlled *Motorcyclist* magazine, and American motorcyclists were for the most part simply unaware of foreign motorcycle affairs, or that the Norton marque had for some years been pre-eminent in international as well as British competition.

Mathews and J.M.McGill, Norton distributor for Canada, were, of course, keenly aware of the international competition picture. They also knew that the AMA and H-D, who controlled it, were dead set against either the importation or even the recognition of any type of foreign machine. When Mathews, intent upon invading the US with a British machine, signified his intention to McGill, who had provided him with official help in his Canadian conquests, McGill, after some reflection, declined to offer help for the Daytona challenge. McGill reasoned that with both popular and official sentiment being hostile to any foreign entry into the American motorcycle competition bailiwick, it would be virtually impossible for Mathews' entry to be accepted in the first place. Added to this, was the expense of transporting both men and machines to Daytona, as well as their maintenance while there.

After some further soul searching, Mathews decided to enter the contest as a private entrant, bearing the expense himself. Accordingly, he sent his official entrance declaration to the appropriate AMA officials, and much to his surprise, was accepted. The late Jack Halford, an immigrant Englishman who was once connected briefly with Reggie Pink's New York import organization and who was at the time well aware of the situation, told the author in an interview in 1964, that the AMA Contest Committee, who, for some inexplicable reason, were unaware of Norton's prowess in international racing, refused to take Mathews' entry seriously. Noting in Mathews' declaration that more than fifty International Nortons had been previously manufactured and sold, (an AMA rule for entering any make of machine) his entry was duly accepted. The Contest Committee's thinking was no doubt further influenced by the fact that foreign machines had never been able to make much headway on the domestic competition scene.

Up to now, it may be remembered that American competition machines, as compared with the sophisticated types already developed in Great Britain and Europe, were essentially crude pieces of equipment. With but limited fork travel, and solid rear ends, both the Indian Sport Scout and the H-D racing machines, both highly modified in open defiance of the original Class C concept, were but rather poor handling vehicles intended to be manhandled around a dirt track, and broadslided through the turns. The lack of rear springing caused the rear wheel to be airborne much of the time under rough surface conditions, and the foot-operated clutches and wide ratio hand-operated gear change mechanism was not conducive to saving time in a pinch where split second gear changes could spell the difference between defeat and victory.

During the late 1930's, H-D competition in the now universal Class C category was centered on a speed version of their somewhat mediocre 45 cubic inch twin, which was ultimately known as the DLDR ('R' for racing) model. Still cursed by coil ignition, some competitors had, by this time, been fitting proprietary magnetos, which obviated some of the historic difficulties encountered with the age old problem of burned out condensers. In response to much prodding from both enthusiasts and dealers, H-D finally brought out a racing version of the 45 D model in 1941, which was known as the WLR ('R' for racing), or more simply, the 'WR'. Still unable to pry from Tom Sifton his private modifications that had made his own modified DLDR models so formidable, H-D's Engineering Department did its best to come up with their own compromise to challenge the former unassailable position of Indian's Sport Scout. While the new WR was but little different from the former DLDR models in having limited travel forks and a solid rear end, its engine's potency had been substantially increased with improved breathing, high performance cams, and magneto ignition, together with a light pattern clutch and gearbox to save weight. As in the case of the now highly developed Sport Scout, its concept was a continuing violation of the original Class C rules.

In contrast to these Yankee crudities, Mathew's Norton was the identical machine, that, after a decade of refinement, had already won sweeping victories both at home and abroad, for example Harold Daniel's TT victory on a special model in 1938. Its superb road holding qualities offered to serious contestants a well proved engine that was by this time almost unburstable under 200 miles of flat out running. With its spring frame that kept the rear wheel more effectively on the ground, together with its four-speed gearbox, a rider could more effectively mate the rather narrow power band of the engine, running 'on the cam', to whatever racing conditions presented themselves. In addition, the hand-controlled clutch and foot-operated gear change could save many valuable seconds over the

Yankee riders who were still running machines that differed but little from those used on American courses since 1915.

This surprising upset caused President Walter Davidson to bitterly excoriate the AMA Contest Committee for admitting a foreign interloper. The late Charles (Chuck) Billings, then Editor of the *Motorcyclist,* also came under his share of criticism from certain AMA officials for his report in which he admitted, if somewhat grudgingly, that certain advanced (in American eyes) British design features gave Mathews a victory over an extremely grueling course.

The Yankee track racers had now been bested on their own grounds, and technical progress had to be postponed due to World War II.

An interesting footnote to domestic motorcycle history in the 1930s period and beyond was the almost total control that H-D exerted over the internal affairs of the AMA. This quite naturally extended to the contents of the *Motorcyclist,* which since 1931 had been published as the official AMA magazine. Editor Billings was a West Coast AMA Commissioner, and of course worked under the direction of E.C. Smith, who in turn answered to H-D's top management.

During the 1920s, when several national trade publications still existed, some of the more widely read motorcycle journalists contributed to all of them, including H.W. Parsons, E.B. Holton, and J.L. Beardsley. While these authors dwelt mainly with historical matters, they were, as rather outspoken men, prone at times to comment upon the general state of motorcycling.

With the general decline of motorcycle journalism and the closing down of all national publications other than the *Motorcyclist,* these authors quite naturally continued to submit articles to the survivor. Under the watchful eye of E.C. Smith, however, any opinions or reporting of events that were not considered in the best interests of H-D were either rejected, or heavily censored. As a result, their offering had simply disappeared by the mid 1930s.

The author, in those days a young medical student, and still somewhat naive regarding the true state of domestic motorcycling, had, in the fall of 1937, submitted a series of three articles to Editor Billings. Based on material provided by the late Charles Markham, staff member of the British magazine *Motor Cycling,* they offered a critical comparison of the engine designs of H-D and Indian. While money was enclosed to pay for the return of the articles, if rejected, nothing further was ever heard of them.

Early the following Summer, the author attended a hill climb in Vallejo, California, in company with the local H-D dealer, Nelson Bettencourt. As E.C Smith was in attendance, the author, with some trepidation, inquired as to the fate of his submissions. Smith, somewhat haughtily, replied that the *Motorcyclist* considered that only their staff members were competent to report on motorcyling affairs. When informed that the author was contemplating the recording of a complete history of domestic motorcycling, Smith stalked angrily away.

The author put the incident in the back of his mind, but later that Fall, he was informed by Verne Guthrie, a former H-D sales representative and presently an automotive journalist, that President Walter Davidson had recently issued a memorandum that no middle management employees were authorized to grant him any interviews. It was further stipulated that the author was not to be granted any further access to the Company premises on Juneau Avenue.

It was Guthrie's opinion that the Davidsons were perturbed that anyone outside the Company might be delving into H-D's affairs for the purpose of recording their history. In any case, to this day the author has been persona non grata in the City of Milwaukee.

The rather bizarre incidence of the censuring of a private person outside the industry for an academic inquiry into American transportation history was further explained to the author by Alfred Rich Child. He stated that in the mid 1920s incidental to a policy and price fixing meeting of the heads of the three surviving manufacturers, President Davidson suggested that the factories should exert control over all news reports involving the industry. The purpose was to conceal the then redundant state of the market and the generally low esteem in which the general public regarded motorcycle matters.

Excelsior and Indian went along with this policy for a time, but the latter, as a public company, was required by law to issue financial reports which revealed the industry's critical situation. Such did not apply to H-D as a closed company, and trade journal editors were importuned to grant prior review and censorship privileges of articles submitted by writers not employed by H-D, under the threat of withholding advertising contracts.

This policy ultimately backfired, as editors and reporters quite naturally valued journalistic integrity, and many ceased featuring articles on H-D affairs as a result. In addition, a growingly sophisticated readership became unimpressed with H-D sponsored sales-orientated anthologies masquerading as "histories" when contrasted with more factual reports available from news media outside the industry, such as business and financial magazines and newspaper reports such as found in the Wall Street and Milwaukee Journals.

Chapter 7

World War Two

WITH THE OUTBREAK OF THE WAR IN EUROPE IN THE LATE SUMMER OF 1939, President Franklin D.Roosevelt alerted the American people and Congress to the need for preparedness. The ever-widening scope of the war tended to indicate that the United States would be drawn in. He was handicapped by his efforts by certain leaders in Congress who, led by an avowed isolationist, Senator Burton K.Wheeler of Montana, pointed to the long traditional American concept of avoiding entanglement in European affairs. The growing menace of German U-boats and their sinking of large tonnages of Allied shipping brought much sympathy for the plight of Great Britain, however, and Roosevelt was at long last able to persuade Congress to supply the British Navy with 50 of our idle, overage WW I destroyers.

In the Fall of 1939, both American motorcycle factories received contracts to supply military machines to the Allied Forces. Indian had already received an order from the French Army for 5,000 Chief sidecar outfits. Shortly afterwards, both factories each received an order for 5,000 solo military machines from Great Britain since the Coventry area, where the Triumph motorcycle plant was located, had just been leveled by the Luftwaffe.

H-D's answer to this order was a heavy duty utility version of the now venerable 45 inch 'DLD' model. Now designated as the 'WLA' ('A' for Army), it was fitted with 18 inch wheels and 4.00 inch or 4.50 inch section tires and wide clearance D section mudguards to facilitate off-the-road travel with a minimum of mud-clogging. To provide added protection to the underside of the engine cases and transmission, a heavy pressed steel plate with channeled edges was bolted under the frame. This fitting was also provided with a rearward extension on the near side to give further protection to the lower run of the rear chain. A low compression commercial type engine, a modified WL type, was installed and provided with enlarged cooling fins to prevent overheating during prolonged, low-speed bottom gear running. An extra large air cleaner was attached to the carburetor air intake, together with a heavy luggage rack fitted with leather panniers, a rifle boot along the fork legs, ammunition boxes, and other military gear.

With its low compression engine, the highly restrictive air cleaner, and the added weight of the military gear, the rather weighted 'WLA' now had a top speed of a little over 50 mph, together with but feeble powers of acceleration. But with plenty of torque for rough going, and its indestructible clutch and gearbox and traditionally rugged H-D construction, the 'WLA' was ideal for its purpose. As a low-powered machine, the traditional primary chain-shedding weakness was now eliminated, and with no other apparent vices the war model gave exceptionally dependable service under appalling conditions of use with but minimal maintenance.

Following the completion of their contracts with the British, both factories were awarded open-ended contracts by the US Defense Department for military machines, together with official authorization for the acquisition of the necessary supplies of iron, steel, aluminum, and other accessories to complete them. The H-D organization was in a much better position to supply large numbers of military machines than was Indian, whose tooling and production facilities had been allowed to become depleted during the lean sales years of the early 1930's. The H-D management immediately expanded its production facilities, leased additional plant space adjacent to the main Juneau Avenue facilities, and hired additional workers for around-the-clock operation. While the bulk of the production was now 'WLA' models, a limited number of 74 inch and side valve big twin sidecar models were also supplied to the armed forces for special services. These differed but little from their former civilian counterparts, being fitted with slightly lowered gear ratios, wide clearance mudguards, and low compression engines. Certain numbers of these were made available to civilian buyers who were able to obtain special government procurement clearance. A limited number of low compression police models were also produced for civilian law enforcement use on the home front. A few 61 inch ohv models were produced on order by the US Navy for Shore Patrol and Coast Guard duties.

The Harley and Davidson families, factory management and production personnel, dealers, and a world wide host of H-D enthusiasts were saddened when on February 7th 1942, H-D's long time President Walter Davidson passed away in his sixty-sixth year. In ill health for several months, his death was attributed to the stresses of overwork due to the company's expanded production for the war effort, together with complications of a liver ailment. His survivors included his wife, Emma, sons Gordon, Walter Junior, and Robert, his brother Arthur, and two sisters, Mrs.Henry W.Marx and Miss Janet Davidson, all of Milwaukee. For all of his adult life, Davidson was vitally concerned with the promotion of H-D motorcycles, first as a consultant in the initial prototype work of his brother Arthur and William S.Harley, and from 1907 as President of the Company after its initial incorporation and formal entrance into the industry. During most of these thirty five years, he was a figure of controversy. Capable of inspiring trust and loyalty in certain company personnel and among its far flung dealership, he was both hated and feared by many who did not see eye-to-eye with his often ruthless manner and arbitrary judgments in managerial decisions. Whatever his personal faults, he became a veritable giant within a long troubled industry. Through the years his role as Company President, both

The WR racing model introduced in the Spring of 1941. It was H-D's answer to the racing Indian Sport Scout. Note the short bottom fork links.

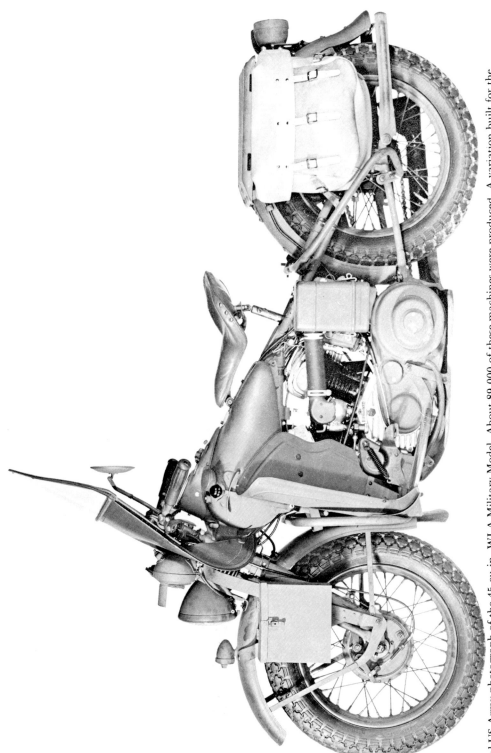

Official US Army photograph of the 45 cu.in. WLA Military Model. About 89,000 of these machines were produced. A variation built for the Canadian Army, the WLC, differed in slight detail, and was fitted with Big Twin forks and front brake assembly.

Engine details of a WLA. This restored example was seen at Visalia in 1974.

at its original organization, survival and ultimate success, can never be overstated as he complemented the pioneer engineering efforts of his brother Arthur, and William Harley. While during the early years he established a reputation as a tight-fisted and often hard-hearted executive, at the same moment he insisted that only an honestly conceived and properly built product was worthy of public sale, as long typified in H-D production, and he held unswervingly to these tenets throughout even the most difficult periods of company history.

While his personal holdings of Company stock were said to be substantial, he had diversified his estate by making large investments in other companies. Among these were the Northwestern Mutual Life Insurance Company and the Milwaukee Gas Light Company. He also had substantial holdings in other industrial firms in the Milwaukee area, his total worth being ultimately estimated as between three and five million dollars. Beginning his career as a working class blue collar artisan, certain of his contemporaries have stated that he acquired a certain polish and sophistication as time went by. No little credit for this was attributed to his wife, Emma, who was a woman of culture and talent.

Davidson was not a pioneer motorcyclist in the strict sense, but he quickly became familiar with his brother's and William Harley's prototypes after the decision had been made to incorporate the venture for formal marketing. His subsequent entrance into competition events has already been discussed, and the numerous trophies he won in these early events are still treasured by the present organization as mementos of H-D's earliest days.

In all fairness to Walter Davidson's memory, it must be stated that as President and titular head of the Company, it was quite naturally his role to make both public and inter-company announcements regarding H-D sales and general policy matters. As many of these were to become highly controversial with both the dealers as well as the riders, Walter quite naturally bore the brunt of much criticism. It should, of course, be stressed that all major Company policy matters were exhaustively discussed by the four Founders, and were implemented only after mutual agreement between the Davidsons and William Harley.

The two surviving Founders, together with the families and heirs of William A. and Walter, almost immediately conferred to select a new Chief Executive for the Company. The details of their deliberations were, of course, secret, but the matter has subsequently been the subject of much speculation upon the part of veteran H-D employees. President Walter was survived by three sons, Gordon, Walter Jr., and Robert. While it is a matter of record that the first two were already employed in various capacities within the Company, neither had shown any real interest in assuming managerial

The King himself. Clark Gable and his 1942 EL. The photograph was taken by the late Joe Walker at a Los Angeles motorcycle meet in the Summer of 1942. Note the period automobiles.

Details of the 1943-44 experimental XA model built at the request of the US Army. It was a frank copy of a utility-type side valve 45 cu.in. BMW used by the German Army. Only 1,000 were ever made. *(George Hays)*.

responsibilities. Robert, the youngest, had already elected to follow a career outside the Company in a field unrelated to motorcycling.

At the same time, the role of William Harley in Company affairs was such that he was already seeking to step down as Chief Engineer, and was in process of grooming his own son, William J., to succeed him. In the light of this fact, it became obvious that his present interests did not lie in the direction of assuming the Presidency of the Company.

Many H-D dealers and enthusiasts speculated whether Arthur Davidson, as one of the original Founders, might now inherit the mantle of Company leadership. In view of the fact that the details of the interfamily discussions were never revealed, a number of former Company employees have offered their own views. Arthur at this time was well over sixty-three years of age, not enjoying the most robust of health. There was also the matter of his drinking problem. Known as an abstainer or an occasional drinker, he periodically went on drinking sprees to return a week or ten days later in disheveled but penitent condition. He continued in his original post as General Sales Manager, where, as reportedly the most personable of the Davidsons, he had garnered a vast circle of loyal friends within H-D's riders and dealer network. Whatever his personal habits, he was shortly to ascend to an equally important post within the domestic motorcycle industry.

The mantle of H-D leadership passed to William Herbert Davidson, the son of the late William A., who was not only a life long motorcycle enthusiast, but held a degree in Business Administration from the University of Wisconsin. He had held various supervisorial and managerial posts within the Company during the between-the-wars period, as well as competing successfully in many competition events, winning the coveted Jack Pine trophy on a modified 'DR' model in 1930.

Another interesting facet of this particular phase of H-D history incidental to the selection of a new President is the fact that William H.'s father, William A., individually held the largest block of Company stock in relation to the other shareholders. This was, of course, now reflected in the position of William H. through his inherited holdings. In any conference within a family-held Company such as H-D, it appears almost inevitable that the stock ownership of the concerned parties affects the voting power. In the absence of any knowledge of the details of the closed deliberations, the whole subject is but a matter of conjecture. While William H. survives today as a retired Chief Executive, he has always refused to comment upon any of these historical proceedings.

During the Fall of the following year, the H-D Company sustained another great loss with the death of William S. Harley in his sixty-third year on September 18th 1943. Noted by his associates to be in a state of increasingly poor health during that summer, he dropped dead of heart failure while sitting at the bar of a local club. As the man almost single-handedly responsible for the development of the original H-D motorcycles, he had remained for many years as a giant within the industry. As a paradox to his conception of the bulk of H-D designs, he was known to relegate their refinement to others within the company who demonstrated their practical mechanical and engineering abilities such as William Ottaway, Arthur Constantine and Joe Petrali. In later years he was seen to withdraw somewhat from the motorcycling sphere, preferring cars to two wheelers. He spent much time in hunting and fishing, as well as his avocation of painting and drawing. A somewhat poetic and introvertive man, he combined the unusual talents of engineering know-how with the abstraction of art. His duties as Chief Engineer were taken over by the veteran William Ottaway, and subsequently relegated to his son, William, who had been his official assistant for the two preceding years.

Indian's long time Sales Manager, James Wright, resigned his position to take a similar position with a manufacturer of machine tools. It is thought that Wright, always a dynamic individual, chaffed at the lack of motorcycle sales activity during the war, and he decided that the critical machine tool sales field, now made vital by war materiel production, offered a more active and lucrative challenge. At a meeting of the AMA's Executive Committee held on January 20th 1944 in the Lexington Hotel in New York City, H-D's Sales Manager Arthur Davidson was named as the succeeding AMA President. It is reported that the Committee was of the opinion that due to the long tenure of office enjoyed by an Indian representative, it was now fitting that an H-D executive ascend to that office. As H-D had for many years enjoyed actual control over the affairs of the AMA, it now had titular control as well. With the ongoing support of long time H-D enthusiast, Secretary-Manager E.C. Smith, AMA control was even more firmly in the grip of H-D.

In the Fall of 1942 United States Army Procurement authorities ordered both factories to produce twin cylinder shaft driven machines based on European design. Apparently greatly impressed with the heavy duty BMW and Zundapp machines employed with much success by Field Marshal Erwin Rommel in his North African campaigns, the US Army considered the domestic development of similar types mandatory to augment this country's already formidable array of motor transport. H-D's Experimental Department's answer was the XA model, a 45 cubic inch horizontally opposed side valve twin with shaft drive and four-speed foot-operated gearbox with hand clutch control. A frank copy of a pre-war utility BMW model, the 'XA' showed much promise as a heavy duty service model, but was

William Hoecker's XA with disc wheels. Only a few of this model were built, and were intended for use in desert terrain. *(Alisha Tamburri)*.

marred by lubrication and valve gear problems which could have been corrected if the Army had standardized the model for series production. As it was, the end of the European conflict signalled the transfer of activities to the conflict with the Japanese in the Pacific theater. In the island terrain, the ubiquitous four-wheel drive Jeep was now considered more practical than the motorcycle, and Army orders for the new machines were cancelled after each factory had produced about a thousand examples. Many H-D enthusiasts looked forward to a refined 'XA' being added to the factory's post war line. This was not the case, however, and a couple of hundred civilianized 'XA's remain today in the hands of collectors of antique and special interest motorcycles.

H-D's contribution to the war effort totalled an incredible 88,000 machines. Most of these were of the 'WLA' 45 cubic inch model, and with continually expanded component part production, additional parts for another 30,000 units were on hand by the fall of 1944. For this effort, the Company was awarded not one of the usual Army-Navy 'E' awards for Excellent Service, but two.

A fortuitous side effect of the American motorcycle industry's war production effort was an enhanced public awareness of motorcycling both at home and overseas where the ruggedness of Yankee machines was amply demonstrated. H-D's advantage here was its two-to-one production volume as compared with Indian. Thousands of newly inducted GI's were taught to ride at the various transportation, motor pool, or armoured division training facilities throughout the country. Many of the country's competition stars were utilized as instructors. American Army machines ultimately ended up in nearly every country in the world, along with other types of American military material. Most riders became immediately impressed with the ruggedness of the Milwaukee product as typified in the 'WLA'. Doubtless its necessarily mild performance created a desire in many riders' minds to own a larger and more powerful civilian big twin model.

As is usually the case in such matters, large quantities of hastily produced military equipment never reached the front lines, and motorcycles ordered by the US Army were no exception. With the cancellation of contracts for military machines in the Spring of 1944, thousands of H-D and Indian machines were released for sale on the civilian market. At a government mandated retail price of $450, about 15,000 'WLA's' and 6,000 Indian 741's were placed on the market during the Summer of 1945. The shaft drive models from both factories were offered for sale shortly afterwards at $500. Large numbers of Yankee machines were released for public sale in England during the same period. Most of the H-D machines available were 'WLA's'. Some of these had seen limited service in Home Defense or military police assignments, but many were still in their original factory crates at various military depots. Large numbers of these were acquired as surplus by such well known dealers as Marble Arch Motors, Pride & Clarke, and others, as well as by F.H.Warr, the veteran franchised H-D distributor. Most of these 'WLA's' were sold as originally supplied, with military gear intact. Some dealers selling such machines offered the option of civilian specification, stripping them of their military gear and refinishing them in original factory colors. Many English owners acquiring such machines even went as far as to order civilian type mudguards to replace the rather austere War Department wide clearance type, and Milwaukee obliged by running off an extra supply of such fittings. The once active H-D Owner's Club of Great Britain ordered substantial numbers of such machines, and many were in use until quite recently.

While H-D's war production was phenomenal, the profits accrued were not great, as the machines were produced on a cost-plus basis of about 10% per unit. In addition, the Company was, in the end, not recompensed for the bulk of their spare-part component units that could have accounted for an additional 30,000 'WLA' machines, although the Company was said to have driven a hard bargain with Army purchasing agents for about one half of this parts surplus. In later years, component parts, mostly 'WLA' engines with generators and carburetors, were to come on the civilian market in the mid-1950's at give-away prices. It was at one time possible to acquire such units for $79.50 each.

In the overall sense, it was now apparent to many knowledgeable people within the trade that in the United States, at long last, a new interest in motorcycling was to emerge, and that the sport was now to enjoy a certain modicum of respectability. As a portent of things to come, Alfred Rich Child, H-D's long time Asiatic Distributor, had resigned his position as Manager of the Overseas Reassembly Division of the Lockheed Aircraft Company, which position he had held since the war, and announced that he would shortly import BSA motorcycles from Great Britain for sale on the American market through a newly-formed company based in New Jersey.

Frederick H. Warr's 1942 WLC W.D. model converted to civilian specification. Note fitting of the 16 inch wheels. Many hundreds of ex-W.D. WLAs, WLCs, and lesser numbers of ex-W.D. 641 Indians are still in daily use in many parts of the world today. *(F. W. Warr)*

Chapter 8

Post~War Problems

THE WAR ENDED IN THE SUMMER OF 1945, AND ALTHOUGH THE ALLIES OSTENSIBLY won an overwhelming victory, subsequent events were to prove that while the war had been won, the peace had been lost.

Aside from the political overtones, which were as yet to be revealed, the United States emerged from yet another World War, even greater than the first some two decades before, with its borders unravaged by enemy action and with but minimal human casualties as compared with both its allies and enemies alike. Both the civilian population and the nation's business and industrial leaders at once envisioned that an almost instant and Utopian prosperity would ensue, due to the now immense pentup demand for consumer goods and the belief that the colossal productive might acquired through the war effort could now supply it. Much actual progress was made toward productive conversion to the civilian market during the Fall and Winter of 1945-46, but other factors were at once to intervene suddenly, seriously curtailing the planned output of consumer goods. With central Europe largely devastated by massive bombing, England prostrate and economically and physically exhausted, and Japan totally annihilated, the United States at once found itself the sole productive nation in a world that was too impoverished to purchase its goods. The US was mindful of the now serious threat of Communism that could well be an attraction to the poverty stricken war-devastated nations, many of which were already well within the Russian sphere following Stalin's duplicity at Yalta.

To counteract this threat, the newly-inaugurated US President, Harry S.Truman, with the backing of majority leaders of the Democratic party in Congress, now proposed that the United States embark on a program of both monetary and industrial aid in the form of vast loans and essential materials for the rebuilding of Europe. Known as the Marshall Plan, it was named for the former US Army Chief of Staff George Catlett Marshall, who was chosen to administer it, and the bulk of the domestic supplies of iron, steel, aluminum and other light metals, machine tooling, synthetic rubber, electrical components, and countless other commodities now under the control of government procurement agencies for shipment overseas. At the same moment, favorable tariff rates were instituted which encouraged the import of foreign goods to be paid for in hard dollars, with which to further strengthen foreign monetary systems.

This massive program, which doubtlessly staved off further Communist advances abroad, brought about great economic hardships at home, where, by this time, most essential civilian goods were in very short supply. The critical transportation industries that supplied railroad rolling stock, automobiles, trucks and critical machine tooling were particularly affected. In order to aid domestic industry as much as possible, essential component materials were allocated to various manufacturers on a quota system, based on their immediate pre-war production.

The American motorcycle industry was at once placed at a critical disadvantage by this state of affairs, as its pre-war production had been minimal. At the same moment, it gave a tremendous advantage to both the overseas motorcycle manufacturers and the growing number of import organizations which came into being to facilitate their sale in the United States.

The sudden dramatic public interest in motorcycles came as a puzzling phenomenon to many old time riders as well as members of the domestic industry, who now noted that trading conditions in the general post-war shortage of goods made for a seller's market. Yet a factual analysis of the situation by both sociologists and economists indicated that this was not surprising. There was presently a vast pent-up demand for luxury and recreational goods, dating back not only to the recent war years, but from the previous decade of the Great Depression. Now that the inevitable post-war prosperity had become a reality, there was plenty of available money for their purchase. Then too, millions of young men, freshly released from the armed forces, sought to make up for the recreational opportunities so long denied them. As far as motorcycling went, countless GI's had been introduced to the sport through service employment, which in turn served to whet their appetites for more luxurious and better performing civilian-type machines. Added to this, the now burgeoning ranks of motorcycle dealers offering new models from overseas made for a greater market penetration through their sheer numbers.

Due to the immediate difficulties in obtaining critical materials, the H-D Company perhaps wisely decided to institute somewhat limited production of their successful pre-war line of models. The top of the line was, of course, the well tried 61 and 74 cubic inch ohv big twins, together with the rugged 74 inch side valver. The venerable 45 twin was still in limited production, with an eye to supplying military and utility machines to their export buyers. The Servi-car was also in production, along with sidecars and package vans. Prices, of course, were greatly advanced, the 61 ohv twin was now retailing at $725 FOB Wilwaukee.

Surprisingly enough, the American manufacturers offered no direct competition to the foreign invaders. The H-D 45 was never the sporting mount as compared with the Indian Sport Scout, and the latter had now been dropped from the line by Indian's new President, Ralph B.Rogers, who, while continuing the popular Chief, was planning to introduce a line of lightweight machines, based on continental lines.

In the meantime, the H-D Company was engaged in encouraging a number of its dealers, who had suspended operations due to the hiatus of the war years, to reactivate their franchises, as well as soliciting the acquisition of new dealerships through advertisements placed in both the trade press and various hobby and outdoor magazines. An enhanced factory advertising campaign was also announced through both the pages of the *Enthusiast* and by direct contact with the established dealers.

In spite of production difficulties due to shortages of essential materials, the American motorcycle industry was able to produce about 19,500 units in 1946, according to the US Department of Commerce reports. While this was substantially more than was reported for 1940, the increase was largely due to the enhanced production of scooters, mainly manufactured by the Cushman Motor Company of Lincoln, Nebraska, with lesser numbers produced by Gladding and Salsbury. While both factories strictly enforced their long standing edict against the franchise holders selling other than their own factory's products, it has been noted that they tended to look the other way in the matter of scooters, and substantial numbers of these, mostly Cushmans, were sold by both outlets. As there was still a shortage of available new automobiles due to the material shortages with a consequent high price structure for used cars, the scooter now attracted a growing number of utility riders, as well as schoolboys seeking cheap transportation, as the smallest sized Cushman now retailed for about $150.

At the end of the war, the Cushman concern greatly enlarged its production facilities, and as a result they were now able to keep up with increasing sales. This happy state of affairs, for some H-D dealers at least, came to an abrupt end in the Spring of 1947 when the factory, through its traveling representatives, informed all retailers that henceforth no more Cushman products could be sold through franchised outlets. Several dealers, especially in the larger cities where scooter sales had been brisk, tended at first to ignore this edict. These rebels were at once notified by the factory that any and all orders for H-D machines would be suspended until they complied. A few, who were known to have extensive scooter sales were ordered to certify, with notarized statements, that they had, in fact, officially severed all franchise connections with the Cushman Company.

Various versions of this episode in H-D history have been related to the author by veteran dealers, along with their own personal opinions as to the reason for this official factory mandate. The most popular story is that a group of Cushman's managerial staff visited the H-D factory in the late Winter of 1947. During the course of their tour of the premises, some of them were heard to adversely compare the now somewhat antiquated Milwaukee facility with their own recently-constructed plant in

A 1947 'Knucklehead' Dresser. In the restoration, modern plastic panniers have been substituted for the period cowhide bags. *(George Hays)*.

Lincoln. Another account has it that with the new lightweight model that H-D was shortly to introduce, which will be subsequently described, H-D's top management now thought it best to remove potential competition for its sales well before its introduction.

Production at Milwaukee now proceeded at a greatly reduced pace, as the Company's material allocations were by necessity based on pre-war production. With a soaring demand for new machines, especially the now popular ohv models, dealers' orders were filled on a quota basis. In spite of production difficulties, the quality and finish of the new machines was excellent. A notable advance was the use of the Parker process in rust-proofing all metal parts most subject to corrosion. The originator of this patented chemical treating process, one Edward Parker, paradoxically enough began his operations in space leased from the Indian Company in Springfield!

In the meantime, foreign motorcycles, mostly from Great Britain, began appearing on the American market in increasing numbers. By the end of 1946, nearly 10,000 units had been sold. Most of these were imported by organizations formed by the handful of brave entrepreneurs who had the temerity to launch these ventures in the late 1930's, when both the machinations of the established dealers and the sub-rosa disapproval of the AMA had all but strangled their efforts. The most prominent of these were Johnson Motors based in Pasadena, California, who handled Ariel and Triumph, and Alfred Rich Child in New Jersey, who now held the BSA import rights for the United States.

While H-D as yet had no comparable model with which to compete with the British singles, the Company rose to the challenge by inaugurating an accelerated national advertising campaign, and at the same moment increased their efforts to strengthen the morale of their dealership. Factory representatives were instructed to spread the gospel of traditional American motorcycling and the type of machine it typified, as well as emphasizing that it was a patriotic duty of all riders to support the American motorcycle industry. Along with this went a warning to all dealers not to undertake the repair of any foreign machines in their premises, or even sell them tires or lubricants. Another somewhat logical reason advanced for buying American machines was that in their heavyweight configuration they were much more suited to general domestic conditions of use and their longevity was already well proved. While this was true, it did not negate the fact that a horde of new riders were enjoying the lightweight single cylinder machines for casual weekend pleasure riding, and that a new group of feminine enthusiasts were now also coming into the fold. H-D was also somewhat hard pressed to gloss over the fact that not a few long time dealers had deserted Milwaukee to sell the newcomers, sensing not only a new and hopefully more viable market, but also perhaps tiring of the traditional oppressive tactics of H-D's management.

The question of the suitability of the imported machines for typical American riding conditions was well taken, as in many cases they were not. The first British imports were generally 21 cubic inch models that were basically ex-War Department types with civilian finish. These included Ariel, Royal Enfield, BSA, and the 350 cc Triumph twin. The first 500 cc (30.50 cubic inch) models to arrive were side valve Nortons, of North African fame! Their initial retail prices were attractive, first fixed at $585 but soon raised about $100 more. This now relatively modest price, together with their light weight, ease of handling, and above all, their featuring of hand-controlled clutch mechanisms and foot shifted gearboxes found them an immediate welcome from many budding US enthusiasts who could never formerly relate to a 700 pound big twin. In passing, it must also be noted that the imports carried but a nominal import duty of about 8%, while American big twins were still having to contend with a 33% to 50% tariff barrier when exported. Some 9,064 machines were imported in 1946, this figure rising to 15,073 in 1947.

While these figures augured well for a revitalized American motorcycle market, all was not lovely in the garden. While the imports offered the advantages mentioned, together with the capabilities of economical running, their generally initial engine size of 350 cc was scarcely powerful enough to cope with the exigencies of long distance high speed travel. They were particularly prone to failure in the popular motorcycling area of the West and Southwest where high summer temperatures were the rule and where hard riding was the essence of the sport. Then, too, the imports were never designed to stand up to the punishment the average rough-riding Yank was used to giving his machine. Particularly vulnerable were clutches and gearboxes, especially to ex-H-D riders, as the British models required careful application and gentle gear changing if any longevity in use was to be expected. The initial problems were somewhat mitigated when the more powerful 500 cc imports became available in the Spring of 1948. Still no match on the road in high speed travel, the Ariel Red Hunter, the Triumph Speed Twin, and a few others of like size offered at least better longevity. A notable exception was the ohc Norton International, which could give a good account of itself in any sort of going, but, as a high priced machine in low volume production, it was rarely seen.

Another problem for the imports was the weakness of many of their dealers. While many pioneer outlets in the foreign field prospered, too many enthusiasts entered the arena with too little capital and less business experience, and many predictable failures occurred. There was also an ongoing problem with obtaining necessary spare parts. Some dealers were forced to cannibalize new machines to keep favored customers on the road. On the credit side of the ledger, a new market unfolded with the coming availability of utility type lightweight machines for the newsboy rider, such as the James, Excelsior (British) and Francis-Barnett, all powered with proprietary 125 cc Villiers engine-gearbox units. These were later joined by the civilian version of the Royal Enfield 125 cc paratroop machine.

Meanwhile, enjoying at long last a seller's market of enthusiasts' inquiries and a backlog of unfilled orders, many H-D dealers were asking the factory whether or not any middleweight machines with which to compete with the foreign imports might not now be forthcoming. Many were chagrined at the official answer that in view of the current production problems, no new models were contemplated. This position was further amplified by statements, mostly through the factory representatives, that H-D had been producing motorcycles for 45 years, and knew better than anyone else what type of machine suited the American rider. Those dealers who persisted in their inquiries, were told that the venerable 45 model might well be advocated as a sales alternative to the ever-burgeoning imports. This was scarcely a logical answer to veteran dealers, who knew well that this model's 500 pound plus weight and 68 mph top speed was scarcely a challenge to a lower cost Ariel Red Hunter or Triumph Speed Twin whose top speed was 20 mph higher.

On the sporting side, there was now the inevitable collision between the AMA Competition Committee and the dealers in foreign imports, who at once challenged the longstanding ruling mandating a 7.5:1 compression ratio for 30.50 ohv singles when competing against 45 cubic inch side valve engines. The Competition Committee's immediate answer was that for the foreseeable future the present ruling would stand. When pressed for an explanation, the official stand of the management of the AMA now, of course, totally dominated by H-D, was that the AMA and its constituent Competition Committee was totally committed to the interests of the American motorcycling, American riders, and American manufacturers. It was further stated that if foreign machines wished to compete on America's home ground, they must do so on traditional American conditions without reference to foreign precedent. This was a bitter pill for the importers to swallow, as the leading overseas contenders such as the Ariel Red Hunter, Triumph Speed Twin, and Norton International models required at least an 8.5:1 compression ratio to allow them to develop their full power, especially if tuned for competition.

Hollister, California, July 4th, 1947. American motorcycling's Day of Infamy. Here an inebriated reveler on his stripped H-D toasts a Time-Life photographer. *(Time-Life Inc)*.

The monotony of the American motorcycling journalistic scene was enlivened in the Spring of 1947 by the launching of a new motorcycle magazine called *Cycle,* which was inaugurated by an enterprising young publisher, Robert E.Peterson, who also had just introduced other motoring publications such as *Motor Trend* and *Hot Rod* to cater to the increasing public interest in automotive progress. The long limpid *Motorcyclist,* which under AMA and H-D domination had traditionally existed as an apologist for the industry, acting principally as its defender, was now challenged by a new publication oriented toward the interests of the consumer. For the first time in the memory of most US motorcyclists, critical evaluations and road tests of currently offered models were actually aired in print.

The domestic answer to this journalistic bombshell was a rather thin magazine, aptly named *American Motorcycling,* launched in Chicago. Heavily backed by both H-D and Indian interests, it emphasized the traditionalist theme of the Yankee big twin and the patriotic obligation to patronize the domestic industry.

In addition, H-D's management sought to strengthen their position by reactivating the regional H-D dealer's associations in various parts of the country, all of which met at least twice a year. Factory representatives constantly impressed upon the dealers the patriotic duty of supporting American products. Practical sales techniques were emphasized in the promotion of accessory sales, where the 45-60% markups were contrasted with the traditional 25% sales markup on the bare machines. This accentuated the 'dresser' theme, where, to customize his machine, the purchaser would add a dualseat, saddle bags, spotlights, and other items which by this time were the style for the typical big twin rider.

H-D was in a most fortunate position in relation to the clubman's market, as the production of the classic Indian Chief had been much curtailed as Indian's new President, Ralph B.Rogers, was preoccupied with the development of two new lightweight models with which he hoped to compete in the market for smaller machines. With the renewed interest in big twin models, the standard clubman's machine was now almost universally a 61 or 74 cubic inch H-D ohv model equipped with windshield, front and rear crash bars, leather saddle bags, a rear carrier for additional luggage, along with whatever extra spotlights and additional chrome gadgets the owner chose to install. This concept was, of course encouraged by the factory, and in any club meeting or semi-private contest, there was inevitably an award for the 'Best Equipped' machine, which could be won by simply loading the model with every available gadget.

Class C racing was somewhat haphazardly revived after the war, and culminated in the first post-war running of the 200 mile Daytona Classic in 1947. Johnny Speigelhoff, of San Diego, won the meet handily on a racing Scout.

An interesting vignette of AMA history emerged from the 1947 Daytona Classic in relation to the barring of a super sports ohc 500 Moto Guzzi from the contest. Its owner, pioneer motorcyclist John Cameron, of Whittier, California, who entered the machine in question, was notified by a member of the AMA Competition Committee that his entry had been disqualified, even though Cameron's entry was accepted before the meet, as required by the rules. Cameron told the author in 1978 that the Moto Guzzi showed such promise during the prerace practice period that the AMA officials were fearful of another foreign victory, such as had occurred with the Norton entry in 1941! Cameron lodged a vociferous protest, but the Committee refused to give him a hearing.

Motorcyclists everywhere, whether clubmen, casual riders, or the new emerging sportsmen favoring imported machinery, were disappointed and chagrined in the Summer of 1947, when a July 4th general clubman's meeting at the village of Hollister, California, was invaded by a group of the so-called 'outlaw' motorcyclists. Over the three day weekend, these worthies terrorized the town, and it took a force of some 500 California Highway Patrol officers, California State Police, and local law enforcement officers to quell the disturbance, and disband the rioters.

The sensational aspects of the incident were at once seized upon by the news media, including *Life* magazine, then the leading news-picture publication, and the roughneck aspects of motorcycling were again emphasized to untold millions of readers. The names of such outlaw clubs as the Booze Fighters, Galloping Gooses, Satan's Sinners, Satan's Daughters, and the Winoes were prominently featured. Dozens of these revelers were arrested for indecent exposure and for relieving themselves on buildings along Hollister's main thoroughfare. The now classic photograph by a *Time-Life* photographer of the drunken rider of a stripped-down ohv model brandishing a bottle of beer appeared on the cover of the July 21st issue. The debacle was again aired on its twenty-fifth anniversary when *Life* again featured the picture on its cover in July 1972. Anguished letters from orderly motorcyclists were subsequently printed by *Life* in their 'letters from the readers' section, including one from actor Keenan Wynn and another from *Motorcyclist* Editor Paul Brokaw, deploring the blatant exploitation of the incident. Both declared that of the 4,000 odd motorcyclists present, only about 500 of that number actually caused the trouble, the balance being mostly sober AMA club members. Whatever the actual details, the incident unfortunately labeled the H-D as the outlaw machine of choice.

The so-called roughneck or 'outlaw' element among motorcyclists, while a thorn in the side of clubmen and orderly private riders in pre-war days had ever been a problem, such had previously constituted a minority within a minority, and up to this point had never presented much more than a minor annoyance. The Hollister incident pointed up the fact that certain antisocial elements within the fabric of the nation were now finding within the motorcycle movement a means of expression of protest within the so-called traditional establishment.

The 'outlaw' motorcyclist concept now constituted a fertile field of speculation for psychiatrists and sociologists of the post-war era, who were also studying the effect of certain of the younger elements of the social spectrum who had been dislocated by their participation in the war. Some of these so-called experts averred that these people were motorcyclists who were expressing their revolt against the organized activities of the dealer-sponsored club oriented meetings. Others claimed that certain antisocial individuals had chosen the iconoclastic entity of the motorcycle to express their general emotions of revolt against the formal social structuring of contemporary American life. Whatever the theoretical background to these assumptions, it ultimately transpired that the outlaw adherents in general gravitated to the American heavyweight 'V' twin as their favored mount, with ownership of H-D big twin machines predominating. Adopting stripped machines without windshields, saddle bags, spotlights, or even crash bars, it may well be assumed that their attitude was one of revolt against the big twin 'dresser' favored by clubmen as well as against the now effete middleweight British imports.

Most of the long established H-D dealers refused to countenance the general unwashed outlaw types as customers, so their repair and service needs soon created numbers of small specialist unfranchised shops. Many of these soon became notorious for dealing in stolen machines or pirated parts.

In the Fall of 1947, two updated versions of the ohv 61 and 74 cubic inch big twin models were announced for the 1948 sales year to replace the 'knuckle head' type which had been in production for a decade. While, as ohv machines, the original model had in large part overcome the overheating problems at high speeds that had been an unfortunate attribute of the 74 and 80 cubic inch side valve models, its all-iron cylinder barrel and head had at times evidenced its own overheating problem, especially in hot weather at prolonged high speeds. The problem of oil leaks around the rocker box coverings had never been entirely solved. To correct these faults and produce a cooler running engine, H-D's Engineering Department's answer was the so-called 'pan-head', with an aluminum alloy cylinder head and an hydraulically-controlled lifter in the ohv mechanims. The 'pan-head' description alluded to the skillet-shaped aluminum cover over the valve mechanism.

While the changed configuration was a theoretical improvement, considerable trouble was experienced with the early models. The oil pump, situated low in the crankcase, now had to force the lubricating oil to the top of the cylinder head through a complex labyrinth of oilways. If the oil pressure was not constant for any reason, the hydraulic lifters failed to function properly, causing a variation in the timing sequence. Practical mechanics at once pointed out that the system could be more efficient and reliable if the hydraulic tappets were placed at the bottom of the push rods rather than at the top, and therefore less subject to timing variation if there was a change in oil pressure. After large numbers of dealers and riders reported both rocker arm failure and serious alterations in the normal valve timing sequence, the factory supplied kits of revised parts in hopes of correcting the difficulties.

A feature of this new design was a shaped felt pad fitted into the top of the 'pan' head which was intended to pick up and hold the oil to give added lubrication to the rocker mechanism. In some cases, amateur mechanics failed to replace this felt on reassembly after a valve adjustment. The resultant noise from the increased resonance in the 'pan' from the rockers was said to be ear splitting!

On November 24th 1947, the H-D Company held a general dealers' sales conference in Milwaukee at the Shroeder Hotel, described in the contemporary issues of the *Enthusiast* as the largest meeting of its kind ever held in the Company's history. Dealers from all over the US attended, as well as a number of overseas dealers.

Sales Manager J.C.Kilbert opened the first meeting, and introduced the last surviving Founder, Vice President Arthur Davidson. Davidson spoke at length of the critical economic international situation and its relationship to the ever-growing inflation. Gordon Davidson, the son of the late Walter Davidson, and now Chief of the Production Department, outlined the Company's projected 1948 production schedule. He stated that he hoped to increase the present year's output of about 20,000 machines to 30,000 for the following season. He reported that the Company was currently in process of enhancing its manufacturing facilities and was acquiring additional tooling to meet this projected goal.

Later in the meeting, Arthur Davidson again gave an address, this time emphasizing the company's general sales policies. He warned all dealers that only company built parts, accessories, and factory-supplied lubricants should be handled by the franchised outlets, and that any retailing of the

Win Young broadslides at a race on the Lincoln Park oval in 1948. His machine is a DLD with a WR racing engine. *(Robert Magill).*

A study in contrasts. A 1947 Ariel Red Hunter and a 1940 EL go over the jump at Lincoln Park. *(Robert Magill).*

products of other suppliers would result in disciplinary action. He next called attention to the vast display of company-manufactured or supplied accessories on view in a large hall adjacent to the meeting room. He pointed out that the generous 45% dealer markup on these items could greatly enhance their profits, and that buyers of both new and used machines be urged to purchase as many of these items as the traffic would bear. He also stated that as the factory had cut its own costs to dealers to the bone to aid in placing H-D in a competitive position in a growingly critical market, the factory's stake in accessory sales to dealers was now a critical factor in Company economics.

Representatives of the Kilbourne Finance Company spoke at length on the promotion of conditional sales contracts written through its organization to enhance the sale of new and late model used machines. Dealers were also advised to utilize the services of this company to floor larger stocks of showroom machines and informed of the favorable insurance rates offered for the protection of machines sold under the terms of these contracts.

Other factory personnel who addressed the meeting were Service Manager Joseph Ryan, Parts and Accessories Manager Harry Devine, Law Enforcement Sales Manager Frank Egloff, and J.C.Kilbert. Kilbert emphasized the importance of developing commercial sales of Servi-car and package truck sales. He pointed to the enviable sales records in this area racked up by Dudley Perkins of San Francisco, Claude Salmon, of near-by Oakland, and Alfred Rich Child of Japan, who had sold large numbers of these units to commercial establishments in the Bay area in pre-war years.

During an intermission following this stage of the proceedings, Law Enforcement Sales Manager Egloff was seen to be holding conferences with various groups of dealers, urging them to learn whether purchasing specifications written into local municipal, country or state ordinances could be strengthened to continue the mandatory retention of H-D machines. He emphasized that the continuation of this strategy would have the advantage of keeping dealers of foreign machines out of the domestic law enforcement business.

E.C.Smith, Secretary-Manager of the AMA was also on hand to render a report on the current status of that organization. He stated that its membership had grown from 4,650 in 1928 to over 50,000 in 1947, which knowledgeable members of the audience immediately concluded was wildly optimistic. He emphasized that dealer support of the AMA was vital to its continuing success, as well as lauding the H-D Company for its role as its most substantial financial supporter. He also mentioned that continuing rider and dealer support of the *American Motorcycling* magazine would be most helpful for the sales promotion of domestic motorcyles. In conclusion, he again praised the role of H-D in its long support of the AMA, and presented its current President, Arthur Davidson, and sole surviving Founder, with a handsome trophy.

A surprise feature of the meeting was an appearance by Chief Engineer William J.Harley, who outlined briefly the various technical improvements that had been incorporated into the post-war range of H-D models. As this segment of the meeting opened, it was noted that two black-draped objects flanked the rostrum. The mystery was soon dispelled by Harley as he announced the introduction of the first two prototypes of a new 125 cc lightweight model. To be cataloged as the H-D 125, the new 175 pound machine was a startling innovation in contrast to H-D's long preoccupation with heavyweight machines. Of basically simple design, it featured a solid rear frame, the girder forks being sprung with rubber band suspension. To further enhance comfort, 3.25 inch section tires were fitted on both wheels. Experienced members of the audience were quick to note that the engine, with its integral three-speed gear box unit, was a frank copy of the German DKW unit built in Germany from the original Schnurle design shortly before the war. This unit was shortly to be seen again from overseas in the form of the BSA Bantam. Both companies had secured the patents through the Allied acquisition of German assets following the war.

Another surprise feature of the gathering was a train trip to the outskirts of Milwaukee, where President William H.Davidson was on hand to greet the dealers and their guests. He explained that the new 260,000 square foot acquisition had just been purchased from the government and, as a former defense plant, could be readily adapted to motorcycle production. He noted that new tooling and equipment would shortly enhance H-D's output, and that over $3,500,000 was being spent on the project. He also stated that the production of 'WR' racing machines was to be expanded, and hoped that dealers would be quick in sponsoring qualified competition riders to counter the growing challenge of foreign machines in motorcycle sport.

The meeting was, in effect, a challenge by the company in throwing down the gauntlet to foreign competition, and at the same time reaffirming the Company's adherence to American motorcycling tradition by featuring the heavyweight 'V' twin. While the new 125 model was indeed a departure from this tradition, the Company showed no inclination to introduce any new models in the 21 and 30.50 cubic inch categories currently supplied by foreign machines.

Quite naturally the affair was billed by reports in the *Enthusiast* as a love feast, but all was not serene. Many dealers had hoped for an H-D scooter to replace the now-denied Cushman that had been

Homer Drown pilots his 1935 VL over the TT course at Lincoln Park in the Summer of 1948. *(Robert Magill)*.

such a good seller on the utility market. A number were also highly critical of the fact that no new models were planned to fill the 350 cc - 500 cc category featured by their most serious foreign competitors.

The story is often told that a number of veteran dealers, concerned by their inability to compete w.th foreign machines with H-D's of like category, met privately with Arthur Davidson, to find out whether the Company had plans to offer such models. At the same time, many of the smaller dealers complained that their quota of machine orders was not being filled in the same ratio as was supplied to the dealers in the larger cities and trading areas. Davidson responded to the first query by saying that no new models were planned because at this time the company was not prepared to spend the considerable sum of money required to build such prototypes. He further stated that during the past forty years H-D had built machines best suited to American conditions, and was therefore in a position to know what type of machine was best suited to the American rider. This was the type of machine the Company intended to produce. In response to the second question, Davidson stated that in some cases

195

dealers in the larger trading areas might be given quota preference because their volume sales meant that they were selling proportionately more machines. Put off by the rather arbitrary attitude, some of the dealers next contacted President William H.Davidson, who, it has been alleged, echoed the same sentiments.

In relation to H-D's conservative policy of adhering to their post-war models, John R.Bond, an automotive engineer who later published and edited the prestigious *Road and Track* magazine, offered his own comments on the matter. As an employee in the Company's Engineering Department during 1946 and 1947, he noted that every encouragement was given to the prototype studies of new or innovative motorcycle designs. While H-D's top management showed much interest in such creative projects, nothing was ever done to incorporate any of them into current or subsequent models.

The following spring, the Company did much to reactivate the H-D Dealers Association in the various geographical sections of the country. While still very much alive as organizations, most of them had naturally languished somewhat during the war years. Factory representatives now exhorted the dealers to redouble their sales efforts, and to aid in counteracting the growing threat of intense foreign competition, to emphasize the patriotic theme of patronizing domestic industry as well as harking back to the traditions of American motorcycling in machine selection.

Sales of foreign machines had become substantial. The general motoring public, up to this time often unaware of the availability of foreign makes, was now treated to a new era in motorcycle merchandizing. Some of the well-financed foreign dealers established extensive showrooms in the larger cities, many of which overshadowed the traditionally shabby housing some of the domestic dealers had long suffered. With a generally broad selection of both light and middleweight machines available to them, potential buyers had a welcome range of choice. Then too, the foreign dealers were under no repressive control from either factories or distributors, and were free to not only retail any make of machine, but could offer a diverse group of accessories from any manufacturer as well.

While the foreign machines up to this point had no domestically produced counterpart, the situation changed somewhat when Indian's new President, Ralph B.Rogers, announced that his company was shortly to introduce a new line of light and mediumweight machines. During this period also, the domestic big twins suffered no foreign competition to speak of, as the few that had been produced overseas between the wars, were not reintroduced in the early post-war years. The two exceptions to this were the Ariel Square Four and the Vincent HRD. The former, a somewhat unorthodox design by Edward Turner was, in effect, powered by two vertical twin engines geared to a common crankcase. While the closely grouped cylinders cooled sufficiently for use on the winding lanes in the mild British climate, this configuration was less than satisfactory over the vast distances and high summer temperatures of the West and Southwest US where motorcycling was most popular. To those few Square Four enthusiasts who persisted, the only possible answer was the fitting of a proprietary oil cooler. The Vincent, a massive 61 cubic inch V twin with a rather curious spring frame and dual carburetors, was capable of far out speeds, but was rather temperamental and difficult to keep in tune. This, with its rather weak lower bearing design, was a machine for the enthusiastic mechanic rather than the casual tourist.

On the other side of the coin, the H-D 125 proved to be a sound machine and was generally well received by schoolboys and utility riders, as well as numbers of adult newcomers to the sport. Ruggedly built in the best H-D tradition, its engine proved both more durable and capable of higher performance than the Villiers-engined James, Excelsior (British) and Francis-Barnet lightweights that had been imported in fair numbers. The 125's 47-49 mph top speed was somewhat better than the James's 40-odd, and was far less susceptible to spark plug fouling. About 10,000 H-D 125s were delivered during the first year.

Great Britain's answer to the Yankee big twins in the speed battle was the enlarging of the classic 500 cc Triumph Speed twin to 649 cc in the new Thunderbird model in 1949. This was soon followed by similar bored out 500's by Norton and BSA. For substantially less retail cost, the British enthusiast now had a machine that could keep up with the Yanks, albeit far less rugged and in need of much tinkering.

It was during this period, when motorcycle journalism was quite naturally expanding with the rising market, that a whole new regiment of aspiring young journalists took to the typewriter. Many of these tried to outdo one another in praise of the now effete imports and in downgrading the native products. As H-D was now the leading producer due to Indian's pre-occupation with some smaller continental-type models, it took most of the brunt of this criticism. Characterized as out of date trucks, crude, overweight, and 'Hawg' like, the Yankee classic was excoriated as an out-of-date dinosaur. This somewhat scurrilous attack was prompted by lack of knowledge and experience of these writers who rushed into print without realizing that they were dealing with two distinct types of machines, having generic origins in separate continents with opposed applications of use.

On the other side of the pond, however, the reaction to the post-war Yankee big twins was reported as most cordial. In a December 1955 issue of the English *Motor Cycling* magazine, published by Temple Press, a road test reported of a 1950 74 cubic inch 'FL' model lent to the staff by a US Army Air Force Sergeant. The author, while commenting on the excessive weight and bulk of the machine, was ecstatic about its effortless high cruising speed, easy starting, and the superlative comfort afforded by the hydraulic fork, softly sprung saddle, and the general air of invincibility engenderd by the large capacity slow turning engine. The conclusion was that the big Yank offered a standard of comfort and enormous power not yet available on the British market.

For the 1949 sales season, H-D enthusiasts were electrified by the announcement that the time tried classic H-D leading link forks were to be replaced on the big twin models by an oil dampened telescopic fork, the first change in H-D suspension in forty years! The new fitting followed the usual telescopic pattern, except that it was, of course, a rather massive fitting. With a wide range of travel, riding comfort was markedly improved, and together with the dampening effect of the time-honored spring seat post and the standard 5 inch section low pressure tires, the effect was such that any present digression into a rear spring frame was entirely unnecessary. Some difficulty was experienced with the earlier models so fitted, however. With soft springs and a long rate of travel, it was possible to spill the machine if a tight turn were made allowing the lower outer end of the standard crash bar to dig into dirt or pavement. The author himself had two narrow escapes from crashing when turning off pavement onto rough desert tracks on a 1950 'FL'. Joe Walker, the local Santa Ana dealer, installed a factory-offered kit that was subsequently developed to slow the rate of oil travel within the fork, which corrected the difficulty. In subsequent sales literature the new models were catalogued as the 'Hydra Glide'.

With the low production of Indian Chiefs in the company's post-war reorganization, the H-D low compression 74 cubic inch 'FL' model became the standard law enforcement machine in the United States, and was widely exported abroad for this use. Its only international competitors in this field were the resurrected BMW opposed twin and the low production copy built in France as the Ratier, neither of which were then produced in any substantial numbers. As a result, probably more Presidents, Prelates, Heads of State, and other dignitaries have ridden with H-D police escort than any other machine! The Police 'FL' was admirably suited to this work, as its low compression engine could be idled for long periods in slow speed traffic work without fouling, yet it could be rapidly accelerated to pursuit speeds as the occasion demanded. While its top speed with full radio and other standard law enforcement equipment was only slightly over 80 mph, this was sufficient during its heyday to overhaul most standard automobiles. Its massive trouble-free drive train and clutch was well suited to standing up to both low speed and start-and-stop usage, and the riders generally commented that its low center of gravity made it very stable and comfortable to ride. A few die-hard municipalities, however, clung to their Indians, mostly through long established tradition, and H-D's Law Enforcement Sales Department was constantly dogging these heretics as a matter of both pride and principle. One of these was the City of New York. Their regiment of pre-war Indian Fours now redundant, they still maintained a vast fleet of Chiefs. The production of this model was terminated in 1953, but some 55 machines were assembled from parts on hand in 1955 by the Tite-Flex Company, the manufacturer of Chiefs since 1951. The purpose of this was to supply these machines to the New York Police Department, whose procurement specifications called for Indian machines. To counter this, H-D assembled two 'FL' models for bidding survey, duly fitted with reversed controls to comply with the left-handed throttle edict, together with a pristine finish in Indian Red Color! This act enraged both the New York Police oficials as well as Tite-Flex, and according to several old timers' accounts, the Atlas Corporation, owner of Tite Flex, filed a patent infringement suit against the H-D Company. The exact outcome of this rather bizarre affair is unknown, but it was long a rumor that H-D paid a substantial sum in damages to Atlas to keep the matter out of court. H-D had the last laugh, however, when the last of New York City's Indians were retired in the late 1950's, and 'FL's' took their place.

By 1950, competition for a now stabilized motorcycle market was keen, with foreign dealers now outnumbering the domestic contingent by a wide margin. While H-D now had a firm grip on both the law enforcement market and the family-oriented club scene, mostly in the Midwest and East, sporting riders and new converts to motorcycling generally preferred the imported machines, particularly in the West and Southwest. The H-D dealers as a group mostly withdrew into their own world, and feigned a haughty disregard for the 'limey' interlopers. Their favorite sales ploy was an appeal to tradition, as well as to the fact that they considered the more lightly constructed overseas offering as flimsily built, particularly in their transmission system. Here they had a point, but a point in common with both the domestic and foreign machines was that they leaked lubricating oil. The imports appeared to shed this fluid from both the engine cases and gearbox, while the Yankees leaked from the ohv mechanism, which even 'panhead' modifications did not entirely cure. One motorcycle journalist was said to have viewed the cumulative problem and stated that an American machine was a motorcycle that weighed 700 pounds, had 63 tail lights that worked, and leaked oil. An imported machine, such as a Triumph, was described as weighing 400 pounds, had one tail light that did not work, and leaked oil! And so the battle raged.

Feeling the marketing pinch, and with a now static dealer representation that made H-D a minority in retail outlets, the Company cast about for other ways to counter the competition. A logical point of attack was the United States tariff system. This allowed, under the Marshall Plan, foreign goods, automobiles, and motorcycles included, a favorable rate of 8%, the hard dollars going to purchase farm products and other commodities. On the other hand, many durable goods produced in the United States, cars and motorcycles included, had to contend with tariff barriers that reached as high as 40%, which all but stifled export trade.

As the majority producer of domestic motorcycles, the H-D Company took the stand that they had a legitimate case for a revision of these policies, and accordingly decided to petition the US Tariff Commission to give substantial protection to the American motorcycle manufacturers. Eric von Gumpert, H-D's veteran Traffic Manager cum Export Manager, was said to have prepared the appropriate briefs, with the assistance of the Company's legal counsel, and accordingly on May 15th 1951, the H-D Motor Company formally petitioned the US Tariff Commission for relief against their foreign competition. In their plea, the Company asked for not only a 40% import duty to be levied on all foreign machines, but also that they be allowed entrance on a quota ratio based on their pre-war shipments, which would in actuality have had the effect of keeping out foreign machines altogether!

In the meantime, the foreign dealers and importers had already formed the British Motorcycle Dealers Association, a rather loosely organized body originally formed to combat the generally hostile policies of the AMA against their products.

When the news of the impending hearings on the tariff matter was relayed to the importers by the Select Senate Committee on Tariffs, the British Motorcycle Dealers Association immediately rose to the challenge. Retaining their own legal counsel, they girded themselves for the forthcoming battle led by one Denis McCormack, then the Triumph importer and President of the group.

The hearings lasted for some three weeks during the month of July, with officials of the H-D Company and their counsel, representatives of the BMDA and their counsel, along with a large group of interested dealers and riders as spectators. Both groups brought examples of their machines to the second floor of the Senate Office Building via the elevator, although it was noted that the full dress 'FLH' was squeezed in with some difficulty.

H-D's counsel presented their case, stating the inequality of the tariff laws currently in force and their effect on the Company. One surprise was H-D's admission that they had suffered serious financial reverses during the post war years, both from impaired production through the mandates of the Marshall Plan, and their non-competitive wage position. H-D, of course, was forced to negotiate with the United Auto Workers local in Milwaukee, while foreign competitors paid on a free-floating scale.

The BMDA presented their case at first through the means of comparing their imports with the domestic product, and pointed to their exhibited machines as being of a size and engine capacity that

The 125, initially designated as such, and marketed as the 'Hummer' after 1955 was H-D's first ever two-stroke. Its engine and gearbox was a frank copy of the German DKW.

was not competitive with domestic products, as nothing similar was then being manufactured in the US.

The keynote speech for the importers was not made by counsel, however, but by Alfred Rich Child, longtime H-D representative in the Orient and presently the BSA importer since 1944, with headquarters in New Jersey. Reading from a prepared spech, Child began his remarks with the re-counting of the long established marketing practices of the domestic motorcycle industry. He alluded to the highly restrictive franchise conditions imposed upon retail dealers, initially both by Indian and H-D, and how the latter had carried matters to the point where none of their dealers could handle any products not procured through company courses. He further described how in refusing to allow their dealers to handle other than their own products, they had effectively removed less productive low volume manufacturers from the field. He went on to state that the US manufacturers, H-D in particular, had refused to develop a market for light and middleweight machines, and at the same time had prevented other manufacturers from attempting to serve this market to the detriment of a large potential for machines of broader appeal. He went on to describe the H-D Company as representing an entrenched monopoly that was not only attempting to force on the American market a machine that had but limited popular appeal, but was now attempting to put a segment of American free enterprise out of business by cutting off their source of supply.

Witnesses at the hearing have told the author varying accounts of the proceedings, but all agree that the H-D contingent, headed by President William H.Davidson, sat in stunned silence following Child's testimony. After some minutes, H-D's legal counsel attempted to impeach Child's testimony concerning his reference to the fact that the late William A.Davidson, Vice President in charge of Production, had been born in Scotland. H-D Company publications often stated that all of the four Founders were born in the United States. Child responded that his statements were based on his personal acquaintanceship with the late William A., and he now challenged H-D to produce evidence that William A. had, in fact, been born in Milwaukee.

As the matter was brought up late in the afternoon, the presiding officer called for an adjournment until the next day, and stated that if H-D, through their counsel, wished to pursue this matter, they could do so the next morning. When the hearings resumed the following morning, H-D's counsel did not again allude to the matter, and it was then assumed by those attending the hearings that perhaps in spite of published company 'histories', they could not, or did not, wish to dispute Child's allegations in the matter.

As an aside to the proceedings, several witnesses later told the author that the members of the BMDA were at some pains to restrain the ebullient McCormack from emphasizing the large volume of sales of foreign machines currently being enjoyed by members of that body in fear it might jeopardize their case. After some deliberation, the Senate Committee rejected H-D's case, and in their subsequent written opinion sustained the position of the BMDA in the matter. This was, of course, a bitter pill for the H-D Company to swallow. Not only had the generally monopolistic practices long carried on by both manufacturers been publically exposed, but H-D itself had now to bear the brunt of this long-known but never before publicized aspect of the American motorcycling picture. As matters stood, H-D was now forced to make its own way in the domestic market without any official change in a somewhat disadvantageous position in tariff protection and competition from foreign machines built by low cost labor.

In his reminiscences concerning his role in the affair, Alfred Rich Child told the author in 1979 that while he regretted having to expose to the public the basic tenets of long-established H-D policies, he felt, after some soul searching, that the future of American motorcycling was in serious jeopardy unless a free and unfettered market could be enjoyed by its sales outlets.

American motorcycle sport got underway somewhat haphazardly, as many former competition stars as well as hundreds of thousands of young soldiers were not demobilized until 1946. As previously noted, the rather hastily organized 200 Mile Daytona Classic was won in 1947 by Floyd Emde, on a Sport Scout. H-D took the trophy in 1948, after inducing Emde to leave the Wigwam and enter the contest on a new 'WR'. The 'WR' had become a formidable competitor after Tom Sifton shared his tuning secrets with the factory engineers.

In general, the early post-war period of motorcycle sport can be well described as a time of conflict between the AMA Competition Committee and the riders of foreign machinery as some rather arbitrary rules had been written into the regulations fifteen years before. The long standing edict that ohv machines of 30.50 cubic inch displacement could have no more than a 7.5:1 ratio was at the heart of the controversy, as the popular British machines such as the Ariel Red Hunter, the Triumph Speed Twin, and small numbers of ohc International Nortons had their performance seriously handicapped by this ruling.

In addition, the Competition Committee arbitrarily refused to sanction road racing types of event, such as had long been popular in Europe and England. Some reports had it that the Committee considered road racing on hard surfaces highly dangerous, much more so than the traditional horse track competition. The lack of such courses in the US, and the difficulties in obtaining official support in closing sections of public roads were also cited. Others, mostly competitors favoring foreign machines, were on record as stating that the general design characteristics of the solid framed H-D 45s and Scouts with their minimal rate of front fork travel, were unsuited for use on such circuits and that the AMA did not wish to inaugurate a new competition class for which domestic machines were initially handicapped.

It was during this time that H-D urged both competition riders and dealers sponsoring such contestants, to field as many machines as possible at major racing events. The effect of this was, of course, to 'bury' a budding foreign machine's rider among enough assorted 'DLDR' and 'WR's', making it difficult for them to either win or place. President William H.Davidson had already authorized the assembly of as many new 'WR's' as the Company's meagre material allotments would allow, and dealers and riders were urged to resurrect prewar 'DLDR' models for the use of budding racing enthusiasts. There were also scattered reports of much gamesmanship on the part of allegedly H-D oriented AMA referees in a number of hotly disputed contests where foreign contestants bitterly claimed that wins or places had been unfairly denied them.

In spite of the formidable challenge from overseas, H-D 45s and Sport Scouts continued to do well in competition. The high torque output of the 45 cubic inch side valvers was such that once a rider was able to build up engine revolutions they were more often than not in winning or placing distance. These machines were particularly formidable on the mile or longer courses. The foreign machines were at their best on the shorter quarter or half milers where their nimbleness and ease of control with foot controlled gearbox and hand-operated clutch were telling factors.

Except for the startling British win in 1941, Daytona remained as the American's V twin domain until 1949, when Manx Nortons again entered the fray. Wiry Dick Klamfoth, an eighteen year old farm boy from Groveport, Ohio, placed first, with the 1941 winner, Canada's ace rider Billy Mathews, coming in a close second. For some reason, the AMA Competition Committee had allowed the Manx racers to enter.

It was theorized by some that H-D now had infinite faith in their modified 'WR's', which had made a spectacular showing at the Langhorne, Pennsylvania Classic the year before. Some previous overheating troubles over a long distance were ostensibly cured by fitting larger valves, together with altered port timing. Another surprisingly generous concession was the raising of the traditional 7.5:1 compression ratio for ohv engines to 8:1, this to take place in the 1950 season. On the other hand, the Nortons were forced to fit kick starters, as US contests were still held under the much flouted Class C rules which forbade run-and-bump starting.

For the 1950 Daytona Classic, Norton fielded a team of four, which included Dick Klamfoth, Billy Mathews, Ernie Roccio, and the ex-Indian rider, Bobby Hill. In an all out effort to win, Norton retained the services of the legendary tuner, Francis Beart, who as an independent entrepreneur had already made a name for himself in preparing winning Nortons in England. In addition, Beart had now the assistance of the famous Indian tuner, James Hill, as the Indian Company now distributed a number of British machines through its newly-formed Indian Sales Company.

On the day of the 200 mile main experts event, a huge fleet of H-D's were on hand, together with a smaller contingent of Indian Scouts, six Triumph entrants, which included the indefatigable Ed Kretz, with Jack Horn and Rod Coates. Also included was BSA with an official team of three, headed by Tommy McDermott, who was said to have a very fast machine, together with three additional private entrants on the same make.

When the race was flagged off, Kretz streaked into the lead. At the 20th lap, Kretz was still in front, followed by Klamfoth and Jimmy Phillips on another Triumph. Kretz was sidelined with a slipping clutch, and Mathews then took the lead, with Klamfoth now just behind followed by Bill Tuman on another Norton. Bobby Hill's Norton was unfortunately out of combat, as he had dropped the machine on the north turn and filled his carburetor with sand. Tommy McDermott on his lightning BSA bored through the pack, but was not able to take the lead toward the finish, coming in third behind Billy Mathews who took first, and Klamfoth who was second. Bill Tuman was fourth, with Ernie Roccio seventh, so the contest was clearly a Norton victory.

Klamfoth was again a Norton winner in 1951, coming in first just 20 seconds ahead of teammate Bobby Hill. In 1952, Klamfoth again scored another Norton victory.

No doubt in consequence of these victories, the double knocker style of ohc valve action was now barred from US competition by the AMA, and H-D set about to design a successor to their once formidable 'WR' which was now clearly outclassed. Indian continued its racing representation with its aged Sport Scouts, but without factory help and the nearing demise of the Indian Company, the Redskin's days were numbered.

Interposed between these years of changed US competition activity, H-D people as well as a host

The Model K 45 cu.in. Sportster of 1953. An attempt to combine a traditional side valve engine with modern suspension, it was handicapped by a lack of power.

of other motorcycling enthusiasts were saddened by the untimely death of Arthur Davidson, the last surviving Founder. On the evening of December 30th 1950, Davidson and his wife were returning to their home in suburban Milwaukee. Making a left turn into the driveway, their automobile was struck head-on by a motorist heading in the opposite direction, reportedly traveling at very high speed. The Davidsons were removed from their mangled vehicle and transported to the nearest hospital, but both were dead on arrival.

The career of Arthur Davidson with the H-D Company is almost too well known to bear repeating. Working with William S.Harley, he helped to develop the first prototype machine, and subsequently was almost solely responsible for building H-D's strong dealer organization through the years. A firm believer in advertising, he constantly kept H-D and its activities at the forefront by means of various forms of publicity. Described by contemporaries as the most personable of the Davidson brothers, he nevertheless shared with his late brother, Walter, an almost paranoic antipathy to competitors. With his total dedication to the cause of H-D for all of his adult lifetime, he was no doubt one of the main factors in its survival through the years, and to its successes, even in the very difficult post-World War II years.

As Arthur Davidson's death left the post of Chief Executive of both the AMA and M & ATA vacant, George D.Gilbert of the Baldwin-Duckworth Chain Company of Springfield, Massachusetts, was appointed to fill this position by the joint Board of Directors.

In the meantime, H-D production and sales proceeded apace, though somewhat inhibited by the material restrictions still imposed by the Marshall Plan. With a loyal following of enthusiasts, most of whom would never own another brand of motorcycle, the Company continued to sell all the units it could produce. While foreign machines showed an enviable reception in the Far West and Southwest, they were less popular in the Midwest and East, where the big twin Yank was still the most favored motorcycle. The 125 proved to be a rugged and dependable machine, and sold well to both aspiring young riders and adults entering the game, as well as limited utility users. Before the end of production, the Company was to sell over 100,000 of this model.

In spite of healthy sales on somewhat restricted production, many dealers still complained that the lack of a middleweight model to compete with the imported machines was inhibiting their market penetration. At the same time the Company still imposed their strict policy of allowing dealers to handle only Company supplied products and accessories, this being enforced by the usual eagle-eyed coterie of factory representatives. In the end, some dealers gave up their franchise in favor of foreign products, but there was one notable exception.

Skip Fordyce was a pioneer H-D dealer in Riverside, California, an important motorcycling center since early post-World War I days. As a genial fellow, and the sponsor of a local motorcycle club, he was immensely popular with riders in general, and built up a lucrative business, with the aid of his attractive wife, Ruth, who was also active in Southern California circles of the Motor Maids of America. Noting the growing popularity of middleweight foreign machines, and a legion of sales lost for the lack of an H-D counterpart, Fordyce electrified the nation's H-D community by taking on the franchise for Triumph machines. He was almost at once chastised by both H-D factory representatives and Milwaukee for this heretical defiance of established Company policy. He was also warned that his long-standing and lucrative H-D franchise was now subject to immediate revocation. Fordyce's reply was to reiterate his position in regard to the lack of a suitable middleweight H-D machine in the Southern California market, and informed the Company that he would continue to handle Triumph whether or not the former edict was enforced. While the Company at this point could well have carried out its threat, Fordyce's long popularity and his past impressive H-D sales record prevailed, and H-D's management capitulated, its head bloody, but unbowed.

In commenting on the incident to the author in later years, Fordyce stated that while he was a lifelong H-D enthusiast, he had at long last become disenchanted with the Company's dictatorial policies. With a large establishment to maintain, and faced with the lack of competitive H-D machines in the now popular 500-750 cc class, he saw no other course than to climb on the band-wagon and secure a franchise for a model that was currently much in demand by a broad segment of new enthusiasts.

In his subsequent discussions with H-D's top management, Fordyce stated that he called their attention to the long-standing flouting of the Sherman Anti-Trust and Clayton Acts dealing with the restraint of trade. He further served notice on H-D that he could well successfully institute legal proceedings against them on these grounds should the matter come to the courts.

Following this incident, he recounted that during the course of the matter he received hundreds of long distance telephone calls and letters from long established H-D dealers from all over the country, most of which both encouraged his stand in the matter and offered him their support.

It was now noted that numerous H-D dealers had the temerity to themselves take on franchises for other makes of machines. As a landmark case, the Fordyce episode at long last heralded the end of

H-D's Golden Anniversary Model of 1953. With its 'panhead' engine and solid frame, its direct lineage to the 1936 61E is clearly evident. *(George Hays).*

the Company's death grip on the activities of their dealers. Many of the more bombastic factory representatives, who formerly could enter a dealer's shop and make him quake in his boots, now adopted a less dictatorial and even jovial manner.

While more and more H-D dealers felt free to take on other makes with impunity, Carl's Cycle Service in Minneapolis was not so fortunate. The proprietor at once took on a BSA franchise without factory reprisal. But when he obtained a franchise for the heavy-duty German Zundapp, and equipped a local Shrine drill team which was formerly 100% H-D mounted, with the Teutonic models, the long-suffering H-D Sales Department revoked his franchise!

In the meantime, the factory's Engineering Department was busy developing two new middleweight models, one a racer, the other a roadster. With the devaluation of the British pound, the retail cost of English machines were reduced some 20% and, at the same time, rising material and labor costs at Milwaukee had mandatorily increased the retail price of H-D big twins to over $1,000, a figure some experts solemnly pronounced was more than any enthusiast would pay for any motorcycle.

The new racing machine which was to replace the now outclassed 'WR' was designated as the 'KR'. Taking a lesson from the obvious British successes with their close-ratio, foot-operated, four-speed gearbox and hand clutch, and their rear springing which aided in keeping the rear wheel more in contact with the ground, the new model featured these improvements. However, and what was regarded as a retrograde step by many, the engine itself followed the long hoary traditions of American competition by being a side valve V twin.

While the early 'KR' models did not develop as much power as the 1941-based 'WR', their performance was enhanced by both the new four-speed gearbox and foreign type control system. The engine itself, subjected to critical scrutiny by the now less sychophantic trade press, was described as a 20th century anachronism. With its spread-out combustion chamber necessitated by its side valve configuration, it developed about 56 hp, but it benefitted from a wide open breathing system and the ability to turn out excessive torque at moderate engine revolutions from a mere 6.5:1 compression ratio. Aside from its archaic engine design, the engine and four-speed gearbox were enclosed in a common case in the modern mode, with the disadvantage that the whole required dismantling to repair the latter. The clutch, an H-D innovation after many decades, was the oil-immersed type.

Teething troubles immediately appeared, and early clutch failure accompanied by over-oiling was partially cured by providing a pressure relief system that allowed removal of excess lubricant. Initial competition use showed that the 'KR' neither handled as well or developed as much power as the former 'WR', and much midnight oil was burned in order to stabilize the telescopic fork and swinging arm frame that was in itself a marked innovation in H-D competition machinery.

In order to give the rider the option of varying suspension to suit various types of competition, the spring frame could be replaced with solid units for certain short track events, where the latter proved to be more practical. This option persisted until the mid-1960's when Dick Mann, a brilliant dirt track exponent, demonstrated that his variations of the swinging arm could result in enhanced performance.

The roadster version of the 'K' model proved to be a mid-twentieth century anachronism. Fitted with a mild touring version of the 'KR' engine/gearbox unit, the new model featured a soft acting telescopic front fork and swinging arm rear suspension. In an attempt to provide the best of both worlds, the modern chassis was mated with the identical side valve engine of the 1920 era. The whole concept, it seems, was to hark back to tradition with the engine, yet give a concession to modernization with a softly sprung ride.

While the new model elicited some hope from the assembled dealers at a factory sales meeting where it was unveiled, the ultimate result was disappointing. In its standard tune, the engine developed insufficient power to provide either enough urge for double riding, now the necessary hallmark of a clubman's machine, nor could it satisfactorily haul a sidecar, and no mounting lugs for such fitting were provided. While some impressive road test results were published by the factory, they proved to be inconclusive during actual conditions of use.

The author was provided with a demonstration machine by the late Joseph Walker, pioneer H-D dealer in Santa Ana, California, for his own evaluation. While possessed of adequate acceleration through the gears, the top speed was a disappointing 81 mph, this with the rider well crouched over the fuel tank. At anything over 60 mph, there was simply no acceleration or hill climbing ability left worth noting. In 1955, after disappointing sales, the engine was bored out to 55 cubic inches in an effort to obtain more power. While acceleration through the lower speed ranges was improved, as was the hill climbing ability, the overall results were not up to expectations. The model eventually was superseded by the 55 cubic inch sportster, of which more later. In the overall sense, the early side valve 'K' models may well be described as the last attempt of America's sole surviving manufacturer to offer a traditional motorcycle in the 45 cubic inch category.

      With the offering of the 'K' type, the venerable 45 inch 'D' model was at last laid to rest. Even in its final years, it was still fitted with the traditional leading link girder forks, and its ultimate role appears to have been the basis for the long running three-wheeled Servi-car model, an established favorite for law enforcement parking control in suburban areas and in limited commercial work.

In 1952, a marked concession to modernity was offered in the big twin models with the offering of an optional foot gear shift and hand clutch control as an alternative to the previous traditional system. The latter was effected by the fitting of a spring loaded servi-mechanism that gave positive clutch control with little pressure from the handlebar lever. The traditional system was generally favored for law enforcement use, as it enabled the officers to continue the use of hand signals when engaged in traffic control.

The classic side valve 74 cubic inch model was at long last terminated in 1952. Not seen in the catalogs since 1948, it had been available on special order. Most of the latter models of the series were in use by police units in Mexico and South America where its sterling attributes of both reliability and ease of maintenance were especially appreciated where skilled mechanical services were at a minimum.

In 1952, the hydraulic valve tappet arrangement in the big twins was altered to place the units at the bottom of the push rods rather than at the top, a change that many practical H-D mechanics considered long overdue. This reduced the chronic oil leaks around the rocker boxes to some degree, but enabled the valves to retain their adjustment for a longer period, as well as reducing tappet noise. Further modifications to the cam action and port profiles resulted in a 10% increase in engine power. While this was welcomed by riders in general, most particularly those who favored sidecar units or long distance solo touring, the added surge caused further problems with inherent V-twin vibration characteristics.

For some years the author enjoyed the ownership of a low compression 1950 'FL' model. As a sturdy and dependable machine, it afforded many thousands of miles of pleasant trouble-free travel. Its engine, however, showed an annoying vibration period at speeds between 55 and 60 mph, which represented a very useful rate of travel. A long time H-D enthusiast suggested that an accessory item was available in the form of a short steel forging that could be bolted just ahead of the engine mounts through the twin sidecar stay lugs that were brazed to lower angles of the twin down tubes. A letter of inquiry to the factory, outlining the author's problem, and requesting information on the fitting in question was, in time, answered. On the letterhead of the Engineering Department, the letter stated that H-D machines were not fitted with engines that were subject to vibration, and that therefore the Company did not see fit to include such an accessory in their line of optional merchandise. In the meantime, an old time H-D mechanic and friend of the author, Maury Biggs, procured the fitting in question from some obscure trade supplier, and its installation did much to improve the machine's running characteristics.

During the 1952-1953 sales season, and in celebration of the Company's 50th anniversary, H-D's advertising emphasized its role in the development of 'V-Power', comparing the now classic ohv twin design with the new contemporary fitting of ohv V-8 engines in the current offerings of Ford, General Motors, and Chrysler automobile manufacturers.

In spite of the ever growing threat of foreign competition in the various AMA sporting events now being promoted in enhanced numbers in every part of the country, H-D was able to make an impressive showing during the 1950's and early 1960's. In the initial days of this era, machines tuned by the inimitable Tom Sifton played a decisive role, beginning with Larry Hedrick's sensational 1950 season on his reworked 'WR'. Sifton correctly reasoned that the low weight of the machine could be a telling factor. His judgement was vindicated with the 126 pound Hedrick's many victories on a specially lightened machine on the mile tracks. Following Hedrick's enforced retirement from racing due to injuries sustained in an automobile accident, Sifton's creations next figured prominently in the scintillating career of Joe Leonard, culminating in his Daytona victory in 1958.

In 1954, the AMA Competition Committee instituted a new point system in tabulating the results of individual wins in order to determine the outcome of the National Championship standings. Up to this time, National Championship status was decided by the results of the races held at the famous mile track at Springfield, Illinois, a 'sudden death' type of affair where the winner was crowned National Champion regardless of previous victories. The new system was based on the individual rider's attainment of points earned through his standing in the various Nationals entered during the current season.

The 'K' model racing machine, introduced in 1952, experienced numerous teething troubles, as well as developing noticeably less power than the latest 'WR's' it was designed to replace. This disadvantage was somewhat overshadowed by the fact that, with its option of a sprung rear frame and four-speed gearbox with foot-operated change and hand operated clutch, its rear wheel spent more time in contact with the ground, and the rider could save valuable seconds in its overall control. As usual, Tom Sifton was largely responsible for its later improved performance, but veteran mechanics criticized the complication of the construction of its unit engine case and gearbox castings that

Some of the members of a Mystic Shrine Motorcycle drill team. Many such organizations standardized on H-D FL and FLH machines.

necessitated a complete dismantling of both to make minor adjustments. It was on a Sifton-tuned machine that Joe Leonard of San Jose, California, won the National Championship in 1954. This victory was somewhat tempered by the fact that BSA took all first five places at Daytona.

The administration of the AMA was changed in 1954, when Carl Swenson, President of the Milsco Manufacturing Company of Milwaukee, replaced George D.Gilbert. At the same time, the veteran Secretary-Manager E.C.Smith, retired and was succeeded by Lin Kuchler, who promised a more aggressive role in the management of AMA affairs. He proposed that a firmer policy be instituted regarding the public relations role in the AMA vis a vis media exposure of sanctioned racing events, to give a more prominent role to advertising motorcycle sport. He was actively supported in this by William (Bill) Tuthill, a pioneer motorist and motorcyclist, who was the proprietor of a museum of racing vehicles in Daytona Beach, Florida. Tuthill voiced the opinion of many that the AMA up to this point had not expended enough effort in the public relations sphere in an attempt to gain recognition for motorcycle sport and to put it more prominently in the public eye. Kuchler immediately sought an enhanced budget appropriation from the AMA's Board of Directors for such a program. After a somewhat prolonged discussion, it was later reported that this conservatively-orientated body declined to advance from its historic isolationist position regarding publicizing motorcycle affairs. After numerous futile attempts to change this rather stagnant policy, Kuchler resigned in 1966.

In the Spring of 1954, the so-called 'outlaw' element in motorcycling at long last found its identity in a motion picture released that spring. Entitled 'The Wild One', featuring Marlon Brando, Mary Murphy, Lee Marvin, and Brian Keith, its plot was loosely based on the events at Hollister, as well as somewhat superficially touching upon the iconoclastic self-indulgent philosophy of the 'rebel' motorcyclist. The production was roundly condemned by numbers of the AMA affiliated clubs, some of whom picketed theaters where the film was exhibited. While by this time most of the outlaw riders were centering their interest on heavyweight American V twins, mostly H-D's, the director of the picture charitably mounted some of his actors (some of whom were actually members of bona fide outlaw groups) on a mixed bag of American and English machines. Brando, the anti-hero, rode a pristine Triumph Speed Twin. Much of the antipathy felt by traditional motorcyclists against the outlaws was based on the fact (aside from some of their alleged antisocial actions) that they cut down many of the fine old classic 61E and UL and ULH models that were growing in value each year as long as they remained in original condition.

In spite of losing the Daytona classic when the one time Indian star, Bobby Hill, won on a BSA, Joe Leonard was able to amass enough points in a series of other events to bring a National Championship to the Milwaukee brand.

In 1957, the ill-fated side valve 55 cubic inch 'KH' model was dropped in favor of a new ohv machine that was catalogued as the 'XL' Sportster. This was, in effect, the same machine, with an ohv version of the 'K', still displacing 55 cubic inches. Critics at once noted that the engine should have been enlarged to the classic 61 cubic inch dimensions as of yore. However, with limited space within the frame, a longer stroked engine would have to be taller to conform to these specifications, and would have necessitated the expense of tooling up for an entirely new model. The new machine was offered in two versions, one a touring type which was in effect a scaled down 'FLH', and a sports type machine that offered magneto ignition. This last was widely heralded as the answer to the need for a middleweight sporting machine. While a weight of about 460 pounds ready for the road made this supposition more or less of a reality, its appeal was somewhat limited by the fact that early examples exhibited high speed steering problems. Starting was also made difficult by the fact that the Edison magneto for some inexplicable reason was not fitted with an impulse coupling. At any rate, the naturally higher performance capabilities of the 'XL' were welcomed enthusiastically by sporting riders, and a new era of H-D model influence was brought into being.

The following year, the venerable 'FL' and 'FLH' models were fitted with rear springing by means of a pair of hydraulically dampened coil springs that supported a pair of swinging arms that had their pivot just behind the seat post. The new model was catalogued as the Duo-glide. Critics at once noted that the forward slanted position of the spring units at once hampered their efficiency. It was also admitted that their more efficient vertical fitting would seriously interfere with the placement of the now traditional saddle bags and/or police radio equipment that had long been carried in paniers on either side of the rear wheel. Had the shock units been placed in the vertical position, this would have created an overwide lateral silhouette. In truth, most big twin enthusiasts had already long been in agreement that with the large section tires, combined with the highly efficient spring seat post, rear springing was not really necessary. On the other hand, it was noted that luggage racks, luggage attachments, carriers and radio equipment fitted to the law enforcement 'FL' models were prone to fracturing after high mileage use. This was attributed to both rear wheel hammer combined with the characteristic vibration syndrome of the V twin engine configuration. The new model was now carried on as the Duo-Glide, and at a weight penalty of some 80 pounds the classic H-D big twin was fitted with rear springing as standard.

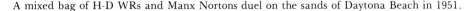

A mixed bag of H-D WRs and Manx Nortons duel on the sands of Daytona Beach in 1951.

This general period in time saw an amazing proliferation of motorcycling literature. Numerous articles in the popular motorcycle press saw capsulated histories of various makes, along with other efforts describing historic or especially thrilling race meets and competition events of the past. J.L.Beardsley, a one-time motorcycling reporter of an earlier day, recounted significant sports events, many of them dealing with the Golden Age of dirt and board track racing.

The late Floyd Clymer, who deserted retail motorcycle sales for the publishing business, issued a large number of reprints of early day motorcycle literature in the form of catalogue reprints as well as books on various aspects of the sport. Much of this informative material was abruptly cut off when it was ascertained that he was publishing reprints of foreign works without benefit of royalty payments to the copyright owners. Among these were the classic works of the Nicholson Brothers, of Saskatoon, Canada, on the subject of motorcycle mechanics and speed tuning, and certain other publications from the Temple Press and Iliffe concerns in Great Britain. A large shipment of these works was impounded at the dock just before transshipment to the States through legal action instituted by the companies concerned.

In the late 1950's, motorcycle drag racing became popular, and had its inception in the Southern California area. Long popular in England, where it was known as sprint racing, the contest was actually an acceleration trial where the winner's time, for the short straightaway course, was tabulated at the end of the run in both elapsed time and mph attained at the finish line. Competition was somewhat loosely categorized into classes based on engine displacement, the most spectacular being the larger or unlimited class which included much modified big twin H-D types. With overboring of the cylinders and much stroking, some of these now exceeded 100 cubic inches and put up fantastic times when fueled with blended spirits.

The first H-D dragster of note was built up by Mike Tucker, featuring a more or less standard 'FLH' that was merely stripped and the engine subjected to special tuning. More radical conversions were built by Joe Smith. Other noted special builders were Ken Tipton and Bob George. Tipton is today the proprietor of an extensive shop dealing in speed equipment, and George gained much notoriety with his double engined H-D special which was known as 'The Beast'. Most of the early day motorcycle drag competition centered around a course situation on an old disused airfield at Pomona, where car contests had been held since about 1950.

The design of these dragster machines had profound effect on the early 'outlaw' type of big twin, which was originally merely a stripped standard model with the front mudguard, windshield, crash bars, luggage equipment, and other detail accessories removed, together with the inevitably bobbed rear mudguard.

With the growing scarcity of big twin models, coupled with the fact that the standard 'FL's' and 'FLH's' now had rear springing fitted as standard, small accessory shops offered their own type of specially-made solid frames as substitutes. Many custom designers considered the sprung frame as a spurious luxury, and were probably correct, considering that its added weight reduced overall performance. At the same time, special, small capacity, lightweight fuel and oil tanks and 'banana' type saddles were being manufactured by small specialist firms to fit such frames. The old 'California Bobber' had become the 'California Chopper', inferring that in the lightening process the machine had been 'chopped', and a new era of motorcycling, based on the pre-war 'outlaw' theme was now at hand.

As far as the so called 'outlaws' themselves went, groups of such riders as were organization minded, gathered into formal groups such as the Hell's Angels, and the later Hessians, Satans, Mongols, etc.. These clubs became legally incorporated groups, and stood ready to institute legal action against newspaper reporters, journalists, freelance authors, and publications that aired their doings should they venture to criticize their activities in print.

Many individual riders, however, who favored individually-styled machines, did not elect to join such clubs, but at the same moment favored the life style and leather-dominated dress of the so called 'outlaw' and later joined the collective designation as 'bikers'.

By this time, the biker machine of choice was now almost universally some older model of big twin H-D modified to the owner's liking. A few old Indian Chiefs were 'chopped', together with a few British machines, notably the Triumph Thunderbird. But by 1960, the H-D was the machine of choice for such conversion.

Up to this point in time, both the H-D Company and its dealers continued to ignore the chopper movement. In most cases, H-D still refused to service or overhaul such machines.

In the meantime, the retail outlets continued to expand as growing numbers of enthusiasts secured franchises for foreign machines. If an aspiring dealer had access to sufficient capital, such were relatively easy to acquire. In addition, the importers in most cases were adverse to their franchise holders handling other makes, in contrast with the long established domestic tradition. Not a few of the still numerous Indian dealers acquired franchises for BSA and Triumph after Indian finally phased out production.

As the result, H-D representation dwindled. While the implications of the Fordyce insurrection had by this time stripped the factory of much of its power over the dealers, the majority as dyed-in-the-wool enthusiasts still sold H-D's exclusively. Although Milwaukee still held a strong position in the touring and traditional AMA club organization areas as well as in law enforcement, its monopoly in the latter field was soon to be challenged by BMW.

Almost unnoticed in the November 1959 issue of Floyd Clymer's *CYCLE* magazine, was an advertisement announcing the introduction of the Honda. Proclaimed as an innovation from Japan, it was a small moped-like machine with a 50cc ohc engine that featured, of all things, electric starting. Its challenge to the market was — 'You meet the nicest people on a Honda'.

A group of AMA club riders, with passengers and luggage, move along a desert highway. The FLs and FLHs were the standard US touring machine up until the late 1960s.

In the summer of 1960, H-D's top management entered into negotiations with the Aermacchi concern of Varese, Italy, in regard to the possibility of a merger between the two companies for their mutual benefit. Aermacchi was currently in financial difficulty in competing in the highly competitive motorcycle market in India. H-D was, of course, losing out on a potentially vast segment of the American market from their previously adamant refusal to introduce any middleweight models. The upshot of the matter was that H-D purchased a 50% interest in Aermacchi. This strengthened the latter through an infusion of fresh capital, and at the same time enabled H-D to offer the American buyer a competitively priced middleweight machine that was produced by relatively low cost labor. At the same time, and to strengthen the marketing position of both, an international trading corporation, Aermacchi-Harley-Davidson S.A. was set up in Zug, Switzerland.

The present Aermacchi organization had its origin from a parent company, Aeronautica Macchi S.p.A., of Milan. This had been in existence since its founding in 1912 as S.A. Nieuport Macchi for the manufacture of aircraft. Several interesting and practical designs were produced in limited numbers before WW I. The factory was enlarged in the early 1930's to produce fighter aircraft for Mussolini's air force. Also produced during the between-the-wars era were some highly advanced single seated seaplane types that gave a good account of themselves in the Schneider Cup races.

The factory was destroyed during WW II by bombing. Following its end, the company then established modest facilities in Varese, with plans to produce ground vehicles only. A few light cars were manufactured in 1946, but after experiencing difficulties in material procurement, the management decided to concentrate on two wheelers. Their first effort was a 125 cc scooter-like machine. In 1956, a four-stroke model called the Chimera was added to the line, with the option of either a 175 or 250 cc engine that had the cylinder positioned horizontally. Aermacchi's Chief Engineer, Alfredo Bianchi, was determined to produce good handling machines in the best Italian tradition,

A Club member 'rides the plank' with his FLH 'Dresser' at an AMA Club field meet. *(George Hays)*.

and to attain a low center of gravity he frankly copied the long popular Moto Guzzi Falcone and Astore models. The 250 cc machine was also produced as a sport model, and with high lift cams and specially tuned with an 8.5:1 compression ratio could easily top 80 mph. First produced in 1957, it enjoyed rewarding popularity with Italian riders, the model being then known as the Ala Verde. In 1960, its name was appropriately changed to the 'Wisconsin' after H-D entered the picture, and when imported to the States early in 1961 was marketed as the 'Sprint'. In this guise it was fitted with a smaller 2½ gallon fuel tank and sports-type mudguards to conform to the contemporary 'street scrambler' type then popular with US riders.

What with the infusion of fresh capital and enhanced production now scheduled for the US market, Aermacchi next inaugurated an accelerated competition program in Europe which did much to enhance its prestige and resulted in increased sales. During 1962 a limited number of racing 250's were built which made a very good showing in the Belgian and Ulster classics. Aermacchis finished well in the German Grand Prix as well as in other contests in France, Spain, and Finland. Aermacchi next fitted a 350 cc engine with a five-speed gearbox, and on a highly tuned model Renzo Pasolini was able to place third in the FIM 350 cc World Championship in 1966. The noted Kel Carruthers made a good showing on the Isle of Man in 1969, his machine being only 1.4 seconds slower through the Highlander speed trap than the fastest Yamaha 350.

After these successes, Aermacchi next developed an ohc racing special, but H-D's management refused to sanction a continuation of this project due to the ever-mounting expense of fielding a large team of racers. Some factory people have since commented that H-D was already committed to a heavy competition program in the States, and felt that victories at home on Milwaukee-built machines had better advertising value. Aermacchi's top management was equally adamant concerning the importance of maintaining the marque's prestige in Europe, as their racing successes had increased sales. But as Milwaukee held the purse strings, Aermacchi was forced to field a limited number of modified super sports machines that cost less to build and maintain. It then appeared that these machines were entered in various international events to prove their mettle to the public rather than seeking outright wins, the latter course involving vast expense.

In spite of the general good quality and performance of the Sprint, it did not fare too well on the American market. The 250 cc class had never elicited much interest in a country with a traditional pre-occupation with large capacity machines. Then too, the dealer-enthusiasts were largely big twin orientated, and many did not take kindly to either a small capacity machine, especially if it was not made in Milwaukee. What with small volume sales, most dealers stocked only a minimum of spare parts, and some buyers were put off the road for long periods while some essential component was on back order.

As a possible competitor for the ever growing numbers of small Japanese machines that were attracting new riders, H-D introduced a 50 cc model built by Aermacchi, known as the Leggero, in 1965. A well-finished lightweight with good performance for its size in the best Italian tradition, it was somewhat handicapped by the traditionally hard Italian seat. Its low speed handling was somewhat impaired by fitting a wide ratio three-speed gearbox in place of the more usual ratio four-speed type offered by the competition. An improved model bored out to 65 cc was offered two years later, but sales were disappointing as the dealers generally did not promote the machine locally, in spite of much factory advertising.

The deservedly popular Milwaukee-built 125 which had subsequently been marketed as the 'Hummer' had been updated in 1953 by fitting a soft acting hydraulic fork and enhanced performance was achieved by boring out the engine to 165 cc. Known as the 'Ranger', it was phased out in 1962 in favor of a new 175 cc two-stroke model that powered the 'Pacer', 'Scat', and 'Bobcat' models developed to cover the now popular market for street scrambler and utility type machines. The former 165 cc model was relegated to powering an off-the-road trail type machine without lighting that was designated the 'Super 10'.

While they were soundly built and rugged machines in the best H-D tradition, these models did not fare too well, as by this time the pre-war DKW design had been decisively outclassed by the latterly developed ohc and two-stroke machines from Japan, which now showed fantastic performance in models of like displacement.

The Company entered the scooter market in 1960 with the 'Topper' model, powered with the well proved 165 cc engine that was fitted with a centrifugal clutch. A ruggedly built machine that was easy for a novice rider to control, it was overly heavy for its power. Sales resistance was encountered when it was ascertained that its engine capacity and power development was insufficient for it to legally negotiate the now ever expanding network of high speed freeways. Selling as it did for $600.00, it suffered in comparison with cheaper oriental motorcycles with higher performance. It was ultimately discontinued in 1964.

The 250 cc Sprint enjoyed some mild popularity as a competition machine, as the AMA Competition Committee, at H-D's request, created a special Novice classification for this capacity. As the 250 class had never been taken seriously by Yankee fans, most of the riders went on to large machines when they attained Amateur and Expert status.

H-D racked up an impressive number of competition wins and top placings during the decades of the 50's and 60's, in spite of serious challenges from BSA and Triumph, the principal opponents. The contemporary trade press, its numbers continually augmented by new publications, featured detailed reports of the dozens of AMA-sanctioned events held each season. Even a condensed digest of these usually spectacular events would fill a large volume.

An exhaustive study of the competition scene of this era reveals that H-D's consistent success was based on a composite of a number of factors. By backing a large number of entrants, in most cases the field could be literally blanketed — which could make it more difficult for foreign machines with usually lesser representation to work their way through the pack to a place or win. The long standing AMA competition rules traditionally favoring the Yank machines in the classic horse track courses, was another telling factor. Added to this was the fact that most of the top AMA officials were past middle aged veterans with long years of service in their tenured positions, and by tradition owed first allegiance to that long H-D dominated body. In addition, the accrued point system established by the AMA in 1954 naturally favored the make that could consistently field large groups of entrants in a majority of the sanctioned contests. Points could be thus accumulated by sheer weight of numbers. On the ever critical financial side, H-D seemed consistently willing to pay the expenses and bonuses to a growing number of established stars as well as budding amateurs. While racing could well be charged off to advertising, it involved the expenditure of a great deal of money. Some Company insiders later averred that the resultant depletion of H-D's cash reserves had a significant bearing on later events. Even so, H-D was able to attract both the loyalty and enthusiasm of a number of talented riders during this period, such as Brad Andres, Mark Brelsford, Walt Fulton, Dan Haaby, Mert Lawwill, Joe Leonard, Bart Markel, Fred Nix, Cal Rayborn, and the great Carroll Reseweber.

In 1954, the first year of the AMA point accrual system, H-D's Joe Leonard won the National Championship, with other Milwaukee riders placing behind him. Brad Andres was top man in 1955, with Leonard coming back to head the field in 1956 and 1957. From 1959 through 1961, the great Carroll Reseweber swept the board, and proved to be one of the greatest American riders of all time. A quiet, taciturn individual of unpretentious demeanor, Reseweber's special gift appeared to be not only his uncanny ability to fathom, but to predict ahead of time and execute the tactical maneuvers of competition riding with such finesse as to be almost unbeatable. Knowledgeable observers were quick to note his centaur-like oneness with his machine, as he swept through almost impassable crowds of riders with an agility that left crowds speechless. His best year was 1961, when he won nearly every contest entered. Added to this were the efforts of H-D's Competition Manager, Richard (Dick) O'Brien, who capably oversaw the vast logistical problems of fielding large numbers of riders.

Reseweber's luck and H-D's fabulous era ran out during the fall of 1962. At a practice period for an end-of-season race at Lincoln, Illinois, a very dusty improperly prepared track saw a pile up of riders that ran into an impenetrable cloud of powdered dirt. The debacle saw one rider killed, several seriously injured, and Reseweber, for a time at death's door, sent into a crippling retirement.

Chapter 9

A Time of Change

THE MOOD OF THE COUNTRY HAD CHANGED MARKEDLY SINCE THE END OF THE immediate post-war era. The thinking had been that with the war's end, conditions would revert to pre-war social and economic stability, now that the depression was safely passed. But such was not to be the case. The Korean episode was a stark reminder that the Cold War was indeed a reality. While the war had ostensibly been won, it was clear that peace had yet to be attained. What with the general disillusionment, the thinking trend was the preservation of the individual, and old values were abruptly challenged. Personal rebellion was the order of the day. In the search for individual truth, the Haight-Ashbury philosophy of doing ones own 'thing' emerged. With less emphasis on things orthodox, motor-cycling as an often iconoclastic release grew in popularity.

By 1960 the motorcycle market had more or less stabilized, with Milwaukee adherents on one hand, and the devotees of British and continental machines on the other. The import dealers maintained a more or less informal coffee clatch club atmosphere, and low pressure selling was the rule where the average customer could be relied on to trade for a new model every other year or so. Harley-Davidson's dealership stood at an estimated 800 outlets, down from the 1,100 odd that serviced the industry when the country lived with but two makes. Assuming a certain hauteur, both the dealers and their customers in most cases withdrew into the other two-wheeled world where Milwaukee was god and H-D was its prophet. Even at this late date, H-D could still count on many middle aged enthusiasts whose experience dated back to the 'J' model days, as well as aging veterans of the belt drive days who would never heretically consider any but the Milwaukee brand. It was almost a cult-like atmosphere, but it was two-pronged. The 'dresser' clubman or Eastern and Midwest clubman were on the one side, and the 'chopper' enthusiast (the term now dignified by the appelation of 'custom') on the other. These were not necessarily outlaw by persuasion, but by those who aped the trend by affecting a cut-down machine, most usually an H-D big twin that sported bobbed mudguards, and without windshield, crash bars, saddle bags, or any other weighty appurtenances. There the matter stood, momentarily uncomplicated by the soon-to-appear invasion from the Orient.

The majority of the custom affectionados were not outlaws in the usual sense, or preoccupied by their unsavory depredations, but rather free thinking Bohemians clothed in leather and iron, who reveled in individualistic freedom and gloried in the macho image.

In spite of this growing trend, modified machines were still unwelcome in most franchised dealerships. Instead, their needs were met by the budding members of back alley mechanics for repair

In 1960, the 125cc 'Hummer' was
updated into the 165cc 'Super
Ten'.

or overhaul and the burgeoning custom accessory manufacturers who could by this time supply nearly everything needed to build up a modified H-D. The only factory items were engines and gearboxes — more often than not war surplus WLA units that were still available. In other cases the custom machines were built up from aged 61, 74 and 80 cubic inch units salvaged from some worn out or junked standard model. As a paradox, H-D cultivated and encouraged the loyalty of the one cult and ignored, if not discouraged, the preoccupation of the other.

As an aside, a minor but significant market in old model spare parts came into being, this for the benefit of over age or antique H-D's. In contrast to Indian, whose traditional policy had always been 'keep 'em on the road' — H-D's sales policy had always been to promote the new models at the expense of maintaining an older example. For this reason, the continued manufacture of current spare parts generally ceased with the termination of any particular model. With this knowledge in mind, many dealers and enthusiasts stock piled essential spares. This was especially true when the 'J' models were phased out in 1929. What with the initial disenchantment with the new 'VL', most of the existing stocks of 'J' parts at the factory were quickly sold to dealers. In addition, and in later years, small specialized firms and individuals began fabricating such hard-to-get items as primary and secondary chain cases, tool boxes, and other sheet metal items.

In the meantime, new converts to motorcycling were being attracted to the advanced designs of the 50 cc and 90 cc moped type machines soon traded up to larger displacement models. Honda was soon joined by Suzuki and Yamaha, who offered a line of small but high performance two-stroke models. This market was further expanded by the entrance of Bridgestone and Kawasaki. Honda next cannily capitalized on the growing interest in larger machines with the introduction of the high performance 250 cc Hawk, together with the 305 cc Dream model that was offered for the benefit of the tourist. Sales were enhanced not only by the high quality of these machines, but with their adoption of electric starting — a heretofore unheard of luxury in two wheelers. Another bonus was their general propensity to be oil tight, a condition generally not experienced with traditional American and British machines. A further telling factor was the reasonable price of the Japanese imports due to their low labor costs which augmented their ability to attain high volume production.

William J.Harley, Walter C.Davidson, and William H.Davidson inspect the first shipment of cycles from Aermacchi Harley-Davidson. The motorcycles are 1961 Sprints.

It was during this period that the use of plastics material in industry to replace certain metal fabrications of higher production cost came into being. In line with this trend, H-D acquired 60% of the stock of the Tomahawk Boat Company, who were presently producing moulded plastics pleasure boats. Boat production continued, along with an augmented line of plastics bodies for the Servi-car, windshields, saddle bags, and other parts. Boat manufacture was carried on until 1965.

In addition, H-D expanded its activities in the manufacture of golf carts, both gasoline and electric powered. The former were fitted with the Dyna-start mechanism. A short time later a line of industrial carriers and in-plant trucks were added to the line. The bodies for these were moulded in plastics, being fabricated in the Tomahawk plant.

Three-wheeled golf carts and utility trucks, manufactured in the Tomahawk Plant. Most models offered the option of either gasoline or electric power.

In the Spring of 1962, a new trade publication called *Cycle World* was launched by Joe Parkhurst, who was both its Publisher and Editor. Parkhurst's endeavor was orientated toward the offering of a more sophisticated journal than had heretofore been seen in the field. Featured were in-depth articles with technical aspects of motorcycle engineering. Also emphasized were searching evaluations of new models as they appeared, along with comprehensive road tests by members of the staff, who were experienced riders. Parkhurst's efforts were generally well received by both the trade and consumers, as his efforts were directed toward the interests of the latter.

An early road test featured the latest H-D 'FLH' model. While noting its generally high quality of manufacture, the tester commented on a number of minor faults, such as a certain heaviness in the gear shift mechanism, heavy steering at low speed, and its now inadequate braking capabilities.

An evaluation of the Sportster resulted in the report that its steering capabilities were somewhat vague when put into a tight turn. Other observations concerned hard starting and critical engine vibration at certain speeds.

In addition, Parkhurst commented editorially on the evergreen question of AMA policies. Taking a strong stand on its undemocratic structure and its long domination by Milwaukee, he called for at least better liaison between its trade management and the ordinary rider. He also commented on the often arbitrary stand taken by the Competition Committee in regard to their control of contestants.

Such frank revelations could scarcely endear Parkhurst to H-D's top management, and it was later alleged that the thinking in Milwaukee was that *Cycle World* was anti H-D. There were several subsequent icy confrontations between representatives of the two organizations when by chance they encountered each other at various trade shows. Parkhurst ultimately offered Milwaukee an olive branch in the Summer of 1964. In an editorial appearing in the July issue, he stated that the magazine and its management were definitely not anti-H-D, nor had it any axe to grind in regard to any make of machine. He restated the magazine's objective policy in regard to quality of product that the industry was producing, and that his main thrust was in promoting the best interests of both the sport and the industry.

Reportedly somewhat mollified, H-D continued to purchase limited advertising space in *Cycle World,* and ill will between the two subsided until a few years later when further controversies relating to AMA policies were aired in the magazine.

H-D volume of sales, as noted in Standard and Poor's Corporation Index reports, rose from $16,390,000 in 1958 to $30,560,000 in 1965. This was not a real increase however, when the ever-rising inflationary factor was taken into consideration, and profits during this period did not increase. As it was now estimated that H-D was currently enjoying but 6% of the retail market, its overall position was precarious at best. It was now painfully apparent that the Company had to review its marketing position, and in any case, required an infusion of new capital. It was accordingly decided that the Company now go public, and for the first time in its history its stock was offered for general sale. The exact details of what next transpired are somewhat clouded. While data regarding the matter was released to Standard & Poor, other individuals have rendered conflicting accounts of the matter.

William G.Davidson in 1969. He shortly afterwards abandoned the formal role as a Corporate Executive and took to the highways of America to personally contact motorcyclists of all persuasions.

According to the former, there were ultimately 1,780 shareholders. On the other hand, and in a rare interview granted to motorcycle journalist Tony Hogg by President William Davidson, the latter stated that there were but 300 shareholders. It is definitely known, however, that of the 53% of the voting shares outstanding, over fifty members of the Harley and Davidson family held this majority. These consisted of not only the direct heirs of the Founders, but also cousins and relatives by marriage, as well as the shareholding estates of deceased members.

A subsequent report of the matter from Standard & Poor, the originally offered 300,000 $20.00 par shares were converted to $5.00 par shares, raising the total to 1,200,000 shares. A group of Wall Street brokers headed by Robert W.Baird & Company, next offered 101,898 shares, 75,000 of which were new financing, priced at $14.75 per share on May 27 1965. The following year a new offering was placed on the market by the Baird group that consisted of 101,543 shares of which 85,000 were new financing, at $18.00 per share, the offering being advertised in the Wall Street Journal on April 4 1966.

In 1965, the 'FL' and 'FLH' Duo Glide models were fitted with electric starting, a somewhat belated gesture in competition with most of the Japanese models which had in some cases been so fitted since 1960. Many veteran enthusiasts at once decried this move as unnecessary, as what with refined field coil ignition systems, starting up the big twins had never been difficult if the correct drill was followed. A starting system from an outside supplier who also had recently developed a similar type for large outboard marine engines was adapted, the whole electrical system being converted to twelve volts. An embarrassing sequel to the introduction of this new model, now cataloged as the Electra Glide, was the fact that the starting system was susceptible to shorting out in wet weather. A new system hurriedly developed in conjunction with the Homelight Corporation resulted in a dependable unit. What with an added 75 pound weight penalty, the already heavy machine's braking capabilities were impaired, as the contact areas had not been increased in some years. To cope with this and the weight of the rear springing, the hp of the engine was increased from 52 to 65. Some riders claimed that the increase in power through modified cam action and increased compression ratios resulted in more severe vibration at certain speeds. Another problem was that the increase in power put undue stress on the main bearings, and it was reported that this traditionally trouble-free item of H-D design was now in some cases prone to failure. The problem was later remedied with the fitting of a larger diameter crank pin. A final difficulty was that the increased power put added stresses on the drive train, so that the standard pattern chain was sometimes subject to breakage. This matter was solved when the suppliers fabricated a heavier chain with larger rollers. In spite of these minor faults, the big twins continued to attract their usual quota of long time enthusiasts. The refined police models were still in strong demand, foreign machines up to this time having made but few inroads into H-D's long traditional market. What with rising prices, however, some government purchasing agents were now complaining that the motorcycles were costing substantially more than the heavy duty 'export' model sedans that for some years had been favorites for long distance highway patrol duties.

Somewhere in the Arizona desert. A relaxed tourist on an FLH slakes his thirst while under way. *(David Rose).*

A serious problem was noted in handling and steering regarding the new Electra Glide models used by the California State Highway Patrol in the Spring of 1967. The State Highway Department had recently cut longitudinal rain grooves on many of the freeway routes on the theory that they aided in reducing the risk of skidding in wet weather. While this practice obviously did not affect the stability of cars, it was rightly hailed as a hazard to motorcyclists, as in some cases it caused the front wheel to oscillate. There were several serious crashes sustained by Patrol Officers taking part in high speed pursuits. It was ultimately ascertained that the oscillation of the front wheel combined with the lack of rigidity in the lower portion of the spring frame units caused a whipping effect that rendered the machines unmanageable at high speed. Factory representatives were hastily dispatched to California to seek a solution to the problem. In the meantime, a private owner, Johnny Eagles of Orange, a highly skilled mechanic and motorcycle engineer, already had an answer to the problem. He theorized that if gussets were welded horizontally along the lower ends of the standing part of the frame, the resultant increase in rigidity could eliminate the vibration. His suggestion was relayed to the factory by Santa Ana dealer Joe Walker, and subsequent models soon appeared with this modification, which cured the trouble.

To cater to the long-standing American interest in high powered motorcycles, a new challenge from Great Britain was forthcoming in the form of beefed up vertical twins. Matchless, Norton, BSA, and Triumph were now offering 650 cc and 750 cc versions of their classic 500 cc models. Offered as an alternative to H-D's growingly popular H-D 883 cc Sportster, they provided high performance at very competitive prices. In spite of the fact that these big machines often leaked oil, suffered from chronic clutch and gearbox problems, and featured tooth-loosening vibration, stalwart young speed enthusiasts bought them in large numbers. Some of these were soon appearing as much modified 'choppers'.

In spite of this competition, H-D carried bravely on. The Sportster was proving to be a popular seller among younger riders who preferred a more agile mount than the 'FL' and 'FLH' models, and were growingly providing a new outlet for customizing. Both the 'Muscle Bike' imports as well as the Sportster came under criticism for their uncertain steering on rough or winding roads, the straight-line point-to-point travel offered by the freeways appeared to obviate the real need for such niceties for the average American enthusiast. An important source of added cash flow to the Company were the golf carts and industrial trucks. The Tomahawk plant's production capacity was augmented for their accelerated assembly, with the aid of the additional capital secured from the stock sales.

In spite of the somewhat sober financial outlook, H-D continued to support a vigorous competition program under the continuing management of Dick O'Brien. Bart Markel followed the great Carroll Reseweber in 1962 to win the National Championship. Roger Reiman took the honors in 1964, with Markel to return as the victor in 1965 and 1966. Ralph White won the Daytona Classic in 1963, with Reiman, who had already taken top honors there in 1961, returning to win again for Milwaukee in 1964 and 1965.

In the meantime, interest in custom machines was growing. Weird and wonderful examples were by this time being featured at cycle shows, and many trade fairs were now featuring custom entries. A new magazine *Street Chopper,* catered for this growing interest, along with other occasional news stand publications of lesser magnitude. The once miniscule custom parts suppliers were now expanding their activities to more commanding proportions, and counterfeit H-D parts were being manufactured in larger quantities. While the retail cost of these were often inordinately high due to low production, bikers put off by the hostile attitude of many of H-D's franchised dealers toward their patronage in most cases overcame this cost differential.

The sedate Servi-car was now somewhat surprisingly coming to the attention of the customizers. A few of these three wheelers had lately come into use for hauling the beer and sleeping bags on group picnics and weekend outings. Iconoclastic designs were soon seen to be fitted in place of the usual box body, such as ornate rickshaw structures or even decorated outhouses.

Custom sidecar bodies also were receiving their fair share of attention. On more than one occasion, the author has noted burial caskets mounted on a more or less standard chassis, the leather and Levi-clad passenger ensconced within the tufted taffeta lining!

In tune with the times, Hollywood favored biker interest by producing motion pictures on this theme. Established stars such as Jack Nicholson, Peter Fonda, John Cassavetes, and Joe Namath were featured in a number of these productions which came to be known in the trade as 'Bikers'. Bona fide custom enthusiasts and biker club members usually were hired either as bit players or to fill in an authentic background.

All in all, the once strong cult-like fervor of H-D enthusiasts of other days was now part and parcel of the biker image. Often a source of embarrassment to both long established dealers and factory alike, H-D was by this time the basis for a custom-cult of its own.

The ultimate in dedication to Milwaukee. A pair of MMA members display their H-D tattoos. *(David Rose).*

In spite of added capitalization and an intensified advertising program, H-D's share of the growing motorcycle market remained more or less static. Top management's next decision was to attempt the sale of the Company to a strong conglomerate. With heavy resources of both capital and extensive advertising capacity, it was hoped that such a sale could infuse new life into the Company. Apparently at this point, H-D's top management was fearful of actual bankruptcy. The financial losses of such an eventuality were enormous, both to the proliferated H-D family group as well as the

The Jammers Company display a part of their ware in an advertisement in *Iron Horse* magazine.

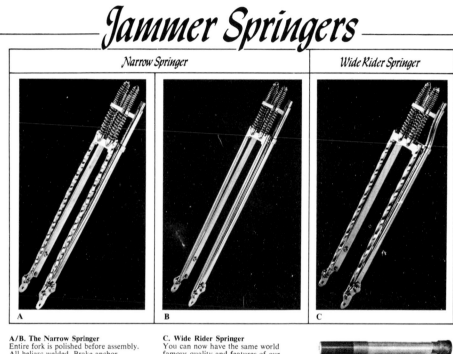

W & S Engineering offer custom-built Sportster parts in an advertisement in *Super Cycle*.

numerous stockholders, many of whom had ventured their life savings. Accordingly, in the Fall and Winter of 1967 and 1968, feelers were put out on Wall Street in an effort to entice firms dealing in registered stocks to consider what H-D liked to term a 'merger'.

It was shortly following these efforts that two giant conglomerates expressed interest through their top management in acquiring H-D. One of them was Bangor Punta, the other, the American Machine and Foundry Company. The adversary proceedings between these two concerns in the forthcoming battle over which of them was to purchase the assets of the venerable Milwaukee Company now forms one of the most complex financial stories ever to be noted in the domestic motorcycle industry.

The Bangor Punta concern, with headquarters at 405 Park Avenue in New York City, was originally known as the Punta Alegro up until 1960. It came into being shortly after WW I, the parent company being the Bangor and Aroostock Railroad, a feeder line which carried mostly farm produce from the interior of Maine. Its Directors acquired additional capital shortly thereafter, and amalgamated with the Punta Alegro organization that owned and operated sugar processing plants in Cuba. As time went on, its holdings were expanded to include leisure time products, such as pleasure boats, camping equipment, emblematic jewelry, fire arms, public security, energy systems, process engineering equipment, fashion fabrics, agribusiness and transportation, to name the most prominent. The total assets of B-P at that time totaled well over $267,000,000 according to reports of Standard & Poor and Moody's Corporation Indexes.

In an ongoing expansion, B-P acquired the Waukesha Engine Company of Milwaukee, a pioneer firm who manufactured gasoline and diesel engines for automotive and industrial uses. David W. Wallace, B-P President, and Nicholas M. Salgo, majority stockholder and Chairman of the Board of Directors, were reported as being most anxious to acquire H-D, not only for the motorcycles, but for the golf carts to augment their present line of leisure products. It was noted that the carts made up about 18% of H-D's current production.

At this point in time B-P already held 28,450 shares of H-D stock, recently purchased, it was reported, from groups of small private owners. It was also alleged that some of the shares had been purchased from dissident members of H-D families who were not interested in the motorcycle business, and wished to cash out their holdings as the Company was now in less than sound condition.

The American Machine and Foundry Company was formerly known as the American Car and Foundry Company, and had been organized in the earlier years of the century to manufacture railroad rolling stock, heavy machinery, and also owned a yacht building and marine engine business known as the New York Yacht, Launch, and Engine Company. In later years it gradually expanded its holdings to include companies building electrical products, bakery equipment, tobacco processing machinery, oil and gas products, and diversified industrial products, recreational products, such as bicycles, rubber goods and bowling products. Its total assets, noted at the time of its initial negotiations with H-D, amounted to $433,567,000.

Also incidental to the proposed sale of H-D's assets was the public declaration of its current financial condition, along with the names of its Board of Directors. This latter named William H.Davidson, President, Secretary-Treasury O.P.Resech, together with Board members A.H.Davidson, J.A.Davidson, R.J.Davidson, W.C.Davidson, W.H.Davidson, J.E.Harley, W.J.Harley, O.P.Resech, and A.W.Williams.

It was also revealed that during the past fiscal year, H-D had purchased from the Eck Foundries, Inc. of Milwaukee, $966,334 worth of raw materials, forgings and castings. An interesting revelation was that William H.Davidson, Walter C.Davidson, and Robert J.Davidson, were listed as Directors of the Eck Company, together with holdings owned by the estates of the deceased Arthur H. and Gordon M.Davidson. It was stated that the Davidson holdings amounted to 43% of Eck's outstanding stock. Some former H-D employees have alleged that at one time or another, the Davidsons actually owned a controlling interest in Eck, but in any case, their holdings gave them convenient control of a critical source of supply for H-D's manufacturing operation. Also significant was the fact that an Eck representative held a seat on the Board of Directors of the AMA.

Other facts revealed were that as of September 30th, 1968 H-D was represented by 650 retail dealers throughout the US and Canada, who were supervised by 23 factory supervisors. During the past five years, 80% of H-D sales were of the larger Sportster and FL-FLH models, an area where foreign competition was less effective. At that date, H-D had approximately 1,700 employees, the production force being represented by unions, the salaried managerial force being non-union. The Company's source of income was listed as the sales of domestically produced motorcycles, the sales of motorcycles imported from Harley-Davidson Aermacchi, the sales of golf carts and industrial trucks, and the profits from a finance organization and an insurance company operated for the benefit of both dealers and customers. A significant item also was that H-D's export sales, outside the US and Canada, now amounted to but 3% of the total production.

On the financial side, it was noted that on $43,000,000 worth of gross sales in 1968, the net profit after taxes was but $1,176,000. While H-D was still in the black, its profit margin was becoming dangerously thin.

AMF's interest in acquiring H-D was essentially that of B-P, namely to augment their respective lines of sporting and recreational equipment. AMF's position in the matter was strengthened by the

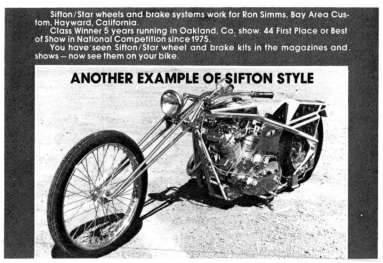

Tom Sifton, the Patriarch of H-D tuners, offers his wares in an advertisement in *Easy Riders*

An original type of five-speed transmission adaptable to all 1936-1979 H-D big twins from Little John Ltd., of Denver, Colorado.

Chairman of its Board of Directors who was also President of the Company, Rodney C.Gott, who had not only been a motorcyclist but was an H-D enthusiast as well. AMF's offer was to purchase H-D on the basis of a merger, in which they not only would acquire the H-D families' controlling interest, but would give the balance of the stockholders one and one half shares of AMF common stock on a tax free exchange. According to information on the matter contained in their offer, AMF would retain the present H-D management, allow them to continue to control and supervise their dealerships, as well as allowing them to be responsible for the development of future models.

To advise both the H-D Company and its stockholders in the matter, H-D retained the Robert Baird organization, reportedly for a fee of $100,000. During the course of the negotiations, AMF's initial offer had been to offer 1.23 shares of their stock in trade, but in learning of B-P's accelerated purchase of H-D shares, they subsequently raised their offer.

It was then noted in various issues of the Wall Street Journal that B-P had acquired 28,450 shares of H-D stock in over-the-counter trading during the latter part of September, 1968, and on through November 8. The first 9,000 shares were pruchased at $25.00 each on September 20th. The following week its purchase of another 7,800 shares saw its price rise to $25.75. During the week ending October 18th, 10,000 more shares were pruchased at $29.75. On the week ending November 8, 850 additional shares were purchased at $30.00.

In the meantime, H-D's management had already informed its stockholders by letter that it favored the proposed merger with AMF. This communication stated that H-D's Board of Directors had already approved a 'letter of intent' to consumate a tax free merger with that Company. Despite this announcement, on October 31 B-P gave notice of a tender offer to acquire at least 150,000 shares of H-D stock at $40.00 per share, net to the sellers. On November 14th, B-P increased its offer to $42.50, and on November 19th withdrew the limitation on the number of shares it agreed to purchase and to acquire any and all shares tendered. The total value of all H-D shares held by B-P now stood at $770,950. B-P's strategy of course was to purchase as many shares as was possible in order to gain the voting rights.

In the meantime, H-D's management continued to communicate with the outstanding shareholders by means of form letters signed by William Davidson, urging that they consider accepting AMF's offer, and advising against dealing with B-P. The main consideration was, the letters stated, that the proposed merger with AMF would involve a tax-free exchange which would not be the case with B-P. What was not mentioned, but subsequently alleged, was that AMF's Rodney C.Gott had assured William Davidson personally that the former would retain the present company management intact and would allow H-D continuing control over their dealership. It was also alleged that if B-P got control of H-D, that it might well put it on the market for sale to others if a profit could be realized.

In rebuttal, B-P issued an open letter in the *Milwaukee Sentinal,* stating their own case in the matter, as H-D had refused to provide them with a list of H-D stockholders for direct communication. This statement, in the form of a full page advertisement, called attention to the fact that AMF had

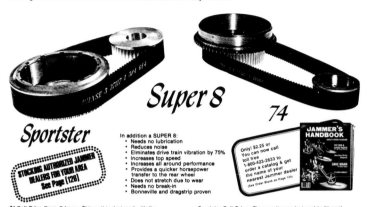

Jammers offer their own version of a custom primary belt drive in the advertising section of *Super Cycle.*

recently declared a loss of $12,547,000 applicable to its common stock through losses sustained incidental to their bowling equipment manufacture. This loss, according to B-P, amounted to 74 cents against each outstanding share, which H-D stockholders would have to assume.

Another allegation was that the $1.35 dividend on AMF shares was substantially less than the $1.80 dividend on the B-P stock which figured in the exchange.

B-P's statement furthermore called attention to the fact that the proposed AMF merger, the equity per share of H-D's stockholders would decrease from $23.03 to $14.13, a loss of 38%. On the other hand, if H-D merged with B-P, the per equity per share would increase 100%, or so they alleged.

Finally, H-D's retention of the Robert W. Baird group was challenged on the grounds that the latter was prejudiced in favor of H-D through their past dealings, together with the fact that they were scheduled to receive a $100,000 fee for their service.

The actual monetary value of B-P's offer would amount in the end to approximately $23,650,000.

According to notices mailed to stockholders, a meeting was scheduled for December 17 1968, at the Milwaukee Athletic Club, stating that the former would be urged to vote for the merger with AMF.

On December 16 B-P, through their legal counsel, filed suit in Superior Court against AMF and H-D, pleading that the two companies had not acted in the best interests of their stockholders in their proposed merger, and also cited that in their opinion, certain regulations of the US Securities and Exchange Commission had been violated.

The next round of this complex battle was that B-P filed notice that they would drop their lawsuit if AMF would increase their offer to H-D stockholders. Ultimately, the actual per share offer of AMF rose to about $42.00.

In the end, the H-D stockholders, both from management's urgings and an increase in their

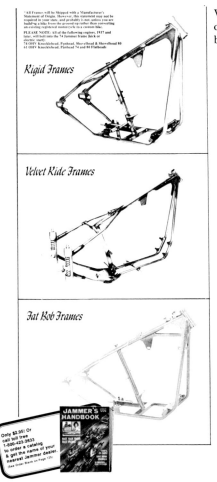

Various types of
custom frame offered
by Jammers.

New stock custom-
cast engine cases for
H-D big twins offered
by S.T.D.
Engineering.

offer, caused the latter to accept AMF's bid, with but token opposition. While the whole affair had been responsible for much controversy and uncertainty among many of the stockholders, in the end it was actually of great benefit. In the bidding against each other, AMF and B-P had driven the value of the stock much higher than it would have been under more normal circumstances. The author has interviewed a number of one time shareholders such as present or retired dealers, as well as others outside the industry who in some cases held substantial blocks of shares. As many of them had originally purchased them at $6.00 or $7.00 per share, the ultimate increase to $43.00 had enabled them to profit handsomely.

The course of the proceedings was widely reported in such leading financial papers as the *Wall Street Journal* and *Barron's*, as well as enjoying exhaustive coverage in the local Milwaukee press. Other leading newspapers such as the *New York Times* and the *Los Angeles Times* also featured comprehensive coverage. The events were widely followed by interested motorcyclists, as this was the first time in Company history that any financial details of H-D's transactions had ever been aired. It was ultimately noted that AMF exchanged 877,671 shares of its common stock, valued at approximately $21,650,000 for all of the assets of H-D.

AMF formally took over the H-D Company in January, 1969. As anticipated, there were no substantial changes in the managerial staff. William H.Davidson remained in office as President, and the present Board of Directors all retained their position. William J.Harley, Vice President in charge of Engineering, John Harley, Parts and Accessories Manager, O.P.Resech, Secretary-Treasurer, carried on as before. The third generation Davidsons were represented by William H's two sons, John A. and William G., the latter in the Design Department. Vice President in charge of Sales, Walter G.Davidson, resigned shortly to pursue other business interests outside the Company.

AMF at once launched an intensive advertising campaign, stressing their line of leisure time products, with H-D prominently featured. A sales blitz in the Pacific Northwest on behalf of their snow-mobiles, ran into difficulties however. The firms of Moore and Pierre, Inc., Kellogg Sales and Service, Inc., and Joe's Snowmobiles, all of Spokane, Washington, filed suit in Federal District Court in Spokane against AMF and H-D as a subsidiary. Asking $35,000,000 in damages, the plaintiffs charged that AMF had breached their franchise agreements and monopolized the sale and distribution of AMF products by setting up competing outlets within the plaintiff's areas of trade. The matter was settled through negotiations between the opposing counsels before the matter came to trial.

At the annual meeting of the Board of Directors of AMA held in Anaheim, California, during the month of February, William M.(Bill) Bagnall, editor and publisher of the *Motorcyclist* was elected President, succeeding William E.Kennedy, a sales executive of the Rex Chain Belt Company of Milwaukee who had held the office since 1965.

In a self-congratulatory editorial announcing the event, Bagnall pledged that he would exert his best effort for the best interests of both the AMA and for motorcycling. In recounting the names of his predecessors, he concurred in the traditional H-D mandate in omitting the name of the AMA's first president, one-time Indian dealer, Douglas Hobart.

And so it was that H-D, sixty eight years after the first prototype motorcycle built by its two founders, saw the light of day, now joined the ranks of the many family-owned business concerns that were lately merging with vast conglomerates.

An official warning from AMF H-D in a current accessory catalog against the use of non-factory replacement parts.

The 'Topper' scooter, marketed briefly after 1960. It was fitted with the 165cc engine and a centrifical clutch.

The 'Super Ten' as the 'Ranger', an off-the-road machine without lighting. First produced in 1962.

The M-50 Lightweight.   227

William Hoecker's 1965 175 cc 'Bobcat'. This is typical of the other two-stroke Pacer and Scat models. *(Alisha Tamburri)*.

Mark King's well-maintained 1969 883 cc Sportster. The handlebars are an accessory item, and the large section rear tire was often substituted to give a softer ride. *(Alisha Tamburri).*

A super Full Dress touring FLH. *(George Hays)*.

Stuntman 'Slide' Sommers puts
his 883cc Sportster through
its paces. *(George Hays)*.

The great Cal Rayborn caught by the cameraman in a split-second manoever. *(H-D Motor Company)*.

Coming out of the north turn. A typical dirt track race somewhere in Middle America.

Leo Payne on his specially-tuned Sportster at Bonneville, where he set a new record for unstreamlined machines at 182.89 mph.

William Herbert Davidson,
the second Chief Executive
of H-D. He served from
1942 through 1973, when
he retired.

William J.Harley shortly before his death in 1971.

William G.Davidson as a youthful enduro
contestant in 1962.

The XR-750, officially launched in the Spring of 1970. It is offered in both road racing or dirt track models with options as to suspension systems and gear ratios. It is a formidable contender on the dirt track at this writing.

The Dirt Track version of the XR-750. *(AMF-Harley Davidson)*.

The extended fork syndrome. A group of customized H-Ds sporting varying styles of front suspension, as seen at the Visalia CAMA Rally in 1972. *(George Hays)*.

A group of MMA club
members at their
annual Santa Claus
Rally, Christmas,
1972. *(David Rose)*.

MMA Club members
on their much
modified H-Ds. *(David
Rose)*.

A group of MMA
members display their
diverse ideas on
customizing along
Santa Monica
Boulevard.

235

A futuristic power rickshaw based on the Model G Servi-car. *(George Hays)*.

A Servi-car much modified and fitted with a large V-8 car engine. *(David Rose)*.

Chapter 10

The AMF Era

THE OFFICIAL DATE OF AMF'S ASSUMPTION OF OWNERSHIP OF H-D WAS JANUARY 7, 1969. It was reported that the Davidsons and the few remaining Harleys were happy to at long last get their money, and that AMF could now look forward to the addition of H-D products to their already substantial numbers of leisure time products. Some of the accounts of AMF Board Chairman Rodney C. Gott's campaign to persuade AMF's stockholders to approve the takeover of H-D emanating from H-D's Publicity Department were somewhat romanticized in picturing Gott as an altruistic enthusiast who was acting as a latter day Moses now dramatically to lead H-D out of its wilderness.

A more factual overview of the matter and the real reason behind AMF's top management's approval of the H-D acquisition was later supplied by Ray Albert Tritten, Gott's immediate successor. AMF's very substantial profits during 1968 and 1969 were such that a large accrual of corporate income tax liabilities had been incurred. According to the vagaries of U.S. Corporate income tax laws, a straight line profit picture could be either reduced or eliminated by the expenses of either internal expansion or the acquisition of other corporations. The $21,000,000 paid for H-D was at once sheltered from taxation, and its acquisition opened the way for further tax loopholes in its operation, as well as adding to AMF's present line of sports-type products.

There were allegations among the nation's financial community that the sudden rise in H-D stock during the negotiations might well have come about through collusion between nominally competing brokers, but these were never serious enough to cause an investigation by the Securities and Exchange Commission.

The first act of H-D's top management following the AMF takeover was to assure both dealers and owners that all present Company personnel were to remain, and that traditional H-D policies were to be maintained. It was now emphasized that with an infusion of fresh capital, H-D's line of products would be shortly expanded. It was also pointed out that an updated advertising and marketing campaign would soon be forthcoming from AMF's vast expertise. The reassurance was to allay the fears of many enthusiasts that motorcycle production might be suspended in favor of other products. At the same time, the output of the gasoline and electric golf carts and three-wheeled industrial trucks was ordered to be expanded to enhance AMF's position in the leisure-time field and otherwise to enhance the cash flow position.

With these pronouncements broadcast to produce what was hoped would be a calming effect   237 outside the factory, AMF's Sales, Marketing and Production executives now addressed themselves to solving the problem of H-D's current position of near insolvency. While noting Board Chairman Rodney C. Gott's enthusiasm for acquiring H-D, AMF's secondary level of top management were at once appalled at the deteriorated state of the Company's fortunes.

The first step in this analysis was to recount the more salient facts of H-D's past history, to determine the reason for the Company's long decline in an era of general economic prosperity, of ever-increasing motorcycle sales and general public interest in motorcycling, and to consider the role of H-D as America's sole surviving domestic manufacturer. The result of these studies was contained within a series of detailed inter-departmental memoranda, major portions of which were made available to the author in the fall of 1982.

In the first instance, the Company was operating in a factory, the main complex of which was based on production concepts developed during the Civil War. These 19th century operations were centrally powered, originally by steam, and latterly by electricity, the machine tooling being activated by a complex system of jackshafts and pulleys via a myriad of leather belting. Their efficiency depended upon being housed in a multi-storey building. This method was woefully ineffective as contrasted with the modern continuous flow system assembly line.

The shortcomings of the Juneau Avenue factory were highlighted in the initial days of the war effort, when production approached 30,000 units per year, the originally-projected capacity of the factory when it was completed in 1920. It was for this reason the Capitol Drive plant was acquired at the close of the war. Being of limited floor area, it was only capable of containing the facilities for assembly of engines and transmissions.

As a closely-held family-owned company, H-D was, in its earlier days, capable of being efficiently managed through frequent conferences among the Founders. However, the ultimate weakness of this arrangement came to light during the period when they began to die off. The control of the company then passed to their heirs, whose proliferation soon complicated top management decisions.

Upon the death of President Walter Davidson in 1942, Arthur Davidson remained as the sole surviving Founder. While young William H. Davidson, William C. Davidson's son, had been elected President, it has often been mentioned through unofficial sources that Arthur was still the power behind the throne. With Arthur's death in December, 1950, this influence quite naturally reverted to a

The 1978 XLCR-1000 Cafe Racer. *(AMF-Harley-Davidson).*

The 1979 FXE 1200 Super Glide. *(AMF-Harley-Davidson).*

relatively large group of children, relatives, heirs of deceased members' estates and other shareholders who now represented voting powers.

Marketing conditions by 1950 had eased somewhat due to the prior fulfilling of material commitments incidental to the Marshall Plant. H-D was producing, by all accounts, between 13,000 and 28,000 units per year, mostly big twins, and they were selling all they could produce as post-war prosperity was now in full cry. While foreign middle-weight machines, mostly British, were racking up impressive sales, H-D was still holding its own market. What with the factory facilities fully utilized, the question now arising was whether to seriously expand Company activities to make way for future product development and prototype work on new models, or to maintain the present range of work within the existing facilities. A decision had to be made whether to maintain status quo by collecting continuing substantial dividends on the traditional machines, or to acquire new facilities with consequent indebtness. In short, the former course was chosen. In addition, the Company was shortly to embark on the rather repressive expedient of petitioning the US International Trade Commission to impose tariffs and import quotas on foreign machines, as has been described, to the extent that such competition would have been all but eliminated!

The Company's marketing target itself was restricted in the sense that it tended to dictate the type of person who should ride H-Ds. In this context it almost mandated that the machine itself, other than law enforcement types, be of the full dress or 'dresser' category. Its rider would then be of restrained temperament and conservative dress.

Such thinking quite naturally put the custom biker far outside the scope of their reasoning, and in their Midwest conservatism anyone who rode a stripped machine in leathers and Levis was at once equated with the excesses of Hollister.

But in the changing marketing conditions following the war, young riders and more recent converts to the sport were buying middleweight foreign machines, the custom chopper cult was growing by leaps and bounds, and the now aging conventional dresser rider was fading from the scene through normal attrition. In addition, the factory-despised biker type was driven to trade with the growing after-market industry that was now profiting in the millions while factory production had fallen to a little over 9,000 units by 1955.

It was also noted that the now-established H-D cultism and mystique was being fostered, not by the dresser riders whom the factory was still courting, but by the iconoclastic, free-thinking rebels who

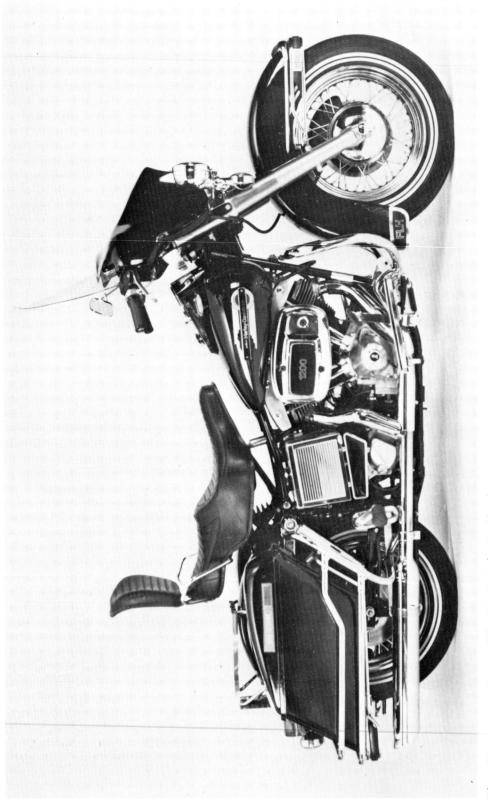

The 1979 FLH 1200 Electra Glide. *(AMF-Harley-Davidson)*

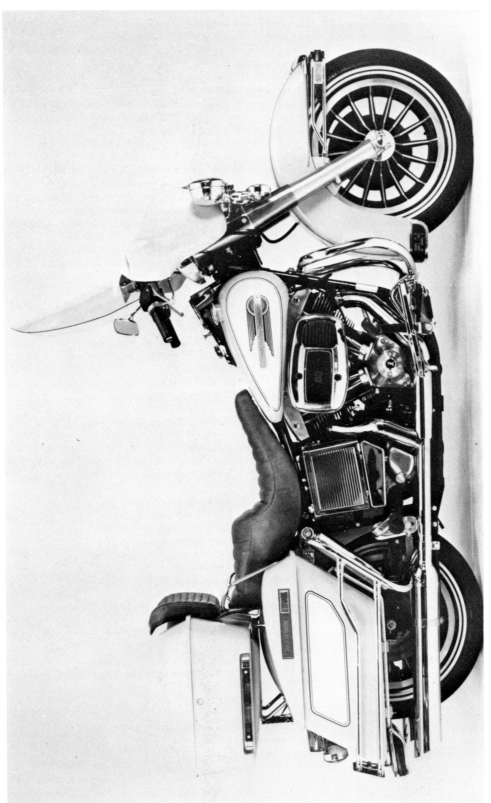

The 1979 FLH with optional frame-mounted seat. (AMF-Harley-Davidson).

reveled in the unconventional and flaunted it from the saddle of a much-modified H-D.

Another fact noted was that in the heat of the post-war motorcycle boom, H-D's top management had become both detached and withdrawn from the realities of the marketplace. The old, self-serving and public-be-damned attitude as personified by President Walter Davidson in the pre-war years was still the order of the day. The Company's take-it-or-leave it hauteur in dealer and customer relationships was even intensified.

As a family company, no outsiders, even those who were latterly responsible for certain significant changes in H-D's basic designs, were ever promoted to positions in top management. It was also true that upcoming young Harleys and Davidsons usually joined the Company at an early age, apparently whether they wished to or not. They also appeared to rise to top managerial positions whether they deserved to or not, and thus created an entrenched bureaucracy that could not be fired. In some cases they were noted to be both inefficient and arrogant.

In another category of AMF's general survey of H-D, outside consultants in automotive and mechanical engineering were retained to analyze the firm's technical position. It was noted that the big twin engine, based on the ohv 61 cubic inch 61E developed jointly by William Ottaway, Joe Petrali, and Hank Syvertson during the winter of 1934-35, had been improved following its 1936 introduction into a fairly efficient and reliable power plant. Certain minor improvements were effected in the 'panhead' version of 1948. But further modifications up through the 'shovelhead' of 1967 to produce a higher power output to cope with the ever-increasing weight of the machines included altered porting and valve timing, cam contouring, and increased compression ratios. These modifications to a long stroke, narrow angle V-twin push rod engine intensified the inbuilt proclivity to vibrate. Due to the shape of the combustion chambers, it was prone to overheating with hard driving, particular in high summer temperatures. These problems, along with the increased weight of the machine, clearly indicated that a redesign of H-D's prime power plant was in order, especially as it had become less reliable and required much maintenance.

It was also noted that with the technical failures of the K and KH models, the ultimate conversion to an ohv type in 1957 had left the Company with no middleweight machine, an offering by British manufacturers that in the 1950s and 1960s had enjoyed the largest sales volume.

The results of this survey were obtained by AMF staff interviews with usually reluctant former members of H-D's top management, senior and retired employees, representative dealers, as well as a cross section of experienced riders in various parts of the country.

Many of the dealers were bitter about the high-handed treatment meted out to them through the years by the Company, along with the fact that no middleweight machines were developed during the intermediate post-war years to compete with foreign imports. H-D's top management had historically abhorred any form of competition from other makes, in an almost paranoic manner. The often-expressed opinion was that the Company's only answer to competition in any form was to simply destroy it if possible.

While the overall conclusions arrived at by AMF regarding H-D's past and by knowledgeable motorcycle people both within and without the industry were in general agreement, in all fairness it must be stated that the censure of H-D's top management in the 1951 decision not to restructure the company was rather harsh. It must be recalled that the original Founders were generally unsophisticated men who launched the Company as a backyard venture, initially working almost single-handedly. Progressing toward a brief period of success during 1917 through 1921, they then were forced to contend with the lean years of US motorcycling. Operating in a strictly marginal industry between the two World Wars with but minimal output, they barely survived the Great Depression by ruthless cost cuting and penny pinching. This later practise, while no doubt necessary in part, was often carried to the extreme in later years, coloring the Company's business image and their relationships with both dealers and customers.

The accelerated demands for increased production due to War Department contracts caused many problems. What with a long-outmoded manufacturing facility that was inadequate for sustained high volume production, a lack of sufficient floor area, and the need for additional machine tooling, it was only through heroic round-the-clock effort that the Company was able to turn out the component parts to assemble about 150,000 units between 1940 and 1944. While this no doubt caused the top management to secure additional facilities on Capitol Drive after the war, it is scarcely likely that anyone then engaged in domestic motorcycle manufacture could envisage that within the decade there would be a tenfold increase in public interest in motorcycling.

It is also somewhat outside the realm of probability to consider that H-D's management would at that point seriously consider totally revising its current production facilities that had served the ongoing marketing demands for the past four decades. With its inherent Midwestern insularity, and a totally inbred family hierarchy that had historically resisted the inclusion of any outsiders for the purpose of enhancing the marketing, sales or production expertise, in the light of subsequent events it

A pleasant interlude in investigative reporting. The author's 1934 74 cu. in 1934 VLD built up from 95% new old stock parts acquired from veteran dealers. It was assembled by Johnny Eagles, with advice from Maury Biggs and Conrad Schlemmer. The improved 1936 nine stud engine was fitted in place of the seven stud 1934 type to avoid blown gaskets. *(Steve Nelson)*

is obvious that H-D's management was simply incapable of formulating a turnaround in long standing policy.

It was also concluded that the Company's traditional policy of maintaining a close veil of secrecy regarding their internal affairs was to conceal the shareholders' policies that were diametrically opposed to the public image that it was expedient to project. It appeared that the Company's long standing tradition of advocating conservative engineering was inspired by the fact that the owners did not want to spend the funds for forward product development or retooling for new designs. This also explained the long standing reluctance on the part of H-D's top management to grant interviews to motorcycle journalists, news reporters, or historians. Their preferred mode of public communications was through self-serving press releases.

In fairness, however, it must be mentioned that some of the Company's problems were caused by circumstances beyond its control. One of these was labor-management relations. The history of the world trade union movement is a complex one, and is beyond the scope of our attention here. Suffice it to say that with the ultimate legalization of collective bargaining, most industrial concerns could anticipate dislocations or cessations of production at or near the time for contract renewal. Large concerns such as automobile manufacturers, coal and gas producers, steel processors and others prudently anticipated such conflicts by adjusting production schedules, marketing programs, and other internal activities to allow for such eventualities. Such were expedient for very large companies with a large cash flow, but obviously brought great hardship to smaller firms, such as H-D. Cessation of production involving several hundred units and corresponding spare parts, along with possible internal sabotage, could and did seriously disrupt H-D's operations. This occurred in the years after 1937 and up to World War II, and several periods during the 1950s and 1960s.

Also, the AMF memoranda apparently did not include mention of President William H. Davidson's policy after 1946 to implement new product development. Former employees have recounted work on new designs following contemporary motorcycle technical progress. That advanced prototype development or production did not take place reflects both the shareholders' policy of maximizing profits and, perhaps, top management's reluctance to interfere with H-D's long-established basic designs in the thought that new designs would not be accepted by H-D's traditionally-minded customers. The details of these internal problems will probably never be revealed unless someone intimately associated with the shareholders' decision comes forward to discuss them.

Another matter of controversy was the current state of the factory's run-down tooling and other

243

production equipment. While this was admittedly inadequate for the work at hand, matters had come to this state of being not without good reason. During the period of the Great Depression after 1930, motorcycle production on the part of both H-D and Indian had remained static for the simple fact that interest in motorcycling had steadily declined in the 1930-40 decade. With reduced sales, and a market sustained by exports of heavyweight V twins to foreign buyers, it made little sense to undertake plant or equipment expansion. In fact, both factories had, before 1941, been utilizing only a small part of their twelve acres of floor space, with large areas of the plants simply closed off or leased to other users. Neither company could have foreseen the War Department demands or the immensity of the global conflict which depleted their slender resources even further. With reduced markets and slender profits, pre-war expansion would have been not only unnecessary but financially imprudent.

AMF's immediate problem was to overhaul the entire Company operation. It was decided for the time being to retain intact the old management structure for purposes of continuity in the public mind. With the infusion of fresh capital, much-needed new tooling was acquired for both the Juneau Avenue and Capitol Drive plants. With increased production, a stepped-up advertising campaign was launched and plans were made to turn H-D's traditional marketing methods in a new direction.

It was also decided to retain the Aermacchi line of light and middleweight machines, although their sales volume had never been encouraging. This had, apparently, been due to indifference on the part of H-D's dealers, together with a lack of public association with H-D in this market, as has been mentioned.

H-D's traditional competition program was carried on uninterruptedly during both the lengthy company sales negotiations as well as during the initial phase of AMF's takeover. The inimitable Cal Rayborn had taken the checkered flag at Daytona in 1968, the first rider to top the magic century mark at a 101.29 mph average, his KR running faultlessly the whole distance. Roger Reiman's KR broke the record at the AMA Time Trial Contest that year at an incredible 149.08 mph. This was notable in that it was attained with an engine that differed but little in detail from the original side valve type models that Indian's Charles B. Franklin had introduced in 1916.

1968 was a banner year for H-D's modern Wrecking Crew. Of a total of twenty-three Nationals entered, H-D took eighteen first places. Cal Rayborn had gone on after his Daytona victory to seven straight wins on the National circuit.

In spite of the success of the continually refined racing K, which had formed the backbone of

The 1979 XLH 1000 Hugger. *(AMF-Harley-Davidson)*.

H-D's competition efforts since the mid-1950s, it was now becoming obvious that its days were numbered. Modern and highly sophisticated designs from the Orient were already making their appearance in the traditional American horse-track type of motorcycle competition and Dick O'Brien of the Competition Department rightly concluded that the last possible horsepower had been wrung from an ancient design.

The overall design of a new racer, provisionally designated as the XR-750, closely followed that of the last Ks in having a double looped frame that had been adapted in 1967. The rear swinging arm was secured against lateral movement by a pair of massive pre-loaded Timkin bearings. A solid rear frame unit was also offered as an option, as preferred by some competitors. In a break with tradition, the 45 cubic inch engine was fitted with overhead valves, and in essence was a sleeved down 883 cc Sportster unit. In spite of its obsolescence, H-D still remained faithful to the V twin as personified by its traditional design configuration. Features were a bore/stroke ratio of 3.005 x 3.291 inches with high domed pistons and large valves. With a cam action that emphasized long duration with moderate ramp action, a rather broad power band between 4800 – 7800 rpm was attained. The maximum torque output at 6200 rpm shows 62 hp.

Anticipating the time required to test the machine and to inaugurate the production, H-D petitioned the AMA Competition Committee in October, 1969, to sanction a new Class C design that now featured overhead valves. That Milwaukee-dominated body at once complied, but at the insistence of some of the non-H-D affiliated members, it was stipulated that at least 200 examples be produced before a final clearance could be granted. H-D at once protested this ruling, as the Production Department did not consider that this many models could be assembled before the opening of the 1970 season. The committee was adamant, however, pointing out that H-D had itself long used the arbitrary production number ploy to keep the more exotic models entered by foreign manufacturers out of US competition. It was stated that if an exception were made in favor of H-D, who had instigated the production rule for their own advantage in the first place, additional ill feeling would be generated in what was already a somewhat tense situation.

The new model had its first public exhibition at a trade show held early in the Spring of 1970 in conjunction with a meet at the Astrodome. Prototype tests had already been conducted the preceding January at Daytona by both Cal Rayborn and Roger Reiman. Both reported that the XR handled as well, if not better, than the last KR models.

The 1980 FXEF 80 Fatbob Super Glide. *(AMF-Harley-Davidson)*.

In the fall of 1969, a new television series gave a sympathetic treatment to the sport of motorcycling in general, and H-D in particular, with the showing of 'Along Came Bronson.' Initially a two-hour motion picture starring Michael Parks and Bonnie Bedelia, it was subsequently made into a series production. The theme was that of a knight errant rider who travelled the California coast and his interaction with people along the way. An MGM-TV production produced by Robert H. Justman and Robert Sabaroff, in association with NBC TV in New York, it featured exceptional cinematography by the late Ray Flin.

The actual logistics of the features were under the direction of Bud Ekins, a one-time noted enduro rider, who built a special sidecar outfit with a seat over the front wheel to facilitate close-up shots of the motorcyclists involved. Parks, as the leading man, rode a new Sportster, which, along with other machines shown in various episodes, was maintained by Ekins. The latter had for some years been supplying motorcycles and riders as well as stunt men for various Hollywood productions.

In order to effect a limited updating of H-D's big twin design, it was decided to incorporate solid state ignition. The conventional gear-driven generator and breaker point distributor was replaced by a pancake-type ac alternator that was positioned on the drive side of the crankcase, inside the sprocket. A rectifier placed just ahead of the forward engine mounts converted the ac to dc.

This move was well in line with that of other manufacturers of automotive equipment, as public sentiment against air pollution was growing. The breakerless solid state type of ignition was stated as effecting more 'clean' combustion, as compared with earlier 'dirty' types.

H-D's improved system proved generally reliable and trouble-free, although many old time mechanics have stated that the original system was easier to trouble-shoot and far more economical to repair. The new system was announced for 1970 for FL and FLH models. It was noted that aftermarket builders of engine cases at once made ready patterns to cast their own replicas.

In 1969 a new Sprint model was forthcoming from Aermacchi with an improved 350 cc engine. The first 250 cc Sprint model introduced in 1961 had evoked only mild interest, for reasons already mentioned. Some favorable publicity regarding it had been forthcoming in 1965 when a torpedo-type streamliner powered with a tuned 250cc engine and piloted by George Roeder attained a speed of

The 1980 XLH 1000 Sportster. *(AMF-Harley-Davidson)*.

The 1980 FXE 1200 Super Glide. *(AMF-Harley-Davidson)*.

177.22 mph on the Bonneville Salt Flats. Sprint fans noted that the enlarged engine gave a better all-around performance, especially in hill climbing. It also had benefited from recent technology incorporated into its design as the result of Aermacchi's active competition program in Europe. It was produced in both Sports and Street Scrambler versions. A well-finished and attractive machine, it unfortunately sold only in small numbers.

During the late 1960s the growing conflict between riders with an interest in road racing and the Competition Committee of the AMA came to a head. The controversy had centered around the participation of AMA licensed contestants in events that were not officially sanctioned by the AMA. This type of competition had long been anathema to that body, as neither H-D nor Indian had ever produced machines that were well suited to other than the horse track type of competition. In fact, such events had been actively discouraged ever since the mid-1930s when foreign machines with a race bred background, such as the Norton, made a few successful appearances on the American sporting scene.

In the post-war years, however, with the increasing number of foreign machines, riders of such, by sheer weight of numbers, had instigated a series of road racing events which were, of course, not AMA sanctioned and were classed as 'outlaw' by that body.

In defense of their interest, several small groups of road racing enthusiasts organized their own associations, the more prominent being Motorcycle Racers Inc. (MRI) and the American Association of Motorcycle Road Racers (AAMRR). Matters came to a head when two well-known riders ran afoul of the AMA Competition Committee. Dick Mann, who currently held the number two position in the Nationals, competed in a road race at Pepperwell, Massachusetts, and was promptly suspended by the AMA for competing in an unsanctioned event. Privateer Gordon Jennings, a motorcycle journalist and a competitor of note, entered a road race at Indianapolis, with the same result. Both protested that no AMA-sanctioned races were being held during the weekends of their alleged transgressions, and both pointed out that they had been loyal supporters of the AMA for some years. During the well-publicized discussions of the matter between various prominent competition riders, as well as trade representatives, much of it in *Cycle World*, many agreed that the AMA was acting in a

The 1980 FLH Classic with sidecar. *(AMF-Harley-Davidson).*

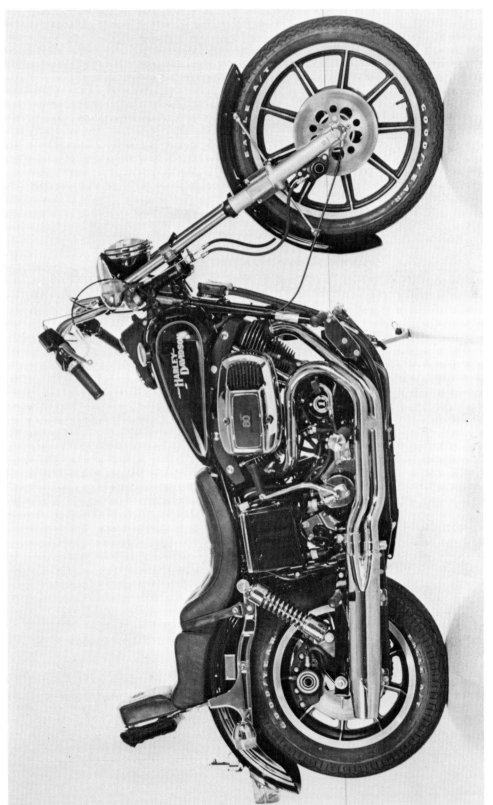

The 1980 FXS 80 Low Rider. *(AMF-Harley-Davidson).*

most arbitrary manner in branding as 'outlaw' a segment of the sport which was by this time attracting increasing interest among motorcyclists as well as spectators. As a result, many people within both the sport and the trade became very bitter toward the AMA.

In a series of articles in *Cycle World* by Assistant Editor Ivan J. Wagar, it was pointed out that if the AMA could not see its way clear to sanction types of competition events that catered to broader public interests, it was then logical that other organizations would come into being to provide them. He noted that for far too long the AMA had existed as a small private club, dominated by H-D and a small circle of their satellite suppliers. He further questioned the long-standing head-in-the-sand attitude of the AMA in neglecting the best interests of riders in general. He also pointed out that it was a real economic necessity that professional riders compete in indoor track races that were currently being held during the winter season when sanctioned AMA events were not forthcoming. The public airing of the matter was later to have much bearing on the coming reorganization of the AMA hierarchy.

In the fall of 1970, H-D introduced a new model based on the classic FL that both startled the club type 'dresser' rider and delighted the ever-growing number of custom enthusiasts. Cataloged as the 'Super Glide', the new machine was basically a stripped FL, without electric starting, fitted with Ceriani-type forks, foot pegs in place of foot boards, and most definitely not intended for a windshield, saddle bags, spotlights, or any of the other excrescences that had long been traditional for the Yankee big twin rider. Factory literature described this model as a big twin with Sportster elements added, while a trade journal characterized it as 'an institutionalized chopper.'

Some factory personnel have reported that its creator, William G. Davidson, the elder son of William H., presently in the Company's Design Department, had been working on the details of such a machine since 1967. It was also reported that he had been an early advocate of a new type of machine that would appeal to the sports hobbyist market. As a friendly and gregarious individual, combining an artistic flair with some engineering background, 'Willie G.' was soon to put aside the sartorial spendor of the traditional executive. Donning the leathers and Levis of the Biker, he sallied forth on the highways and beer bars to mingle freely with the riders of the custom-chopper cult. This activity was said to have been instigated by AMF's Sales and Marketing Department. It was now painfully obvious that H-D's former austere detachment from the desires of a large number of their enthusiasts had not only lost sales, but had driven them to trade with the custom equipment manufacturers whose sales volume was now measured in millions.

The 1980 FXWG Wide Glide. *(AMF-Harley-Davidson)*.

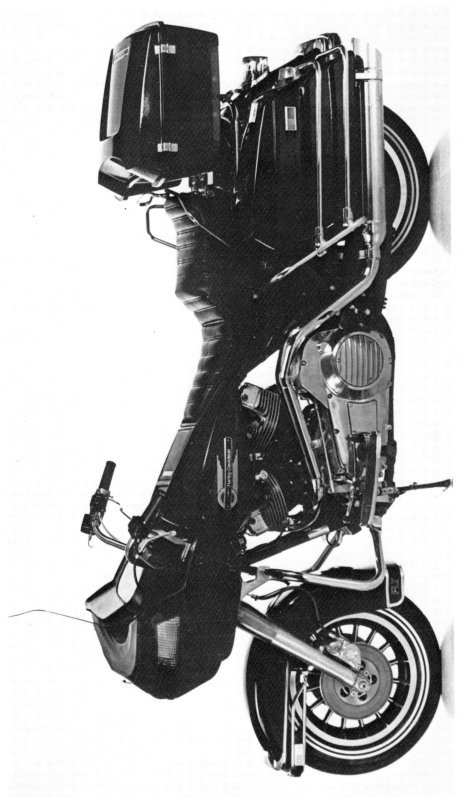

The 1980 FLT Tour Glide. H-D's first new top-of-the-line model in forty five years! This modernized V twin features a five speed transmission, improved suspension and steering, frame mounted fairings with twin headlights, and a totally enclosed rear chain in an oil bath case. (*AMF – Harley-Davidson*).

Neither the factory nor Willie G. could take all the credit for the introduction of custom-styled machines, however. A number of dealers in the Southwest and West had, for a couple of seasons, been building such models in their own shops from either older machines taken in trade, or from fleet purchases of condemned Police models from law enforcement agencies. As the late 1960s had been a critical era of declining H-D sales, the dealers no doubt felt forced to enter the custom field on their own.

AMF-H-D expanded their advertising activities, and in slick Madison Avenue style couched their appeal in new generation language. A new identifying logo was adopted: a broad ribboned number '1' which carried a simulation of the American flag, together with the slogan 'The All American Freedom Machine.' The '1' no doubt was meant to refer to H-D's recent victories in the big Nationals, with the emphasis that H-D was an all-American product. The term 'freedom' was an apt reference to the freedom of self-expression that motorcycling can provide, now reinforced by recognition of the free-swinging 'biker' cult.

What with the infusion of fresh capital, and an augmentation of H-D's engineering staff by AMF production specialists, the output of machines was almost at once doubled, but the effort was complicated by the physical limitations of the 19th Century Juneau Avenue factory and its now obsolete tooling.

The increased costs and advancing overheads at once mandated an increase in factory prices. Many dealers and owners were shortly alarmed by three such price raises within the first year of AMF control. Critics noted that the suggested retail selling price of H-D big twin models seemed to be approximating that of a well-equipped full-size Chevrolet sedan.

These increases, whether warranted or not, were especially critical to the fortune of H-D's export markets, as the relatively higher selling price of the large V twins already imposed a serious sales problem. The export of American vehicles of all types had been markedly reduced since the close of World War II due to changing worldwide economic conditions, as will be subsequently discussed. Dealers visiting the factory were now heard to comment that AMF appeared to have recruited an excessive number of clerical and middle management employees which might well account for the AMF claim of soaring overheads.

While a certain air of renewed confidence in H-D's future had been imparted by the AMF takeover, problems in production almost immediately appeared. With the speeding up of the assembly line, it became apparent that the quality control with which H-D's top management had always concerned itself was now deteriorating. With the restricted areas available for working on an enhanced number of machines, the units were pushed through without either adequate time for careful assembly, or checkouts while the machines were on the line.

Another problem was that during this period a number of veteran production foremen and other experienced employees elected to retire. This severely interfered with production quality.

In consequence, a large number of machines were crated and shipped to dealers that showed various product defects, or even, in some cases, had vital components missing. The dealers at once lodged strong complaints, demanding warranty reimbursement for the shop time required to make the machines operable. H-D's new management policy was now, curiously enough, that the responsibility of final machine checkout was upon the dealer. The net result was that the interpretation of warranty responsibility was now in the hands of the factory. Only in cases where the dealer could prove that a part or parts were visibly defective or actually broken could the dealer hope to receive reimbursement for expended shop time.

This situation naturally infuriated most of the dealership, who had been originally apprehensive of a change in H-D ownership. While in the past H-D had experienced a number of problems with various newly-introduced models, the overall quality of their major components had usually been above the average of the general motorcycle industry. Veteran dealers had previously reported that at certain periods under the original management quality control problems were experienced during 1952 and 1957. In correcting certain problems in production during these years, the factory's official position was that labor troubles were the cause.

During the 1970-71 episodes some factory officials had stated that some veteran employees resented liaison AMF production people overseeing the assembly lines, and that actual sabotage of machines had occurred. In any case, many of these initial problems were corrected by the 1973 season. The damage had been done, however, and riders and dealers began talking privately about the difference between 'Milwaukee' and 'AMF' machines. Pointed remarks were made regarding the present quality of paint finishes, and not a few dealers scrubbed the AMF labels off the tank sides.

The Harley and Davidson families and dealers and enthusiasts everywhere were saddened by the news on August 23, 1971 that William J. Harley had died in his 59th year. Reported as being in ill health for some months previously, his condition was aggravated by the complications of chronic diabetes. As the son of the real father of H-D, he had literally grown up in the Juneau Avenue factory.

Starting at the bottom in the shipping department at the behest of his father, who saw to it that he learned every phase of H-D production, he was by 1957 a Vice President and head of the Engineering Department. Not the least of his practical education, in addition to his college degree, was the ongoing tutelage from his father and others on the staff such as William Ottaway and Hank Syvertson, who had enjoyed years of experience in both theory and trial and error. Veteran employees have stated at various times that of all the second generation H-D family members who joined the Company, he was the most suited by both temperament and ability, as well as desire, to carry on in a top managerial position.

Harley is described as being cautious and conservative in his outlook on engineering matters, and more inclined to formulate his designs on the well-proven works of others, whether from within or without the Company. His first design was the adaptation of the classic DKW 125cc engine-gear unit to produce the first ever H-D lightweight – the 125cc Hummer. This was later modified to evolve the 165cc Teleglide and later, the Scat, Pacer, and Bobcat models. His most notable design was, of course, the 45 cubic inch K model, later enlarged to 55 cubic inches as the KH, a rather curious mixture of traditional and modern that was greeted with mixed emotions by H-D enthusiasts. The ohv Sportster model which was based upon it was, in its final form, alleged to have been taken from a 1000 cc J.A. Prestwich pushrod V twin of 1934. A lifelong motorcycle enthusiast, Harley grew up in the 'J' and 'Peashooter' eras, and, as a young man, conducted much of the road testing and practical evaluation of the 61E and continuing EL series.

In later years he was President and a Director of the Aermacchi operation after its management was reorganized following acquisition by H-D. He was also the Chairman of H-D's Swiss international marketing affiliate. The President of Italy presented him with the Order of Merit, an honor historically accorded to nationals of foreign countries who contributed to Italy's economic and social betterment. In addition, he served the usual tours of duty by the H-D family members as a Director of the AMA and the M&ATA.

Another family transition in 1971 was the resignation from the Company of Walter Davidson, Jr. who informed associates that he 'didn't like being told what to do.' Filling various minor executive offices as a young man growing up in the Company, he had been, since his uncle Arthur's death in 1950, a Vice President and Sales Manager. He was a frequent speaker at central and regional Sales and Dealers' meetings, as well as making appearances at Daytona and other big National race meets. He tirelessly promoted H-Ds 'name brand' loyalty, and the American V twin concept. While wholly

The 1980 FXB Sturgis. *(AMF-Harley-Davidson).*

Interior of the Rodney C. Gott Museum. *(AMF-Harley-Davidson).*

committed to H-D's traditional production format, not a few dealers and riders considered him as personifying the general ineptitude and arrogance of some of H-D's second generation executive management whose inability to grasp the realities of a changing market ultimately caused the Company to fail under its original ownership.

Walter Jr's tenure of office since the early post-war years represented perhaps the most stormy period of H-D's history. The dealers assumed a more independent position following the well-publicized Fordyce revolt. Most of them were constantly importuning the factory for new and updated designs to meet the competition, or were adding other brands to their stock to fulfill customer demands. To meet the competition from the growing aftermarket boom, many were also stocking outside products whose prices were far more competitive. A number of dealers had dropped their H-D franchise in favor of other makes, attested by the fact that H-D's roster had dropped from a 1941 high of over a thousand down to about six hundred in the early 1960s.

Through it all, Walter Jr. continued to stoutly defend the Company's position in producing only 'American' type motorcycles, emphasizing its policy of serving the dealers only, and reaffirming the factory's right to be the arbitrary judge of warranty reimbursement claims.

After the AMF takeover, his constant rehashing of old Company shibboleths was somewhat embarrassing to some of AMF's younger executives, as they considered them relics of the bad old days of domestic motorcycling. A particular source of controversy was his ongoing public statements favoring antisemitism, then no longer a popular advocacy in an age of growing ethnic tolerance. He continued to associate himself with H-D affairs after his separation from the Company, and still attended race meets and regional rallies that favored H-D riders up until his death in 1979.

In an analysis of H-D production by AMF's staff, it was soon determined that the big twin types, especially in the 'dresser' FL and FLH models, were rather complex machines and expensive to produce. While the Company had lately emphasized the fact that in an age of growing complexity H-D was still a basic machine, such was not actually the case. In fact, their 'basic' design, a slightly updated copy of their 1930s products, was actually quite complex when compared to such contemporaries as the Excelsior Super X or the Indian Chief models whose simplicity was due to the fact that they were conceived by mostly two designers: Arthur A. Constantine and Charles B. Franklin. On the other hand, the H-Ds were evolved as a 'bits and pieces' entity from the efforts of a series of factory engineers. The author, who has had the opportunity to closely observe the ground up restoration of several 1930s makes, can attest to the fact that a mid-1930 H-D has nearly twice as many parts as does a contemporary Indian Chief.

The York facility is a single storey 800,000 square foot building that was built during World War II as a defense plant. It was acquired by AMF in 1964 and converted for the manufacture of certain of the Company's leisure time products. In adapting it for motorcycle manufacture, a 1,000 foot main assembly line was laid out, with component part assemblies feeding into it at appropriate intervals. The conversion was undertaken by a crew of specialists under the direction of John Nowak, a thirty-five year veteran of H-D's long time production staff.

It was decided to retain the Capitol Drive plant in Milwaukee for the continued manufacture of engines and transmissions. These are completed to the testing stage, and then shipped to York in the Company's own trucks. Plastic components are still made in Tomahawk, and also trucked to York.

The famous museum was subsequently shipped to York where it is housed in a special building. Board Chairman Rodney C. Gott, as a lifelong H-D enthusiast took personal charge of this project, and it was later named in his honor.

The Juneau Avenue plant now houses the main executive offices and a part of its cavernous interior is used for storage. Guided tours are no longer conducted here, nor at the Capitol Drive plant, but the York facility offers two public tours daily when the plant is in operation.

The York facility is situated just east of the industrial City of York, and is located adjacent and just north of the famous Pennsylvania Turnpike in a park-like setting of 232 acres. A substantial number of AMF's former labor pool formed the original nucleus of H-D's new production force. It is suggested in York there existed a more harmonious labor situation than in Milwaukee, where the Company experienced numerous difficulties with the former AFL-CIO group. The Company's production force in York is, at this writing, represented by the Mechanics and Aerospace Workers Union. The average wage of production workers in 1978 was reported as being $6.00 per hour. By 1983 this had risen to $9.00.

Shortly after the inauguration of the expanded production facilities, the Company announced the offering of the most comprehensive line of models in H-D's history. This was partly due to AMF's continuation of the Aermacchi line, in the hope that an expanded advertising campaign might enhance its sales. For a hoped-for market penetration to counter the growing horde of Oriental two strokes, H-D offered five Aermacchi models. The X-90 was a portable, small-wheeled minibike weighing but 126 pounds, equipped with lighting to make it street legal. The Z-O was fitted with the same gearbox unit and was of the street-scrambler type. The SR-100 was a high-clearance, motocross model with long travel suspension and a highly tuned 100 cc engine. To enhance its rather narrow power band, it was fitted with a five-speed gearbox. These two models were subsequently refined and carried forward as the Baja and Rapido, respectively, and for their size exhibited an amazing power output.

Two updated 350 cc Sprint models filled the middleweight category. The SX was a trials machine with knobby tires and a new five-speed transmission. The SS-350 was similar, except that it was fitted as a street machine. A heavier frame with twin down tubes steadied the steering in answer to reports that the frames of earlier models were prone to flexing.

The Harley-Davidson Sportster was entirely redesigned, with a longer, taller and heavier frame which now accommodated a new engine of 61 cubic inches. It was offered in two models, the XLCH-1000 being a sporting type, and the XL-1000, a touring model with electric starting. The former version had been alluded to in review and test descriptions as being somewhat intermediate, as if the designers were not sure whether the Sportsters were a scaled-down FL or a sports model in their own right. The new models were now most definitely not oriented toward the 'dresser' category. The fitting of an electric starter to the XL model countered objections in some quarters that the machines could be hard starters.

The classic FL models now featured an improved oiling system and hydraulic brake controls which somewhat enhanced their recent lack of stopping power. This last had been made much of road tests conducted on FLs in several trade magazines in the late 1960s. With more and more weight being added every few seasons to this venerable model, and the fact that its braking system had not been updated in decades, riders not fully conversant with the machine's stopping capabilities had sustained a series of accidents. In 1972 a disc brake was fitted to the front wheel, with the rear being so accommodated the following season, this contributing somewhat to the updating of this ancient design. New color combinations and slight changes in trim were executed by Willie G. Featured also were new plastic windshield fairings and streamlined luggage carriers catering to the interests of the tourists, the FL's traditional customers.

The new Super Glide was a stripped down FL with the Ceriani-pattern forks of the Sportster and was designated as the FX-1200, the forerunner of an upcoming line of X models. As road tested by *Cycle World*, it was noted that it exhibited all of the long familiar FL characteristics as a somewhat heavy steering ponderous machine with the usual 'clunk' shifting gearbox. The tester noted that the big, slow-turning engine gave the traditional high torque urge at moderate rpm for comfortable cruising speeds up to about 70 mph when any higher speeds brought about a vibration syndrome that was highly uncomfortable. Noting the overall design was a concession to the now familiar custom chopper type, the FX was heralded as initiating a new trend in the more usual reactionary H-D design format. A subsequent option in later models was the fitting of an electric starter, which caused some raised eyebrows among custom enthusiasts as somewhat undermining its macho image.

The XR-750 was offered as two distinct models. One was a dirt track machine, with a choice of gear ratios and suspension systems to suit the individual rider. The other was a road racer, with an enveloping forward fairing and a streamlined tail section. It was advertised as being capable of 160 mph with the improved aluminium engine.

The Company was able to achieve some public notoriety with an XR when the well-known motorcycle daredevil, Robert 'Evel' Knievel selected the model as a replacement for his Italian Laverda machines. The Company supplied him with three machines along with technical advice. Following his ill-fated attempt to make a rocket-assisted jump over the Snake River Canyon in 1973, he became involved in a felony complaint by a reporter whom he assaulted with a baseball bat. With the resultant unfavourable publicity, H-D withdrew its support.

A more pleasant adjunct to H-D publicity was the motion picture, 'Electra-Glide in Blue', featuring the adventures of the talented actor, Robert Blake, as a motorcycle patrolman. As a riding enthusiast, Blake had previously gained much critical acclaim in the controversial film 'In Cold Blood', as well as portraying a tongue-in-cheek detective in a long-running TV series featuring a white cockatoo as his pet.

The domestic motorcycle market, which had been expanding somewhat unevenly since the Oriental invasion of the early 1960s, underwent explosive growth after 1970. 1973 proved to be the year of greatest sales – one million five hundred thousand units – and this figure was not topped again within the decade. Experts claimed that the post-war baby boom had by that time provided sufficient young people to form the backbone of this market. Due to H-D's enhanced production, the Company sold over 50,000 machines, a creditable showing over past years, but in reality a miniscule part of the vast numbers of total machines sold.

In spite of the general boom in motorcycling, the Aermacchi models did not sell well. As has been mentioned, most of the dealers were not oriented toward light or middleweight machines, and many

The AMF-H-D Assembly Plant at York, Pennsylvania. *(AMF-Harley-Davidson)*.

did not wish to tie up flow capital in large numbers of these models and their concomitant parts. The general public had quite naturally never associated H-D with small motorcycles, and, too, it was rather incongruous that H-D, long an adamant foe of foreign imports, was now pushing the sales of such with the H-D label fixed on their tank sides.

Now that H-D production had at long last reached more respectable proportions, a new and sinister note crept into the proceedings. The capacity of the production line had lately reached 365 machines per day, working two shifts, which, allowing for normal operation, would indicate a yearly output of about 60,000 units. This production, relating it to the size of the operation and the number of line stations utilized, caused production to move at such a speed that proper quality control was impossible.

This, of course elicited a storm of protest from the dealers, as, historically in the domestic motorcycle industry, machines received from the factory had always been subjected to both quality control in assembly and at least a nominal test run whether actually on the road or simulated on a test bed. As many dealers operated small establishments with a staff of only one or two mechanics, this diversion of their time from normal repair work seriously upset their cost schedules where a day or two's time had to be allocated to setting up and repairing a brand new machine. Further problems were noted when it was found that major components such as engines or transmissions or both were inherently faulty and, in some cases, could not be made to function properly even after extensive overhauling. It was noted that mismatched crankcase halves could not be made oil tight, or that valve guide orifices were improperly machined and prevented valves from seating correctly. Transmission parts were sometimes inaccurately machined, either precluding shifting gears, or making it impossible to find neutral, all indicating quality control problems in the Capitol Drive plant as well. These cumulative faults were to further complicate factory-dealer relationships in the ongoing vexing problem of warranty reimbursement to the dealers.

During the initial period of the AMF reorganization of H-D, many owners and not a few dealers were questioning AMF's top management about the possibility of an updating of H-D's line of models, or even the introduction of new models in the near future, based on the advertising copy released by AMF promising a strengthening of the H-D operation. At length AMF's management leaked quasi-official statements to the effect that what with the payment of 21 million dollars for H-D, and the 30-odd million in additional facilities for the York factory, plus new tooling, any further expenditures for forward products or prototype work was at that time not possible.

With the general increase in motorcycling interest, the custom accessory and aftermarket business boomed. The ongoing increase in the retail price of H-D parts encouraged outside suppliers to enter the market with counterfeit copies at more competitive prices. The list of suppliers based in Taiwan continued to grow. It was now relatively easy to construct one's own big twin with aftermarket components.

257

A heavyweight 80 cu.in. V twin, assembled from aftermarket parts manufactured in the US, Taiwan and Hong Kong.

A new trend in customizing was the emergence in the late 1960s and early 1970s of the extended fork. Some unknown customizer extended the fork legs to present a somewhat reared back and rakish appearance. As subsequent enthusiasts began outdoing each other in raising the front end, the next step was to increase the rake of the head lug. This not only allowed the fitting of even more extended forks, but became mandatory to maintain a semblance of stability. In the beginning of this trend a rake of about 45° was established at the expense and complication of altering the standard frame. The custom manufacturers almost immediately entered the field with special frames, mostly of the rigid type with the rake already built in, and often with the option of several lug angles. The earliest extended forks were usually pre-1948 girder types that had been extended by welding in additional tubing. The custom manufacturers designed their own types as original fabrications of various lengths and patterns. Some were based on the original H-D design; others were based on the British girder pattern with a single compression spring. In most cases a special front wheel was required. These were usually of 21-inch diameter with a 3-inch section tire. Most were fitted with a brake to make them street legal, some of the internal-expanding type inside the hub.

The extended fork posed problems in steering and handling and was often downright hazardous when negotiating tight turns. As the chopper was generally a straight line freeway machine, this was not too critical if the rider came to a near shut-down when rounding a curve or turning into a right angle.

The subsequent custom-type machines based on the Super Glide and produced by H-D featured extended forks, but without the extreme rake or length of the early examples. Most of these today show a 33° to 35° rake. With careful balancing, stability and cornering appeared satisfactory.

During H-D's transitional period, two separately-published paperback books appeared which purported to deal with Harley-Davidson history. The first was published under the direction of AMF but with no author's credit given. It offered a brief digest of the Company's early years, as already published at various times in past issues of the *Enthusiast*, together with brief, non-technical descriptions of various models produced through the years, and a summary of H-D's more outstanding competition successes. As a typical in-house offering it quite naturally omitted any of the more controversial aspects of American motorcycle industry, such as sales and marketing problems, relations with competitors, or various debatable incidents involving H-D's position with the AMA. Considered by most critics as an advertising effort, it was mainly circulated through dealer outlets.

The second book, written by Maurice Hendry, an Australian enthusiast, and published by Ballantine Books, was said to have been produced with official factory co-operation. It was markedly similar to the former AMF production in avoiding controversial issues, and, in addition, the text showed evidence of heavy censorship. Offered mostly through dealers, its bland and self-laudatory content attracted only slight interest.

A significant event in H-D history occurred in 1973 when President William H. Davidson announced that he would retire from active service on September 30th. Associates have reported that during recent months he had become somewhat detached from Company affairs and was no doubt tired of playing the role of figurehead in an organization he no longer controlled and one whose new direction he questioned. With his retirement he officially rang down the curtain on some forty-five years of continuous participation in Company affairs. Officially joining the Company in 1928, he became a member of the Board of Directors in 1931. He was also elected Vice President in 1937, following the death of his father, William A., in 1937. With the death of his uncle, Walter C., in 1942, he became President, although it was said that he walked in his uncle Arthur's shadow until the latter was killed at the end of 1950. In his elevation to the ultimate position of Company leadership, he was considered well qualified through both education and experience. It is also suggested that his position within the managerial hierarchy was strengthened by the fact that he controlled the largest block of Company stock through inheritance.

In addition to his substantial H-D share holdings, he also became involved in a number of outside business interests. Among these were his holdings in the Seventh District Federal Reserve Bank in Chicago, and the Eck Foundry Company in Milwaukee. He was also active in civic affairs, such as the United Fund, and was also appointed as a member of the Economic Development Division of the State of Wisconsin. Long active on Boy Scout work, he was awarded membership in the Order of the Silver Beaver for his volunteer work.

A man of some sophistication, he was more suave and diplomatic than his more bombastic uncle. Yet he could be forceful and adamant if occasion required. Following his retirement he was reported to have incorporated a substantial portion of his holdings into the Harley-Davidson Foundation, the usual tax-saving ploy of large corporate shareholders.

In later years he was known to have relented somewhat in the restrained reserve that H-D had always exhibited toward the trade press in general and motorcycle historians in particular, and he granted several personal interviews.

In the ever-controversial question of H-D's historic domination of the AMA, Davidson stated quite frankly that that body could never have survived its 1925 financial crisis had not the Company elected to underwrite its financial requirements. In the matter of the long time pre-occupation of the AMA with the 45 cubic inch side valve engine, he stated that it was the only machine for many years available for competition. Had the AMA not emphasized such a readily available stock model as the basis for a competition machine, then any sort of motorcycle competition during the lean years of the late 1920s and early 1930s would have been non-existent. As far as the restrictive rule on the compression ratio maximum enforced on the 500 cc ohv imported machines is concerned, Davidson was reported as stating that the AMA did not think it was obligated to completely obliterate all chances of the domestic products competing against imported machines.

As an interesting aside to these comments, Davidson's sentiments in the matter were echoed from a rather surprising source. In 1948, Steve Lancefield, the noted British speed tuner, stated in an interview published in *The Motor Cycle*, that in his opinion the AMA rules were equitable to the point that British machines, even though of differing design, had a fair chance to compete. He further stated that while the AMA was protecting its own side valve machines, the British had been protecting their own type of machine by banning the fitting of superchargers and the use of special fuels. This restrictive attitude was placed in force after Georg Meier had won the Isle of Man Senior TT with a supercharged BMW in 1939.

William H. Davidson's rather passive attitude toward H-D's declining sales after the initial private sale of the Company's stock in 1965 has been the subject of much speculation on the part of enthusiasts, dealers and certain veteran employees. The historic efforts to supply the needs of law enforcement bodies were carried forward, as were appeals to the 'dresser' riders whose numbers were markedly declining. While it was now obvious to everyone connected with motorcycling that the custom biker type of rider was dominating the current demand for the heavyweight big twin, the Company continued largely to ignore them. As a result, the aftermarket accessory market grew amazingly with each subsequent sales season.

Some light was shed on this subject in the spring of 1983, when two former Midwestern dealers, once prominent in H-D affairs, independently offered to share their opinions with the author in exchange for his promise to protect their anonymity. A part of their knowledge was gathered from their long association with the Company and its managerial personnel, as well as the fact that they both purchased H-D stock during the time it was offered to selected people outside the Company.

It was their shared opinion that the surviving members of the Harley and Davidson families, together with various heirs of deceased relatives and their estates, had more or less tacitly agreed as early as 1963 that it might be better for all concerned that the Company be sold. At this point in time, all the original Founders were long gone, and, indeed, most of the second generation were either deceased or had resigned. As a point of fact, many of this group had never evidenced a consuming interest in Company affairs, as witnessed by the arrogant attitude assumed by some of them that indicated a negative attitude to the operation. Then, too, as a closely knit and clannish family group, outside people were never admitted to the inner circle of top management, and at this point there were no emerging family members with either the technical or managerial abilities to move the Company forward in an industry that was becoming increasingly complex and competitive. On the financial side, what with long obsolete plant facilities and the continuing outmoded designs, it would have taken an inordinately large commitment of funds to revitalize the Company. This was especially brought home with the failure of the stop-gap expedient of bringing in the Aermacchi designs which had not achieved the desired results for reasons already explained. At this point the financial requirements or desires of the second generation and their heirs had been satisfied, and it might well have been considered pointless to carry on into an uncertain future replete with capital risks.

The question as to just why the Company had refused since the mid-1930s to update its designs may well have its answer in matters of finance. After precariously weathering the depression, sales had stabilized in the post-war era. With a seller's market between 1945 and 1955, profits had been rewarding and the tooling up for completely new models would have entailed an enormous expense. As long as there was still a ready market for the slightly modified ohv 61E and its 74 cubic inch derivative whose tooling had long ago been amortized, the course of action where the profit motive was uppermost was clear. This explains why the old basic H-D was 'improved' only very conservatively with bits and pieces added on, and only then when such had been demanded by enthusiasts for some seasons.

This ongoing Company policy was emphasized to the author by Joe Petrali in an interview in 1972, when he recalled a conversation with the late Walter Davidson, Jr. in the late 1950s. In discussing the contemporary state of the market, Petrali suggested that H-D might well have been in a better competitive position regarding the influx of British middleweight machines if an updated 30.50 cubic inch model C single with overhead valves had been introduced in place of the 125 cc DKW lightweight just after World War II. Davidson replied that the matter had been considered, but that the profit margin on the 125 worked out to be porportionally greater on a costing basis, and what with moderate tooling costs included, the idea of a larger single was dropped. It is today interesting to contemplate how the course of US motorcycling history could have been altered at mid-century with the introduction of such a machine.

While this Company policy might well be a source of anguish for dedicated cultist-enthusiast H-D fans, it is a fact that the original Founders were unsophisticated mechanics, less interested in the niceties of engineering theory than they were in producing a practical vehicle suitable for the work intended and one which could be built to a competitive price and produce a reasonable profit. In this they succeeded very well. It must also be remembered that in a capitalistic free society any operation must be accomplished with a profit, and, as the sole owners of the Company, the Founders and their heirs had the right to proceed in any manner they thought best suited to their personal interests.

It was unfortunate, however, that the original Founders and later second generation owners had not been more circumspect in concealing their self-serving attitude from public view. Veteran dealers have been heard to remark how, in the consummation of every business transaction, however small, Company officials were continually applying an almost paranoic emphasis on the fact that their corporate interests were always uppermost.

A further thought in this regard, and one often touched on by veteran dealers and riders, is that H-D's earlier management always seemed to be handicapped in their relationship with others of the industrial community and the motorcycle industry in particular, by the lack of that often indefinable personal attribute known as 'class.' The coarse manners and profane speech of Walter Davidson, the cold austerity of William H., and the intemperate public statements of Walter Jr. were in startling contrast, for instance, to the personalities of Indian's executives, such as the boyish charm of Frank J. Weschler, the courtly manners of the aristocratic Russell Waite, or the suave sophistication of multi-millionaires E. Paul duPont and Ralph B. Rogers.

With William H's retirement, an AMF production executive, John H. O'Brien was installed as President of the H-D Division. It was next decided that the Juneau operation should be moved to a facility already owned by AMF in York, Pennsylvania, as already mentioned.

When official news of the impending change in manufacturing locale was forthcoming, H-D's union labor force became much concerned, as some 700 jobs at Juneau Avenue would then be eliminated. In spite of the fact that the Capitol Drive plant was to be retained as the engine assembly plant where over one thousand employees were employed, the unions called a strike. AMF President Rodney C. Gott at once ventured the opinion that all of H-D's operation might well be transferred to Pennsylvania, where union militancy was less pronounced. Failing this, he further stated AMF would be doing well to rid themselves of H-D altogether.

During 1972 and 1973 AMF's Sales and Marketing executives analyzed H-D's dealer organization with an eye to strengthening their marketing position. The dealers in the larger cities came under particularly close scrutiny both in the matter of the physical aspect of their showrooms and their sales methods as well. Dealers were encouraged to either update their often run-down buildings, or move into new or better quarters within their franchise areas. When the efficiency of their selling practises was in question, suggestions were made as to changes in tactics. Those who did not at once comply, or who were not receptive to change, were put on notice than when their franchises came up for the usual annual review they would be dropped. Not a few veteran dealers lost their franchises in this manner, including such long time stalwarts as Marion Dedricks of Seattle and Joe Walker of Santa Ana.

In addition, numerous aging or senile dealers with decades of representation were dropped when it was ascertained that they were no longer physically or mentally able to pursue aggressive sales activities. Many, but not all, of these had existed in small towns or remote locations. As possible younger replacements, the Company solicited new dealers through advertisements placed in trade and hobby magazines, stating that many new and potentially profitable locations were becoming available.

At this point, the Company was facing increasing competition from the Japanese importers which were not only growing in numbers, but also in ever-increasing dealer representation. They were seriously challenging the FL models in both the touring and law enforcement fields with high-powered machines whose sophisticated design and high performance capabilities far overshadowed the venerable American classic. A telling advantage in their favour was their low maintenance requirements and the fact that they did not require top overhauls at 15,000 to 20,000 miles as did their Yankee counterparts.

In spite of the competition, H-D sales held fairly steady, with over 70,000 units assembled during 1973. Economic conditions were generally good and what with consequent high employment, sales of automobiles, household appliances and other durable goods were at an all time high.

The archaic FLH model was carried forward to accommodate the fiercely loyal but now aging and dwindling group of 'dresser' and club-type enthusiasts who had formerly been the historic supporters of the marque. Increasing emphasis was now placed on the Super Glide and Sportster models to accommodate the growing numbers of custom biker riders who were now weaned from 'chopping' old classic models. Sales in this area were helped by the fact that custom enthusiasts could now purchase machines from a dealer and take advantage of sales contract purchase with monthly payments without having to pay cash for aftermarket components for home assembly.

The production supervisors and work force were, by now, much concerned about deteriorating quality control, as most craftsmen in whatever line invariably take pride in their work. It was obvious that to maintain proper quality control a second production line was required to have both the line speed and the work load providing more time for both assembly and final finish. The AMF management, however, stated that there were insufficient funds to bear the expense of duplicating the line, and added to this problem the present production volume had to be maintained to reach sufficient volume to balance costing. The upshot of the matter was that it was now mandated that the machines would be shipped 'as is' from the line in the best finished state that could be accomplished under the circumstances. It would be then up to the dealers to attend to any unfinished details upon receipt of the machines.

While this, of course, was a very high-handed method of turning out a supposedly finished product, the problem did not begin and end at York. With engines and transmissions being completed at the Capitol Drive plant in Milwaukee, the 'hurry up' schedule there was resulting in engine and transmission parts being subject to inaccurate machining and assembly as well.

Veteran employees have related how a 'hospital' unit was set up at the end of the assembly line in an attempt to rectify the problems in the worst of the defective machines. Aside from this, a more serious problem was that of the 'ghost' machines – units that had some serious defect in a vital component, such as either engine or transmission, or both, and which could not be made to run properly by even the heads of the engineering staff or chief mechanical tuners. Most of these anomalies were due to inaccurate machining within these components. In such cases, the defective parts were discarded and the cycle parts dismantled and recycled through the production line.

The consternation on the part of the dealers in having to accept a product that was now averaging over 50% of defects can only be imagined, yet they had no recourse as long as they wished to retain their franchise. Most of them relied heavily on repair and overhaul work for the major portion of their income. The necessity of having to devote much shop time to rebuilding new machines, in addition to the usual set-up procedures, was an economic hardship, especially in the smaller establishments. Another problem was that of factory reimbursement for warranty work. Under the new AMF policy of expecting the dealers to make final running adjustments to new machines, it became a matter of individual interpretation as to the extent of liability the factory was to assume according to the degree of maladjustment encountered. The dealers were clearly not happy with the current state of affairs, but the factory, which always had the final decision in such matters, appeared unwilling to tender reimbursements unless the machine in question was a 'ghost' with an unworkable or non-functioning engine or transmission.

An additional problem to both riders and dealers was that late in 1974 a very substantial increase in wholesale and retail selling prices was announced by the factory. Added to this were even proportionately higher costs of spare parts. It was often stated that with the retail cost of an FLH at $4,000,00, its component parts, if purchased over the counter, would cost the buyer about $20,000,000. In consequence, the sale of aftermarket parts manufactured by outside suppliers boomed, with the factory still campaigning against their use.

In the fall of 1973, the governing body of the AMA was reorganized. The change had been gradual over the preceding two or three years, mostly from the pressure from the growing power of the dealers of the dealers representing the ever-increasing numbers of Japanese machines, as well as from splinter groups of competition riders who rebelled against the arbitrary AMA Competition Committee. These people saw no reason why they should continue to support an organization that had long been almost solely oriented toward the interests of H-D. As it was, the competition picture had already changed radically. Spectator interest in road racing, long an anathema to AMA, was growing to the point where most of the newly inaugurated events were in that category. In addition, California's District 37, one of the most active groups in the country, was threatening to secede from the AMA, as were a number of New England clubs. The various splinter groups of competition riders no longer interested in the traditional AMA horse track type of racing were now promoting their own events.

The AMA Executive Committee was expanded from eight to ten members, retiring the former majority that had consisted of H-D and its satellite representatives and bringing in new blood. Its first step was to vote the AMA as an FICM affiliate, which would allow certain US races to count on points for International Championships. Formula 750 events held in the US could now also be a part of the FICM calendar. After some prolonged negotiations, the AMA's petition to the FIM was accepted, and the International Six Days Trial was next scheduled to be held in the Berkshire district of New England. This was a notable step in international motorcycle competition relations and marked the first time since 1923 that American motorcycling had returned to the fold of the international body.

In commenting on the reorganization of the AMA in an editorial in the November 1972 issue of *Cycle World*, Associate Editor Ivan J. Wagar, long a crusader for a modernized AMA, stated that at last the latter was no long a private club dominated by H-D and a small clique of their suppliers, but was now truly representative of all people interested in motorcycling, whether trade competition riders, or more casual private owners.

As far as the internal affairs of the AMA itself were concerned during the 1969-1973 period, which represented the end of H-D domination, a later Secretary-Manager, Ed Youngblood, revealed that its affairs were in a state of utter chaos. The organization was over one million dollars in debt through mismanagement, along with a sudden decline in membership. It was ascertained that the former President and Board had exhibited a woeful lack of initiative in promoting growth, together with a neglect of the average road riding member in favor of traditional horse track racing which had long been H-D's main forte.

During the ensuing years, the number of AMA Executive Board members was increased from eight to ten and then twelve. Its makeup was soon to include representatives from *Cycle World* and *Cycle Sport* magazines, as well as from Honda, Kawasaki, Suzuki, and Yamaha. New trade and aftermarket suppliers formerly excluded by H-D were also included. The incoming 1973 President, J. R. Kelley, head of KK Motorcycle Supply, who succeeded H-D's 1969 appointee, William Bagnall, pledged that the new AMA would henceforth attempt to serve the best interests of all segments of motorcycling.

In the following editorial in *Cycle World*, Ivan Wagar complimented the H-D contingent for gracefully relinquishing their former majority position on the AMA Board in order that the AMA could now proceed in a democratic manner. He noted that John Davidson retained his seat as the H-D representative, and that John Harley agreed to retain his position as AMA secretary. He further stated that the new Board harbored no ill will toward long time AMA competition officials such as Aub LeBard, Pete Colman, Walt Fulton, or Earl Flanders, and that their many years of dedication to the cause of motorcycling were deeply appreciated. He also hoped that many of the long-standing animosities that had existed could now happily be forgotten.

With the broadened representation within the AMA, retail dealers of the Japanese imports now urged their old customers as well as the buyers of new machines, to join the AMA as private riders, and such representation increased accordingly.

As a result of this long overdue revamping of the AMA, its effectiveness for the benefit of motorcyling in general increased markedly in the ensuing decade. Private owner representation, never before permitted, was effected through the institution of a Rider Council drawn from private owners within the geographical AMA Districts. A special committee was formed to counteract the ignorant and often misguided efforts of certain state and national legislators to penalize motorcycle riders by ill-advised restrictive local or national legislation detrimental to the sport. This committee has successfully challenged certain restrictive ordnances banning motorcycle riding in certain public parks or scenic recreational areas laid down by short-sighted municipal or state law enforcement bodies. It has also successfully challenged a ridiculous law that suggested that safety belts should secure the rider to his machine, and a motorcycle design that steered from the rear wheel!

Motorcycle sales in all categories increased rapidly during this period. The Japanese manufacturers expanded their extensive line of models to include increasing numbers of heavyweight machines. H-D's accommodation of the custom chopper type of machine was well received, although critics noted that the only updating was cosmetic in that the same old vibrating self-destructive V twin engines requiring high maintenance and having traditional 'clunk' shifting gearboxes were merely transferred to chopper-style frames.

The custom accessory aftermarket from outside suppliers boomed, with many of these shamelessly pirating the outline and form of the H-D patent logos and trade marks to label their products. The Company continued their warfare against these people with advertisements condemning their use. The 'chopping' of older model H-Ds diminished in favor of individual building up of customized machines from aftermarket parts. While most of the new generation H-D riders were now in the custom category, the old FLH models as slightly refurbished machines from the late 1930s were carried forward to accommodate the diehard 'dresser' enthusiasts, numbers of whom still carried on in individual club organizations catering to this interest.

The custom-chopper-biker movement and the later H-D enthusiast interested in the 1970s custom factory offerings have been well served in the journalistic sense during the later years. The earlier publications were *Street Chopper* and *Custom Chopper*. These magazines gave further impetus to

The author with his FLHT. This is a modified FHT marketed to satisfy those traditionalists who consider the latter too radical a change from the classic FLH. For 1985, it was cataloged as the Electro-Glide. (*Steve Nelson*).

the movement by forming a medium for an exchange of ideas and the dissemination of technical knowledge dealing with the common eccentricities of H-D engines as well as methods of modifying standard machines. While some of the data dealt with the customizing of British or Japanese machines, the bulk of the interest was centered on H-D. These publications have also been involved in the promotion of trade fairs and shows devoted to customized machines, with heavy subsidies from various independent aftermarket manufacturers who exhibit their wares. To attract private entrants, prizes were awarded for various categories of customizing as well as mechanical excellence.

Three more recent magazines in the field are *Easy Riders*, *Supercycle*, and *Iron Horse*. All vigorously promote the free swinging biker life style and are fanatically pro-H-D. Deriding the Oriental imports appears to be a matter of ongoing policy as they are referred to as 'rice-grinders' or 'rice mills'. They stress the patriotic necessity for buying an American product that is rich in long standing tradition and in this latter concept usually feature a section of their magazines devoted to old photographs of models of days long past. In an interesting advocation of the big V twin they imply that such offers 'safe' power, in contrast to the 'dangerous' power of the late model Oriental large capacity machines. While admitting that the top speeds and acceleration of the latter are far and above that of current H-Ds, they suggest that the low down torque capabilities of the latter offer more effective performance at 'safer' and more satisfying speeds.

Featured also in these blunt but sophisticated and effectively-written publications are in-depth articles dealing with technical and design subjects, as well as repair and overhaul outlines. Also noted are highly explicit articles dealing with various sexual mores, together with eye-catching nude female figure studies, and in-mail beauty contests featuring photographs of the readers' 'Ole Ladies'.

Not the least of their emphasis is on individual biker freedom. They support the free-thinking policies of the loosely organized Modified Motorcycle Association (MMA) as well as *ABATE*, another biker group which constantly campaigns against restrictive laws aimed at motorcyclists and, most particularly, compulsory helmet laws.

The scope of this segment of motorcycling interest is attested by the fact that the cumulative audited monthly circulation of the five leading biker publications by 1980 reached nearly one million copies per month.

By this time, the general public had come to more or less accept the presence of the biker element as a matter of course, realizing that the Levis and leather appearance did not necessarily have a sinister import. However, both the public at large and the H-D Company itself were united in their condemnation of certain T-shirt and coat patches that utilized certain profane expressions of either the biker philosophy or adulation of H-D itself. In spite of this, the factory encouraged the ongoing cult-like fervour of the average biker toward H-D. Willie G. continued to solicit biker interest by his presence at the Daytona meetings during the Championship races and at the bikers' traditional summer meeting held annually at Sturgis.

In the meantime, AMF had never been able to put H-D in a satisfactory position as a viable division of its industrial empire. According to the most accepted reports, AMF had poured upwards of 35 million dollars into H-D, and had yet to realize equitable profits or to overcome the problems of quality control for the production of a satisfactory product.

The immediate problem appeared to be that AMF had acquired H-D in the now traditional conglomerate intent of converting an ailing company into a viable operation by updating manufacturing capability and creating an enlarged or mass market in a simultaneous effort. But in this case there was not a potential mass market for H-D in the usual sense as it was basically an obsolete product line, (the Aermacchi line aside), that historically catered for traditionalist enthusiasts. AMF was then competing in an expanding marketplace where machines from the Orient whose vast worldwide markets provided the capital for continuing updating and development of high technical machines for a new generation of motorcyclists who had no allegiance to 'tradition'.

As far as the Aermacchi machines went, they were already outdated as basically 1950s products, and by the 1970s were no longer competitive in either technical development or retail price with an ever-growing horde of similar displacement Japanese machines.

In attempting to modernize H-D's former archaic production methods, AMF was faced with developing techniques of both assembly line production and supply of components to suit, and in proper sequence. There was also the problem that as a formerly hand-assembled product, H-D machines had long been built by individual craftsmen who, in most cases, had worked out, in conjunction with their veteran supervisors, detail techniques and improvements which were never formally included in production directions or printed shop procedures. With the normal attrition by death and retirement of these employees, new production workers faced a bewildering problem of trying to figure out why certain parts of a 'Milwaukee' machine worked fine where those of a 'York' H-D would not.

Added to these problems was the now decades-old truism that industrial products made in the

United States could never compete pricewise with those made overseas for the simple reason that the high standard of American living mandated a wage structure that was never competitive.

While AMF's top management has been somewhat loath to talk about the Company's H-D experience, the author was subsequently able to obtain interviews with several of the people involved on the promise of preserving their anonymity. From their cumulative statements it was learned that both AMF's Board of Directors as well as the formerly enthusiastic Rodney C. Gott had become disenchanted with the H-D acquisition early in the game. Saddled with long outdated 1930s designs as a result of H-D's 'profits before progress' policy, the make faced a fast-dying market of die-hard 'dresser' clubmen types as well as a more or less static cultist contingent whose loyalties were more emotional than due to the excellence of the product. As a somewhat complex machine to produce, its fabrication was dependent on a labor force that could never be competitive with that of the Orient, and, unlike them by tradition, viewed its relationship with management as an adversary proceeding.

The problem of production costing and quality control already priced out of sight as far as its competition was concerned, was bound up in the complexities of corporate financial structuring. In an organization formed from a group of autonomous divisions, each segment must perforce show equitable profits within its own sphere of activity. With financial obligations to shareholders, no corporation can long take profits from one division to bolster the fortunes of an ailing one. As H-Ds profit picture had never been other than marginal, AMF's Board of Directors simply had not the reserve capital available to overhaul the York operation to the extent required to correct all its difficulties.

Accordingly, in the mid-1970s, AMF, through various financial and industrial agencies, began putting out cautious feelers that the H-D Division was available for purchase. Ultimately a number of Midwestern heavy equipment and agricultural implement manufacturing concerns were contacted, including Fuqua Industries, Caterpillar, John Deere and Company, and several others, but with no takers.

Walter H. Halsted, who had for three decades been involved in both the wholesale and retail selling of heavy equipment in the Midwest told the author in 1982 that any firm purchasing H-D would put itself on the horns of a dilemma. With H-D's established policy of adhering to outdated designs, any purchasers with serious intention of engaging in the manufacture of motorcycles would have to completely start over again with both new designs and new plants, a formidable undertaking in the face of Oriental costing and technology. At the same moment, with H-D's designs now frozen into tradition, its present buyers were mostly antique enthusiasts who would simply not accept modern designs with the H-D label on the tanksides.

In any case, the Company was presently facing a crisis with its customers, many of whom were now giving vent to their strong feelings in the trade press regarding the current poor quality of H-D machines together with their own experiences with unreliability. Factory relationships with dealers were still in controversy, as the former still had no established policy on warranty reimbursement. Many dealers complained that invariably individual claims were settled in the financial favor of the factory, leaving them to bear the expenses of replacement parts and labor costs which they considered as factory defects in the first place.

H-D's former prominence in motorcycle sport declined after 1970, as technically advanced racing machines developed by Honda and Yamaha began to dominate the big Nationals, such as Daytona. H-D's last win was in 1969, with Honda's first victory in 1970. Yamaha won every year through the 1970s and into the early 1980s with their highly developed two-strokes.

H-D's XR models, while highly developed by the legendary Richard O'Brien, were ultimately outclassed as to both speed and power. The technical limitations of a pushrod V-twin were at long last no match for either sophisticated two-strokes or four valves per cylinder ohc four strokes that could rev up to 12,000-15,000 rpm. O'Brien was reported as requesting funds to develop a new high performance opposed twin, but was told that under present circumstances such could not be made available.

Yet the XRs continued to make a good showing in the traditional horse track events, as the torque characteristics of the V twin were at their best in such events, particularly in the mile. Jay Springsteen was then gaining prominence as H-D's star rider.

Now freed from H-D's dominance, the revitalized AMA promoted all types of motorcycle competition. Much encouragement was given to this, along with publicity oriented toward touring, all being now covered in the enlarged official magazine *The American Motorcyclist*.

The subject of domestic motorcycle competition since 1950 is a vast one, and space considerations preclude a comprehensive coverage in a single volume primarily dealing with the history of one make of machine. This specialized subject has been well covered in the book, *American Racing Motorcycles* by Jerry Hatfield, who has devoted many years of study to the complexities of the matter. Not only is the subject of American motorcycle competition thoroughly covered, but technical development of the machines as well. The details of H-D's participation are included and the interaction with foreign machine owners and their makers. The extensive ongoing conflicts and controversies between the H-D dominated Competition Committee and the owners and manufactuers of other makes also receives attention.

It was during this period that H-D, in common with the nation's other industrial concerns, faced steeply rising operational costs from OPEC's sudden escalation of the price of crude oil. H-D was particularly affected, as the plastic components from Tomahawk and the engines and transmissions from Milwaukee were transported in company trucks over the 700-odd miles to Pennsylvania for final assembly.

Viewing the sudden changes in the world's economic picture, Rodney C. Gott and his Board of Directors now thought to reassess their position in relation to the production of bowling alleys, sports equipment, sailing boats, and motorcycles, and considered the fact that perhaps a reversion to heavy industry products might be more in line with changing trends.

It was at this point that Ray Albert Tritten, AMF's Vice-President, and slated to succeed Rodney C. Gott as Chairman of the Board, hired Vaughn L. Beals, Jr. as Vice-President in charge of H-D's Engineering Division. Tritten, had, of course, been privy to all H-D's troubles, and had noted with alarm the constant turnover of engineering personnel who had found it not within their abilities to solve H-D's problems of quality and cost control, material acquisition, and the maintaining of a suitable production force. It is also alleged that Tritten hoped that if Beals could not turn H-D around far enough to satisfy AMF's management, he could at least make it attractive enough to attract another buyer!

A Canadian by birth, Beals held both bachelor and master's degrees in engineering from the Massachussetts Institute of Technology, and had spent some years in the aerospace industry. He later headed the Sales Department of Cummins Diesel Engines, paradoxically inaugurated three decades before by Ralph B. Rogers, a one-time President of Indian. A few years later, he resigned from Cummins to form his own manufacturing company devoted to producing logging equipment in the Pacific Northwest.

To further strengthen H-D's technical staff, a young AMF engineer named Jeffrey L. Bleustein joined the Motorcycle Division in 1975. The holder of a PhD in Engineering from Columbia University, he was for a time an instructor at Yale University's Engineering Department. He joined AMF in 1971 as a technical consultant for various of the AMF diversified divisions, before being assigned to H-D specifically. A new policy inaugurated by Bleustein and backed by Vaughan Beals was to recruit a staff of professionally-trained engineers with diversified backgrounds, a situation which had not heretofore been a part of H-D strategy. It was hoped by AMF's Vice President Tritten that some of H-D's more pressing problems, such as the development of new products and the enhancement of production techniques, could now go forward.

H-D's progress during this period was somewhat inhibited by a rapid turnover of staff. Ongoing internal dissensions saw a number of chief executives come and go. Following John H. O'Brien, John Davidson, Vaughn Beals, Gus Davis and Charles L. Thompson took turns at heading the Division. In the end, it was Beals who took charge under AMF's ownership.

In spite of all the personality conflicts and other distractions that took place during the later 1970s, it was generally agreed that forward product development, heretofore put aside through costing difficulties, was paramount if the Company was to survive. The classic top-of-the-line FLH big twin, a slightly warmed-over replica of the 1936 61E, was to be superseded by a new model. This now venerable machine, still revered by aging dresser enthusiasts as THE H-D, and hailed by chopper-custom fans as the classic American motorcycle for individual modification, had long been derided by H-D critics as the typical example of Milwaukee conservatism. While it was in fact over four decades old and had been updated along the way by bits and pieces engineering, it was an historic example of motorcycling conservatism. In spite of the sporting and recreational outlets that motorcycling can provide, actual buyers have long tended to be conservative in their outlook when considering which make to select. When Great Britain's motorcycle industry was enjoying its Golden Age and world wide sales between the wars, many new and unorthodox designs that were hailed by automotive engineers and forward-looking journalists as brilliant and revolutionary, were simply ignored by buyers. The works of Granville Bradshaw, with his ABC shaft drive twin, and later oil and liquid-cooled engines, quickly fell by the wayside. Other notable failures were the car-like all enclosed two-wheelers of Cyril Pullin, along with dozens of other obscure makes with unorthodox engine configuration offering technical advancement.

The situation in the United States was even more proscribed due to the very limited motorcycle market. Here, the unorthodox prototype fared even worse and none ever made it into production. As a result, motorcycle engineering in the States became almost static. The 1912 Excelsior was still basically similar in 1924. The Indian Scout as designed originally in 1912 was recognizable in the very last Indian Chiefs assembled in 1955. H-D's long running J series merged with the VLs in 1930 to themselves integrate with the EL, UL and FL machines. As the sole surviving US make, the FL series became the ultimate in the cult aspect of motorcycling.

A serious problem occurred in connection with it, however, in the late 1960s. What with succeeding modifications to wring more power out of this ancient design in order to cope with its ever-increasing weight, the power band shifted in favor of higher engine revolutions. The four-speed gear box had to be mated to the engine in ratios sufficient to get it moving from rest and provide some acceleration through the gears, resulting in a lower gearing. The new result was that when driven at speeds upwards of 55 mph the engine appeared to be both overworking and vibrating excessively. To relieve this discomfort some aftermarket suppliers, almost simultaneously, devised a drive train made up of armored toothed rubber belting. Some of these systems consisted of final drive only, but some included the primary also. While such a conversion necessitated changing the whole sprocket system into pulleys, the result was an almost unbelievably smooth-running machine that effectively isolated the engine vibration from the rider. While most of these conversions were fitted to built-up custom-type machines, not a few were fitted to dressers for the added comfort of the touring rider.

While aftermarket suppliers were fond of emphasizing that their inventions of the past, such as hydraulic forks, hand clutch and foot gear shifts, rear springing, disc brakes, etc. were taken up by the factory only after being introduced by themselves, the factory always blandly stated that as conservative engineers they never inaugurated any new features without sound reasoning. Such were included only by sufficient public demand.

The 61 cu. in ohv Sportster first produced in 1971 was carried forward in two models. The XLH Super H was more or less of a touring model with a 3.8 gallon fuel tank and electric starting. Its companion model was the XLCH Super CH with kick starting and the smaller 2.2 gallon 'peanut' type fuel tank. In actuality, the Sportster was never much of a touring model due to its rather severe vibrating tendencies from its long stroke, high revving engine. The most popular model was the CH type, welcomed by street cruisers and café racing types who wanted a hot performer for more casual riding. Even a young rider in top physical condition could only ride one for fifty miles or so without the necessity of dismounting in order to recover from the 'pins and needles' syndrome induced by its vibration. Some of the earlier XLCHs were fitted with Edison magnetos that for some reason were not fitted with impulse couplings and had the reputation of being very difficult to start, especially when cold.

In 1976 H-D's advertising format was altered when AMF retained the prestigious New York advertising firm of Benton and Bowles to handle all of AMF's recreational lines. H-D's Sales and Marketing personnel at once took exception to the arrangement as they were of the opinion that Benton and Bowles were subordinating H-D's motorcycling specialty to general sporting goods interests and others AMF products. This thought was substantiated by the fact that AMF's corporate office in Connecticut issued strict guidelines as to the form and content of ad copy to all their divisions. Added to this certain of AMF's officers were to approve of all copy before publication.

As H-D had its own sales promotion department, it retained its own local agency to produce sales literature, brochures, display items, etc. It also hired another agency to produce radio and television commercials, these being aired regionally and paid for on a co-operative basis by both the factory and the area dealers involved. The Company preferred these latter promotions as they could clearly exert more direct control over both the content and areas of coverage.

An example of lack of communication between H-D and AMF occurred when the former's advertising manager placed an ad in *Easy Riders*, then, as now, the largest circulating biker magazine and most fiercely pro-H-D. AMF's top management was at once appalled by this, stating that it was not the proper format for an AMF subsidiary. The copy was withdrawn after one insertion.

A former Benton and Bowles executive told the author in 1983 that the factory-dealer co-op plan grew to nearly $2 million by 1978. This increase in volume displeased AMF's top management as Benton and Bowles was by prior agreement to receive a flat annual fee with all advertising commissions being rebated to AMF. As the large sums being expended by H-D in their own programs prevented AMF from getting the rebates, it then ordered H-D to run all their co-operative programs through Benton & Bowles. With the onset of the economic recession in 1980, AMF ordered that all the recreational subsidiaries select and manage their own advertising campaigns.

In the mid-1970s the domestic motorcycling manufacturing picture changed with both Honda and Kawasaki establishing their own facilities in the United States. Honda purchased a large tract of land adjacent to Marysville, Ohio, and built a large plant for the assembly of both cars and motorcycles. As domestic Japanese laws forbade the sales of machines over 750 cc in that country, it was therefore logical to assemble machines of large capacity within the country of their intended market. The GL 1000 series which became known as the Gold Wing, GL 1100, and Aspencade models after their initial introduction in 1975, as well as certain other over 750 cc models, were then assembled in Ohio, engine and drive trains being shipped from Japan.

Kawasaki inaugurated manufacture of their KZ series machines in Lincoln, Nebraska. They almost immediately brought forth their KZp 1000 Police Special to challenge H-D's long monopoly in the United States. As early as the late 1960s certain US law enforcement bodies began buying small quantities of Japanese machines for evaluation as by this time inflationary conditions in the US had driven the cost of an H-D FLH to about twice that of the standard heavy duty Dodge Polaris sedan. In addition, Kawasaki was also in competition with the Italian Moto Guzzi machines in this field as, during the past three years, fair numbers of Police 850cc models had been purchased by various State as well as local law enforcement bodies for evaluation.

As a somewhat light machine fitted with an 85 hp across-the-frame four cylinder multi-valve short stroke ohc engine, there were initial problems with frame fracture and steering accuracy. The company, however, continued to improve the model soliciting ongoing suggestions from riding officers themselves, and, within a couple of seasons it developed into a very satisfactory machine for this use. With an all up weight of just over 500 pounds and a top speed in fifth gear of nearly 130 mph, its powers of acceleration were almost unbelievable. In addition, it required only minimum maintenance such being mostly lubrication and a change of engine oil and spark plugs at 5,000 mile intervals. Mileages of 40-50,000 and more were frequently recorded before any serious repairs were required. This was in direct contrast to H-D police models which were suggested to require full checkovers every 2,500 miles. It has often been stated by the heads of various law enforcement bodies that high ongoing maintenance costs were ultimately, in their eyes, H-D's downfall as the machine of choice. Those problems were aggravated during the initial AMF days when quality control problems manifested themselves.

H-D police machines continued to be sold, however, if in even smaller quantities. Most departments in the East, Northwest and Midwest continued to use limited numbers of motorcycles but these were not subjected to hard usage like those of the West, Southwest and Far West as they were ridden but four or five months out of the year because of weather conditions. In these areas, they were seldom used for patrolling freeways and expressways which reduced the rigor of the demands made upon them still further. Many of these departments continued to purchase H-Ds, even at a cost penalty, because of long traditions of use, and many officers preferred them due to their center of gravity being lower than the newer across-the-frame fours. Even in areas where the Oriental or Italian machines became the machines of choice, in many cases a few of the older H-D models were kept for use in parades and other patriotic displays where it seemed more prudent to show only American-made machines as escorts.

In 1976 and 1977 the very moderate public interest in 250cc class racing was enhanced by the introduction of the Aermacchi-designed 76-RR liquid-cooled racing model. As a well-designed high performance machine, it offered much encouragement to those desiring to enter competition riding in the novice class. After a number of individual engine and gearbox units were assembled late in 1977, the series was discontinued.

1977 also saw the introduction of a new variation of the Sportster – the XLCR. This model featured the standard engine and gearbox unit of the Sportster fitted to a lightweight triangulated space type frame, cast alloy spoked wheels and a small European type front fairing. This design, said to have been the work of Willie G., was intended to perhaps capture domestic interest in an increasingly popular type of sports machine that was finding favor with Sunday morning 'café racer' types.

Produced for two seasons, the model was not a commercial success. In the first instance it was immediately perceived as not following the classic Sportster lines; as 'not being a real Harley.' Secondly, the light double loop tubular frame was insufficiently heavy to dampen the more severe aspects of the long stroke Sportster's engine vibrations. The result was that even the most physically athletic of the younger riders, who habitually preferred the model, could only ride a few miles at a time before having to dismount to recover from the effect of the hammering. The author recalls seeing an XLCR with one of the front down tubes completely fractured just below the head lug. The owner stated that he did not intend to repair this as the machine handled better and seemed to transmit less vibration in this condition! This model was discontinued after something over 3,000 units were produced.

In 1977 another event occurred which was to have further repercussions on H-D history. One Carl T. Wicks of Long Beach, California, a long-time H-D enthusiast who was also a professional airline pilot and then owner of a motorcycle escort funeral service, met with a small group of H-D enthusiasts to form the nucleus of what was soon to become the Harley-Davidson Owners' Association, Wicks' idea was to unite all H-D owners, whether dresser or custom type rider, under a common banner of interest. In the face of H-D's then current production difficulties, he hoped to attain a better rapport between the factory for the interests of the average private owner as well as to offer technical aid in the solving of some of the make's more glaring deficiencies. Like many another enthusiast he was

In June, 1981, the new owners and full time employees of Harley-Davidson pose for an official portrait. Standing (from left) are: John Hamilton, Dr. Jeffrey Bleustein, Kurt Woerpel, Chris Sartalis and William "Willie G" Davidson. Seated (from left) are: James Paterson, Timothy Hoelter, David Lickerman, Peter Profumo, David Caruso, Ralph Swenson, Charles Thompson and Vaughn Beals. (*Harley-Davidson Motor Company*).

becoming appalled at the horror stories abounding concerning the many purchasers of new machines who were seeing them disintegrate after a few miles on the road, or who found themselves stranded in out of the way places due to the failure of some component.

In the initial phase, Wicks met with William Dutcher, then the head of AMF's Publicity Department, and Joe Walker, one-time owner of an H-D dealership in Santa Ana, California, in the hope of obtaining the blessing of the factory as well as possibly some financial support.

Dutcher was reported as favoring the idea of such an organization but was non-committal as to whether any official support might be forthcoming. After some consideration, Wicks went forward with his organization plans and established a club magazine which was known as the *Gear Box*. With no other support, Wicks persuaded a number of the more prominent after-market producers and wholesalers in the Southern California area to buy advertising space and obtained their backing for both technical and organizational advice as members of his Board of Directors. In time most of the seventeen H-D dealers in the Los Angeles basin agreed to offer their support. In most cases they not only purchased advertising space in the club magazine, but offered club members a 10% discount on certain parts and services.

In order to expand the organization, Wicks induced certain enthusiasts who travelled widely throughout the west and other parts of the country to act as area representatives in the recruitment of new members. In this and other programs Wicks contributed substantial sums out of his own pocket in promotional activities and soon numerous chapters extended throughout Northern and Southern California as well as Texas and Pennsylvania.

It was subsequently determined that the factory took a rather dim view of these proceedings. The *Gear Box* articles featured technical articles dealing with H-D's more glaring problems, together with recommendations for the use of alternative after market components, and this certainly did not meet with factory approval. The factory for a time maintained a quasi-official relationship with the HDOA and sent press releases regarding new models or technical changes for publication in the magazine.

The export situation regarding the overseas sales of domestic motorcycles changed markedly after WWII. What with Europe and Japan economically prostrate, and with currency exchange problems and tariff barriers existing in other parts of the world, the export of American goods came to a near standstill. This was a potentially severe blow to the domestic motorcycle industry as between the wars from 45 to 55% of its yearly production had been exported. While both H-D and Indian always officially denied these high figures, no doubt wishing to conceal the pathetic state of the home market, the US Department of Commerce statistics confirm the true state of affairs.

As it was, small numbers of H-D FL Police models and WL types were exported to Mexico and South America, along with a handful of Indian Chiefs during the early post-war years. But with increases in tariff barriers and the relatively strong position of the dollar, the export of H-D machines, now the sole US survivor, remained insignificant until the late 1950s.

In the meantime, the overseas demand for heavyweight American machines was partially filled by the presence of vast numbers of WLAs, WLCs and Indian 641 WD models that were either left behind or allocated through Lend Lease to Allied countries in various far-flung theaters of war. These were kept in service through the large stocks of spare parts that usually accompanied their allocation to the various military establishments.

As it was, thousands of these machines were still in active use up until the mid-1960s and the occasional discovery of additional small supplies of spare parts in out-of-the-way places keeps small numbers of these veterans on the road to this day.

The Japanese market for H-D's was revived in the mid-1950s when Richard Child reactivated the business started by his father, Alfred, in 1924. Some competition was present in the form of the Japanese Rikuo models, now in very limited post-war production, but local enthusiasts soon came to prefer the Milwaukee-built product.

Frederick W. Warr, the son of Frederick C., who originally imported H-D's to Great Britain in 1930, reactivated the family business in 1952, operating from modest premises in the London suburb of Fulham. Similar operations were set up in Amsterdam, Brussels, Paris, and Stockholm, as well as Australasia, South Africa and the South Seas, for the benefit of servicemen bringing over American products to members of the armed forces both tax and freight free. (The Fred Deeley organization in Canada was also reactivated.) This extended the need for repair and service facilities, several depots for which soon appeared in Germany where the bulk of US service personnel are stationed.

H-D's original export business was conducted from the main offices in Milwaukee, but under AMF a separate export division, H-D International, was located in the AMF headquarters in Connecticut. Various overseas importers have reported that actual contact with this office was more often than not an uncertain proposition.

In actual practise, however, the more formal overseas import agency facility with satellite dealerships seldom exists as originally structured. This rather surprising situation was discovered by the author in the years between 1980 and 1984 when he undertook extensive world travel in order to study the world's motorcycle business situation in general and H-D in particular.

To begin with, most of the importers handle a diverse line of trade goods and do not deal exclusively in motorcycles. On many occasions after the mid-1950s H-D's production was sporadic due to fluctuations in the home market. This was because of strikes and material procurement difficulties. This affected both the supply of machines and the more critical spare parts. Then, too, many retailers considered that the importers often added excessive commissions for trans-shipping the product, adding to the already exorbitant costs of certain import duties, freight and added excise charges. For these reasons, many foreign H-D outlets began to obtain machines and parts as individuals, travelling to the US to buy up used and leftover machines from dealers, as well as new and used spare parts and after-market products. In addition, numbers of enthusiastic riders and mechanics, never officially connected with formal import suppliers, have set up individual non-franchised repair and sales outlets on their own. Most of these official or unofficial dealers have connections with certain US franchisees who are happy to obtain extra income from a ready market for the inevitable unsold new machines of any year, together with an outlet for used machines and spare used parts.

In the investigation of this rather odd marketing situation, which is virtually unknown in the United States, the author came across many unusual and even humorous situations.

Fred H. Warr in London, a forthright, independent, and totally cordial individual, related that due to the recent problem of obtaining spare parts, and otherwise communicating with H-D's top management, he had sought both independent suppliers and dealers for machines and parts and had, in fact, developed a lucrative alternative in building up WLC type machines from left-over parts stock purchased in quantity from speculators following the end of the war. With a parts stock sufficient to build up about eighty machines, Warr predicted that he could remain in business for many years in this activity alone.

Warr's import agreement with H-D had been cancelled during the early AMF days when he refused to move to enlarged and more modern premises. The agency was then awarded to Coburn and Hughes of Luton, Bedfordshire. As Warr had already established his own product sources, his business went on as before.

A somewhat humorous situation exists in Amsterdam. The notorious Reeperbahn, Holland's famous red light district, is situated in a long alley off the main city square. The buildings on either side are fitted with large windows, and behind each lounges an attractive young lady seeking customers. The end of this alley is bisected by a canal with access to the other side provided by a bridge. At its end there is a large non-franchised H-D outlet reputed to be the headquarters of the Dutch Hell's Angels group. On either side are more lady-of-the-evening establishments. When asked about the suitability of the location, an habitué told the author that as the alley is a popular tourist attraction, the advertising value for H-D is priceless!

Australia, New Zealand and Tasmania are served by a formal import agency, but at least half of the ongoing H-D sales are effected through independent operations. Enthusiasts are building frames, fuel tanks and many other components locally, with various new or used engines, transmissions and other after market parts imported from the United States.

Peter Hanson, in Copenhagen, has one of the largest non-franchised establishments in Europe and caters for US Armed Forces enthusiasts stationed in Germany. His supply sources are several large dealers in the US as well as the usual aftermarket outlets both in the US and Taiwan.

Many parts and machines are sent from US sources to overseas buyers in disassembled condition, to avoid paying import duties where possible. Many are shipped along with other finished goods in shipping containers and, in many cases, the shippers do not declare motorcycle components as a separate entity in the cargo manifest.

A limited but no less sinister source of parts and machines for overseas outlets is from stolen items. Most of these appear to go through Mexico, being trans-shipped through either Vera Cruz or Tampico to European ports where customs officials can be persuaded to look the other way.

It must be emphasized that the total numbers of H-Ds sent overseas is not large, especially when compared with the world-wide Japanese machine sales. But, as the same moment, there are H-D enthusiasts in far-flung corners of the globe who are dedicated to the brand and will go to extreme lengths to secure machines.

On December 17, 1976, the Harley and Davidson families and friends were saddened by the death, from cancer, of John E. Harley, son of Founder William S., in his sixty-first year. After attending Notre Dame college, he entered the Company as a draftsman in 1939. Called into service in WWII, he was assigned to an armoured division as an instructor. Discharged as a Major in 1945, he returned to the Company and served in various service and engineering capacities. As an inheriting stockholder he joined the Board of Directors in 1949 and was appointed Manager of Parts and

Accessories in 1957. While he never held a major office in the company, he was an active motorcyclist and attended most of the competition meets. Accompanied by his wife, Kay, he toured extensively on EL, FL, and FLH models. His son, John E. Jr., born in 1945, joined the Company in 1975 at the Capitol Drive plant as a Production Expediter.

During the mid-1970s, H-D production and sales followed the contemporary boom in domestic motorcycle sales that was approximating million unit sales during those years. In the peak years of 1975, H-D records indicate that they shipped a total of 75,000 units. This fell to 61,000 in 1976 and 45,000 units in 1977. Compared with foreign imports, mostly from the Orient, H-D's share of the market hovered around 5% to 6%. It was noted that the majority of production now centered on the Sportster and FX models, confirming that the custom-biker type of machine was dominating their market penetration. The growing production of large Oriental types, dominated by the Honda GL 1000 model, now assembled in Ohio, along with other large capacity machines by Yamaha and Suzuki, was invading the dresser-tourist market formerly dominated by the H-D FLH models.

At this point AMF Board Chairman Rodney C. Gott, in preparing the Corporation's annual report, stated that AMF might well be advised to develop more strength in their industrial products than in leisure-time goods such as sailboats, bicycles, sporting goods and motorcycles. Much of their disenchantment with the latter was sparked by a prolonged strike in 1974 by H-D production employees over cost of living raises that had caused a three month loss of production. Then, too, the increased cost of fuel to haul engines, transmissions, and plastic parts from Wisconsin to York necessitated another round of retail price increases which further penalized H-D's already unfavorable marketing position. It was now at long last realized that not only was there not a mass market to be developed for H-D products, but that their basic design was such that they could never be mass-produced economically.

In an analysis of H-D's costing problems, AMF's top management believed that they might well have a case to substantiate the thought that the size of the US market, then its largest single motorcycle outlet, had led the Japanese to dump their excess production. John Davidson, who had then succeeded Gus Davis as H-D President, was ordered to implement action through the Federal Trade Commission for the relief of H-D.

AMF's financial experts were hard put to arrive at definitive conclusions in the matter, as machines over 750cc were not allowed to be manufactured in Japan and were now being assembled in Ohio and Nebraska. Using complicated formulae, AMF's Accounting Department concluded their surveys on marketing comparisons of the Japanese pricing structures that tended to prove actual dumping operations penalized H-D's marketing costing up to nearly 50%.

On this basis, AMF's attorneys prepared briefs that were submitted to the International Tariff Commission to sustain H-D's contention that the Japanese should be ordered to either raise their retail prices or else pay increased duty on machines shipped to the USA.

During the lengthy hearings held in Washington, D.C. during the summer of 1978, the opposing counsels presented their briefs. In order more fully to investigate the domestic marketing position, the Commission ordered H-D to allow certain of their dealers to offer their own testimony on the problem.

This proved to be fatal to H-D's position. Most of the dealers were bitter over their Company relationships concerning H-D's poor quality control and conflicts over warranty reimbursements. In addition, as H-D had included their line of lightweight Aermacchi machines into their marketing analysis, the dealers testified to their long-standing resentment of being pressured into handling a line of machines they believed should never have been introduced in the first place.

Also mentioned was the fact that H-D had acquired an interest in the ailing Aermacchi firm at a give-away price of $260,000 as a stopgap measure to cover up their reluctance to expend their own internally-generated profits on improving their manufacturing facilities in Milwaukee and that this was more of a money-saving gesture than an attempt to expand H-D's line of products.

In this same vein, it was further mentioned that in most dealers' opinion, the Aermacchi line was obsolete in design in the first place and that the Italian subsidiary had not kept their products technically competitive with the Japanese.

At the end of the lengthy hearings, which cost AMF a great deal of money, the Commission decided that while some degree of dumping by the Japanese had occurred, it had not materially harmed H-D. It further commented that H-D had injured its own status in the market place by not keeping its products up to date. Described by experts in Tariff Law as probably one of the most complex cases ever to come to a hearing, the voluminous testimony encompassed nearly four large volumes.

Perhaps one of the greatest benefits of the hearing from the dealers' standpoint was that it almost at once terminated the import of Aermacchi machines. The division was subsequently sold to another Italian financial combine, and ultimately became the Cagiva concern which today builds both proprietary two-stroke engines and gearboxes for other assemblers as well as complete machines.

Shortly afterwards, H-D's Engineering and Marketing Departments approached AMF's new Board Chairman, Ray Albert Tritten, who had succeeded the now-retired Rodney C. Gott, saying it was now mandatory to update H-D's obsolete line of machines. What with the termination of the Aermacchi line, poor sellers though they were, the waning sales of big twin machines would depress the Company's market penetration even further. Tritten somewhat reluctantly agreed, and, as a stop-gap measure, the ancient shovelhead engine was given an increased cylinder capacity of 81 cubic inches. The larger capacity engine was first fitted to the FLH models, and was gradually integrated into the FX series, the last 74 cu/in. types being fitted to the Wide Glide models in the summer of 1979. In the meantime, prototype work was inaugurated on a new top-of-the-line model, as well as on an updated 80 cu.in. engine.

Another problem the Company had to face late in 1978 was the more stringent regulations imposed upon the automobile industry by President Carter, through Joan Claybrook, Head of the National Highway Transportation Safety Council, in the matter of reducing toxic exhaust emissions. This was effected by a program of experiments which resulted in larger air cleaners, restricted intake breathing, and the mandatory use of non-leaded lower octane fuels. At the same time, Tritten, under continuing pressure from AMF's Board of Directors, was making plans to change the Corporation's emphasis from leisure-time products to heavy industrial products, oil and gas production, and general industrial services.

The point suggested by AMF's forward product engineers was perhaps well planned, as by the end of 1979, the world economic picture was changing. The OPEC nations' sudden increasing of crude oil prices greatly upset the world's economy, especially among Third World countries whose well-being was presently dependent upon loans from the International Monetary Fund. Much of these funds, originally borrowed in the late 1960s or early 1970s, had already been expended on futile social or industrial programs, and, in many cases, had been embezzled by unscrupulous leaders. These nations, once more in dire straights, were now facing prohibitive costs for energy and certain industrial processes dependent upon fossil fuels.

In the meantime, the Oriental motorcycle factories were continuing with high production, even though the world market for their products had now softened. Their offering to the US included an ever-increasing number of high tech models, now mostly in the 600 to 700cc classes and upwards, and in bewildering profusion.

H-D's model line now included two 74 cu. in FLHs, an 80 cu. in. FLH Anniversary Model, 74 cu. in FX Super Glides in both kick start and electric starting models, the XLCR Café Racer, a 250cc two-stroke track machine and limited numbers of the XR 45 cu. in. Flat Tracker. In 1979 the line was expanded to include 74 and 80 cu. in. Police models, and a Fat Bob FX with a five gallon fuel tank.

With the ever-increasing prices of all models and concomitant spare parts, the aftermarket manufacturers, such as Gary Bang, Drag Specialties, Jammers and Harley Nostalgia greatly expanded their own parts offerings, most of which were made independently in either Japan or Taiwan, and could be retailed at substantially lower than factory prices.

Due to pressure from the Japanese, H-D concentrated on their name brand loyalty theme, and numerous H-D oriented outings and field meets, especially among biker devotees, featured the sledge hammer destruction of some still viable Japanese models as a part of the festivities.

Along with the factory's efforts to revive patriotic nostalgia for an American product, there was still the vexing problem of quality control. Dealers reported that many machines as received required extensive adjustment. It was also noted that the average H-D required a top overhaul within the first 5,000 miles due to broken piston rings, warped valves and other component defects.

The new FLT model announced in the spring of 1980 was a distinct improvement over the long-obsolete vibrating, gear clunking, muffler dragging, heavy steering FLH it was destined to replace. A newly-designed frame positioned the head lug behind the steering head, which lightened the steering. To contend with the age-old V-twin vibration problem, the engine was mounted so as to flex in a longitudinal direction, effectively isolating this motion from the rider, now officially recognized at long last as 'drive train feedback.' To this end the footboards were flexibly mounted also. Best of all, a new five-speed gear box offered a more rational mating with the torque characteristics of the engine. With the fifth gear functioning as an overdrive, a comfortable 60 mph required only about 2,900 rpm, a vital factor in prolonged engine life.

Another new model was an FX type custom-style machine that featured rubber belts for both primary and secondary drives. These toothed belts, developed for H-D by the Gates Rubber Company, were said to have longer life than conventional chains due to their flexibility. Their silent running was also commendable but their main function was to help dampen engine vibration, a feature pioneered several seasons before by several aftermarket concerns who offered conversion sets to fit later model FH and FX machines. The author was able to test ride one of the first of these machines, now offered as the 'Sturgis' model, and noted at once the commendable smoothness of the drive train.

These new models were described as being the work of Erik Buell, of the newly-revitalized Engineering Department under the direction of Vaughn Beals.

AMF Chairman Ray Albert Tritten was now faced with the acute problem of the corporate position of AMF in relation to the H-D operation considering the general dissatisfaction among the members of his Board of Directors concerning its future. With the continuing problems of ever-rising manufacturing costs, the retail prices of the machines had been raised to the point that they were now far outside the competitive market, yet the profit margin was still a miniscule 3-4%, a fact AMF's stockholders found difficult to accept.

There was also an impasse in the fact that in spite of numerous feelers extended to various manufacturing firms throughout the Midwest regarding the sale of the H-D Division, there were no takers. It was subsequently learned that lack of forward product development during the post-war period had indicated that the owners had been more interested in profits before progress, and that more forward-looking manufacturers did not fancy taking over an obsolete line of products that would necessitate a complete restructuring of the Company.

As a last resort, Tritten, now facing an ever-declining dealer roster and an abysmal lack of public confidence among long-suffering H-D enthusiasts, conferred with Vaughn Beals and others of H-D top management regarding their cumulative buy-out of the Company. It was reported that Beals had already stated that he felt confident that H-D could be best managed if separated from AMF, and, indeed, had proved, with the help of Charles Thompson, to be the Division's most competent head.

After numerous conferences in the fall of 1980, papers of intention were filed in February, 1981, indicating that a new group would initiate a takeover.

In the new organization, Beals was to act as Board Chairman, with Thompson as President. Other participants were listed as Jeffrey L. Bleustein, John Davidson, William G. Davidson, Timothy K. Hoelter, David Caruso, Peter L. Profumo, James Paterson, Ralph Swenson, and David R. Lickerman. Complete details of the transaction were not disclosed, but it was generally described as a highly leveraged operation. AMF demanded approximately 80 million dollars for their H-D holdings which was loaned by a consortium of four banks headed by New York's Citicorp. In addition, AMF were said to have subordinated their interests in the three assembly plants and their equipment to insure the deal. Each of the participants was said to have contributed from $75,000 to $150,000 of their own funds as personal guarantees. The biggest problem of the financing was, of course, the exorbitantly high interest rate in force at the time.

AMF's top management were greatly chagrined at their 11½ year failure to get H-D off the ground. This was heightened by the fact that they had been highly critical of what had been described as H-D's former archaic manufacturing methods and inept public relations policies, yet, in the end, AMF had done but little better. While their purchase of the Company had, of course, saved it from oblivion, public confidence in H-D quality was badly shaken, and, pricewise, its products were now well outside the mainstream of the American market.

Several former AMF executives have offered varying opinions as to the actual causes of the H-D fiasco. Some incriminate inept management, such as William H. and John Davidson's lack of expertise in inaugurating modern production. They also fault John H. O'Brien, recruited from American Motors, who launched an expensive and ill-starred export program with headquarters in Switzerland. Gus Davis appeared to have ongoing personality conflicts with both H-D's personnel and AMF's management.

Others blame a lack of continuity in management to AMF's adherence to the long-standing policy of paying low wages to middle management personnel. This practise appeared to have been inaugurated in H-D's earliest days when even the top management shareholders tool but modest salaries. This was supposed to discourage middle management from seeking raises, all of which was reflected in the dividends accrued to family members at the end of each fiscal year.

In the end H-D's problems centered on the lack of a strong departmental management with a clear understanding of the current motorcycle market and effective production methods, together with inconsistent communication with the parent company.

AMF Board Chairman, Ray Albert Tritten, commenting on the H-D fiasco in 1982 following his retirement, stated that the Company had erred in acquiring H-D as the manufacturer of obsolescent products which had but little market left and had been milked of its capital by its original owners.

In a copyrighted article in the September, 1982 issue of *Nations Business*, he further stated that AMF should have divested itself of H-D as early as 1965 when it became apparent that it was not possible to develop a viable market for H-Ds. He described the Company as an albatross around AMF's neck that had absorbed excessive capital that should have been allocated to more viable and profitable divisions.

During AMF's problems with H-D, the trade press was remarkably restrained in its coverage of the situation. This was no doubt due to H-D's position as a traditionalist American manufacturer and the industry's sole survivor, together with the fact that the Company was assuming a progressively less decisive role in the domestic market. Oblique observations on the matter were usually seen in "Letters to the Editor" sections, where the occasional complaint from owners of "lemon" H-Ds were aired. Balancing these were comments from stalwart, diehard enthusiasts stressing the patriotic necessity of supporting the domestic industry.

In spite of cash flow and profit problems, AMF consistently supported H-D's traditional role in AMA competition, centered mainly on dirt track racing. Under the direction of Dick O'Brien, one-time pre-war stock car racer and tuner, the high torque capabilities of the XR racers were exploited to the limit. On the long-established point system, Mark Brelsford gained top honors in 1972. Gary Scott placed second in 1974, gaining first place in 1975. Jay Springsteen's ascendancy came in 1976, extending through 1979 when Randy Goss became Grand National Champion in 1980.

The attraction and mystique of the American style V-twin motorcycle had been the subject of continuing speculation among motorcycle journalists ever since the early post WWII period. The cult-like fervor by which it has been embraced by a substantial number of riders of varying persuasions leads many observers to speculate how individuals incorporate the free spirit of motorcycling into their own private realm of fantasy. The emotions appear to cross the spectrum of pure enjoyment into a dedicated lifestyle that expresses their summation of life's philosophies.

It is certain, too, that the passage of time has at last endowed the sport of motorcycling with enough longevity now to reinforce it in another of America's long list of traditions and the artifacts that accompany them. The American V-twin, as personified through nearly three generations of enthusiasts, is solidly entrenched within the thinking of even those who have had only a passing interest in the sport.

Becoming popular as it did in the days just before WW 1, the V-twin is personified by Harley Davidson and Indian. These makes have joined the McCormack reaper, the Singer sewing machine, the Springfield rifle, the Concord stagecoach, the Model T Ford, the Curtis Jenny, the magnificent motor cars of August and Frederick Duesenberg, and the Stearman biplane, as enduring examples of Americana. With the demise of Indian at mid-century, H-D now carries the torch alone as the sole survivor.

Chapter 11

A New Beginning

JUNE 1, 1981, WAS ACCLAIMED AS THE OFFICIAL DATE UPON WHICH THE NEW group was to assume control of Harley-Davidson. Posters, banners, and other advertising material had previously been distributed to dealers for public display, proclaiming that the Company was now reverting to 'family' ownership.

The new corporate roster indicated that Vaughn L. Beals, Jr. was to act as Chairman of the Board, with Charles Thompson as President. A last minute change in the list of participating owners was the deletion of John Davidson, who, it was alleged, decided that he did not wish to risk his capital in the new venture. Many members of the Midwest industrial community noted that it was, indeed, a courageous undertaking for anyone to take over Harley-Davidson in the face of their now sadly depleted fortunes.

As an inaugural gesture, an ambitious advertising campaign in the trade press was launched stating that the new company's aims were to produce... 'motorcycles by the people, for the people,' and stressed the patriotic theme of supporting a veteran American industry. A barrage of factory communications promised a new direction from the reorganized company in marketing and enhanced dealer co-operation, an intimation that the 'profits-before-progress' policy of the original management, perforce carried on by AMF, would now be superceded by an aggressive program of updating present products and the development of new models.

The new Company was reorganized into three divisions: Harley-Davidson, Milwaukee; Harley-Davidson, York, and Harley-Davidson International, the last an export division based in Connecticut in quarters leased from AMF that still housed their head offices.

In a number of general press releases, and in statements to the trade press, Chairman Beals suggested that as a now closely-held autonomous company, staffed by people dedicated to the future of H-D, a single-minded approach to H-D's long-standing production and marketing problems could now restore the Company to its rightful place in the domestic motorcycle industry.

Long time members of the industry admired Beal's optimism in the undertaking of the almost monumental task of rehabilitating H-D, but it was understood that he was relying on both the underlying cultist appeal of many enthusiasts for the name, together with the loyalty of many veteran dealers as the foundation of his efforts.

Observers within the trade had previously noted that the latest techniques in overall management and production had never been instituted, even in the later AMF days. William H. and

John Davidson were cited as having never understood the intricacies of 20th Century production . The ineptitudes of John O'Brien and Gus Davis had later been complicated by a lack of ongoing close liaison with either AMF's Board Chairman Rodney C. Gott or Ray Albert Tritten, who themselves had apparently never made serious attempts to recruit top production experts other than Vaughn Beals, until it was almost too late.

The most pressing problem was, of course, that of quality control, complicating dealer-factory relationships. Most dealers interviewed by the author during this period produced warranty claims in amounts anywhere from five to thirty thousand dollars for a one year period which were still in dispute.

The next problem was that of repairing deficiencies in production, for, with H-D's retail prices now at astronomical heights, AMF's net profit on the whole operation had barely topped 3%.

Faced with the herculean task of reorganizing the whole company, the only significant event of the latter part of 1981 was the symbolic mass ride of most of H-D's new owners, members of top management, and sone non-factory enthusiasts, from York to Milwaukee in July to celebrate H-D's return to its ancestral home. Production proceeded as before without as yet any interruptions, and racked up a total of 41,600 units for the year. It was later alleged by some that this sales volume, in spite of worsening world economic situation, enabled the new owners, in a prudent gesture, to reimburse themselves for their personal funds initially invested to the tune of $1,350,000.00.

During the opening months of 1982, an aggressive legal campaign was inaugurated aimed at citing the large number of unfranchised garages and repair shops, said to total well over 3,000 establishments across the country, for the unauthorised use of H-D trade marks and logos. Cease and desist letters were also sent to large numbers of aftermarket manufacturers and dealers also accused of illegally using Company insignia. What with the ever-growing scope of activity involving H-D parts and accessories, such practises had assumed serious proportions. During AMF's latter days their suppression was not undertaken seriously, due to the general chaotic conditions within the Company during this period.

It was during this time that Charles Thompson had the misfortune to sustain a severe heart attack and it was announced officially that he was taking a leave of absence from the Company.

The impact of the growing worldwide economic recession ultimately had its effect upon the United States early in 1982. Triggered by the OPEC nations' drastically increased prices for fossil oils in the mid-1970's, its effect was now compounded by economic and political conditions within the

H-D's Superbike, the XL1000 Special. This 120 mph speedster was fitted with dual carburetors, high lift cams and a tuned exhaust engineered by Jerry Branch. About 1,500 units were produced during 1983 and 1984. It was discontinued in 1985. *(Steve Nelson)*

(Steve Nelson)

H-D's 1984 and 1985 top seller, the FXST Soft Tail. The top hinged rear frame is fitted with gas-assisted shock absorbers placed under the gearbox. The 'clean' look is reminiscent of the 1950s custom choppers. *(Steve Nelson)*

United States itself. Succeeding Congresses, long dominated by a liberal majority, had historically indulged in massive deficit spending for various lavish social programs designed to benefit certain special interest groups as well as buying votes to keep the incumbent Democratic Party in power. In order to keep somewhat abreast of these often wasteful programs, punitive income and other taxes were raised to astronomic proportions. This vast infusion of Federal money into the economy had set off an inflationary spiral that seriously eroded the dollar and forced interest rates upward to unprecedented heights. This at once hampered individual buying power as well as business progress. President Jimmy Carter, a political anachronism who had barely won the election in 1976, proved ineffectual in handling the crisis. A general revulsion against these unsound fiscal policies was seen in the election of 1980 when Ronald Reagan, a long-time advocate of conservatism and former Governor of California, was swept into office in a landslide victory.

The new Conservative coalition took immediate steps to lower taxes and reduce Federal spending, but the damage had been done. By 1982 the country entered a period of economic recession. As a result, the sale of all durable goods and especially luxury items suffered, motorcycles being among the first to be affected. This situation was now compounded by economic conditions in Japan. As a highly industrialized nation, production of a myriad of products had soared after Japan 's post-war recovery. Coupled with this, Japan's unique industrial system fostered labor-management relations which were highly cooperative, a distinct reversal of the usual adversary mode present in the United States and most of Europe. In order to foster the paternalistic role of industry in protecting the worker, Japanese management maintained high production and voluntarily took reduced profits in order to do so. This general overproduction resulted in a surplus of goods that were now dumped at modest prices on the world markets, including motorcycles, of which U.S. buyers purchased some 800,000 units in 1981. With reduced markets the Japanese simply carried on as usual with the result that the vast numbers of new machines shipped to the U.S. were stored in warehouses adding to the numbers of unsold machines already on hand since 1981.

Various people within the industry estimated that by the autumn of 1982 approximately 1,400,000 surplus machines of all Japanese makes were on hand; an incredible number. The author was inclined to agree with this figure after gaining access to various warehouse complexes across the U.S. and Canada, where football field-sized buildings were seen to be crammed to the ceilings with crated machines of all capacities up to 1100 cc.

The effect upon the retail sales of domestic motorcycles was, of course, dramatic. The importers were ordered to clear the surplus stock by any means, and with dealers swamped with heavy inventories, blitz selling at giveaway prices was the order of the day. Machines in the larger capacities ordinarily selling for over $3,000 were now offered for $2,000, with smaller types priced accordingly. The American Honda Corporation was able to protect most of its dealers by offering their own financing, but Yamaha, who had already undertaken enhanced production in a futile effort to catch up with Honda, faced disaster. Yamaha dealers were forced to cut their out-the-door prices proportionately lower, and, in spite of some Company backing, many closed their doors.

These trading conditions quite naturally caused a drop in sales of the larger machines assembled by Honda and Kawasaki in their American plants, and, in consequence, they were forced to lower their prices to almost ridiculous levels. With the glut of new machines in every capacity, the market for used machines was almost wiped out.

While H-D had never been priced competitively with any of the imports, the general condition of the market inevitably took its toll, and the York plant cut production back to the capacity of one day shift where previously it had run on two for the past decade. The sales of European machines, such as BMW, Ducati, Laverda and other similar makes of large capacity suffered as well.

In the midst of these problems, H-D's management now offered the Sportster model with a new all-welded frame. This was done to both enhance its overall handling, which historically had been at its best in straight-line freeway travel, but which also substantially lowered its overall weight to under 500 lbs. This move pleased Sportster fans, as it improved performance and made the machine more pleasant to ride, even in spite of its inherent severe vibration.

One of the difficulties of the now widespread economic dislocation was the high interest rates which, while coming down somewhat in the face of the tightening money supply by the Reagan administration, were still pegged at exorbitant levels by finance organizations offering to carry consumer sales contracts. In most cases, automobiles and other durable goods faces rates of from 20 to

H-D's answer to the late Twentieth Century. The all-new FXRT Sport Glide with the 1984 Evolution engine, five-speed transmission, and integral fairing and saddle bags. In 1989, the model was cataloged as the Convertible, with quickly detachable windshield and bags. *(Steve Nelson)*

22%. In consequence, motorcycles as a luxury item were further penalized.

As a defense, in the early summer of 1982 H-D offered the XLX-61 model Sportster at a reduced price of $3,995.00, plus local sales tax and license fees. To effect this the factory cut its own markup and the dealers were now expected to substantially lower their own 20% profit. But with the blitz sales of 750 cc class Japanese machines offered at prices nearly half those of the Sportster, public response was, to say the least, a disappointment.

With a month long plant shutdown earlier in 1982 to reduce investory, and falling sales all over the country, H-D now suffered a severe cash flow problem. H-D dealers, in many cases overloaded with machines eating up their own flooring costs in bank interest, now offered all models for sale at nearly their own factory cost to relieve a serious situation. Sales competition was particularly fierce in southern California's Los Angeles and San Diego areas, the historic site of the largest U.S. motorcycle market. With about twenty-one dealer outlets in this area, serious buyers could almost write their own ticket.

Vaughn Beals, in an unprecedented move contrary to H-D's secretive policies, announced to the trade and general press that the country's oldest motorcycle manufacturer was now in dire straights and faced imminent bankruptcy.

In this statement he was not alone, as many other manufacturers, most particularly in the automotive field were also complaining. The popular theme in the midst of the now serious economic recession was that some steps should be taken to limit the import of Japanese and other Oriental imports, particularly in the automotive and electrical fields as such goods had been encroaching on U.S. markets in ever-growing numbers. Organized labor was especially perturbed at the widespread loss of industrial production jobs, and demanded both an import quota system as well as domestic content laws to protect U.S. employment.

In order to concentrate the Company's emphasis on motorcycles, Vaughn Beals had already ordered the sale of the manufacturing rights to H-D's gasoline and electric powered golfcarts and industrial vehicles. These were purchased by a small specialist firm in Ohio. The production of the long running Servi-Car had already been discontinued in 1973 when AMF found that inflationary costs mandated its retail price at $3,500.00, considerably more than that of contemporary sedan cars, causing a serious drop in sales. So it was in 1982 that production was concentrated solely on two wheelers.

Beals' immediate reaction to the drastic fall in motorcycle sales was to cut the scope of company operations. In the autumn of 1981, about two hundred clerical jobs were eliminated, and during the following spring sixteen hundred of H-D's remaining 3,800 employees were laid off. Among them was young John Harley, Jr., who had joined the Company in 1977 at the Capitol Drive plant and had risen to the post of Production Expediter, representing the last of the Harley family on the Company roster.

For further economies, Beals ordered all executive and middle management salaries frozen, eliminated employee pension contributions and limited health care benefits. In addition, he announced that all production would be suspended at intervals in order to clear out surplus finished machines on hand.

In the meantime, many dealers were still complaining of quality control problems and were deluging the factory with ongoing warranty disbursement demands. In answer, Beals announced that the factory was now inaugurating a new streamlined "Material on Demand" policy of controlling inventory stocks, which would also facilitate a new policy of stricter quality control as machines were assembled.

The problem of carrying an inventory of bought-out components required in general manufacture had long been an important factor in industrial management. It had been the practise at H-D to carry large stocks of components in order to insure that production during normal demand would not be interrupted. While this was prudent in one sense, it mandated the tying up of millions of dollars of capital, and had lately been one of the problems AMF had faced in contending with cost and profits projections.

This improved "Materials as Needed", named MAN, had already been described in several trade production periodicals, and was elaborated on in an article in *Automotive Industries* with quotations from H-D's Vice President in Charge of Production, Tom Gelb and Plant Manager James Lucas. It was stated that the main goal was to involve more of the production force in quality control on the assembly line, rather than by a small group of overseers, a practise already in place in Japan. Under AMF H-D has begun to utilize this system, but Lucas stated that a more effective use of assembly workers was now in operation.

With MAN the emphasis was changed from batch production to mixed mode on the assembly line. In the former practise the final line work force would shift from 90 to 140 people, depending on the model at hand. With mixed mode final line strength remains constant due to an ever-changing mixture of models being built. With the assemblers on the same work station during their shift they attain more proficiency and can identify personally with all the models running through and can better cope with any problems in assembly that may arise.

The MAN "just in time" system was defined as including set-up reduction, flow processing, lead time reduction, inventory reduction, stable schedules with consistent daily production, employee involvement, MAN parts card control, statistical process control, and preventive maintenance.

In the matter of critical set-up time, Gelb stated that this had been reduced to six steps: placing main line set-ups to off-the-line preparation, reduction of unnecessary movements, eliminating nuts and bolts and basic machine adjustments, the standardization of dies, tooling and fixtures, and the use of block gauges for adjustments. These innovations providing for a continuous flow operation are described as reducing the need for a back up inventory as much as 75%. The Milwaukee engine and gear plant was also reorganised along the same lines, with consequent enhanced efficiency and quality control.

It was noted that under Vaughn Beals' management, H-D began enlarging its professional engineering force, reaching an ultimate peak of 269 persons. Product research expenditures were to reach 5% of yearly sales, a distinct innovation in traditional H-D procedure.

At this juncture, the author, noting the need to update H-D's ongoing history, wrote to Chairman Beals for an interview in order to explore the Company's current situation. It was hoped that by this time, as a revitalised Company under new management, H-D would at long last take a rational look at its own position in the domestic motorcycle history. In due time a refusal was received along with Beals' statement that the Company preferred to write its own version of its own history!

H-D's model line was carried on nearly as before, except that the Sturgis variation of the Wide Glide no longer had its primary belt drive, and the name designation was dropped. The reason was that much trouble had been experienced in this unit, with heavy belt wear and numerous instances of breakage. This evoked much controversy among the aftermarket suppliers who claimed that the

California State Highway Patrolman Steve Thompson with an FXRTP Police model. H-D sold 131 of these units in January, 1984 to the State of California at a subsidized bid of $4393.00 each. *(Steve Nelson)*

H-D exhibited this Suzuki-Katana type machine with a Sportster engine gear unit as a prototype machine at the International Motorcycle Show in Cologne, Germany in September, 1984. It was stated that none will be available in the United States. *(Hans Muth)*

factory version was inferior to their own, and cited several seasons of success with their own products.

The FLT model was promoted as the ultimate touring machine, with its dual headlights and large wind fairing which was frame mounted. This latter, which had space for a radio, tape deck, and CB radio fixtures, along with integral traffic signals, imparted a certain heaviness to the steering which took getting used to, although the steering itself was much improved by the altered position of the head lug.

The most important update, however, was the new five-speed gear box, its $4,500,000 tooling cost a legacy of AMF's final overdue attempt to update the line. This effectively overcame the problems of the four-speed box of the FLH in more efficiently mating itself to the power band of the engine, enabling the rider to cruise at 60 mph speeds with but 3,000 rpm.

An improvement over the classic FLH, many an old-time enthusiast resisted the FLT as a radical change that "wasn't a Harley-Davidson."

As motorcycle sales in general were falling everywhere, the Company instituted further economy measures, and the former extensive advertising coverage in the major trade magazines was temporarily suspended.

In a series of releases to the Associated Press, Chairman Beals restated the precarious position of the Company, and claimed that the over-supply of Japanese machines, especially in the larger categories, and the ongoing dumping of them on the American market, was seriously eroding H-D's sales. A number of feature writers in various articles in the leading newspapers across the country elaborated on H-D's situation, and no little public sympathy was forthcoming for the country's sole surviving motorcycle manufacturer, especially as so many other industries were suffering from Oriental competition.

In the autumn of 1982, H-D issued another Company 'history'. This showed an almost identical format to the 1969 edition offered by AMF, but with a slight revision of the last section to include information on the 'buy back' and formation of the new company. With a 62-page content and about 120 stock H-D photographs, it followed the usual in-house sales promotion theme.

In November, another press release announced that H-D was shortly to file a petition with the U.S. International Trade Commission for relief from alleged unfair foreign competition. Many veteran Harley-Davidson dealers and others with long experience in the trade at once offered the opinion that H-D might well now be embarked on yet another attempt to throttle the importation of all types of foreign machines, such as was seen in the 1951 and 1978 bids to seek government protection for H-D products. As it was, all that could be noted at this point was the filing of an intent, as H-D's legal counsel and staff began preparing briefs for the new hearing which was scheduled to take place the following January.

In the meantime, and incidental to H-D's rather bizarre export situation, a corporation known as Pacific International, a subsidiary of the franchised Long Beach Harley-Davidson dealership, petitioned the courts for voluntary liquidation. It was revealed that this corporation had been formed several years previously for the express purpose of exporting new machines to both Japan and Australasia. Several hundred units had been involved in the transaction in an ongoing series of overseas shipments. But in the absence of a firm contract agreement with the buyers to accept a prearranged quota of machines, or provisions for advance payments, a softening of the Far Eastern market had resulted in Pacific International ending up with a $2,000,000 inventory of warehoused machines. Faced with high interest rates on their financing, and with no immediate buyers, bankruptcy was inevitable. The H-D motor Company at once revoked the parent dealership's franchise, terminating the whole operation.

A somewhat similar occurrence had been noted in the Harley-Davidson West affair, where, earlier in the year, the owner of the Marina Del Rey, California, dealership had won a $7,300,000 judgment against both AMF and Harley-Davidson Motor Company. A six-member jury decided, after a three week trial in U.S. District Court, that White Plains, New York-based AMF and the H-D Motor Company of Milwaukee, had interfered with the business relationships between Talbot Enterprises, Inc., owners of H-D West, and its customers. The defendants later filed an appeal, and the higher court reduced the damages to $800,000.00.

The Talbot Group, through blitz sales, extensive advertising, and cut rate retail prices had not only built up an enviable sales record in the seacoast resort city, but had established an international sales organization that exported several hundred machines a year to both Japan and Europe, the latter through an outlet based in Rotterdam. Self-described as 'The World's Largest Harley-Davidson Dealer', Talbot had captured about one-third of H-D's export business formerly covered by the Richard Child franchise in Japan.

The whole operation came to light when Talbot requested H-D to ship a part of its orders to East Coast warehouse facilities to avoid their freight costs through Pacific ports. After 1980, Talbot had expended $200,000 on expansion, but H-D refused to deliver the balance of some 1,500 machines ordered for the 1981 sales year and then attempted to service Talbot's customers themselves. The Company's allegation was that Talbot had been infringing on its own foreign outlets nominally serviced by H-D's International Sales Division.

A spokesman for Talbot told the author that their operation had come into being because H-D had not been able to maintain a satisfactory line of communication or machine shipments with their export agents, and had been particularly inefficient in the shipment of spare parts.

AMF and the newly-organized H-D Motor Company prorated the damage costs between them, and, of course, terminated Talbot's franchise. The latter cleared its remaining stocks of both machines, spares parts, and shop equipment through sales to adjacent dealers.

Through the balance of the year, the factory fired off a series of communiqués to their dealers, stating that what with greatly streamlined operations and a reduction in their labor force, the Company was now prepared to weather the current economic depression.

As it was, the general motorcycle market continued in a generally depressed state. The holders of franchises for Japanese machines continued their blitz sales of surplus stocks at giveaway prices, some of which actually dated back to 1981. The factories were, in many cases, propping up their ailing dealers in many volume sales locations, but in spite of this many closed their doors.

H-D was particularly hard hit as their offerings were by necessity priced far outside the mainstream of the contemporary motorcycle market. Another debilitating factor was that H-D's lately traditional sales profile of blue collar customers were the hardest hit by the recession as so many heavy industries employing them were now either closed or subjected to heavy employee layoffs.

Another stumbling block was that of the interest rates now in effect on conditional sales contracts. While President Ronald Reagan, through drastic cutbacks in government spending combined with lower tax rates, was by this time reducing both inflation and the prime bank interest rates, conditional sales contracts on durable goods were always much higher. With these standing now at an average of 21%, the cost of the more popular big twin H-D models could now total fantastic proportions on the usual forty-eight month contract. A composite of dealers reports of this situation to the author revealed that seven out of ten bona fide H-D buyers could not qualify due, in most cases, to their own reduced financial circumstances.

In the meantime, Chairman Beals continued to send out press releases describing the Company's difficult position, which was then augmented by feature articles by reporters in the general news press following the same theme. Observers within the industry stated that Beals was no doubt hoping to gain public sympathy for the forthcoming tariff hearings where the Company sought increased protection against the Japanese imports. This may well have been a timely strategy as there was by this time much public sentiment favoring other tariff barriers against Japanese automobiles, machine tools, electronic products and other goods that were seen to be taking U.S. jobs particularly from labor union interests. While both the Reagan administration and the Congress were in sympathy with much of this public sentiment, this was tempered by the memory of how the Smoot-Hawley Act of 1930, instituted to protect U.S. industry during an economic depression, had, in the end, along with tariff walls erected by other industrial nations, served to augment rather than relieve the world-wide hard times by inhibiting the free flow of international trade.

In relation to the matter of the flood of Japanese goods, many knowledgable mechanics, both professional and amateur, had come to question the widespread employment of Japanese parts on H-D products which had been gradually increasing over the past decade. These included throttle and starting mechanisms, electric switch controls, Keihin carburetors, Showa front and rear suspension units, Hitachi starting motors as well as ignition systems, traffic signals, speedometers and tachometers, and other small parts. Also included were wheel assemblies, both wire spoked and cast alloy, some of the latter being imports from Italy. The Company response to this was to state that in recent years all automotive products included about 50% outside components bought from specialized firms. As there were presently no domestic firms manufacturing such items, it was incumbent on the Company to purchase them wherever their volume production made their costs competitive and that Japan was the logical choice.

Harley-Davidson's petition for relief under section 201 of the Tariff Code was scheduled for January 15, 1983, presided over by three hearing officers who had overseen the serving of subpoenas on all parties concerned, including representatives and legal counsel for the four major Japanese motorcycle manufacturers involved.

Many within the domestic motorcycle industry were taken off guard by the news of the formal hearing, as it was generally supposed that the 1978 decision had answered most of the questions raised by H-D in regard to the scope of foreign competition. Some veteran dealers and others who recalled the 1951 hearings again voiced the oft-repeated opinion that H-D was up to its historic policy of attempting to meet competition by simply destroying it. However, as will be seen, H-D this time resorted to a different set of tactics.

In its petition H-D declared that as the sole surviving U.S. manufacturer and as a specialist in producing heavyweight machines, the mass importation of Japanese products of over 700 cc had caused serious inroads into the market, as their retail prices were half or less than possible with a domestically-manufactured product. They, therefore, limited the scope of their complaint to the over 700 cc category, exempting those below it. In addition, imports from Great Britain, Germany, and Italy whose individual numbers were less than 4,000 machines from each manufacturer were also exempted. This served to exclude Triumph, BMW, Ducati, Benelli, Laverda and Moto-Morini whose individual importations had been well below this number for several seasons past.

In presenting their case, H-D through their counsel suggested that a sliding scale of import taxes should be levied for five years to enable H-D to inaugurate, through their own reorganized operation, an improved and updated line of products that could render them a more substantial footing in the over 700 cc market and enable them to be more competitive.

In addition, H-D had lined up a carefully selected coterie of witnesses, both dealers and laid off Company employees, to elaborate on the hardships encountered through their loss of livelihood through H-D's diminished share of the market, and who could be relied on not to use the hearing as a forum to air their past or fancied grievances against the Company, as had been the case in 1951 and 1978.

The Japanese were less well represented as the respondents. With the staggering figures indicating their present and recent imports, together with the fact that H-D had presently but less than 5% of the U.S. retail market, the enormity of their marketing advantage could not be denied. Also, their legal counsel were less effective than H-D's as they had each hired their own lawyers and appeared to have no co-ordinated defense. Some observers voiced the opinion that theirs was almost a *nolo contendere* position.

A prominent expert witness in the matter, called by the government to aid in clarifying certain internal industry matters, was Gordon Jennings, long-time motorcycle journalist and one-time competition rider. His role was to play devil's advocate in inducing H-D to reveal some of their own internal problems. He suggested that H-D had long lagged far behind the contemporary motorcycle market, in the historic 'profits-before-progress' policy of the original owners, and that the Company under AMF had barely been able to hold their own in the marketplace, even under more prosperous times. He also queried H-D's witnesses concerning the recent serious problems of quality control and their unenviable record through the late 1970s and early 1980s of 50% to 80% final product defect. 285

H-D's representatives admitted the presence of these and other problems, but stated that with new ownership and the application of advanced engineering and production techniques, the Company was now making progress toward both new product designs and more efficient production. It was also stated that in view of present market conditions, the Company needed breathing space to perfect and introduce new products and that with the present glut of Japanese machines offered at giveaway prices the Company simply could not survive unless some government intervention was forthcoming to control and regulate Japanese imports.

It was further stated that H-D's 1982 production of about 31,000 machines represented the financial breakeven point in dollar income, the factory now running at 50% capacity. To contend with this, it was stated, managerial and production personnel had been cut to the bone. In again referring to Japanese competition, and emphasizing the matter of dumping, it was also noted that starting in 1980 with the Yamaha Virago models, custom chopper-type Yankee styling was being adapted to compete in H-D's traditional marketplace.

After a three-week hearing whose testimony was to fill nearly three volumes, and which cost both sides a great deal of money, the case was concluded and the three commissioners withdrew to deliberate the case. At the end of March, the following decision was rendered: Japan had in fact been guilty of excessively loading the American market with a large backlog of machines at less-than-cost retail prices. A tariff of 45% was to be added to the regular 4.4% rate previously in force on all machines over 700 cc. This rate was to be applied on all machines over 6,000 units from all four Japanese manufacturers. This rate would drop to 35%, plus 4.4% the second year on all imports over the number of 7,000, dropping to 25%, plus 4.4% over 8,000 machines the third year, and 15% plus 4.4% over 9,000 machines the fourth year, and 10% plus 4.4% over 10,000 machines in the fifth year, the program ending at that rate in 1987. As noted, the low volume British and European imports were exempted. Also exempted were imported spare parts, machines already landed and units assembled by Honda and Kawasaki in their American plants, these being considered as domestically-produced.

The Commission duly made its recommendations to President Reagan who by law had the ultimate approval and who immediately signed the order to become effective on April 15, 1982.

This decision was greeted with mixed emotions by the domestic motorcycle industry the majority of whom had not taken H-D's claims seriously. However, Chairman Beals had gone to the effort of enlisting public opinion already in sympathy with some protection for domestic industries, as well as recruiting such Wisconsin legislators as Senator William Proxmire to plead his case in Washington before the hearings took place.

Some critics pointed out that with at least a million Japanese units of all capacities on hand it would be some time before enough new machines would be imported to make the effects of the increased tariff felt. Others thought that the importers could spread the tariff charges over their entire range of machines to the extent that retail prices in general would not be unduly affected.

The Japanese were particularly bitter about the new ruling. Sadanori Yamanaka, Minister of International Trade, stated that his country felt like retaliating in some manner but would withhold any such action at present.

In an extensive trip through Japan during the winter of 1984-85, the author was able to confer with several highly placed members of the Japanese industry. It was their contention that their industry had already leaned over backward to avoid overwhelming H-D. Honda had deliberately refrained from introducing their standard law enforcement model, a much modified Nighthawk, into the U.S., along with a Servi Car-like three wheeler based on the discontinued H-D 'G' model. Both Yamaha and Honda had gone on record as offering but a token competition in the heavyweight races sponsored by the R. J. Reynolds Tobacco Company as the Camel-Pro series which began in 1974. The Japanese were also of the opinion that President Reagan had rendered his decision based on the use of H-D as a stalking horse to emphasize the need to warn their country to voluntarily apply a quota system for U.S. exports.

As an aside to the tariff matter, im March, during the Commission's deliberations, a consortium of Japanese companies offered H-D a loan of $20,000,000 along with what was termed 'technical advice.' This offer was immediately turned down by Chairman Beals who deemed it 'unacceptable.'

In the meantime, H-D continued its legal battle against a myriad of accessory and novelty firms who were continuing to incorporate H-D trade marks and logos into their products without official permission or licensing. What was hoped to be a landmark action was filed in California's Central U.S. District Court against Troy Enterprises, a San Fernando Valley-based firm doing business as 'Joe's Motorcycle Novelties.' Following a judgment for $15,000 to be levied against that firm, H-D's general counsel, Tim Hoelter, stated that a long legal precedent of protecting a firm's officially registered trade was re-emphasized. The Company also announced that it stood ready to license any legitimate firm to officially use H-D insignia on miscellaneous types of products. At the same time, other firms found to be using H-D logos were being mailed a series of 'cease and desist' letters warning them of their

A long time favourite with the custom cruiser enthusiast, the Low Rider model now with the E2 Evolution engine. *(Harley-Davidson Motor Company)*

infringement.

Early in 1983, H-D announced through its then Marketing Director, Clyde Fessler, that a new Company-sponsored organization was being formed to cater to new H-D buyers and other H-D owners, this to be known as the 'Harley Owners Group' (H.O.G.). The initial membership fee was set at $30.00 per year, the first year being given free with the purchase of a new machine. Featured activities included an exclusive 'Fly and Ride' motorcycle rental service in Florida and Hawaii, a limited option highway retrieval service from adjacent dealers in case of a breakdown, a nation-wide register of stolen motorcycle listings, exclusive meetings and rallies for members only, and other benefits.

On a trip to Los Angeles Fessler found it expedient personally to inform Carl Wicks, Harley Davidson Owners' Association founder and President that the Company was shortly officially to take over the functions of that organization. In an angry exchange of opinions, Wicks stated that the Company should then purchase the rights to the HDOA *Gear Box* magazine, membership roster and mailing lists, advertising contracts and other functions that Wicks had originally organized by spending his own funds. Fessler stated that the Company's position was that it had the right to form its own organization under its sole control and that it was not about to pay anyone anything for any privately formed H-D groups. This episode quite naturally ended any casual relationship formerly enjoyed between them. Some prominent HDOA members subsequently told the author that the Company had come to resent the substantial sponsorship offered them by numerous aftermarket manufacturers and suppliers outside the Company sphere.

Persistent rumors circulating throughout the industry for a couple of years regarding projected new high tech motorcycles were given credence with the leaking of information concerning the Nova models. It appeared that the new machine had been designed in Germany with automotive engineers at Audi-Porsche designing the engines and drive trains. These were to be wide angle, multi-valve liquid cooled modular types capable of being built in 500, 750, and 1,000 cc sizes, featuring five- and six-speed gear boxes and both chain and shaft drive. In semi-official announcement it was learned that the Company hopefully planned to enter the high tech market in competition with the Japanese with an entirely new range of machines. While prototypes were said to have been tested, actual production was awaiting an improvement in H-D's current straightened financial circumstances.

The author paid a visit to the York assembly plant in the spring of 1983. The lack of a huge overhead spare parts warehouse system was noted, outside components being flowed into the assembly system via the 'MAN' procedure recently placed in force. About one thousand production workers manned the single assembly line which accommodated all models currently in production in an intermixed mode. Careful attention to quality control was much in evidence and the line was stopped whenever any difficulties arose with a machine. With the drastic drop in production since 1981 the plant was running on a single day shift turning out an average of 165 machines of all models. Production foremen stated that this was the full shift capacity if proper quality control was to be maintained. This was the main topic of conversation and several management people contrasted the current batches of well-finished machines now coming off the line with the AMF days. It was suggested that if production demand increased, a second shift would be required to increase output.

It was also mentioned that the Company was shortly to make an all-out bid to recapture some of their lost law enforcement machine sales and the author was shown a variant of the FLHT model arranged to be fitted with police equipment, as well as an FLH modified for the same purpose.

In the autumn of 1982, H-D's top management decided to introduce a new Sportster model. The sales of these machines had been somewhat uneven in several seasons past as, being unsuited for touring, they had become an out-and-out custom Biker or 'cruising' type, to employ a newly-coined term. While offered as a lower priced 'entry' model to the H-D line of big twins, the Roadster variants with the more sensible 3.4 gallon fuel tanks appeared to have a lessening appeal also, even with lowered prices.

Noting the mild popularity of the Sportster as a high performance type, H-D rightly concluded that a new model based on the XR-750 cc racing machines might have enhanced appeal for the super-sporting riders. In adapting the Sportster to this category, the impracticability of offering a detuned racing model for street use was noted as this would entail a necessary redesign of the whole machine. Serious consideration of the project was inaugurated in the autumn of 1982.

In consultation with Dick O'Brien it was decided to adapt the cylinder heads of the 750 cc racer to the standard Sportster, which would then include dual carburetors and a tuned dual exhaust system, together with altered camshafts of high lift, long duration profile, along with other high performance features.

In the translation, however, it was soon found that numerous other modifications were in order. These included new cylinders, iron instead of alloy as in the racer, increased cooling fin area, decreased valve angles to allow for a flatter combustion chamber, and modifications to the valve gear.

The actual modifications and innovations to the all-important combustion and gas flow characteristics were worked out by Jerry Branch, founder and owner of Flowmetrics, Inc. a machine shop and testing laboratory located in Cypress, California, which, for many years, had enjoyed a national reputation for the ultimate in sophisticated and high tech internal combustion engine development. It was also noted that Branch had finalized much of the development of the original ohv XR, although H-D had not at the time revealed his involvement in the matter. Branch was engaged to assemble the new heads, which meant porting and polishing the ports and combustion chambers, shimming the double valve springs to the correct height and fitting the titanium collars and keepers.

Intended as a low volume production, it was thought that Branch's small volume capacity shop would have no difficulty in making up the limited number of heads required which could then be shipped in sequence to Milwaukee for final engine assembly in the Capital Drive plant. Unfortunately, difficulties presented themselves. The ports, as cast by the Eck Foundry in Milwaukee were so cored that the orifices were only of lead pencil size diameter, necessitating much added machine work when received by Flowmetrics. This caused immediate production slowdowns with other complications. As Branch's operation got underway in January 1983 Branch immediately demanded that corrections be instituted at Eck and undertook an almost daily series of long distance phone conversations with H-D's engineering department. But nothing happened. So Branch hired additional machinists, at the same time dispatching each day's production via air freight to Milwaukee by nightly trips to the Los Angeles International airport.

In addition to these difficulties there were further problems with the new model. When prototypes were exhibited at various regional dealers' meetings, the general enthusiasm was such that dealers at once placed intended orders for many more machines than were originally projected for production. The factory had originally intended to set the retail price at $4,995.000 with an additional $800 – $900 cost for a speed kit, also worked out at Flowmetrics, in case the machines were intended for competition. But with the unexpected dealer enthusiasm, it was decided to raise the prices. This was first pegged at $5,995.000, then ultimately at $6,995.00. This move at once caused consternation among the dealers due to the recession-caused drop in general motorcycle sales and the difficulties in financing what sales there were in the face of high interest rates. There was but little room in the $5,900.00 factory cost (based on the $6,995.00 retail price) to give the dealer scope to manoeuver in the current retail discounting chaos.

Also, the new model did not live up to its promised high performance capabilities in its standard over-the-counter guise. H-D reported a 70 hp output on their dynamometer, but this was taken off the drive sprocket under optimum laboratory conditions. Branch's more realistic analysis of a standard

Factory and aftermarket progress in 1985, the 'hard tail' custom frame by the Santee Company mated with the Evolution engine. *(Santee Industries)*

assembled machine was that it developed 56 hp, this reading taken off the rear wheel. Thus, the first few machines that were delivered were at once a disappointment, for, in spite of all their special features, performance was scarcely better than that of the standard Sportster models.

Branch, in the meantime, had worked out a speed kit that, with some sophisticated modifications to both the engine and exhaust system, would make nearly 100 hp, with consequent enhanced performance. The upshot of the matter was that the customer simply received a stock performing XR-1000 for $6,995.00, plus local sales and license taxes, and could only obtain the anticipated performance by spending about $1,000 more for the special equipment.

The author was presented with a demonstration machine for testing by a Los Angeles dealer which had been especially tuned and fitted with Branch's custom modifications. The power and acceleration and top speed were shattering. A lack of raw courage prevented wide throttle running on a deserted country highway, but a tweak of the twist grip at 85 mph would lift the front wheel!

In July of 1983, H-D announced the publication of its fourth version of its own history within recent years, billed as 'An Official Eighty-Year History.' As reviewed by several trade magazines it was described as not being a history but rather an anthology of H-D events and a celebration of the Company's better days. Written by David K. Wright, reportedly under the direction of H-D's publicity department, it contained a large number of heretofore unreleased factory photographs and much detailed information on both production figures through the years as well as an outline of the Company's complex range of past and present models. While a typical in-house offering that avoided any pertinent issues, it was nevertheless of value for those interested in detailed model data and for enthusiasts interested in restoring old machines.

Later in 1983, and for evaluation purposes, the author purchased an FLHT model that was advertised as a 1983¹/₂ offering. Identical to the previously offered FLT, except for the lighter fork-mounted fairing, it illustrated the improved suspension, handling, and other advanced features heralding H-D's new era of development. The paint, chrome, and fiberglass detailing was of very good quality. Thoughtful inclusions were the totally-enclosed rear chain drive with an oilbath case, an oversize twelve volt car type battery, and a gutter arrangement around the fuel filler cap on the tank to drain off spilled gasoline. The disc brakes offered very effective stopping power. The most outstanding feature was the five-speed gear box which mated well with the engine and gave an effortless 65 mph cruising speed at a minimal 3,100 rpm, the epitome of big V twin performance offering long engine life. Minus features were the rather high seating position of 32 inches which precluded riders under 5 foot 10 inches in height, and a 'starving' front cylinder valve tappet which periodically let forth distressing noises.

The big news of 1983 was the announcement of the newly-designed E-2 evolution-type engine, rumors of which had been emanating from the factory for some time, the original design work having been undertaken during AMF ownership. While the crankcases were as before, the top end, such as cylinders, heads, and other parts from the base gaskets up were brand new.

Of the same classic cylinder and displacement dimensions, the alloy cylinders carried shrunk-in iron liners, promising better heat dissipation than the supplanted shovelhead, with 75% cooler running. The old domed pistons were replaced by flat top Mahle types, which gave a smaller and more efficient combustion chamber with the valves now inclined at a lesser angle. To avoid heat distortion, the cylinder hold-down bolts were made to extend full length through both the heads and barrels.

The camshaft lift and duration sequences were plotted through a computer, together with the use of high speed strobe equipment. Cam action matched the higher port velocities and faster combustion chamber filling of the new head design.

An improved valve gear featured large rollers to better control the cam lobe surface speeds. Oil feed was effected by lightweight, hollow shaft one-piece push rods which promised reduced stress and longer valve train life.

The breakerless electronic ignition system featured dual automatic advance and retard curves. A Magnavox control module containing two different microprocessor mapping circuits was controlled by the pulses from the speed cup to regulate the advance and retard sensors. As a totally electronic unit, the system was described as being maintenance free.

Claiming 10 to 15% more power development than the previous shovelhead design, along with cooler running and enhanced fuel economy, the E2 was described as satisfying traditional H-D enthusiasts as to its overall appearance, yet at long last bringing a modern dimension to the top-of-the-line 80 cu. in. V twins. But with the traditional 45 degree cylinder angle, and the consequent uneven firing sequence, coupled with the old forked connection rods, the engine was still subject to vibration.

The new engine was stated to have cost the Company $15,000,000 for development and about 500,000 miles testing, much of it in a laboratory as well as on leased facilities at the race track in Tallegada, Alabama.

The new engine was offered in an entirely new model or machine – the FXRS Sport Glide. The design, based on the customer biker or cruiser style of machine, featured such FLT and FLHT components as the recently introduced five-speed gear box, totally-enclosed oil bath rear chain, as well as Elastomer flexible engine mounts, gas-assisted shock absorbers, and anti-dive levelling elements built into the front suspension. In addition, the E-2 engine was now standard in the FLHT, and FLT models.

The new model was intended to fulfil two categories; the style of the custom-type cruiser with touring features such as the short bikini type fork mounted fairing and fiberglass carrying panniers.

As an entirely new and updated model largely designed through computerized development, an innovation in H-D practises, it quite naturally attracted much attention from both riders and others in the industry. Road tests by staff experts from the leading trade magazines were unstinting in their praise for the FXRT, heralding it as the beginning of a new twentieth century era for H-D.

The author was supplied with a demonstration machine through the generosity of a prominent Los Angeles basin dealer. With nearly five hundred miles of travel over varying road conditions he could only agree that the overall handling, suppressed vibration syndrome, comfort, and road handling combined with enhanced acceleration and high crusing speed capabilities indicated a superior machine. While the relatively slow turning engine combined with the 700 lb. plus weight of the motorcycle precluded 140 mph top speeds and rocket-like acceleration, the performance in hand was more than adequate for all average riding conditions. Best of all, with enhanced engine power, the FXRT could be cruised for indefinite distances at speeds of 75 to 80 mph in hot weather without danger of overheating, a condition not found with the old shovelheads.

Coincidental to the introduction of the new model, the factory announced that it had expanded its new 'Materials as Needed' component acquisition by concluding a contract with the Milwaukee Milsco Manufacturing Company to effect over $11,000,000 in economies through inventory reduction and a decrease in setup times. At the same time, dealers generally were happy to note that in recent months enhanced quality control had materially reduced warranty reimbursement claims.

All in all, H-D was now receiving congratulations from both the industry and enthusiasts, and Chairman Beals was given much acclaim for both his administrative ability and his engineering expertise in turning H-D around in such a relatively short period of time.

In August, 1983, H-D concluded an agreement with the Rotax concern in Austria, manufacturers of proprietary gasoline, industrial, marine, ultralight aircraft and motorcycle engines, to supply a limited number of engine-gearbox racing units. With the new AMA ruling allowing 500cc

The Trihawk three wheeler. One of the more promising of the type purchased by H-D in 1984 after it had already been placed in limited production. Its high power-to-weight ratio makes it a startling performer. *(The Trihawk Corporation)*

powerplants in the Short Track Class, H-D decided to expand its scope. An all-aluminum alloy single cylinder four-stroke unit with a five-speed transmission developing 52 hp at 8,000 rpm was introduced.

Ron Woods Racing Products of Costa Mesa, California, built up twenty-five chassis sets, utilizing fiberglass for fuel tanks and seat frames, resulting in an all up machine weight of 250 lb. Five units were retained by the factory for their own riders, the balance being offered for sale to qualified competition riders. Additional engine units were stated to be available on order, according to the demand.

In order to offer competition to the ever-expanding number of aftermarket suppliers supplying retrofit H-D parts, the factory announced a new and extensive line of similar offerings as 'Eagle Iron' accessories. These lower-priced units were purchased from the same Taiwanese and Japanese sources as utilized by the aftermarket, and were offered as a sideline to the standard factory parts supplied from Milwaukee and York.

The economic picture had brightened considerably in the U.S. by the end of 1983. With a lowering of individual income and corporate taxes and reduced spending by the Reagan administration, together with holding down the inflationary spiral, business and marketing expansion helped to reduce unemployment. The general motorcycle business, however, was still indeterminate as the market was already saturated with cut-rate Japanese machines as the surplus stocks in storage were released. These on-hand stocks were not subject to the increased tariff; American Honda and Kawasaki were raising their output and H-D appeared not to have been able to materially suppress this competition. Chairman Beals publicly stated that while H-D had lost money in 1982 and 1983, 1984 was to be the critical year in H-D's survival plan.

At the year's end H-D was reported by the R.L Polk organization to have shipped just short of 28,000 units. Chairman Beals was stated to have said that this drop from the previous year was partly due to the softening of H-D's export market, as the strengthened U.S. dollar had raised foreign prices to astronomical heights. This also meant that individual exporters with their lower operating costs could still exploit this market to their advantage. As the Canadian dollar softened, sales there declined as well.

During a survey trip to South America in the autumn of 1983, the author noted that such former strong markets in Mexico, Brazil, Argentina, Chile and Venezuela now had domestic content laws that mandated foreign imports be assembled locally with native labor, favoring Honda and Yamaha who complied by establishing native assembly plants.

In November H-D announced that it was testing prototype machines to enter competitive bidding in the State of California for supplying machines for the State Highway Patrol, the first time H-D had competed in this field since 1974, at which time the new model KZp1000 Kawasaki machines had been selected.

An event occurred at the end of 1983 that was to have subsequent unfortunate repercussions in factory-dealer relations. During the early 1970s the U.S. Government had become concerned with the growing problems of air pollution. Automotive emissions were incriminated to a large degree after extensive research, and the Office of Environmental Protection had suggested strong laws mandating exhaust systems that would ameliorate this condition.

The State of California, as a populous industrial state with vast numbers of motor vehicles, had an acute problem with smog, especially adjacent to the larger cities and most particularly in the Los Angeles area. It, therefore, passed more stringent laws governing emissions than those of the Federal EPA. Motor vehicles intended for sale in California were required to fit special exhaust suppressors.

The State governing body also included motorcycles in their mandate, and suggested that after 1983, catalytic convertors be installed on all large motorcycles. Members of the industry at once launched a strong protest, claiming that the hanging of a heat-producing device on a two-wheeled machine could be most hazardous to the rider and could be a fire hazard to adjacent people or objects. After a number of hearings, the authorities agreed to reduce their requirements, but, at the same time, large capacity machines such as H-D's would have to be fitted with gasoline vapor suppression canisters by 1984.

The factory, claiming preoccupation with new product development, stated it could not comply with this mandate on the date specified. In order to get around the law and supply its dealers with new machines at the same time, the factory informed the dealers that they would be required to both order and pay for their 1984 stock requirements and that the non-canister equipped machines would then be registered at 1983 models.

This mandate aroused a storm of protest from California dealers. While the mandated equipment was not a great issue, the fact that they would have to raise considerable capital to floor a whole year's supply of machines in one operation was a hardship, not to mention the large expense of paying current high interest rates on bank loans for a whole year. To ease this hardship, H-D offered a flooring assistance plan.

In January, 1984, prototype police model machines were shipped to selected dealers while the factory prototype was undergoing evaluation by the California Highway Patrol. The model used was, quite naturally, the new E-2 FXRT, now designated as the FXRTP. A prominent Orange County dealer loaned the author one of his two models for a road test. To enhance performance a 40 mm carburetor was substituted for the standard 38 mm, the exhaust system was relieved somewhat, and the sensor governing engine revolutions was removed. Already noted as a good handling machine, the speed tuning improved the overall performance.

Another police model, the FLHTP, similar to the author's personal machine, but with the E-2 engine, was also road tested. While its performance was less spectacular due to its greater weight, it handled well, and, in the author's opinion, was well suited to suburban patrol duty.

In order to meet CHP performance specifications, which included 100 mph top speed and the attainment of 80 mph in 18 seconds from rest, the FXRTP required the fitting of a specially-designed plastic fairing, as without this the machine could only attain 96 mph. With the fairing, the top speed was 107 mph.

The CHP ultimately purchased 155 FXRTPs at the low bid price of $4393.00. The offering was rumored to have been subsidized by H-D, the Company in effect losing $385.00 on each unit so anxious were they to enjoy the prestige of having CHP representation. The official bid was some $200.00 under that of Kawasaki who still enjoyed the bulk of U.S. law enforcement patronage.

On the subject of law enforcement motorcycles, the city of Torrance, California, had been unique ever since 1967 in utilizing Sportster type machines. Since that time it had kept on charge a fleet of about twenty-five Sportsters adapted for suburban patrol. David Good, the retired head of the Traffic Division, told the author that in the opinion of a number of veteran motorcycle officers, this model was useful and reliable and economical as long as it was not subjected to the rigors of freeway patrol involving high speed pursuit. A further advantage was its lower first cost when compared with the standard FL type big twins. The Sportsters were terminated in favor of Kawasaki KZps in the autumn

The ultimate aftermarket creation is Motorcycle Nostalgia's American Eagle, fitted with its Super Vee engine. Its internals are made up of standard components from the 350 cu.in. Chevrolet engine, such as piston assembly, camshaft, oil pump etc. All cycle parts are of diverse manufacture from Taiwan, Korea, Japan, as well as the U.S.

of 1984, however, when a group of new H-D's were found to have insufficiently hardened crankpins which resulted in early mileage lower end failures.

In the late spring of 1984, the XR-1000 model was discontinued after about fifteen hundred units had been delivered to dealers. Sales had been disappointing due to the unrealistic pricing and lack of publicity on Jerry Branch's tuning alternatives, as mentioned. A year later, many examples still remained in dealers' showrooms. In the opinion of many, the fiasco need not have occurred had the whole matter been more judiciously handled. Noting the fantastic performance in what was a basically sound machine of the supersports type, and its good showing in the recently inaugurated big twin races, many enthusiasts predicted that within a decade or two the XR's would join the 1928-29 two-cammers as a much sought-after classic.

A surprise offering that spring was the Soft Tail, an FX model that featured a rear suspension system with the spring units concealed under the engine plates giving the 'clean' look of a 1950s custom chopper. The suspension was the invention of William Gray, an aftermarket and accessory dealer of St. Louis from whom the Company bought the patent rights. With a solidly-mounted engine, offering traditional H-D vibration, and a four-speed gearbox with a kickstarter, the whole package offered H-D nostalgia. Harking back as it did to the early custom chopper types, it soon became H-D's sales leader.

It was not noted that the popularity of the Soft Tail and other FX models far outstripped the H-D FLT-FLHT dresser market, touring devotees not concerned with nostalgia now seeming to prefer the Honda Gold Wing models with their turbine-like smoothness and low maintenance requirements.

After 1980, domestic automobile manufacturers turned in ever-increasing numbers to the front wheel drive configuration. Already well established in Europe, this offfered increased traction in mud and ice, more positive steering, enhanced room in the passenger compartment, economy of production, as well as much weight saving by eliminating the long drive shaft and rear axle differential.

In the search for reduced weight and further economies, some experimenters next turned to the three-wheel design which had been out of favor for several decades. Several promising prototypes designs featuring converted motorcycle engines received some publicity, but the most promising appeared to be the Trihawk. This was designed by race car engineer Robert McKee, and financed by millionaire sportsman and capitalist Lou Richards. After some three years of prototype testing, the finalized design was assembled in a small factory in Dana Point, California. The car was designed around the French Citroen 1299 cc flat four air-cooled engine that for several seasons had powered the GSA model. The frame and suspension followed race car practise. Most of the components were bought out accessories, including the hydraulic braking system which was from Renault.

With an all up weight of 1,300 lbs. and with 80 hp in hand, the performance was sprightly, to say the least, with 0 to 60 mph possible in under ten seconds. The author was treated to a demonstration by Production Manager John Ingram, which proved that the Trihawk could offer bugs-in-the-teeth motoring, à la Lotus 7 or the TC MG. A super loud exhaust conjured up the air of the Grand Prix circuit, aided by the five-speed transaxle transmission. With a $12,000 price tag, the Trihawk might best be described as an expensive toy rather than a utility vehicle.

A surprise announcement in the autumn of 1984 was that H-D had purchased the manufacturing rights to the Trihawk. No plans were revealed to market it through regular H-D dealers, and it was noted that sales were being made through both the factory itself and three franchised outlets, although at the time production was about eleven units a month. In November it was announced that former Marketing Director, Clyde Fessler, had been appointed Sales Manager for the new Division.

A surprise new FX variant at mid-season was the Disc Glide which featured a solid spun alloy disc wheel at the rear, reminiscent of similar accessory fittings of the 1920s. Said to have been the brain child of Willie G., it could not be sold in California, being a 1984 model with inadequate emission controls.

As a hoped-for aid to sales, the Company negotiated with the Ford Motor Company to include H-D products within their finance coverage, which later was extended to cover Yamaha products as well. While the interest rates were no lower than the standard 22%, its policies on buyer qualification were said to be more liberal. Some dealers later complained that Ford would, in some cases, limit individual dealer participation to a $100,000 ceiling.

A mid-year specification change in all big twins was a new oil-immersed clutch assembly, an innovation in H-D's historic dry plate type. The change was noted as offering lighter control lever action, as it formerly took excessive hand pressure to operate. This, combined with more candle power for the headlight, went along with the detail upgrading and improvements inaugurated in the product line by the new Company. The Company also announced that for 1985 most, if not all, of the FX and FT line would be fitted with Gates rubber belts in place of chains for the secondary drive. Aside from the 1980 Sturgis model, since dropped, belt drive had been fitted to the venerable FLH 1981,

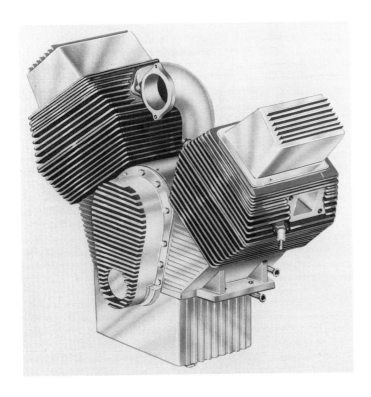

The Super Vee 93 cu. in 100 hp engine designed by Dick Crawford, noted race car tuner, for Motorcycle Nostalgia. Apart from the cylinder and crankcase castings, most of the internal parts are of Chevrolet V-8 origin. *(Steve Nelson)*

ostensibly to aid in correcting its vibration problems. Following that year, a chain was only optional on the FLHP models. The Company claimed silent running, reduced vibration and longer life. While obviously cheaper to manufacture, belts entailed greater replacement costs and complication, as, with no detachable link, the suspension unit on the drive side required dismantling.

A factory press release at midyear announced that H-D had just negotiated a defense contract for the U.S. Navy for 39 million dollars for the manufacture of shell casings. Another pending contract was for the assembly of small jet engines for the powering of target drone aircraft. It also stated that the company was fabricating cable systems for computers. It was noted that 400 laid off workers at York were now rehired. Industry leaders were quick to perceive that the dollar volume from diversification would help to offset the current static state of the motorcycle market, and would no doubt enable H-D to show a profit for the year.

In spite of the welcome improvements in H-D's product line as well as a decided upturn in quality control, many dealers were now taking exception to certain Company policies. One was the ever-rising cost of spare parts, accessories, and the suggested retail price of new machines. The traditional 20% and 25% dealer markup on Sportster and big twin models had already been reduced from 20% to 16%. But the latter figures were no longer realistic as with H-D selling prices already far outside the range of the competition, most dealers were now forced to offer heavy discounts to move any machines. This caused a further drop in their already dismal profit picture.

Another trading difficulty described to the author related to a Company practise of differing price structuring applied to various areas of the country. In one area the suggested retail for an XLX Sportster was set at $3,995.00. In another area, it might be set at $4,500.00, but with a very small dealer markup allowed in any case. Such a policy enabled a serious buyer to simply travel to whatever location offered the lowest price.

Further difficulties experienced in this profit squeezing were that with the current depressed motorcycle market, few dealers could afford to accept Japanese machines as trade-ins, making sales all the more difficult.

Another constantly discussed problem was the ever-spiralling price of new machines. Some dealers stated that the increases since 1980 were far above the official annual inflation rate of 4%. When queried about the problem, factory representatives invariably pointed to rising operating and production costs. But, as a closely held private corporation not obligated to publish any financial reports or profit and loss statements, the whole matter remains in the realm of conjecture.

In the May 1984 issue of *Cycle Guide*, it was reported that a group of H-D dealers were contemplating the formation of a H-D Dealers' Alliance organization to act as a collective bargaining agency with the H-D Dealers' Council, the official factory department dealing with franchisees.

The State of California ultimately mandated fuel vapor suppressors for all over 700 cc motorcycles sold in that state after January 1, 1984. In the spring of 1984 a group of southern California dealers filed a class action lawsuit against the Company, charging an abrogation of their original franchise agreements involving dealer retail markups, aas well as negligence in providing legal emission suppressors as required by law.

In discussing the matter with the author, a prominent dealer in the area stated that with an increased 1984 suggested retail price for the Wide Glide model of $7799.00, as an example, and a dealer's cost of $6462.00, enforced retail discounting might entail a gross profit of only $400.00, depending on the driving of a hard bargain to make a sale. He further stated that his own protestations to the factory elicited a long standing traditional H-D policy statement that the factory served only its dealers and that the dealers' relations with the buying public were their own affair.

Factory representatives ultimately held a number of meetings with dealer groups in an effort to iron out their differences, including a week-long session held during the month of August in Reno. It was ultimately agreed that the matter should be submitted for arbitration to the Sales and Marketing Division of the Department of Motor Vehicles. This government body regulates the automotive industry as to its business practises in an effort to prevent unfair competition as well as offering consumer protection. Both the dealers and factory representatives agreed that a prolonged court battle would be both time-consuming and expensive.

The State arbiters ultimately agreed that the factory had erred in not fitting the suppressive devices in time and that the back dating of 1984 machines had imposed a financial hardship on both dealers and consumers. The State then suggested that the two parties agree to the holding of a special sale with rebates to customers. In compliance with this order a sale for the month of November was announced, offering rebates of $1,200.00 on big twins and $800.00 on Sportsters. One half of the cost would be borne by the dealers and one half by the factory. Payment of the latter's share was effected by crediting the dealers' spare parts account.

While the sale, which was widely advertised, resulted in a modest public response, it was only in force throughout the southern California area, and many dealers in other parts of the State were of the opinion that it gave an unfair advantage in sales to the participants.

In commenting upon the affair to the author, several dealers expressed regret, stating that in their opinion the matters in dispute should have been settled before things got out of hand. Others stated that perhaps the episode would cause H-D's top management to take a more realistic view of the dealers' problems than had been the case in the past. It was also stated that the lack of proper communication between the dealers and management was complicated by the constant turnover of personnel in Milwaukee, together with the fact that present personnel appeared to be constantly shifted from one department to another. Other opinions had it that, in the end, the problem of the overpricing of the top-of-the-line models had yet to be solved and that, due to management policies, the dealers' profit margin was constantly diminishing..

With the generally critical state of the domestic motorcycle industry in 1984, there was much speculation as to just how H-D's six hundred odd dealers were surviving, especially after it was apparent to many that profits were 50% below normal. After a nationwide survey conducted in the spring of 1984 comprising numerous confidential interviews with representative dealers, the author came up with what may well be the answer.

Approximately 40% of H-D's franchised dealers also handle at least two makes of Japanese machines. What with a broadened range of machines in all displacement categories, often augmented by the inclusion of ATVs as well as outboard motors, snowmobiles, water jet skis, and sometimes other types of sporting goods, sufficient dollar volume is attained to make the operation profitable. The gross income from H-D sales alone was reported as comprising from 13 to 20% in these operations.

About 30 to 35% of the larger and generally long established exclusively H-D dealerships are operated by either individuals or corporate organizations who had previously (and prudently) extended their holdings into other areas of business or investment endeavor. In many cases, these have prospered to the extent that under the vagaries of the 1984 income tax laws, dollar losses from an unprofitable business can be translated into a money-making tax saving for the profitable one! This explains the presence of the gleaming, well-stocked showrooms that carry on with few customers.

Some of the owners of these subsidized operations complain that they are under constant pressure from the factory to mount more aggressive sales campaigns. In some cases, they complain of threats to franchise another dealer in a nearby location. This had been described as factory policy to 'wake up' dealers who are thought to be too complacent.

A few of these subsidized dealer operations in populous locations offer new machines at a substantial discount, advertise locally as volume dealers, take a minimal markup to induce volume

Two views of the 883
Evolution Sportster engine.
With alloy cylinder heads
and barrels,
hydraulically-controlled
valves, flap topped pistons
and a diaphragm-controlled
clutch, reduced operating
temperatures and increased
power and performance are
anticipated. The 1100cc
model was enlarged to
1200cc in 1989. All of the
Evolution engines were
designed by an engineering
team headed by John Favel,
formerly with
Norton-Villiers. The
flowmetrics were designed by
Jerry Branch.
(*Harley-Davidson Motor
Company*)

sales, and rely largely on a heavy customer traffic to stimulate increased accessory and service sales.

The last dealer category is the small volume, lightly-staffed operation located in small or outlying rural communities that enjoy very low overhead in minimal premises. Some of these are often after-hours and weekend operations, the proprietor also holding unrelated full time employment. Such shops usually stock only a handful of new machines, offer repair service on all makes, and sometimes undertake mechanical work unrelated to motorcycling. Many of these shops specialize in building up custom big twin machines using aftermarket parts. Many of these shops also act as agents for export operations and supply used parts or partially dismantled derelict machines. The scope of these operations diminished after 1982 due to the high value of the dollar against foreign currencies.

By 1985 it was noted that both the quality and range of aftermarket or retrofit parts increased markedly. This was no doubt due to the widespread demand for competitively priced spare parts, but also due to an increase on the part of both independent shops and mechanically inclined individuals who were fabricating replica big twins. The average 1985 price of sufficient parts to build such a machine ranged between $4,300.00 and $5,000.00.

During the winter of 1984 and 1985 two aftermarket firms were reported as testing newly-designed prototype engines intended as substitutes for the originals, in either stock H-Ds or built-up machines.

The first to announce was Steve Iorio of Motorcycle Nostalgia in Huntington Beach, California. His engine was a wide-angle liquid-cooled V twin of 93 cu.in. displacement that was based on the front portion of the well known 350 cu.in. V-8 Chevrolet. This was made to fit in the standard H-D frame and mate up with the standard drive train. The thought was to build a high performance but reliable engine that could be sold both intact or in parts for owner fabrication. The use of mostly standard Chevrolet parts, such as pistons, connecting rods, valves, etc. was stated as offering an 80% saving in cost.

H-D's veteran Competition Manager and ace tuner Dick O'Brien elected to retire in 1984, returning to South Carolina, his first love, tuning stock car racing engines. His successor, Clyde Denzer, stated that at present the company had no plans to experiment with any new engine designs. He further stated that H-D's decision to continue with the Camel Pro and other competition programs in 1985 would depend on whether or not Honda would enter their new RS 750 ohc V twin track machine.

For the 1985 sales season it was noted by the industry that the four principal Japanese manufacturers were each offering new 'just under 700 cc' tariff-beater supersports models. These multi-cylinder machines, weighing on an average of 500 lbs. were capable of top speeds of from 110 to 120 mph. Their average purchase price was around $3,000.00 in the then current discounting practise. It now appeared that the stored backlog of Japanese machines dating back to the 1981-1982 overproduction had at last been cleared.

By 1984 all of H-D's big twin FX and FT models had been refined to the point where they were possessed of both adequate performance, within the parameters of V twin design, and reliability and uniform high quality. It was at this point that some factory announcements indicated that H-D might seek a new direction in sales and marketing. Via the trade press it was learned that the company was actively seeking additional financing for final prototype and product development as well as assembly facilities for the now much-publicized Nova models, indicating that H-D was interested in penetrating the high tech motorcycle market.

At the International Motorcycle Show held that October in Cologne, Germany, H-D exhibited a continental-type machine designed by German engineer Hans Muth that closely resembled the 1982 Suzuki Katana. It had a Sportster engine/gear unit installed, although it was frankly described as a static mockup, H-D representatives stated that as a prototype it was intended to test potential sales reactions. They also stated that H-D was contemplating establishing a branch in Germany to manufacture and market a proposed line of H-D machines. Several articles in the German press also elaborated on this theme, and stated that H-D was seeking both to market a line of machines in Europe and that the company was negotiating with German banks to raise capital to finance the venture. The proposed line of machines was stated as not being planned for availability in the U.S. and that H-D proposed to eliminate their 'outlaw' image.

Knowledgable observers within the industry questioned both the proposed Nova emphasis as well as the efficiency of the German project, as in 1985 principal H-D sales were in the custom biker 'cruiser' category. The author, who travelled extensively through Europe at various times during the 1980s can attest that most of the H-D machines observed were of the custom cruiser type.

In the spring of 1984, the Harley Davidson Owners Association under President Carl Wicks strengthened its executive staff and revitalized the *Gearbox* magazine. New chapters were formed in southern California, Texas and Pennsylvania. While the HDOA now showed continuing growth, contact between it and the factory remained minimal and the HDOA was no longer on the list of

Harley-Davidson's headliner for 1986 – the 883 Evolution Sportster. What with enhanced performance and an overall weight reduction to 466 pounds, this new model was heralded as an 'entry level' machine priced at $3,995.00 to attract new converts to traditional American motorcycling. It was accompanied by a more expensive identical model bored out to 1100cc, priced at $5345.00. This was superseded in 1988 by a higher powered version bored out to 1200cc. *(Harley-Davidson Motor Company)*

officially-approved H-D affiliated organizations.

During the winter of 1984-85 Jerry Branch's Flowmetric Corporation was commissioned by the factory to analyze and restructure the E-2 Evolution engine's performance capabilities. After the usual intensive research, Branch reported that a substantial increase in power output had resulted. Branch's method of testing and his subsequent internal modifications to both engines were publicized in booklets and were made available to those interested in supersports type performance. H-D's intentions regarding the production of a specialized high performance F model were not revealed following Branch's suggested modifications. It was during this period that Branch stated that a number of disappointed XR-1000 owners brought in their machines for his speed kit conversion.

Along with the new improved models and perhaps changing factory policies, the interest in H-D's models of the past follows the general trend of interest in all makes of antique motorcycles. Due to the past three decades of production by aftermarket suppliers, most contemporary enthusiasts are familiar with all of H-D's variants going back to the 1936 61E. These old 'knucklehead' 61s are a favorite with restorers as the smaller capacity engines can be statically balanced to make them run very smoothly. What with the later availability of replica mudguards, fuel tank halves, instrument nacelles, and other retrofit parts, many big twins of the 1950s and 1960s that were once 'chopped' have been brought back to original specification.

In 1983 a pleasant interlude to the author's investigative reporting of motorcycling history was the acquisition of sufficient unused old stock parts from veteran dealers' collections to make up a 1934 74 cu in VLD. This was carefully assembled by Johnny Eagles, and as an essentially new machine, it is an interesting recreation of the days of classic American motorcycling. After being run in, it was on exhibit for a year at Richard Pinney's Santa Ana, California, H-D agency.

In February, 1985, James Marcolina, formerly a factory traveller and presently in charge of dealer recruitment, sent a form letter to all H-D dealers stating that the factory was now aware of the need for improved relationships with their dealers. Included was a questionnaire which was to be anonymously prepared and which invited any and all criticisms of past or present factory policies. Dealers interviewed told the author that they hoped that the long deteriorated relationships with the factory might now be corrected if top management could take a more sympathetic and realistic attitude toward the dealers' problems.

On February 28th, the R.L. Polk Company, the leading US statistical reporter of automotive product production and motor vehicle registrations announced that H-D's 1984 output was 28,361 units. Of the total motorcycle type vehicles sold that year, 1,190,000, H-D's share was 3.67%. While the over-the-million total was said to be rather high in the face of 1984 market conditions, the surprising number of off-the-road All Terrain Vehicles (ATV) accounted for the figures.

During the annual Daytona races held during the first week in March, H-D made an excellent showing with four machines placing in the Battle of the Twins (BOTT) races, a special event for modified under-1000 cc twin cylinder machines. The winner was Gene Church, whose machine, an HOG-sponsored entry, was tuned by Don Tilley.

In April, Japanese automobile manufacturers announced a projected 24% increase in the export of cars to the US over the preceding year. This at once brought forth a strong protest from domestic industrial and labor leaders for further regulation of Oriental imports, and there were several media references to H-D's contention that certain US products needed ongoing tariff protection.

During May the Harley-Davidson Owner's Association underwent a general reorganization with the resignation of Carl Wicks as President and the installation of former Technical Director E.L. Stillman in his place along with the election of a new Board of Directors. As several new chapters were now in process of being formed in both Northern California as well as in Florida and Texas, the membership roster was expanding.

Stillman at once opened negotiations with H-D's Publicity Department in view of gaining some official recognition for the H-DOA, but what with its autonomous control of its own editorial policies and advertising content, such was not forthcoming.

At the same time, the author was appointed as the H-DOA's official H-D historian, with the stipulation that he continue to record the ongoing events of H-D history as well as H-DOA organizational activities.

Also during May the author conducted another survey in the southern area of the country, comprising the eleven states of the old Confederacy. Its purpose was to interview a representative group of motorcycle dealers regarding the current status of sales and marketing.

Motorcycle sales in this part of the country are historically below those in other areas on a comparative basis due to lower wage and salary scales, with H-D sales following the same pattern. In Florida and Texas, however, with large population and more viable economies, general motorcycle sales were improved, as were H-D sales, these latter states being traditional H-D strongholds.

Many H-D dealers commented favourably on the Company's improved quality control and that the evergreen warranty reimbursement problem was now less critical. Many also concurred in the recent Company announcement offering to improve dealer relationships. At the same moment, there were complaints concerning the critical attitudes of certain young traveling sales and marketing experts from Milwaukee who had lately been accusing the dealers of not more aggressively implementing sales and marketing programs. Most of the dealers were of the opinion that these young men were both unaware of H-D's past history as well as its unique position in the marketplace as an enthusiast's machine which precluded conventional "hard" selling tactics.

During the spring of 1985, there were no new announcements concerning the status of the Trihawk project, except that in March the assembly operation was moved from Dana Point to Milwaukee, where it was stated that future manufacture was to take place. In April, however, H-D dealers received a formal factory announcement that the whole project was being terminated. Insiders claimed that the critical state of the Company's finances mandated a retrenchment.

In June the author made his annual survey trip through Europe to study current trends in the motorcycle market. Oriental domination everywhere was noted except in Italy, where a substantial protective tariff protects the domestic manufacturers. In Germany it was learned that H-D's projected entry into the continental market had not yet been implemented. An official of the Deutschbank stated that what with BMW's long standing position being seriously threatened by highly competitive Japanese models, the times were not auspicious for substantial market penetration by a new competitor.

Most of the H-D machines noted in Germany were ether Milwaukee-built examples of custom cruiser models or built-up examples from aftermarket components. These are mostly owned by US service personnel stationed at the NATO installations, who purchase the machines via the government agency that delivers them tax and freight-free.

With the increase recently in duty on imported motor vehicles in both Norway and Denmark to 115% of their landed cost, retail sales of new H-D machines is at a standstill. Import duties of 50% are still in force in Sweden, and a handful of new H-D's are sold each year in Stockholm.

H-D's import agent in France is located at 30 Rue Chapelle in Paris. In Austria, Daimler-Steyr-Harley-Davidson-Puch is located in Vienna at 3 Rosenwald NE. But with 60% tariff in force in both countries, only about a dozen machines per year are sold in both countries.

No Western-made vehicles of any kind are imported into Eastern Bloc countries. Due to the general poverty of the inhabitants, only a modest number of utility-type lightweight machines and mopeds are to be seen. Most of these are of Czechoslovakian manufacture, such as the CZ. Some assembled makes fit Sachs and Puch engine gearbox units built there under license.

Motorcycle sales in Great Britain are mostly Oriental, but a strong market for rebuilt and refurbished British-built classic makes of the post-World War II era appears active. About thirty five to fifty new Milwaukee built H-D's a year are sold through either Coburn and Hughes or Frederick H. Warr each year. The latter still does a brisk business in converting surplus WLCs to civilian specification. A newcomer in this field is Ian Cottrell of Weymouth, who also stocks aftermarket parts from the US.

A more recent development in Great Britain is the appearance of a number of firms offering aftermarket parts with which custom-type "cruiser" style machines can be fabricated. "Chopper"-type frames are offered with sharply raked fork head lugs, with various options on the type of engine that may be fitted whether Japanese or Harley-Davidson. These appear to be supplying a growing market demand in England as well as in Holland and Belgium.

Back in the US, the Company carried forward into the early summer the "Real Steel Days" sales campaign announced earlier that spring. In this a prospective purchaser was offered coupons worth $800.00 toward either a reduction in the price of the machine, or an equal value of machine accessories or motorcycle clothing. At the same moment, it was emphasised that this special offer as well as the actual trade value of the coupons was to be dependant upon the degree of participation that individual dealers were prepared to offer.

The Sportster model, which appeared in its final form in 1957 as an ohv model following the dropping of the ill-fated K and KH models, ultimately resulted in a heavyweight type of machine that appealed to a certain segment of the American market. Possessing as it did a number of design flaws, particularly in the valve gear, and having an inherent vibration syndrome that proved to be somewhat self-destructive to the engine itself, let alone the physiognomy of the rider, it proved to be too unreliable as a tourer. It ultimately found its place as a café racer or street cruiser for short distance riding, and as a rorty big twin it enhanced the macho image of many dedicated biker types who embraced it as an enhancement of their life style.

Many H-D dealers and enthusiasts had suggested for many years that an improved and updated model could well expand the Sportster's appeal as well as attracting a new segment of the market.

H-D's top management apparently agreed, and after first improving the top-of-the-line big twins with the new Evolution engine introduced in the fall of 1983, work proceeded on an updated Sportster.

The results were announced to dealers on April 30th on a confidential basis, with the statement that trade media announcements would be publicly aired on July 1, with deliveries to dealers scheduled for shortly afterwards.

The descriptive literature stated that the new model, provisionally described as the 883 Evolution Sportster, was a complete redesign, with over half of the engine parts changed to create an engine similar to the 80 cu. in. twin. Included were alloy cylinder heads and barrels, a revised hydraulic valve gear, flat topped pistons, and other changes calculated to enhance power development and improve longevity, counteracting the Sportster's historic reputation as a temperamental machine requiring excessive maintenance. Enhanced performance was indicated by the lowered weight of the new model, down to 466 pounds.

Described as a new attempt at an "entry level" machine aimed at new first time H-D converts who might well wish to participate in traditional American motorcyling, the retail price was set at $3,995.00. Past experience with special sales on the previous Sportster models indicated that at the price public response had been favorable. In addition, with a dealer's mark-up of 20%, the latter now had some room to manoeuver within the trade-in sphere as well as having some leeway to offer some discounting as might be felt necessary.

Most enthusiasts and dealers interviewed expressed both approval as well as optimism over H-D's latest move. They predicted that increased sales volume, now critical to the Company's ongoing prosperity, could well result from the offering of an updated model that could, through its reasonable price structuring, greatly broaden H-D's market penetration for 1986.

In the technical sense, the new Sportster now has a cylinder displacement reduced to 883 cc from the former 997 cc model offered since 1971. The Company states that this was done as a measure of economy for the prospective new owners, as most domestic insurance companies offer a reduced premium rate for machines under 900 cc.

With altered valve configuration and flat top pistons, the Evolution Sportster runs cooler and shows less vibration, being modelled after the 80 cubic inch E2 models introduced in the Fall of 1983. Even with reduced cylinder displacement the new engine appears to develop the same power as the iron engine models it replaced. A near-identical model bored out to 1100cc was offered concurrently, priced at $5345.00, with a softer dual seat. For 1988, this model was superseded by one whose cylinder dimensions were increased to 1200cc.

The 883 model was well received, and soon proved itself as a reliable and dependable machine with low maintenance requirements. Its sales appeal was at once enhanced with a "buy back" program that featured an agreement between the factory and participating dealers where the purchaser had the option of trading his 883 after a year's time for a full credit of its original retail price on a new big twin 80 cubic inch machine of any model. In these cases the factory shared with the dealer the difference between $3995.00 and the eventual sale price of the 883 as secondhand. What with this and the attraction of the new model, 10,000 units were sold the first year,

As tested by the author, the reduced vibration of all Sportster variants was clearly apparent. The 1100 and the subsequent 1200cc models exhibited impressively enhanced power, but vibrated severely at speeds over 65 mph. What with the availability of improved accessory dual seats and fuel tanks enlarged to 3.2 gallon capacity, these models offer possibilities for moderate speed touring. While it was obvious that the performance of all the Sportster models would have been enhanced by the fitting of a five-speed gearbox, factory officials have pointed out that the machines were built down to a price to enhance H-D's marketing penetration. Even so, more closely spaced gear ratios improved their performance in 1987. Added to this, other improvements included altered valve cam action, larger carburetors, and heavier fork legs to stiffen their steering.

In July, 1985, *Motorcycle Products* magazine noted that H-D had been awarded a new contract by the Defense Department for another 110,000 shell casings for naval ordinance worth $19\frac{1}{2}$ million dollars. It was also stated that 250 former employees at the York facility had been rehired as a result. This assured needed cash flow for another season at least.

Don J. Brown, a former motorcycle journalist and later a motorcycling market analyst of Hancock-Brown Incorporated, reported that the motorcycle market for 1985 showed a 20% drop for 1985. This was blamed on the 1981–1983 glut of Japanese imports and the consequent discount warfare. H-D's marketing position was strengthened, however due to product improvement, and its share of the over 850cc heavyweight market rose from $12\frac{4}{2}$% to $16\frac{4}{2}$% by the end of 1986, even though its total production was but 4% of the market with the production of 32,000 units.

In August, H-D received some valuable nationwide publicity for its participation in the refurbishing of the famous Statue of Liberty in New York harbor that had been carried out through public contributions. The Company sponsored a two-pronged transcontinental ride led by President

Vaughn Beals and Willie G. Davidson from Los Angeles to New York. For this event, a limited number of FL type machines were offered with special finishes as Liberty Edition models at a premium price, the override being donated to the statue restoration fund. For a fee, private riders were invited to join the official entourages for either all or any portion of the cross-country journey.

At the termination of the Liberty Ride early in September, a large delegation of H-D riders gathered in the park adjacent to the Washington monument in Washington, D.C, following a parade through the streets of the Capitol. In an impressive display of H-D enthusiasm, observers were quick to note the characteristic brake squeal of the pre-1970 models!

Additional funds were raised when the officials' machines and riding jackets were auctioned off at premium prices. Accompanying promotional press releases stressed H-D's patriotic participation as a pioneer free enterprise undertaken and the relation of the freedom of motorcycling to the Liberty theme. H-D's participation received much acclaim in the general news media.

Another motorcycling event that received national publicity in the late Fall of 1985 was the celebration of the one hundredth anniversary of the inauguration of motorcycling. The American Motorcyclist Association sponsored a ceremonial dinner in the Anaheim Convention Center at Anaheim, California, on November 10. In attendance were the top officials of H-D, as well as the United States executives of Honda, Kawasaki, Suzuki, and Yamaha. Also included among the invited guests were current World Champions Bubba Shobert and Freddie Spencer, past competition stars such as Jim Davis and other pioneers. Also recognized were past and present motorcycle journalists, including the author. Keynote remarks were offered by U.S Congressman Glenn Anderson, a pioneer motorcyclist, as well as by Nicolas Rodil del Valle of the FIM.

A feature of the gathering was the presentation of a replica of Gotleib Daimler's first-ever motorcycle, reconstructed by Ray Behner and Jim Carlton. This spectacular affair was organized and arranged by Ed Youngblood, current President and Chief Executive Officer of the AMA.

Chapter 12

The Rebirth of Harley-Davidson

THE RENAISSANCE OF THE HARLEY-DAVIDSON MOTOR COMPANY HAD ITS ACTUAL beginning with AMF's Board of Directors' member, Ray Albert Tritten, engaging a new group of upper management and augmenting the technical staff in 1975. While Board Chairman, Rodney C. Gott, had promoted H-D's acquisition by AMF, his expectations of its successful operation had not materialized due to unfortunate circumstances as noted. Not only had AMF's Marketing Department judgement been at fault in attempting to inaugurate mass production in an outdated factory, but a succession of four division Presidents showed a lack of managerial abilities, as well as a failure to understand modern production techniques, which was compounded by the ineffectual overall co-ordination of communication with AMF's top management.

The removal of assembly operations to a modern factory at York in 1973 was a forward step, but entailed a year or two of organizational problems including the training of a new labor force. During this period Gott's health problems brought about his early retirement, leaving his hand-picked successor, Tritten, with the reins.

It may also be recalled that Tritten, along with other AMF Board members, had not shared Gott's enthusiasm for adding the ailing H-D to their roster of leisure-time product companies. Fueling their doubts was that the Company was a deteriorated operation marketing obsolete products in the hands of owners who had a history of exploiting their dealers and customers. But, in spite of their lack of enthusiasm, it was obvious that a revitalization was essential as an alternative to terminating production. The move to York was the first step.

In spite of AMF's early problems, it will be recalled that improvements had already been made to the top-of-the-line big twin models. The designing of the so-called "cone" engine for 1970 with its solid state ignition was to bring H-D in line with the growing trend for "clean" engines to comply with governmental pressure for reduced toxic emissions. The crankshaft-mounted alternator also made for a much quieter engine through the elimination of the generator cam gear. The fitting of hydraulically-activated disc brakes front and rear during 1972 and 1973 eliminated the reluctance of the big twins to be brought to a stop. A further improvement to the FLH models was the introduction of a secondary belt drive that was not only cleaner than the chain but, more importantly, aided in reducing the ever-present problem of vibration.

Subsequent forward product development included the introduction of the Buell-designed FHT model, an update of the FLH which featured a new five-speed gearbox, a flexibly-mounted engine,

Richard F. Teerlink, H-D's Chief Finance Officer, who was promoted to the office of Company President in March 1987. Overall Company operations are headed by Vaughn L. Beals, Jr., Chairman of the Board of Directors. *(Harley-Davidson Motor Co.)*

and sprung footboards which did much to isolate vibration from the rider. This model, introduced for 1980, represented the first serious modernization of H-D's top-of-the-line model in 48 years, and involved the development of high tech tooling to machine the gear cases.

305

Another updated 1980 model produced under AMF ownership was the Sturgis, based on an FX custom cruiser type fitted with both primary and secondary belt drives in a further attempt to cope with vibration.

It was during this late 1970s period that Tritten continued his efforts to improve H-D's product and production position by authorizing prototype work on updated engines, as well as forward plans for marketing strategies in conferences with what was to become known as the Beals group concerning their future purchase of H-D. Incidental to this forward planning it was later revealed that this was to include an enhanced advertising and marketing program, improvement of the accessory line, the establishment of a factory-sponsored owners' group, the licensing of H-D's trademarks for use with unrelated merchandise, as well as vigorous prosecution of their ongoing unauthorized use by certain aftermarket suppliers.

While at the time these activities were naturally not given publicity, Tritten's role in H-D's ultimate recovery was never revealed, although his efforts form an important segment of Company history.

The news of the impending "buy out" in February, 1981, and its consummation the following June was generally well received by H-D's long suffering dealers, who agreed that the company's prospects for recovery might well be enhanced under a sole proprietorship dedicated to motorcycle manufacture. As a further encouragement, the travelling factory representatives at once informed the dealership that revitalization plans were already well underway, but, of course, at this early date the specifics were not forthcoming.

Meanwhile, the dealers were in the compromising position of having to make do with the present range of models, as well as having to cope with the adverse economic conditions. These included rampant inflation and exorbitant interest rates brought on by the imprudent fiscal policies of the Carter Administration and increasing industrial unemployment from foreign competition. An immediate problem was the dumping of vast numbers of Japanese motorcycles at cut-rate prices due to that country's surplus production in line with government policy of maintaining full employment at any cost.

H-D's new management at once launched an advertising campaign emphasizing the Company's role in traditional motorcycling and chiding the Oriental competitors who copied H-D's basic design format. In a series of well-timed press releases, the Company's precarious position in the marketplace was frankly discussed, pointing up the fact that yet another American industry was being unfairly undermined by foreign competition. It subsequently transpired that this was part of a planned strategy to stimulate public sympathy for projected tariff relief.

The above factors all combined to penalize the economic position of the dealership. Added to this, they were attempting to market long obsolete products that were priced well above the competition and were suffering from severe quality control problems resulting in product defect.

Most dealers were now forced to offer substantial discounts from the suggested retail prices set by the factory, which usually included waiving the dealer setup and freight charges. Two other pressing problems were the insistence of the factory in setting inventory quotas, as well as reducing the dealer markup on new machines and spare parts and accessories which were instituted at the time of the tariff relief authorized by the U.S. Tariff Commission in the Summer of 1982. In response to dealer protest against these measures, the factory representatives informed them that the factory's present financial position mandated them, and that the Citicorp lenders were also closely supervising Company policy. These mandates were further reinforced by Company representatives during the various dealers' meetings held periodically in many parts of the country.

Up to this point the factory's relationship with its dealers had been handled by a division known as the Dealers' Advisory Council. While nominally considered as a democratic body with representative dealers serving as officers, most dealers have reported that in their opinion this body's actions were, in fact, stagemanaged by the factory in co-operation with certain selected dealers who were known to be most co-operative with factory policy. Instances were cited where the discussions of dealers' problems in meetings were sidetracked in favor of promoting factory agenda. In return, it was alleged that certain "pet" dealers were given special preference in the allocation of popular new models and accessories as well as in the controversial differential area pricing on certain models.

During the Summer of 1983, a group of dealers from the Eastern and Midwestern regions met informally to discuss their problems and to speculate on a course of remedial action. The upshot of these discussions resulted in an organizational meeting held in September, 1983 in Kansas City where the National Harley-Davidson Dealers Alliance was formed. A pro tem Board of Directors was appointed by the charter members in attendance. Their immediate function was to formulate a charter, incorporate the Association, recruit new dealers and attempt to work with the factory with a view to solving some of their most serious problems.

During the initial and organizational meetings of the Alliance, various dealers alluded to a

National Harley-Davidson Dealers Alliance

Dear Fellow Harley-Davidson Dealer,

Do you consider your business to be as operational and profitable as it was a few years ago? Is it harder to make a profit, with mail order retailers, backyard repair shops and reduced margins being in style? Most of us feel the constraints of fewer sales at narrower profit margins. Trade-ins are harder to appraise because they now seem to depreciate monthly due to the Japanese manufacturers discounting the glut of non current product.

A group of dealers (The National Harley-Davidson Dealers Alliance) have acknowledged the need for unity and analysis of the situation we find ourselves in.

We are not a group of dissident dealers out to make trouble for our manufacturer, as it would only result in long term trouble for ourselves and our supplier; but to the contrary, we are a group of very concerned dealers, highly interested in the welfare and future existence of our businesses. Our main goals are first and foremost to have a harmonious and cooperative atmosphere with the factory, to get our former profit margins restored (before they deteriorate further) and to discuss and negotiate some of their programs and procedures.

We think if you'll carefully analyze the 1984 Bonus Bucks program with its reduction from 25% to 20% mark up, the mandatory trade acceptance and rampant deluge of expensive trinkets of the sample program, during slow cash flow periods of our seasonal business; it will only indicate the factories' drive for their greater profitability. It simply increases inventory levels of merchandise and also your debt load through increased floor plan levels. If Spring 1984 isn't a banner sales event, first the dealer and then the factory will be in serious financial difficulties.

The Pro-Tem board of directors of the Alliance have been appointed by the charter members who attended the formation meeting in Kansas City in late September 1983. It is their job to formulate a charter, incorporate the association, keep the dealers informed, and work with the factory on the more serious concerns.

An election of officers and board members will be conducted at the first opportunity to hold a National Harley-Davidson Dealers Alliance annual meeting.

The previous dealer representation (The Dealer Advisory Council) were advisors on programs and products at the factories direction and discretion.

The formulation and growth of the National Harley-Davidson Dealers Alliance is more sympathetic and in tune with your actual needs and concerns from a dealers standpoint.

The Alliance needs your support and input now to strengthen the organization by your contribution and involvement to join in membership.

The Alliance is your organization, designed by your fellow dealers, for the common good of all Harley-Davidson Dealers.

Please show your support for this organization by your membership, just as the dealers who are formulating the Alliance have shown their concern for you, in vast contributions in time, effort and dollars, on their part to insure your future business livelihood through a reasonable, organized and unified form of negotiation between the dealers network and factory

To those dealers that still don't understand the Dealers Alliance or its objectives; please contact the district Alliance representative in your area or Al Muth (phone 715-284-4725) Black River Falls, Wis. He will be glad to give you the name of your district Alliance rep.

To join the National Harley-Davidson Dealers Alliance:
The dues are $100 for 1 year dues, $200 for 2 years.
Send to: Al Muth Harley-Davidson Sales
       Route 4
       Black River Falls, Wis. 54615
Al is our (BONDED) treasurer.

Protem Board of Directors
National Harley-Davidson
Dealers Alliance.

P.S. Something to think about.
If you're not part of the answer, you may be part of the problem.

Al Muth Harley-Davidson Sales   •   R.R. 4, Box 277   •   Black River Falls, WI 54615

A serious controversy developed between the Harley-Davidson factory and its dealership over certain belt-tightening procedures initiated during the Company's recovery period during 1982 and 1983. The H-D Dealers Alliance was formed by a group of dealers to act as an independent collective bargaining agency, in order hopefully to improve the dealers profit situation after the factory had reduced their mark-ups on machines, parts and accessories.

number of grievances involving factory policies and procedures. Among those mentioned was the fact that the present owners had paid too high a price for the Company and that they were contending with excessive debt servicing. Also under fire was the so-called "Bonus Bucks" program that tied dealer markups to sales performance, which, in reality, eroded their profit margins. The "Nova" project for the development of a new high tech model was criticized as being ill-advised, being outside the mainstream of traditional H-D interest, but involving the expenditure of funds that could have been better allocated to relieve the dealers' present low profit picture. Also questioned was the differential area pricing scale on some models that was said to unfairly favor certain dealers over others. Mandatory inventory requirements also came under fire as causing financial hardship when many of the past season unsold models were still on hand consuming flooring space. Of particular notice was the fact that allegations were rife that Chairman Beals, during the initial complaints of dealer hardships, had publicly stated that many of them were inept in the management of their franchises and lacked expertise in retail selling. While agreeing that the Company was presently in a precarious financial position, it was generally acknowledged that an unduly large burden had been foisted on the backs of the dealers.

In the initial organization of the Alliance, funds contributed by charter members present were used to print and circulate a brochure among the seven hundred or more dealers in the U.S. and Canada. In enumerating certain grievances, the petitioners stated that they had no wish to harm or impede the best interests of the Company, but only wished to strengthen it. At the same time they stressed the fact that the Company could not surmount its present problems without a strong and profitable dealership network.

Charter members of the Alliance who were elected as officers and Board of Directors included, as a pro tem body: James Wismer, Westminster, California, President; W. Glenn Steele, Bloomfield, New Jersey, First Vice President; James Fischer, Phoenix, Arizona, Second Vice President; Rose Schoch, Stroudsburg, Pennsylvania, Secretary; Al Muth, Black River Falls, Wisconsin, Treasurer. Board members included Recil Cox, Asheboro, North Carolina; Dudley Perkins, San Francisco; Ray Worth, Belton, Missouri; Ronnie Helms, Elkridge, Maryland; Michael Gutteridge, Danville, Illinois; Gene Walker, Salem, Oregon; Ivan Smith, Oklahoma City, Oklahoma, and Bob Ricciuti, Westland, Michigan.

The country was divided into eleven geographical districts, with an area representative appointed to each to act as liaison between the dealers and the Alliance. These included Charlie Renny, Mt. Clements, Michigan; Leo Kuelbs, Fort Worth, Texas; John Brinkworth, Buffalo, New York, and Dick Martin, Phoenix, Arizona. The yearly dues were set at $100.

With the subsequent interest shown, and the affiliation of nearly three hundred dealers, a form letter was mailed to all dealers on May 9, 1984, announcing a general membership meeting to be held June 4 at the Midway Lodge in Milwaukee. For those unable to attend, it was suggested that comments be forwarded to the Area Representative.

At this time, copies of digests of the initial Alliance meetings, and correspondence to dealers were forwarded to the author as being pertinent to the preservation of ongoing Harley-Davidson history.

In the meantime, the factory management had become well aware of details of the Alliance organization. Chairman Beals immediately issued a statement that the factory would not recognize any dealer organization other than the factory-sponsored Dealers' Advisory Council.

On the same dates as the Alliance meeting on June 4 and 5, the Dealers' Advisory Council met in Milwaukee. At a poorly-attended meeting, Bill Cleary, a long-time dealer in Savannah, Georgia, was elected President. It was later reported that after a number of questions regarding factory policy were ignored in favor of a previously prepared agenda, a number of dealers walked out of the meeting.

In a form letter sent to the dealers dated June 27 and mailed from Savannah on Cleary's letterhead, Cleary announced his election. He also stated that while it was now evident that numbers of dealers had lost confidence in H-D's management, it was hoped that a new policy of openness was to be inaugurated. H-D Board member, Dave Caruso, was stated as being now committed to holding seminars with various groups of dealers to discuss the status of the Company. It was also stated that Cleary had been given the opportunity to examine the Company's financial statements for the years 1981 through 1983. It was concluded that the Company's current situation was, indeed, critical.

Meanwhile, the Southern California H-D Dealers' Association, representing 23 dealers in the current most active motorcycle market in the U.S., met on June 24 in Palm Springs, Ca., chaired by its President, Charles (Chuck) Holinda of El Cajon. After a spirited discussion of current problems, which were reduced factory markups and factory insistence that new model inventory requirements be met in the face of the dealers' backlog of the current year's unsold stock, Holinda mailed a letter dated June 29 to the factory, with copies to each member of its Board of Directors. Copies were also sent to the local factory representatives outlining the Association's requirements before any orders for 1985 models could be submitted. These included a demand for a restoration of their lost profit margin, that the leftover vehicles still in dealers' stocks be evaluated before setting 1985 requirements, and abolition of the ''Bonus Bucks'' program that had been tied to sales performance.

While Chairman Beals had been adamant in refusing to enter into negotiations with the Alliance, quasi recognition was accorded by David K. Caruso, VP in charge of Marketing who, on July 5 mailed a 14 page statement to the dealership outlining some of the factory's production problems, with a cover letter stating that at the June 4 meeting of the Dealers' Advisory Council certain of the factory's more controversial policies had been discussed. Omitting any reference to the Alliance, he urged that dealers bring their questions to the factory-sponsored organization.

Still not mollified, the Alliance Board of Directors sent another mailing that Autumn, calling for a First Anniversary meeting to be held November 26 and 27 at the Best Western Motel in Waltham, Mass. It was stated that future Alliance meetings would be held in various other locations in the country in order to maximise general dealer participation. It was also mentioned since the recent factory-sponsored dealers' meeting announcing the 1985 models, H-D's management had attempted to intimidate certain dealers against joining the Alliance or participating in its activities, citing threats to withhold certain best selling models, the delaying of shipments of critical spare parts, or even cancellation of their franchises.

Meanwhile, H-D's recovery had its initial impetus with the introduction in the late Fall of 1983 of the updated 80 cubic inch Evolution engine, intended as the sales leader for the 1984 season. These were fitted to only a few models, however, these being the FLT, FLHTC, and FXRT and FXRTP police. The majority of the 1984 big twins were still fitted with the iron engines to clear out the stock on hand. H-D's largely conservative customers had adopted a "wait and see" attitude, and it was not until the 1985 sales season that they had proved themselves through their obvious technical superiority.

In the interim, the dealer members of the Alliance were still expressing their disapproval of the reduction of their profit margins, condemning the "Bonus Bucks" program, and were particularly critical of the financial burden of carrying excessive inventory of new machines when they already had an unsold surplus.

To emphasise their contentions, the Alliance Board of Directors sent a comprehensive question-naire to all dealers soliciting their opinions on various aspects of factory-dealer relations such as product pricing, product quality, factory marketing programs, HOG financing, warranty reimbursement and dozens of others. With a clear majority of the dealers responding, it was learned that 84% of the factory's policies did not meet with general approval. Another rather surprising fact was that 65% of the respondents stated that if there was any way they could quit the motorcycle business without excessive capital loss they would be willing to do so. A similar survey conducted by *Dealer News*, a trade magazine circulated exclusively among motorcycle retailers and suppliers, elicited an almost identical response.

In commenting on the unsatisfactory state of factory-dealer relationships, it must be emphasized that such conflicts within industry are not unique to the motorcycle trade in general or Harley-Davidson in particular. The ultimate theoretical goal of any manufacturing organization is continuous, uninterrupted production serviced by retail outlets which ensures a continuous cash flow to provide financial stability. Such is never the case in reality as the seasonal fluctuation in sales makes this impossible. This is particularly true in the motorcycle market and other lines such as clothing, sporting goods, and certainly with automobiles. In the latter, various marketing gimmicks are resorted to as off-season sales stimuli, such as reduced retail prices, factory-shared rebates, special financing rates, and blitz advertising. Such campaigns are generally seen at the end of a sales season to reduce unsold inventory.

It is also true that the history of industry is replete with incidents where a manufacturer utilized the assets of its dealership during periods of financial crisis or distress. This has been true in the transportation field, as witnessed by the recollections of Charles P. Sloan, one time President of General Motors; Walter P. Chrysler, William Crapo Durant, Lee Iacocca, and, recently, by Robert Lacey in his comprehensive history of the Ford Motor Company. All of these firms at one time or another have been known to alleviate certain of their financial and marketing difficulties from the assets of their dealership.

By 1985, however, H-D's position improved from the introduction of the Evolution engines, which by this time were being fitted to all the big twins and were now proving themselves through enhanced performance, reliability and reduced maintenance. While a few teething problems in the early models such as loose drive sprockets, valve gear maladjustment and oil pump failures occurred, these were quickly corrected. Numbers of former customers who had been turned off by the Company's past products were now returning to the fold.

Certain members of the Alliance, however, were still airing their grievances. The problem of excess inventory was still involving many dealers. Then there was now the rumor that the Company was planning to sponsor the opening of motorcycle boutiques in various strategically placed shopping malls that would carry motorcycle accessories, spare parts and numerous unrelated products that were franchised to feature the H-D logos. Further criticism was levelled at the Company for the money expended on both the ill-fated Nova and the Trihawk automobile project, the complainants stating that these funds should have been utilized to the dealers' financial advantage. Another item of controversy was the Eagle Iron program. This consisted of the stocking of lower cost retrofit spare parts by the factory for resale to dealers. These were usually sold through the aftermarket industry and manufactured mainly in the Orient. The Alliance at once took exception to this, stating that by dealing with the factory they were forced to pay an extra markup over and above what was usually charged when they dealt directly with the original sources.

This protest was met head on by the factory through Dr. Jerry Bluestein who, in a form letter mailed to all dealers, stated that with the present state of financial affairs, the factory was in dire need of the additional profits from Eagle Iron sales.

During this period, Vaughn Beals continued to refuse to recognize the Alliance as a dealers' bargaining agency. However, he was no doubt kept well informed through the dealers' conveyance of their complaints through ongoing contacts with the factory travellers. One of these young, newly-hired representatives, once told the author that he had been greatly taken aback during his initial calls at the bitterness that was being expressed regarding factory management.

The Harley-Davidson Dealers' Alliance held its third annual meeting July 8, 1985 in Columbus, Ohio, with 75 delegates from the eleven geographical districts in attendance. Among matters discussed was the result of the recent Alliance and *Dealer News* surveys that showed that 80% of the respondents were dissatisfied with factory policies. Also discussed was the matter of excess inventory, most of the dealers reporting that they had six to eight months' supply on hand with additional shipments of new models expected within a matter of weeks.

In spite of official factory rejection of the Alliance, a representative, Jim Marcolina, head of Dealer Relations, was on hand to answer questions. President James Wismer emphasized that an analysis of dealer financial position from 1979 through 1983, as compiled from a nationwide survey, showed a steady decline in profits during this period. He noted that while the factory's financial position had lately improved, the dealers' decreased profit picture was bound to cause a drop in dealer representation.

At its peak the Alliance membership reached over 340 dealerships. Those most active consisted mostly of mainly newly-franchised shops that were somewhat lightly financed, with their future at risk in their problems with a soft retail market and their problems with the factory. Most of the long-established dealerships, many of whom had become corporate enterprises with the advantage of lucrative, non-related holdings, were less vocal, but most were in total sympathy with their peers who were not so fortunate.

The situation was further complicated when the factory announced that it was in process of cancelling the franchises of about 65 dealers as their poor sales records made them an unprofitable burden. Many, but not all of these, also held franchises for other makes, as well as stocking an extensive inventory of aftermarket accessories.

One of these dealers dropped was Vance Griffitts of Inglewood, California. Griffitts told the author in the Summer of 1986 that over the years he had averaged sales of 25 to 35 H-D units per year, carried a substantial parts stock and retained a Harley-Davidson mechanic. But with declining sales, and a 10 machine inventory of unsold models, he could not justify the financial outlay to stock 20 more. Upon his refusal to reorder, his franchise was cancelled.

In the meantime, with continuing public acceptance of the improved models, the factory enhanced its advertising campaign, stressing H-D's stellar role in traditional American motorcycling and deriding Oriental attempts to reproduce the Milwaukee format. HOG activities were accelerated, with numerous regional rallies and tours offered, frequently coinciding with national AMA competition events.

While the first year's HOG membership was free with the purchase of a new machine (with the dealer defraying the cost) the new member was urged to renew the next year's membership for $30. This was raised to $35.00 in 1987. The HOG organization proved to be an effective means of promoting a spirit of fraternity and camaraderie among Harley riders, and by 1985, Steve Piehl, its factory director, announced that no fewer than 63,000 members were enrolled. As an adjunct, a woman's organization known as Ladies of Harley was formed, with separate yearly dues and a special magazine for their benefit that complemented the quarterly HOG publication known as "Hog Tails." The original factory publication, *The Enthusiast*, continued to be circulated to all H-D owners, regardless of their HOG affiliation.

By the mid 1980s a number of diverse social and economic factors had greatly influenced the course of domestic motorcycling. The previous dumping of large numbers of Japanese machines at giveaway prices had saturated the market, along with giving a false public impression of their value. With many of these models in short production runs, the second-hand and trade-in market was in chaos, complicated by the problem of obtaining spare parts.

The general decline in public interest in motorcycling was attributed to a number of factors not present during the initial boom in sales during the 1960s and 1970s. Aside from the fact that Japanese production cost increases precluded the continuing manufacture of low-cost entry-level machines, there were other diverse factors involved. By the mid-1980s there were numerous recreational outlets available not present in earlier years. These included health spas, aerobic exercising, jogging, expanded growth of winter sport and ski resorts, tennis, golf, and racketball facilities and enhanced opportunities for water sports, skin diving, snorkelling and jet skiing. Motorcycling was now overshadowed by such competition. In addition, the youthful members of a growingly affluent middle class were now preferring cars to motorcycles.

While domestic motorcycle sales totalled over one million units in 1987, the inclusion of nearly half a million All Terrain Vehicles (ATVs) and scooters indicated that bona fide two wheelers' sales had been dropping steadily since the boom years of the seventies.

In the meantime, ongoing changes in the U.S. economy were affecting the general marketplace. President Ronald Reagan's 25% cut in personal income taxes in 1981 that was to reduce the ruinous interest rates and resultant 17% inflation inherited from the Carter Administration, produced the desired lowering of both and was a stimulant to business in general. But at the same time, the Congress, controlled by the Democrat party, refused to reduce spending for vote-producing "pork barrel" projects in their home districts. This thwarted Reagan's attempts to cut government spending, and the result was an ever-growing deficit that consumed vast sums in interest payments. The high value of the dollar hampered the sale of exports, and the country further suffered from a huge trade imbalance. In an attempt to reverse this trend, Treasury Secretary James A. Baker III met with representatives of the six principal Western trading nations to arrange a free floating dollar. One serious effect of this was to at once cause an increase in the cost of Japanese vehicles, as the dollar to yen ratio plumetted to 150 from the previous 268. The consequent rise in the retail price of Japanese motorcycles, especially in contrast to the recent dumping prices, saw an overnight drop in sales and many dealers handling these makes were soon forced out of business.

On January 15, 1986 H-D announced that it was refinancing its indebtedness to the Citicorp Bank consortium with a 45 million dollar loan from the Heller Finance Group of Chicago, an institution controlled by the Fuji Bank of Japan. In addition, a further 10 million dollars was borrowed from the Wisconsin State Employees Retirement Fund. Company employees later reported that Heller's loan commitment was insufficient to clear the Citicorp obligation, and that the additional funds were raised from extensive lobbying by Company management to stem the loss of jobs taking place in that state. It was later found that Citicorp declined to extend its five year loan commitment to H-D in 1981 due to its problems with large loans now in arrears in South America.

The situation in regard to Grand Prix formula racing as typified at Daytona had changed drastically since the 1970s. H-D was forced out of the picture through lack of funds for forward design development, and private entrants were seriously handicapped when the vast sums available to the Japanese firms enabled them to dominate.

In order to create enhanced public interest in the Daytona fixture, the AMA created a modified supersport class for 1,000 cc twins which stimulated the entrance of H-D's XR-1000 on the part of Gene Church, as well as Italian Ducatis and certain of high performance Japanese models. Through extensive tuning, Church was able to make a credible showing during the 1985 and 1986 seasons. The use of the XR models somewhat overcame the redundancy of the former XR-750s, the redoubtable Dick O'Brien having wrung the last available power from this now outdated design. H-D enthusiasts were at once encouraged with the possibilities of this popular fixture which was designated as the "Battle of the Twins (BOTT)".

Incidental to H-D's 1985–86 recovery program was the extension of a licensing program awarded to manufacturers of unrelated products featuring the H-D trademarks and logos. A broad variety of novelty items was introduced such as glassware, crockery, athletic goods, jewelry, adult and infant wear, toys and even the tentative offer of a H-D cigarette in arrangement with P. Lorillard Tobacco Company, making a grand total of over 65 such items. In addition, the Company expanded its offerings of motorcycling clothing as well as a broad range of accessories and "dress up" items for machines. All of these franchised products carried premium price tags.

Also offered was a service to customize the color finish of fuel tanks at extra cost for new machines. In addition, a line of speed equipment known as "Screaming Eagle" products was offered. In this some four stages of enhanced tuning were included, ranging from a $289.00 Kerker-designed silencing system to $3450.00 engine conversions featuring high performance carburetors, modified flowmetrics, high compression pistons and extended camshaft ramp duration.

Also noted was ingoing litigation aimed at non-franchised use of H-D logos and other diverse products, as well as retrofit parts. Legal action was instituted against Harley-Nostalgia of Huntington Beach, California for both the long-time use of the name as well as certain of their product labelling. A proposed $15,000.00 damage claim was ultimately waived in an out-of-court settlement in which the proprietor, Steve Iorio, agreed to the prior submission of catalog material for Company clearance.

Another legal controversy erupted while the Company was still under the partial control of the Citicorp group. This involved one Stephen Denali who had been retained by the Company to negotiate a retail financing agreement with the Ford Motor Company. Denali charged that as a free-lance contractor he had been arbitrarily displaced by Company management before he had concluded his contractural agreement with Ford, thus vacating his commission. During the prolonged legal manoeuvering the matter was aired at length in the *Milwaukee Journal,* with both Denali and the Company mailing form letters to the dealership, each stating their position in the matter. Denali ultimately attempted to force Citicorp to reveal certain details of the Company's then critical financial situation, with the veiled suggestion that it was facing bankruptcy. The matter was ultimately settled out of court with the Company awarding an undisclosed financial sum to Denali. Observers were of the opinion that the Company capitulated due to the disturbing nature of the newspaper publicity.

The Buell RR1000 Battle twin offered in 1987. Eric Buell, one time competition rider and former H-D designer, designed this street-legal machine around the XR1000 engine and gearbox unit. Most of its cycle parts are stock components. Built to compete in the AMA-modified Supersport class, it is sold and serviced by a limited number of franchised H-D dealers. The fairings were removed for this photograph. For the 1989 and 1990 sales season, the 1200cc Evolution engine was substituted. *(Erik Buell)*

In the early Spring of 1986, Erik Buell, the talented designer and motorcycle engineer who was responsible for several of H-D's updating innovations, such as the FLT model and the later air-activated anti-dive front suspension units, announced his resignation from the Company. He stated that he wanted to pursue his own personal design projects in the motorcycle field, which turned out to be the creation of a supersports-type racing machine with a Sportster type engine and gear unit. As a one-time competition rider, Buell's intention was to create an American-type machine to compete in the Superbike class.

In order to defeat the inevitable astronomical cost of a ground-up design, Buell utilized mostly readily available stock components, the majority of which were of domestic origin. To comply with Superbike competition rules, Buell would have to create a street legal machine as to exhaust noise level, emission controls, and even turn signals. It was also mandated that at least 50 examples had to be offered to qualify the machine for competition under AMA rules. Working in a modest plant in Mukwonago, Wisconsin, Buell was able to announce the completion of his project by the spring of 1987, and, along the way, kept the author appraised of his progress.

The power plant selected was the iron XR1000 engine and gearbox unit. While the Evolution Sportster engine was available and weighed 35 lbs less, it was somewhat short on power. The XR mill had hand-polished, three port cylinder heads of the venerable XR750 as developed by Jerry Branch, developed considerably more horses, with possibilities of extended tuning, and was readily available as H-D had a surplus on hand.

The Buel RR1000 in competition trim with full fibreglass fairings. The fairing around the front wheel is a recent innovation in racing machinery. *(Erik Buell)*

The disadvantage was that the XR1000 was extremely noisy, somewhat temperamental, required much maintenance, and was subject to severe vibration. In engineering the Bimoto-type frame, Buell mounted the engine with flexible mounts consisting of a series of ball-jointed struts at either end of the crankcases and on the cylinder heads.

Having previously raced Yamaha's TZ750 machine, as well as Honda's RS500, Buell adhered to similar dimensions with a 55 inch wheelbase. The forks were 41mm Marzocchis and featured an electric-pneumatic anti-dive system with a triple clamp assembly. The rear shocks were gas-assisted units developed by Works Performance, being placed under the engine cases due to the short wheelbase. Named the RR Battletwin, early examples bettered quarter mile measured times against both the Ducati Paso and Ducati F-1, being 123 mph versus 122 for the Paso and 118 for the F-1.

With a realistic suggested retail price of $12,999 that allowed for an equitable dealer markup, about 20 H-D dealers made arrangements to floor examples and perform the 2,500 mile interval service maintenance. With renewed general interest in modified Supersports machines that were street legal, the Battletwin created a resurgence of American participation in the BOTT class.

The Evolution-engined 883 Sportster proved to be a successful model, with the technical improvements in power plant that somewhat reduced vibration, enhanced its reliability and lowered maintenance requirements. About ten thousand units were sold the first season, its $3995.00 price tag making it attractive as an entrance level H-D at less than half the cost of a big twin.

A deluxe model was soon offered, with wire-spoked wheels, a more comfortable dual seat, and extended color options, for about $400 extra. In 1987 a Hugger model was added, with its rear suspension arranged to lower the seat height to 27 inches in deference to both short-statured riders and to attract a growing number of feminine riders.

The 1100cc model offered concurrently with the original 883 enjoyed some popularity with former Sportster enthusiasts who demanded more power, but it showed an enhanced vibration at speed over 60 mph. For 1988, this model was superseded by a bored-out 1200cc model. Ths Sportster line was then updated with larger carburettors, more closely spaced gear ratios, and 39 mm Showa forks that were less prone to flex than the previous 35mm types. With the fitting of the softer accessory dual seat, windshield, and the available accessory 3.2 gallon fuel tank, the Sportster had possibilities as a touring mount.

As a basically stark and functional machine, the Sportster represented a model built down to a price but typifying the traditional no-frills concept that pleased many H-D enthusiasts.

On May 15, 1986, all H-D dealers were confidentially notified that the Company was in process of qualifying itself with the Securities and Exchange Commission as a public company and was shortly to offer shares for public sale. It was also noted that the owners were buying up an additional 280,000 shares presently owned by others than the original buy-out owners. The initial stock offering was announced as amounting to 1,400,000 shares that was then raised to 2,000,000 when the formal announcement was made on June 27, at a price of $11.00 per share. In addition, $70,000,000 in unsecured subordinated notes or warrants were offered at $12\frac{1}{2}$% interest, payable semi-annually beginning Jan. 1, 1987.

The initial offering was handled through the brokerage firm of Dean Witter Reynolds, being sold through the American Stock Exchange. It was also available, under the rules of the Securities and Exchange Commission, from other leading brokers such as Merrill-Lynch, Shearson-Lehman, Lazard Freres, Salomon Brothers, Smith Barney, E.F. Hutton, etc.

The entire issue was sold out by August 1. Chairman Beals announced that thousands of loyal Harley owners and dealers had rallied to support the Company, but, according to later official reports, the actual number of shareholders was but 3,400, the bulk of the offering being held by a few large investors. As predicted, the stock was quoted at $6.50 a few weeks later, but by Autumn it had risen to around the net purchase price.

Under the rules of the Securities and Exchange Commission, the Company was obliged to issue a frank statement of the Company's financial status and certain details of its internal affairs, the first time in history its inner workings were ever made public. According to the 26-page prospectus, it was

7. & 8.) Holiday Rambler Corporation® acquired by Harley-Davidson, Inc. in December, 1986, manufactures premium motorhomes and travel trailers. The Imperial™ travel trailer and a Presidential™ motorhome are pictured here.

9.) Aviator, a division of Holiday Rambler Corporation, converts full-size vans and mini-vans.

10.) Nappanee Wood Products division combines the time-honored values of individual pride and quality workmanship with state-of-the-art technology in creating the finest of custom cabinetry for the home and for commercial use.

11.) Whether it's parts for surgical equipment, recreational vehicles, musical instruments, or industry, B&B Molders, Inc., the precision injection-molded plastics subsidiary of Holiday Rambler Corporation, can manufacture the necessary components.

12.) Utilimaster,® a subsidiary of Holiday Rambler Corporation, makes truck bodies for Ryder Truck and has received major orders from Interstate Brands and Purolator Courier.

13.) Commercial walk-in vans like this one for Eagle Brand Snacks are also manufactured by Utilimaster®

Various products of the Holiday Rambler Corporation, acquired by the Harley-Davidson Company in December 1986.

stated that the Company did not anticipate any expansion of motorcycle sales, but it was emphasized that the Company enjoyed a unique position in the heavyweight machine market, and that since its extensive product improvement, its share of the over 850cc market had increased from $12\frac{1}{4}$ to 19%.

The prospectus also showed in its financial statements since 1982 H-D's critical position in the 1981 to 1983 years, with 48% of its more recent profits accrued from a contract to supply the U.S. Navy with 500 lb. bomb casings. Salient details of H-D's financial condition are noted in the Appendix, and those interested may obtain a prospectus available from any leading brokerage firm.

In August, it was announced that F. Trevor Deeley, holder of the exclusive H-D Canadian import rights, had been appointed as a member of the Company's Board of Directors. While Deeley's holdings amounted to but 2,000 shares, the appointment was described as a move to strengthen H-D's marketing activities in Canada.

That Autumn H-D shares made a slow climb to about $13. In November, it was announced that the Company had purchased the Holiday Rambler Corporation, an Indiana-based concern manufacturing recreational motor homes, specialized truck bodies, and prefabricated household cabinet work. It was a highly profitable operation; the owner was willing to sell due to advancing age at a price of $155,000,000. H-D's acquisition was described as a highly leveraged operation, with a down-payment of $35,000,000, the balance to be paid out of future profits. H-D's Chief Financial Officer, Richard F. Teerlink, a certified public accountant who joined the Company in 1980, stated that diversification into more profitable products than motorcycles had become critical to enhance cash flow.

Following the purchase of Holiday Rambler, H-D stock continued to rise. It was later suggested by some brokers that certain of the large investors were privy to inside information that H-D's projected diversification was a marked stimulus to the original sales, but these allegations were never proved.

In March of 1987, Company press releases announced that Teerlink had been promoted to the Presidency of H-D's motorcycle division. Vaughn L. Beals, Jr., as Chairman of the Board, remained as Chief Operations Officer overseeing all H-D operations, with the motorcycle operation now comprising 35% of total sales income.

It was during this period that the US Congress was still being importuned by certain labor groups to impose protective tariffs on certain foreign goods, which agitation had been ongoing ever since President Reagan took office in 1981. Both Reagan and certain members of both political parties in Congress had opposed the idea, citing the dangers to the general economy in instituting a trade war, and harking back to the stifling of international trade in the early 1930s from such tariffs which worsened the effects of the Depression.

But certain groups, not unnaturally, such as operators of such industries as iron, steel, automotive, shipbuilding and software products, electronics and computers, along with many labor unions, were constantly seeking government relief from what they termed unfair competition from lower paid offshore labor forces. In the light of such severe competition, many industries were able to revamp their operating procedures for enhanced efficiency and improved quality control, most of which was now based on Oriental methods, along with better utilization of labor with the so-called "team" approach to production. Many trade unions opposed such changes, which they claimed were infringing on seniority and other labor rights.

In defense of his free trade policies, President Reagan was constantly citing examples of domestic industrial progress, of which Harley-Davidson's turnaround was a prime example. The Company was still much in the public mind since the tariff relief awarded them in 1982, but which imposed a five-year time limit to enable them to make themselves more competitive on world and domestic markets.

In a preliminary agreement between the White House and H-D's top management, public recognition of the Company's recovery by a Presidential visit was then arranged. On May 6, 1987, President Reagan and a few of his staff members paid a two-hour visit to the York facility. After a brief tour of the plant, Reagan made a short address to the assembled employees, complimenting both them and the Company's top management for their co-operative efforts in improving H-D's product line and implementing state of the art techniques. He stressed the fact that American industry could gain parity in world markets through proper application, and that H-D's efforts exemplified such possibilities.

While the Presidential visit was largely political, this in no way diminished the Company's recent accomplishments.

Observers were quick to note that John Drinkworth, newly-elected President of the H-D Dealers' Advisory Council, was invited to share the podium with other Company officials, H-D Dealers' Alliance President James Wismer being conspicuous by his absence.

Two new models received immediate acceptance from H-D enthusiasts. In January, 1986, the Heritage Softtail model with concealed rear springing, and fitted with the shrouded FL type fork was

First offered in January 1986, the Heritage Softtail is a novelty model that is a near replica of the 1949 FLH. It is basically a 1985 Softtail fitted with FL-type fork. Its fuel tank and instrument nacelle are also nostalgic. With a broad appeal to H-D traditionalists it was an instant success. *(Harley-Davidson Motor Co.)*

Another favorite with H-D traditionalists is the FLHS, first offered in 1987. As a stripped model with crash bars and saddle bags only, it can be fitted with accessory equipment optional with the buyer. *(Harley-Davidson Motor Co.)*

introduced. The effect was to form a replica of the Company's 1949 HydraGlide FLH, as the "clean" rear portion simulated the old solid frame design. The machine's nostalgic appeal was immediate and its initial production run of 1,700 machines was quckly sold. The author purchased one for testing and evaluation and found it to be a good handling machine with its shallow fork angle and commendably low center of gravity. A very handsome machine, its appearance was often complimented by casual passers-by, not a few of whom enquired if it was a restoration of an older model!

Another model well within the nostalgia ambiance was the FLHS, introduction in 1987. This was, in effect, a stripped FLHC, with front and rear crash bars and the usual plastic pannier saddle bags offered as standard. This again recalled the classic FLH models. A strong selling point was its somewhat reduced price of $8545, and the opportunity for the buyer to ride it "as is", or "dress" it with accessory windshield, passing lights, scoot boot, etc. in the optional custom accessory tradition of H-D.

For 1988, the product line included the two new models as described above, as well as the three updated Sportster models, and three sidecar machines, the FLHT and FLHTC as well as the FXRT. These could be fitted with an updated sidecar retailing at $3995. A total of nineteen variants based on the two basic models were available, together with options for some 88 variants of detail trim, paint color, and accessory adaptation.

The performance-enhancing features announced for 1988 including altered camshaft profiles and larger carburetors were not made available to California buyers, as the more powerful engines did not meet the stringent emission limits mandated by the laws of that State – the strictest in the nation.

H-D's stock made a dramatic rise in value during the opening months of 1987, and its shares qualified for sale on the prestigious New York Stock Exchange. Vaughn Beals and a group of Company officials celebrated this event with a triumphal group ride down New York's Fifth Avenue.

By August 1987 the shares had doubled in original value to $24.00 indicating actual profit of nearly one hundred million dollars (on paper, at least) to the shareholders. But on October 19, 1987, the soaring rise in value of all publicly traded shares plummeted overnight in the worst stock market debacle since the crash in 1929, the Dow Jones average dropping 508 points. The infamous "Black Monday" was blamed on a wave of heavy speculation, together with the catastrophic effects of much illegal inside trading, the perpetrators of which were soon being indicted by Government attorneys. H-D's stock fell drastically, now being valued at less than its original $11.00 price. With some recovery noted in the opening months of 1988, H-D's shares finally rose to around $12.00 by March of 1988.

By April 1st, the value of H-D's shares rose dramatically, and at that point reached $21.00. This reflected the earning power of Holiday Rambler, as well as general investor confidence in the Company's management.

As an aside to the later public airing of the recent details of H-D's financial position mandated by its stock offering, the facts of the Company's early-day financial structuring, a closely-guarded secret during the days of family ownership, at long last came to light. Alfred Rich Child, in the late Autumn of 1985, with, perhaps, some premonition of his own mortality, undertook to review and initiate a cataloging of his vast file of personal records and papers. Among them was a collection of documents once supplied to him by the late Crolius S. Lacey which had somehow been forgotten. Lacey, one of H-D's earliest employees and its first Advertising Director, had given Child both copies of H-D's listings of its shareholders, the amounts of ownership, and an outline of its methods of financing, together with letters of explanation.

It appears that during the between-the-wars period, there existed a total of 39,995 shares of stock, arbitrarily valued at between $25 and $35 per share according to majority vote. In order to maintain control of the operation, the Davidson family members, with William S. Harley as a minority shareholder, always kept at least 21,000 shares. But what was not generally known was that shares were offered to both certain Company employees with access to private capital, as well as other individuals outside the Company. The principal shareholders were, of course, the various Davidsons: Walter, William A., Arthur, Margaret, Janet, and Elizabeth Davidson Marx, whose holdings totalled 23,254 shares. A surprising revelation was that William S. Harley's holdings of 2,548 shares represented less than 5% of Company ownership. Other of the more well-known minority participants included Charles H. Lang, early-day dealer and owner of the patents to H-D's two-speed hub gears, and Crolius S. Lacey.

A previously little-known fact revealed was that one Frank L. Wood, a wealthy resident of Milwaukee and a local capitalist, together with certain members of his family, owned a total of 5,256 shares.

Also revealed in the Lacey documentation was the fact that there was much trading of shares between individual owners. Minor prospective shareholders were offered them at certain fixed amounts, with future repurchase agreements at previously agreed profits. In this way the Company was able to raise needed ongoing operating capital without recourse to commercial banks and their higher interest rates, a practise which the founders were reluctant to follow.

Lacey also stated that shareholders' meeting were generally of the closed or "star chamber" variety and were open only to the immediate family members who held the balance of voting power. President Walter Davidson was reported as stating that the fewer people who were privy to Company policy, the less chance of having such information leak out. An exception to this rule was that Frank L. Wood was included in such conferences, and that interdepartmental memoranda were forwarded to him, no doubt in deference to his extensive financial involvement.

Lacey concluded that the Davidsons' almost paranoic preoccupation with secrecy was due to the fact that it was considered that the family's public position would be compromised if it was known that a substantial amount of the Company's financial structure was in the hands of numerous individuals outside of the small circle of the Founders and their families. These were given almost exclusive prominence in material published by the Company or in press releases.

During the post World War II years, the shares increased both in value and number due to accelerated company activity, and through several stock splits. The usual dividends were 10% and sometimes 12% per annum. When the Company was sold to AMF in 1969, a number of the heirs of long-time shareholders profited handsomely.

While this information in recent years has become more or less esoteric, it is interesting to note the early day details of the Company financing, especially as it was by tradition a closely guarded secret. For those interested in statistical detail, a sample listing of shareholders in the between-the-wars era is included in the Appendix. A complete and detailed set of documentation today resides with the estate of the late Douglas Sisson, a nephew of Lacey.

Alfred Child made the foregoing information available to the author in January, 1986. His private motivation in reviewing his historical files was timely, and he passed away quietly in his sleep the following month, well into his 95th year.

The decline of the dollar, which by 1988 had become critical, was now responsible for the acceleration of the export of H-D's. While the retail price of big twins, the preferred export model, by 1988 had stabilized at around $15,000, there were still sufficient enthusiasts who could afford to buy them. In 1987, approximately 1,600 units were sold in Canada, 1,200 in Western Europe through the export depot in Raunheim, Germany, and 1,300 in Japan, with lesser numbers to Australasia and a few other foreign countries. In addition, there was a credible number of both used and new machines exported through private and dealers. FX model machines to complement the "biker" mode in foreign countries are the biggest sellers, except in Japan where dressers are preferred.

The retail and trade-in value of the now obsolete iron engine models dropped appreciably after the introduction of the improved Evolution models, as was to be expected. Most enthusiasts today prefer such as rebuilt and "blueprinted" models which helps to reduce their traditional vibration syndrome.

Factory-dealer relationships have somewhat improved with H-D's product updating. This along with the firming of the domestic market has seen a marked reduction in warranty reimbursement problems. Dealers' markups for both new models and spare parts and accessories have been increased but have yet to regain the long enjoyed 25% and 100% figures.

Many dealers have stated that H-D's management keeps its dealers more or less at arm's length in being communicative on general policy matters. Individual dealers surveyed in various parts of the country vary in their views on Company relationships; some stating that the situation is one of detente, all the way to a state of uneasy truce. With the principal Company emphasis latterly focussing on diversification of product, some have expressed the opinion that the factory may well be less compromising toward their dealers' positions.

In the matter of diversification, during December 1987 and January 1988, various announcements appearing in the trade press announced another corporate acquisition. The North Atlantic Treaty Organization for some years had utilized German-built Maico motorcycles for military use by its ground forces. This was adapted from their 500cc street scrambler type two-stroke, capable of extensive off-road operation. With the demise of the Maico concern, the void was filled by Armstrong Competition Motorcycles Ltd. in Great Britain who offered a similar machine fitted with a 500cc or a 600cc ohc four stroke engine-gear unit made by Rotax in Austria. H-D's purchase of Armstrong provides further Company expansion, although whether or not these machines are to be manufactured in the U.S. was not announced.

During the latter 1970s and into the 1980s domestic motorcycling faced certain image problems. Certain of the general public as well as many within the industry took issue with the proliferation of high tech Oriental supersports machines of sophisticated design that were capable of top speeds of 160 mph and three second zero to sixty acceleration. The appalling number of fatal accidents, many of them of solo nature where the rider simply lost control, continuously noted in the general media, brought much public sentiment against two-wheeled motoring.

Another point in question was the high accident rate especially among juvenile operators, involving All Terrain Vehicles (ATVs) in off-road situations. Most of these were connected with the tricycle-type machines marketed in various cylinder capacities by the Oriental manufacturers. With over 900 fatalities and 350,000 reportable accidents within the past five years, there was a strong movement among consumer groups for their banning by law from public sale. Through the efforts of the American Pediatric Association and the U.S. Consumer Protection agency, the Attorney General filed a class action suit against the manufacturers of three-wheeled machines. In spite of the latter's protestations that accidents were the fault of the operators, the sale of the trikes were banned, the order to take effect February 15, 1988. As the four-wheeled quadricycle type was not involved, the manufacturers at once concentrated on this type of ATV, with an announced program of safety orientation promised with each sale.

In regard to the ultra-fast Superbikes, the manufacturers suggested that more stringent licensing requirements on the part of the States and more rider education was needed. These suggestions were aimed at countering proposed legislation from Congress to impose a horsepower-to-weight ratio mandate, sponsored by Senator John Danforth of Missouri. It was later learned that Danforth had gathered his statistics from reports by an amalgamation of accident insurance companies that had sought eventually to ban the sale of motorcycles altogether! After a storm of protest from the industry as a whole, Danforth withdrew his bill, partially because it was the industry suggestion that more extensive rider education might well be in order.

A spokesman for the Japanese manufacturers stated that for 1988 smaller and less powerful entry level sports-type machines were being introduced, and that more such models were to be offered during the 1989 and 1990 sales seasons.

The co-called biker life style was also under some condemnation from certain of the more conservative touring riders, who resented the image of the long-haired, bearded and often tattooed individuals whose leather-and-Levi presence had become more and more identified with heavyweight motorcycling on the largely custom-cruiser types of machines, most of whom favoured H-Ds.

This attitude was by this time somewhat outmoded, as the general public had developed a tolerance for the free-swinging individualistic life style of such riders. This was aided by the fact that the great majority of bikers had proved themselves to be law-abiding, socially responsible citizens who adhered to a live-and-let-live philosophy. Their public image was enhanced by their support of various charities, such as Muscular Dystrophy research, providing toys for underprivileged children and donating blood to Red Cross banks.

An unfortunate aspect of motorcycling had long been emphasized by certain motion picture producers, who for several decades had cast bikers in unsympathetic roles involving gang activity, along with various types of sadistic behaviour. Concerned with this image, the AMA conducted a survey in 1987 of films released since the 1953 production of "The Wild One" starring Marlon Brando, the first of an ongoing series of "biker" pictures. The results, published in the August issue of *"American Motorcyclist"*, listed about 70 such films released through the years, starring such actors as Lee Marvin, Jack Nicholson, Peter Fonda, Joe Namath, William Smith, Robert Walker, Jr. and others. It was also noted that certain action-type serial programs tend to feature biker types as villains.

In spite of the falling motorcycle market, the AMA has enjoyed sustained support from motorcyclists of all persuasions, not only for their campaigning against unfair treatment from Hollywood, but also for their support of various groups such as the MMA and ABATE and affiliated riders' associations in their drives against compulsory helmet laws and certain access restrictions in parks and recreational areas.

On the positive side, motorcycling in general and H-D in particular has received much publicity from the exploits of Malcolm S. Forbes, Jr. In inheriting of the prestigious *Forbes* magazine and a six hundred million dollar fortune from his late father, Forbes has been the unabashed exponent of the personal enjoyment of great riches. As a dedicated motorcyclist he has been described as "the world's oldest biker" at age 68, owning a stable of about 75 machines of all makes, of which about 25 are various H-D models. With a group of free-swinging friends, self-styled as "the Capitalistic Tools", Forbes has obtained diplomatic permission to undertake motorcycle tours of both mainland China and the Soviet Union. He has also commemorated his exploits with a large fleet of custom-made hot air balloons, a recent addition being a huge simulation of a Heritage Softail model.

Forbes has also received much publicity through his acquaintance with actress Elizabeth Taylor who has been persuaded to ride an 883 Sportster painted her favorite shade of purple. In an interview on national television with talk show hostess Oprah Winfrey, Miss Taylor described Forbes as her good time biking companion and stated that she was a HAWG fan.

H-D has been able to successfully combine its sales, marketing and HOG promotional activities to encompass the broad spectrum of H-D interests. Their extensive advertising displays in the trade magazines emphasise both the functional simplicity of their products and their role in traditional

WOULD YOU SELL AN UNRELIABLE MOTORCYCLE TO THESE GUYS?

We don't.

THINGS ARE DIFFERENT ON A HARLEY.® HARLEY-DAVIDSON

CYCLE

A Harley-Davidson advertisement that appeared widely in the trade press during 1987 sparked much controversy among some enthusiasts who disputed the image presented. However, about 80% of H-D interest is centered on the bike mode. Among these adherents are members of the MMA, ABATE, as well as such fraternal groups as the Hell's Angels, Bandidos, Hessians, Mongols, Chosen Few, to name several

American motorcycling. HOG rallies catering to the conservative devotees are hosted by Chairman Beals and members of his middle management team clad in tennis sweaters and designer slacks. The now traditional Bacchanalian biker gatherings, such as Sturgis, with accompanying nude female beauty pageants, wet T-shirt contests, along with big beer belly and tattooed contenders are attended by the bearded Willie G. Davidson dressed in Levis and leathers.

A surprise announcement of a new model was made at a special meeting held on March 24 at the Newporter Inn in Newport Beach, California, to which members of the trade press were invited. The

The FXSTS 'Springer' model, announced in April 1988 as the 85th Anniversary machine to commemorate the Company's founding. Its overall resemblance to a 1950s custom 'chopper' emphasises H-D's commitment to the traditions of American motorcycling. *(Harley-Davidson Motor Co.)*

FXSTS, as it was designated, was unveiled by Willie G. It was the regular Softail model but in the FX style and fitted with an updated replica of the two-legged girder fork, as formerly fitted to all H-D products between 1908 and 1948, when it had been superseded by the hydraulically-controlled Hydroglide type.

With extended front fork legs fitted with a 21in front wheel, and with the concealed Softail-type rear springing, the whole aspect of the new model conveyed the ambiance of the long classic custom-type 1950s 'chopper' as built from traditional aftermarket components.

Hailed by Willie G. as yet another manifestation of the Company's allegiance to the nostalgia of American motorcycling, it was noted as being a celebration of the Company's 85th Anniversary. It was also announced that a limited production run of 1,250 units was planned, with a suggested retail price of \$10,600.00.

Observers at once remarked that another modernized antique could be easily produced by fitting shortened fork legs together with a 16in front wheel and a classic FL type mudguard, to create a 1936 replica of the classic EL series that had been launched in that year.

In addition, the program featured a slide show with the computerized graphics of a new 61 cu. in. V twin racing engine that the Company was currently developing which would have double overhead camshafts and multi-valve cylinder heads. This was apparently to herald a new era of H-D's competition participation, in addition to its contribution of the XR1000 engine-gearbox unit to the Buell-designed 'Battletwin'.

A note of controversy was interjected into the proceedings when Joe Minton, a motorcycle engineer and the technical writer who had latterly been contributing articles to the trade press describing Jerry Branch's developmental work on his refinement of H-D's XR1000 and Evolution engines, circulated among the assemblage. In a series of conversations with individual attendees, he took issue with H-D's top management in its refusal to accord Branch and his Cypress, California-based Flowmetrics organization public recognition for his important contributions to the Company's resurgence.

In the midst of the general enthusiasm for the Springer model, some dealers and technical experts questioned its safety qualifications in relation to the solid-legged fork. Some veteran riders recalled the handling problems encountered in the old racing models during high speed running in the days of the old Wrecking Crew. These apprehensions were somewhat allayed by Joe Minton, who stated that in his opinion the fork was safe enough if the bearing assemblies were kept properly adjusted and lubricated.

In June, it was announced that the Company was seeking permission for the Securities and Exchange Commission to issue another two million shares of common stock. Its purpose was to raise additional capital to further retire some still outstanding Company obligations. At this point, the stock was being quoted at $ 24.00. Observers commented that further acquisitions of profitable non-motorcycling subsidiaries might also be contemplated.

It was noted following Willie G's announcement of new racing engines that the Company did not at the time actually have any prototype designs in progress. The only prototype work presently in hand was in the hands of Jerry Branch, who had partially completed a multi-valve V twin air cooled 61 cu. in. engine under development in Cypress. The Company was reported as undergoing a revitalization of their Racing Department, which had languished following the retirement of the veteran Dick O'Brien. This was no doubt sparked by the poor showing at the 1988 Daytona Races where H-D's entrant was a non-starter due to mechanical problems and disagreements among the staff regarding tuning methods. At the time of this writing, Branch states that it would take until at least 1990 to bring new racing machinery into place.

The most prominent Company activity was an Eighty-fifth Anniversary celebration and rally held in Milwaukee in June, featuring carnival-type entertainment, socializing with Company officials, and demonstration rides of the 1989 models. Company participation was also planned in the August rally at Sturgis, the long traditional biker's conclave, as well as numerous summer activities for the benefit of HOG members.

The annual Sturgis Rally, now almost an exclusive H-D affair, saw 40,000 enthusiasts gathering for a typical biker celebration. County officials as well as the organizing committee co-operated in attempting to control public displays of nudity. Such were now limited to private gatherings throughout the week.

A late announcement for 1988 was the offering of the Springer fork and wheel assembly as a replacement for the standard hydraulic fork on certain FX models from 1984 onwards, re-emphasizing the 1950s chopper theme. The rather high price of $1,795.00 for the unit was described as necessary to recover prototype costs. Early in 1989, the price was raised to $2195.00, increasing costs being cited.

Management personnel, dealers, and many friends were saddened at the death of Charles Thompson in October, 1988, who had been forced to retire from the Company in 1983 following a heart transplant. A former dealer in Louisville, Kentucky, before joining the Company in 1969 under AMF management as National Sales Manager, he was elected President in 1980. He had been active during the buy-out proceedings in 1981 with the rest of the Beals group.

The alarming drop in overall motorcycle sales during 1988 prompted the Motorcycle Industry's Council, comprising the four Japanese manufacturers along with H-D, to seek ways and means of reviving the market. $400,000.00 was raised to fund marketing studies, with the conclusion that family participation with special emphasis on feminine recruitment should be emphasized. H-D shortly afterward dropped out of the program, its management contending that it had already inaugurated such a drive with its general advertising and in its newly launched *Ladies of Harley* magazine. In addition, for three seasons past, it had selected an attractive young lady rider as *Ms Harley-Davidson* to aid in the promotion. Subsequently publicity in both the *Enthusiast* as well as in *Hog Tales* carried on this theme.

While the Japanese manufacturers, who still commanded the majority of motorcycle sales, cut back production, H-D had actually increased its output in response to its increasing leadership in its exclusive heavyweight class. The 883 Sportster showed increased popularity and by the end of 1988 was the most popular selling individual model in the US market.

A new model launched in January 1989 was an FL variant, the Electro-Glide Ultra Classic. With a twin headlight, frame-mounted fairing, it was equipped with a stereophonic sound system, optional hand or helmet-mounted intercom system, computer-controlled cruise control, self-cancelling turn signals, air suspension, and connections for a citizens band radio. A new 32 ampere hour alternator and an increased capacity starting motor were also fitted, in common with the other FL and FX models, together with an enlarged five gallon fuel tank to enhance cruising range. While H-D had

The top of the line model for 1989 was the limited production Electraglide Classic with electronically-controlled cruise control, stereophonic sound equipment, rider and passenger intercommunication equipment and provision for a citizen's band short wave radio. This model was Milwaukee's answer to similarly equipped Japanese heavyweight touring models. (*Harley-Davidson Motor Co.*)

been emphasizing in their advertising that they featured purely functional machines, this new departure was stated as being offered to allow H-D to cover the entire spectrum of the market and to compete with the current high tech Japanese tourers.

Another new model launched later that year was a variant of the FXRT Wideglide, the Convertible. In its original form, this machine was more or less a hybrid custom chopper type fitted with a peanut fairing and plastic saddle bags in order to double as a tourer. As such it had not caught on well, and it was thought that as a new offering with a quickly detachable windshield and bags, its dual role could now be more or less defined as such.

In March, 1989, the suggested retail price of the 883 Sportster was raised to $4195.00, inflationary manufacturing costs being cited. Still a fair price for a machine of its displacement, it was noted that in its Evolution form, over 30,000 of the model had now been sold.

An official announcement from the factory that month told of a reorganization of H-D's top management. Jim Paterson, a production executive, was elevated to the Presidency of the Motorcycle Manufacturing Division. Richard F. Teerlink was promoted to head all of H-D's manufacturing activities, in which was included the Holiday Rambler Division, various defense contract operations, the engine casting contract for Briggs and Stratton and plumbing accessories for the Kohler Corporation. Vaughn L. Beals, Jr., remained in the top spot as H-D's Board Chairman, with authority over all operations. Inside information from certain factory personnel included the allegation that Beals were relieved that he was no longer obliged to attend certain functions that featured biker excesses.

What with the now substantial H-D activity, journalistic attention was accelerated. Paisano Productions, publisher of *Easyriders*, the pioneer biker magazine, along with several additional offerings, reported overall monthly sales of over 400,000 copies. An *Easyrider* spin-off, *Iron Horse*, that was circulated east of the Mississippi, accounted for 100,000 copies more, as did *Outlaw Biker* and *Supercycle*. A more restrained publication, *Hot Bike*, resurrected from the defunct *Street Chopper*, now offered by McMullen Publications, also showed rapid growth. These offerings now overshadowed the so-called "straight" publications such as the long running *Cycle*, *Cycle World*, *Motorcyclist*, and the official AMA magazine, *American Motorcyclist*.

Hog Tales, H-D's official quarterly HOG publication devoted to the activities of that organization was briefly incorporated into another newly founded biker magazine, *American Iron*, which featured a somewhat restrained format. But when the factory learned that the aftermarket firm of Custom Chrome had a substantial financial interest in it, the *Hog Tale* contract was withdrawn, and it reverted to its separate format. This move was reported as being due to certain ongoing legal difficulties between the two firms involving Custom Chrome's alleged infringement upon H-D's patented trademarks.

As could be expected, a substantial number of new books dealing with H-D subjects appeared during 1988 and 1989 in the wake of the resurgence of H-D interest. These included *The Motorcycle That Built A Legend, Harley Racers, Illustrated Harley-Davidson Buyers Guide, Harley-Davidson Photographic History* and *Inside Harley-Davidson*. These books generally dealt with the technical details of past models, and in addition to many photographs had much material garnered from factory printed catalogs and repair manuals. They are of value in catering for the ever increasing interest in the overhaul and restoration of old machines.

Eric Buell's Bimoto-type supersports Battle Twin fitted with the twin carburettor XR-1000 engine-gear units saw the projected assembly of fifty units completed in 1988, with twenty seven of them being sold to Japanese enthusiasts. In the Spring of 1989, Buell announced that with newly enlarged facilities, a production run of two hundred machines was contemplated for the 1989 and 1990 sales season. The 1200cc Evolution Sportster engine unit was to be fitted to the new models, citing both the shortage of the XR parts as well as the greater tractability and dependability of the Evolution units.

Dealers reported that the sale of new machines remained generally firm during the Winter and early Spring of 1989, together with the profitable sales of the factory-supplied accessories, clothing, jewellery, toys, and extensive novelty items bearing the H-D franchised trademarks, which were premium priced and carried a high retail markup. There were complaints from some quarters that certain best selling FX and Heritage models were in short supply due to their diversion by the factory to the export market. Many dealers took the position that domestic dealers should have preference in this regard, noting their financial sacrifices made on the factory's behalf during the lean years of 1982–1984.

At a factory-sponsored press conference held in Pomona, California, in June, the dealers were assured that their allocations would receive more careful attention in the future. It was also stated that the factory was viewing present marketing conditions with caution, noting the generally depressed state of sales. The thought was that over-production and a backlog in dealer's stocks would inevitably lead to retail discounting, a condition that had caused much hardship during past years.

In a subsequent visit by the author to the York facility, a production supervisor stated that while daily output had been gradually increased from 165 to about 210 units per day, such could be easily cut back should market conditions demand it. The advantage of this flexibility was that sales and production could be kept at parity, and that the factory could point to the fact that they were "selling all they could make".

However, in spite of H-D's resurgence in a depressed market, and the glowing reports of H-D sales in some trade magazines, many dealers reported that by late Spring and Summer of 1989 they were overstocked with unsold models. In consequence in late Summer many resorted to special sales where 1989 machines on hand were offered at discounts of from 10% to 12%, with 20% discounts on related products.

On the sporting scene, Grand Prix racing in the Camel-Pro series sponsored by the R.J. Reynolds Company continued to draw large crowds in spite of the general decrease of public interest in motorcycling. Many non-motorcycling fans were attracted to the vicarious thrills of motor sport. By this time, however, it was obvious that private entrants could no longer compete with the factories financially, what with the vast expense of fielding a team requiring sophisticated maintenance facilities and attendant mechanics. The old truism was in evidence that those willing to spend the most money would inevitably be the winners. Then too, the individuality of the sport was lost when technological progress mandated that one make of machine was virtually indistinguishable from the other.

The most popularly supported sports spectacle was now motocross, as the promoters could attract large crowds to the athletic stadiums where artificial terrain could be constructed, and the venue readily lent itself to television viewing. In addition, the specialized machines in the various displacement classes were available for "as-is" purchase.

Dirt track racing, long the mainstay of American motorcycle sport, went into a decline, as no machines especially built for this were available on the general market, and the costs of engineering and custom building had become prohibitive. In an attempt to revive the sport, H-D in co-operation with the AMA promoted the idea of a Supersports class of both road and track racing, utilizing the 883 Sportster, with firm rules regarding the limited extent of modifications to the machines, such as wheels, tires, and suspension with radical engine tuning restricted. To date, this class has not attracted much attention, and some sceptics recalling the Class C days opined that the class could quickly metomorphisize into high priced racing specials as before.

The limited dirt track activity had been dominated by Honda ever since 1982, who had swept the board with their specialized V twins. They dropped out of the running in 1988, with the thought that after such a long run of success, they had nothing more to prove. H-D at once saw the opportunity to again enter their traditional venue, and with a factory-sponsored team on resurrected XR-750s to compete with a stellar field of riders, such as Chris Carr and Scott Parker. Entering all the major Nationals, Parker with Carr just behind garnered sufficient points to win the coveted Number One plate. Harley-Davidson also did well in the 600cc class, but the significance was somewhat downgraded as the badge-engineered Rotax-engined specials with Woods frames were not regarded as Milwaukee irons.

H-D continued to strengthen their bonds with their adherents through the HOG organization, whose membership grew to well over 90,000 by 1989. A comprehensive program of nationwide rallies was put into place, featuring most of the now traditional biker entertainment, along with the encouragement of exhibiting restored antique models. Levi-and leather-clad factory personnel mingled with the crowds, emphasizing that H-D was ever ready to listen to the preferences of their customers as to suggestions for new models and accessories.

Worthwhile charitable participation was the now long-running factory supported program of raising funds to combat muscular dystrophy, featuring "love rides" in various parts of the country, where a substantial individual contribution would allow clubs and other groups to join with factory personnel. A ride from Glendale, California to nearby Malibu drew a crowd of several thousand in November, 1989.

At the close of 1989, the estimated domestic motorcycle sales had declined from 715,000 in 1988 to 535,000 units. This included scooters, mopeds, and ATVs. The latter category showed a surprising popularity, with the now legally mandated quads seeing wide use in commercial applications and in agriculture. In an extensive trip through the Western states in the Summer of 1989, the author saw large numbers in use on cattle ranches and farms for such utility uses as herding livestock, running fence lines, irrigation systems, and even in light duty cultivating. Small capacity scrambler type motorcycles were also much in evidence. While quads are not street legal, they are used in winter on rural roads to negotiate heavy snow conditions.

In 1989, H-D sold approximately 37,000 units domestically, with about 7,000 more going to export markets. While the former figure is small compared with the total market, its domination of the heavyweight market is significant with 57% of the sales of the over 850cc category, and 43% of the over 650cc market. These figures showed an increase over the year before.

H-D's export sales expanded, with the growing interest in the biker movement in Scandinavia, Central Europe, and in Australia and New Zealand. A sales increase was noted in Great Britain, with an expanded import organization now in place. H-D's mistique is evidenced in the growing number of overseas fraternal type clubs, with nearly 100% H-D participation.

Significant growth of sales was also noted in Japan, where the Balcomb Trading Company managed by Richard Child had expanded activity. Unlike the rest of the export markets, the Japanese favor "dresser" type machines over the FX custom cruiser models. In addition to the factory effort, several private firms engage in parallel export, purchasing left-over FL models from dealers. There is also much activity in the export of used models.

An interesting adjunct to domestic sales have been the building of special machines by the dealers in their own shops, to offer an optional choice for the custom enthusiast. In addition to the touring versions of the 1200cc Sportsters already mentioned, a sporting version of both models has been offered, utilizing special parts made by a newly organized aftermarket firm, the White Brothers in Sacramento. These allow the lowering of the machine by shortening both the forks and the rear shock absorbers, which appears to improve the handling.

Another favorite type of customizing has been applied to Heritage Softail models, with the fitting of fat bob tanks, solo seats, and special paint jobs, which with the use of 1940s tank badges has revived the 1950s look. What has been described as the ultimate classic H-D has been the fitting of Springer fork assemblies to Heritage Softails, with replica pre-1949 mudguards having side stays to attach to the girders. These also have solo saddles, special paint jobs, fat bob tanks, and 1930s style glue-on decals. The factors frowns on fitting 16in wheels in Springer forks, however, as there are doubts concerning the handling. In October, the factory send out a form letter to the dealer's mechanics, and while not actually forbidding the conversion, warned them not to ride or road test the machines.

The 1990 model range announced in October included no less than twenty two machines along with a sidecar. These were all permutations of the four main configurations, the FL's, FX's, Sportsters, and the Heritage series. A new model was the Fat Boy, a Heritage-based design that featured a special

Erik Buell's latest design is the 1990 Westwind, a high-performance two-seat street machine fitted with the vibration-damped Evolution Sportster engine that combines with the latest in state-of-the-art suspension. Production is limited to 200 units with a $14,350 price tag. *(Erik Buell)*

silver paint finish, aluminum disc wheels, a bobbed front mudguard, and a line of special accessories to accompany it. In common with other Heritage models, the rear suspension unit was now fitted with an adjusting device to vary the spring rate. The suggested premium retail price was $14,000.00.

The factory-sponsored official history written by David Wright was updated in a second edition in 1987. With an apparent realization that a growingly sophisticated readership was disenchanted with analogical sales material, H-D for the first time in its long history sponsored a book that dealt wth actual facts involving Company affairs. *Well Made in America*, a 226 page offering published by McGraw-Hill and written by Peter C. Reid, a motorcyclist and an authority on industrial management, deals with the recovery period of H-D history.

This work is arguably somewhat slanted toward featuring the role of Board Chairman Vaughn Beals in the Company's recovery. The important part played by AMF Chairman Ray Albert Tritten in originally recruiting Beals and a new group of professional engineers to turn the company around is not mentioned. The important role the dealer organized Harley-Davidson Dealers Alliance played in influencing ongoing relations with the factory is not mentioned either: the substantial number of prominent dealers involved being dismissed as insignificant.

Another publication appeared in 1990: *The Big Book of Harley-Davidson*. Featured were a large group of factory photographs accompanied by much early day material garnered from past issues of *The Enthusiast*, along with a large section devoted to reprints of past factory advertising copy.

By 1989 the Company that once stood on the brink of financial disaster and was at risk of foreclosure by Citicorp bankers was showing a remarkable recovery. Reports to the shareholders showed a gross income of $750,000,000 from combined operations, a 9% increase over the preceeding year. The motorcycle sales increased by $14,000,000, which included a 10% increase in exports.

Left: The Fat Boy model, introduced for 1990. Based on the Heritage Softail, it features silver gray finish, specially designed saddle bags, a custom dualseat and alloy disc wheels, all for a premium suggested retail price of $14,000. Some experienced tourists have questioned the handling of the machine in side winds. *(Harley-Davidson Motor Co.)*

Public confidence in the Company was evidenced throughout 1989 by a rise in the value of its shares to $28.00. By January, 1990, this has increased to $38.00, due to the news that a large industrial conglomerate was seeking to take over H-D. As a strengthened company with promising growth potential due to its diversified products, such an eventuality was now an ongoing factor for H-D to consider.

A press release in November, 1989 revealed that Malcolm I. Glazer, President of the First Allied Corporation had issued a statement to the effect that his company now held 6.24% of H-D stock. It had also requested a clearance from the Security and Exchange Commission to acquire up to 15% of H-D's total shares, and was also seeking a seat on the Board of Directors. It was noted that First Allied held large blocks of shares in various diversified industries, including substantial holdings of railroad stock acquired through government sales of portions of the Amtrack system.

H-D was reported as being less than cordial to First Allied's intent, but as a public company, management had surrendered certain of its controlling rights should a substantial number of shareholders exert voting pressure.

During January and February of 1990, releases to the motorcycle trade press announced the introduction of a new H-D powered supersports model by Erik Buell. Known as the RS 1200 Westwind, the new machine featured passenger accommodation with a seat over the rear fairing incorporating a folding backrest. The Westwind somewhat belies its big twin antecedents by being rather small and compact, with 17 inch wheels on a 55 inch wheelbase and weighing but 435lbs.

Fitted with an Evolution Sportster engine and gearbox, the Westwind had a 40mm Keihin carburettor and a compression ratio of 9:1, along with a Supertrapp exhaust system. The claimed top speed as stock was 109mph, but more power was available with modifications through H-D's Screaming Eagle performance components.

Buell paid special attention to the isolation of traditional Sportster engine vibration from the rider by providing ball joint attachments in the frame which allow the engine to move within its own plane.

The well engineered Westwind with its announced production of 200 units offered the sporting rider an American V-twin engine combined with state of the art chassis construction for the ultimate in high speed travel.

The motorcycling world in general, and H-D in particular, was saddened by the sudden death from a heart attack on February 23rd, 1990 of Malcolm S. Forbes. His well publicized exploits on a world wide basis with his associates called the Capitalistic Tools brought spectacular attention to motorcycling, and the year before he had received a special award from the AMA for his contributions to the sport. Among the hundreds of people attending his memorial service at New York's Episcopal Cathedral were many from the sporting and entertainment world as well as politicians and members of government. His noted companion, actress Elizabeth Taylor, subsequently announced to the press that they had planned to marry.

At almost the same moment, an unauthorized biography of Forbes written by a Wall Street Journal investigative reporter, Christopher Winans, and published by St. Martins Press entitled *The Man who Had Everything* appeared on the market. Forbes' image was somewhat clouded by the revelation that for some years he had engaged in relationships with various young men. The Forbes family was subsequently embarrassed by the apprehension of a young health spa trainer, George Warnock, who had attempted to extort $250,000 from the estate in exchange for his silence regarding allegations about his former relationships with the publisher of *Forbes Magazine*. These unfortunate events were quite naturally a source of embarassment to both the top management of the AMA as well as Harley-Davidson.

The annual Daytona 200 had for several years past become less oriented towards racing and more towards a motorcyclists' convention, with emphasis on biking socialization, it being estimated that the event was 90% supported by H-D owners. What with the recent trend in nostalgic motorcycling, the newly instituted Vintage Races featuring old time machines was drawing increasing interest. H-D's top management was now encouraging the Big Twin contests for the benefit of 883 Sportster participation in a possible revival of the former Class C concept. To this end, the factory announced that new XR-75 racing engines would now be available in limited quantities for private purchase at $6995.00.

Both the AMA and H-D had also noted that private support of competition had dwindled, largely because high tech racing machines were now almost entirely being entered under factory sponsorship due to the high costs involved. The AMA noted that the number of active competition licenses had dropped to less than five hundred.

The factory sponsored HOG continued to expand under the leadership of Steve Piehl, and by 1991 had increased membership to 130,000. HOG emphasised social events for H-D owners

The aftermarket supplier, Storz Performance of Ventura, California, founded by the former H-D factory competition rider, offers numerous custom designed high performance accessories including components to create a road going replica of Milwaukee's classic XR track and TT racers. Available are special Italian forks, wheel assemblies, exhaust system, fuel tank, tail piece, lights, and other components. *(Photo Credit: Storz Performance)*

such as field meets, charity runs, and group touring. Paisano Publications, which promoted *EASYRIDERS* magazine and other related biker publications, sponsored area field meets under the banner of **ARROW** (Associated Road Riders of the World) which featured mild types of riding stunts for owner participation, with appropriate prizes for winners.

During the Spring the factory continued its aggressive policy of warning various aftermarket manufacturers of H-D accessories to desist in their use of representations of factory patented logos on their products, as well as purchasing advertising in trade magazines urging owners to use only factory derived spare parts. It also expanded its own penetration of the accessory market with additional products to encourage the customizing of machines, long a hallmark of H-D ownership. This program was enhanced by the issuing of an expanded 100 page catalog sent to all registered owners.

One of the Company's outside suppliers of custom exhaust systems, Christy Dello of Corona, California, inaugurated a successful $7,166,000 lawsuit against the Company in January, 1991. Dello claimed that the Company had agreed to purchase $250,000 worth of equipment from his firm, but backed out of the deal after he had borrowed heavily to tool up to fill it, driving him into bankruptcy. The Company counsel, Timothy Hoelter, argued that the employee who originally made the agreement was no longer with the firm, which then nullified the deal, but the jury was unconvinced and awarded the judgement to the plaintiff.

During the Spring of 1990 the Company enjoyed an ever increasing number of export sales: the biker syndrome receiving added converts in England, Europe, Australia and New Zealand, along with increased dresser interest in Japan. Hells Angels chapters were also proliferating in these countries, along with similar but unaffiliated fraternal type biker clubs as well.

The parent Hells Angels chapter and national headquarters in Oakland, California, saw its organization in some disarray with the murder of its incoming President, Michael O'Farrell, as the result of a fight with a member of the Aryan Brotherhood in a beer bar in San Leandro. O'Farrell was to have succeeded the veteran Ralph M. "Sonny" Barger as titular head of the group.

With a healthy increase in sales, H-D's top management made plans to enhance their production capabilities at the York facility, and announced a $20,000,000 expansion of the painting department. The growing strength of H-D's market SGW value of their outstanding shares increased to $58.00, and in the financial report issued to the stockholders in May 1990 a two-for-one split was indicated.

The annual motorcycle convention in Sturgis, South Dakota held in May 1990 was the largest ever, and as a fifty year anniversary of the event was as usual predominently an H-D affair. It was estimated that nearly 300,000 riders were in attendance for the week long celebration. The national media was quick to note that there were at least a dozen deaths from various causes, along with numerous arrests for drunkeness and drug abuse, together with about two hundred injuries. The trade magazines along with the official AMA publication were quick to point out that these episodes would be the norm for any such public gathering of this magnitude, whether motorcycle related or not.

To exploit the growing cult value of the Harley-Davidson name, the Company recently expanded their licensing of unrelated products that bear their patented color schemes and logos and which include jewelry, toys, various garments, as well as toiletries and perfumes. Another expansion has been in the clothing field, and the Company distributes a wide range of Levi and leather type goods in various designs in the now traditional biker mode. A separate department under the Harley-Davidson Motor Clothes designation encourages dealers to expand their apparel departments.

The nostalgic theme of American motorcycling as personified in contemporary motorcycle design has brought about an enhanced public interest in antique Indian machines, with substantial numbers of reworked or newly fabricated models forming a limited but now growing industry. There has lately been much speculation concerning the ownership and legal status of the Indian trademarks in the U.S. The situation in Canada has been less clearly defined however, and in the Fall of 1990 one Robert Dell, a professional Indian restorer in Marion Bridge, Nova Scotia, made application to the Patent Office in Ottawa to acquire the legal rights to the Springfield logos. Unknown to Dell, H-D in a move to expand their licensing activities had already applied to the same authorities for the rights to the Indian trademarks in Canada. While H-D had contested Dell's application, the authorities decided in the latter's favor on the basis of his Canadian citizenship and his position as a bona fide producer of Indian restorations and replica components.

For the late 1990 and early 1991 sales seasons, both the 883 and 1200cc Sportsters were updated. The entry level $4359.00 883 XLH was continued as a stripped model with its original chain drive, small solo saddle, and restricted instrumentation and chrome plating. The 883 Hugger model at $4800.00 featured buckhorn handlebars and shorter rear shock absorbers which lowered its seating position. A deluxe version was fitted with a newly designed belt drive, wire wheels, and a dual seat as standard. As an optional fitting on past XL machines, a belt drive conversion was made available from the accessory group as a $499.00 extra. The 1200cc model as a bored out version was offered with similar specification at a base price of $6095.00.

Both the 883s and 1200s for 1991 were fitted with five speed transmissions. This long awaited improvement was added to allow highway cruising speeds with reduced vibration; the latter long a hallmark of Sportster operation. In this modification the engine was redesigned with a new clutch, a revised valve tappet and cam gear system, and redline engine revolutions reduced from 6000 to 5200.

While the rear suspension with its limited travel gave a somewhat hard ride, which could be somewhat alleviated by fitting a seat with additional padding.

A production foreman at the York facility told the author that as a response to economic recession that beset the country during the Fall of 1990, the upgrading of the Sportsters to,, hopefully, fulfil at least partially the role of the more expensive big twin as a touring machine was a logical marketing strategy.

The author concurs with this theory, if a Sportster is fitted with the optional 3.2 gallon fuel tank and is cruised at speeds under 65mph. The handling of these models is enhanced by the fitting of an aftermarket lowering kit, such as that supplied by the White Brothers.

The domestic motorcycle market underwent several changes during 1990 and 1991. Sales statistics for 1990 showed a 24% decrease from 1989, there being but 266,000 bona fide motorcycles and 51,000 scooters sold. The decrease in the former is said to be due to the declining sales of the Oriental supersports models. The total is also affected by the reclassification of All Terrain vehicles, which are now four wheelers through government mandate, the three wheelers being phased out, and the former now being grouped with automobiles in sales statistics.

Harley-Davidson's position in the market has lately been enhanced, through both the improved public acceptance of the Evolution models which gives the Company over 60% of the domestic heavyweight market. A new trend has been the growing numbers of upscale buyers who have embraced the biker mode as a new hobby. More enthusiasts who inhabit the "straight" world during their regular avocations now assume the "biker" ambiance during weekends, and these economically upwardly mobile newcomers are not only able to pay the high prices for a new machine but often spend several thousand more dollars on custom equipment. More than a few of the veteran biker types resent the growing numbers of these effete newcomers who crowd into the traditional "outlaw" watering places!

Production at the York facility presently totals about 260 units per month, an output justified by both the firmness of the domestic market and the recent surge in exports. It is stated that about 30% of 1991 production is for export and not a few dealers have complained that foreign distributors are receiving first preference in their orders of the best-selling models.

Of special interest is H-D's position in Japan, where Richard Child's Balcom Trading Company has lately been importing increasing numbers of F1 dresser type machines which are favored in that country. Attendant to this enhanced popularity, Uniphoto Press International of Toyko in 1989 entered into an agreement with Haynes Publications to produce a Japanese language edition of this work for the benefit of Far Eastern enthusiasts.

An entirely new top-of-the-line FX model introduced in 1991 to complement the big twin line is the Sturgis FXDB, a revival of a model briefly produced in the early 1980s. The new model has the standard primary chain drive, unlike the former all belt drive model, and incorporates a number of distinctive changes. A two point engine isolation mounting is fitted which insulates the rider from engine vibration. An altered frame with a single seat post exposes the battery and oil tank; the latter a simulated case that houses the electrical components. The real oil tank is mounted underneath the frame and therefore requires shorter feed lines. The final belt drive is mounted outside the frame tubes and the belt can be changed without removing the suspension units. Also included for the first time in recent years is a fork lock built into the steering head and actuated by the ignition key. The Sturgis in standard form has the engine and transmission cases finished in matt black, although a deluxe chrome trimmed version is also available. Factory personnel have indicated that the updated Sturgis frame may be included in the design of future variations of the FX model line.

Factory production was halted during the first two weeks of February 1991 by a strike of the production workers represented by the Aero Space and Sheet Metal Workers Union. Stewards informed the author that the union had foregone demands for increased wages in view of the Company's distressed position in the market during 1982 and 1984, but that management had failed to live up to its promise to increase hourly rates once the Company recovered. Then there was also the allegation that certain of the workers were subjected to excessive overtime

The Sturgis model, reintroduced for 1991, with isolastic engine mounts, repositioned oil tank, built in fork lock and the final belt drive assembly placed outside the frame for easier servicing and replacement. *(Photo Credit: Harley-Davidson Motor Company)*

demands. At any rate, a compromise was affected whereby the hourly wages were to be increased by 14% to around $13.00 over a three year period.

Both production workers as well as shop stewards have told the author that among the senior production workers at York there is some smoldering resentment relating to the original establishment of the facility and stemming from the days of AMF management. While the latter owners already owned the plant, H-D's production was moved from Milwaukee to take advantage of the lower wage scales acceptable in Pennsylvania due to the then high unemployment and loss of jobs there from the decline of their smokestack industries.

At any rate, the wage scale is being improved, although the rates are still somewhat lower than those enjoyed by workers in the automobile industry.

The FX and FL Evolution big twins have been subjected to detail improvement along the way, with the fitting of wet plate clutches and a repositioned control attachment, improved electrics, and a larger capacity starting motor.

The overall picture of motorcycling in general in the United States is somewhat clouded, due to the recent drop in sales and increasing interference from insurance companies in raising their rates, along with restrictive safety regulations regarding mandatory helmet laws and environmentalists advocacy of the closing of off-road venues. U.S. Senator Deconcini recently advocated the formation of a special law enforcement group to police fraternal biker groups, alleging organized crime connections.

In spite of this, the firm condition of Harley-Davidson in the market place is enhanced by the loyalty of enthusiasts, good public acceptance of updated models, the attraction of new customer groups, and now increasing worldwide interest in custom-cruiser type machines.

At the moment, the nostalgia factor in motorcycling is enhanced by the Company's policy of producing replica type machines that appear to be the backbone of serious enthusiasm for Milwaukee products.

Left. The ultimate in Milwaukee nostalgia. The White Brothers Accessory company of Garden Grove, California, offers a lowering kit, altered Springer fork, solo seat, fuel tank name plate badges and other items to recreate a 1940's big twin from a late model Heritage Softtail. *(Photo Credit: White Brothers)*

Appendix 1

The Excelsior Motorcycle

THE EXCELSIOR MOTORCYCLE WAS A DISTINCT MAKE OF MACHINE THAT WAS produced independently of any other. Its brief history is included here as it was significant in its survival through 1931, as was its role as the smaller of the so called 'Big Three' manufacturers that formed the bulk of domestic motorcycle production during the pioneer and vintage periods. Many of Excelsior's activities and some of the men responsible for certain of the designs were at one time or another connected with both Harley-Davidson and Indian.

The make had its beginning sometime early in 1905 in connection with a small manufacturing company in Chicago, Illinois. What fragmentary information is available indicates that it was founded by a small group of early day motorcycle enthusiasts who were impressed with the design efforts of one Walther Heckscher, a French-Jewish mechanic with some engineering background. He had gained some prior experience in Europe at the turn of the century with early variations of the engine designs of De Dion and Bouton.

Heckscher, who in the early 1900's was most probably unaware of the prototype experiments of Harley and Davidson, had independently arrived at the same conclusions: namely that the conversion of standard heavyweight roadster pedal cycles to motorcycles by the simple expedient of fitting an engine and driving mechanism did not result in a satisfactorily rugged machine. It was during this period that he built at least three prototypes from the ground up, with more substantial components that were infinitely superior to the many bicycle conversions already being marketed, this being the 'clip on' era.

Heckscher's ultimate effort followed the then standard design with a De Dion type single cylinder engine fitted into a diamond-type frame. The fuel tank was carried above, between the twin top tubes, with cannister type containers carrying the ignition batteries, tools, and lubricating oil, clipped to the frame in various positions. The single-speed drive via a flat belt and pulleys was fitted with the then standard belt tensioning device that also served as a primitive clutch, a spring loaded pulley activated by a handle. The standard bicycle pedaling gear was retained to afford both initial starting and braking power, with a coaster hub in the rear wheel. The substantial frame carried a loop at its lower forward end to accommodate the engine cases, and was further distinguished by a spring fork with twin fixed and movable legs in a parallel position, to which the wheel axle was fitted in a leading link configuration. The machine was built of substantial materials, and Heckscher's version of the now familiar De Dion engine proved more rugged and reliable than many of its contemporaries.

Using his prototype as a demonstrator, Heckscher attracted the interest of a small group of enthusiasts who were able to raise sufficient capital for him to set up production facilities in a small machine shop in Chicago's South Side. But with limited funds and with almost no sales or marketing facilities, the infant company, whose name is now forgotten, was only able to build and sell about sixty machines during 1905 and 1906, most of them in the immediate area.

It was during this period that Ignatz Schwinn was considering motorcycle manufacture as a sideline. A German immigrant bicycle mechanic, he had founded a growingly successful manufacturing concern in that city during the world wide boom in the then newly-developed safety bicycle. In casting about for a suitable design, the story goes that he quite by chance discovered Heckscher's somewhat ineffectual efforts to produce what was proving to be a satisfactory machine. Already it had gained a measure of recognition in the Chicago area. The upshot of the matter was that Schwinn offered to purchase the manufacturing rights and to engage Heckscher to oversee production.

The deal was consummated early in 1907, the first 300 or so machines being assembled as originally produced, the only visable change being the name 'Excelsior', selected by Schwinn, painted in script on the tank sides. Extensive advertising of the new product, along with its inclusion into the franchises of selected members of the already far flung dealer organization soon made the Excelsior a prominent make within the now rapidly expanding domestic motorcycle industry. From what fragmentary information is available, Heckscher remained with Schwinn but a short time, then resigning and fading into history. The reason for this is unknown, except that the somewhat eccentric Schwinn was remembered as a difficult man to get along with.

Schwinn's small engineering staff refined the machine further, which underwent expanded production during 1908 and 1909. Sales were now extended into Schwinn's vast export market, with outlets in Europe, Africa, and Australasia.

In 1910, a 50 cu.in. V twin model with mechanical inlet valves, in the so-called 'pocket valve' configuration was offered to compliment the original single cylinder model, which somewhere along

The first Excelsior 30.50 cu.in. belt drive single. These early 1907 models were identical to the 1906 machines as designed by Walther Heckscher. *(Antique Motorcycle Club of America).*

The first Excelsior twins offered for 1910 and 1911 were of 50 cu.in. displacement, and had single geared belt drive. This example is owned by George Twine. *(Antique Motorcycle Club of America).*

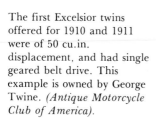

the line had its engine size adjusted to conform to the international half liter 30.50 cu.in. displacement. The twin was also a belt driver with parallel leg leading link suspension, but featured a heavier frame.

The two model range was continued through 1911, and in 1912, the engine size of the twin was increased to the now standard 61 cu.in. displacement. The Company was now actively supporting competition, this being the era of the wooden 'motordromes' that were being built along the lines of the similar 'velodromes' that had been catering for bicycle racing. It was during this year that a limited production close-coupled racing machine was offered for public sale at the bargain price of $250.00. Its performance was comparable to similar models now being offered by Indian, Thor, Flying Merkel, and a few others who were supplying machines for this growingly popular spectator sport. The Excelsior became a formidable contender in racing circles, with Lee Humiston being the first rider to break the magic 100 mph speed barrier on December 30, 1913, at the mile board oval at Playa Del Ray, a resort suburb of Los Angeles. Humiston went on in the opening months of 1913 to establish a number of records that stood for several years thereafter.

In 1913, the single was dropped from the line, production being concentrated on the 61 cu.in. twin which, as a roadster model, was now fitted with all-chain drive, but was single geared with a clutch mounted on a countershaft just behind the engine. In 1914, a two-speed version was also

The 1912-1914 Excelsior twins were of 61 cu.in. displacement, and featured single gear chain drive with an Eclipse type clutch. This 1912 model was restored by AMC Founder Ted Hodgdon. *(Antique Motorcycle Club of America)*.

offered, with a planetary gearset. Both machines were now fitted with heavier fork, the suspension being effected by a quarter eliptic scroll-ended leaf spring almost identical to that already used by Indian.

In 1915, a three-speed model was offered in place of the two-speeder, this with the now standard sliding gear transmission and clutch that was also introduced this season by Harley-Davidson, Indian, and other leading makes. In addition, a new two-stroke ultra-lightweight model was also introduced. This was a rather crude looking machine with a 250 cc engine, somewhat like the contemporary English Villiers, with single geared flat belt drive. It featured a cylindrical fuel tank clipped under the single top tube, with a cartridge-type spring fork activated by a horizontal coil spring fitted to the top of the head lug. While possessed of somewhat limited performance, it was a transportation bargain at a price of $125.00.

During the 1914 competition season, Excelsior's rivals, Harley-Davidson and Indian, had developed more potent speed machinery, and a new designer was engaged to improve engine performance.

J.A.'Jock' McNeil was a recent immigrant from Scotland who had already gained a measure of racing fame as both a rider and practical engineer. He had made a name for himself with a series of machines of his own design that appeared at various board track meets fitted with 61 cu.in. '90 bore' V twins then being marketed as proprietory units by J.A.Prestwich in England. In addition, McNeil was

CONCENTRATED QUALITY
The
EXCELSIOR LIGHT WEIGHT
$135.00

A motorcycle for the masses. For the business and professional man, the office and factory worker, the man who has reached the age when dignity and personal comfort are of paramount consideration, the boy in the transient period between the bicycle and high speed motorcycle, for every one, regardless of size, age or other consideration, who desires a convenient, economical and efficient means of personal transportation, the

EXCELSIOR LIGHT WEIGHT

stands preeminently the *real light weight* motorcycle.

The motor is the highest development in two stroke, three port construction with but three moving parts.

No gears, valves or complicated timing mechanism, automatic lubrication without pump or piping.

Speed control by throttle only.

Two speed gear with handlebar control.

Combination chain and belt drive.

Simple, Comfortable and Noiseless Spring Seat; Drop Forged Nickel Steel Spring Fork; Foot operated brake on belt rim.

Our catalog describing six models now ready.
Write for it today.

Excelsior Motor Mfg. & Supply Company
Office and Factory, 3703 Cortland Street, Chicago

You get quick results from advertisers when you mention MOTOR CYCLE ILLUSTRATED.

Excelsior's first excursion into the lightweight field was in 1914, with a single geared 250 cc belt drive model. An improved two speeder was offered in 1915, as shown here. A smooth running machine, its very mild performance attracted few buyers. It was withdrawn from the line the following year. *(Excelsior Motor Company)*.

The famous 17-3 model that was in production from 1915 through 1919, with but detail improvements. It featured a three-speed gearbox, electric lighting, and a gracefully streamlined fuel tank, the first of its kind in the United States. *(Excelsior Motor Company)*.

Excelsior's famous short-coupled racing model was first offered in 1914, and was based on the factory model ridden by Lee Humiston for the first 100 mph record made in December, 1913. Its performance was later improved by J.A.McNeil, who originated the 'Big Valve' configuration that was later a standard feature of all Excelsior twins. *(Excelsior Motor Company)*.

actively engaged in engineering work for other private owners. He was also retained by the Joerns Manufacturing Company of Minneapolis, Minnesota, to refine the very advanced 61 cu.in. overhead camshaft Cyclone designed by Andrew Strand, which was then suffering from numerous teething troubles. McNeil's efforts enabled their riders to rack up some sensational wins during the 1915 and 1916 seasons, after which the company foundered due to inept management and financial problems.

McNeil's efforts on behalf of Excelsior resulted in the famous 'Big Valve' model, featuring valve diameters of 2 ⅛ inch which greatly improved induction and exhaust porting, adding some 30% to their power output. This new engine was next added to the roadster line as an option, but became standard the following year, albeit in somewhat detuned form.

Competition riders gaining further laurels for Excelsior during this period included Carl Goudy, his lesser known brother, Bill, Lee Creviston, Bill Leuders, Roy Artley, Bob Perry, Joe Wolters, and later, Maldwyn Jones, an already established star for his past performances on Flying Merkels and Harleys. In the Fall of 1915, Carl Goudy made a sensational win at the 300 mile race at the Maywood, Chicago oval.

For 1915, the 61 inch twin had its appearance enhanced with the fitting of a handsomely contoured fuel tank, a marked improvement of the more usual slab sided types of the competition. The overall appearance of these models was such that one would not look out of place when compared with the domestically-produced models of two decades later.

Excelsior machines were always handsomely finished, with rich pearl gray paintwork highlighted by maroon tank panels outlined in gold striping and gold lettering on the name transfers. Scarlet pinstriping in the form of small arrows extended along the fork tubes, and small control parts as well as the cylinder barrels were nickel plated. For the 1917 season, and through 1919, the paint finish was changed to military olive drab, but retaining the maroon tank motif.

An outstanding model was the 17-E for 1916, which featured deeper sectioned mudguards, with full valances on the front wheel. An all-electric model with a Nidco lighting system was offered, although many experienced motorcyclists still preferred the well-proved acetylene Solar system with the gas tank fitted on a bracket over the handlebar lugs. Many law enforcement bodies were now specifying Excelsior big twins, whose utility had been enhanced during the last two seasons by a line of sidecars.

Excelsior machines were also purchased in limited numbers by the War Department, and gave good service both during General Pershing's 1916 Mexican campaign, as well as during overseas operations in World War I. These later models were subject to continuing detail improvement, along with a strengthened clutch and drive train.

The lightweight model was continued by 1916 in two versions, the original single gear, along with a two-speed model that was fitted with a two-speed sliding-dog type transmission integral with the engine, the final drive still being by flat belt. Selling for an increased price of $140.00, its already mild performance was somewhat hampered by its now increased weight. Never an overpopular seller in an age when the heavyweight V twin was the favored American motorcycle, it was not reintroduced for 1917.

Excelsiors were never produced in large numbers, even though the make was now established as a member of the 'Big Three', along with Harley-Davidson and Indian. In 1912, the Company announced that 40,000 machines were then on the road, both at home and overseas. In 1919, it was stated that 100,000 Excelsiors had been marketed, with substantial numbers going to export.

In the immediate post-war continuance of long distance record breaking, Wells Bennett, the enthusiastic Portland, Oregon, Excelsior dealer, bested the 1915 Three Flag record made by

The 17-C model as updated in 1920 by Arthur Lemon. Henderson Four forks were fitted to rationalize production, but many enthusiasts felt that their heavier pattern upset the handling. A few 74 cu.in. models were built in 1921. With the emphasis on Henderson production, less than 300 of these machines were produced between 1920 and 1924. *(Antique Motorcycle Club of America)*.

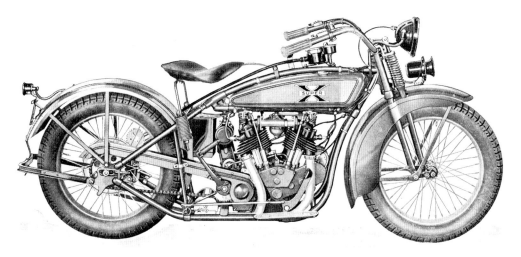

The first Super-X 45 cu.in. model introduced late in 1925, which was designed by Arthur Constantine with some help from Joe Petrali. The engine and gearbox unit had been designed in 1924 as a proposed new Harley-Davidson Model, but now appeared with modified Henderson cycle parts. A front brake was fitted in 1928. *(Excelsior Motor Company).*

Cannonball Baker on an Indian, this being the run from the Canadian border to Tijuana, Mexico. In the seesaw running of this course by other makes, Bennett set up new times in this event during 1918 and 1919. In 1920, he won the Los Angeles 'sealed top gear' run to Bakersfield, with a time not equaled until years later.

Another noted Excelsior star of this era was Roy Artley, who rode a racing 'Big Valve' at Los Angeles's famed Ascot Speedway during 1918 and 1919. Artley had previously represented the marque during the famous Southwestern Desert Races held annually, except for the war years, between San Diego and the hazardous roads to Phoenix, Arizona.

Following the Armistice, McNeil designed a new racing engine for Excelsior based on the former Cyclone design, featuring overhead camshafts. As an all-ball bearing motor, with many advanced features, it proved to turn out fantastic power. The racing shop assembled about a dozen engines, one of which was fitted to a standard track machine which factory rider Bob Perry had shipped to Los Angeles for testing on the Ascot Speedway. On January 2nd 1920, Perry was killed when the machine went out of control in a power slide and through the fence. The story goes that Schwinn, who had long considered Perry as a son, in his grief destroyed the remaining engines. There appears to be some doubt concerning the validity of this fact, however, as team members Wells Bennett, Joe Wolter, as well as Jock McNeil as a private entrant, continued to race the cammers on the West coast. Another private owner, Waldo Korn, was also known to compete on a cammer, for which he had a spare engine.

As a footnote to this affair, cammers based on the original design were built in small numbers by the Reading Standard concern, who had purchased moulds to make the engine castings from the now defunct Cyclone concern. The Company suspended production in 1922 due to financial difficulties, and after an abortive attempt at reorganization in 1924, finally expired for good.

As Schwinn had now made the decision to suspend official factory support, private entrants still riding Excelsior machines fared less well than did Harley and Indian riders who still enjoyed factory sponsorship.

In 1917, Schwinn purchased the manufacturing rights to the Henderson four, and took on its originator, William Henderson, together with his brother, Thomas, and Arthur Lemon, who was the former's engineering protege. Following a series of disagreements with Schwinn over the latter's insistence on changing the Henderson's basic design, William and his brother resigned, to organize the Ace Motor Company, with Lemon remaining to become chief of Excelsior's Engineering Department. The Ace venture figured in the complex metamorphosis of the original Henderson design through the Ace period and on to the development of the Indian four, which history has already been exhaustively explored in the Author's companion work on the Indian motorcycle entitled *The Iron Redskin* (G.T.Foulis/Haynes Publishing Group).

The new Chief Designer, Arthur Lemon, updated the twin for 1920. The traditional pearl gray finish was now a dark blue, matching that of the four cylinder Henderson which had carried this color since its acquisition from the original designer. The twin was now fitted with the same fork as the Henderson, which was of trailing link type with forward curving fixed legs and activated by an enclosed oil dampened coil spring.

As the four had been a popular seller, the factory now concentrated most of its efforts to its production, and according to the best available information, only about 300 twins were assembled between 1920 and 1924, many of which were exported. In 1921, a 74 cu.in. version was built in small numbers, intended for sidecar and commercial work.

In 1922, Arthur Lemon was able to convince Schwinn that official company sponsorship of competition should be reinstated. He proposed the development of the 21 cu.in. class, which was admittedly safer for the riders than either the 61 or 30.50 cu.in. classes. Schwinn finally acquiesed, and two lightweight competition machines were built. These were ridden by Paul Anderson, a highly skilled rider, and Maldwyn Jones, a one time Flying Merkel and H-D exponent. AMA President Douglas Hobart, a one time Indian employee, inveigled the Contest Committee to sanction the new lightweight Class, and incurred the wrath of Harley-Davidson as that company at the time had no comparable machinery.

In 1922, Maldwyn Jones had considerable success in hill climbing, entering a 74 cu.in. twin in numerous events, together with Eddie Ryan, the enthusiastic San Pedro, California, Excelsior dealer.

Arthur Constantine, an automotive engineer who had been employed by Harley-Davidson since 1920, resigned from that Company late in 1924, and immediately joined Excelsior. He brought with him his design for a then new class of middleweight motorcycle with a 45 cu.in. engine, which he had developed while in H-D employ, but which had been rejected by H-D's top management. Constantine was able to sell Schwinn the idea of putting it into production. In its final form, however, it utilized certain Henderson components, such as frame members and fuel tank, in the interests of rationalized production. Cataloged as the 'Super-X', as a high performance machine of moderate weight and reasonable selling price, it became immediately popular, within the limitations of the then stagnant domestic market.

During the prototype development of the Super-X, the youthful Joe Petrali joined Excelsior's Engineering Department. With an already established competition reputation which was augmented by his legendary skills in speed tuning, he was able to convince Schwinn that he could contribute much to the Company's design progress. Petrali was also anxious to work with Constantine, for whom he had great admiration.

With Schwinn's somewhat grudging approval, about a dozen racing versions of the Super X were assembled, having close-coupled frames and blanked off gearboxes to conform to the current rules mandating direct drive for track and speedway work. A factory-sponsored racing team which, in addition to Petrali, included Charles 'Red' Wolverton, Bill Minnick, and Bob Sirkegian, together with some private participation by Jock McNeil, hung up a series of notable victories. Petrali also racked up a number of notable records at the board oval at Altoona, Pennsylvania, during 1926 and 1927.

At Schwinn's suggestion, Constantine updated both the Super-X and Henderson for the 1929 sales season, resulting in resurrecting of his original 45 cu.in. design. With its bulbous fuel tank and general appearance it now followed Harley Davidson lines, as well as the new four 'K' models which had a new pocket valve type 80 cu.in. engine. During the two previous years, Excelsior's interest in the

The last Super-X model, produced between 1929 and 1931, as updated by Arthur Constantine. It bore a distinct resemblance to contemporary H-D machines. The machine shown is a 1930 Sports Model, with enlarged porting and extra cylinder finning. Owned and restored by Dewey Bonkrud. (*Alisha Tamburri*).

21 cu.in. class waned, as what with his racing activities, Petrali had not had the time or opportunity for development.

The factory also built a few ohv hill climb specials, with which both Petrali and Gene Rhyne won a number of National Championships. Interest in the Super-X was enhanced with the optional offering of a 61 cu.in. version. Its overall appearance was unchanged, and the increased displacement was effected by enlarging the cylinder dimensions.

The Company suspended all motorcycle production in the late Spring of 1931, the reason given by Schwinn being the now worsening worldwide economic depression. Another, and perhaps more obscure reason, was the technical failure of a number of the 1931 Hendersons due to the fitting of inferior electric components in order to cut production costs. A limited number of both models were assembled from parts on hand during the summer of 1931, an activity which finally came to a halt in the Fall. Most components still on hand passed to the hands of the Ballack Company, also of Chicago, who continued to supply Henderson and Super X enthusiasts for many years thereafter. The great Cortland Street plant was now wholly given over to bicycles.

Petrali now joined Harley Davidson, and was for some years their only professional rider, as well as making important contributions to their technical progress. Constantine went on to engage in free-lance industrial engineering projects, and was for some years associated with the Bendix organization. In 1945, he became a consultant for Indian, in a program that attempted to salvage their ill-fated Torque based lightweight motorcycles.

There was much consternation on the part of Super X and Henderson enthusiasts when the news of suspension of production was announced, but domestic motorcycle sales were in the doldroms, and the exigencies of the depression were such that both Indian and Harley-Davidson were hard pressed to keep afloat.

Both models were never produced in other than limited numbers, and never enjoyed extensive dealer representation. As in the case of their competition, a large portion of the output went to the export field, and when world markets declined, Excelsior's now limited domestic sales could not sustain economic production.

The demise of Excelsior represented the end of a motorcycling era in the United States, which had begun with such promise in the early years of the century. For the ensuing two decades, American motorcycling dwindled to become a very minor entity on the domestic transportation scene.

In again referring to Schwinn's acquisition of Heckscher's operation, some possible additional information in the matter came to the author's attention in 1984. It has been suggested that this came about through the latter having previously contracted with Schwinn to provide the machine's frame sets, as Heckscher's manufacturing facilities were somewhat limited. Being lightly financed, he fell behind in his obligations for them, and in the end, Schwinn acquired his operation through foreclosure. As all the old Company records of this period were long ago discarded by Arnold, Schwinn and Company, the actual details of the matter will probably never be wholly resolved.

Appendix 2

A General Guide to the Descriptive Designation of Harley~Davidson Models.

A GENERAL GUIDE TO THE DESCRIPTIVE DESIGNATION OF HARLEY-DAVIDSON MODELS

Year	Piston displacement	Type of engine	Model name or popular name	Factory designation
1903	26 cu.in	De Dion-Bouton atmospheric inlet valve	none	Inconsistent numbering under 2500
1904-1918	35 cu.in	As above until 1910. Pocket valve thereafter	Silent Grey Fellow	5-35, 9A, 9B, 9E
1909-1929	61 cu.in	4 stroke pocket valve twin	Sixty-One	F, FE, J, JE, JD, JDH
1919-1922	37 cu.in	Horizontally-opposed 4 stroke twin	Sport Twin	W, WJ
1922	74 cu.in	Pocket valve twin to 1929		JD
1930	74 cu.in	Side valve twin to 1936		V, VL
1936-1952	61 cu.in.	ohv twin	Sixty One 'Knuckle-Head'	61E, EL FL
1941-1980	74 cu.in	ohv twin	Seventy-Four Hydra-Glide Duo-Glide Electra-Glide Super-Glide 'Pan-Head' 'Shovel-Head'	U, UL, FL FLH, FX, FXE
1936	80 cu.in	Side valve twin	Eighty	VLH

1937-1941	80 cu.in.	side valve twin (cradle frame)	Eighty	UH, ULH
1926-1934	21 cu.in.	side valve single ohv single	Peashooter	A, AA B, BA
1929-1934	30.50 cu.in.	side valve single	Baby Harley	C, CM
1929-1952	45 cu.in.	side valve V twin	Forty Five	D, DL, DLD, R, RL, RLD, W, WL, WLD, WLDR
1932-1974	45 cu.in.	side valve V twin	Servi-Car	G, GE
1942-1943	45 cu. in.	side valve Flat Twin	H-D BMW	XA
1947-1953	125cc	single cylinder two-stroke	Hummer	M-125, S, ST
1953	165cc	single cylinder two-stroke	Teleglide	53-ST
1960	165cc	single cylinder two-stroke	Super Ten	60-BT, 60-BTU
1962	165cc	single cylinder two-stroke	Ranger (Trail version of Super Ten)	62-BTU
1960-1964	165cc	single cylinder two-stroke (scooter)	Topper	60-A 60-AU
1952-1953	45 cu.in.	side valve V twin	K	52-K
1954-1956	55 cu.in.	side valve V twin	KH	54-KH
1957-1970	55 cu.in.	ohv V twin	Sportster XL	57-XL
1971-	61 cu.in.	ohv V twin		XL-XLCH
1961-1966	175 cc	single cylinder two stroke	Pacer, Scat, Bobcat	BT, BTU BTH
1961-1969	250 cc	single cylinder ohv 4 stroke, inclined cyl	Sprint	C.H.SS
1965-1967	50 cc	single cylinder two-stroke	50, Leggero	M-50
1967-1972	65 cc	single cylinder two-stroke	65, Leggero	M-65
1968-1979	125 cc	single cylinder two-stroke	Rapido	ML, MLS, SS, STX
1969-1979	125 cc 175 cc 250 cc	single cylinder two-stroke		SS, SX
1969-1976	350 cc	single cylinder ohv 4-stroke, inclined cyl.	Sprint	SS, SX
1971-1977	100 cc	single cylinder two-stroke	Baja	MSR

MODEL DESIGNATION OF HARLEY-DAVIDSON MOTORCYCLES FROM 1908 THROUGH 1929

Year	Model	Twin or single belt or chain drive	Ignition	NACC hp rating	Motor numbers (left base of cylinders)
1908	4	single belt	battery	3.90	Under 2500
1909	5	single belt	battery	4.34	

1909	5A	single	belt	battery	4.34	All 1909 numbers
1909	5B	single	belt	battery	4.34	2500 to 4200
1909	5C	single	belt	magneto	4.34	Models 5B-5C 26in. wheels
1910	6	single	belt	battery	4.34	All 1910 numbers
1910	6A	single	belt	magneto	4.34	4200 to 7600
1910	6B	single	belt	battery	4.34	
1910	6C	single	belt	magneto	4.34	
1911	7	single	belt	battery	4.34	All 1911 numbers
1911	7A	single	belt	magneto	4.34	7600 to 10,000 and are
1911	7B	single	belt	battery	4.34	followed by letter A
1911	7C	single	belt	magneto	4.34	models 7B and 7C
1911	7D	twin	belt	magneto	7.20	have 26in. wheels
1912	8	single	belt	battery	4.34	
1912	8A	single	belt	magneto	4.34	All 1912 numbers 10,000
1912	8D	twin	belt	magneto	7.20	and up followed by AB,
1912	8E	twin	chain	magneto	8.68	BA, or B
1913	9A	single	belt	magneto	4.34	10,000 up with letter C
1913	9B	single	chain	magneto	4.34	10,000 up with letter D
1913	9E	twin	chain	magneto	8.68	10,000 up with letter E
1913	9G	twin	chain	magneto	8.68	10,000 up with letter E
1914	10A	single	belt	magneto	4.34	number with letter CF
1914	10B	single	chain	magneto	4.34	number DG or G single speed
1914	10C	single	chain	magneto	4.34	number DG or G two speed
1914	10E	twin	chain	magneto	8.68	number EH or H single speed
1914	10F	twin	chain	magneto	8.68	number EH or H two speed
1914	10G	twin	chain	magneto	8.68	number EH or H two speed fore car
1915	11B	single	chain	magneto	4.34	number with J single speed
1915	11C	single	chain	magneto	4.34	number with J two speed
1915	11E	twin	chain	magneto	8.68	number with K single speed
1915	11F	twin	chain	magneto	8.68	number with K three speed
1915	11G	twin	chain	magneto	8.68	number with K fore car
1915	11H	twin	chain	generator	8.68	number with LT single speed
1915	11J	twin	chain	generator	8.68	number with LK three speed
1916	16B	single	chain	magneto	4.34	number with L single speed
1916	16C	single	chain	magneto	4.34	number with L three speed
1916	16E	twin	chain	magneto	8.68	number with M single speed
1916	16F	twin	chain	magneto	8.68	number with M three speed
1916	16J	twin	chain	generator	8.68	number with LM three speed
1917	17B	single	chain	magneto	4.34	number with 17S single speed
1917	17C	single	chain	magneto	4.34	number with 17S three speed
1917	17E	twin	chain	magneto	8.68	number with 17T single speed
1917	17F	twin	chain	magneto	8.68	number with 17T three speed
1917	17J	twin	chain	generator	8.68	number with L 17T three speed
1918	18B	single	chain	magneto	4.34	number with 18S single speed
1918	18C	single	chain	magneto	4.34	number with 18S three speed
1918	18E	twin	chain	magneto	8.68	number with 18T single speed
1918	18F	twin	chain	magneto	8.68	number with 18T three speed
1918	18J	twin	chain	generator	8.68	number with L18T three speed

'J' type single cylinder models were discontinued after 1918, but a few models were assembled to special order during 1918-1919, presumably from left-over spare parts. These were unsequentially numbered, as were about 26 machines assembled during 1920.

All models were fitted with 28in. wheels, except as noted, from 1903 through 1918.

Engine numbers between 1903 through 1907 were under 2500, but were not sequentially numbered.

Belt drive singles were discontinued after 1914, but a few more were assembled during 1915 and 1916, presumably to special order and made from left over spare parts. These were unsequentially numbered.

Year	Model	Cyls.	Ignition	NACC hp rating	Motor numbers (left base of cylinders)
1919	19F	twin	magneto	8.68	number preceded by 19T or 19A three speed

1919	19J	twin	magneto generator	8.68	number preceded by L19T or L19A three speed
1920	20F	twin	magneto	8.68	number preceded by 20T three speed
1920	20J	twin	generator	8.68	number preceded by L20T three speed
1921	21F	twin	magneto	8.68	number preceded by 21F three speed
1921	21FD	twin	magneto	9.50	number preceded by 21F three speed
1921	21J	twin	generator	8.68	number preceded by 21J three speed
1921	21JD	twin	generator	9.50	number preceded by 21JD three speed
1922	22F	twin	magneto	8.68	number preceded by 22F three speed
1922	22FD	twin	magneto	9.50	number preceded by 22FD three speed
1922	22J	twin	generator	8.68	number preceded by 22J three speed
1922	22JD	twin	generator	9.50	number preceded by 22JD three speed
1923	23F	twin	magneto	8.68	number preceded by 23F three speed
1923	23FD	twin	magneto	9.50	number preceded by 23FD three speed
1923	23J	twin	generator	8.68	number preceded by 23J three speed
1923	23JD	twin	generator	9.50	number preceded by 23JD three speed

The 9.50 hp designation beginning in the Fall of 1921 indicates the 74 cu.in. motor. The 61 cu.in. was bored out from 3 5/16in. to 3 7/16in.

The 37 cu.in. opposed twin cylinder 'Sport Twin' model manufactured from the Spring of 1919 through the Fall of 1922 had the engine number prefix 'M' for the magneto-equipped model, and 'MJ' for the electrically-equipped machines that were fitted with head and tail lights. The numbers ran from 100 through 8000, but were not in sequential order.

A limited number of these machines were assembled in 1923 and 1924 for export, principally to England and Australasia, where the model had enjoyed a better acceptance than it received in the United States. The prefix on these engines was either 'E' or 'EX'. The numbers were at random.

1924	24FE	twin	magneto	8.68	number preceded by 24FE three speed. Aluminum pistons
1924	24FD	twin	magneto	9.50	number preceded by 24FD three speed. Cast iron pistons
1924	24FDCA	twin	magneto	9.50	number preceded by 24FDCA three speed. Aluminum pistons
1924	24 FDCB	twin	magneto	9.50	number preceded by 24FDCB three speed. Iron alloy pistons
1924	24JE	twin	generator	8.68	number preceded by 24JE three speed. Aluminum pistons
1924	24JD	twin	generator	9.50	number preceded by 24JD three speed. Cast iron pistons
1924	24JDCA	twin	generator	9.50	number preceded by 24JDCA three speed. Aluminum pistons
1924	24JDCB	twin	generator	9.50	number preceded by 24JDCB three speed. Iron alloy pistons
1925	25FE	twin	magneto	8.68	number preceded by 25FE three speed
1925	25FECB	twin	magneto	9.50	number preceded by 25FECB three speed
1925	25JE	twin	generator	8.68	number preceded by 25JE three speed
1925	25JDCB	twin	generator	9.50	number preceded by 25JDCB three speed

All above 1925 models had iron alloy pistons

1926	26F	twin	magneto	8.68	number preceded by 26F
1926	26FD	twin	magneto	9.50	number preceded by 26FD
1926	26J	twin	generator	8.68	number preceded by 26J
1926	26JD	twin	generator	9.50	number preceded by 26JD

All above 1926 models had iron alloy pistons

1927	27F	twin	magneto	8.68	number preceded by 27F
1927	27FD	twin	magneto	9.50	number preceded by 27FD
1927	27J	twin	generator	8.68	number preceded by 27J
1927	27JD	twin	generator	9.50	number preceded by 27JD

All above 1927 models had iron alloy pistons

1928	28F	twin	magneto	8.68	number preceded by 28F. Iron alloy pistons
1928	28FD	twin	magneto	9.50	number preceded by 28FD. Iron alloy pistons

1928	28J	twin	generator	8.68	number preceded by 28J. Iron alloy pistons
1928	28JD	twin	generator	9.50	number preceded by 28JD. Iron alloy pistons
1928	28JXL	twin	generator	8.68	number preceded by 28JXL. Dow metal pistons
1928	28JDXL	twin	generator	9.50	number preceded by 28JDXL. Dow metal pistons
1928	28JDH	twin	generator	9.50	number preceded by 28JDH Twin Cam. Dow metal pistons
1929	29D	twin	generator	6.05	number preceded by 29D. Side valves. Dow metal pistons
1929	29F	twin	magneto	8.68	number preceded by 29F. Iron alloy pistons
1929	29FD	twin	magneto	9.50	number preceded by 29FD. Iron alloy pistons
1929	29J	twin	generator	8.68	number preceded by 29J. Iron alloy pistons
1929	29JD	twin	generator	9.50	number preceded by 29JD. Iron alloy pistons
1929	29JDH	twin	generator	9.50	number preceded by 29JDH Twin Cam. Dow metal pistons.
1929	29JDL	twin	generator	9.50	number preceded by 29JDL. Dow metal pistons

The JDH twin cam, or 'Two Cam' models had distinctive engine cases that were not interchangeable with the standard single cam models

MODEL DESIGNATION OF SINGLE CYLINDER MODELS — 1926 THROUGH 1937

1926 & 1927	Model A	magneto	3.31 hp	number preceded by A, side valves. Iron alloy pistons
1926 & 1927	Model AA	magneto	3.31 hp	number preceded by AA, oh valves. Aluminum pistons
1926 & 1927	Model B	generator	3.31 hp	number preceded by B, side valves. Iron alloy pistons
1926 & 1927	Model BA	generator	3.31 hp	number preceded by BA, oh valves. Aluminum pistons

The A, AA, and B and BA Models were of 21 cu.in. displacement.

| 1928 & 1929 | Model C | generator | 5.50 hp | number preceded by C, iron alloy pistons |
| 1928 & 1929 | Model CM | magneto | 5.50 hp | number preceded by CM, aluminum pistons |

The C and CM models were of 30.50 cu.in. displacement.

The magneto-equipped 21 cu.in. export model was designated as AAE, and was fitted with handlebar clutch control, foot pegs, and flat-type bars. The battery-equipped export model was as above, cataloged as BAE.

The standard 21 cu.in. single first offered in 1926 had a wheelbase of 56½in. and weighed about 280 lb. The later versions had 2in. less wheelbase with a shorter and somewhat more bulbous fuel tank.

The 1926 and 1927 models were fitted with 3;30x20in. clincher tires.

The 1928 and later models were fitted with 3;30x19in. drop center tires.

The Model C 30.50 cu.in. single first cataloged in late 1928 weighed about 365 lb. and had a 57½in. wheelbase. The tires were 4.00x18in. drop center.

In the Fall of 1931, the Model C shared the same chassis with the newly updated 45 cu.in. twin. Its weight was now about 430 lb.

The competition 21 cu.in. 'Peashooter' was designated as the Model S. Its wheelbase varied from 52 to 54in. and it weighed about 190 lb. Its specially-built ohv engine featured pressure oil feed to all bearings except the wrist pin, and had a sodium-cooled exhaust valve. Two port cylinder heads were optional. The Model SA had an optional barrel-type carburetor. Tires sizes were 28x2¼ clincher.

The competition 30.50 cu.in. model of 1934 was designated as the CAC, and was fitted with oh valves. Designed for alcohol fuel only, it had a 14½:1 compression ratio, and was said to develop 45 hp at 6,800 rpm. Optional tire sizes were 28x2⅜ in. clincher or drop center. Total weight was about 230 lb.

A 21 cu.in. side valve stationary industrial engine was offered briefly in 1931, designated Model CG. It had a stub shaft on both sides of the crankcase.

MODEL DESIGNATION OF 45 cu.in TWIN-CYLINDER MACHINES 1928 THROUGH 1952

In regard to the model designation of the 45 cubic inch side valve models, there are some discrepancies in descriptive nomenclature. As introduced to the line late in 1928, they were provisionally cataloged as the 'R' models. Later designation from the best available information is as follows:

D	Low Compression	1929-30-31
DL	High Compression	
DLD	High Compression	'Sports Special Solo'. It was fitted with a 74 inch twin carburetor, large intake manifold and one extra plate in the clutch.
R	Low Compression	This was the 1932-36 series, with the generator changed to horizontal type, and featured large diameter valves.
RL	High Compression	
RLD	High Speed Model	
W	Low Compression	This was the 1937-51 series, with circulating oil system, cooling fins on engine cases, and had the same fuel tank halves as the '61 E'.
WL	High Compression	
WLD	High Speed Model	
WLDD		Introduced in April 1939, as the 'WLD Special'. Had deep finned aluminum cylinder heads and larger cylinder finning. In 1940 its designation was returned to 'WLD'.
WLDR		Racing model introduced in 1940 This was usually known as the 'WR'
WR		Racing models. A few ohv machines were built as road racers for use in Europe, as well as factory-owned hill climb machines.

MODEL DESIGNATION OF HARLEY-DAVIDSON SIDECARS FROM 1915 THROUGH 1925
(These units were all supplied by the Rogers Company)

Code	Year	Model	Frame number
	1915	11 L	100 L to 3500 L
	1916	16 L	3500 L up
	1917	17 L	numbers preceded by 17 L
	1918	18 L	numbers preceded by 18 L
	1919	19 L	numbers preceded by 19 L
Jenny	1920	20 L	
Joy	1920	20 QL	
Meadow	1921	21 L	The frame numbers on all
Mimic	1921	21 LR	models from 1920 through
Mister	1921	21 QL	1925 were preceded by
Pen	1922	22 L	these symbols. They were
Pie	1922	22 LR	stamped on either the top
Plot	1922	22 QT	or the rear of the back axle
Purity	1923	23 LT	tube.
Puritan	1923	23 QT	
Repand	1924	24 LT	
Rescue	1924	24 QT	
Slant	1925	25 LT	
Slash	1925	25 QT	

Sidecar units offered after 1925 were manufactured by Harley-Davidson, and their frame numbers and symbols were non-sequential. Body styles were identical from 1926 through 1930. Models offered from 1931 through 1939 had a lowered chassis and more streamlined bodies.

Model U or V is a generator-equipped 74 cu.in. with standard compression ratio
Model U, VL or VLD is a generator-equipped 74 cu.in. with high compression
Model E refers to the 61 cu.in. ohv medium compression
Model EL refers to the 61 cu.in. ohv high compression
VLH or U to H 80 cu.in. high compression
VHS or UHS 80 cu.in. medium compression.

The letter C used in conjunction with models F, J, JD, or V indicates a heavy-duty low compression commercial type motor, generally fitted to sidecar or package truck models

The foregoing data has been compiled from extensive model designation published at various times in factory literature, and it must be emphasized that there are many discrepancies between it and the model and engine numbers of actual machines. In some instances the engine numbers are out of sequence in many machines produced through the years, and sometimes the letter designations follow an inconsistent pattern.

Old machines are often found to have been altered or updated with the fitting of later type parts. Similar engines fitted to like models then naturally show differing numbering. Most early engines as overhauled were fitted with aluminum or Dow metal pistons in place of the original cast iron type.

This data can therefore be used only as a general guide.

COMPETITION RECORDS FROM 1919 THROUGH 1950

Record	Name	Machine	Track or Course	Date	Time	MPH
Board Track — Solo—Class A—61 cu.in. motors						
1 mile	Jim Davis	IND	Beverly Hills, Cal.	Apr 17, '22	:32.53	110.67
5 mile	M.L.Fredericks	IND	Salem, N.H.	Sep 18, '26	2:37.60	114.21
10 mile	Joe Petrali	H-D	Laurel, Md.	Sep 7, '25	5:23.80	111.18
20 mile	Jim Davis	H-D	Fresno, Cal.	Oct 2, '25	11:50.60	101.32
25 mile	Joe Petrali	H-D	Laurel, Md.	Sep 7, '25	14:08.40	106.07
50 mile	Otto Walker	H-D	Fresno, Cal.	Feb 22, '21	29:34.60	101.44
100 mile	Joe Petrali	H-D	Altoona, Pa.	Jul 4, '25	59:47.20	100.36
Board Track — Side Car — Class A — 61 cu.in. motors						
10 mile	Sam Riddle	IND	Sheepshead Bay, N.Y.	Oct 11, '19	8:15.60	72.64
25 mile	F.J.Scott	'ND	Altoona, Pa.	Jul 4 '25	18:35.40	80.68
50 mile	Bill Minnick	H-D	Altoona, Pa.	Jul 4 '25	37:34.20	79.85
1 Mile Dirt Track — Solo — Class A — 61 cu.in. motors						
1 mile	Ralph Hepburn	IND	San Luis Obispo, Cal.	Nov 5, '22	:39.60	90.91
5 mile	Ralph Hepburn	IND	San Luis Obispo, Cal.	Nov 5, '22	3:26.20	87.29
10 mile	Ralph Hepburn	IND	San Luis Obispo, Cal.	Nov 5, '22	6:59.80	85.76
25 mile	Ralph Hepburn	IND	San Luis Obispo, Cal.	Nov 5, '22	18:02.00	83.11
50 mile	Fred Ludlow	H-D	Syracuse, N.Y.	Sep 19, '21	38:52.13	77.19
200 mile	Ralph Hepburn	H-D	Dodge City, Kan.	Jul 4, '21	137:54.00	87.02
300 mile	Ralph Hepburn	H-D	Dodge City, Kan.	Jul 4, '21	210:03.00	85.69
1 Mile Dirt Track — Solo — Class A — 30.50 cu.in. motors						
1 mile	John Seymour	IND	Syracuse, N.Y.	Sep 19, '25	:44.20	81.26
5 mile	John Seymour	IND	Syracuse, N.Y.	Sep 19, '25	3:43.76	80.45
8 mile	Jim Davis	H-D	Syracuse, N.Y.	Sep 13, '24	5:59.39	80.14
10 mile	John Seymour	IND	Syracuse, N.Y.	Sep 19, '25	7:30.04	80.00
15 mile	John Seymour	IND	Syracuse, N.Y.	Sep 19, '25	11:19.60	79.45
20 mile	Paul Anderson	IND	Syracuse, N.Y.	Sep 13, '24	15:07.80	79.33
25 mile	John Seymour	IND	Syracuse, N.Y.	Sep 19, '25	19:15.65	77.91
1 Mile Dirt Track — Solo — Class A — 21.35 cu.in. motors						
5 mile	Miny Waln	IND	Bakersfield, Cal.	Apr 12, '31	3:34.60	83.88
10 mile	Joe Petrali	H-D	Syracuse, N.Y.	Aug 31, '35	7:20.90	81.65
15 mile	Joe Petrali	H-D	Syracuse, N.Y.	Aug 31, '35	11:10.85	80.50
20 mile	Curly Fredericks	IND	Syracuse, N.Y.	Aug 31, '29	15:21.40	78.14
25 mile	Joe Petrali	H-D	Syracuse, N.Y.	Aug 31, '35	18:44.52	80.11
1 Mile Dirt Track — Side Car — Class A						
1 mile	Floyd Dreyer	IND	Toledo, O.	Aug 14, '21	:51.60	69.77
5 mile	Ralph Hepburn	H-D	Syracuse, N.Y.	Sep 13, '24	4:04.31	73.68
10 mile	F.J.Scott	IND	Toledo, O.	Jul 26, '24	8:25.00	71.29
25 mile	Floyd Dreyer	IND	Toledo, O.	Aug 14, '21	21:47.00	69.18

½ Mile Dirt Track — Solo — Class A — 30.50 cu.in. motors

1 mile	John Seymour	IND	Winchester, Ind.	Jul 22, '23	:54.00	66.67
3 mile	Otto Pechar	IND	Torrington, Conn.	May 30, '25	2:46.40	64.89
5 mile	John Seymour	IND	Winchester, Ind.	Jul 18, '23	4:39.40	64.41
10 mile	Paul Anderson	EXC	Winchester, Ind.	May 18, '23	9:39.00	62.18

½ Mile Dirt Track — Solo — Class A — 21.35 cu.in. motors

3 mile	Tuffy Jacobs	IND	Ascot Speedway	Apr 27, '30	2:30.40	71.79
5 mile	Joe Petrali	H-D	Hamilton Speedway	Jun 21, '31	4:18.08	69.75
10 mile	Joe Petrali	H-D	Hamilton Speedway	Jun 21, '31	8:35.20	69.88

½ Mile Dirt Track — Side Car — Class A

1 mile	Lester Foote	H-D	Greeley, Colo.	Sep 16, '20	1:13.60	48.91
5 mile	Bill Minnick	H-D	Frederick, Md.	May 30, '24	5:34.00	56.89
10 mile	Floyd Dreyer	IND	Pittsburgh, Pa.	Oct 10, '21	11:11.20	53.64

Non-Competitive Board Track Records — Solo — Class A — 45 cu.in.

1 mile	Joe Petrali	S-X	Altoona, Pa.	Jul 2, '26	:33.44	107.65
5 mile	Joe Petrali	S-X	Altoona, Pa.	Jul 2, '26	2:53.70	103.60
10 mile	Joe Petrali	S-X	Altoona, Pa.	Jul 2, '26	5:57.50	100.70

Straightaway — Solo — Class A — 40 cu.in. motors

1 mile	Bobbie Turner	TRI	Daytona Beach, Fla.	Feb 19, '51	:27.88	129.24

Straightaway — Solo — Class A — 61 cu.in. motors

1 mile	Rollie Free	VIN	Bonneville, Utah	Sep 11, '50	:22.99	156.58

Straightaway — Solo — Class A — 30.50 cu.in. motors

1 kilo	John Seymour	IND	Daytona Beach, Fla.	Jan 12, '26	:19.34	112.63

24 Hour Record

Fred Ham	H-D	Muroc Dry Lake, Cal.	Apr 8, '37	1825.2 miles	76.05

1 Mile Dirt Track — Solo — Class C — 45 cu.in. motors

5 mile	Larry Hedrick	H-D	Springfield, Ill.	Aug 20, '50	3:39.11	82.15
8 mile	Art Hafer	IND	Milwaukee, Wis.	Aug 25, '40	6:00.58	79.87
10 mile	Kenneth Eggers	H-D	Springfield, Ill.	Aug 20, '50	7:17.06	84.66
15 mile	Larry Hedrick	H-D	Milwaukee, Wis.	Aug 26, '50	10:50.72	82.99
20 mile	Horace Travis	H-D	Du Quoin, Ill.	Sep 4, '49	14:41.98	81.52
25 mile	Larry Hedrick	H-D	Springfield, Ill.	Aug 20, '50	18:01.71	83.20
50 mile	Lester Hillbish	IND	Syracuse, N.Y.	Aug 26, '39	39:15.59	76.42

½ Mile Dirt Track — Solo — Class C — 45 cu.in. motors

3 mile	Bill Miller	H-D	Richmond, Va.	May 29, '49	2:49.38	63.76
5 mile	Bobby Hill	IND	Jacksonville, Fla.	May 8, '49	4:39.38	64.43
7 mile	Paul Albrecht	H-D	Shreveport, La.	Oct 29, '50	6:48.40	61.74
8 mile	Johnny Butterfield	H-D	Richmond, Va.	Oct 1, '50	7:30.34	63.95
10 mile	Paul Albrecht	H-D	Richmond, Va.	May 29, '49	9:15.35	64.82

Dirt Track Speedway — Solo — Class C — 45 cu.in. motors

100 mile	Jimmy Chann	H-D	Langhorne, Pa.	Sep 4, '49	68:53.45	87.09
200 mile	Louis Guanella	H-D	Oakland, Cal.	Oct 27, '40	141:45.55	84.64

Straightaway — Solo — Class C — One Mile

40cu.in.	Bobbie Turner	TRI	Daytona Beach, Fla.	Feb 20, '51	:30.43	118.40
45cu.in.	Fred Ludlow	IND	Bonneville, Utah	Sep 25, '38	:31.27	115.12
74cu.in.	Fred Ludlow	IND	Bonneville, Utah	Sep 25, '38	:29.81	120.74

The above record tabulations, incomplete through the years shown, were compiled from contemporary trade and sports reports. They differ markedly from the official AMA records as published in later years. After H-D came into control of the AMA after the mid-1920s, it was alleged by some that many of the earlier tabulations were altered, and in some cases records attained by other makes of machines were deleted, or the results changed.

Most of the early records tabulated when American motorcycle sport was under the auspices of the Federation of American Motorcyclists, from 1909 through 1920-21, were lost during the organization period of the AMA. The only source of these today are the fragmentary data available from that published in contemporary trade publications.

Harley-Davidson Stockholders and their Holdings as of September 30, 1930

Certificate Numbers	Name	Number of shares	
1-32-52	Walter Davidson	6830	25/100
6-33-54	William A. Davidson	5779	25/100
5-34-53-88	Arthur Davidson	6538	20/100
51	Margaret Davidson	467	40/100
20-36-75	William S. Harley	2548	65/100
10-37-64	Frank L. Wood	1956	90/100
68-87	James A. Stone	77	20/100
26-27-39	Charles H. Lang	708	40/100
30-38	James L. McGee	700	
11-41-78	George E. Dortmann	720	60/100
13-42-70	J.J. Balsom	425	
31-43	Minnie Becker	233	45/100
12-44	Henry Milk	350	
28-45	Crolius S. Lacey	166	70/100
14-46	James G. Daily	350	
15-47	Mrs. James G. Daily	350	
25-48-17-55	Janet M. Davidson	1820	49/100
56-57	Elizabeth Davidson Marx	1820	49/100
18-50-89	Crystal Heyfel	60	
58	Annie H. Wood	500	
59	Robert Arthur Wood	400	
60	Lillie Wood Manson	400	
61	Jessie Wood Sincere	400	
62	Matha Wood Wolff	400	
63	Cary Wood Thomas	400	
77	Leo H. Wohl	50	
76	Max W. Wohl	50	
79	Francis H. Muelier	23	
80	Lawrence G. Rigner	26	
80	Charles R. Fisher	1	
82	Millie C. Fisher	1	
83-84-85-86	Milton Chaisin	40	

This list of Harley-Davidson Motor Company shareholders is typical of such listings for the years of 1920 through 1941. The holdings of the Harley and Davidson family members remain more or less constant, along with such minor shareholders as Charles H. Lang and Crolius S. Lacey. The prominence of Frank L. Wood and other members of his family are noted, holding a total of 4456 shares, and explains why he was usually included in policy-making decisions. The names of the balance of the various minor shareholders are subject to variation.

It is noted that of a total of about 39,000 outstanding shares, the Harley and Davidson families always retained at least 21,000 shares, giving them majority control of the Company operations.

The control of the Company reverted to their heirs following the deaths of William A. Davidson in 1937, Walter in 1942, Arthur in 1950, and William S. Harley in 1943. These heirs, including the estates of various deceased members, retained control of the Company until it was sold to the American Foundry Company in 1969.

SELECTED FINANCIAL DATA

	1986	1985	1984	1983	1982
	(In thousands, except share and per share amounts)				
Income statement data:					
Net sales	$ 295,322	$ 287,476	$ 293,825	$ 253,505	$ 210,055
Cost of goods sold	219,167	217,222	220,040	194,271	174,967
Gross profit	76,155	70,254	73,785	59,234	35,088
Operating expenses:					
Selling and administrative	51,060	47,162	47,662	36,441	37,510
Engineering, research and development	8,999	10,179	10,591	9,320	13,072
Total operating expenses	60,059	57,341	58,253	45,761	50,582
Income (loss) from operations	16,096	12,913	15,532	13,473	(15,494)
Other income (expense):					
Interest expense	(8,373)	(9,412)	(11,256)	(11,782)	(15,778)
Other	(388)	(338)	(311)	188	(1,272)
	(8,761)	(9,750)	(11,567)	(11,594)	(17,050)
Income (loss) before provision (credit) for income taxes, extraordinary items, and cumulative effect of change in accounting principle	7,335	3,163	3,965	1,879	(32,544)
Provision (credit) for income taxes	3,028	526	1,077	906	(7,467)
Income (loss) before extraordinary items and cumulative effect of change in accounting principle	4,307	2,637	2,888	973	(25,077)
Extraordinary items and cumulative effect of change in accounting principle	564	7,318	3,578	7,795	–
Net income (loss)	$ 4,871	$ 9,955	$ 6,466	$ 8,768	$ (25,077)
Average number of common shares outstanding	5,235,230	3,680,000	3,680,000	3,720,000	4,016,664
Per common share:					
Income (loss) before extraordinary items and cumulative effect of change in accounting principle	$ 0.82	$ .72	$ .79	$ .26	$ (6.61)
Extraordinary items and cumulative effect of change in accounting principle	0.11	1.99	.97	2.10	–
Net income (loss)	$ 0.93	$ 2.71	$ 1.76	$ 2.36	$ (6.61)
Balance sheet data:					
Working capital (deficiency)	$ 39,937	$ 16,245	$ 16,756	$ 13,003	$ (28,786)
Total assets	327,196	114,092	99,207	88,980	85,766
Short-term debt, including current maturities of long-term debt	18,090	2,875	2,305	2,136	40,734
Long-term debt, less current maturities	191,594	51,504	56,258	57,666	35,072
Total debt	209,684	54,379	58,563	59,802	75,806
Stockholders' equity (deficit)	26,159	4,622	(6,323)	(12,789)	(21,975)

5. SHORT-TERM FINANCING

Notes payable represent floor plan obligations of Holiday Rambler which are secured by inventory. The line of credit available under these arrangements is $22,200,000 at December 31, 1986, of which $8,133,000 was unused.

Under the terms of a dealer floor plan agreement with ITT Commercial Finance Corp. (ITT) Harley-Davidson has agreed to indemnify ITT for any loss, as defined, that it may incur in connection with the sale or disposition of merchandise it receives as a result of dealer default or other defined events. At December 31, 1986 and 1985, approximately $76,000,000 and $80,000,000, respectively of receivables were subject to the agreement. Harley-Davidson has not incurred any significant losses under the agreement since its inception.

Harley-Davidson has also entered into a trade acceptance agreement with ITT which will expire on June 1, 1987. Under the terms of the agreement, Harley-Davidson received cash from ITT in the amount of 100% of certain eligible accounts receivable at the time of sale. On June 1, 1987, Harley-Davidson is obligated to repurchase all unpaid balances from ITT. At December 31, 1986 and 1985, trade acceptances of $6,677,000 and $5,265,000, respectively, were subject to this agreement.

Harley-Davidson has a retail motorcycle finance agreement with Ford Motor Credit Corporation (FMCC). In accordance with the agreement, repossession losses are shared. Harley-Davidson's annual liability for the excess losses, as defined, is limited to 3% of the aggregate amount financed during the year. Harley-Davidson has not incurred any losses under this agreement since its inception.

Holiday Rambler has had an agreement since 1984 with American Acceptance Corporation to provide wholesale floor plan financing to the Company's dealers. Under this agreement, Holiday Rambler guarantees payment of amounts floored. At December 31, 1986, the amount guaranteed totaled approximately $7,900,000. Holiday Rambler has not incurred any material losses from the repurchase or guaranty agreements and currently anticipates no material losses.

At December 31, 1986, Holiday Rambler estimates that it is contingently liable under repurchase agreements for an approximate maximum of $9,200,000 to lending institutions that provide wholesale floor plan financing to Holiday Rambler's dealers. Holiday Rambler's loss exposure on repurchase is limited to the difference between the resale value of the vehicle and the amount required to be paid the lending institution at the time of repurchase.

6. LONG-TERM DEBT

Long-term debt consists of the following:

	December 31,	
	1986	1985
	(In thousands)	
Harley-Davidson:		
12-1/2% Subordinated Notes due 1996 (a)	$ 70,000	$ —
Revolving credit loan (b)	—	49,457
Refinanced debt (c) (d)	—	
Capital leases (e)	6,291	2,802
Other	542	2,120
Total Harley-Davidson long-term debt	76,833	54,379
Holiday Rambler:		
Revolving credit loan (f)	7,012	
Term loan (f)	55,000	
Subordinated term note (g)	50,000	
Other	6,772	
Total Holiday Rambler long-term debt	118,784	
Total Company long-term debt including current maturities	$195,617	$54,379

Harley-Davidson

(a) On July 15, 1986, $70,000,000 of unsecured Subordinated Notes were issued which will mature on July 15, 1996 and bear interest at 12-1/2% per annum, payable semi-annually, beginning January 15, 1987.

The Subordinated Notes are redeemable at Harley-Davidson's option subject to various limitations at various redemption prices plus accrued interest to the date fixed for redemption. The Subordinated Notes cannot be redeemed prior to July 15, 1989.

The payment of principal and interest on the Subordinated Notes is generally subordinated to the payment in full of all Senior Indebtedness of Harley-Davidson whether now outstanding or incurred in the future.

(b) On July 23, 1986, Harley-Davidson entered into a restated loan and security agreement with several financial institutions which provides for revolving credit loans up to $45 million based upon percentages of eligible receivables and inventory. This agreement substantially amends the prior loan and security agreement dated December 31, 1985. Borrowings under the agreement will be secured by a security interest in all receivables, inventory, equipment, deposit accounts, real property and general intangibles. Borrowings are due January 1, 1988 but Harley-Davidson may request an extension annually.

ELECTION OF DIRECTORS

Six directors will be elected to hold office until the next Annual Meeting of Stockholders and until their successors have been elected and have qualified. The persons named in the accompanying proxy will vote all shares for which they have received proxies for the election of the nominees named below unless contrary instructions are given. In the event that any nominee should become unavailable, shares will be voted for a substitute nominee unless the number of directors constituting a full board is reduced. Directors are elected by plurality vote.

The names, ages as of April 1, 1987, and principal occupations for the past five years of these nominees and the names of public companies of which they are presently serving as directors are set forth below:

Name	Position
Vaughn L. Beals, Jr.	Chairman, President, Chief Executive Officer and Director
Frederick L. Brengel	Director
F. Trevor Deeley	Director
Richard Hermon-Taylor	Director
Michael J. Kami	Director
Richard F. Teerlink	Vice President, Chief Financial Officer, Treasurer and Director

Vaughn L. Beals, Jr., 59, became Chief Executive Officer of the Company in 1981. He has served with the Company since 1975, and prior to 1981 served as Corporate Vice President and Group Executive of the AMF Motorcycle Products Group.

Frederick L. Brengel, 63, has been a director of the Company since March, 1987. He is the Chairman and Chief Executive Officer of Johnson Controls, Inc., a leading manufacturer of automated building controls, automotive seating, batteries and plastics. Mr. Brengel is also a director of the Heil Co., a manufacturer of bodies and hoists, tanks, and solid waste systems, First Wisconsin Corp., a bank holding company, First Wisconsin National Bank of Milwaukee, Rexnord, Inc., a manufacturer of mechanical and electronic industrial components and equipment, and Wisconsin Bell Inc.

F. Trevor Deeley, 66, has been a director of the Company since July, 1986. He is Chairman and Chief Executive Officer of Fred Deeley Imports, the largest independent motorcycle distributorship in Canada and the exclusive distributor of the Company's motorcycles in Canada.

Richard Hermon-Taylor, 45, has been a director of the Company since July, 1986. Mr. Hermon-Taylor was a Vice President and board member of the Boston Consulting Group, a management consulting firm, until 1986 and is now an independent management consultant.

Michael J. Kami, 63, has been a director of the Company since July, 1986. Mr. Kami also serves as President of Corporate Planning, Inc., a management consulting company, which he founded in 1966.

Richard F. Teerlink, 50, has served with the Company in his present capacity since 1981. Prior to joining the Company, he held similar positions with Herman Miller, Inc. and RTE Corporation. Mr. Teerlink is a certified public accountant.

COMPENSATION AND OTHER TRANSACTIONS

Cash Compensation

The compensation of each of the five most highly compensated executive officers of the Company, and of all the executive officers of the Company as a group, for services rendered to the Company during 1986 was as follows:

Name of Individual	Capacities In Which Served	Paid and Deferred Cash Compensation
Vaughn L. Beals, Jr.	Chairman, President and Chief Executive Officer	$ 386,000
Richard F. Teerlink	Vice President, Chief Financial Officer and Treasurer; President and Chief Operating Officer - Motorcycle Division	$ 248,000
Thomas A. Gelb	Vice President - Operations	$ 212,000
Peter L. Profumo	Vice President - Program Management	$ 203,000
Jeffrey L. Bleustein	Vice President - Parts and Accessories	$ 180,000
All Executive Officers as a Group (6 individuals)		$ 1,390,000

Short Term Incentive Plan

The Company adopted a Short Term Incentive Plan for its 1986 fiscal year. Under this plan additional compensation is paid to participating employees, including executive officers, based on overall Company performance. The plan is open to employees in certain salaried grades approved by the Company. The plan pays cash bonus compensation of up to 50% (70% in the case of Mr. Beals and, in the case of Mr. Teerlink, 60% of base compensation paid on or after March 15, 1987) of base compensation, depending on the position level of the participants and the Company's overall performance, including levels of accounts receivable and inventories and income from operations, during 1986. There are approximately 80 employees eligible for participation in the plan.

Thrift Incentive Plans

The Company also maintains a Thrift Incentive Plan for Salaried Employees. Under this plan employees with one year of service may save up to 15%, but not in excess of $30,000, of their 1986 income before taxes (7% and $7,000 for 1987 income) pursuant to Section 401(k) of the Internal Revenue Code. The Company may, if it elects, also contribute up to 50% of the first 6% of savings. The Company made no matching contributions in 1986 and does not plan to make such contributions in 1987.

Bibliography

Publications and photographs publicly circulated by the Harley-Davidson Motorcycle Company

The Archives of the Hendee Manufacturing Company
The Archives of the Indian Motocycle Company
The US National Museum, Department of Transportation
The United States Congressional Record
The United States Department of Commerce
The Reports of the United States Senate Select Committee on Tariffs
The United States Department of Justice, Bureau of Prisons
The Federal District Court, Denver, Colorado
The Superior Court of Cook County
The Superior Court of Monroe County
The Detroit Public Library
The Milwaukee Public Library
The Los Angeles County Public Library
Bibliotica Nationale, Mexico City, Republic of Mexico
Motor Cycle Cavalcade, by Ixion (Canon B.H.Davies), Iliffe
Vintage Motorcycles, by James Sheldon, Batsford
The World's Motorcycles, by Erwin Tragatsch, Temple Press
Motorcycles, by Victor Page
Vintage Motorcycling, by M.A.Bull
The Golden Age of the Fours, by Theodore Hodgdon, Bagnall
The Story of the TT, by G.S.Davison
Standard & Poor's Corporation Index
Moody's Corporation Index
Barron's Weekly
The Motor Cycle
Motor Cycling
The Motorcyclist
Motorcycling Illustrated
The Western Motorcyclist and Bicyclist
Cycle World
Cycle
Custom Chopper
Street Chopper

Iron Horse
Supercycle
Automotive Illustrated
Motor Age
The World's Automobiles, by G.N.Georgano
The New York Times
The Los Angeles Times
The Milwaukee Journal
The Milwaukee Sentinal
The Wall Street Journal
The Journal of the Antique Motorcycle Club
The Official Journal of the Vintage Motor Cycle Club
The Journal of the Classic and Antique Motorcycle Club
Robert W.Baird & Co., Incorporated
The First Boston Company
The Atlas Corporation
The Baldwin Chain Company
E.I. duPont De Nemours
Delco, Incorporated
The Firestone Tire & Rubber Company
Bangor Punta Incorporated
American Machine & Foundry Company
The Goodyear Tire & Rubber Company
The Wisconsin Historical Society

Index

Abate 252
Ace 75, 89, 90, 93, 95, 118, 310
Aermacchi-Harley-Davidson 209, 222, 239, 243, 244, 253, 260
Aeronautica Macchi S.A. 210
Alexander, J.Worth 106
Allchin, T.R. 50
Allen, Irwin D. 50
Alzina, Hap 55, 116
American Association of Motorcycle Road Racers 238, 247
American Car and Foundry 221
American Machine and Foundry Co. 111, 221, 223, 226, 237, 238, 242, 243, 244, 245, 252, 255, 257, 258
American Motorcycle Association 50, 100, 103, 104, 106, 110, 122, 130, 131, 134, 135, 136, 140, 165, 170, 172, 173, 188, 189, 198, 200, 202, 206, 209, 211, 212, 216, 224, 225, 226, 238, 239, 242, 243, 245, 246, 247, 250, 252, 260, 262, 263
American Motorcycle Mfrs. Association 35, 50
American Motorcycling 190, 194, 266
Anderson, Paul 310
Andres, Brad 212
Antique Motorcycle Club of America 106
Appeal Mfg. & Jobbing Co. 68, 69
Appel, George 49
Arena, Sam 110, 135, 137, 164
Ariel 188, 189, 199
Armstrong, Earle 34, 36
Artley Roy 38, 52, 69, 152, 308, 309
Aurora Automatic Machine 29
Automobiles Rally 64
Automotive Industries Illustrated 57, 59

Bagnall, William 226, 263
Baird, Robert W., and Co. 217, 223, 224
Baker, Erwin 'Cannonball' 27, 34, 38, 49, 75, 90, 135, 308
Baker, James A. III 311
Balcom Trading Company 88 · 325
Balinski, Lou 136
Bangor Punta 221, 223, 224, 225
Barclay, Alvin 38
Barnes, Austin 156
Barron's 225
Barr, Frederick 23, 31, 84
Bauer, Louis J. 103

Beal, David 257
Beals, Vaughn 267, 275, 277, 281, 282, 283, 284, 286, 290, 305, 308, 314, 315
Beart, Francis 136, 200
Beardsley, J.L. 208
Bedell, Alan 38
Bendix, Victor 35, 92
Bendix Mfg. Co. 35, 88, 92, 312
Bennett, Wells 46, 49, 61, 75, 308
Bettencourt, Nelson 174
Bianchi, Alfredo 210
Bicycling World 25
Bigsby, Paul A. 140
Billings, Chet 136, 174
Bleustein, Jerry 267, 310
BMW 209
Boido, Lorenzo 27
Bond, John R. 196
Boston Globe 38
Boyd, Harold 40
Boyd, Glen 33
Bradshaw, Granville 267
Brant, Harry 37
Branch, Jerry 288, 289, 294, 312–319
Brando, Marlon 319
Brelsford, Mark 212, 276
Briar, Bill 33, 38
Bridgestone 214
Briggs, George 100, 103, 104
Brinck, Eddie 124
Brinkworth, John 308, 318
British Motorcycle Dealers Association 198, 199
Brokaw, Paul 190
BSA 188, 196, 199, 200, 204, 207, 208, 218
Buckner, Leonard 52, 53
Budelier, Rich 55, 68, 69, 95, 96, 97, 98, 118, 159
Buell, Erik 275, 312, 313, 324, 328
Burns, Albert 'Shrimp' 52, 53, 60, 123
Butler Bros. 21, 63
Butler, Thomas C. 43

Cable, Charles 80
Cable Company 79
Callow, A.R. Ltd 71
Cameron, John 190
Campanale, Ben 163, 164
Carl's Cycle Service 204
Carpenter, Bill 135

Carr, Chris 325
Carriker, Jud 123
Carruthers, Kel 211
Carter, President Jimmy 274-279
Caruso, David 275
Caterpillar Tractor 266
Cato, E. Raymond 118
Chamberlain, Clarence 21
Child, Alfred Rich 69, 70, 79, 80, 82, 83, 86, 87, 88, 106, 107, 108, 130, 131, 140, 184, 188, 194, 199, 271
Child, Richard 86, 88, 256, 284, 317, 325
Chrysler, Walter D. 309
Church, Gene 311
Claybrook, Joan 274
Cleary, Bob 308
Cleland, Charles 57, 58
Cleveland 42, 45, 55, 63, 67, 71, 77, 90, 101
Clymer, Floyd 37, 38, 40, 46, 114, 115, 159, 208, 209
Coates, Rod 200
Coffman, A.B. 50
Coleman, Pete 252
Connelly, William 150
Constantine, Arthur R. 69, 82, 93, 94, 102, 104, 109, 118, 124, 182, 255, 310, 312
Cook, Charles 75, 106
Cooper, H.D. 115
Corrento, Sam 37
Coulter, Harry 75
Cox, Recil 308
Crandall, Harry 37, 38
Creviston, Lee 308
Crocker, Albert G. 29, 97, 123, 140, 156
Crolius, Lacey 24
Cropp, Warren 61
Cummings, Bill 135
Cunningham, Walter 33
Cushman Motor Co. 156, 186, 194
Custom Chopper 263
Cycle 190, 209
Cycle Guide 295
Cycle Sport 250
Cycle World 216, 242, 244, 247, 250, 263
Cyclone 36, 263, 307, 309

Danforth, Senator John 319
Daniel, Harold 173
Dauria, Fred 150
Davidson, A.H. 222
Davidson, Arthur 14, 15, 18, 21, 26, 31, 35, 40, 42, 43, 46, 53, 55, 66, 68, 69, 70, 73, 77, 87, 94, 95, 102, 109, 111, 125, 127, 131, 170, 176, 179, 182, 191, 194, 195, 202, 238
Davidson, Douglas 50, 51
Davidson, Gordon 109, 176, 191, 222
Davidson, John A. 222, 225, 250, 267, 273, 274, 277, 278
Davidson, Robert 176, 182, 222
Davidson, Walter 15, 22, 23, 24, 29, 37, 49, 60, 64,

69, 71, 72, 75, 77, 95, 100, 102, 103, 104, 106, 114, 119, 125, 127, 133, 134, 135, 140, 143, 156, 157, 159, 162, 172, 174, 176, 179, 202, 238, 245
Davidson, Walter, Jr. 84, 109, 176, 225, 253, 255, 260, 261
Davidson, William A. 18, 19, 23, 39, 44, 63, 71, 73, 90, 94, 140, 146, 148, 182, 199, 243, 245, 259
Davidson, William C. 17, 222
Davidson, William G. 225, 242, 244, 245, 247, 252, 253, 257, 259, 265, 275, 320
Davidson, William Herbert 71, 182, 194, 196, 199, 200, 217, 222, 223, 225, 242, 245, 259, 260, 275
Davis, Gus 267, 278
Davis, Jim 47, 52, 53, 60, 66, 92, 123, 124, 162
Davis Sewing Machine Co. 63
Dayton 35, 36, 39
Dealer, The 26, 40, 56
De Dion 14, 15, 17, 23, 25, 29, 89, 107, 259
De Long, Everett 89, 90, 92
Deeley, F. Trevor 315
Deere, John 266
Denali, Stephen 312
Derkum, Paul 27
Devine, Harry 82, 194
Dixon, Freddie 50, 51, 75
Dodds, Jack 38
Dormoy, Etiene 100
Douglas 45
Dreyer, Floyd 60
Dunlap, Walter 21
Dunlop, Paul 155
du Pont, E. Paul 116, 118, 126, 155, 261
Durant, William Crapo 56, 118, 309
Dutcher, William 271

Eagles, Johnny 218
Easy Rider 265
Eck Company 222, 246, 259
Edwards, Ted 163
Egloff, Frank 194
Ekins, Bud 239
Emblem Motorcycle Company, The 35, 40, 63, 66
Emde, Floyd 190, 199
Enos, R.W. 47, 51
Enthusiast, The 40, 52, 60, 66, 134, 150, 152, 158, 186, 191, 194, 259
Eros Mfg. Co. 95
Excelsior 21, 24, 27, 31, 33, 34, 35, 36, 37, 38, 39, 40, 42, 46, 47, 49, 52, 53, 55, 57, 58, 59, 60, 61, 62, 67, 68, 75, 77, 89, 92, 94, 95, 100, 102, 108, 111, 116, 120, 124, 303, 304, 305, 306, 307, 308, 309, 310, 311, 312

Fagan, Herbert 156
Farmer, Weston 100
Favel, John 297
Federation of American Motorcyclists 22, 42, 49, 50
Federation of Western Motorcyclists 50

Fédération Internationale Motocycliste 52, 250, 263
Feilbach 39
Fenwicke, Red 136
Fessler, Clyde 287, 294
First Allied Corporation 327
Fischr, James 308
Flanders 39, 122
Flanders, Earl 159
Fletcher, Jack 46
Flin, Ray 246
Fonda, Peter 319
Foote, Lester 53
Forbes, Malcolm S. 319, 328
Ford, Henry 27, 35, 56, 70
Fordyce, Ruth 202
Fordyce, Skip 202
Fowler, L.E. 63, 64
Francis-Barnett 189, 196
Franklin, Charles B. 35, 53, 63, 101, 102, 128, 237, 244, 255
Fredricks, M.K. 'Curly' 38, 52, 60, 61, 92, 124
Free, Rollie 137
Frodsham, Jack 155
Froman, Daniel 66
Frugoli, Joseph 75, 76, 106, 108, 140
Fugii, Colonel 87
Fugua Industries 266
Fuji Bank 311
Fukui, Genijiro 80, 82, 86
Ful Floting 26
Fulton, Walt 212, 252

Garst, Paul 33
Geer, Harry O., Company 20
Gelb, Tom, 281, 282
George, Bob 208
Gerberick, Royal 72
Gilbert, George D, 202, 206
Glaser, Malcolm I. 327
Gonzales, George 168
Goss, Randy 276
Gott, Paul 33, 37
Gott, Rodney C, 223, 238, 243, 255, 266, 267, 278, 304
Goudy, Bill 264
Goudy, Carl 33, 36, 307, 308
Graves, Morty 36, 38
Gray, William 294
Grey Light Car Co., The 64
Griffith, Virna 166
Griffiths, Vance 310
Guthrie, Verne 55, 68, 174
Guanella, Louis 137
Gutteridge, Michael 308

Haaby, Dan 212
Hadden, L.D. 35
Hadfield, Al 49
Halford, Jack 173
Halsted, Walter 266

Ham, Fred 150, 152
Hansen, Peter 272
Harding, Warren G. 65
Harley-Davidson Motor Co. 14, 17
Harley, John E. 222, 225, 250, 263, 272
Harley, Jr., John J. 281
Harley, William J. 137, 182, 194, 222, 225, 242, 252
Harley, William S. 14, 15, 18, 20, 23, 25, 29, 35, 53, 62, 89, 90, 92, 93, 137, 148, 176, 179, 182, 202
Hartley, L.W.E. 136
Hatfield, Jerry 266
Hayes, Tommy 164
Heath, Ed 100
Heckscher, Walther 303, 304, 312
Hedrick, Larry 205
Hedstrom, Carl Oscar 13, 14, 20, 35, 37, 92
Heller Finance Group 311
Helms, Ronnie 308
Hemmis, C.W. 110
Hendee, George M. 14, 18, 21, 56, 92
Hendee Mfg. Co. 14
Henderson, 26, 31, 46, 63, 67, 71, 89, 90, 93, 95, 98, 102, 116, 118, 120, 152, 166, 310
Henderson, Thomas W. 35, 310
Hendry, Maurice 259
Hepburn, Ralph 47, 49, 52, 53, 60, 61, 62, 66, 92, 123, 124
Herb, Joe 110
Herrington, A.W. 40
Hicketheir, R.J. 157
Higley, Walter 47, 52, 53, 60
Hill, Bobby 200, 207
Hill, James 146, 200
Hobart, Douglas 50, 100, 102, 226, 310
Hodgdon, Theodore A. 131
Hoelter, Timothy K 275
Hogg, Edwin 46
Hogg, Tony 217
Holinda, Charles 308
Holmes, Art 27, 29
Holtz, Roy 43
Honda 214, 256
Horn, Jack 200
Hot Rod 190
Houghton, Dewey 122
House, Red 135
Humiston, Lee 305, 307

Iacocca, Lee 309
Ince, Dick, 162
Indian 14, 17, 20, 21, 24, 25, 26, 27, 31, 33, 34, 35, 36, 37, 38, 39, 40, 42, 44, 47, 49, 52, 53, 55, 59, 60, 62, 63, 67, 71, 75, 77, 79, 89, 90, 92, 93, 98, 104, 108, 111, 112, 115, 119, 120, 166, 168, 170, 196, 200, 239, 244, 259, 305
Indian News, The 153
Ingram, John 294
Iorio, Steve 298, 311

Iron Horse 265
Iver Johnson 21, 40, 63, 67, 71, 77

Jacobs, K.H. 35
Jahnke, Irving 34, 37, 38
James 189, 196
Jefferson 21
Jennings, Gordon 242, 247, 285
Joerns Mfg. Co. 307
Johns, Don 36, 37, 38
Johnson, R.D. 135
Johnson, William E. 155
Jones, Brothers 67
Jones, Hap 143
Jones, Maldwyn 34, 52, 53, 308, 310

Kawasaki 214, 269
Kelley, Jimmy R. 164, 250
Kelley J.R. 263
Kennedy, William E. 226
Kerle, Roy 72
Kuelbs, Lea 308
Kilbert, J.C. 191, 194
Kilbourne Finance Co. 170, 194
Klamfoth, Dick 200
Klaus, Van Peterson and Dunlap 21
Klemenheimer, Walter 46
Korn, Waldo 52, 61, 310
Koto Trading Company 80
Kretz, Ed 137, 163, 164, 172, 200
Kroeger, Emil 14
Kuchler, Lin 206
Kunce, Frank 53

La Follette, Senator Robert M. 95
Lacey, Crolius S. 317, 318
Lacey, Robert 309
Lancefield, Steve 260
Lang, Charles H. 317
Latour, John 141
Lawson, H.J. 13
Lawwill, Mert 212
Le Bard, Aub 263
Lemon, Arthur 90, 310
Leonard, Joe 205, 206, 207, 212
Leopold, B.F. 95
Leuders, Bill 308
Le Vack, Herbert 51
Lickerman, David R. 275
Lightner, Frank 27
Lindstrom, Windy 110, 163
Long, John 27
Long, Lester 127
Long, Ray 163
Longman, Frank 50
Los Angeles Times 225
Louderback, J.Harold 97

Lucas, James 281
Ludlow, Fred 36, 47, 49, 52, 60, 61, 62, 64, 69, 95, 123, 152, 172

Madera, Francisco I, 40
Mann, Dick, 239, 247
Marcolina, Jim 310
Markel, Bart 212, 219
Markham, Charles 174
Marks, Don 52
Marsh Cycle Co. 14
Marshall and Illsley 27, 44, 71
Martin, Dick 308
Marvin, Lee 319
Matchless 218
Mathews, Billy 173, 200
Mavrogordato, M.N. 75
McCall, John 164
McClellan, Harold 97
McCormack, Denis 198, 199
McDermott, Tommy 200
McGill, J.M. 173
McGraw Hill 327
McIntyre, Noel 190
McKee, Robert 294
McLaglan, Victor 166
McLay, James 18
McNeil, J.L. 305, 307, 309, 310
Meacham, Al 38
Meier, Georg 247
Meock, Frank 27
Merkel 21, 24, 27, 33, 39, 101, 305, 308
Michealson 35
Miller, Theodore 70
Milwaukee Journal 257
Milwaukee Sentinel 223, 257
Minneapolis 39
Minnick, Bill 124, 310
Mitzell, Howard 162
Modified Motorcycle Association 265
Mossman, Putt 163
Moto-Guzzi 190, 210
Motor Cycle, The 260
Motorcycle and Allied Trades Association 52, 100, 103, 106, 125, 130, 202, 243
Motorcycling and Bicycling Illustrated 63
Motor Cycling 25, 197
Motorcycle Illustrated, The 25
Motorcycling Review 25
Motorcyclist and Bicyclist Illustrated 50, 57, 59
Motorcyclist,The 25, 122, 131, 136, 140, 141, 163, 170, 174, 190, 226
Motor Trend 190
Muir, John 46
Muth, Al 308
Muth, Hans 298
Mummert, Harvey 100, 101

Namath, Joe 319
National Harley-Davidson Dealers Alliance 306
Newman, Bob 52, 53

Neracar 67, 71, 77
New York Times 116, 225
Nichiman H-D Sales 87
Nicholson Bros. 208
Nicholson, Jack 319
Nieuport Macchi 210
Nippon Jidoshe K.K. 79, 80
Nix, Fred 212
Nordberg, George 23, 31, 84, 90
Norton 189, 190, 196, 199, 200, 218, 239
Nowak, John 255

O'Brien, John H. 261, 267, 275, 278
O'Brien, Richard 219, 245, 255, 266, 267, 276,76, 288, 298, 311
O'Conner, John J. 56
Okura, Baron 79, 80
Ollerman, Frank 24
Orient 14
Orient-Aster 14
Ormonde 69
Orput, R.J. 38
Ottaway, William 29, 31, 32, 33, 34, 35, 36, 37, 38, 39, 47, 51, 61, 62, 92, 137, 148, 182, 242, 253

Pacific Motorcyclist and Bicyclist 122
Pacific Motorcyclist 29
Packard, James Ward 64
Parker, Edward 188
Parker, Scott 325
Parks, Michael 246
Parkhurst, Joe 216
Parkhurst, Leslie 'Red' 33, 36, 38, 47, 49, 52, 61
Parsons, H.W. 50, 57, 59, 60
Pasolini, Renzo 211
Paterson, James 323
Patterson, Dr. W.S. 33
Pechar, Al 124
Pennington, E.J. 13
Penton, John 150
Pepper, George 135, 136, 163
Perkins, Dudley 136, 194, 308
Perry, Bob 34, 36, 52, 308, 309
Pershing, General John 40, 308
Peterson, Robert E. 190
Petienpol, B.H. 100
Petrali, Joe 100, 102, 110, 122, 123, 124, 134, 136, 137, 140, 143, 156, 157, 159, 162, 172, 182, 260, 310, 312
Phillips, Jimmy 200
Pierce, George N., Co. 18, 26
Pike, Roland 136
Pink, Reggie 109, 155, 173
Pope, 14, 18, 21, 24, 27, 31, 33, 36, 129
Pope, Colonel 14, 39
Pope, Don 60, 61
Prescott, Ray 57, 58
Prestwich, J.A. 82, 133, 253, 305
Prince, Jack 24, 36, 37, 47, 52, 92

Prufumo, Peter L. 275
Pullin, Cyril 267

Rasmussen, Thomas L. 106
Rathbun, Harley 46, 118
Rayborn, Cal 212, 237, 238, 244, 245
Reading Standard 17, 21, 24, 35, 40, 55, 57, 59, 63, 68, 71, 77, 310
Reagan, President Ronald 279, 284, 286, 311–315
Reid, Peter C. 327
Reiman, Roger 219, 237, 238, 244, 245
Remy 40, 49, 72
Renny, Charlie 308
Resech, O.P. 222, 225
Reseweber, Carroll 212, 219
Rhyne, Gene 110, 312
Ricardo, Harry 37, 101
Riccuiti, Bob 308
Richards, Leslie D (Dick) 50, 57, 58, 60, 63, 66, 114, 115
Richards, Lou 294
Riddoch, I.P. 51
Rife, Archie 123
Rikuo 87, 88
Risdon, C. Will 55, 64, 68, 95, 96, 97
Road and Track 196
Robinson, Dorothy 166
Robinson, Earl 150, 166
Roccio, Ernie 200
Roche, Jean 100
Rochester Cycle Supply 20
Rochester Harley-Davidson 130
Rodenburg, Rody 135
Roeder, George 246
Rogers Company 67, 95
Rogers, Ralph B. 186, 190, 196, 261, 267
Ross, Robert 106
Royal Enfield 188, 189
Ruhle, William J. 69
Ryan, Eddie 310
Ryan, Joseph 43, 84, 194

Salgo, Nicholas M. 221
Sakurai, Morikichi 82, 84
Salmon, Claude 106, 194
Sankyo Company 80, 82, 84, 86, 88
Schaeffer, Art 159
Schebler 23, 24, 62
Scherer, Julian C. 'Hap' 40, 46, 49, 51, 57, 59, 60, 66, 69, 73
Schickel 40, 63, 67, 71
Schoen, Rose 308
Schrak, W.G. 35
Schroeder, Martin 34
Schunk, Pop 136
Schwinn Bicycle 21
Schwinn, Ignatz 39, 52, 61, 89, 116, 118, 124, 304, 309, 310, 312
Scott, Gary 276
Senter, O.B. 114, 115

Seymour, Johnny 60, 61, 124, 143
Shidle, Norman 57, 58, 59
Sifton, Tom 136, 162, 163, 173, 205
Sirkegian, Bob 310
Skinner, Kenneth 13
Sloan, Charles P. 309
Smith, E.C. 106, 131, 152, 172, 182, 194, 206
Smith, Ivan 308
Smith, Joe 208
Smith, Ray 27
Smith, William 319
Sparks, Art 162
Speigelhoff, Johnny 148, 190
Springs, Hammond 60
Springsteen, Jay 276
Strand, Walter 263
Stratton, Alvin 33, 34
Steele, Orrie 110, 162
Steele, W. Glenn 308
Street Chopper 219, 263
Sullivan, T.S. 38
Supercycle 265
Super-X 102, 104, 109, 110, 112, 145, 152, 153, 312
Suzuki 214, 250, 256
Swenson, Carl 206
Swenson, Ralph 275
Syvertson, Hank, 137, 141, 242, 253

Tancrede, Babe 163
Taylor, Elizabeth 319
Taylor, Lee 33, 34
Teerlink, Richard F. 305, 315, 323
Temple, Claude 50, 51, 75
Terpenning, TNT 110
Thomas, E.R. Co. 14
Thompson, Charles K. 322
Thor 14, 17, 24, 27, 33, 36, 39, 40, 305
Tiffany, Sarter 101
Tipton, Ken 208
Tite-Flex 197
Torres, Ben 27
Toscani, Fred 136, 143, 159
Trailblazers 98, 159, 162
Tritten, Ray Albert 267, 274, 275, 278, 304, 306
Triumph, 188, 189, 197, 198, 199, 200, 206, 208, 218
Tucker, Mike 208
Tuman, Bill 200
Turner, Edward 155
Tuthill, William 143, 206

Underhill, Robert 24
Urquehart, Guy 55

Vanderkoff, Van 40
Van Order, A.F. 95, 96, 97, 98
Villa, General Francisco (Pancho) 40
Vincent HRD 196, 256
Von Gumpert, Eric 31, 46, 47, 67, 80, 198

Wager, Ivan J. 242, 263
Wagner 14, 21
Waite, Russell 261
Walker, Gene 38, 52, 53, 60, 308
Walker, Joe 197, 204, 218, 261
Walker, Otto 36, 37, 38, 47, 49, 52, 60, 61, 123
Walker, Robert Jr. 319
Wallace, David W. 221
Wall Street Journal 225
Waltham Mfg. Co. 13
Warner, Paul 'Speck' 38, 53, 60
Warr, F.H. 98, 184, 271, 272, 301
Watkins, Ray 27
Watson, Duncan 31, 46, 50, 67, 75, 98
Waukesha Engine Company 221
Weishaar, Ray 34, 37, 47, 52, 53, 60, 61, 123
Weistrich, David 69, 70
Weitzell, Harry 27
Welborn, E.E. 37
Wells, Billy 31
Weschler, Frank 53, 60, 63, 66, 73, 74, 76, 77, 92, 95, 102, 103, 123
Western Bicyclist and Motorcyclist, The 25, 49
White, Ralph 219
Whiting, Randolph 150
Whiting, Walter W 46, 114
Williams, A.W. 222
Wicks, Carl T. 269, 287, 298
Wilson, Woodrow 42, 43
Winfrey, Oprah 319
Wismer, James 253, 308, 315
Wolter, Joe 34, 38, 61, 308, 309
Wood, Frank 317, 318
Wolverton, Chas. 310
Worth, Ray 308
Wright, David K. 289, 327
Wright, James A. 103, 104, 106, 109, 126, 131, 155, 170, 172, 182

Yale 39
Yamada 80
Yamaha 214, 250, 256
Yerks, A.W. 34

Zimmerman, Harry A. 129, 130
Zundapp 182, 204